Applied Enterprise JavaBeans™ Technology

Kevin Boone

Sun Microsystems Press
A Prentice Hall Title

Prentice Hall PTR
Upper Saddle River, New Jersey 07458
www.phptr.com

ISBN 0-13-044915-6

9 780130 449153
94999

For information regarding corporate and government bulk discounts please contact:
Corporate and Government Sales (800) 382-3419 or corpsales@pearsontechgroup.com
Or write: Prentice Hall PTR, Corporate Sales Dept., One Lake Street, Upper Saddle River,
NJ 07458.

Sun Microsystems Press Publisher: *Myrna Rivera*
Editorial/Production Supervision: *Donna Cullen-Dolce*
Executive Editor: *Greg Doench*
Marketing Manager: *Debby vanDijk*
Manufacturing Buyer: *Alexis Heydt-Long*
Cover Design Director: *Jerry Votta*
Cover Design: *Nina Scuderi*
Compositor: *Lori Hughes*

10   9   8   7   6   5   4   3   2   1

ISBN 0-13-044915-6

Sun Microsystems Press
A Prentice Hall Title

To my family

Contents

Author's note

My first computer was a Sinclair ZX-80, and I'm only slightly ashamed to admit it. The ZX-80 was supplied in kit form, and had one kilobyte of RAM. To make it do anything interesting at all, you had to program it laboriously in machine code, by entering the hexadecimal values of the instructions and data. This was such a common passtime (honestly) that you could buy books on it, with titles like "How to Program Your ZX-80 Laboriously in Hexadecimal." With this mastered, you could make the little machine do all manner of fascinating things: play chess, calculate your income tax return, synthesize speech, and anything else to which a 2 MHz processor could turn its attention. This was only true, of course, if you had an obsessive attention to detail, a pathologically good memory, and nothing much else to do. Machine code was—and remains—powerful, flexible, and staggeringly unpleasant to use for a project of any significant complexity.

The first computer software that I got paid to write was totally different. It ran on GEC microcontrollers and was written in the obscure 'Ladder Diagram Language.' With this language, the programmer 'drew' a simulation of an electrical system, complete with switches, relays, motors, and lamps. Ladder Diagram Language was the opposite of machine code: It was so abstract that it had no procedural semantics at all. The programmer simply denoted a vague wish that, for example, pressing button 'A' would bring about the activation of motor 'B,' if it wasn't too much trouble, thank you. This was all very well until it became necessary to express a concept like 'flash lamp B twice with a one-second pause.' The language simply didn't have the expressive power for this.

The development of programming languages and techniques can be seen as an attempt to find the best balance between abstraction and flexibility. If a system of software development is truly flexible, it is likely to be expressive at such a low level that it is difficult to use for anything substantial. If it is very abstract, then common requirements and operations are expressed very easily, but there is not sufficient power to handle other, less predictable, requirements.

Enterprise JavaBeans (EJBs) is a technology that—in its intended domain—may just have the balance between abstraction and flexibility about right. EJBs are models of business processes and objects. They are abstract enough to relieve the developer of many of the tedious minutiae of business application development (transaction management, concurrency control, enforcing security), while at the same time allowing operations to be expressed with the flexibility of the Java programming language. You wouldn't want to use EJBs to implement an air-traffic control system or a heart pacemaker, but that's OK: No one is suggesting that you should. EJBs are ideally suited to a small range of application types that just happen, at present, to be exceptionally important. I am talking, of course, about datacentric, business-process-driven, secure, transactional, distributed systems, a category which includes almost all e-commerce applications.

EJBs, when properly understood, make the development of this type of system much easier. The EJB framework abstracts away the low-level details, leaving the developer free to concentrate on the application itself. The component-based framework supports—or at least does not actively hinder—code reuse and modularity. Being based on open standards, the architecture makes it possible to integrate EJBs with legacy systems and applications of other types. All in all, EJBs are the right tool for the job.

The downside to all this is that EJB development takes some getting used to. There are many complexities to master and pitfalls to avoid. For example, the interaction between the EJB container and the EJB implementation itself is complex and subtle. When something creates an entity EJB and calls a method on it, the EJB container calls up to seven different methods on the EJB implementation, and typically more than 20 distinct, documented internal operations are carried out. And this does not include the undocumented, vendor-specific operations that are concealed inside the container. When I am teaching this subject, a description of this sequence of operations is nearly always followed by a question: Why does it have to be so complicated? The reason is very simple: The EJB architecture is complicated so that *clients* of EJBs can be straightforward; and clients of EJBs can be other EJBs. In other words, EJBs—in conjunction with their containers—are very good at encapsulating complex operations and providing simple interfaces to them. As we shall see, EJBs present a very simple interface to their clients; a Java object calls methods on an EJB in almost exactly the same way as on another ordinary Java object. It is worth bearing this fact in mind when wading through the material on transaction management, for example, in Chapter 9.

There are now quite a number of EJB textbooks that describe the fundamental principles of EJB development very well. I wrote this book because there are none that answer the kinds of questions that people who came to my courses were asking. These were questions like, 'How can I use a remote debugger while developing an EJB application?' and, 'How can a transaction rollback be made to encompass changes in instance variables as well as database operations?' Incidentally, you will find the answers to these questions on pages 441 and 260, respectively. Actually, I wrote this book because I spent four months living in hotels while teaching EJB courses all over Europe, and I needed something to keep me out of the bars in the evenings, but that's beside the point.

I hope that you find EJB development as profitable, useful, and above all, rewarding, as I do. I hope that this book helps in some small way to make this the case.

Kevin Boone, London, November 2002

About the author

Kevin Boone is one of Sun Microsystems' most senior educators in the UK. He has over 15 years of experience as a professional software developer and is also a qualified teacher. Between 1986 and 1998, Kevin worked as a software engineer for a number of private and public sector organizations, contributing to projects ranging in size from heart pacemakers to electricity generating plants. His work on computer modelling of brain activity led to a Ph.D. in 1996 and a desire to adopt a more academic role. Since becoming a full-time educator in 1998, Kevin has developed and taught courses in software development using Java and C++, object-oriented modelling, and, of course, Enterprise JavaBeans. Since joining Sun in 2000, Kevin's main responsibility has been for the delivery and preparation of courses on J2EE and e-commerce platforms. He is particularly involved in the development of the EJB teaching curriculum. Kevin remains an active developer and contributes to a number of open-source projects, including the Linux kernel.

Preface

About this book

This book has two main purposes. First, it provides Java developers with all the information they need to author robust, powerful, secure EJB applications. Second, it provides guidance on, and interpretation of, the *EJB Specification*, focusing particularly on Version 2.0. It also describes some of the more important technologies that are associated with EJBs: JNDI, JDBC, JMS, and Web components.

My experience teaching EJB technology and advising on EJB projects has shown that it is relatively easy for an experienced developer to gain the skills necessary to begin working with EJBs. There are many courses, textbooks, and tutorials that provide support at this introductory level. The problem is that they don't provide the developer with sufficient information to make a success of demanding, critical applications. Failure of EJB projects to manifest the benefits that are claimed for the technology is often the result of an incomplete understanding of the more subtle aspects of the technology. These include such matters as the behaviour of an EJB server under load, the use of transaction boundaries to drive synchronization between the EJB and a database, and the impact of different database administration strategies on the EJB server's resource management systems. The experience necessary to overcome these problems can be gained by practice, of course, but a better approach, I believe, is to develop a really comprehensive grasp of the underlying technology before beginning work on expensive projects.

This is where this book comes in: It describes EJB technology and the development of EJB applications in detail, starting from first principles and continuing to systems supporting distributed database transactions and a comprehensive security policy. The emphasis throughout is on accuracy, depth, and comprehensiveness, rather than on simplification. Where it is necessary for developers to gain the full benefit of using EJBs, the book even describes aspects of the EJB technology that are normally said to be 'transparent' to the developer. These include—among other things—the generation and operation of the automatically generated EJB proxies and how these interact with the developer's code; how database connection pooling works (and therefore how to optimize database connection efficiency); how to handle transaction rollbacks in session beans; how the container deals with name resolution and cross-references; and the operation of bean-instance pooling systems.

All these topics are crucial to the development of mission-critical applications, but are covered superficially, if at all, in other books.

Despite its technical depth, this book assumes no initial knowledge of EJBs or related technologies. It begins with very simple examples, and explains step-by-step how to code, compile, assemble, deploy, and test them using the *J2EE Reference Implementation*. To illustrate more sophisticated EJB features, the book uses a substantial, real-world application, for which complete source code is provided.

At the time of writing, the EJB community is being stirred by the introduction of the first products to support Version 2.0 of the *EJB Specification*. This version includes a number of substantial enhancements: message-driven EJBs, a new query language and persistence management scheme, and numerous smaller improvements. All these features are covered in depth in this book.

Intended readership

This book is written for professional software developers who expect to work extensively with Enterprise JavaBeans, or are already doing so. Although it assumes no prior knowledge of the subject, it goes into the technology in considerable depth. In order to make full use of the book, the reader will need to have

- a high degree of familiarity with the Java programming language,

- a working knowledge of networking, TCP/IP, and the Java sockets abstraction,

- sufficient familiarity with UML to understand basic class, collaboration, and use-case diagrams,

- a working knowledge of relational database management, particularly SQL, and an understanding of the need for transaction management,

- a sound foundation in object-oriented software engineering concepts,

- some familiarity with the XML language, and

- a willingness to come to grips with a variety of rather complex software tools that will be initially unfamiliar.

Although I assume that the reader is familiar with the Java language, I have included appendices that describe important, less well-known features of the language, such as reflection and serialization. These are key technologies that underlie the operation of EJB systems. In addition, while assuming basic familiarity with database technology, this book describes in detail more advanced features like distributed transaction management, as these are subjects with which many Java developers have little experience.

This book is part textbook and part reference book. Like a textbook, material is presented—as far as possible—so that each new topic builds on earlier topics. I say, 'as far as possible,' because some compromises have been necessary. This is an

EJB book, and readers will doubtless want to see examples of EJBs fairly early in the text. However, there is a great deal of background and related material that the developer must master to be able to develop EJB applications. This includes JDBC, JNDI, and transaction management. Ideally these subjects would be introduced first, but I felt this would not be appreciated by readers. However, I have resisted the temptation to hide these things in appendices, or in 'advanced topics' chapters, and placed them as early in the text as I felt readers could stand. These topics are all vital to a full understanding of EJB technology. If you study the *EJB Specification*, you will see that it contains references to databases and transactions on almost every page. Therefore, like a reference book, I have anticipated that the reader will not want to read every chapter word for word before going on to the next chapter. Some of the material presented will probably only become meaningful when the reader has begun authoring EJB applications.

How to read this book

At risk of sounding glib, I recommend reading this book from start to finish. As has been discussed, the material of each chapter builds on preceding chapters. However, because each chapter covers its topic in considerable depth, you may prefer to skim some chapters rather than studying them in detail before going on. This is fine, but bear in mind that the chapters were not written to be self-contained, and you may find it necessary to flip back and forth to support this approach. I recommend that you do not skip the chapters on JNDI, JDBC, and transactions, however eager you may be for more EJB material. While it is possible—at a pinch—to master session EJBs without a detailed understanding of databases and transactions, this will be difficult for message-driven EJBs and impossible for entity EJBs.

Ten common EJB myths debunked

A number of commonly held misconceptions about EJBs sometimes deter software developers and project managers from making the transition to EJB-based application development. This is a shame because, although EJBs won't be suitable for all applications, it will be suitable for many, and one should not reject a strategy for the wrong reasons. Similarly, companies often adopt the use of EJB technology in haste, because their staff do not understand the full implications of such a decision. I should like to take the opportunity to dispell some of the myths about EJB technology early in this book.

Myth 1: EJB is just an extention of JavaBeans It is often said that Enterprise JavaBeans is an extension of JavaBeans technology. Despite the similar names, these technologies actually have very little in common, at least as far as the practicalities of development are concerned. There are philosophical similarities, but this is little consolation to a developer who has to move from one technology to another.

The similarities center on the notion of 'properties'—a Java class has a property if it exposes methods that allow some data to be read or written. For example, if a Java class exposes the methods

```
public void setName() {...}
public String getName() {...}
```

then it can be said to have a property 'name.' Whether the class itself internalizes the representation of the String name is irrelevant for these purposes. This is much is true for EJB and JavaBeans, but not much more.

I have often heard developers say that they would like to become involved in EJB projects, but think they should 'work up to it gradually' by way of JavaBeans development. This is unfortunate because—apart from an increased familiarity with Java programming in general—experience with JavaBeans will probably not make it easier to develop EJB applications. There simply isn't enough common ground. To learn to develop EJB applications, start by writing EJBs.

Myth 2: EJB development is trivial, as the container does all the work
The EJB container provides services to the EJBs which greatly simplify the development of enterprise applications—of particular importance are transaction management and security. However, it is still possible to develop EJB applications that are unreliable and offer poor performance if the underlying technology is poorly understood. The interaction between the EJB container and the developer's code is complex and subtle, and takes some time and practice to understand.

Myth 3: EJB applications are inherently portable EJB applications are more portable than those based on most other application development frameworks. In particular, being based on open standards means that there is good cross-vendor compatibility. There are, however, three problems with the assertion as it stands.

First, it is only true if the developer follows the guidance of the *EJB Specification* quite closely. It is possible to write nonportable EJBs either by ignorance or design.

Second, the *EJB Specification* recognizes that vendor products will probably offer facilities beyond the demands of the Specification, and that these facilities will have to be configured somehow. Vendors are allowed to have their EJB assembly tools include vendor-specific information in the deployable JAR and EAR packages. Many products will not function without this information, which won't be available if the package has come from a different product.

Third, not all EJB servers are equally fastidious about enforcing the restrictions imposed on EJBs by the *EJB Specification*. Some servers, for example, permit EJBs to read and write local files. It is difficult to move an application from a product that takes a tolerant line on these things to one that is strict.

In summary, the provisions of the *EJB Specification* mean that it will nearly always be possible to port an EJB application from one server to another. However, it may take a good degree of skill, and familiarity with both products, to accomplish this.

Myth 4: CORBA can do the same things as EJBs CORBA is an infrastructure for distributed objects, which has some overlap with EJB technology. However, CORBA is not an application framework. It does not remove the developer's need to get involved in the mechanics of transaction management and security. It does specify how transaction context and security context is to be propagated in method calls between servers, but does not stipulate how this information is to be used by applications. EJB servers can be based on CORBA standards, and offer services which extend the CORBA paradigm, rather than competing with it.

Myth 5: Java is slow Java applications are slow to start up, compared with native-code applications, because of the overhead of initializing the JVM (Java virtual machine). When just-in-time compilation is used, Java code is not significantly slower in execution than native code *in the kinds of applications to which EJBs are suited.* Of course, if one has an axe to grind, it is always possible to find some piece of code that shows a particular language in a bad light. C++ enthusiasts, for example, may assert—correctly—that C++ code outperforms Java in standard performance benchmarks. This is of little interest to EJB developers, because the standard benchmarks tend to involve operations such as matrix multiplication, that are unlikely to be implemented in EJBs. An EJB server may be relatively slow to start up, but once it has started, the EJBs are executed essentially as native code.

Myth 6: EJB applications are slow *Badly written* EJB applications are slow. Common sense and an understanding of EJB-container interaction should allow good performance to be achieved. There are, it is true, substantial overheads involved in method calls on EJBs. But it is not sensible to compare a piece of software written using EJBs with one written to run entirely in a single process. The latter may well be more efficient under light load, but the inherent scalability of EJB applications allows much better performance under heavy load (as the single-process solution probably won't scale at all).

Myth 7: EJBs support XML As we shall see, the *EJB Specification* has little to say about the use of XML with EJBs. It only mandates the use of XML for deployment descriptors (configuration files). EJBs are being used ingeniously with XML, but only by dint of the efforts of developers. There is an increased interest in the use of XML for passing data between EJBs, and a number of general-purpose implementations of systems that automate this are available, but it is not intrinsic to the *EJB Specification*. It is possible to expose EJB functionality as Web services, and use XML-RPC to make the method calls. However, this is part of the Web services development model, not the EJB model.

Myth 8: The *EJB Specification* is opaque and impenetrable; EJB servers operate by smoke and mirrors The Specification is certainly not light reading, but neither is it incomprehensible, and it is essential for serious developers to have a copy handy. One of the goals of this book is to assist in the interpretation of the Specification, and you will see frequent references in the text to sections of that document.

Similarly, although the operation of an EJB server is complex, there is no black magic involved. Indeed, creating efficient EJB application requires a detailed understanding of the interaction between the EJB server and its EJBs.

Myth 9: EJBs are general-purpose, and can be used for any kind of application While not strictly incorrect, it is probably fair to say that EJBs excel in certain areas, rather than in others. EJBs are well-suited to distributed, datacentric business applications. They would be inappropriate for real-time systems or for applications where the advantages of scalability and security are not significant enough to outweigh the overheads of the distributed infrastructure.

Myth 10: It is possible to develop EJBs without knowing much Java On the contrary, I wouldn't recommend even starting EJB development unless you have a good background in Java. For the classroom courses that I teach, I normally recommend that participants have two years of Java development experience. People with extensive C++ experience can usually pick up EJB development quite easily as well, because many of the object-oriented concepts of Java and C++ are similar.

Chapter overview

Here is a summary of the material covered in this book.

EJBs in context This introductory chapter describes the goals and requirements of EJB technology and what you—the developer—can expect to gain by using it. It explains how EJBs fit into other distributed programming paradigms (like CORBA), and into the wider 'J2EE' model of application development. The chapter includes an outline of the other services that a J2EE-compliant application server is expected to provide and which EJBs can use (e.g., JavaMail, JMS). There is a brief discussion of the development philosophy that underlies the *EJB Specification*, including the roles of the developer, assembler, and deployer, and how the EJB model—appropriately used—can enhance code reuse and improve reliability.

Distributed objects This chapter describes the principles that underlie distributed programming in Java and form the technological foundation for the EJB architecture. We begin by describing the process of Remote Method Invocation (RMI) and how we could, if we wished, develop an RMI framework from the ground up. This will be illustrated using outline source code for such a system.

This discussion will highlight some of the challenges that face the developer of an RMI framework, and how these have been tackled in the standard Java RMI scheme (and, indirectly, in the EJB architecture). Again, we will use source code examples to demonstrate how these things work in practice. Finally, we will discuss the overlap between Java RMI and EJB RMI, with particular emphasis on protocols (like IIOP) that allow interoperability between these systems and others.

Overview of EJB technology This chapter describes EJB technology in outline and provides an overview of the interaction between the EJB, the client, and the EJB container. It also describes the *EJB objects* and *home objects*, and explains why the use of these constructs—although perhaps somewhat confusing at first—ultimately simplifies the development of substantial software projects.

We begin by examing how an EJB is seen by its clients, which may be synchronous, using RMI, or asynchronous, using messaging. We then discuss the Java entities that make up an EJB, the home interfaces, local interface, remote interface, and implementation class, and how they are packaged with a deployment descriptor to make a complete EJB.

The chapter concludes with a discussion of the techniques that commercial EJB products may use to optimize performance and increase reliability.

As it is an overview, this chapter does not provide any complete examples of EJBs, and could lead readers into thinking that the subject is more complicated than it really is. Moreover, to avoid fragmenting the text, I have included material in this chapter that, although part of an outline of the technology, is rather more complex than you may wish to see on a first reading. If you are impatient to see an EJB working and look at some real code, you may prefer to read Chapter 4 first. You may find that this helps to put some of the more complicated parts of this chapter into perspective.

A first EJB This chapter will describe the practical details of writing, compiling, deploying, and testing EJBs. We start with the simplest of simple EJBs: The example in this chapter is a stateless session bean, with only two methods accessible to clients. For purposes of illustration, we will describe this process for the *J2EE Reference Implementation* Version 1.3. For other products, the assembly and deployment process will be different, but the coding will be the same.

Introducing the case study This chapter introduces a case study—the *Prestige Bike Hire* application—that will form the basis for many of the examples used throughout the rest of this book. The case study is of a system for managing the business of a motorcycle rental firm. The system maintains bookings for rental vehicles, calculates hire costs, and maintains customer accounts. The chapter presents the client's requirements and outlines the architecture of the system that will be constructed. This case study has been chosen because it is complex enough to require the use of a number of EJBs of different types and demonstrate security and transaction management, but is not so large that we can't present most of the relevant source code. Subsequent chapters of the book will examine different EJBs from this case study in detail.

Session EJBs We have already discussed the basic principles of session EJBs and seen a very simple example. In this chapter, we will examine the session EJB in much more detail. We start with stateful session EJBs, as their life cycles are conceptually simpler. We will discuss, in particular, issues relating to instance management: activation, passivation, and timeout. We then move on to stateless session EJBs, explaining how the EJB container can optimize performance by pooling instances and the implications that such pooling has for the developer. We will see these principles at work by analyzing the behaviour of the session EJB from Chapter 4 in detail. Finally, we present a more realistic session EJB example and give some practical guidelines on using session beans in applications.

Developer's guide to naming and JNDI While previous chapters have shown in outline how EJBs and their clients use JNDI to find home interfaces, this chapter describes the JNDI system in more detail. We start with an outline of the JNDI architecture, and describe some of the key terms and concepts used in JNDI programming. This is followed by a description of the use of JNDI by EJBs and their clients, including the distinction between the server-wide namespace and the 'local' namespace provided for each EJB. This will lead to a discussion of the use of the 'java:comp/env' prefix in name lookups; this is an issue about which many developers and, sadly, some container vendors are unclear. Finally, to provide a detailed description of the JNDI architecture, there is a complete implementation of a JNDI interface to a set of objects stored in a file. This is provided for those readers who need a very thorough understanding of JNDI, perhaps to support EJB container extensions.

It is easy for an EJB developer to forget that JNDI was designed not as a support service for EJBs, but to simplify access from Java programs to naming and directory servers (rather as JDBC is used for database access). Much of JNDI is intended to support this more general usage and is not directly used in EJB development. However, EJB developers are increasingly being called on to use the more general features of JNDI in their applications to support such features as user and group management.

JDBC and databases This chapter presents an overview of the JDBC specification, particularly as it applies to EJB development. Readers who are already familiar with JDBC in other environments will find its use within EJBs similar to their previous experience; however, there are some small technical differences that have profound practical consequences, as we shall see. We will discuss how the container provides `DataSource` objects that allow clients to open and close database connections, and how the database connections are, in fact, container-supplied proxies for real connections. This will lead to a discussion of connection management and connection pooling, and how to author EJBs to take advantage of these facilities. Finally, we look at some practical techniques for improving the modularity and manageability of database access procedures in EJBs.

Transactions This chapter explains how to make use of the transaction management features offered by the EJB architecture. It describes the basic principles of transactions and the standard features that are supported by the EJB architecture. We then discuss the appropriate uses of bean-managed and container-managed transactions including the `SessionSynchronization` interface in stateful session EJBs. The concepts of this chapter will be demonstrated using both simple test EJBs and a practical example from the *Prestige Bike Hire* application. Finally, for readers with an interest in the underlying technology, there is a description of the roles of the transaction manager and resource managers, and the protocols by which these components communicate with one another and with the EJB container.

Message-driven EJBs Message-driven EJBs are new in Version 2.0 of the *EJB Specification*. This chapter begins with a discussion of enterprise messaging in general, with a particular focus on the practical benefits of this technology. We then discuss the JMS specification and the general procedures for sending messages using the JMS API. This leads to a discussion of the problems of asynchronous communicaton in the EJB architecture, which is essentially a request-response system, and how the use of message-driven EJBs can help in development of asynchronous services. We then discuss the development and use of message-driven EJBs themselves, illustrated by examples from the *Prestige Bike Hire* application.

Entity EJBs This chapter analyzes entity EJBs in more detail. It starts by describing the life cycle of an entity EJB and how the container manages the instance pool to handle database tables of arbitrary size. This will include a discussion of the container's manipulation of primary keys, including cases where the primary key is not a simple database field and has to be modelled as a class. We then discuss methods that the container can use to keep the instance variables in sync with the database tables, and the implications these techniques will have on the efficiency of the EJB. This chapter covers those aspects of entity EJB development that are relevant to both bean-managed and container-managed persistence. Later chapters will deal with each of these techniques in depth.

Bean-managed persistence When using bean-managed persistence, the developer writes the Java code that synchronizes the EJB's internal state with the underlying database. This chapter describes in detail how to accomplish this. We begin by summarizing the developer's responsibilities, then describe step-by-step how to code, compile, assemble, deploy, and test a fully featured entity

EJB, which supports reads, writes, insertions, and deletions, single-object finders, multiobject finders, and home methods. The example also presents the use of data access objects (DAOs) to decouple the EJB implementation from the data store. Finally, the chapter provides some advice on how more complex constructs like persistent associations can be handled using bean-managed persistence.

Container-managed persistence Container-managed persistence (CMP) is a technique for allowing the EJB container to handle all the synchronization between the entity EJB and the underlying persistent storage device, usually a relational database. This chapter describes how to make use of CMP in both the EJB 1.1 and EJB 2.0 models. The chapter starts with a description of some of the issues that any persistence management scheme must address. It then describes how these issues were tackled in the EJB 1.1 scheme. Examination of some of the problems with the EJB 1.1 model allows an insight into the way in which the EJB 2.0 CMP model, although complex, solves many of the problems that prevented a wide uptake of CMP in EJB 1.1. We finish with a description of some practical examples from the *Prestige Bike Hire* application.

EJB practicalities This chapter discusses some practical matters that may be of interest to the EJB developer, such as the use of remote debugging tools, IDE capabilities, problems with EJB server configuration, and portability.

Design, patterns, and good practice This chapter discusses higher-level design issues in the EJB architecture and provides general guidance on building efficient, maintainable EJB applications. Some of the matters it describes are fairly technical, such as the effect on the application when exceptions are thrown from one EJB to another, while others are more pragmatic, like the use of design patterns.

Security This chapter describes how to secure EJB applications, and the implications that EJB technology has for enterprise-level security. It explains how to make use of the security features offered by the EJB server and how EJB security is integrated with authentication features offered by Web-based applications and application containers. We start by describing the philosophy behind the J2EE security architecture and the EJB security model. We then discuss the use of declarative security, which allows security policies to be implemented in the deployment descriptor without coding. Declarative security will not always be sufficient on its own, and the developer will have to put some security procedures into code. We discuss the benefits and implications of doing this. As an illustration of these concepts, we will see how different types of authentication and encryption can be applied to a simple EJB application. Finally, there is a discussion of how EJB security fits into the wider scope of enterprise security and of recent developments in secure, interoperable RMI protocols.

EJBs and the Web layer This chapter describes in outline how to implement a Web-based user interface to an EJB application, focusing specifically on the issues of integrating EJBs to servlets and JSP pages. The chapter begins with a brief overview of the techniques that are available for server-side generation of dynamic content, particularly servlets and JSPs. It then describes how servlets and JSPs can initialize, locate, and use EJBs. Where stateful session EJBs are used, this requires synchronizing EJB instances to the servlet session; this technique is described in detail. Finally, we discuss the additional complexities involved in building an application in which the Web components are not hosted in a application server, but in a standalone JSP/servlet engine.

Connectors and resource adapters This chapter provides a brief introduction to resource adapters and the J2EE connector architecture (JCA). This architecture allows the developer to integrate support for arbitrary external resources into the EJB container. We begin with an example of an application that would benefit from the use of a connector. We then describe the JCA API in outline. Most of this chapter is concerned with the implementation and analysis of a specific resource adapter, which provides EJBs with access to a stock quote server; the API is described in detail with reference to this example. We then move on to a discussion of the proposed 'common client interface.' Finally, there is a brief explanation of the principles of transaction management and security management within resource adapters.

In addition, there are appendices on installing and testing the case study application, Java techniques that may not be familiar (such as serialization and reflection), the *J2EE Reference Implementation*, and the fundamentals of public key cryptography and SSL.

Getting started with EJB development

To develop, compile, package, deploy, and test EJB applications, you are going to need at least the following software:

- Standard Java development tools. The ones you use already will almost certainly be adequate, although there are an increasing number of products that have additional support for EJB development (e.g., tools for synchronizing the content of the various Java classes and interfaces that make up an EJB).

- An EJB server or application server. This book refers to the *J2EE Reference Implementation*, but any product with full EJB 2.0 compliance will run the examples. If the product you normally use does not offer full compliance, there is no reason why you should not run the Reference Implementation as well. It is free of charge, after all.

- Tools for packaging EJBs and generating the XML deployment descriptors. These may be supplied with the EJB server, or you could use a general-purpose XML editor and the `jar` utility in conjunction with makefiles or Ant scripts.

- The EJB API documentation and Specification (which may be supplied with the EJB server, or you can download from `java.sun.com/products/ejb`).

I don't recommend that readers begin to learn EJB development using one of the heavy-duty, commercial application servers, for the same reason that novice pilots do not train in jet airliners. Commercial-grade application servers are optimized for supporting large client bases with short response times and high availability. These products do not sell on the basis of their ease of use or their powerful development tools (yet). In addition, they tend to be quirky, and slow to start up and shut down. Instead, I suggest using the *J2EE Reference Implementation* from Sun Microsystems (guidelines for obtaining and installing this latter product may be found in Appendix F). The reason I recommend this particular EJB implementation—apart from the obvious one that it is free—is that being a reference implementation, it should comply fully with the *EJB Specification*. It has a powerful specification checker that tests the compliance of the developer's code, making it a very useful educational tool. In addition, this is almost the only product currently available that is guaranteed to support all the new EJB 2.0 features, such as message-driven EJBs, the new connector API, and the extended container-managed persistence model. Moreover, the Reference Implementation is available for many hardware and operating system platforms. I have used Linux and Solaris for creating and testing the examples in this book, but instructions for operating the Windows version of the Reference Implementation are also given where there are differences. There should, of course, be no differences in the EJB code itself. All the examples in this book were tested with the *J2EE Reference Implementation*, Version 1.3.1.

The Reference Implementation is supplied with a simple SQL database engine called *Cloudscape* (supplied by Informix, Inc.), and this has been used for all the examples that require database support, in preference to a commercial database, for the same reasons as discussed above.

This book does not advocate the use of particular interactive development environments (IDEs) and illustrates all compilation and execution operations using a command line and Ant build scripts. If you normally use an IDE, it will almost certainly be fine for EJB work. However, while I accept that many developers like to use IDEs, I feel that they conceal from the developer certain complexities which *must* be fully understood for EJB work. A case in point is the use of the class search path and the relationship between package names and directory structures. EJBs run in a different environment from the one in which they were compiled, and therefore incomplete understanding of these issues is a major cause of frustration for new EJB developers.

The state of the art

At the time of writing, there were at least 14 vendors offering EJB servers or application servers with EJB support. These vendors range in size from small specialist firms to global giants like Oracle. This number will almost certainly increase; there is very broad industry support for EJB. This book is based on 'final release 2' of Version 2.0 of the *EJB Specification*, which was current at the time of writing.

The fact that there has been a second 'final release,' means, we assume, that further 'final releases' are not ruled out. Should such changes impact the material or the source code in this book, updates will be posted on the supporting Web site: `www.kevinboone.com/ejb_book`.

At the time of writing, the first draft of the proposed Version 2.1 of the *EJB Specification* had just been published. At present, no EJB product supports any of the new features, and there was no settled date by which the new specification would be ratified. As a result, I have decided not to include EJB 2.1 features in the text; the specification is almost certain to change by the time you read this. Instead, I have included a brief discussion of the EJB 2.1 proposals in Appendix A.

What's new in EJB Version 2.0?

For readers who are already familiar with Version 1.1 of the *EJB Specification*, here is a summary of the features that are substantially different in the new version, and where they are described in this book.

- A new type of EJB, the *message-driven EJB*, has been introduced. These EJBs have neither home nor remote interfaces; their methods are called in response to the arrival of messages from an asynchronous messaging service. See Chapter 10.

- EJBs can now interact in a nondistributed way, to avoid the overheads of remote method invocation. To support this, the EJB developer must provide two additional interfaces, the 'local interface' and the 'local home interface.' These are analogues of the traditional remote interface and home interface, and are used to generated intra-JVM calling proxies rather than distributable proxies. For more information, see page 57.

- Entity EJBs can now make use of an entirely new container-managed persistence strategy, which improves significantly on the EJB 1.1 model. This new strategy specifies how persistent associations are managed, as well as persistent properties, and separates properties from instance variables. See page 408.

- The new CMP scheme is supported by a new query language *EJB QL*, whose job is to decouple the EJB logic from the database implementation. See page 408.

- Entity EJBs can now expose methods to clients that do not rely on a specific EJB being created or located. They are called through the home interface (local or remote), and are therefore called *home methods*. See page 351.

- The mechanism of *principal delegation* is now clearly defined in the *EJB Specification*. The deployment descriptor can now be used to specify the security role and principal that will be propagated from one EJB to another. See page 508.

- The mechanisms for interoperability are now more rigidly defined. A whole chapter of the the new *EJB Specification* (Chapter 18) is dedicated to these new requirements, which mandate techniques for naming, transaction context propagation, and security context propagation, among other things.

Notes on the text

In this book, I have used the following typographical and notational conventions.

- Names of programming entities (classes, variables, keywords) that appear in the text are given in a typewriter font, `like this`.

- SQL statements use capital letters with Roman font for the keywords, and ordinary lower case for table and column names: "SELECT * FROM ORDERS WHERE id=100".

- Source code listings are shown with light grey background with line numbers and with Java keywords highlighted, like this:

```
for (int i = 0; i < 10); i++)
    print(this);
```

The line numbers are, of course, not part of the listing but are provided for ease of reference in the text.

- User interface actions are given in abbreviated form, in quotation marks; for example: 'File-Deploy' means "select the 'File' menu (or button) and then the 'Deploy' submenu (or button)".

- Where a command to be entered on the command line, or in a script or batch file, is too long to display on one line, I have used the backslash symbol to represent a continuation onto the next line, like this:

```
This is really\
one line
```

Most Unix systems will let you use the backslash symbol in this way on the command line or in shell scripts; some Windows systems will not. If your system does not, you will need to concatenate all the lines displayed into one long line.

- References to specifications are given like this: [EJB2.0 x.x], where 'x.x' is the section number. The term '*EJB Specification*' on its own should be taken to refer to Version 2.0, unless otherwise stated.

- EJB 2.0 introduces the ability to specify intra-JVM method calling and defines new interfaces and proxies to support this. For brevity, in this book I will not distinguish the different types unless it is crucial to an understanding of the

matter at hand. Therefore, the term 'home interface' will refer to both local
and remote home interfaces, 'EJB object' will refer to the (remote) EJB object
and the EJB local object, and 'remote interface' will apply to both the remote
interface *and* the local interface. This is because the *EJB Specification* does
not provide a term that refers collectively to the local and remote interfaces. In
practice, there should be no confusion, because the different types of interface
and proxy are used in the same way.

Source code

Full source code for all the examples in this book can be found on the accompanying
Web site, `www.kevinboone.com/ejb_book`. In the same place, you will find details
of the sources available, information about the structure of the source trees, and
hints on compiling and deploying using the `Ant` build tool.

Acknowledgments

I would like to thank my manager at Sun Microsystems, Kevin Streater, for making
it possible for me to use the resources of the company—time and equipment—in the
writing of this book. I am also grateful to my other colleagues at Sun, particularly
Steve Ferris, Tim Rault-Smith, and Zahir Hussein, for their help, encouragement,
and criticism. The students who have attended my classes on EJB development also
deserve a mention—their continual challenges to my own knowledge of the subject
have made me strive always to increase my own expertise and to find new ways to
explain difficult concepts. But most of all, I should like to thank Rachel, my wife,
for her tolerance and support while I was spending every evening hunched over the
keyboard. And, of course, thanks to Bryony and Max, my children, without whom
this book would have been finished much sooner.

Chapter 1

Enterprise JavaBeans™ in context

Overview

This introductory chapter describes the goals and requirements of EJB technology and what you—the developer—can expect to gain by using it. It explains how EJBs fit into other distributed programming paradigms (like CORBA), and into the wider 'J2EE' model of application development. The chapter includes an outline of the other services that a J2EE-compliant application server is expected to provide and which EJBs can use (e.g., Java-Mail, JMS). There is a brief discussion of the development philosophy that underlies the *EJB Specification*, including the roles of the developer, assembler, and deployer, and how the EJB model—appropriately used—can enhance code reuse and improve reliability.

1.1 Enterprise JavaBeans: what are they, and what do they do?

Let's start by examining the answer to this question as provided by the most authoritative source, the *EJB Specification* itself:

> "The Enterprise JavaBeans architecture is a component architecture for the development and deployment of component-based distributed business applications. Applications written using the Enterprise JavaBeans architecture are scalable, transactional, and multi-user secure. These applications may be written once, and then deployed on any server platform that supports the Enterprise JavaBeans specification."

This definition makes a number of important assertions, which are worth considering in more detail.

1

"...a component architecture..." The distinction between 'component-based' and 'object-oriented' development is not a strict one, and you will see EJBs referred to as 'distributed components' and 'distributed objects.' I take the term 'component' in EJB technology to mean a piece of software that is self-contained, has well-defined functionality, and fits into some kind of application framework. It is this latter point that probably makes the term 'component' more applicable than 'object' in EJB technology.

The application framework is exemplified by the *EJB container*, a concept about which we will have much more to say later. EJBs depend for their very existence on their container; it regulates all aspects of their lives, including their communication with other EJBs [EJB2.0 6.2]. This is not the restriction that it first appears, because the use of the container has profound advantages, as we shall see.

EJBs can be viewed as simple objects: They expose methods, and these methods can be called. Like ordinary objects, the methods take arguments and can return values. Unlike ordinary objects, EJBs can be distributed across different hosts, and the architecture takes care of the communication. When a client makes a method call on an EJB, it is in fact making that call on the container, which acts as a proxy, as we shall see.

"...distributed business applications..." What is a 'business application'? This is a very broad term, but we can identify certain characteristics that most business applications will exhibit. First, there is a reliance on data, often in volume, and with strict measures to protect the integrity of that data. Most business applications make use of relational databases. Second, many business applications have large numbers of users, often geographically distant from the application host. Third, business applications often integrate systems of different types, from different vendors. Some of these systems will be 'legacy' systems—that is, based on obsolete software and protocols, but needing to be retained. EJBs can make use of messaging services, connectors, and other techniques for access to legacy systems. The EJB infrastructure has interoperability as one of its core requirements [EJB2.0 19.2]. Applications are 'distributed' when components can be hosted on different servers. The ability to distribute components has important implications for fault tolerance and load sharing, as we shall see.

It is worth pointing out at this point that, under EJB 2.0, not all EJBs have to be capable of distribution. The developer is at liberty to author EJBs such that they are only accessible to calls from other EJBs in the same JVM. This makes access more efficient at the expense of limiting load balancing and fault tolerance. We will have much more to say about this issue later.

"...scalable..." An application is scalable if the system that hosts it can be expanded or upgraded to support a higher client load, without significant modification to the software. Scalable does not necessarily mean 'high performance,' despite a common belief that this is the case. EJB applications support scalability because they lend themselves to distribution; they support high performance because they allow the sharing of resources and minimize overheads, as we shall see.

"...transactional..." Where business applications are datacentric, the integrity of the data is of paramount importance. This means that access to the databases, and often to other resources, will be transactional—that is, consist of operations that must succeed or fail as a group. We will have much more to say about this issue in Chapter 9, as transaction management is a key feature of the EJB infrastructure, particularly in a distributed environment [EJB2.0 19.6].

"...multi-user secure..." Business applications will need to be able to identify their users, and allow access to the data only to defined users. Information about which users are allowed which operations is often not part of the application, but stored in some sort of user database (e.g., an LDAP directory server). Security is an integrated part of the EJB framework, as described in Chapter 16.

"...written once, and deployed on any server..." With care, EJB applications can be made quite portable (but see below). The use of the Java language ensures portability not merely at the source-code level, but at the binary level. This makes it appealing for vendors to author EJB components that are general-purpose and can be integrated into other applications. A requirement to distribute source code would discourage this. Provided that the EJB author is careful to follow the Specification, the interaction between the EJB and its container should not depend on the container vendor. The EJB architecture is designed to support the use and integration of components from different vendors, by such means as using a standard (XML-based) configuration scheme for components.

In summary, EJBs are Java™ software components that run in a framework that supports distribution, load sharing, fault tolerance, security, and transaction management. To their clients they 'look like' ordinary Java objects, and can be used similarly.

In a more pragmatic sense, EJBs are components built from Java program classes and interfaces. In particular, each EJB has at least one class, which provides the application functionality, and, where direct interaction by clients is allowed, two or four interfaces, which specify which methods are to be exposed to clients. These Java elements are packaged into a standard Java JAR file along with a *deployment descriptor*, an XML file that provides configuration information to the server. Each JAR file can contain one or more EJBs. In practice, we tend to use graphical tools for building the JAR and XML files.

1.2   EJBs in the enterprise

EJBs, for all their power and flexibility, are most useful in conjunction with other components of an enterprise application. The J2EE model of enterprise application development—which is described in more detail below—sees EJBs as implementing the bulk of the application's business logic and data management. In this model (Figure 1.1), EJBs occupy an architectural 'tier' between the enterprise data sources (relational databases, directory servers) and the presentation elements (clients using Java, servlets, etc). Centralizing the application's business logic in EJBs allows a variety of different clients (including clients via CORBA protocols) to make use of that logic and decouples the application from the specific representation of its data in the enterprise data sources.

The rest of this section describes in more detail some of the J2EE™ and non-J2EE technologies with which EJBs are likely to interact. These interactions are summarized in Figure 1.2. Some of these technologies are sufficiently important that they have their own chapters in this book.

1.2.1   J2EE technologies

Java 2 enterprise edition (J2EE) is not a technology in its own right; it is an umbrella specification that dictates how a number of other Java technologies are to intraoperate. Not all of these are relevant to EJB developers, but those that are (particularly JNDI™ and JDBC™) are described in detail in this book. Others (JSP and servlets, for example) will be described briefly. For completeness, this section describes in outline all the technologies that are part of the J2EE group. It also describes some important non-Java technologies.

JavaIDL

JavaIDL is a Java implementation of the CORBA interface description language (IDL). IDL is a language for specifying the methods of an object and their properties that is independent of the programming language. JavaIDL is a set of classes, which maps IDL data onto Java stubs that support the IIOP protocol.[1] On the whole, EJB developers don't need to be too concerned with JavaIDL, except where EJBs need to make explicit calls on CORBA ORBs. In most cases, the intricacies of JavaIDL are encapsulated—where necessary—in code generated by the EJB server vendor's tools.

JAF

JavaBeans activation framework (JAF) is a specification for mapping content handlers to arbitrary data types (typically MIME types). JAF gets only a brief (one-line) mention in the *J2EE Specification*; it is included because the JavaMail API has a dependency on it. EJB development is not likely to involve direct use of JAF.

---

[1]IIOP is described in detail in Chapter 2.

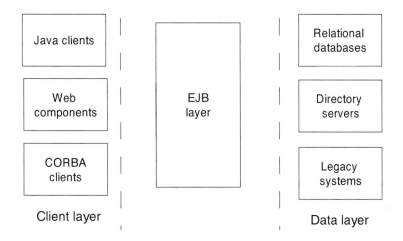

Figure 1.1. A simplified view of the J2EE application model; EJBs are central to this model, implementing the business logic and data management.

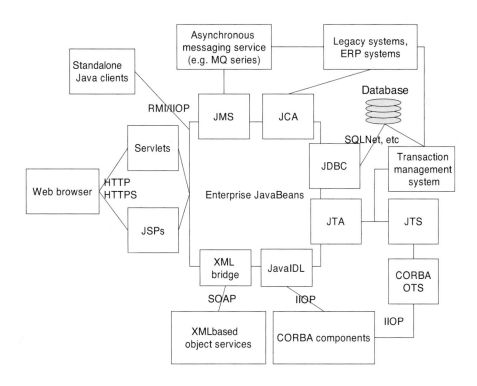

Figure 1.2. EJBs in relation to other enterprise application technologies.

JCA

The J2EE Connector Architecture (JCA) is a relatively new addition to the J2EE standards. It defines a specification by which application servers can allow the components they host to get access to external resources, particularly legacy systems. The term 'connector' is used to describe any piece of software that allows this. At present, the major commercial EJB products all have their own proprietary ways of implementing connectors and often provide a range of connectors for popular data management systems, like IBM's *CICS* or SAP *R/3*. The problem is that not only are the connectors themselves proprietary and nonportable, the EJB code that makes use of them will only work with that vendor's connectors.

The JCA is an attempt to standardize the provision of connectors. A JCA-compliant product is portable across application servers and provides a uniform method of access for EJBs; thus the EJB code is also portable.

Providing a connector architecture is not straightforward. The systems that are connected may well have transactional semantics and need to be integrated with the transaction management system of the EJB container. In addition, it may be necessary to propagate the security context of the EJBs' caller into the connector. The JCA takes care of these issues and others.

At the time of writing, few commercial products are available that support JCA. The *J2EE Reference Implementation*, however, provides an implementation of it that can be used to experiment with the technology. JCA is described in more detail in Chapter 18.

> Gotcha!
>
> The abbrevation 'JCA' is also used to denote the 'Java Cryptography API,' but in this book, 'JCA' will never be used in this sense, so there should be no confusion.

JDBC

JDBC is a specification and API for providing Java program classes with access to relational databases in a vendor-neutral manner. We will have much more to say about this later (mainly in Chapter 8, but it is discussed extensively in other chapters as well).

JNDI

Java Naming and Directory Interface (JNDI) was originally intended to fulfil the same role with respect to directory servers that JDBC does for database servers. That is, it is a specification and API that allows Java code to query and update a directory server. JNDI is still widely used for this, especially with LDAP directory servers (see page 178), but it has an additional role in the J2EE architecture. Here the JNDI API is used to retrieve classes that provide access to resources. These resources may be EJBs, database connections, simple data elements, mail servers, and many others. While information about the resource may be stored in a directory server, it may equally not be. The use of JNDI for this purpose is to avoid introducing a new API just for looking up resources. JNDI is extremely important to EJB development, and the whole of Chapter 7 is devoted to it.

JSP

Java Server Pages™ (JSP) are HTML or XML documents with embedded programmatic content. They are increasingly used for providing a Web-based user interface to EJB and database applications. In practice, JSPs are translated into servlets (see below), and have more-or-less the same properties and capabilities. JSP is an alternative technology to Microsoft's *Active Server Pages* (ASP) and to other server-side Web scripting technologies like PHP.

JTA

Java Transaction API (JTA) is a set of related APIs for Java components to communicate with the various components of a transactional system. In particular, there are APIs for use by application components, transaction managers, and resource managers. An EJB product is required to support the JTA APIs [EJB2.0 17.1.3] to the extent required to allow EJBs to demarcate transaction boundaries. The product can support the other APIs as well, and it would certainly improve interoperability to do so, but at the time of writing, many commercial products do not provide such support. The implication is that if an EJB product is to take part in a distributed database transaction, it must use database drivers provided by the vendor of the EJB product, not the database. This issue, along with others relating to the use of JTA, is discussed in detail on page 287.

JTS

Many developers misunderstand the role of the Java Transaction Service (JTS), and its relationship to JTA. In fact, JTS is *not* part of the *J2EE Specification* (at least in Version 1.3), and EJB products are not required to support it [EJB2.0 17.1.3]. So what is it, and why is it important? The CORBA Object Transaction Service (OTS) Specification defines how transaction context can be propagated between distributed objects. This allows objects on different hosts to take part in the same distributed transaction. This is also a goal of EJB technology: If one EJB calls a method on another and the caller is part of a database transaction, then it should be possible for database work done by the called method to be encapsulated into the same transaction as the caller.

JTS specifies the interface between JTA (the transaction management methods that applications will use) and the low-level CORBA OTS. A JTS-compliant EJB product should allow EJBs to intraoperate seamlessly with CORBA components, at least in so far as transaction management is concerned. Although JTS is a specification, Sun Microsystems provides a full implementation of that specification; when developers talk of 'using JTS,' they often mean 'using Sun's implementation of JTS.'

As CORBA integration becomes increasingly important in EJB technology, JTS may become more widespread. At present, most commercial products use proprietary techniques for propagating transaction context between EJBs.

JMS

Java Messaging Service (JMS) is a Java interface to asynchronous messaging products like IBM's *MQ Series*. JMS is becoming very important, as it provides an elegant way for EJB products to integrate with legacy systems. Version 1.3 of the *J2EE Specification* and Version 2.0 of the *EJB Specification* both add increased support requirements for JMS, and a compliant application server must provide not only an interface to a messaging service, but the actual infrastructure of a messaging service as well. The JMS architecture and its integration with EJBs, is discussed in detail in Chapter 10.

JavaMail

JavaMail is a specification for Java components to send and receive email messages in a vendor-neutral way. Although it is a specification and not an implementation, in practice most developers who are using it are actually using Sun's implementation, which provides support for SMTP, IMAP, and POP3 mail protocols. EJBs can use JavaMail to send email messages, as described on page 584.

Servlets

Servlets are Java program classes that extend the functionality of a Web server. When a Web browser makes a request that corresponds to a servlet, the Web server calls the class's `service()` method. This method must generate content (usually HTML or XML) to be conveyed back to the browser. Servlets and JSPs are widely used to provide a Web interface to an EJB application; this technique is discussed in detail in Chapter 17.

1.2.2 Related technologies

CORBA

Common Object Request Broker Architecture (CORBA) is a set of standards for allowing objects to interact in a distributed environment. In a sense, this is what EJB technology aims to do, and it is often thought that EJB and CORBA are competing technologies. There is indeed an overlap between what EJB servers do and what object request brokers do. The EJB developers have neatly sidestepped this issue by integrating some of the CORBA specifications into EJB. In particular, the IIOP protocol, which CORBA uses for communicating method-call information over a network, must now be supported by compliant EJB products. There is, of course, more to CORBA than remote method calls; Sun's developers have been

very busy integrating other CORBA services into the Java environment. This is
particularly evident in the development of JTS. The details of CORBA are beyond
the scope of this book, although we will discuss those aspects that overlap with
EJB technology (page 37).

The CORBA and IIOP specifications are defined and maintained by the Object
Management Group (OMG), a large consortium of vendors and other interested
parties. The size of the OMG means that its standards have very broad support,
but it can take a long time to adapt to changes in technology. One vendor that is
notably absent from the OMG is Microsoft, which has its own proprietary techniques
for distributed computing, such as DCOM (see below). The relationship between
EJB and CORBA is set out in detail in [EJB2.0 19.5].

DCOM, COM+, .NET

Microsoft's Distributed Component Object Model (DCOM) and its successor
COM+ are proprietary distributed object technologies from Microsoft. They are
central components of Microsoft's integrated enterprise application framework called
'.NET,' which includes a distributed transaction infrastructure, messaging services,
Web components (based on ASP), and a database server.

While there are undoubtedly advantages to building a system from a set of
products by a single vendor (there should be minimal problems with interoperability,
for example), there are disturbing disadvantages as well. The most obvious of these
is the difficulty of integrating products from other vendors. Another problem is
Microsoft's continued unwillingness to produce versions of their products that run
on Unix platforms; the majority of enterprise applications are deployed on Unix-
based systems, even if something else is used for development.

Although Sun has not escaped criticism for its attempts to maintain control of
the Java and J2EE standards, these standards are fully publicized and anyone can
sell products that support them. The problem with Microsoft's offering is that the
same company controls both the products and the specifications. Being in a position
to do this puts a vendor at a huge advantage. Consider, for example, the task of
producing integrated development environments (IDEs) to support the production
of enterprise systems. It should be fairly clear that producing such tools is much
simpler if everything the tools will work on is a product from the same vendor.
If it proves to be impossible to achieve what is desired by users of the tools, no
problem: We can change the underlying technology. This is simply not an option
with a standards-based platform. Spare a thought for those brave souls who develop
integrated development tools for J2EE: The tools must be able to generate and
maintain code that complies with about 20 different open standards, all of which
are developing rapidly under the pressure of about 100 major vendors. This is why
it remains true that integrated tool support for J2EE is underdeveloped.

Use of Microsoft's distributed component technology does not preclude integration with EJBs. Part of Sun's J2EE support is a set of products that enable non-
Java software to be clients of EJBs. These products, known collectively as client
access services (CAS), currently support Microsoft COM and ActiveX clients (see
`developer.java.sun/developer/earlyAccess/j2eecas`). Essentially these prod-

ucts use IIOP bridging technology, in which COM interactions are translated into IIOP interactions.

XML

Extensible markup language (XML) is probably the most widely hyped, least understood of all the current enterprise technologies. In fact, XML is extremely simple; the cleverness is in the use which is made of it.

XML is a general-purpose language for describing data. Superficially an XML document resembles HTML, in that sections are demarcated using tags. What goes in and between these tags is entirely at the discretion of the developer, provided that basic syntactic integrity is maintained. This allows the format to be adapted to suit a large number of applications. In addition, the structure and content of the tags can be described formally in a document type definition (DTD), which allows the receiver of an XML document to ensure that the document is structured in a way that can be interpreted.[2]

XML owes its success to a number of factors:

- It enjoys wide industry support. Among other things, this means that XML parsers and document assemblers are widely available.

- It is a completely open standard.

- The basic structure of an XML document can be checked against its DTD. This is particularly important in business-to-business applications, where the sender and receiver of a document may be very different kinds of business and may not work closely together.

Organizations involved in business-to-business (B2B) e-commerce are particularly excited about XML. To see why, consider that at present the majority of B2B transactions are carried out using proprietary EDI (electronic data interchange) services. These services are run by a small number of specialist providers, and are funded by subscription. In addition, many transactions are not carried on the Internet, but on private EDI networks, also maintained by specialist providers. The use of these services can be extremely expensive. In addition, the data formats used in EDI are often proprietary, and subscribers can easily by locked into a particular provider. With this background, it's easy to see why XML, which is open, flexible, and can readily be carried on a public network (with suitable encryption), is taking the B2B world by storm.

Although XML as a standard is well-supported, this does not necessarily mean that two XML-enabled applications can exchange data; this is one of the most widespread misconceptions about XML. To exchange data, the applications must at a minimum agree on a common DTD. As the use of XML has increased, large numbers of 'standard DTDs' have been defined by various industries. There are, for example, standard DTDs for data as diverse as livestock trades, *curricula vitae*, and

---

[2]The *XML Specifications* use the term 'XML schema' rather than 'DTD'; I have 'DTD' in the text as it remains the more commonly used by developers at present.

interactive teaching materials. Having agreed on the DTDs, the collaborating organizations must agree on a protocol by which the XML documents will be encoded and transmitted.

So what does all this have to do with EJBs? The answer at present, sadly, is 'not much.' The *EJB Specification* only stipulates the use of XML for deployment descriptors (files that specify configuration data to the server). There's nothing to stop the developer coding EJBs that use XML for data interchange, but there is no built-in support for this. In particular, there is widespread interest in using XML to carry objects in EJB method calls (techniques for doing this are discussed on page 42) but EJB products aren't required to provide any support; it's up to the developer to implement it.

1.3   Why use EJBs?

It is possible to write applications that support distribution, transaction management, and security without using EJBs. There are many such applications in use already. So what advantages do EJBs have to offer over other techniques?

- The EJB developer works within the EJB framework to take advantage of its built-in support for features like transaction management and security; once understood, little developer effort is required to make effective use of these features. With suitable servers, EJB applications can even make use of features as sophisticated as distributed transaction management with *no coding whatsoever*.

- EJB 2.0 introduces a very powerful persistence management scheme, which supports not only persistent data, but persistent relationships between objects. It takes a while to get used to, but once mastered, this revolutionizes the development of persistent application objects. Again, very little coding is required to implement such objects.

- The EJB framework presents the EJB with a managed operating environment. For example, the framework ensures that an EJB instance is never executing in more than one concurrent thread,[3] so the developer does not have to be concerned about the effects of concurrency on data integrity. The container is also responsible for memory and resource management, so EJB developers don't have to be concerned with these issues.

- EJBs can make use of the full range of Java APIs and class libraries. It is relatively straightforward to code an EJB that parses XML, sends email, and communicates with directory and database servers via standard APIs like JDBC and JNDI.

- EJBs isolate database implementation from the application's business logic. If we use entity EJBs, for example, as models of the underlying data, then the

---

[3]It's a bit more complex than that, because we can use transaction locking to allow concurrent access with compromising integrity. See page 476.

use of that data is decoupled from its internal representation. This leads to increased ease of maintenance and portability of code. We can also use EJBs as interfaces to legacy systems, with similar advantages.

- EJBs are very accessible to Web components such as servlets and JSPs. There are a number of products available that support these components in the same application framework (typically called *application servers*). This makes it straightforward to provide EJB applications with a Web-based user interface and, perhaps, provide Internet access to the application.

1.4 The EJB philosophy

The *EJB Specification* is based on a small number of fundamental principles, an appreciation of which will help the developer to understand why the Specification has the form that it does.

EJB applications are loosely coupled This is discussed at [EJB2.0 5.4]. The *EJB Specification* was designed from the outset to support the integration of components from different vendors. For example, EJBs refer to other components and services to which they have access by arbitrary names. These names can be mapped onto real names without modifying program code. This allows EJBs to be authored without detailed knowledge of the environment in which they will be used or of the other components with which they will interact. In traditional software engineering, this principle is called 'loose coupling.' A loosely coupled system is easier to test and maintain, and its components are easier to reuse.

The Specification distinguishes carefully between the role of the 'component provider' and the 'application assembler,' even though in practice these may be the same person or people. As we shall see, an 'application assembler' is someone who builds an application from separate EJBs, perhaps from different sources. The assembler's roles include resolving naming conflicts between the different components and ensuring that transactions are propagated between components correctly. These factors are largely controlled declaratively—in XML files—not in Java code, allowing applications to be assembled without code changes.

EJB behaviour is specified by interfaces The clients of EJBs do not, in principle, need access to the EJB implementation code itself, either at compile time or runtime. An EJB's interaction with its clients is specified *entirely* in terms of Java interfaces. These interfaces expose the methods that clients can call, and thereby set out a 'contract' between the client and the EJB. Developers who work with systems that do not enforce this strict separation between 'interface' and 'implementation' sometimes find the use of interfaces a burden in EJB development; nevertheless, it increases portability and modularity, and makes it easier to support integration with non-Java components (in which interfaces may be specified using IDL, for example).

EJB applications do not manage resources As far as possible, EJBs get access to external resources (databases, legacy systems) through their container. It is the container's job to manage these resources and make the access as efficient as possible. In most cases, the container will implement resource-sharing and pooling schemes to support this. The programmer does not have to worry about resource allocation and deallocation. The EJB container itself cannot be configured or managed through API calls. It is the administrator's responsibility to configure resource sharing policies, not the developer's.

The container supports the application developer This is particularly important where persistence management and transaction co-ordination is required. When Version 1.1 of the *EJB Specification* was current, developers were loathe to use container-managed persistence (CMP). In Version 2.0, the CMP strategy has been radically revised. It is now possible to define container-managed relationships between objects as well as container-managed persistent data. These features are straightfoward to use when fully understood and significantly ease the development process. However, for these advantages to be fully realized, the developer must 'buy in' wholeheatedly and develop in the spirit of the EJB model.

EJB applications are tiered Although it is sometimes necessary to divert from this goal for reasons of efficiency, EJB applications are easiest to manage if a strict tiered architecture is followed. The fact that there were two types of EJB in Version 1.1 of the *EJB Specification* made it quite natural to adopt a two-tiered model: the client-facing tier based on session EJBs, with entity EJBs deployed between the session tier and the back-end data sources. Don't worry if the terms 'session EJB' and 'entity EJB' are not clear at the moment: We will have much more to say about these, and the tiered model in general, in Section 15.1.1.

The session tier is the API to the application Ideally, the entire business logic of the application should be encapsulated within its EJBs and exposed via the outermost tier. In most applications, this tier will consist of session EJBs, message-driven EJBs, or both. Thus, the session tier can be seen as the 'API to the application.' This interpretation favours the view that the application consists of services that are exposed through the outermost tier of EJBs. Clients that wish to get access to the services can do so, supplying input and rendering output as they see fit. If this logic is followed to its conclusion, then it becomes a very straightforward matter to provide a range of different types of client for the same application. It also tends to decouple some of the internal business logic from the needs of the client, particularly that related to access to the back-end services.

Not all Web-based applications will benefit from being developed using EJBs. However, there is a tendency for developers of Web applications to have business logic in servlets, even when they are using EJBs. This reduces the effectiveness of the tier model and couples the servlet tier to the data model, leading to reduced ease of maintenance.

The entity tier is the API to the data sources If the session tier is the 'API to the application,' then the entity EJB tier is an 'API to the database.' What this means is that the entity tier hides the back-end datasources behind an object-oriented (or at least component-oriented) facade. This tier therefore exposes back-end functionality via the methods of its EJBs. There should therefore be little or no business logic in this tier. If this is taken to its logical conclusion, the application's business logic in the session tier is completely decoupled from the data representation. Again, this increases ease of maintenance.

There are sometimes good reasons for not following this architectural blueprint strictly, usually related to performance. Of course, imposing a new layer of abstraction in a system *always* leads to some performance penalty, however small. In earlier versions of the *EJB Specification*, and products that implemented it, it was probably fair to say that the performance penalties were more severe than they should have been. For example, using entity EJBs strictly to iterate a large database table could be breathtakingly slow. Recent changes to the *Specification* allow the purity of the tiered architecture to be upheld with relatively little degradation in performance, if the developer is careful.

1.5   EJB roles

An interesting feature of the *EJB Specification* is that its requirements are largely divided into different 'roles.' When reading the Specification, it is therefore quite clear to whom the various requirements correspond.

Component provider The component provider [EJB2.0 25.1] is a software developer who authors EJBs. These EJBs may be destined for a particular application, or they may be general-purpose or part of a software library. The EJB author may not know the names of the EJBs with which it is to interact although, of course, their method specifications must be known. Similarly, the EJB author may not know the names of external resources like databases. The Specification indicates how the component provider uses the XML deployment descriptor to indicate that these EJBs and resources are required, and the names by which it has referenced them.

Application assembler The application assembler [EJB2.0 25.2] is someone who builds an application out of component EJBs. The same person or people may be operating in this role as are fulfilling the component provider role, but the Specification is quite clear that the two are distinct jobs. The application assembler resolves references between EJBs, unifies the references to external resources, and packages the components into a single file ready for deployment. It is slightly confusing for the newcomer to EJB development that most of the graphical tools used for building EJB applications don't distinguish between what they are doing in the provider role versus in the assembler role. It often appears that the developer is supplying redundant information or information that is duplicated; this is because the deployment descriptor being built does support the notion of a separate provider and assembler, even if they are in practice the same person.

Deployer The deployer [EJB2.0 25.3] takes a file from the application assembler that contains the EJBs and other components required for the application and installs it on the server, making appropriate customizations for the site. These customizations include replacing database references with real database information, mapping the security roles in the application onto real users and groups in the organization, and supplying values for other configuration parameters.

Server vendor The server vendor supplies EJB server products. An EJB developer should not assume that the sections in the *EJB Specification* that deal with the responsibilities of the server vendor are not of interest. On the contrary: The server sets the operating environment of the EJB, and this section of the *EJB Specification* gives the developer an insight into what environment the EJB can expect.

Administrator An administrator [EJB2.0 25.4] is a person responsible for the maintenance and performance tuning of an application.

Tool provider A tool provider authors EJB packaging and deployment tools.

1.6   EJB products

To construct EJB applications, you will need an EJB server, or something that includes an EJB server. This section discusses the features you can expect an EJB server to have—in addition to support for the *EJB Specification*, of course—and lists some products that are currently available.

1.6.1   Features of EJB products

The EJB architecture was developed to support large, critical (high reliability), distributed applications. It is the responsibility of the EJB server vendor to provide a product that allows this goal to be met. The *EJB Specification* has little to say about the ways in which it will do this. In practice, containers normally use some or all of the following strategies.

Load sharing

In many large systems, a single server—however powerful—will not be able to support the total load of the application. In any case, one large system is less effective than two smaller ones at handling failures. In practice, therefore, all commercial EJB products are able to distribute load between servers.

Gotcha!

Strictly speaking, to claim J2EE compliance for a product, a vendor must be able to produce the results of standard J2EE compliance tests. Not all vendors do so, but this does not necessarily mean the product is noncompliant or inadequate. Moreover, even demonstrable compliance says little about the product's support for load balancing, fault tolerance, or other features likely to be important in an enterprise application. What is worse, some of the compatibility tests are not very demanding and are easy to pass. This allows some vendors to claim compliance and yet have a product that is weak in certain areas. In short, don't assume that all EJB products that carry the stamp 'J2EE compliant' are equivalent. Determine the features that are important to your projects, and ask vendors what support is provided for each feature.

As a client's first access to an EJB service is via a name-service lookup, coarse-grained load sharing can be implemented at the point in which the EJB's factory object is looked up (more about factory objects later). Each successive request for the same EJB factory can be directed to a different server, with the EJB itself distributed on all the servers. This process can be governed by the name lookup service (on the server), or by the client. In the latter case, typically the work will be done in a proxy on the client, so that the developer does not have to code the client differently.

Such a strategy is straightforward to implement and can work reasonably well where the number of clients is large and the load imposed by each client relatively small. With a small number of demanding clients, load can easily get out of balance, as there is no opportunity for rebalancing once the factory object has been located.

Alternatively, we can balance at the method call level, if EJBs are pooled or the instance variables of unpooled EJBs can be synchronized across servers. This allows more rapid adaptation to changes in load, but is complex to implement.

In practice, load sharing is much more complicated than it first appears. The reason is that some EJB components—notably stateful session EJBs—have state that is meaningful to a client. This means that requests from the client cannot be distributed arbitrarily. Instead, they must either be bound to the server on which that client's state is stored, or we must provide a method for synchronizing the state across servers. This issue will be discussed in more detail later, when we look at failover strategies.

Needless to say, the method of load balancing will depend on the server vendor but, if you follow the rules set out in the *EJB Specification* and the guidance given in this book, this should not present a problem.

Resource pooling

The most common form of resource pooling is database connection pooling, which is supported by all commercial EJB products. This topic is discussed in detail in Chapter 8. The purpose of resource pooling is to allow large numbers of Java objects to have access to a small number of instances of a shared resource. In the case of database connections, these are computationally expensive to open and resource-hungry to maintain. A connection pooling scheme allows the mapping of a large number of 'virtual' connections onto a much smaller number of real connections to the database. The J2EE scheme defines a method for access to shared resources that abstracts away from the underlying resource management system. This means that, to a large extent, the Java code required to interact with the resource is the same as it would be without the application server. However, resource pooling schemes work best if the code does not hinder their operation, so an understanding of their operation is advantageous.

Failover and redundancy

In critical applications, we need to be sure that if a single server fails, the application itself can continue to operate, albeit at reduced performance. Any load sharing system will allow a degree of fault tolerance; it is the ability to handle a failure *with no loss of service* that distinguishes such a scheme from true 'failover.' In order to achieve a failover with no loss of service, clients must continue to be able to interact with the EJB application without interruption. This is straightforward for EJBs that have no client state, but where state is involved there is more to it. We have already seen that we could avoid the problem of state in load sharing simply by binding incoming client requests to the server that is carrying the client's state. For failover, this simply won't do: We must find a way to synchronize the state.

The problem is that, unlike servlets (page 549), EJBs do not keep their state in nice, neat packets. The state of an EJB is in its instance variables, and the instance variables of its instance variables, and so on. Synchronizing these efficiently is a far from straightforward job. Happily, it's a job for the server vendor, not for the application developer.

A number of EJB products are now able to offer failover support for stateful session beans. Typically, the EJB instance that is most up-to-date has to be serialized, and the serialized version recreated on each participating server. For maximum reliability, this needs to happen after every method call that changes an instance variable. Clearly, this could be very inefficient if used carelessly.

1.6.2   Integration

Many enterprise-scale EJB products also offer impressive support for other distributed component technologies, notably CORBA. In addition, an EJB product is likely to be a part of a larger application server that includes some or all of the following:

- support for other J2EE components, such as servlets and JSPs;

- a distributed transaction manager;

- a relational database;

- a directory server;

- a messaging service.

In addition, many products provide vendor-specific extensions that allow EJBs to integrate with popular back-end systems like SAP *R/3*. The problem with vendor-specific extensions is, of course, that the EJBs that use them are not portable across servers. JCA is starting to alleviate this problem, by providing a cross-platform technique for interfacing with arbitrary data sources.

1.6.3   Platform support

If an EJB server is written entirely in Java (a few are), then it may be possible to produce a truly platform-independent product. In reality, this is unusual. Most products either include native machine code components or communicate with other services that are themselves platform-specific. In practice, vendors typically support a small number of platforms, often limited to Sun Solaris on Sparc platforms, and Microsoft Windows NT on Intel-based PCs. Only a few vendors (notably IBM) support an impressively large range of platforms. At the time of writing, support for Microsoft Windows 2000 and Linux, for example, was scant.

1.6.4   Vendors and products

There are a number of products on the market that support EJB applications, as well as a number of open source EJB servers. However, there are relatively few dedicated EJB servers commercially available. Normally, one has to buy a product that supports EJBs as part of a wider set of functionality. Commercial products that support EJBs tend to fall into two groups.

- Database engines with EJB support. Many vendors with strong reputations in the relational database field are producing EJB products that integrate with their databases. Typical examples are Oracle's *8i* and *9i* and, to a certain extent, IBM's *WebSphere*.

- Well-established application servers whose vendors have embraced the J2EE model and adapted their products to support EJB. Examples include the *SunONE Application Server*[4] from Sun Microsystems, and products from Pramati and Gemstone.

Another group, which is currently small but likely to expand, is products from vendors of development tools and IDEs (e.g., Borland's *Inprise*).

---

[4]Formerly *iPlanet Application Server*.

Knowing a product's background gives some clue to the areas in which it is likely to excel. For example, a product from a database vendor should be able to offer a high degree of optimization of database performance. A product from an IDE vendor should offer ease of development. Of course, all products, regardless of heritage, should support the functionality required by the *EJB Specification*.

Table 1.1 lists some of the products available that include support for EJB 1.1 or later. This list was probably not exhaustive at the time it was written, and it certainly won't be exhaustive by the time you read it.

When considering the price of an EJB product, bear in mind that a product that supports the full range of J2EE services (servlets, JSP, etc.) is almost certainly going to be more expensive that a dedicated EJB server. If it includes a database and a distributed transaction manager as well, then it is likely to be very expensive indeed.

1.7   Summary

EJBs are Java software components that run in a framework that supports distribution, load sharing, fault tolerance, security, and transaction management. The developer works within this framework to make the use of these features relatively straightforward. EJBs can use Java APIs like JDBC and JNDI to interact with external resources and can interoperate with other distributed object architectures, such as CORBA. The EJB framework is designed to support the notion of building an application with components from different vendors. The specification distinguishes between the 'component provider' and the 'application assembler,' even though these may, in practice, be the same person or group of people.

Effective use of EJBs requires that EJB server products be widely available. At the time of writing, there are a large number of vendors with products that support EJB 1.1, and a small—but growing—number that support EJB 2.0.

Vendor	Product	Contact URL	Evaluation support	Notes
Allaire Corp.	JRUN	www.allaire.com/products/jrun	Free developer version	All java
IONA	iPortal	www.iona.com/products/ip/ip-ipas_home.html	Free 30-day	
Evidian	JOnAS	www.objectweb.com	Open Source	
Gemstone Systems, Inc.	Gemstone/J	www.gemstone.com/products/j	Free 30-day	
Borland, Inc.	Inprise	www.inprise.com/appserver	Free trial version	Supports the connector API
Persistence Software, Inc.	Power Tier	www.persistence.com/powertier	Free 30-day	
Pramati Software, Inc.	Pramati AS	www.pramati.com	Free 30-day	
Sybase, Inc.	EA Server	www.sybase.com/product/easerver	Free 60-day	
BEA, Inc.	WebLogic	www.weblogic.com	Free 30-day	World's bestseller; EJB2.0 support
Sub/AOL	iPlanet application server	www.iplanet.com	Trial versions on request	
(open source)	jBoss	www.jboss.com	Open source	Very popular open source EJB server
Unify Corp.	eWave	www.ewavecommerce.com	Free single-user	
Oracle Corp.	Oracle 8i/9i	www.oracle.com	Trial versions for some platforms	Very wide platform support
IBM Corp.	WebSphere	www-4.ibm.com/software/webservers/appserv	Free 60-day	Very wide platform support

Table 1.1. Some products that support EJB technology.

Chapter 2

Distributed objects and RMI

Overview

This chapter describes the principles that underlie distributed programming in Java and form the technological foundation for the EJB architecture. We begin by describing the process of Remote Method Invocation (RMI) and how we could, if we wished, develop an RMI framework from the ground up. This will be illustrated using outline source code for such a system. This discussion will highlight some of the challenges that face the developer of an RMI framework, and how these have been tackled in the standard Java RMI scheme (and, indirectly, in the EJB architecture). Again, we will use source code examples to demonstrate how these things work in practice. Finally, we will discuss the overlap between Java RMI and EJB RMI, with particular emphasis on protocols (like IIOP) that allow interoperability between these systems and others.

2.1 What are distributed objects?

In its most general sense, the term 'distributed objects' refers to an object-oriented architecture in which collaborating objects are located on different computers. Data and instructions are exchanged over a network. The computers may be in the same room or on different continents (Figure 2.1). In EJB 2.0, EJBs do not have to be capable of distribution (for efficiency reasons), but it is envisaged that most EJBs will support distribution to allow the server to provide load balancing and fault tolerance. Therefore, we assume in this chapter that EJBs are to be treated as distributable. In addition, this chapter assumes that if there is a distinction between 'objects' and 'components,' it is not important as far as distribution technique is concerned.

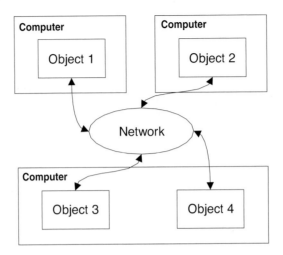

Figure 2.1. The principle of distributed objects: objects on different computers exchange data and instructions over a network.

This chapter is concerned primarily with synchronous forms of distributed object interaction. Asynchronous techniques are discussed in Chapter 10.

2.2   How objects can communicate

Distributed objects can communicate in whatever method is most convenient for the developers and suits the needs of the application. The developer may implement a custom client-server protocol to be carried over TCP/IP or use one of the many pre-existing techniques. A common strategy is to use one of the general-purpose schemes that allow one object to call methods in another object. These schemes are called by the generic term 'remote method invocation' (RMI), but this term is also used by Java programmers to mean a *specific* scheme and protocol, as will be described. The basic principle of RMI is shown in Figure 2.2.

EJBs are distributed components and can call methods on one another over a network. In order to understand the system of RMI used by EJBs, we will begin by seeing how a simple RMI system can be implemented from scratch in a few lines of Java. Although simple, this implementation will bring out the issues that RMI designers have to deal with and give a better understanding of why the EJB RMI scheme takes the form that it does.

2.2.1   A socket-based remote object server

A *very* simple technique for allowing one object to call a single method on another, passing a single `String` parameter and accepting a `String` return value, is shown in Listings 2.1 (server) and 2.2 (client).

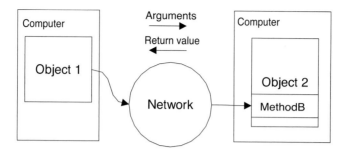

Figure 2.2. The principle of RMI: Objects call methods on other objects, with parameters and return values being passed over a network.

Listing 2.1: SocketsTestServer.java.

```
     package com.kevinboone.ejb_book.sockets;
     import java.net.*;
     import java.io.*;

 5   /**
     This is the server class for the Sockets example.
     (c)2002 Kevin Boone
     */
     public class SocketsTestServer
10   {
     /**
     The method 'test' is the only method that the client
     can call in this simple example. It takes one String
     parameter and returns a String result.
15   */
     public String test (String s)
       {
       System.out.println ("Called method 'test()'");
       System.out.println ("String parameter is: " + s);
20     return "Hello from remote";
       }


     /**
     The main method
25   */
     public static void main(String[] args)
       {
       // Create an instance of this class, on which to
       //   call methods as instructed by the client
30     SocketsTestServer socketsTestServer =
         new SocketsTestServer ();

       try
         {
35       ServerSocket s = new ServerSocket(1098);
         // Listen for client requests in an endless loop
         while (true)
           {
```

```
40            try
              {
              System.out.println ("Waiting for client call");
              // Listen for client connection
              Socket s2 = s.accept();
              System.out.println ("Client connected: "
45                + s.getInetAddress());
              // Get a buffered reader from the client socket s2
              BufferedReader bis = new BufferedReader
                (new InputStreamReader(s2.getInputStream()));
              // Read a string from the client
50            String line = bis.readLine();
              System.out.println ("Data from client: " + line);
              // Call the method 'test()' on this class
              String response = socketsTestServer.test(line);
              // Give the response back to the client
55            s2.getOutputStream().write (response.getBytes());
              s2.close();
              }
            catch (Exception e)
              {
60            System.err.println
                ("Caught exception: " + e);
              e.printStackTrace(System.err);
              }
            }
65      }
      catch (IOException e)
        {
        System.err.println
          ("Caught IO exception while initializing server socket: "
70        + e);
        e.printStackTrace(System.err);
        }
      }
}
```

Listing 2.2: SocketsTestClient.java.

```
package com.kevinboone.ejb_book.sockets;
import java.net.*;
import java.io.*;

5   /**
    This is the test client for the SocketsTestServer class.
    (c)2002 Kevin Boone
    */
    public class SocketsTestClient
10  {
    /**
    The 'main' method calls the method 'test' in the remote
    object. It does this by creating a socket connection
    and passing a parameter that will be picked up by the
```

```
15  server for the remote object
    */
    public static void main (String [] args)
      {
      try
20      {
        System.out.println
          ("Creating socket connection to remote");
        Socket s = new Socket ("localhost", 1098);
        System.out.println
25        ("Sending parameter to remote's 'test' method");
        s.getOutputStream ().write ("Hello\n".getBytes ());
        // Get a buffered reader from the socket
        BufferedReader bis = new BufferedReader
              (new InputStreamReader (s.getInputStream ()));
30      // Read a string from the server
        System.out.println
          ("Reading reponse from remote");
        String line = bis.readLine ();
        System.out.println ("Response from remote: " + line);
35      }
      catch (Exception e)
        {
        System.err.println ("Caught exception: " + e);
        e.printStackTrace (System.err);
40      }
      }

    }
```

Hint

Full source code for this example may be found in the accompanying source package, in the directory `sockets`.

The 'remote' class has one method, `test()`, which simply prints its argument and returns a `String` result. The class also has a `main()` method, which implements a simple socket-based server. The server listens on port 1098 (in this case). When a client opens a connection to the server on this port, the server reads one line of data from the client and passes this to the `test()` method. The return value from `test()` is written back to the client, and the client is then disconnected (by closing its socket).

The 'client' class opens a socket connection to the server and passes the `String` argument to the server class over the network.

This output from the server is shown in Listing 2.3, and the client in Listing 2.4.

Listing 2.3: **Output from the 'remote object server' class** SocketTestServer.

```
     Waiting for client call
     Client connected: 0.0.0.0/0.0.0.0
     Data from client: Hello
     Called method 'test()'
   5 String parameter is: Hello
     Waiting for client call
```

Listing 2.4: **Output from the 'client' class** SocketTestClient.

```
     Creating socket connection to remote
     Sending parameter to remote's 'test' method
     Reading reponse from remote
     Response from remote: Hello from remote
```

What would we have to do to make this simple example into a 'real' remote method invocation strategy? Here are a few of the more obvious requirements.

- The client should be able to select which method it will call on the remote object, rather than being hard-coded to call a specific method.

- The client should be able to call remote methods with any method signature.

- The client should be able to find the remote object by specifying its name, rather than by an IP port number. At present, only one remote object can listen on a particular port, and the client needs to know which port supports which object.

- In the simple scheme, the remote object needs to be instantiated on the server before the client can call methods on it. Ideally, we need the client to be able to instantiate objects as well as call methods.

- Neither the client nor the remote object should have to manipulate network sockets directly, nor manage the communications protocol directly. Instead, these low-level operations should be encapsulated inside helper classes. If the use of the helper classes can be made transparent to both the caller and the target object, so much the better.

- The remote object should be able to determine the identity of the client and accept or deny calls based on this information.

A further practical requirement is that the protocol should be, as far as possible, language-independent. It should be possible, in an enterprise application, for objects written in C++, for example, to call methods on objects written in Java.

Let's see how we might extend the simple scheme described earlier to satisfy these requirements. There are some more subtle, complex requirements for an RMI scheme that has to work in the enterprise environment (such as propagation of transaction context), but we will discuss these later.

2.2.2   Handling multiple methods and argument lists

First, we need a technique for the client to be able to call different methods on the remote object, and to pass different arguments. We could use Java serialization for this.[1] Rather than passing simple `String` instances from the client to the server, we could use serialization to pass a more complex object. This object would contain the name of the method to call and the parameters to be passed. A simple example is shown in Listing 2.5. Passing the parameters as an array of `Object`s allows arguments of any type to be passed, provided that they are serializable.[2] The requirement that the arguments be serializable is a fairly fundamental requirement of all Java-based RMI schemes, as we shall see. However, using serialization as the transport mechanism would not be ideal for an enterprise RMI scheme, as it would be difficult to support non-Java objects.

Listing 2.5: **A simple example of a class that could pass method-call information from the client to the remote object.**

```
   public  class  MethodCallHelper
      implements  java.io.Serializable
   {
   String  methodName;
 5 Object[]  arguments;

   //  'get'  and  'set'  methods  here ...
   }
```

So when the caller calls the remote method on the target object, it would first create an instance of `MethodCallHelper` and insert the arguments into the `arguments` instance variable. It would also write the name of the desired method into the `methodName` parameter. The next step would be to serialize this object into a byte array. If all the arguments are serializable, this would result in a `byte[]` that could be passed over the network to the target object. This would then deserialize the byte array into a `MethodCallHelper` and use the information in it to make a call on the appropriate method. Similar techniques could be used to handle the return value from the remote object to the client.

Of course, there are a number of things that could go wrong during this process. Most fundamentally, the remote object may not be instantiated and accepting network connections, or the network connection may not be sound. In addition,

---

[1] Java serialization is described in detail in Appendix E.

[2] We could pass primitive data types by using the standard wrapper classes—e.g., an `int` could be passed as an `Integer`.

the arguments specified by the client may not match those accepted by the called method on the server. Even if the remote method can be called, it may throw an exception. This exception would need to be delivered to the client. This implies that the communication protocol needs to be able to handle not only return values, but also the serialization and deserialization of exceptions. These issues complicate the protocol, but do not require any fundamental changes to the strategy.

So it appears that it would be relatively straightforward to develop a scheme that allows clients to call arbitrary methods on the remote object, and to pass arbitrary arguments. In practice, most schemes currently available for passing method-call information on the wire use binary data, which is not human-readable. It is therefore unhelpful to present an example of the data format. However, there has been a recent upsurge of interest in using XML as the data carrier, and XML formats are human readable. An example is presented later in this chapter (page 42).

2.2.3   Finding the remote object

In our simple scheme, clients determine which remote object to call by specifying the IP port number on which the remote object is listening. A better scheme would be for the client to be able to locate the remote object by its name. Here is a simple solution: Clients communicate with a central name-lookup service, which accepts the name of an object and returns the host and port number on which it is listening. When a number of remote objects are instantiated, each registers itself with the naming service and gets back a port number. The remote object then listens for connections on that port. Clients contact the naming service, and get the host and port number that was supplied to the remote object. Then the client can call the remote object by making a network connection using that host name and port.

This strategy allows objects to be distributed on multiple computers, all served by the same naming service. Then clients can find remote objects regardless of the server on which they are deployed. It also allows a simple load sharing scheme to be implemented, as the naming service could return the IP numbers and ports of different servers in rotation.

With these modifications, we will have implemented a simple *object request broker* (ORB). An ORB is simply a service that makes objects available for remote method calls. An ORB will typically support a number of different classes and their instances, and integrate a name lookup service.

A naming service that can return host names and port numbers is a simple solution to the problem of locating remote objects, but it isn't very elegant. There are better ways to do this, as we shall see later.

2.2.4   Instantiating the remote object

In the simple RMI scheme we have been discussing, the client can only make calls on an object that has already been instantiated on the server. What shall we do if we want the client to be able to instantiate remote objects?

Probably the simplest scheme is to allow the server that is running the name-lookup service to instantiate the remote class when a client requests the location of that remote object. Additionally, we could extend the `MethodCallHelper` class to carry information about whether the server should create a new instance or return a reference to an existing instance if one has already been instantiated. Alternatively, we can use *object factory pattern*. An object factory is an object that has the responsibility of creating new instances of a particular class. The factory itself is always instantiated within the ORB. When a client wants to create a new object of a particular class, it calls a method (typically called `create()` or `new()`) on the factory for that class. In addition, the factory may provide methods to delete objects that are no longer required. The EJB architecture uses this pattern: The factory objects are called *home objects* in the *EJB Specification*. When a client wants to call a method on an EJB instance, it first locates the home object for that EJB and calls its `create()` method. The home object creates the new instance,[3] and returns to the client a reference that can be used to call methods on it.

2.2.5 Abstracting the protocol implementation

For the convenience of developers, and to allow for portability and protocol independence, the implementation details discussed above should be hidden—as far as possible—from the developers of the collaborating objects. That is, the development of both the client and the remote object should be very similar to the development of any other Java class. A simple approach is to put all the Java code that is not specific to a particular object into a set of generic helper classes. For example, in Listing 2.1 we could have the 'server' object inherit from a general-purpose 'object server' class, so that its `main()` method could handle requests to call any method, not just one. This method could use reflection[4] to determine whether the method can be called or not, using the parameters supplied by the client. This would make the whole process independent of the object itself. On the client side, we could wrap up the socket creation and communication in a separate class. In practice, such a class is called a 'stub.' The concept of a stub is very important in RMI and EJB, and will be discussed in much more detail later.

2.3 Java RMI

This section discusses Java RMI, a particular implementation of RMI that is supported 'out of the box' by the Java JDK.

2.3.1 Java RMI principles

You may remember from the previous discussion that the term RMI—strictly speaking—means remote method invocation *by any technique*. The simple, sockets-based approach described in the previous section could qualify as an RMI scheme,

---

[3]An 'instance' of an EJB is not necessarily an instance of a Java class, as we shall see. Later in the book, I will argue that 'EJB instance' is not necessarily even a helpful term. For now, the term is used because it is familiar to Java developers.

[4]Reflection is described in detail in Appendix D.

albeit a limited one. When Java developers use the term RMI, however, they are usually talking about a specific RMI scheme, supported by tools and libraries provided with the Java JDK.

> ### Hint
>
> 'Java RMI' is a particular implementation of a remote method invocation scheme. It does *not* mean 'RMI done in Java,' at least in this book. Here, the term RMI means 'remote method invocation' in a general sense. Where I wish to refer to the specific implementation of RMI that is supported by the Java JDK, I will always use the term 'Java RMI.'

We will discuss RMI with reference to a specific example, code outlines for which are provided at the end of this section.

> ### Hint
>
> Full source code for this example may be found in the accompanying source package, in the directory `rmi`. Please refer to the README file in that directory for instructions on how to compile the source code, generate stubs, initialize the RMI registry, etc.

In Java RMI, the remote object is manipulated on the client by means of an interface called, unsurprisingly, the *remote interface*. The remote interface defines the methods on the remote object that the client is to be able to call. Suppose, for example, that the remote object contains one method, `test()`, which is to be called by clients (it may have any number of 'private' methods—that is, methods accessible only within the same JVM). The interface would be defined as shown in Listing 2.7. The construct `extendsRemote` is used to indicate that this object is intended to be made available for RMI; it has the consequence that a reference to the object is passed by reference over the network, not by value, as will be described.

The remote object is defined to implement this interface, for example:

```
public class RmiTestServer implements RmiTest
  {
  // ...
  public void test ()
    {
    // ...
    }
  }
```

A software tool called `rmic` (RMI compiler) takes this remote class and generates 'stub' and 'skeleton' classes to accompany this interface. In the example listed, we run `rmic` like this:

```
rmic com.kevinboone.ejb_book.rmi.RmiTestServer
```

This would generate two new classes, `RmiTestServer_Stub` and `RmiTestServer_Skel`.

These classes contain the communication protocol support needed for the client to be able to make calls on the remote object, with no knowledge of the protocols used. The specification of the stub `RmiTestServer_Stub` is shown (in outline) below:

```
public final class
     com.kevinboone.ejb_book.rmi.RmiTestServer_Stub
   extends
     java.rmi.server.RemoteStub
   implements
     com.kevinboone.ejb_book.rmi.RmiTest,
     java.rmi.Remote
{
public RmiTestServer_Stub (java.rmi.server.RemoteRef);
public java.lang.String test(java.lang.String)
   throws java.rmi.RemoteException;
}
```

There are two crucial features of this class.

First, it is defined to implement the remote interface `RmiTest`. This means that, on the client, an instance of the stub can be assigned to a variable of type `RmiTest`. Thus the client manipulates the remote interface, and the stub is invisible.

Second, it has exactly the same signature for the `test()` method as the remote object itself. We know this is the case, because the remote object had to implement the remote interface. So, if the client holds a reference to the stub, it knows that if it calls the `test()` method on the stub, the call will be compatible with the `test()` method on the real remote object. A client that does this is shown in Listing 2.8.

When the server class starts up, it registers itself with the RMI registry, like this:

```
java.rmi.Naming.rebind
   ("//localhost/RmiTestServer:1099" , rmiTestServer );
```

(For this to work, the `rmiregistry` naming service must be running on the server.) Then the client can obtain a reference to the remote interface by calling

```
Object o = Naming.lookup("//localhost:1099/RmiTestServer" );
```

This call tells the `Naming` class to look for the remote class `RmiTestServer` in the naming service on `localhost`, which is listening on port 1099 (this is the default port for the Java RMI name-lookup service). The naming service finds the remote object, instantiates a stub that is initialized with the remote's own host and port number, and returns that stub to the client. The client can then assign it to a variable of class `RmiTest`, like this:

    RmiTest rmiTest = (RmiTest)o;

This cast will fail, of course, if object 'o' is not really assignable to `RmiTest`. This would happen, for example, if the `lookup` call was supplied the wrong name. It will also happen if the client's JVM cannot load the stub class or its helpers because it can't find them. This issue will be discussed in more detail below.

From this point on, the client can call methods on the object `rmiTest` almost exactly as if it were calling methods on a local object.

What else must the remote object provide, other than the implementation of the method `test()`? If we define it to extend the standard RMI class `java.rmi.UnicastRemoteObject`, then it doesn't have to do much (see Listing 2.6 for the full example). The `main()` method should instantiate the class, and its default constructor calls the constructor in `UnicastRemoteObject`. This constructor starts a new thread that instantiates the skeleton. The skeleton listens for incoming calls from clients and forwards them to the remote object itself. `main()` should also register the object with the naming service, so that it is available to any clients that are allowed to use it.

Listing 2.6: **RMI object server** `RmiTestServer.java`.

```
     package com.kevinboone.ejb_book.rmi;
     import java.rmi.*;
     import java.rmi.server.*;

 5   /**
     This is the object server for the RMI example.
     (c)2002 Kevin Boone
     */
     public class RmiTestServer
10      extends UnicastRemoteObject
        implements RmiTest
     {
     /**
     This simple class does not need a constructor, but must
15   provide one because its superclass has a non-inheritable
     default constructor
     */
     public RmiTestServer() throws RemoteException
        {
20      super();
        }

     /**
     The main method registers the name of the object in the RMI
25   registry, making it available to clients.
     */
     public static void main(String[] args)
        {
        if (System.getSecurityManager() == null)
30         {
```

```
        System.setSecurityManager(new RMISecurityManager());
        }
      try
        {
35      RmiTestServer rmiTestServer  = new RmiTestServer();
        Naming.rebind("//localhost/RmiTestServer", rmiTestServer);
        System.out.println("RmiTestServer bound in registry");
        }
      catch (Exception e)
40        {
        System.out.println
          ("Caught exception while initializing: " + e);
        e.printStackTrace();
        }
45    }

    /**
    This method is the only one exposed to clients. We know this
    because it is exposed in the remote interface 'RmiTest'.
50  */
    public String test(String s)
      {
      System.out.println ("Called RmiTestServer.test()");
      return "Hello from the remote object";
55    }
    }
```

Listing 2.7: **Remote interface** `RmiTest.java` **for the object server.**

```
    package com.kevinboone.ejb_book.rmi;
    import java.rmi.*;

    /**
5   This is the remote interface that exposes the method
    'test()' on the class RmiTestServer to the client.
    (c)2002 Kevin Boone
    */
    public interface RmiTest extends Remote
10  {
    /**
    This simple method merely prints some progress information.
    Note that it must be declared to throw RemoteException as
    well as any application−defined exceptions that the
15  implementing class may throw
    */
    public String test (String s) throws RemoteException;
    }
```

Listing 2.8: **Test client** `RmiTestClient.java` **for the object server; note that it manipulates the remote object only through the remote interface.**

```
package com.kevinboone.ejb_book.rmi;
import java.rmi.*;

/**
This is the test client for the RmiTestServer class. It
finds the class in the remote registry, and then calls its
'test()' method.
(c)2000 Kevin Boone
*/
public class RmiTestClient
{
public final static String RMI_NAME = "RmiTestServer";

/**
Get a reference to an object of class
'RmiTestServer' and execute its 'test()' method
*/
public static void main (String[] args)
  {
  System.out.println ("Installing security manager");

  // To use remote stub downloading, we _must_ install a
  // security manager. This usually implies a security
  // policy file be installed
  System.setSecurityManager (new RMISecurityManager());

  System.out.println ("Finding remote class");

  try
    {
    Object o = Naming.lookup("//localhost:1099/RmiTestServer");
    System.out.println
      ("Object returned by lookup is of class "
      + o.getClass());
    RmiTest rmiTest = (RmiTest)o;
    String s = rmiTest.test("hello");
    System.out.println ("String returned from remote is: "
      + s);
    }
  catch (NotBoundException e)
    {
    // We get this exception if the RMI registry cannot
    // find the name of the object requested
    System.err.println ("Connected to RMI server, but name '"
      + RMI_NAME + "' not bound in server");
    }
  catch (RemoteException e)
    {
    // We will get this exection for a variety of reasons,
    // including the RMI server not being available
    System.err.println ("Caught a RemoteException! " + e);
    e.printStackTrace (System.err);
    }
  catch (java.net.MalformedURLException e)
    {
```

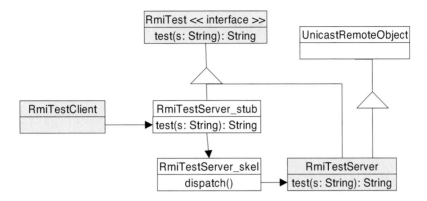

Figure 2.3. Class structure for the simple RMI example described in this section. This diagram shows logical, rather than physical, interaction, but it is important to realize that the communication between the `RmiTestServer_stub` and `RmiTestServer_skel` is potentially a network interaction, rather than an intra-JVM method call.

```
        // This should never happen, as URL is hard-coded
        System.err.println
          ("Caught a MalformedURLException: " + e);
        }
60    }


}
```

In this simple example, the class `RmiTestServer` must be instantiated before calls are made on it by clients. Java RMI *does* provide a scheme by which clients can instantiate remote objects ('activation'). However, this scheme is very different to the one provided for EJBs, so I won't describe it here.

The structure of the 'RmiTest' application is shown in the UML diagram Figure 2.3.

Note that both the stub and the remote object implement the remote interface. The remote object runs in a JVM with a security manager of class `RMISecurity` `Manager`. Using the security manager's configuration file, we can specify which clients are allowed to make calls on the remote object. However, the mechanism for this is not at all similar to that used by EJBs, so to avoid confusion we won't discuss that here either.

The output from the server when a client makes a call is shown in Listing 2.9. This output from the client is shown in Listing 2.10.

Listing 2.9: **output from the RMI object server class** `RMITestServer`.

```
[exec]  RmiTestServer  bound  in  registry
[exec]  Called  RmiTestServer.test()
```

Listing 2.10: **output from the test client class** `RmiTestClient`.

```
   Installing  security  manager
   Finding  remote  class
   Object  returned  by  lookup  is  of  class  class
      ejbook.rmi.RmiTestServer_Stub
5  String  returned  from  remote  is:  Hello  from  the  remote  object
```

What does the stub do? When the client gets the stub from the naming service, the `Naming` class gets an instance of `java.rmi.server.RemoteRef`,[5] which identifies the remote object. This reference is passed to the constructor of the stub and, when the client calls the method `test()`, the stub simply delegates that call to the remote reference, which passes the details over the network to the skeleton. The skeleton deserializes the arguments and calls the method `test()` on the remote object.

> Gotcha!
>
> The use of Java RMI is subject to Java security manager restrictions; a common problem when beginning RMI development is to forget to configure the security manager. The details are beyond the scope of this book: Please refer to the source code package for examples of security policy files and the JVM arguments required to reference them.

2.4 Stubs

In Java RMI, and most other RMI schemes, the use of stubs is crucial. The stub encapsulates code that conceals the specifics of the RMI protocols (of which more later) from the client object (and also the developer, with any luck). The client code should ideally never have to refer directly to the stub. Java RMI makes this possible by having the stub implement the remote interface, which means it can be manipulated in place of the remote object.

---

[5]Strictly speaking, it gets an instance of something that implements `RemoteRef`; the reference is defined by an interface.

However, confusion often arises in both RMI and EJB development over the correct use of stubs. The stub classes, whatever they are, need to be made available to the client. The simplest way to do this is to distribute the files generated by `rmic` (or whatever our particular stub generator is) along with the client. Java RMI supports a somewhat cleverer approach: remote stub downloading.

When the remote object in a Java RMI application registers itself with the naming service, it also indicates the URL from which the stubs can be downloaded. When the client uses `java.rmi.Naming` to find the location of the remote object, the `Naming` object can bring about a process that downloads the stubs onto the client from the URL that was specified during registration. This means that the client need not necessarily have access to the stubs until runtime.

Runtime stub downloading is a clever technique, but not all RMI protocols support it, as we shall see.

2.5   RMI protocols

You may have noticed that nowhere in the previous discussion were details of the communications protocol discussed. This is because the standard Java RMI API is essentially protocol-independent. When a client makes a lookup for the remote object, it gets back a reference to a stub that supports whatever protocol that remote object is prepared to accept. There are, in practice, two protocols in widespread use by Java developers: JRMP and IIOP. However, techniques based on XML (such as SOAP) are becoming increasingly important. This section describes these protocols in outline.

2.5.1   JRMP

The earliest communications protocol used in Java RMI was Java Remote Method Protocol (JRMP). This protocol is proprietary to Sun Microsystems and was developed specifically for Java RMI. It has the advantage of being very simple and therefore imposing little network overhead. For enterprise applications, however, it has two major drawbacks. First, it is Java-specific, and therefore cannot be used to integrate with components written in other languages. Second, it does not provide a mechanism to supply transactional context along with a method call. This latter limitation precludes the use of JRMP as a carrier for transactional method calls. The IIOP protocol suffers from neither of these limitations—as we shall see—but, being a language-independent protocol, has little support for Java features like distributed garbage collection.

2.5.2   RMI/IIOP and CORBA

IIOP is the protocol used by CORBA clients for remote method calls. CORBA is a specification for ORBs that are language-independent and vendor-neutral.[6]

---

[6]This book will not attempt an in-depth discussion of the CORBA architecture or the IIOP protocol because there are already good books on this subject (see, for example, Orfali and Harkey (1998) *Client/Server Programming with Java and CORBA* in the bibliography) and because EJB development does not require a detailed knowledge of these matters.

However, the mechanism by which EJB clients find and communicate with EJBs is derived directly from Sun's implementation of IIOP client support, as we shall see. It may help in the understanding of EJBs to see the way in which the *EJB Specification* is derived from earlier work.

Sun Microsystems is one of the founder members of the Object Management Group (OMG), and therefore integration of Java RMI with IIOP has received quite a bit of attention. The result is a scheme called 'RMI/IIOP'—usually pronounced as 'RMI over IIOP.' The Java JDK (Version 1.3 and later) is supplied with a standard API for RMI/IIOP, structured in a very similar way to standard Java RMI. This API does not handle the IIOP protocol itself; all the classes in the API are simply vendor-neutral wrappers for a vendor-specific IIOP implementation. This makes the API slightly more complex than is the case for standard Java RMI. In addition, to use RMI/IIOP, you will also need a full IIOP implementation for the RMI/IIOP classes to use. This also is supplied with the JDK, but the details are not documented (this is as it should be; the developer should not need to be concerned about the details). When developing EJBs for an application server or a commercial EJB container, you can expect the IIOP implementation classes to be different from those provided with the JDK. You may also find that the vendor provides its own versions of the basic API classes as well.

We will now consider the differences between RMI/JRMP and RMI/IIOP from the perspective of the client and the remote object.

RMI/IIOP clients

As far as an RMI client class is concerned, it makes little difference whether it is using JRMP or IIOP for communication with the remote object: Most of the details are concealed in the stubs. The stub generator `rmic` supplied with the JDK[7] can generate IIOP stubs, as well as JRMP stubs; the only difference is in the command line:

```
rmic −iiop com.kevinboone.ejb_book.rmi.RmiTest
```

The main differences for the client are (1) in the way that name lookups are carried out and (2) that it is now no longer the job of the name lookup procedure to load stubs for the remote object (there is a new method call for that).

The RMI/IIOP implementation uses JNDI (of which much more later) to obtain the remote reference. So rather than:

```
Object o = Naming.lookup("//localhost:1099/RmiTestServer");
```

we now have:

```
javax.naming.Context context
    = new javax.naming.InitialContext();
Object o = context.lookup("RmiTestServer");
```

---

[7]This feature was first introduced in JDK 1.3.

It is important to appreciate that in the new example, the argument to `Context.`
`lookup()` is *not* a URL of any kind. It is simply a name. This is to allow the client
code to be independent of the location of the naming service. If desired, a naming
service URL can be specified as an item in a `Hashtable` that is provided to to
the `InitialContext` constructor (see Chapter 7 for a full discussion). Also, in this
hashtable we can provide the name of the class that forms the interface to the
underlying service provider (as it probably won't be the standard RMI registry).

So the full lookup call may look more like this:

```
Hashtable ht = new Hashtable();
// Specify the class that supports the underlying name service
// (in this case, Sun's CORBA naming service)
ht.put ("java.naming.factory.initial",
  "com.sun.jndi.cosnaming.CNCtxFactory");
// Specify the URL of the naming service
ht.put ("java.naming.provider.url",
  "iiop://localhost:1099");
javax.naming.Context context
  = new javax.naming.InitialContext(ht);
Object o = context.lookup("RmiTestServer");
```

This looks much more complicated than the standard RMI example, but this
complexity is to allow for flexibility.

Another significant difference is that instead of simply casting the result of
`lookup` into an object of the appropriate type, we now use a method call to do this.
This is because the `lookup()` call can now return other objects, not just remote
references, so it isn't appropriate that stub loading should be carried out here. Thus
the output of `lookup()` may not be a stub. So rather than:

```
RmiTest rmiTest = (RmiTest)o;
```

we have:

```
RmiTest rmiTest = (RmiTest)
  javax.rmi.PortableRemoteObject.narrow
  (o, RmiTest.class);
```

The real purpose of this 'narrow' operation[8] is to make a stub available on
the client that will be suitable for the object returned by `lookup()`. This process is
poorly understood by new (and not-so-new) EJB developers, so it is worth spending
some time understanding what is going on here.

Like all the RMI/IIOP API classes, the `PortableRemoteObject` class does not
do any real work itself. It is simply a protocol-independent proxy for the vendor-
supplied 'delegate' class that does the real work. This will be something that implements the `javax.rmi.CORBA.PortableRemoteObjectDelegate` interface, but beyond that the details lie entirely in the hands of the IIOP platform vendor. What
the vendor's code should do is to ensure that a stub is loaded and made available

---

[8]The term 'narrow' means to assign an object to a variable whose type is one of its subclasses. A
'widening' conversion—assigning a subclass to its superclass—will always succeed, but narrowing
can fail if the objects are not really assignable. Most developers use the term 'downcast' rather
than 'narrow,' but 'narrow' is the term the Specification uses.

that is suitable for the object returned by `lookup()`, whatever that happens to be. In other words, if the result of `Context.lookup()` is not a stub that implements the remote interface, the vendor's implementation is given the opportunity to create or load one.

As an example, the *J2EE Reference Implementation* provides a `PortableRemote Object` delegate class called `com.sun.corba.ee.internal.javax.rmi.Portable RemoteObject`. This class has a `narrow()` implementation that works as follows.

When presented with the name of a remote object, the J2EE implementation of `Content.lookup()` will either return a valid RMI/IIOP stub for the remote object or a CORBA remote object (that is, a class derived from the CORBA class `org.omg.CORBA.portable.ObjectImpl`).

The `narrow()` operation first performs some basic checks (like that the object to be narrowed is non-null), then checks to see whether the result of `lookup()` is already a valid RMI/IIOP stub for that object. It does this by testing whether the object can be assigned to a variable of the specified remote interface type. If it can, then the stub is valid and loadable, and is returned unchanged.[9]

In the example above, if the result of `context.lookup()` is a stub that implements the `RmiTest` remote interface, this test will succeed, provided that the stub class is available on the client, and `narrow()` will simply return the stub unchanged. That is, in this circumstance the `narrow()` operation has no effect.

If the result of `lookup()` is not a stub, then the `narrow()` method will attempt to find and load a stub for it. It does this by getting the name of the remote object, prefixing with '_' and adding the string '_stub'. It then attempts to load a class with this name.

If it can do this, the stub is instantiated and returned. If not, the `narrow()` method fails.

So, in summary, the `narrow()` method has no effect when the `lookup()` returns an RMI/IIOP stub that implements the remote interface and can be used directly by a client. It this is not the case, then the `narrow()` operation will attempt to load a suitable stub and return that to the client.

RMI/IIOP remote objects

In EJB development, it is unusual to create an RMI/IIOP remote object directly (the EJB container does that), so I'll be brief.

For the remote object, the main differences between Java RMI and RMI/IIOP are:

- Remote classes generally extend `javax.rmi.PortableRemoteObject`, rather than `java.rmi.UnicastRemoteObject`.

---

[9]A consequence of the way this test is done is that 'narrow()' will often succeed on things that are not stubs or remote interfaces at all. As we shall see, the `lookup()` method is also used to find things like database connection factory classes. Attempting to 'narrow' a database connection factory will usually succeed and return itself. As a consequence, a lot of developers have gotten into the habit of 'narrowing' everything that comes out of `Context.lookup()`. This is an error, and such code is likely to be nonportable.

- Registration of the object with the naming service is also done through JNDI, rather than through the RMI registry. In the server object, rather than using:

```
java.rmi.Naming.rebind
  ("//localhost/RmiTestServer", rmiTestServer);
```

we would use:

```
javax.naming.Context context
  = new javax.naming.InitialContext();
context.rebind("RmiTestServer", rmiTestServer);
```

When a client does a name lookup for the remote object, information is passed over the network in the form of a CORBA *Interoperable Object Reference* (IOR). It is the job of the client-side implementation to convert the IOR into a valid stub that will allow method calls to be made. The IOR contains the hostname and port number of the ORB that will satisfy requests for method calls for that object. The client stub will typically then make a direct TCP/IP connection to that host and port, and pass method-call information. The problem with this strategy is that, in a complex, distributed environment, the hostname that satisfies the name lookup request may not be the same as the hostname on which the name lookup was made. In other words, a single client request is not satisfied by a single host/port combination. This has profound implications for enterprise security because of the impact it has on the configuration of firewalls. This issue is discussed in detail in Chapter 16 (page 535). The difficulty of implementing IIOP-based wide-area communication has led to increased interest in alternative RMI schemes based, for example, on XML.

2.5.3   SOAP, XML-RPC, and 'RMI over SOAP'

One of the things that makes IIOP more complex that JRMP is that it has to be interoperable—that is, it implements a system for encoding objects for transmission across a network in a vendor-neutral and platform-independent way. In an enterprise application, this interoperability is likely to be very important. However, as we have seen, there are significant problems with IIOP when the Internet is used as the carrier.[10]

It might be helpful to take a step back at this point, and review what is required from an RMI scheme. Remember that 'RMI' is a generic term for any technique that allows method calls to be made over a network, and does not in itself specify any communication protocol. Whatever RMI implementation is used, the information sent from the client to the server must be sufficient to allow the server to carry out the following actions:

- locate the object on which the method is to be called;

- identify the method itself;

---

[10]The same problems apply to JRMP, but are less well-documented, because JRMP is not normally used for wide-area RMI.

- specify the arguments to be passed to the method, which may themselves be objects.

The data returned from the server must be capable of

- supplying the return value from the method, which may itself be an object, and

- indicating any errors that occurred in the method invocation.

In addition, of course, the implementation should conceal its low-level operation from clients, typically by using stubs and skeletons.

It should be clear that one of the most significant problems in the design of an RMI scheme is that of encoding objects in an interoperable way. Now, one of the most compelling features of XML is that it can be used to encode arbitrary objects in just such a way. It happens that there is already an emerging standard for encoding objects and simple data types as XML documents: Simple Object Access Protocol (SOAP). SOAP is supported by a number of major vendors, including IBM, Microsoft, and Sun Microsystems, and is likely to be increasingly important. SOAP is a scheme for encoding data (objects, primitives, and arrays) as XML. However, the *SOAP Specification* does suggest methods for encapsulating SOAP documents into HTTP messages (which gives us the transport protocol) and for formulating RPC (remote procedure call) information in the SOAP document. Thus, SOAP provides most of what is required for an interoperable RMI scheme. When SOAP (or similar formats) is used to carry method-call data between objects, this is commonly referred to as 'XML-RPC,' where RPC stands for remote procedure call, essentially the same thing as RMI.

The use of HTTP (or, more likely, HTTPS) as the transport protocol overcomes one of the main problems of IIOP, that of poor firewall support. Using XML allows the implementation to take advantage of the XML parsers that are already available and have built-in facilities for checking document structure.

At the time of writing, there are a number of a SOAP implementations in development. The Apache (`http://xml.apache.org/soap`) version is probably the most widely used, although Sun's recently introduced JAX-RPC (`http://java.sun.com/xml/jaxrpc`) is likely to be significant as well. It is now possible to contemplate the use of 'RMI over SOAP,' because tools are starting to appear that can generate SOAP-compatible stubs and skeletons, as well as the SOAP infrastructure itself.

As an illustration, let's consider the 'interest calculator' EJB that will be presented in Chapter 4. This has an method of the following form:

```
public double getInterestOnPrincipal
    (double principal , double interestPerTerm , int terms);
```

which calculates the interest payable on a certain sum of money (`principal`) at a certain rate of interest per financial term (`interestPerTerm`) for a certain number of terms (`terms`).

When this method call is made using RMI/IIOP, the wire data format will be binary and not particularly meaningful to human readers. However, when the call is made using the Apache SOAP implementation, the method call information is translated into this XML document:

```
<env:Envelope ... >
  <env:Body>
    <ns0:getInterestOnPrincipal>
      <double_1  xsi:type="xsd:double">100.0</double_1>
      <double_2  xsi:type="xsd:double">10.0< /double_2>
      <int_3  xsi:type="xsd:int">10</int_3>
    </ns0:getInterestOnPrincipal>
  </env:Body>
</env:Envelope>
```

This document (an 'envelope' in SOAP jargon) specifies that the method call `getInterestOnPrincipal()` is to be called and passes three primitives as parameters: two `doubles` and an `int`. The SOAP specification sets out the sizes and ranges of these data types, and some conversion may be required to a particular platform's native data types. As a result of the method call, the remote object sends back a further envelope:

```
<env:Envelope ... >
  <env:Body>
    <ns0:getCompoundInterestResponse>
      <result  xsi:type="xsd:double">159.37424601000026</result>
    </ns0:getCompoundInterestResponse>
  </env:Body>
</env:Envelope>
```

This envelope states that there is one result (return value) of type `double`, with the specified value.

These examples of SOAP have only shown method calls being made where the arguments and return values are primitives, but the specification does cater to composite (e.g., object) types as well.

You will notice that the XML fragments presented above do not identify the object that will be the subject of the method call nor where that object is hosted. This information is not part of the *SOAP Specification*, but a network protocol issue. When we are using SOAP with HTTP, then typically the HTTP request will identify (by the URL) the object that is to be the target of the call. The client-side stubs, or load-balancing framework, are responsible for generating the HTTP request on to an appropriate host.

The ability to call methods on distributed objects using HTTP requests carrying XML is one of the main features of the 'Web services' development model. In effect, the example above demonstrates how to expose the 'interest calculator' EJB as a Web service. Of course, the Web services model has other features, including the ability to declare services in a searchable registry and the ability to pass objects over messaging services. A full discussion of Web services is, regrettably, beyond the scope of this book, but well worth following up if you have the opportunity. The combination of Web services and EJB technology is likely to be very important in future. Indeed, the draft of the proposed Version 2.1 of the *EJB Specification* includes provision for directly exposing EJBs as Web services (see Appendix A for a brief discussion).

2.6 Security

You may have noticed that an important feature of distributed computing—security—has escaped mention in this chapter. In fact, this issue is sufficiently complex that a whole chapter (Chapter 16) is devoted to it.

2.7 Enterprise JavaBean RMI

Enterprise JavaBeans are Java components that are designed to run in a distributed environment. EJBs communicate with one another, and with their clients, using an RMI scheme, just as other distributed objects do. From the previous section, you will have gathered that there are already well-developed APIs for Java RMI (which are not very different, no matter what underlying protocol we use): The RMI scheme used by EJBs is based firmly on the RMI/IIOP API. This means that clients will use a JNDI `lookup()` call to locate the EJB and get a stub on which it can make method calls. The stub marshalls the arguments and communicates with a skeleton, which carries out the real method invocation. The use of stubs and skeletons, the process of marshalling and unmarshalling of arguments, and the use of JNDI are all exactly as in RMI/IIOP. Indeed, the *EJB Specification* states in a number of places that argument types and return values must be compatible with RMI/IIOP [e.g., EJB2.0 7.10], as must the class and interface structure itself (e.g., remote interfaces can have superinterfaces).

The main difference between making method calls on RMI remote objects and on EJBs is that clients can never call EJB methods directly. EJBs are encapsulated within an EJB container, and access to the EJB instance itself is made through the container's proxies. These proxies intercept all method calls and pass them on to the EJB itself. The stubs that the client uses actually call methods on the proxies. As in all good RMI schemes, the action of the stubs is transparent to the client. The use of proxies has very beneficial effects for the EJB developer, as we shall see.

Another difference between EJB RMI and Java RMI is that there is a standard method by which the client instantiates new remote objects. There is also a standard technique by which the client can get a reference to an EJB that already exists.

Although remote method calls on EJBs are made using a similar API to that used by RMI/IIOP clients, EJB client-server communication does not have to be based on RMI/IIOP in EJB 1.1, although this is recommended [EJB1.1 13.1]. Using RMI/IIOP has the advantage of allowing EJBs to interoperate with CORBA components, but for purely internal communication (e.g., between servlets and EJBs), vendors are free to use whatever protocols they see fit. However, the *J2EE Specification* and EJB 2.0 [EJB2.0 19.5] say that EJB containers must be *able* to support IIOP. So, for example, the iPlanet application server uses a proprietary protocol (called 'KCP') for communication from EJB to EJB, or servlet to EJB, but uses

RMI/IIOP to support standalone clients or CORBA clients. Most vendors now use RMI/IIOP throughout. What the *EJB Specification* does say [EJB1.1 9.3.9] is that the RMI communication protocol should be able to support remote references that are valid for "a long period of time," and ideally should remain valid across a server crash. It also says that the arguments passed to EJB methods, and their return values, should be compatible with RMI/IIOP.

It is important for an EJB developer to understand the limitations imposed by the use of IIOP as the RMI protocol (or at least, the compatibility with IIOP). The most obvious of these is that objects will be passed by value, not by reference, unless special measures are taken. There will be many occasions where this limitation is very significant. You may wish, for example, to pass a reference to an `OutputStream` to an EJB, and have the EJB stream data back to the client. This is fiddly to implement, because Java streams are not serializable and can't be passed by value. This problem can be overcome by implementing proxy remote objects that encapsulate the behaviour of a stream but can be passed by reference. This requires the generation of stubs and skeletons from the proxies, among other things.

2.8   Summary

RMI is a general term for any scheme that allows distributed objects to call methods on one another, passing arguments and accepting return values. Ideally an RMI scheme should be transparent to both the caller and the called object. The use of stubs (on the caller side) and skeletons (on the called side) helps to accomplish this. A number of RMI schemes are available to the Java developer, which use well-defined protocols to pass arguments and return values, as well as to propagate exceptions from the called object to the caller. The all-Java JRMP protocol is supplied with the Java JDK, but has limitations that make it less than ideal for enterprise applications. CORBA's IIOP overcomes these limitations, at the expense of increased complexity. Neither of these protocols is well-suited to wide-area (Internet) RMI, because of the difficulty of configuring firewalls to support them. Increasingly, developers are turning to XML-based object passing schemes for wide-area distributed applications. At the time of writing, SOAP is the most likely to become an established technique, and complete 'RMI over SOAP' implementations are just starting to become available.

Chapter 3

An overview
of EJB technology

Overview

This chapter describes EJB technology in outline and provides an overview of the interaction between the EJB, the client, and the EJB container. It also describes the *EJB objects* and *home objects*, and explains why the use of these constructs—although perhaps somewhat confusing at first—ultimately simplifies the development of substantial software projects.

We begin by examing how an EJB is seen by its clients, which may be synchronous, using RMI, or asynchronous, using messaging. We then discuss the Java entities that make up an EJB, the home interfaces, local interface, remote interface, and implementation class, and how they are packaged with a deployment descriptor to make a complete EJB.

The chapter concludes with a discussion of the techniques that commercial EJB products may use to optimize performance and increase reliability.

As it is an overview, this chapter does not provide any complete examples of EJBs, and could lead readers into thinking that the subject is more complicated than it really is. Moreover, to avoid fragmenting the text, I have included material in this chapter that, although part of an outline of the technology, is rather more complex than you may wish to see on a first reading. If you are impatient to see an EJB working and look at some real code, you may prefer to read Chapter 4 first. You may find that this helps to put some of the more complicated parts of this chapter into perspective.

3.1 The client's view

In this book, we will encouter some rather complex, and perhaps even intimidating, technology. To put it into context, I would like to begin by discussing how an EJB is seen by its clients. We will see that this is, in fact, quite straightforward. This is important, because EJBs are usefully viewed as providers of services to their clients: A service can be as complex as the needs of the application demand, but the provision of the service must be simple. For example, when I wish to make a telephone call, I know that I have to interact with the telecommunications system in a simple, well-defined way: I dial a number on the handset. This is my interface to the provision of the service. What happens inside the telephone exchange is doubtless very complex, but as a user of the service, this is not important to me.

As we have discussed, and will describe in more detail later, EJBs have two sorts of clients: synchronous clients and messaging clients. Synchronous clients invoke services on EJBs by calling methods on them, perhaps over a network connection. Such clients may be standalone Java programs (or perhaps programs written in other languages), servlets, JSP pages, or other EJBs. The EJBs that support synchronous access are the 'session' and 'entity' EJBs, which are described in much more detail below. Messaging clients obtain services by posting messages into a message service monitored by the EJB server. Messaging clients are serviced by message-driven EJBs, which will be the subject of Chapter 10.

We will see that both of these kinds of clients obtain a straightforward interface to the services of the EJB.

3.1.1   Synchronous clients

A fundamental principle of the EJB architecture is that synchronous EJBs (that is, session EJBs and entity EJBs) are used much like ordinary Java classes. We will see that entity EJBs represent persistent objects and have to be synchronized to a data storage medium (e.g., a relational database); even here, these details are invisible to the client. Such an EJB looks like an ordinary Java object, albeit with persistent state. By way of illustration, this chapter will make use of a simple EJB that calculates interest repayments.

Hint

The EJB used as an example for this section is described in full in Chapter 4, along with step-by-step instructions on how to compile, assemble, and deploy it, and to test it using a test client.

In general, an EJB's synchronous clients will interact with the EJB in a straightforward Java sense.[1] The listing below is an extract from the test client for the 'interest calculator' EJB, which is listed in full on page 96.

```
Interest interest = getInterest ();
double principal = 10000.0;
```

---

[1] For simplicity, I assume in this chapter that an EJB's clients are Java objects. This need not always be the case: EJBs can be invoked from C, C++, and even Microsoft Visual Basic with the appropriate adapter.

```
double rate = 10.0;
int terms = 10;
System.out.println ("Interest = $" +
    interest.getInterestOnPrincipal (principal, rate, terms));
System.out.println ("Total = $" +
    interest.getTotalRepayment( principal, rate, terms));
interest.remove();
```

The client calls a method `getInterest()` (described below) to obtain a reference to the EJB. It then calls methods on it, just like any ordinary Java class. Finally, it calls `remove()` on the EJB instance to signal that it has finished using it.

Now, in reality the client and the EJB are likely to be located on different physical hosts. Note that this is not apparent in the code: The client is not concerned whether the EJB is on the same host, a different host in the same room, or on the Moon; the code is the same in all cases. Of course, the variable `interest` in the listing above cannot reference the real remote object. The Java language has no built-in support for remote references. Clearly, it has to be a proxy of some kind. The identifier `Interest` does not, in fact, refer to a class, but to an interface. The interface will be implemented by a proxy that has the capability of communicating with the remote object. In this way, the low-level details of the RMI procedure are completely invisble to the client. As we shall see, `Interest` is the remote interface for the EJB.

So, from a Java language perspective, an EJB is manipulated through a set of interfaces. These interfaces specify the behaviour of the EJB and form a contract of service between the EJB and its clients. The interfaces are produced by the EJB developer and distributed to clients that require access to the EJB. Clearly, a Java class cannot call methods on an interface unless there is, somewhere, a class that implements that interface. However, this class will be generated automatically by the server's tools. As far as the client is concerned it calls methods on the interface.[2]

The *EJB Specification* defines two kinds of interfaces: the 'local view' and the 'remote view.' The local view interfaces are used by clients that will be located in the same JVM as the EJBs they are calling, while the remote view interfaces will be used by all other clients. An EJB can be provided with both sets of interfaces, and they can provide access to the same functionality, or different functionality, as the developer sees fit. We will have much more to say about the distinction between the local view and the client view, both later in this chapter (page 57) and throughout the book.

Whether we are using local or remote access, two different interfaces are required for method of access. The *home interface* (or 'factory interface') exposes functions that allow clients to obtain references to EJBs, create new EJBs, and remove redundant EJBs, while the *remote interface* and *local interface* provide access to the methods of the EJB itself. In this book, I refer to the remote interface and the local interface collectively as 'business method interfaces.' You may care to consider

---

[2]The *EJB Specification* actually uses this expression: "call method X on the interface Y." This is rather dubious terminology from the point of view of a Java purist, but it does serve to reinforce the message that it is the interface that is important, not the implementation.

whether these two sets of methods could, in fact, be expressed usefully on the one interface. This matter is discussed along with the technicalities of RMI in Chapter 2.

Gotcha!

The terminology used in describing interactions between EJBs and their clients is a potent source of confusion. This is because the client's view of 'instantiation' of an EJB is different to what happens in the JVM on the EJB server. In this book, I have followed two conventions in an attempt to reduce the problem. First, I never described the client as 'instantiating' an EJB. Instantiation is something that happens to a specific Java class. The JVM hosting the EJB may, or may not, instantiate one or more Java classes in response to the client's request. So I always talk about the client 'creating,' 'finding,' or 'removing' an EJB. Second, where something *is* instantiated, I have tried—to the extent compatible with reasonable brevity—to say exactly what class is instantiated. So, when something instantiates an instance of the EJB's implementation class, this is what the text will say, unless it is plainly obvious. In this book, I avoid terms like 'instantiates an EJB' because an EJB is not simply a class.

To begin an interaction with an EJB, its client must first of all obtain a reference to something that implements the home interface (we will discuss what this 'something' is later). We can then call a method on this interface to create or locate the required EJB. This is probably the only part of a client's interaction with an EJB that is substantially different from the interaction between Java objects in the same JVM. According to the *EJB Specification* [EJB2.0 6.2.1], the client uses JNDI to get a reference to the home object. In the `Interest` example, this logic is encapsulated in the `getInterest()` method, which looks like this:

```
InitialContext initialContext = new InitialContext();
Object o = initialContext.lookup ("Interest");
InterestHome home = (InterestHome)
   PortableRemoteObject.narrow (o, InterestHome.class);
return home.create ();
```

The interface between JNDI and EJBs is described in much more detail in Chapter 7. For the moment, notice that the key operation is the call to the `lookup()` method on the `InitialContext()`. The argument to this method provides the name of the EJB, as it is known to the EJB server, and the call returns something that

implements the EJB's home interface, `InterestHome`.[3] The client can then call the
`create()` method to get a reference to the EJB itself. More accurately, it gets a
proxy that implements the remote or local interface. We will have more to say about
the home object, and other server-side proxies, later in this chapter.

With a local client view, the client code is even simpler because the 'narrowing'
operation is not required:

```
{ejb.overview.client.view.session}
Context context = new InitialContext();
Object ref   = context.lookup("MyEJB");
MyEJBHome home = (MyEJBHome) ref;
```

The object returned by the `lookup()` operation will always be in the same JVM
as the caller and does not need to be narrowed.

3.1.2   Asynchronous (messaging) clients

Message-driven EJBs have fewer Java elements than the other types. Because they
don't take part in RMI, or indeed in any synchronous access by clients, they don't
have interfaces of any type. Instead, the developer registers the EJB with a particular message queue or message topic hosted on a message broker. A client interacts
with the message-driven EJB by posting a message to it. This is important, because
a messaging client is asynchronous with respect to the EJB application: When the
client has posted its message, it can continue without waiting for a response. The
EJB can then pick up the message and handle it in its own time. Asynchronous
clients are useful in business-to-business operations, where the the applications may
have to be loosely coupled.[4]

The client code needed to interact with message-driven EJBs is somewhat more
involved than that for a session or entity EJB (but not much more), so we defer an
example until later.

3.1.3   Client view: summary

We have seen that an EJB presents a straightforward interface to its clients. Session
and entity EJBs appear to the client as ordinary Java objects on which method calls
can be made, while message-driven EJBs appear simply as message queues or topics.
To obtain this simplicity, the EJB infrastructure is actually rather complex, and it
is to this that we must turn our attention next.

---

[3] In fact, it gets back something that can be 'narrowed' to something that implements the home
interface. This is described in more detail on page 39.

[4] The term 'loosely coupled' will appear time and time again in this book. It is a very important
concept in software engineering, because loosely coupled systems tend to be easier to manage and
maintain. In brief, a system exhibits loose coupling when its components interact with few, well-
specified interactions, rather than sets of interactions in which data is passed back and forth. To be
able to operate asynchronously, the client and the server must agree strictly on the format of the
data that is passed and cannot engage in dialog. This leads naturally to loose coupling. While we are
on the subject of software engineering, it's as well to introduce another, related concept: *cohesion*.
High cohesion is bad: It means that the components of the system have complex dependencies on
each other.

3.2   Fundamentals of the EJB architecture

An EJB is essentially a software component on which method calls can be made, and which can itself make calls on other components. These calls may be made over a network. In this sense, EJB technology is similar to Java RMI and CORBA. However, there are some defining features of EJBs that make EJB development rather different from (and easier than) other techniques for developing distributed applications. In Version 2.0 of the *EJB Specification*, EJBs are allowed to interact using local calling semantics, as well as distributed, RMI-like techniques.

Here are some other important features of the EJB architecture.

The client's view of an EJB is defined strictly by interfaces As we have already seen, synchronous clients can call only those methods exposed by the EJB's interfaces. In the *EJB Specification*, the interfaces are collectively referred to as the *client view*. Each EJB publishes 'factory' interfaces and 'business method' interfaces (usually, but not necessarily, one of each). The factory interfaces expose methods that clients can use to create, locate, and remove EJBs of that type. The business method interfaces define all the methods that clients can call on a specific EJB after it has been located or created through the factory interface. The term 'business method' is a generic one used to describe any method that a client can call on a specific EJB, and does not have to be related to 'business' in the dictionary sense.

Figure 3.1 shows in outline the interaction between EJBs, with the interfaces forming the points of contact in all cases.

It is important for the developer to understand that *anything* that makes method calls on an EJB is a client of that EJB, and interacts with it via its factory and business method interfaces. This applies even in the case where multiple EJBs interact within the same JVM. Enforcing this model allows the EJB infrastructure to provide important services transparently. If we are sure that the EJBs must be in the same JVM, then we can use local home and local interfaces, rather than remote home and remote interfaces.

In Java, as in most programming languages, an interface is simply a specification of method signatures; it does not indicate how the methods are to be implemented. Obviously something has to implement the interfaces. You may be surprised to learn that in EJB technology the interfaces are *never* implemented by a class authored by the developer. They are implemented proxy objects generated dynamically by the server vendor's tools.

EJBs are isolated and supported by an EJB container Although EJB clients make method calls as if they were directly on the EJB, in fact the method calls are on proxies which delegate to the EJB's implementation class. These proxies, and their supporting classes, form the *EJB container*.[5] The client

---

[5]It is a moot point whether these proxies are considered to be part of the EJB container or something that interacts with the EJB container. Server vendors seem to have strong opinions on this, but it makes no practical difference to the EJB developer.

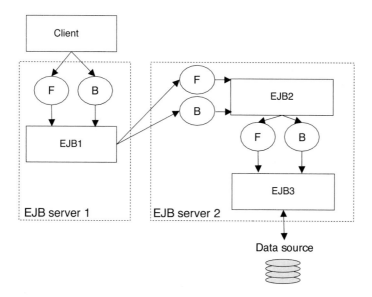

Figure 3.1. The interactions between EJBs and their clients are defined in terms of interfaces. Each EJB has a factory interface ('F') and a business method interface ('B'), as discussed in the text. When EJBs make method calls on other EJBs, even in the same JVM, then the calling EJB is a client of the target EJB and can call only those methods exposed by the interfaces.

never calls EJB methods on the implementation directly, even if the client and the EJB are actually on the same server, or even in the same JVM. This strategy allows powerful features like distributed transaction management to be provided transparently, and provides for pooling of implementation instances to increase efficiency.

Message-driven EJBs are not called directly by clients at all, and don't have container proxies in the same sense. Instead they are called directly by the container when it receives a message for a queue or topic in which the EJB has registered an interest.

The container encapsulates the EJB and acts as its security manager. It also provides general services to the EJB, as we shall see. The notion of the container and its proxies is illustrated in Figure 3.2.[6]

---

[6] A common design choice for an EJB server vendor is to implement the home object and the EJB container as the same Java class, or set of classes. So common is this strategy that in some places the *EJB Specification* is written as though it were mandated. For example, the sequence diagrams that show the interaction between the various components of the architecture show the EJB implementation class being instantiated by the home object, not by the container under the control of the home object. Again, the distinction is an academic one and should not trouble developers unduly.

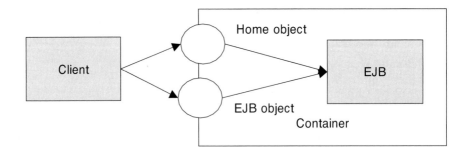

Figure 3.2. The notion of the EJB container as a proxy for the EJB: the client calls methods on the home object and EJB object, which delegate to the implementation itself. The process is transparent to the client. There are different home objects and EJB objects for local and remote access, but the purpose of these objects is essentially the same

Because the methods on the EJB proxies will delegate to methods on the EJB itself, the proxies must be generated to match the EJB—that is, the proxies will be specific to the EJB they serve. The vendor of the EJB server will provide tools to support this generation, which will typically take place when the EJB is deployed to the server.

Gotcha!

The terms 'EJB server' and 'EJB container' are not well-defined in the *EJB Specification*, and are used by developers somewhat interchangeably. In this book, a 'server' will be taken to mean a process of some sort, providing a set of low-level services that may be shared by any number of EJBs. A 'container' refers specifically to the supporting class or classes that encapsulate and manage an EJB.

The EJB container provides an illusion of a single-threaded environment The developer of an EJB should not have to be concerned about concurrency and thread management; in fact, it contravenes the *EJB Specification* [EJB2.0 24.1.2] for the developer to include code to handle these issues. The container ensures that the EJB is never called re-entrantly,[7] so the developer can code the EJB as if it were used in a single-threaded environment. This issue is a subtle one, and is discussed in more detail on page 476.

---

[7]With entity beans, concurrent access is allowed for different transactions; it is assumed that the transaction manager or database will enforce the appropriate locks to prevent loss of data integrity [EJB2.0 10.5.11]. This issue will be discussed in detail in Chapter 9.

The EJB container manages database transactions It does this even when the transaction spans multiple servers. There is a mechanism for specifying the transactional behaviour of EJBs outside of program code, although limited programmatic control of transactions is permissible as well.

The EJB container manages access and security Security attributes specify which methods on which EJBs are accessible to which groups of users. No coding is required, although limited programmatic intervention is allowed. The EJB server must provide a mechanism for end users to identify themselves to the application (e.g., a 'login' dialog box) or be able to access authentication from a Web browser in a Web application. The EJB developer should never have to code authentication procedures.

Creation and location of EJBs is standardized There is a well-defined way for the client to create new EJBs or to find existing ones. It does this on the factory interface, which it finds by doing a JNDI lookup on the EJB name. Having found the interface, the client can call its `create()` or `find()` methods to create or locate new EJBs. When it does this, it gets a reference to a proxy, not to the the EJB itself. The client manipulates the proxy exactly as if it were the real EJB, but the proxy carries out other functions (transaction management, for example) as well as delegating method calls to the EJB.

Instances can be pooled for efficiency When a client creates an EJB, it is really creating a 'conceptual EJB,' not an instance of a Java class. The EJB container may pool instances of the implementation class and give the client a reference to an existing instance when the client asks to create an EJB. Allowing the container to pool instances can lead to enormous gains in efficiency. Again, this is transparent to the client, but the developer must be aware of the circumstances in which pooling is permitted. Proxy instances may also be pooled in some circumstances.

The container manages resources EJBs get access to external resources—such as databases and messaging systems—through the container. The container can pool, share, and manage these resources on behalf of the EJBs, in a way that is transparent to the EJB developer. In this way, we get all the benefits or a resource sharing scheme, with few of the disadvantages.

There is a standard deployment process There is a specified, standard way for the EJB to be packaged and transferred to the server. This process is called *deployment*. Any EJB server that complies with the *EJB Specification* [EJB2.0 23] must be able to accept an EJB packaged in the correct way, regardless of the platform on which it was developed and tested.

3.3   Types of EJB

Version 1.1 of the *EJB Specification* [EJB1.1 4.3] defined two types of EJB: the *session EJB* and the *entity EJB*. Version 2.0 introduces a third type, the *message-driven EJB* [EJB2.0 4.3]. It is possible to envisage EJB applications where the EJBs don't fit neatly into any of these categories, but in practice one of these types can be adapted to suit most jobs. As there are separate chapters on each of these EJB types, the discussion here will be an outline only.

3.3.1 Session EJBs

A session EJB is a nonpersistent object: Its lifetime is the duration of a particular interaction between the client and the EJB. The client normally creates an EJB, calls methods on it, and then removes it. If the client fails to remove it, the EJB container will remove it after a certain period of inactivity. Session EJBs are subdivided into 'stateful' and 'stateless' types. A stateless session EJB is shared amongst a number of clients, while a stateful session EJB is created for a specific client and not used by any others. The use of stateless EJBs offers efficiency advantages but, of course, it is not always possible to use them.

Session beans are defined and described in Chapters 5–7 of the *EJB Specification*, and discussed in detail in Chapter 6 of this book.

3.3.2 Entity EJBs

Entity EJBs represent persistent objects: Their lifetimes are not related to the duration of interaction with clients. In nearly all cases, entity EJBs are synchronized with relational databases. This is how persistence is achieved. Entity EJBs are always shared amongst clients: A client cannot get an entity EJB to itself. Thus, entity EJBs are nearly always used as a scheme for mapping relational databases into object-oriented applications.

Whereas a client normally creates a session EJB and removes it after use, clients normally look up an existing entity EJB. Creation of an entity EJB corresponds to adding new data items to the application (e.g., adding rows to database tables).

An important feature of entity EJBs is that they have identity—that is, one can be distinguished from another. This is implemented by assigning a primary key to each instance of the EJB, where 'primary key' has the same meaning as it does for database management. Primary keys that identify EJBs can be of any type, including programmer-defined classes.

Entity beans are defined and described in Chapters 8–13 of the *EJB Specification*, and discussed in detail in Chapter 11 of this book.

3.3.3 Message-driven EJBs

A message-driven bean acts as a consumer of asynchronous messages: It cannot be called directly by clients, but is activated by the container when a message arrives. Clients interact with these EJBs by sending messages to the queues or topics to which they are listening. Although a message-driven EJB cannot be called directly by clients, it can call other EJBs itself.

Message-driven EJBs are the only type that do not follow a strict request-response interaction with clients. They are defined and described in Chapters 14 and 15 of the *EJB Specification*, and discussed in detail in Chapter 10 of this book.

3.4   Distributed and local EJB semantics

Clients of EJBs interact only with the container's proxies, not the EJB implementation itself. This applies whatever a client happens to be, even if it is itself an EJB in the same application. Typically, the client locates the proxy that implements the factory interface and makes a `create()` or `find()` call on it. This factory proxy then provides the client with a reference to a proxy that implements the business method interface, which the client then uses for all subsequent method calls.

In EJB 1.1, all calls on these proxies were considered to be network (RMI) calls, even when EJBs were located in the same JVM. EJB 2.0 allows for the provision of both remote and local (same JVM) proxies, as will be explained later. There was thus only one type of factory interface—called the home interface—and one type of business method interface—the remote interface.

In EJB 2.0, an EJB can be developed to support 'local' clients as well as distributed clients. A local client is one which is located in the same JVM as the EJB. This is quite a radical change from the all-RMI strategy of previous EJB versions. This section discusses the changes in the Specification, and the implications these will have for developers. Local clients can be provided with a different client view from distributed clients, and therefore another set of factory and business method interfaces is required. However, local clients still only interact with the EJB through proxies.

The inclusion of support for the local client view was not without controversy and has extremely wide-ranging implications for the developer. To understand why, it is helpful to know a bit about the way the *Specification* developed.

3.4.1   History

In Version 1.1 of the *EJB Specification* and its predecessors, EJBs were, by definition, distributable components. The developer could author EJBs without concern for how they would be physically distributed; all method calls were RMI calls. This model had a certain elegance and purity. The RMI strategy demanded the use of call-by-value semantics, which had the effect of decoupling the caller and the target. The ability to pass references to other objects as arguments is powerful, but makes it more difficult to maintain the caller and the target separately. With strict call-by-value, the author of an EJB could always assume that a method could act upon its arguments without side-effects on the caller.

However, there were problems with this strategy if efficiency was required more than purity. If all method calls were treated as RMI operations, each would involve a network channel set-up operation (e.g., TCP/IP connect), and marshalling and unmarshalling of arguments. Although EJB containers can, and do, act to optimize where calls are known to be within the same JVM, the call-by-value method—required to support RMI operation—prevents efficient argument passing within the same JVM. To obtain good efficiency while maintaining the purity of the application model, we learned to author EJBs with 'coarse-grained' client views. Each EJB provided its clients with a small number of complex methods, rather than a larger number of simpler methods. Because fewer method calls were required, the network overhead was kept manageable.

This use of a coarse-grained API was particularly unsuitable for entity EJBs. As we shall see, it is often the case that entity EJBs have relationsips (associations) with other entity EJBs, and these relationships may involve one EJB being dependent on another. As a dependent EJB can only be manipulated through its 'owner,' the close coupling between the owner and the dependent requires an efficient method-calling strategy and the use of a fine-grained API.

When EJB 2.0 was in draft, it was proposed that a lightweight calling mechanism be introduced to support the use of dependent entity EJBs. Various possibilities were examined, but in the end, consensus arose in favour of allowing entity EJBs to provide their clients with both a 'local' view and a 'remote' view. The remote view would be the same as the existing, RMI-based client view, while the local view would be provided by forcing the location of the client and the EJB into the same JVM. Thus EJBs could make intra-JVM calls on one another and thereby pass arguments by reference. For tightly coupled, associated entity EJBs, this is the right thing to do. There was no proposal to weaken the role of the EJB container, and the container proxies would still be interposed between client and EJB.

Having laid the groundwork for the local client view of an EJB, there was no *technical* reason why it could not be extended to session EJBs. There was, and remains, far less agreement on the validity of this technique with respect to session EJBs. Even purists of component-based development could accept—with some reluctance—the need for a lightweight calling strategy between EJBs that were, by their very nature, tightly coupled. But session EJBs should rarely be tightly coupled to their clients, and the use of local calling semantics is less acceptable here. Not everyone who was involved in the development of the EJB 2.0 specification was agreeable to this change; I myself opposed it quite vocally. Whatever arguments exist on each side, EJB 2.0 does currently support the use of intra-JVM, call-by-reference on session EJBs.

3.4.2   Implications

In EJB 2.0, an EJB can be designed to support either distributed clients or local clients or, theoretically, both. The methods exposed to these clients may be the same or different. In all likelihood the methods will be the same if both distributed and local client views are provided, but it is unlikely that a single EJB will need to support both local and remote clients.

Advantages of distributed client-EJB interaction

- The EJB server can direct method calls between different servers to provide load sharing. This allows a larger client load to be supported without any particular developer intervention. The ability to do this is one of the most useful features of the EJB architecture, and one that the developer should not sacrifice lightly.

> Gotcha!
>
> Clients are, on the whole, not affected by whether they are using the EJB's distributed view or local view. Similar procedures are used to locate, create, and invoke the EJB. However, there are some quite important exceptions that are thrown from the EJB container in the event of an error. The developer needs to be a bit careful about this.

- The call-by-value semantics means that the EJB is decoupled from its clients, and the developer does not have to worry about the side-effects of manipulating the arguments passed by clients. Although we can achieve the same effect with a call-by-reference (e.g., the target object can clone its arguments), it relies on the self-discipline of the developer.

- Provided that we can find a way to distribute the internal state of an EJB (difficult, but not impossible), the EJB server can provide fault-tolerant access to EJBs. If one EJB server fails, its load can be picked up by another. This is only possible with distributed calling semantics.

Advantages of local client-EJB interaction

- Local interaction is much faster, as the overheads of network interaction are significantly reduced.

- Despite the closer coupling implied by call-by-reference, sometimes we need call-by-reference for architectural reasons. For example, a client may wish to pass a reference to an output stream to an EJB and have the EJB stream data back as it becomes available. This is very awkward if there is no call-by-reference mechanism.

- As all method calls are local, the developer does not have to be concerned with handling exceptions (usually defined as `RemoteException` and its sub-classes) that may arise at the transport level. For example, the client does not have to deal with the situation that arises if the target EJB is unobtainable because its server is not responding.

3.4.3   Local and distributed interaction: summary

I tend to believe that we (developers) don't yet have sufficient practical experience with the local client view to understand its full implications. No doubt the outstanding issues will be worked out as more projects start to make use of EJB 2.0 techniques. At present, my feeling is that EJBs should support local clients only for the purpose for which they were originally developed: improving the efficiency of interaction between dependent EJBs and their 'owners.' With container-managed persistence, as we shall see, developers have little choice, as the container will expect to see a local client view of a dependent EJB.

It is important to remember that the local client view is available *only* to clients running in the same JVM as the EJB container hosting the target EJB. In some application servers, the servlet engine may be colocated with the EJB container, and therefore accessible—in theory—to a local client view. In other products, the EJB server may be in a separate JVM, or even on a separate host. This means that, in practice, the local client view is only going to be appropriate for EJB-EJB interactions. In particular, the use of standalone test clients necessitates the provision of a distributed client view.

3.5   Anatomy of an EJB

When authoring a session or entity EJB, the developer must provide at least three Java `.class` files: two interfaces that expose the methods of the EJB that are accessible to clients, and an implementation class (often called the 'bean class' or 'EJB class'). We need two interfaces because one exposes the factory methods of the EJB (`create()`, `find()`), while the other exposes the business methods that can be called on the specific EJB. In EJB 1.1, all EJB method calls were RMI calls, and only one pair of interfaces was required, the home interface and the remote interface. Of these, the former exposed the factory methods, and the latter the business methods.

As we have discussed, in EJB 2.0, to support the notion of intra-JVM EJB interaction, the developer can choose whether to specify a 'local' view, a 'remote' view, or both. When the local view is used, the factory methods are exposed by an interface called the local home interface, and business methods by the local interface. These interfaces and their relationships are summarized in Table 3.1. Although the names of the remote view interfaces have changed between EJB 1.1 and EJB 2.0, their functions have not, and neither has the Java code required to define them. All the interfaces are described in more detail later.

On a practical note, the factory interfaces tell the container how to implement the factory proxy, while the business method interfaces fulfill the same function for the business method proxy. These objects are described later in this chapter. Where we are providing a remote view, the interfaces also tell the server how to generate the stubs and skeletons needed to support RMI.

For a message-driven EJB only the implementation class is necessary.

All classes and interfaces must be supplied in a JAR file with a particular structure (see below).

As we shall see, the implementation class must provide implementations not only of the methods exposed by the interfaces, but of the life cycle management methods, which are called by the EJB container, not the client.

The correspondence between the interfaces and container-generated proxies is shown in Figures 3.3 to 3.5. These diagrams are for reference, rather than study, so please don't try to memorize them (yet!).

EJB usage	EJB 1.1 interface	EJB 2.0 interface	Exposes
Distributed interaction	Home interface	Remote home interface	Factory methods
	Remote interface	Remote interface	Business methods
Local interaction	n/a	Local home interface	Factory methods
	n/a	Local interface	Business methods

Table 3.1. Interfaces supplied by the EJB developer in EJB 1.1 and EJB 2.0. It is unusual for both distributed and local interfaces to be provided for the same EJB.

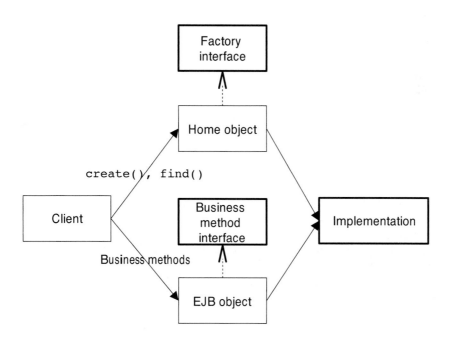

Figure 3.3. The relationship between the factory and business method interfaces in general. Bold boxes indicate Java classes or interfaces supplied by the EJB developer. The proxies will be generated automatically by the server vendor's tools.

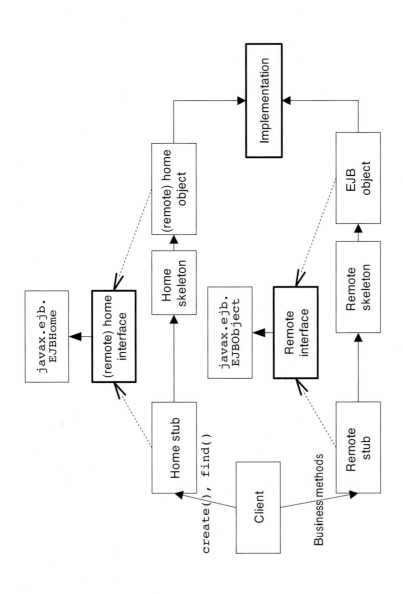

Figure 3.4. The relationship between the factory and business method interfaces in the remote client view. With EJB 1.1, this is the only view available.

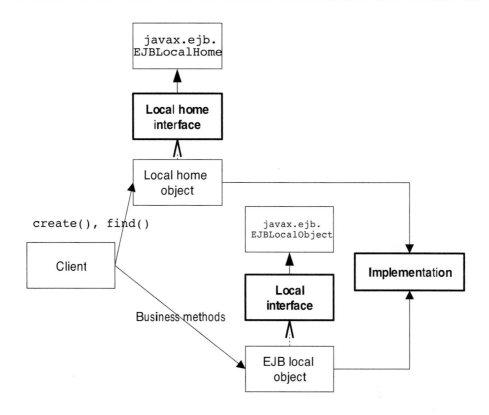

Figure 3.5. The relationship between the factory and business method interfaces in the local client view. Note how much simpler this model is than Figure 3.4, as a result of the absence of RMI support classes.

Along with these three .class files, the EJB developer must provide at least one other file: the *deployment descriptor*. This is an XML file that contains information about the structure of the EJB.

3.5.1   Business method interfaces

Session and entity EJBs need a business method interface,[8] which will expose to clients the business methods they may call. Message-driven EJBs don't have clients in the strict sense, and therefore don't need a business method interface.

When the EJB provides a local client view, the business method interface is provided by the *local interface*. For the remote client view, it is provided by the *remote interface*. Despite the different names, these interfaces have exactly the same function: to expose business methods on the EJB to clients. Each method that the client will call on the EJB must be specified in the remote or local interface. Local interfaces are new in Version 2.0 of the *EJB Specification*. It is unlikely that both a

---

[8]In principle, both local and remote versions could be supplied, but this is unusual.

remote and a local interface will be required for the same EJB, but where both *are* provided, they will probably expose the same methods.

For example, if the EJB is to have a method `withdrawFunds(double amount)`, which can throw an exception `InsufficientBalanceException`, then it would be defined in the remote interface like this:

```
public void withdrawFunds(double amount)
  throws RemoteException,
    InsufficientBalanceException;
```

As in Java RMI, methods in the remote interface must be defined to throw `RemoteException`, because the class that actually implements the remote interface (the remote stub; see below) will need to be able to throw this exception. In addition, the remote interface must declare any other exceptions that can be thrown from the EJB's methods. In the local interface, the definition would read:

```
public void withdrawFunds(double amount)
  throws InsufficientBalanceException;
```

That is, there is no provision to throw `RemoteException`. This is because the local interface is used only for intra-JVM calls; no stubs are required and there is therefore nothing to throw this exception.

All EJB remote interfaces must be subinterfaces—direct or indirect—of `javax.ejb.EJBObject`. Local interfaces must be subclasses of `javax.ejb.EJBLocal Object`.

When the EJB is deployed, the deployment tool or the EJB server will use the remote interface to generate a proxy for the EJB called the *EJB object*.[9] It will use the local interface to generate a proxy called the *local object*.

3.5.2 Factory interface

The factory interface of a session or entity EJB exposes the methods that the client can call that relate to life cycle management of the EJB. These methods do not necessarily correspond to method calls in the implementation class: They may be handled entirely by the EJB container. With distributed client view, the factory interface is formally called the *remote home interface*, while with local client view, it is the *local home interface*. Because EJB 1.1 only supported distributed clients, there was no concept of a 'local home interface.' Thus the terms 'factory interface' and 'home interface' were synonyms. For simplicity, this book follows that same pattern, and the term 'home interface' refers to either factory method. I will use the terms 'remote home interface' and 'local home interface' only when it is necessary to distinguish between them. Such circumstances will be rare, as the remote and local home interfaces fulfill exactly the same purpose.

---

[9]The term 'EJB object' and the names of the other proxies are, in fact, colloquialisms that don't appear in the *EJB Specification*. The Specification simply refers to these objects by the names of the Java interfaces they implement. While this is undoubtedly logical, most developers and publications use the colloquial terms and this book will do likewise.

The home interface (local or remote) can specify two types of method: 'create' methods and 'find' methods. These relate to the two ways in which the client can get a reference to an EJB: It can create a new one or find an existing one. For example, all stateless session EJBs must specify the following method in the remote home interface:

```
public [remote] create()
  throws RemoteException,
    javax.ejb.CreateException;
```

where [remote] is the type of the remote interface. This method creates an EJB, and returns to the client a reference to the EJB object that acts as the EJB's proxy.

For local home interfaces, the equivalent is:

```
public [local] create()
  throws javax.ejb.CreateException;
```

where [local] is the type of the local interface. In this case, the EJB server returns a reference to the the local object that acts as the EJB's proxy.

To accompany the method definitions in the interface, the implementation class must provide a method, `ejbCreate()`, that matches each `create()` in the home interface.

All remote home interfaces must be subinterfaces—direct or indirect—of `javax.ejb.EJBHome`, while local home interfaces must be subinterfaces of `javax.ejb.EJBLocalHome`.

When the EJB is deployed, the deployment tool or the EJB server will use the home interface to generate a proxy called the *home object*.

Message-driven EJBs don't need a home interface.

3.5.3   Implementation class: session and entity EJBs

In a session or entity EJB, the implementation class provides implementations of the methods specified in the business method interface, and perhaps of those in the factory interface. The quotes around the word 'implementations' are there because, however odd it sounds at first, the implementation class does not `implement` either of these interfaces in the Java sense. That is, if we are providing a remote client view (as we usually will be) where the home interface is `MyHome` and the remote interface `MyRemote`, we will *not* write code like this:

```
public class MyImplementation implements MyHome, MyRemote
```

Instead, it is the container-generated stubs and proxies that will implement the home and remote interfaces. Of course, the implementation class must provide code that supports the methods specified in the interfaces. We will see how this is done later.

In addition to the business and factory methods provided for the benefit of clients, this class must implement the methods that will be called by the EJB container during life cycle management. For example, there will be method calls that indicate when the implementation class instance is created and destroyed.

Methods that are called by the EJB container are usually referred to as *callback methods* or *life cycle methods*.

The implementation class must implement `javax.ejb.SessionBean`, `javax.ejb.EntityBean`, or `javax.ejb.MessageDrivenBean`, depending on whether it is a session, entity, or message-driven EJB. Thus implementations must be provided for all the methods in these interfaces, although in many cases the method bodies may be empty.

3.5.4 Implementation class: message-driven EJBs

A message-driven EJB's implementation has no business methods. The container calls the `onMessage()` method when a message arrives. These EJBs have no home or remote interface, and no home object or EJB object is generated. However, like session and entity EJBs, the message-driven EJB's implementation class must handle the callback methods that are concerned with life cycle management.

3.5.5 Deployment descriptor

The deployment descriptor provides configuration information to the EJB server. Information in the descriptor includes the following:

- the display name: the name of the EJB displayed by deployment tools;

- names of the classes that the EJB requires: implementation, interfaces, and primary key class, if any;

- the type (session, entity, message-driven) and subtypes (stateful, stateless, etc.);

- security attributes (see Chapter 16);

- transaction attributes (see Chapter 9);

- configuration ('environment') variables (see Chapter 7);

- EJB cross-reference information;

- resource reference information (e.g., names of databases used).

The deployment descriptor is an XML file, and the *EJB Specification* [EJB2.0 21] states exactly what its syntax should be. In addition, it specifies that the deployment descriptor must be a file called `ejb-jar.xml` in a directory `META-INF` in the JAR file.

The format of the deployment descriptor is not particularly complex, but it can be quite lengthy. While it is straightforward to construct the file manually for simple applications, most serious development work will require the use of software tools. Most developers use graphical tools supplied by the vendor of the EJB server, which are often part of an integrated EJB assembly and deployment tool. For that reason, this book will not have much to say about the deployment descriptor in the text, but a brief overview is presented in Appendix B. More interested readers should refer to [EJB2.0 23] for full details.

3.5.6   EJB class naming conventions

Because the deployment descriptor defines the roles of the `.class` files that make up the EJB, the names used for the implementation class, home interface, and remote interface are arbitrary. However, it is sensible for clarity to adopt a naming convention that indicates immediately what the different classes and interfaces do. A convention that is widely used, and that I have followed in this book, is to base the class and interface names on the EJB name. For example, if the name of the EJB is to be `Booking`, then the names would be:

Home interface	`BookingHome`
Remote interface	`Booking`
Bean class	`BookingBean`

In particular, the remote interface has the same name as the EJB, as this is the name that will be manipulated most frequently in client code. Of course, none of this applies to message-driven EJBs, as they don't have home or remote interfaces. There is, as yet, no widely established naming convention for the local home interface or local interface.

3.6   Principle of operation: session and entity EJBs

When the EJB is deployed, the server and the deployment tools inspect the factory interface and generate the appropriate (local or remote) home object. 'Generation' in this context means that the home object is produced as Java source code, which is then compiled into a Java class. The resulting home object class is then instantiated, and its name made available for clients to look up. The server also generates the EJB object from the remote interface, but does not necessarily instantiate it at this point. The implementation class is made available on the server, but this also is not instantiated.

So when an EJB is first deployed, and whenever the server is restarted, the client can expect to see a home object instance in place for each EJB. The interaction diagram of Figure 3.6 shows a simplified, general interaction between the client, the container, and the implementation class. In later chapters, we will see how this interaction is managed for specific types of EJB. Note that this overview does not depend on whether the client is using the local or distributed client view of the EJB.

1. The client does a name lookup to find the home object; the name lookup service returns a reference to the home object (with the distributed client view, it actually returns the home stub—that is, a stub configured to communicate with the home object).

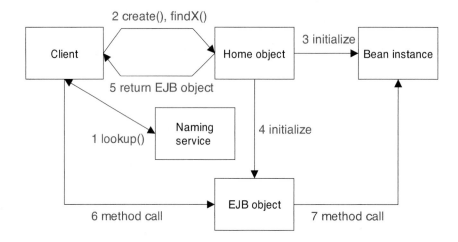

Figure 3.6. Basic principle of operation of a session or entity EJB.

2. The client calls a 'create' or 'find' method on the home object, according to whether it wants to create a new EJB or find an existing EJB. Only entity EJBs are subject to 'find' operations.

3. The home object, in conjunction with the container (if these aren't the same object), initializes an instance of the implementation class. This may involve creating a new instance or finding a free instance in the pool. In either case, an instance is made ready for use.

4. The home object or container initializes an EJB object for the selected EJB. Again, this may be a new instance or a pooled instance.

5. The home object returns to the client a reference to the EJB object. With distributed operation, this is actually the remote stub—that is, a stub connected to the EJB object.

6. The client calls whatever methods it needs on the EJB object.

7. The EJB object checks the credentials of the caller, creates a new transaction if necessary, and delegates the business method call onto the implementation. If the EJB object creates a new transaction, it will attempt to complete it before returning control to the caller.

   The client can make repeated business method calls on an active EJB reference: For each call, the container repeats the sequence of operations described in step 7.

3.7   Principle of operation: message-driven EJBs

Figure 3.7 shows the basic principle of operation of a message-driven EJB.

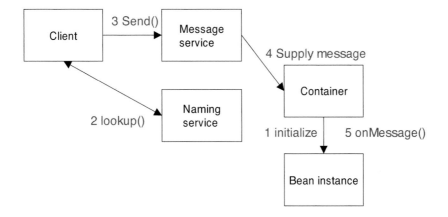

Figure 3.7. Basic principle of operation of a message-driven EJB.

1. The EJB container initializes a pool of instances of the EJB's implementation class.

2. The client looks up the queue or topic to which the desired EJB is listening.

3. The client posts messages to this queue or topic.

4. The messaging service supplies the messages to the EJB container.

5. The container calls the implementation's `onMessage()` method.

3.8   The EJB container and its proxies

In Java RMI,[10] the clients of a remote object did not call methods on the remote object directly. Instead, they call methods on a stub, which passes the method call information over the network to the 'skeleton,' which calls the method on the remote object. The EJB model extends this notion by introducing the idea of the EJB container as an additional element in the interaction. The container has two main functions:

- It intercepts all method calls made by the client and carries out various actions (concerned with security and transaction management, among other things) before delegating them to an instance of the implementation class itself. That is, the container provides proxies that isolate the EJB's implementation class from its clients.

- It provides general services to the EJB, such as database connection pooling.

---

[10]Here we are using the term 'Java RMI' to mean the specific form of RMI supported natively by the JDK; it does not mean 'RMI done in Java,' which could, of course, include EJB interactions.

3.8.1   Container proxies

As we have seen, a remote client of a session or entity EJB makes calls on stubs that implement the home interface and remote interface. These stubs communicate with the home object and remote object, which can be considered part of the EJB container. These proxies then delegate the method calls to the EJB where necessary. Because the EJB server does not know in advance what methods will be provided in your EJBs, it can't provide general-purpose proxies. Such proxies must be generated for each new EJB that is deployed. The server vendor will provide tools to do this, usually at deployment time. The relationship between the proxies and the stubs is show diagrammatically in Figure 3.4.

Where do the home interface and remote interface fit into all of this? The only Java class that *must* implement the home interface is the stub that the client uses to communicate with the home object. Similarly, the stub for the EJB object must implement the remote interface. These stubs must implement the interfaces, because the client will call methods on the stubs via the interfaces. At compilation time, the client will likely not have access to the stubs themselves, but at runtime we can be sure that they will implement methods that the client will call.

However, there is no need for the (remote) home object or (remote) EJB object to implement any of the EJB developer's interfaces. These proxy objects have methods that are called by the skeletons—in a vendor-specific manner, not directly by the client. They therefore don't need to implement any of the EJB's interfaces. They *may* implement them, if the server vendor believes that this is helpful to the implementation of the server, but it is irrelevant to the EJB developer.

If it is irrelevant, why have I mention it at all? The reason is that many introductory textbooks and courses describe the home object as an implementation of the home interface and the EJB object as an implementation of the remote interface. This supports the view that the client 'calls methods on the home object' or on the EJB object. This oversimplification obscures the roles of the stubs and skeletons, and the fact that client-EJB interactions using the remote client view are always network operations, with the overheads and complexities that this entails.

We will now consider the functions of the home object and EJB object in more detail. Unless otherwise stated, the comments in this section apply equally to the proxies supporting the local and distributed client views.

The home object

As we have already seen, the home object for each EJB is instantiated as soon as the EJB is deployed, or whenever the server is restarted. The home object must be available at all times, as the client will use it to get access to the EJB.

The home object is responsible for responding to 'create' and 'find' calls from the client. When the client calls a 'create' method, the home object brings about the creation of an instance of the implementation, if necessary (or returns one from the pool). It also causes an EJB object to be instantiated, if necessary. When the client makes a 'find' call, the home object either locates the EJB itself or delegates the find call to the implementation. These issues will be discussed in more detail in later chapters.

With distributed interaction, the class on the client that encapsulates the communication between the client and the home object is called the *home stub*.

The EJB object

In this section, the term 'EJB object' refers to both remote and local EJB objects.

The EJB object acts as a proxy for the EJB's business methods. When the client makes a call on a business method, it is actually making the call on to the EJB object, which carries out two important actions before calling the method itself. First, it checks whether the client is authorized to call the requested method. If not, it throws an exception. If the call is allowed, the EJB object checks whether a new transaction needs to be initiated (based on the transaction attributes supplied by the developer).

After calling the method on the EJB, the EJB object attempts to commit any transaction it started before the call.

It is important to understand that there is not necessarily a one-to-one relationship between EJB object instances and implementation class instances, nor is there a one-to-one relationship between clients and EJB objects. Failure to understand this principle is a major cause of errors in EJB development. The relationship between the instantiation of EJB objects and implementation class instances will be discussed in more detail in the chapters on session EJBs and entity EJBs.

An important feature of the EJB object is to provide the EJB with the illusion that it is running in a single-threaded environment. This relieves the developer of the need to include thread management and synchronization code. The techniques it uses to do this are discussed in Chapter 6.

With a remote client, the class deployed on the client that encapsulates the communication between the client and the EJB object is called the *remote stub*. Local clients don't use stubs, as the interactions are in the same JVM.

3.8.2   'EJB skeletons'

In Java RMI, the client and server endpoints of the remote method protocol were supported by a stub and a skeleton. It was the skeleton that made the method calls on the remote object. It did this directly at the behest of clients, without interacting with any supporting infrastructure. For example, the skeleton would never take it upon itself to determine whether the caller was allowed to make the method call. In a sense, the stub and skeleton were nothing more than a mechanism to conceal the networking operations.

With EJBs, the situation is more complicated. Between the network and EJB implementation class, two types of supporting functionality are required. First, we have to encapsulate the network operations, as for Java RMI. Second, we need to fulfil the contract between the proxy objects and the implementation class. This contract says, for example, that the proxies can initiate database transactions, carry out security checks, and so on.

All this means that the proxy objects—the home object and EJB object—are *not* merely skeletons in the Java RMI sense. However, there is no logical reason why skeleton (networking) functionality cannot be embedded into these objects along with their other responsibilities. That is, the stubs on the client could communicate directly with the proxies, which would fulfil this 'dual role.'

Of course, this is only possible if there is good collaboration between the authors of the software that generates the stubs and those of the software that generates the proxies. This is likely to be the case only when both of these entities are generated by software from the same vendor.

To allow for increased flexibility, and to allow different RMI protocols to be supported with the same proxies, most vendors have chosen to implement separate skeletons for the EJB proxies, rather than allowing the proxies to be skeletons as well. In a scheme of this sort, when the client calls an EJB method, it calls the method on the stub, which communicates with the skeleton, which then calls a method on the proxy, which calls the EJB method. This slight increase in overhead is compensated by an increase in flexibility.

3.8.3   Container services

As well as its role in isolating EJBs from their clients, the container provides various services to the EJB. One of the most important of these is database connection pooling. When an EJB wants to make a connection to a database, it gets this connection from the container, not from a JDBC driver manager. This allows the container to pool database connections, and share them between different clients. With this strategy, an EJB application can support many clients while using only a few database connections. Database connection pooling is described in more detail in Chapter 8.

An EJB relies on its container for access to all external resources, not just database connections. This principle allows the container to manage resources efficiently while maintaining the scope of transactions and propagating security contexts, as will be discussed later. The problem with this strategy is that it can lead to problems, when EJBs need access to resources of a type that the container did not anticipate. This is by no means an uncommon situation: EJB applications frequently need access to legacy systems, networked services, or hardware devices.

Most EJB server products provide an extension API, which developers can use to extend the functionality of the container. The problem with this approach is that it is vendor-specific: Applications that rely on extension APIs will not be portable. The *J2EE Connector Architecture*—recently finalized—provides a vendor-independent mechanism for extending an EJB container to deal with nonstandard external resources. The connector API is described in detail in Chapter 18.

3.8.4   EJB instance pooling

The EJB architecture is designed, as far as possible, to allow the EJB container to pool instances of the implementation class and share them amongst clients. By doing this, we avoid the overhead of creating and garbage-collecting the large number of instances that would otherwise be required to support large client volumes.

Instance pooling is usually managed by EJB objects in collaboration with other parts of the EJB container (Figure 3.8). In the simple scheme shown, a single, shared EJB object is managing two implementation instances on behalf of a number of clients. It is important to remember that the EJB object must prevent an instance of the EJB's implementation class from being entered by more than one thread at a time, so the object must have a notion of which instances are serving clients at any given time. If the EJB object is itself pooled or shared, and can accept multithreaded calls from skeletons, then it must itself must be thread-safe. When a client calls a method, the EJB object will make a call on one of the instances of the implementation class, if one is available. Otherwise, it will simply wait until an instance is free. This does impose a delay on the response to the client, so clearly there is an advantage to having enough instances that clients will not usually have to wait long. On the other hand, the server hardware cannot support an arbitrarily large number of active threads, so there may not be any advantage to having a very large pool. 10–30 instances seems to work well for most practical applications.

The developer cannot assume that the EJB container will direct a client request to any particular instance in the pool.[11] The client may well find that if it calls the same method twice, the second call involves a different instance than the first. Clearly this will have implications for designers. These implications for different types of EJB will be described in detail in later chapters.

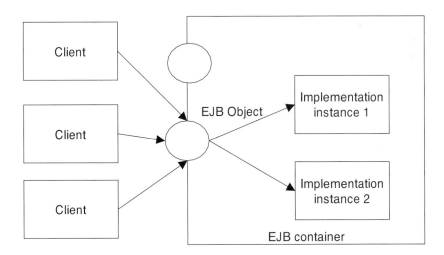

Figure 3.8. Instance pooling with a shared EJB object. See text (Section 3.8.4) for details.

---

[11]With stateful session EJBs, as we shall see, clients may assume that the instance variables *retain their values* between method calls; this is not *quite* the same as assuming that the method calls go to the same instance. The reason it is not quite the same is that in a fault-tolerant environment, the EJB container must be able to synchronize EJB instance variables between servers.

Not all EJB types can be pooled. In particular, it is difficult to pool stateful session EJBs, as we shall see.

3.9 Overview of the EJB API

You may prefer to have a look at the example of a complete EJB in the next chapter before reading this section. Although this information is important, you will be able to follow what is involved in constructing and testing an EJB without this.

To ensure a uniform API between the EJB, the container, and the clients, the various parts of an EJB are required to implement certain interfaces. The most important of these are described briefly here. All these interfaces and their methods will be explained in more detail later in the book.

3.9.1 EJBHome and EJBLocalHome

All remote home interfaces must extend `javax.ejb.EJBHome`, while local home interfaces extend `javax.ejb.EJBLocalHome`. No special effort is required on the part of the developer to implement the methods specified in this interface; the developer's home interface is implemented by the container's proxies, which are generated by the server vendor's tools, usually at deployment time. The methods in `EJBHome` are summarized in Table 3.2. EJB clients can call any of these methods, as well the 'create' and 'find' methods defined by the developer, and they are handled by the home stub in conjunction with the home object and the container. `EJBLocalHome` only defines the method `remove()`, and is therefore much simpler. This reflects the comparative simplicity of local EJB interaction.

Note that the `EJBHome` interface specifies 'remove' methods but no 'create' methods. This is because the `create()` methods have arbitrary parameter lists, and must therefore be specified in the developer's home interface, rather than in a general, API-level interface. `remove()` always takes no arguments.

3.9.2 EJBObject and EJBLocalObject

All remote interfaces—required to support the distributed client view—implement the `EJBObject` interface, and therefore the client can call these methods on the EJB reference obtained from the home object, as well as any methods defined in the remote interface itself. As was the case for the `EJBHome` interface, the methods specified by `EJBObject` are not implemented by any part of the EJB; they are implemented by the remote stub, which is generated automatically. Table 3.3 summarizes the methods specified by `EJBObject`. `EJBLocalObject` supports a subset of these methods, appropriate to intra-JVM operation.

3.9.3 SessionBean

This interface is implemented by all session EJB implementation classes. As these methods will be discussed in much more detail in Chapter 6, only a brief description is given here (Table 3.4).

`EJBMetaData getEJBMetaData()`	Returns an `EJBMetaData` object that provides information about the structure of the EJB, including the names of the Java classes that form its home and remote interfaces, its primary key (if applicable), and the type of the EJB. This method is not commonly used in application programs, but may be useful for development tools.
`HomeHandle getHomeHandle()`	Returns a `HomeHandle` object that is a serializable version of the home stub. The client can pass the handle to another client or use it to store a reference to the home object in a file. This method is rarely used, because any client can get a reference to the home object by doing a JNDI lookup.
`void remove (Object pk)`	Removes the EJB with the specific primary key. This method is only meaningful for entity EJBs, as session EJBs don't have primary keys.
`void remove (Handle h)`	Removes the EJB with the specific handle. Don't confuse an EJB handle with a home handle; an EJB handle identifies a specific EJB. This method can be used on both session and entity EJBs. In practice, it is more convenient to remove an EJB through its remote interface, as described below.

Table 3.2. The `EJBHome` interface.

The `SessionBean` interface extends `EnterpriseBean`, which has no methods but extends `java.io.Serializable`. Thus all session EJB implementation classes are serializable by default.

3.9.4 EntityBean

This interface is implemented by all entity EJB implementation classes. As these methods will be discussed in much more detail in Chapter 11, only a brief description is given here (Table 3.5).

The `EntityBean` interface extends `EnterpriseBean`, which has no methods but extends `java.io.Serializable`. This all entity EJB implementation classes are serializable by default.

`EJBHome getEJBHome()`	Returns a reference to the home object for the EJB. Technically, what we get is a reference to a home stub, on which we can make remote calls on the real home object. This method is seldom used, as we can always get a reference to the home by doing a JNDI lookup.
`Handle getHandle()`	Returns a `Handle` object that identifies the EJB object and is serializable. Note that if we try to serialize the EJB reference itself (that is, the result of calling 'create' or 'find' on the home interface), this may fail; this is because the instance is really a stub, not a real object. Stubs may encapsulate active network endpoints, and are therefore not *guaranteed* to be serializable (see page 486). If we want to serialize an EJB reference, we can get the `Handle` and serialize that. After deserialization, we call `getEJBObject()` on the handle to get a real EJB reference. A particular use for EJB handles is to store a reference to an EJB within an `HttpSession` object in a servlet. This allows successive client interactions with the servlet to use the same EJB.
`Object getPrimaryKey()`	Returns the primary key for the EJB, if applicable. This method is only meaningful for entity beans, as only entity beans have primary keys. This method is of limited use in EJB applications, as the EJB developer will probably provide a mechanism for clients to get the data represented by the primary key.
`boolean isIdentical (EJBObject o)`	Determines whether the EJB is identical to another one. The notion of 'identicality' is well-defined for entity beans: Two EJBs are identical only if they have the same primary key. Identicality is less well-defined for session beans: The *EJB Specification* says that for stateful session beans, they are identical if two references are both associated with the same implementation class instance (unlikely in practice). For stateless session beans, this method always returns `true`, as by definition stateless session beans are indistinguishable. These issues are described in more detail in Chapter 6.
`void remove()`	Remove the EJB.

Table 3.3. The `EJBObject` interface.

`void ejbActivate()`	This method is called by the EJB container on the implementation when it has reactivated the EJB from its 'passive' state. See page 149 for more details. This method is never called on stateless session EJB, and is often empty even in stateful session EJBs.
`void ejbPassivate()`	This method is called by the EJB container on the implementation when it is about to be set into its 'passive' state. See page 149 for more details. This method is never called on stateless session EJB, and is often empty even in stateful session EJBs.
`void ejbRemove()`	This method is called by the EJB container when the implementation is no longer required. The container will then release its reference to the instance, and the garbage collector will eventually delete it and reclaim its memory.
`void setSessionContext (SessionContext sc)`	This method is called by the container immediately after creating the instance of the implementation. The method is passed a `SessionContext` instance which the EJB should store. Later it can use this object to obtain information about transactions and security.

Table 3.4. The `SessionBean` interface.

`void ejbActivate()`	This method is called by the EJB container on the implementation when it has reactivated the EJB from its 'passive' state. See page 330 for more details.
`void ejbPassivate()`	This method is called by the EJB container on the implementation when it is about to be set into its 'passive' state. See page 330 for more details.
`void ejbRemove()`	This method is called by the EJB container when the client calls `remove()` on the EJB reference. The EJB should remove the data that corresponds to this EJB. The container does not remove the instance (as was the case for session EJBs), as it can be reused with a different set of data.
`void setEntityContext (EntityContext sc)`	This method is called by the container immediately after creating the instance of the implementation. The method is passed an `EntityContext` instance which the EJB should store. Later it can use this object to obtain information about transactions and security.
`void unsetEntityContext()`	This method is called by the container immediately before being made eligible for garbage collection. That is, it is the last method that the container will call on the implementation.

Table 3.5. The `EntityBean` interface.

3.9.5 EJBContext, SessionContext, and EntityContext

Objects that implement `SessionContext` and `EntityContext` are passed to an EJB's first initialization method as soon as the container creates it. This method is `setEntityContext()` for entity EJBs and `setSessionContext` for session EJBs. Both these interfaces are derived from `EJBContext`, and it is this superinterface that specifies most of the methods. The purpose of these interfaces is to allow EJBs to find out various things about their operating context, particularly the caller's security attributes and (in entity beans) the primary key.

The `EJBContext` interface is explained briefly in Table 3.6, `SessionContent` in Table 3.7, and `EntityContext` in Table 3.8.

You may have noticed that the method `getEJBObject()` appears (identically) in both `EntityContext` and `SessionContext`, even though these interfaces have a common superinterface.

3.10 EJB rules, standards and limitations

The *EJB Specification* sets out many rules about how an EJB's implementation class and its interfaces should be coded. These can be divided into the following general groups.

Common sense For example, methods on a remote interface should be public (nothing would work properly otherwise), and EJBs should not attempt to use graphics operations to produce output (who would see it?).

Not obvious, but clearly necessary when understood For example, an EJB should not use writable static instance variables. This is because the EJB server may pool instances of the EJB's classes in *different JVMs*. It would be awkward to keep the static instance variables synchronized between different JVMs.

Required to help container developers meet the *EJB Specification* The rules about thread management are in this category. EJBs are not allowed to manipulate threads, because this would make it almost impossible for the EJB container to maintain a single-thread model for EJBs.

Contested Some restrictions on EJBs are contested by many EJB developers and container vendors. For example, EJBs are prohibited from reading or writing files through the local filesystem. The *EJB Specification* merely says that file operations are "not well suited" to business data processing. Others have argued that it should be up to the EJB developer to decide what programming techniques are suited to the application.

There is not enough space in this book to list and describe all the rules and standards that EJB developers should follow (that, after all, is what a 500-page specification is for), and in any event, many of them are unlikely to be relevant in practice (e.g., EJB methods should not be `final`). The more important issues are discussed in Chapter 14.

`Principal` `getCallerPrincipal()`	Returns an object that implements the `javax.security.Principal` interface, which provides information about the entity (person or thing) that is calling this method. If the EJB is being called outside of an authenticated client container (e.g., the application does not provide a log-in procedure), then this method returns the `Principal` 'guest.' `Principal` has one useful method: `getName()`. There are some issues associated with this method that the developer needs to be careful about. See Chapter 16 for full details.
`EJBHome getEJBHome()`	Gets the home object for this EJB or, rather, a client stub that implements the home interface and can communicate with the home object. Thus, if this result is passed to another EJB, that EJB can call methods on the home object via the container, rather than making direct Java method calls within the JVM. Why is this important? In a distributed environment, the EJB that the reference is being passed to may not be on the same server, and therefore not in the same JVM. Thus, the result from `getEJBHome` is a safe way for an EJB to pass its home interface to other EJBs. The EJB can also use it to find or create other EJBs of the same type.
`EJBLocalHome` `getEJBLocalHome()`	Gets the local home object for this EJB, if it provides a local client view. The object returned is a local reference to an object in the same JVM, not a stub.
`boolean` `isCallerInRole(String role)`	In brief, this method determines whether the caller of the method is able to play a specific security role. EJB security is largely based on the idea of roles, more than user IDs or groups. Determining and setting up security roles is a key part of EJB application design. This is a very important topic, and it has a whole chapter (Chapter 16) devoted to it.
`boolean getRollbackOnly()`	An EJB can call this method to determine if it is currently involved in a transaction that has already been set to roll back. This issue is covered in detail in Chapter 9.
`void setRollbackOnly()`	If this method is called, any transaction that is currently in progress will be rolled back rather than committing. See Chapter 9.
`UserTransaction` `getUserTransaction()`	Returns an object that implements the `javax.transactions.UserTransaction` interface. Using this object, an EJB can begin, commit, and roll back transactions. See Chapter 9.

Table 3.6. The `EJBContext` interface. Note that deprecated methods are not shown.

80

EJBObject getEJBObject()	The object returned by this method—which will implement the `javax.ejb.EJBObject` interface—is the equivalent to the `this` reference in nondistributed programming. That is, if an EJB wants to pass a reference to itself to another EJB, or to a client that is not in the same JVM, it should pass the result of `getEJBObject()`, and not `this`. What the caller will actually get is a stub that can be used to make remote method calls on the EJB. This is *extremely* important. Remember that under IIOP objects are passed by value, not by reference. If an EJB passes `this` to another EJB, and that EJB is not in the same JVM, then the recipient will get a *copy* of the EJB implementation, not a reference to it. Making method calls on this copy will only affect the copy, not the real EJB.
EJBObject getEJBLocalObject()	If the EJB provides a local client view, this method returns a reference to the local object. This object can be used in the same was as the `this` pointer.

Table 3.7. The `SessionContext` interface. This is a subinterface of `EJBContext`, so the session EJB has access to the methods in `EJBContext` as well.

EJBObject getEJBObject()	Has exactly the effect as `SessionContext.getEJBObject()`. See above for discussion.
EJBLocalObject getEJBLocalObject()	Has exactly the effect as `SessionContext.getEJBLocalObject()`. See above for discussion.
Object getPrimaryKey()	Returns the primary key for this entity. The primary key uniquely identifies entity EJBs of the same class.

Table 3.8. The `EntityContext` interface. This is a subinterface of `EJBContext`, so the entity EJB has access to the methods in `EJBContext` as well.

3.11   Assembly and deployment

In almost all software development exercises, the computers used to develop the software are not the same as the ones that will be used to run it when in service. Unlike most other forms of software development, the format in which EJBs are packaged for transfer from a development system to a production system is standardized: EJBs are packaged into EJB-JAR files, which are in turn packaged into an EAR file. The EJB server is required by the *EJB Specification* to be able to take a correctly formatted EAR file from any source and install the EJBs it contains. Many products allow EJB-JAR files to be deployed without constructing an EAR file, which is convenient during development. This process, whether applied to EJB-JARs or to EARs, is called *deployment*.

An EAR file can contain EJBs from a number of different sources, produced by different developers. When these EJBs are combined into a single application, it may be necessary to resolve name mismatches between EJBs and satisfy references to external databases, among other things. This process is called *application assembly*.

While deployment and assembly are different processes, most vendors allow both to be carried out with the same software tool. Therefore, many developers don't distinguish sharply between assembly and deployment tools. When we talk of a 'deployment tool,' we usually mean something that can do assembly as well. The term 'assembly' is also used for the packaging of classes into an EJB and the construction of a deployment descriptor.

During deployment, the vendor's tools will normally construct the home and remote objects, and the home and remote stubs. The latter should be made accessible for standalone clients.

> Hint
>
> Having set up the structure and contents on the EJB-JAR file, deployment to the server ought to be a trivial job, whether using scripts, command-line tools, or vendors' graphical tools. If you modify and recompile the EJB classes, updating the EJB-JAR and redeploying to the server should also be trivial. If it requires more than, say, four mouse clicks or two commands, ask the vendor why this is. If you don't get a straight answer, ask for your money back. Deploying an EJB is not rocket science, and should not present a problem for a modern software tool.

3.11.1   The EJB-JAR file

An EJB file is simply a Java JAR archive, with a particular structure. The class files are organized in the JAR to reflect the package hierarchy, as usual, while deployment descriptors are placed in a directory called `META-INF`. If we have an EJB called

'BankTeller,' for example, whose classes are in the package `com.acme.ejb` and have been named according to the convention described above, then the EJB-JAR will have the following format:

```
com
    acme
        ejb
            BankTeller.class
            BankTellerHome.class
            BankTellerBean.class
META-INF
    ejb-jar.xml
    (other descriptors)
```

Note that the *EJB Specification* allows EJB server vendors to provide facilities to configure their products in ways that are not mandated (or, at least, does not forbid this). For example, the *EJB Specification* has nothing to say about load sharing, but this is a key feature of all commercial products. This kind of information cannot be placed into the standard deployment descriptor `ejb-jar.xml`, as the format of this file is strictly defined. So most vendors expect additional deployment descriptors. Ideally, the absence of these additional descriptors should not prevent the application from operating, although its performance may not be optimal. In practice, however, many vendors' products simply don't work at all without this extra information. This is one of the reasons why the cross-platform compatibility promised by EJB technology is not as easy to realize as may be hoped.

3.11.2   The EAR file

The EAR file contains a number of EJB-JAR files, along with WAR files that contain Web components (servlets, JSP pages, etc).

If the EJB-JAR file described above was called `bankteller.jar`, and this was the only EJB-JAR in the application, then the EAR file would have the following structure.

```
bankteller.jar
META-INF
    application.xml
    (other descriptors)
```

The deployment descriptor `application.xml` contains the following information:

- the display name of the application;

- a list of the EJB-JAR and WAR files that are to be deployed;

- application-wide security roles (see Chapter 16).

Again, the *EJB Specification* allows the vendor to use deployment descriptors in addition to the standard one to convey product-specific configuration information.

It is also conventional to include in the EAR file any additional class libraries that the application requires (that are not part of the EJBs).

3.11.3 Dynamic proxy and stub generation

It should be apparent by now that the home object and the EJB object/local object play key roles in EJB technology. Because these objects are proxies for the EJB, the methods they implement will usually depend on the methods in the EJB they serve. Thus, it is not practical for the EJB server to use general-purpose home and EJB objects. These objects will usually be generated dynamically at deployment time. In addition, the home stub and remote stub will also need to be generated, along with skeletons, if they are used.

The strategy used by most vendors is for their deployment tool to inspect the factory interface and business method interface of each EJB, using Java reflection, and construct the home objects, EJB object, EJB local object, and stubs as Java source files in a temporary directory. These source files are then compiled, and the classes inserted into the appropriate place in the server's CLASSPATH.

The stubs are required by clients of the EJBs, so these must be made available to install on the client. The usual approach is for the deployment tool to package these up into a JAR file (called, for example, `clientstubs.jar`) and allow the deployer to select where they should be saved. Although Java RMI supports automatic stub downloading (see page 36), this technique is rarely used by EJB products, and it is normal to distribute the stubs along with the other client code.

3.12 Configuration

Most applications will need to be configured after development to suit the needs of a particular customer. Even if the application is custom-written for a particular client, it is inconvenient if small changes in settings require recompilation of the application.

Outside of the EJB domain, a number of approaches are used to supply configuration information to applications: configuration files (various formats), environment variables, command-line arguments, database tables, etc. The *EJB Specification* defines exactly one way to supply configuration information to EJB applications [EJB2.0 20]. The configuration information is placed into the deployment descriptor, in the form of 'environment variables' (not to be confused with operating system environment variables, although their purpose is similar). Each variable has a name, a type, and a value. EJBs read these values by making JNDI name lookups, as will be described in Chapter 7.

The *EJB Specification* calls for this information to be processed only at deployment time [EJB2.0 20.2.4]. After deployment, changes in the environment variables require a redeployment. However, most EJB products do have mechanisms to change the environment variables after deployment. Such mechanisms are invariably vendor specific, and usually undocumented.

3.13   Summary

EJBs are distributable components that operate in the environment of a container. Clients of session and entity EJBs get access to the EJBs via proxy objects that are part of the container. The proxies are normally generated dynamically when the EJB is deployed to the server. The use of proxies and the container allow uniform methods for imposing security and managing transactions, with limited effort on the part of the developer. Clients of message-driven EJBs interact with the container by sending messages through a messaging service. For all types of EJB, the EJB server will attempt to optimize performance and reliability. The techniques it uses to do this should be mostly transparent to the developer. There are a number of EJB products on the market, and this number will almost certainly increase. Commercial products usually offer facilities in addition to these demanded by the *EJB Specification*, such as load balancing and resource pooling.

Chapter 4

Creating and deploying a simple EJB

Overview

This chapter will describe the practical details of writing, compiling, deploying, and testing EJBs. We start with the simplest of simple EJBs: The example in this chapter is a stateless session bean, with only two methods accessible to clients. For purposes of illustration, we will describe this process for the *J2EE Reference Implementation* Version 1.3. For other products, the assembly and deployment process will be different, but the coding will be the same.

The EJB example used in this chapter is straighforward, but more complex than the usual 'hello world!' examples. It is designed to calculate compound interest repayments on loans, and is therefore called 'Interest.' The Java class files will be in the package `com.kevinboone.ejb_book.interest`. We will also create a simple command-line test client for the EJB, which will be a class called `InterestTestClient`, in the same package. Because the test client is a standalone Java program, we must provide a distributed client view (using remote factory and business method interfaces). There is no compelling reason to provide an additional local client view, but we shall do so anyway for the sake of illustration. The EJB has only two methods, and the same methods are exposed in both the remote and local views.

So the classes to be created (all in the same package) are:

Remote home interface	`InterestHome`
Local home interface	`InterestLocalHome`
Remote interface	`Interest`
Local interface	`InterestLocal`
Implementation class	`InterestBean`
Client	`InterestTestClient`

Hint

Many developers are using the 'Ant' build tool to automate the compilation, assembly, and deployment process. An Ant project is divided into 'targets,' which can have dependencies on each other. Ant uses an XML file, `build.xml`, to specify the dependencies and how to resolve them by carrying out operations. Unlike 'make' and similar tools, Ant and `build.xml` are platform-independent. In this chapter, we will look at the use of individual command-line operations as well as Ant, as not everyone is familiar with Ant. However, it is well worth the effort of getting to know Ant for this type of work. For more information, look at the Ant Web site: `jakarta.apache.org/ant`.

4.1   Setting up the source tree

Full source code for this example may be found in the source code package on the book Web site (`www.kevinboone.com/ejb_book`) in the directory 'interest.'

In what follows I will use the abbreviation '[root]' to mean the root (top) of your source tree; this will, of course, be a directory of your choice. Now there are, of course, many ways to structure a Java source tree, each having their own adherents. For EJB work, my preference is to divide the source tree into three parts: one part for the code that is only ever deployed on the server; one part for code (interfaces and utility classes) that must be the same on both the client and server side of the distributed interaction; and one part for test clients. For Web applications, there will be additional directories for the Web components. All the examples in this book follow this pattern. Within each part of the source tree, the directory hierarchy will follow the same pattern as the package hierarchy, as usual. There will also be a `target` directory (similarly structured) to store the compiled output and a `doc` directory for Javadoc output.

This chapter assumes that there will be a source directory structure, as shown in Figure 4.1.

At the [root] level of the source tree, there is the Ant build script, `build.xml`. This will be used to compile the various parts of the EJB at the command line (in this simple example, one could use command-line tools manually, but it's easier with Ant if you have it).

This source tree may look rather complicated for such a simple EJB, but it's just as well to get into good habits with this kind of development. Separating server-side classes from shared classes makes it much easier to coordinate the development effort, because an EJB's clients should have no dependecies on the server-side code at all. When we look at the *Prestige Bike Hire* application case study, which has

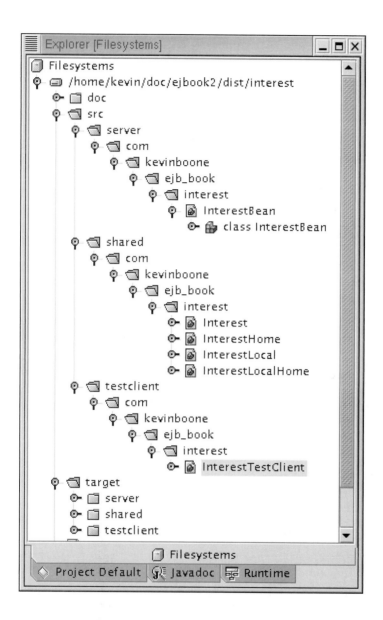

Figure 4.1. Layout of the directory structure for the `Interest` EJB. The `src` directory contains three sections, for client-only code, server-only code, and shared code. The `target` directory has three similar subdirectories, which will be used to hold the compiled classes. In case you were wondering, this screenshot is of the 'Explorer' utility from the *Forte for Java* IDE tool.

several hundred source files, the benefits of a structured approach to source layout will be very apparent.

4.2   Coding the EJB and test client

4.2.1   The (remote) home interface

As this is a stateless session bean, the home interface is straightforward: It specifies exactly one no-argument `create()` method. The home interface is shown in Listing 4.1

Listing 4.1: **Home interface for the 'Interest' EJB.**

```
   package com.kevinboone.ejb_book.interest;
   import javax.ejb.*;
   import java.rmi.*;

 5 /**
   (Remote) home interface for the 'Interest' EJB
   (c)2002 Kevin Boone
   */
   public interface InterestHome extends EJBHome
10 {
   /**
   Create an instance of the EJB
   */
   public Interest create()
15   throws CreateException, RemoteException;
   }
```

Points to note include the following.

- The interface extends `javax.ejb.EJBHome`, as required by the *EJB Specification* [EJB2.0 7.10.5].

- The `create()` method is defined to be able to throw `javax.ejb.Create Exception` and `java.rmi.RemoteException`. Conventionally, the implementation's `ejbCreate()` method will throw a `CreateException` if the EJB cannot be initialized. The `RemoteException` is necessary because the home stub implements this home interface, and the stub's `create()` method may need to throw `RemoteException`.[1]

- Both the interface itself and the `create()` method are `public`.

---

[1]This is a fundamental Java rule. A subclass that overrides a method in its superclass cannot throw exceptions that were not defined in the superclass. This does not apply to runtime exceptions, which are not defined in a `throws` clause.

4.2.2 The local home interface

The local home interface in Listing 4.2 is also simple, and has exactly the same structure as the remote home interface (see Listing 4.1).

Listing 4.2: **Local home interface for the 'Interest' EJB.**

```
    package com.kevinboone.ejb_book.interest;
    import javax.ejb.*;
    import java.rmi.*;

5   /**
    (Local) home interface for the 'Interest' EJB
    (c)2002 Kevin Boone
    */
    public interface InterestLocalHome extends EJBLocalHome
10  {
    /**
    Create an instance of the EJB
    */
    public InterestLocal create ()
15    throws CreateException;
    }
```

Points to note include the following.

- The interface extends `javax.ejb.EJBLocalHome`, as required by the *EJB Specification* [EJB2.0 7.10.8].

- The `create()` method is defined to be able to throw `javax.ejb.Create Exception` but *not* `java.rmi.RemoteException`. The logic here is that as this is not a remote object, it should not throw a remote exception.

- Both the interface itself and the `create()` method are `public`.

4.2.3 The remote interface

The remote interface exposes to the client the methods that it may call. In this simple example, we will have two methods. These methods will throw no exceptions. This leads to the very simple remote interface shown in Listing 4.3.

Listing 4.3: **Remote interface for the 'Interest' EJB.**

```
    package com.kevinboone.ejb_book.interest;
    import javax.ejb.*;
    import java.rmi.*;

5   /**
    Remote interface for the 'Interest' EJB
```

```
     (c)2002 Kevin Boone
     */
     public interface Interest extends EJBObject
10   {
     /**
     Calculate the interest payable on a certain principal, at a
     specified (percent) interest rate per term, for a specific
     number of terms
15   */
     public double getInterestOnPrincipal
         (double principal, double interestPerTerm, int terms)
       throws RemoteException;

20   /**
     Calculate the total amount payable on a certain principal,
     at a specified (percent) interest rate per term, for a
     specific number of terms
     */
25   public double getTotalRepayment
         (double principal, double interestPerTerm, int terms)
       throws RemoteException;
     }
```

Here are some points to note.

- The interface extends `javax.ejb.EJBObject`, as required by the *EJB Specification* [EJB2.0 7.10.6].

- The business methods are defined to throw `java.rmi.RemoteException`, although the methods' implementations will never throw this exception. The reason is the same as for the home interface: The remote stub[2] may throw a `RemoteException`.

4.2.4   The local interface

The local interface exposes to local clients the methods they may call. In this simple example, the local interface has the same methods as the remote interface (Listing 4.4). In reality, we probably don't want to supply both local and remote interfaces for the same EJB.

Listing 4.4: **Local interface for the 'Interest' EJB.**

```
     package com.kevinboone.ejb_book.interest;
     import javax.ejb.*;
     import java.rmi.*;

5    /**
```

---

[2]The 'remote stub' is the stub on the *client* that implements the remote interface. Despite the name, the remote stub is local to the client.

```
     Local interface for the 'Interest' EJB
     (c)2002 Kevin Boone
     */
     public interface InterestLocal extends EJBLocalObject
 10  {
     /**
     Calculate the interest payable on a certain principal, at a
     specified interest rate per term, for a specific number of
     terms
 15  */
     public double getInterestOnPrincipal
         (double principal, double interestPerTerm, int terms);

     /**
 20  Calculate the total amount payable on a certain principal,
     at a specified interest rate per term, for a specific number
     of terms
     */
     public double getTotalRepayment
 25      (double principal, double interestPerTerm, int terms);
     }
```

Here are some points to note.

- The interface extends `javax.ejb.EJBLocalObject`, as required by the *EJB Specification* [EJB2.0 7.10.r76].

- The business methods are not defined to throw `java.rmi.RemoteException`. The reason is the same as for the home interface: The interactions are not 'remote,' but intra-JVM.

4.2.5   The implementation

The EJB implementation class must provide an implementation of the business methods specified by the remote interface and local interface, and an `ejbCreate()` method to match the `create()` method in the home interface. It must also provide implementations of all the methods that are specified by the `javax.ejb.Session Bean` interface, but none of these will do anything useful in this simple example. The source for the implementation class is shown in Listing 4.5.

Listing 4.5: **Implementation for the 'Interest' EJB.**

```
     package com.kevinboone.ejb_book.interest;
     import javax.ejb.*;

     /**
 5   Implementation class for the 'Interest' EJB
     (c)2002 Kevin Boone
     */
     public class InterestBean implements SessionBean
```

```
     {
10   /**
     Keep a reference to the session context object; actually we
     don't need it in this simple example, but we usually do
     */
     protected SessionContext sessionContext;

15
     /**
     Calculate the interest payable on a certain principal, at a
     specified (percent) interest rate per term, for a specific
     number of terms
20   */
     public double getInterestOnPrincipal
         (double principal, double interestPerTerm, int terms)
       {
       log ("Called getInterestOnPrincipal");
25     return principal * Math.pow
           ((1 + interestPerTerm / 100.0), terms) - principal;
       }


     /**
30   Calculate the total amount payable on a certain principal,
     at a specified (percent) interest rate per term, for a
     specific number of terms
     */
     public double getTotalRepayment
35       (double principal, double interestPerTerm, int terms)
       {
       log ("Called getTotalRepayment");
       return principal * Math.pow
           ((1 + interestPerTerm / 100.0), terms);
40     }


     /**
     setSessionContext is called by the container on
     initialization; conventionally we store the passed
45   reference to a SessionContext object
     */
     public void setSessionContext
         (SessionContext sessionContext)
       {
50     this.sessionContext = sessionContext;
       log ("Called setSessionContext");
       }


     /**
55   ejbCreate is called on initialization. In this example it
     need not do anything.
     */
     public void ejbCreate()
       {
60     log ("Called ejbCreate");
       }
```

```
     /**
     ejbRemove may be called when the container tidies up the EJB
65   instance pool (stateless session) or when the client calls
     remove() (stateful session). In this example it need not do
     anything.
     */
     public void ejbRemove ()
70     {
       log ("Called ejbRemove ()");
       }


     /**
75   ejbActivate is associated with memory management in stateful
     session EJBs; in stateless sessions it is never called
     */
     public void ejbActivate ()
       {
80     log ("Called ejbActivate ()");
       }


     /**
     ejbPassivate is associated with memory management in stateful
85   session EJBs; in stateless sessions it is never called
     */
     public void ejbPassivate ()
       {
       log ("Called ejbPassivate ()");
90     }


     /**
     Dump a message to standard out, and thereby to the server's
     log mechanism
95   */
     public void log (String s)
       {
       System.out.print ("Interest: ");
       System.out.println (s);
100    }
     }
```

Here are some additional points to note.

- The `ejbCreate()` method takes no arguments. This will always be the case for stateless session beans.

- The `ejbActivate()` and `ejbPassivate()` methods will never be called; only stateful beans can be passivated by the container. If the container wants to free resources by removing stateless beans, it can simply remove them, as they have no state to passivate. This issue is discussed in more detail later (page 149).

- In this example, all the methods, even those that don't do anything, call the method `log()` to generate some debugging output. Using a single method for this makes it easy to switch off debugging output when the bean is fully tested. Debugging EJBs is much less straightforward than other kinds of Java code, so providing copious debugging output will be useful. Some more elegant ways of controlling debugging output are presented later. Note that the `log()` method is implemented in this case as a simple call to `System.out.println()`. Where will this output end up? This will be server-specific, but with the *J2EE Reference Implementation* it will either go to a log file or to the console (command line) window that is running the server.

4.2.6   The test client

As this EJB only has two methods, and they do similar things, there is limited functionality to test. The simple test client shown in Listing 4.6 creates an instance of the EJB and calls both of the EJB's methods.

Listing 4.6: **Test client for the 'Interest' EJB.**

```
    package com.kevinboone.ejb_book.interest;
    import javax.ejb.*;
    import javax.naming.*;
    import javax.rmi.*;
5   import java.rmi.*;

    /**
    Test client class for the 'Interest' EJB
    (c)2002 Kevin Boone
10  */
    public class InterestTestClient
    {
    public static void main (String[] args)
        throws Exception
15    {
      Interest interest = getInterest ();
      double principal = 10000.0;
      double rate = 10.0;
      int terms = 10;
20    System.out.println ("Principal = $" + principal);
      System.out.println ("Rate(%) = " + rate);
      System.out.println ("Terms = " + terms);
      System.out.println ("Interest = $" +
        interest.getInterestOnPrincipal (principal, rate, terms));
25    System.out.println ("Total = $" +
        interest.getTotalRepayment( principal, rate, terms));
      interest.remove ();
      }

30  /**
    Get an instance of the Interest EJB. Note that the
    EJB-specific stuff is wrapped up in this method,
    so that the main logic can just be plain Java
    */
35  public static Interest getInterest ()
```

```
          throws CreateException , RemoteException ,
             NamingException
          {
          InitialContext  initialContext  = new  InitialContext ();
40        Object o = initialContext.lookup ("Interest");
          InterestHome home = (InterestHome)
             PortableRemoteObject.narrow (o, InterestHome.class);
          return home.create ();
          }

45
       }
```

Here are a few points to note about the test client.

- To find the EJB's home object, the client first instantiates a JNDI naming context, using the default constructor. This will work if the defaults used by the naming service are appropriate for your system. For the *J2EE Reference Implementation*, the defaults will be correct if the client can contact the server using the hostname 'localhost' and the naming service is listening on port 1050. If the client and server are running on the same machine, this is likely to be the case. Your server vendor's documentation should tell you whether the naming context needs additional information. If the naming service is not running on the same machine as the client (as is likely in practice), the client needs to supply some more information to JNDI (Chapter 7).

- The client uses `PortableRemoteObject.narrow()` to convert the result of the lookup operation into an RMI stub, as described on page 39.

- The client does not have to use `narrow()` on the result of the `create()` call on the remote interface. In fact the `narrow()` call will be embedded inside the `create()` method, so it is still called, but not explicitly.

- The client calls `remove()` on the remote object when it has finished with the EJB. As we shall see, however, the server does not remove the bean instance or call `ejbRemove()` on it at this point.

4.3   Compiling the EJB and test client

In this section, I assume that you have modified your system's class search path so that the EJB API classes are searched by default (the procedure for doing this with the *J2EE Reference Implementation* is explained in Appendix F). If this is done properly, then you should be able to run the command

```
javap javax.ejb.EJBHome
```

at the command line and get a listing of the methods on the `EJBHome` interface, rather than an error message. If you have the source-code package and would rather

use Ant, edit the file common/build.properties to indicate the location of the API
JAR file.

With the directory structure described above, we could compile the Java files at
the command line like this on a Unix system (Windows equivalent to follow):

```
% cd [root]
% javac -d target/shared/ \
src/shared/com/kevinboone/ejb_book/interest/*.java
% javac -d target/server/ \
src/server/com/kevinboone/ejb_book/interest/*.java
% javac -d target/testclient/ \
-classpath $CLASSPATH:target/shared \
src/testclient/com/kevinboone/ejb_book/interest/*.java
```

(Remember that the backslash character means a continuation on the same line.)
This compiles EJB interfaces, implementation, and the test client. Notice that to
compile the test client, we have had to extend the classpath to include the 'shared'
components, so that the compiler can find the EJB interfaces, which are referenced
by the client. Note also the use of the '-d' switch to tell the compiler to put the
output into different directories. This isn't strictly necessary, but it's helpful in large
projects, because the EJB developers only need the 'shared' parts of each other's
EJBs at compilation time.

The equivalent on a Windows system is:

```
c:\> cd [root]
c:\> javac -d target\shared\ \
src\shared\com\kevinboone\ejb_book\interest\*.java
c:\> javac -d target\server\ \
src\server\com\kevinboone\ejb_book\interest\*.java
c:\> javac -d target\testclient\ \
-classpath %CLASSPATH%;target\shared \
src\testclient\com\kevinboone\ejb_book\interest\*.java
```

Remember that [root] is the notation used in this book for the top of your source
tree, wherever that happens to be. On a Windows system, you probably won't be
able to type the backslash character to continue on a new line, but will have to type
a very long line for each javac invocation.

After running this command, and assuming that the compilation succeeded, we
will have a target directory structure like this:

```
[root]
   src
      ...
   target
      server
         ...
```

```
shared
    ...
testclient
    ...
```

When we package the class files into a JAR—as will be described below—the directories [root]/target/... will serve as top of the package hierarchy.

If all this command-line stuff is too much like hard work and you have the source-code package and Ant, then you can compile like this:

```
cd [root]
ant compileshared
ant compileserver
ant compiletestclient
```

If even this is too much, the same can be achieved with one command:

```
ant compile
```

And then you're ready to package.

4.4   Starting the J2EE Reference Implementation server

If you are using something other than the *J2EE Reference Implementation*, the following will not apply. Your vendor's documentation should describe how to start and stop the server.

Before you can deploy an EJB, the J2EE server must be running. In principle, it is possible to assemble EJBs without having the server running, but the deployment tool usually attempts to contact the server when it starts up. So starting the J2EE server first allows the deployment tool to start up more quickly, even if you don't intend to deploy anything immediately.

Whatever your normal working practices, I strongly recommend that your start the Reference Implementation server from a command line, not from a menu or a file manager. This allows the debugging output to be seen in the console. Otherwise you will have to make use of log files, a far less convenient process. The procedure for starting the server will depend on the directory in which it is installed, but will normally be something like this on a Unix system:

```
% cd /j2sdkee1.3.1/bin
% ./j2ee -verbose
```

and like this on a Windows system:

```
c:\> cd \j2sdkee1.3.1\bin
c:\j2sdkee1.3.1\bin> start j2ee -verbose
```

A typical output from from the J2EE server when it is started is shown in Listing 4.7.

Listing 4.7: **Typical console output from** `j2ee -verbose`. **The exact output
will depend on how your system is configured, but the key point is that
the server is not ready to receive requests until 'J2EE server startup
complete' is displayed.**

```
     Naming service started:1050
     Starting JMS service ...
     Binding :
       <JMS Destination :
 5        jms/Queue,javax.jms.Queue>
     Binding :
       <JMS Destination :
          jms/Topic,javax.jms.Topic>
     Binding :
10     <JMS Cnx Factory :
          TopicConnectionFactory,Topic,No properties>
     Binding :
       <JMS Cnx Factory :
          jms/QueueConnectionFactory,Queue,No properties>
15   Binding :
       <JMS Cnx Factory :
          QueueConnectionFactory,Queue,No properties>
     Binding :
       <JMS Cnx Factory :
20        jms/TopicConnectionFactory ,Topic,No properties>
     Starting web service at port:8000
     Starting secure web service at port:7000
     Apache Tomcat/4.0-b1
     Starting web service at port:9191
25   Apache Tomcat/4.0-b1
     J2EE server startup complete.
```

4.5   Assembling and deploying the EJB

This step consists of packaging the EJB class files, along with an XML deployment
descriptor, into a JAR archive. It is perfectly possible to do these steps manually,
using command-line tools or Ant build scripts. However, the tricky part for begin-
ners is the construction of the XML file, which is not intuitive. Most EJB server
vendors provide graphical utilities to package the files and create deployment descriptors, and I will assume that is how we will proceed here. When you gain more
familiary with EJB development, you may find it quicker to use build scripts.

The *J2EE Reference Implementation* does not allow EJB-JAR files to be deployed directly (although the *EJB Specification* allows products to do this if the
vendor wishes). Instead, it deploys 'applications.' In this context, an application is
an EAR file containing one or more EJB-JAR files. The EAR file can also contain
'WAR' files, which contain servlets, JSP pages, and static Web content.

So with the Reference Implementation, we would normally create a new application (i.e., a new EAR file) for each new development exercise. We can then create EJB-JAR files for the EJBs, with more than one EJB to a JAR if you prefer.

Gotcha!

The *J2EE Reference Implementation* is under continuous development, and may have changed somewhat since this chapter was written. Don't be concerned if the output from the deployment tool does not look exactly like the screenshots in this chapter.

4.5.1 Create a new EAR file

To begin the process, use the 'File-New Application' menu command, and select the full path and name of the EAR file to be created (see Figure 4.2). Note that the location (directory) of the EAR file is irrelevant as far as assembly and deployment is concerned: The EAR file is really only a convenient place to build up the application until it is deployed on the server.

In the same dialog box, you can enter the 'display name' of the EAR. This display name is only used by assembly and deployment tools; it is not used by clients.

After creation of the EAR file, the deployment tool will display an icon for the new application, but there are no application components as yet (Figure 4.3).

Figure 4.2. Creating a new EAR file for the interest EJB. Note that it does not matter where this file is located relative to the other files in the application.

Figure 4.3. The appearance of the deployment tool after an empty EAR file has been created.

4.5.2   Add an EJB and create a JAR file for it

The classes and XML files that make up EJBs are not stored in EAR files, but in EJB-JAR files, which reside in EAR files. Some EJB tools allow JAR files to be created and deployed independently of EAR files. The *J2EE Reference Implementation*, however, insists on creating an EAR file, even if there is only a single JAR file in it.

The menu command 'File-New enterprise bean' will begin the creation of a new EJB. If this is the first EJB in the application, it will also create a JAR file to contain it. For subsequent EJBs, you will be able to choose whether to create a new JAR to contain the new EJB or use an existing one. I would suggest that EJBs that are designed to function together should be contained in the same JAR file. Otherwise, they should be packaged separately to aid reuse.

With the *Reference Implementation* deployment tool, the initial configuration of EJBs is done step-by-step, using something called the 'Enterprise Bean Wizard.' The first page of the 'Wizard' is shown in Figure 4.4. On this page, we can enter basic information about the new EJB and the new JAR file. Note that JAR files also have display names; the display name is not used by clients, but only by EJB assembly tools.

Having entered the basic information, you will have the opportunity to enter the files that will go into the JAR. At a minimum, these will consist of the EJB's home interface, remote interface, and implementation class. In a real application, there may be a number of supporting classes as well. In this example, we have both local and remote client views, so there are four interfaces in all. Start the process by clicking the 'Edit' button, navigate to the appropriate directories, and add the classes that are required (Figure 4.5).

On the next page, we can specify the type of the EJB and the classes that will play the roles of remote interface, home interface, and implementation (Figure 4.6) class. Note that it is up to you to make the right choices, and it isn't straightforward

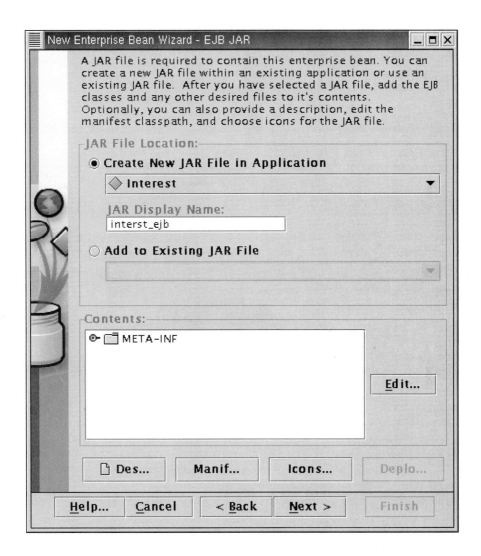

Figure 4.4. The first page of the 'Enterprise Bean Wizard.' As there is no JAR file in the EAR file yet, a new one will be created. Fill in the 'display name' for this new JAR. Note that the 'display name' is not the JAR *filename*; the filename is arbitrary (and is chosen automatically), as the JAR file is contained within the EAR and is not intended to be deployed separately. The 'display name' is what will be displayed by graphical tools like this one.

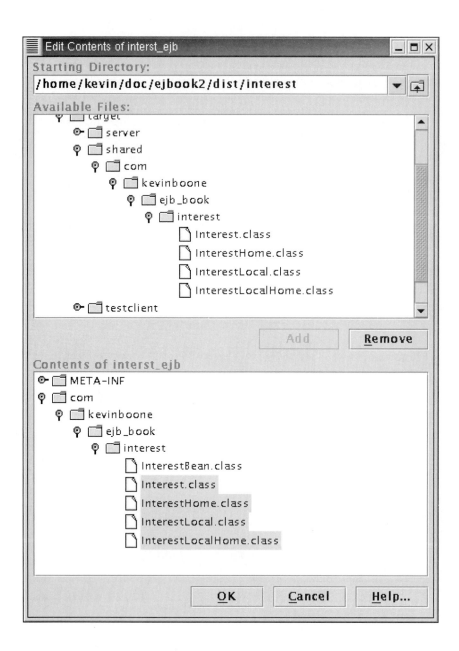

Figure 4.5. Now we have to select the files that are to go into the new JAR. There are two sets of files in this example: the interfaces, which compiled into `target/shared` (shown expanded in the top pane of Figure 4.5), and the implementation, which compiled into `target/server`. These classes are in fact defined to be in the same Java package, and the deployment tool is smart enough to figure this out (note package structure in the bottom pane of Figure 4.5).

104

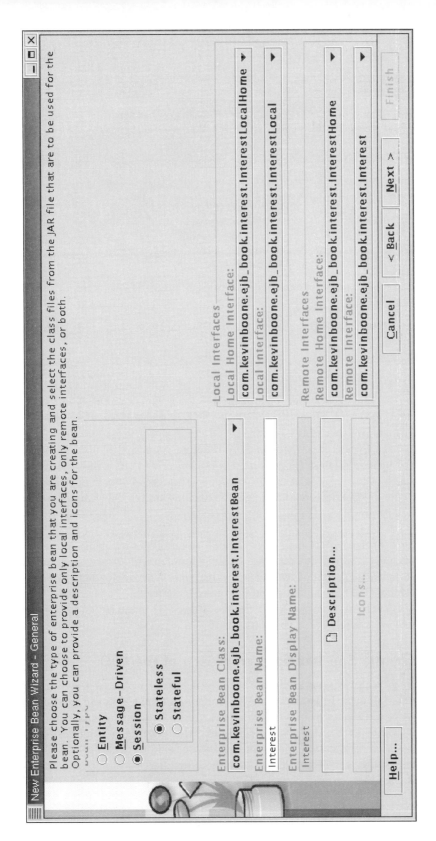

Figure 4.6. Specifying basic information about the EJB: its classes and interfaces, and what it is to be called. Notice that the EJB has a 'name' and a 'display name,' but *neither* of these names are necessarily the one that will be used by clients.

105

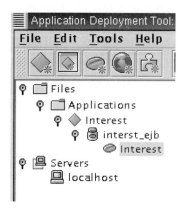

Figure 4.7. Successful assembly: We see the EAR, the JAR, and the EJB itself (the 'coffee bean' icon).

to change them later if you make a mistake. Some EJB tools try to figure out which roles are played by the classes you select, but the *J2EE Reference Implementation* requires the developer to do this.[3] Note that the 'EJB name' and the 'display name' can be different, and neither of these is the JNDI name that the client will look up. In other words, the EJB is identified by three different names. It is my practice to make all three the same unless there is a good reason not to. As will be seen, the JNDI name does not formally exist until deployment time, so in a team development effort, it may not be possible to make the JNDI name match the EJB's internal name (of which, more later). In any case, we can't enter the JNDI name on this page.

We can click 'Finish' after this stage, because none of the information entered on the next six pages is relevant for this simple example (and, in any case, it can always be entered later). After creating the EJB entry, the deployment tool will show the EAR file, the JAR file, and the EJB itself (Figure 4.7).

This EJB is now ready to be verified: Use the 'File-Save' menu command to save the EAR file and the JAR files it contains.

4.5.3   Verify the Specification compliance of the EJB

At this point, it is good practice to use the verifier tool to check the EJB for Specification compliance. It is important to understand that because an EJB is composed of several class files, it is possible to write EJB code that has structural mistakes that cannot be spotted by the compiler (which works at the class level). This is why we need verification tools. As well as more subtle technical problems, the verifier will quickly spot the following common mistakes:

---

[3]For example, it could use reflection to determine the superclass or superinterface of each of your selections. An implementation class will implement `SessionBean`, `EntityBean`, or `MessageDrivenBean`; other heuristics could be used for the other components.

1. methods specified in the remote interface that don't have matching methods in the implementation class;

2. `create` and `find` methods in the home interface that don't have corresponding `ejbCreate` and `ejbFind` methods in the implementation class;

3. exceptions thrown from the methods in the implementation class that are not declared in the remote interface;

4. the home interface not extending `EJBHome`, or the remote interface not extending `EJBObject`.

To start the verifier, use the 'Tools-Verify' menu command. The verifier window will open and display the name of the component to be verified. Note that we can't verify individual EJBs: The tool works on files. In this case, it makes no difference whether we select the EAR file or the JAR file to verify, as there is only one EJB in the application. We need to see the verifier tool say, 'There were no failed tests,' before proceeding to deploy the application.

When you become more familiar with the verifier, you may find it more convenient to run it from the command line and have the results written into a file. The command-line version is simply a shell script called `verifier` (Unix) or a batch file `verifier.bat` (Windows).

Hint

The Reference Information deployment tool does not always write transaction policy information into the XML file, unless you specifically go to the appropriate page in the EJB property sheet. This is harmless, because the server will use defaults, and if you changed from the defaults, the tool would have written the information anyway. It does mean, however, that sometimes the verifier will complain about missing transaction attributes, which can be disconcerting. Normally, viewing the transactions page of the EJB property sheet, followed by saving the EAR file again, will fix the problem.

4.5.4   Deploy the EJB

Begin the deployment process by selecting the 'Tools-Deploy' menu command, which will bring up the first deployment dialog box (Figure 4.8). The first time we deploy, and any time that we change any of the method signatures in the implementation class or interfaces, we will need to select the 'Return Client JAR' item, and specify the name of the JAR file to be generated. The file will contain the client-side stubs

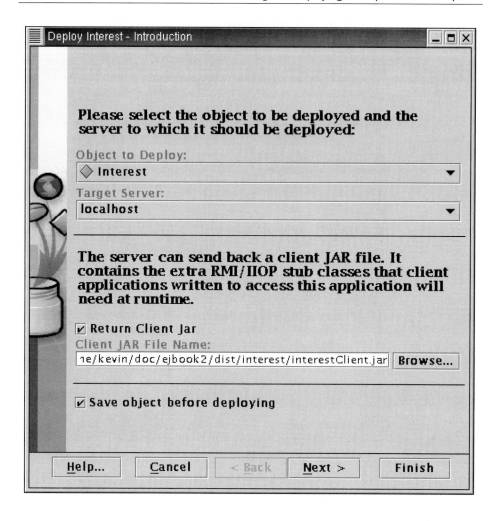

Figure 4.8. Starting the deployment: We need to select 'Return client JAR' here, because the JAR generated will contain the stubs needed by the client.

that will be generated by the server. It does not matter where this file is stored, but it will need to be added to the CLASSPATH of the client when it is executed. In this example, I have chosen the path

```
.../interest/interestClient.jar
```

and this will be specified in the Ant build script or on the command line when running the client.

In the next dialog box (Figure 4.9), we get the chance to fill in the JNDI name of the EJB. Note that we could have done this earlier by selecting the EAR file in the left-hand pane, and then selecting the 'JNDI names' tab on the right-hand pane.

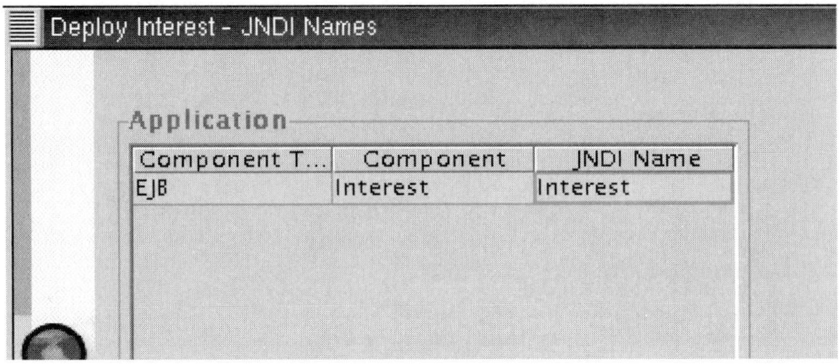

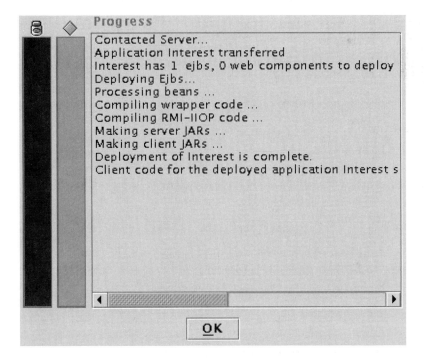

Figure 4.9. Specifying the JNDI name. This is the name that the test client will look up to get access to the EJB.

As we haven't done this so far, the JNDI name of the 'Interest' EJB will initially be blank. In the example, I have made the JNDI name the same as the EJB name as there is no compelling reason to do otherwise.

If the deployment is successful, the deployment tool will display the messages shown in Figure 4.10.

Figure 4.10. Success.

> Hint
>
> If you modify and recompile any of the Java classes in an EJB, you
> will need to tell the deployment tool that you have done this. Use
> the menu operation 'Tools-Update files,' which should produce a
> list of the classes that it has detected changes in. Then deploy
> again. Alternatively use 'Tools-Update and deploy,' which car-
> ries out both steps together. In normal circumstances, you should
> never have to repackage an EJB manually because its code has
> changed.

4.5.5   Deploying at the command line

The previous steps package up the EJB classes into an EAR file and then deploy it.
But what happens if you just want to deploy an existing EAR file? The Reference
Implementation deployment tool provides two options. First, you can open the EAR
file in the tool (File-Open) and then deploy it at described above. This is useful for
viewing EAR files from other sources. Second, you could deploy directly from the
command line, like this:

```
deploytool -deploy interest.ear localhost
```

or, if you have Ant:

```
ant deploy
```

4.6   Testing the EJB

Executing the test client will fully test the EJB, as it only has two methods. The
important thing to note when running the test client is that the CLASSPATH must
allow the JVM to find the stubs that were generated by the deployment tool.

To run the test client from the command line on a Unix system, we need a
command like this:

```
% cd [root]
% java -classpath $CLASSPATH:target/shared/:\
target/testclient/:interestClient.jar \
com/kevinboone/ejb_book/interest/InterestTestClient
```

or on a Windows system:

```
c:\> cd [root]
C:\> java -classpath %CLASSPATH%;target\shared;\
target\testclient;interestClient.jar \
com\kevinboone\ejb_book\interest\InterestTestClient
```

As before, the notation [root] means the source root directory, whatever that is. Remember that during compilation, we elected to have the client's .class files generated in the target/testclient subdirectory, so that needs to be on the CLASSPATH. Also on the CLASSPATH are the client stub JAR file produced by the deployment tool (interestClient.jar in this case), the location of the shared interfaces, and the CLASSPATH environment variable itself. We are assuming that the CLASSPATH environment variable references the JAR file containing the J2EE classes themselves, typically j2ee.jar. Note that the EJB implementation class is *not* locatable on the classpath of the client, as this would normally be deployed only on the server.

The test client should produce the output shown in Listing 4.8. At the same time, the EJB produces the output shown in Listing 4.9, which appears in the console that is running the J2EE server.

Listing 4.8: **Output from the test client.**

```
 Principal = $10000.0
 Rate(%) = 10.0
 Terms = 10
 Interest = $15937.424601000024
5 Total = $25937.424601000024
```

Listing 4.9: **Output from the EJB when the test client is executed.**

```
Interest : Called setSessionContext
Interest : Called ejbCreate
Interest : Called getInterestOnPrincipal
Interest : Called getTotalRepayment
```

Note the sequence of operations that the EJB container follows when it initializes the EJB. First the constructor is called (this happens when the EJB container calls newInstance() on the EJB implementation Class object; see Appendix D for details of this 'dynamic instantiation'). Then the container calls setSessionContext() and ejbCreate(). At this point, the EJB is ready to be called by clients. When the client calls the business methods on the remote stub, then the EJB container calls the corresponding methods on the EJB implementation class.

If you run the test client again, you will notice that only the business methods get called on the EJB. The construction and initialization are skipped. This is because stateless session beans—as we shall see—are held in a pool by the container, and new instances are not created for each client or each method call.

We will examine the behaviour of this simple EJB in much more detail in Chapter 6.

4.7   Troubleshooting

Here are a few points to consider if things don't work properly.

- If the client displays messages of the form 'cannot connect to ORB,' 'connection refused,' or 'can't find SerialContextProvider,' then the most probable explanation is that the J2EE server is not running or did not initialize completely.

- There are a number of reasons why the J2EE server will refuse to start up. First, the user account running it may not have write permissions in the part of the filesystem that the server uses for temporary files. The server will usually produce a helpful error message in that case. Second, in order that the server can be executed by unprivileged users, it listens on general-purpose IP ports (that is, with numbers greater than 1024). However, there is nothing to stop other software from using these ports as well. On both Unix and recent Windows systems, the command `netstat -a` will tell you if this is the case. On some Linux systems, there is a potential port conflict with Gnome over port 1050, in which case one or the other will have to be reconfigured. Third, the server needs a working network interface, even if the computer is not connected to a network, and it must be able to resolve the IP number of the computer by its host name. A loopback interface should be fine if you don't have a real network.

  However, there may be problems—particularly with Windows 2000—if the IP number changes from time to time. This is rather troublesome on systems that use DHCP to set IP numbers. Normally this problem can be fixed by ensuring that the network name of the computer maps onto the loopback address (127.0.0.1), not the actual network IP number. The usual symptom of this problem is that the initialization hangs up after initializing the Web container, and never displays 'startup complete.' You may need to consult a Windows networking guru if you have problems of this sort.

- Error messages about missing classes that are part of the EJB class library probably result from failing to include `j2ee.jar` on the CLASSPATH. Specify this on the command line or in the CLASSPATH environment variable. Most likely you will see this:

```
Exception in thread "main"\
    java.lang.NoClassDefFoundError:\
    javax/naming/Context
```

- If you get `ClassCastException` when running the client, it is usually because you don't have the client stub JAR on the CLASSPATH. This error arises from within the `PortableRemoteObject.narrow()` call, when it tries to cast the object returned from `lookup()` (that is, the home stub) into the home interface type. To do this, it has to be able to load the home stub.

4.8   Summary

In this chapter, we discussed how to code, compile, assemble, deploy, and test the simplest of simple EJBs. We saw how the methods in the home interface and remote interface were realized in the EJB implementation class, and how and when the EJB container called those methods. The purpose of this chapter was to show that, despite the complexity of the underlying technology, development of EJBs is not that difficult. The problem is that when EJB-based applications become more complex than this simple example, developers really do need to understand the technology: That's what the rest of the book is about.

Chapter 5

Introducing the case study

Overview

This chapter introduces a case study—the *Prestige Bike Hire* application—that will form the basis for many of the examples used throughout the rest of this book. The case study is of a system for managing the business of a motorcycle rental firm. The system maintains bookings for rental vehicles, calculates hire costs, and maintains customer accounts. The chapter presents the client's requirements and outlines the architecture of the system that will be constructed. This case study has been chosen because it is complex enough to require the use of a number of EJBs of different types and demonstrate security and transaction management, but is not so large that we can't present most of the relevant source code. Subsequent chapters of the book will examine different EJBs from this case study in detail.

5.1   About the case study

To make the EJB examples in this book as realistic as possible, I have used a substantial application for demonstration purposes. Most of the EJBs that will be discussed in later chapters will be components of this application.

Hint

Complete source code for this application is available from the supporting Web site: `www.kevinboone.com/ejb_book`. Installation instructions may be found in Appendix C.

The application is a booking, charging, and stock management system for a motorcycle rental company called *Prestige Bike Hire*. It demonstrates the following features of EJB technology:

- the application of session, entity, and message-driven EJBs, including more complex entity functionality, like composite and sequential primary keys;

- the use of a strictly 'tiered' EJB model;

- interfacing to a legacy system using asynchronous messaging, with message flow in both directions;

- container-managed transactions;

- distributed transactions that encompass disparate data sources: relational databases and messaging services;

- container-managed persistence with container-managed relationships, using the EJB 2.0 persistence model;

- the use of the EJB QL query language;

- declarative and programmatic security, with container-managed authentication;

- interfacing EJBs to servlets and JSPs using a 'model-view-controller' paradigm.

To demonstrate all these features, the application is necessarily complex, and the rest of this chapter is dedicated to explaining its various components and how they fit together. There are 12 EJBs, implemented in over 60 Java classes, a large[1] number of database tables, and two message queues. In addition, the Web application that forms the user interface consists of about 50 Java class and 40 JSP pages.

Despite its complexity, the reader should not lose sight of the fact that this example is artificial and contrived for this book. I have tried to make it as much like a real enterprise application as possible, subject to the following limitations.

- The application has been chosen to demonstrate as many EJB features as possible, rather than demonstrating optimal design. For example, it could be argued that if one had the freedom to design a database schema from first principles, and the data would only ever be manipulated by EJBs, there are few good reasons to use composite primary keys.[2] However, because EJB developers need to know how to handle such structures, I have contrived an example in the application. In general, where it was necessary to choose between explanatory power and design optimality, I have chosen the former.

---

[1] See below for why it is not helpful to say exactly how many database tables are involved!
[2] This concept is described in detail on page 353.

- The EJBs have been implemented in a way that is as portable as possible, so that they can be used on any platform. In particular, I have avoided the use of stored procedures, selective locking, vendor-specific security APIs, and a number of other features that may be relevant in a production application. Although not used in the case study, these issues are important and are discussed in detail in the text.

5.2 About the 'business'

Prestige Bike Hire is a small, but growing, firm that specializes in the rental of luxury and sports motorcycles. Most of the company's customers are motorcycle enthusiasts, and rent many different motorcycles over an extended period of time, usually for relatively short periods of time (a week or less). To make it easier for these core customers to do business, the firm operates a 'membership' scheme. At enrollment, potential customers submit their details—which have to be verified by staff, not by computer—and these are kept on file. From then on, customers can rent motorcycles without further paperwork. Customers are charged against their credit cards when bookings are made.

Prestige Bike Hire is not an independent company, but is a subsidiary of a larger vehicle hire firm. However, it is completely autonomous, except that financial transactions between the company and its customers are processed using the parent company's financial apparatus, of which we will have more to say later.

Currently, the company operates out of a single, large business premise in North London and has a small staff: two administrators, three workshop staff, and a manager. Administrators take telephone reservations from customers and advise on the availability of particular motorcycle models. They do this using a manual card index system, where each motorcycle has a card on which are entered reservations for a particular times. This system works perfectly well, except that the only way customers can find out whether a vehicle is available is by telephone. Availability is dictated not only by customer reservations, but by the need for servicing.

The workshop staff deal with repairs and servicing, checking motorcycles out when customers collect them, and checking them back in when they are returned. They also help out with bookings and telephone enquiries when required. The manager deals with enrolling new customers and handling unresolved financial transactions.

At any time, the company has about 100 motorcycles in its fleet. Of these, about 30 will be on loan to customers, about five in the workshop being serviced or repaired, and other 65 unused. This poor utilization of assets is of concern to the business. It costs about $3,000 to maintain a motorcycle for a year, so the cost of underutilization is about $150,000 per year. The firm's owners would like to increase the proportion of vehicles that are earning money at any time, by making it easier for customers to make reservations. If more vehicles are on loan at any given time, the likelihood of a vehicle being available at any given time is reduced. Therefore, to avoid customer frustration, the business needs to provide a rapid way for customers to determine availability. Both of these tasks (making reservations and checking availability) need to be accessible over the Internet using a Web browser.

At present, none of the firm's operations are handled by computer, because when it was set up, the customer base and vehicle stock was sufficiently small that business could be handled using paper records. For example, the firm uses a card index for customer details and another card index for vehicle details. While this system is perfectly functional, it does limit the ways in which the firm can do business with its customers.

5.2.1   Vehicle availability

Vehicles are available for rental whenever they are not reserved by another customer or withdrawn for service. Typically, servicing takes one day every month. Rental periods may include public holidays, but bookings can't start or end on a public holiday, as there will be no staff on the premises to check the motorcycles in or out. As the company has more than one motorcycle of each type that it handles, the new system must enable reservations to be made by motorcycle model, while maintaining records internally on a machine-by-machine basis. We do not want customers to have to specify the exact motorcycle they wish to rent. Similarly, if a customer wants to know the availability of a particular motorcycle at a given time, he or she wants to know if *any* motorcycle of that type is available.

5.2.2   Financial transactions

Currently, the staff of *Prestige Bike Hire* do not handle financial transactions directly. Instead, they use the parent company's financial infrastructure, which is based on a legacy mainframe application. The manager sets up accounts for new customers by telephoning the finance department and supplying credit card, name, and address details. At the close of business every day, one of the administrators uses a terminal and modem to enter the details of the charges that have been incurred by customers that day and any refunds that may be due to them. These charges are recorded by the mainframe application and used to charge the customers' credit cards and issue invoices.

The problems with this scheme are obvious: It is time-consuming and prone to error. The new system should automate this task, by communicating credit-card transactions directly to the mainframe. The problem is that this system is only available at certain periods of the day, and is designed to process orders in batches.

The proposed solution to this problem is to use a messaging service as an intermediary between the *Prestige Bike Hire* application and the legacy system.[3] As customers make bookings, their credit card details are placed into a message queue. The mainframe application will be extended to accept orders from the messaging service at certain times of day. Each message will have to take the following form:[4]

---

[3]An alternative, also J2EE-compliant, might be to use a JCA connector to interact with the legacy system using whatever networking protocols it supports, as discussed in Chapter 18.

[4]Although this is a contrived example, it isn't all that different from the data formats expected by credit card charging services like CyberCash.

```
our_ref=2/1065740400000
name=Fred Bloggs
address=1 Skid Row, East Dogpatch, London
card_number=4564564562224562
card_type=Vista
cost=385
```

In this message, the our_ref field is not meaningful to the legacy system, but will be echoed back to the application in the acknowledgement. This will enable us to keep track of which transactions have been acknowledged. After processing the credit-card transaction, the legacy system sends back an acknowledgement message in a similar format:

```
your_ref=2/1065740400000
response_code=0
info=OK
```

The response_code field indicates whether the charge was successful or not, while the info field provides extra information.

Because the charging process is asynchronous, the end user will not be expected to wait for an acknowledgement from the legacy system before getting a response from the application. However, it is envisaged that some credit card transactions will fail owing to insufficient funds, for example. For this reason, when the user makes a reservation, it remains 'provisional' until the legacy system has acknowledged.

5.3   Goals of the application

The new application is to handle the administrative recordkeeping of the *Prestige Bike Hire* company and make it possible for customers to do business using the Web. A Web browser interface will also be used for internal administrative operations.

In outline, the Web interface should make it possible for customers to browse the stock of available motorcycles, place and cancel reservations, and maintain their own customer profiles. Staff should be able to carry out these tasks, in addition to checking in and checking out vehicles, viewing the status of financial transactions, and managing the stock. In addition, the application should dispatch credit-card transactions to the messaging service and process acknowledgements as they arrive.

5.4   Design architecture

5.4.1   Use-case analysis

In the design of any complex computer system, a key task is the discovery of users and their requirements and responsibilities. Many designers like to use use-case diagrams to show these findings. Such a diagram shows *actors*—users—and *use-cases*—services or functionality. The use-case model is a high-level view of the structure of the system and, as such, should probably not be too detailed.[5]

Users, actors, and roles

In our application, actors are determinable from the groups of staff and customers that already exist. We have already identified managers, administrators, workshop staff, customers, and 'others.' We have also suggested that the administrators and workshop staff are likely to make similar use of the system, and perhaps don't need to be separate actors. Similarly, the 'others' group has access only to the static Web content of the application, not to any of the programmatic functionality, and perhaps does not need to be identified as an actor at all. This suggests that the actors can be assigned as `manager`, `administrator`, and `customer`.

Hint

In J2EE, security policies are specified in terms of 'abstract security roles' (see Chapter 16). A role is not exactly the same as an actor in a use-case model, but it is a good starting-point to assume that each actor is embodied as a security role.

Use-cases

Determination of the use-cases requires an investigation of the functionality to be provided. It appears that there are three sorts of services that will available to all actors:

- services related to making bookings for motorcycles, which may include communicating booking costs to the legacy financial system;

- services related to searching, and viewing details of, the motorcycle fleet;

- customer management services, such as editing customer credit card details.

These will form use-cases 'booking management,' 'fleet management,' and 'customer management,' respectively. All of these use-cases will be available, to greater or lesser extent, to all actors. However, there are a number of other services that are available only to the more privileged users. These include

- services related to enrollment of new customers, and

---

[5]A description of use-case modelling and related techniques is quite beyond the scope of this book. A comprehensive treatment of use-case modelling and other UML techniques in J2EE application development may be found in Ahmed and Umrysh (2001)—see page 691 for full details.

- adding and removing motorcycle stock, and changing the status of individual bikes as they are rented and returned.

Some designers would see these as separate use-cases, but I have chosen to represent them as extensions of other services instead. The enrollment service may be seen as an extension of the general customer management service available to all users, while the stock add/remove and check in/check out services may be seen as extensions of the fleet view/search service. These use-cases will be referred to as 'enrollment,' 'add/remove stock,' and 'check in/out,' respectively.

Assigning use-case functionality to actors

Before the use-case model can be elaborated, we need to consider how the various actors will make use of the specific use-cases.

Customer An ordinary customer will be able to carry out the following interactions with the various use-cases:

- make a reservation of a vehicle for himself (booking management);
- view his own reservations (booking management);
- view available motorcycles and their descriptions (fleet management);
- modify his own details (customer management).

Administrator This actor covers both administrators and workshop staff, who need to use the application in similar ways. This actor can take part in the following interactions, as well as those for the `customer` actor:

- making a reservation on behalf of any other customer (e.g., a telephone booking) (booking service);
- viewing reservations for vehicles made by customers (booking service);
- marking vehicles unavailable for rental, and checking them in and out (check in/out service, sub-use-case of fleet management);
- updating details of other customers (customer management).

Manager The `manager` actor takes part in the following interactions, as well as those of the `customer` and `administrator` actors:

- enrolling new customers (customer service);[6]
- purchasing and adding new vehicle stock (add/remove stock service, sub-use-case of fleet management).

---

[6]Customers should perhaps be able to enroll themselves as well. See Chapter 17 for a discussion of the implications of such support on portability.

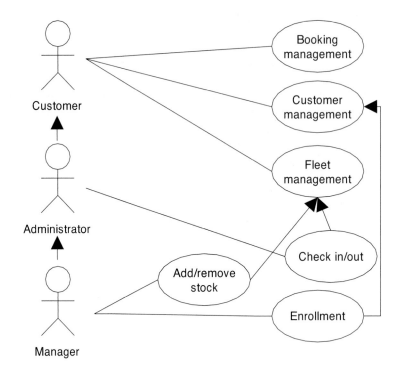

Figure 5.1. Use-case model for the *Prestige Bike Hire* application. See text for details.

It simplifies both requirements, analysis and software development, if actors can be generalized. That is, there are identifiable requirements that are common to multiple actors. In this application, the types of use that will be made of the system by the various actors are very similar; they differ only in the access rights held over data. For example, we expect customers to be able to make bookings for motorcycles for themselves, while administrators can make bookings on behalf of other customers. These are not really different tasks, just different security restrictions. This means that we can simplify the use-case model by denoting `manager` a subactor of `administrator`, and `administrator` a subactor of `customer`. With these simplifications, we arrive at the use-case diagram of Figure 5.1.

5.4.2   Mapping use-cases to EJBs

It is generally considered good practice to encapsulate client interaction within a small number of highly abstract EJBs. These in turn make use of lower-level EJBs. The client-facing EJBs are typically session EJBs, for reasons that will be discussed later. It is unusual to expose entity EJB functionality directly to clients.

So, we will begin by assuming that the three main use-cases in Figure 5.1 are represented by three EJBs: `BookingManager`, `FleetManager`, and `CustomerManager`. Between them, these EJBs will contain the bulk of the application logic.

In addition to these EJBs, we will need entity EJBs to model the persistent data elements of the application, and some utility EJBs to avoid embedding general-purpose functionality in the EJBs that represent use-cases. This is discussed in more detail below.

5.5   Design philosophy

Because this application is designed for educational, rather than production, purposes, we can avoid constraints that may exist in the real world. The most important of these is that we have no pre-existing data model, so we can allow the application server to construct one. This means that the design of the entity EJB tier can be closer to real object-oriented concepts than perhaps might normally be the case. Other design choices include the following.

- We will use only EJB 2.0 container-managed persistence for the entity EJBs. Although this persistence technique has a relatively short pedigree, it offers both performance and simplicity advantages over the alternatives (see Chapter 13).

- The application will be built in a strict tiered architecture, with clients getting access to the application through a relatively small number of EJBs. There will be no direct access to entity EJBs or the back-end database from the Web tier.

- The Web tier itself will be architected using the Jakarta *Struts* model, according to so-called 'model 2' principles. We will have more to say about this in Chapter 17. The relevance of this decision at this stage is that it compels us to think of the EJB tier as the 'model' part of a 'model-view-controller' architecture. This means that the EJBs should embody the business logic of the application, but should not dictate the flow of interaction between the user and the application. Instead, we view the EJBs as forming an API or a collection of services to clients. A consequence of this decision is that application security (authorization) will be implemented at the EJB tier. That is, the EJB security policy will control which users are allowed to do what. But because the EJB tier has no control over the flow of user interaction, we will ask the Web tier to authenticate the user when it is apparent that the user is about to do something that is subject to a security constraint. This is a standard technique, and is discussed in more detail in Chapter 16.

- As this is an educational example, we will not go to the trouble of logging every transaction with every user, as we might have had to in a production system.

These considerations lead to an overall architecture as shown in Figure 5.2.

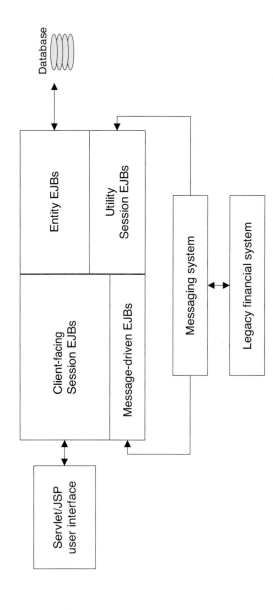

Figure 5.2. Overall architecture of the *Prestige Bike Hire* application. Note the strict tiered approach, with EJBs divided into client-facing and nonclient-facing groups; there are no entity EJBs in the client-facing group.

> ## Gotcha!
>
> The *J2EE Reference Implementation*, although admirable in many ways, does not support the mapping of pre-existing database schemas onto entity EJBs. Some commercial products do offer such functionality. This is why we have not discussed the database schema in this chapter: We have no control over it. In practice, the *Reference Implementation*'s persistence manager will create a database table for each EJB and a table for each container-managed relationship (of which, more later). Although the mapping scheme is comprehensible, it is not completely transparent, and it is easier to make progress with this software if you treat the database schema as a 'black box' under the control of the application server. In a commercial undertaking, we frequently won't have this luxury, and the database mapping capabilities of the EJB product will be of some importance.

5.6   EJB design

There are many ways in which the structure of Figure 5.2 could be rendered as a collection of EJBs. The decisions to be taken do not differ in principle from the decisions taken in any other component-oriented design exercise. As always, one will consider the issues of coupling, cohesion, code-reuse, ease of maintenance, and ease of testing, among other things. As in any object-oriented design, one must decide how rigorously EJBs are to correspond to real-world entities in the application domain. There are, however, some issues to consider that are specific to the use of EJBs.

- When should functionality be encapsulated into an EJB, and when is the class the more appropriate unit of organization? EJBs lend themselves to reuse, but so do Java classes, appropriately organized. As with ordinary programming in Java, it can be helpful in the long term to abstract out commonly used functionality into separate EJBs. For example, in the *Prestige Bike Hire* application, we have an EJB called `Mailer` that has the capability of sending email messages. This functionality could instead have been provided in a utility class and called from other EJBs in the ordinary Java sense. A point for consideration when using EJBs is that when a software module is supplied as an EJB, rather than simply as a class, there is a well-defined way to supply configuration data (in a deployment descriptor). Moreover, the use of an EJB allows the methods to have their own transaction attributes. The importance of this last point will be explained in Chapter 9.

- There is a tendency among developers to assign entity EJBs to match existing database tables. However, the relational data model that pre-exists may not be an ideal foundation for an object-oriented model. When container-managed persistence is used, the degree to which the entity EJB design can diverge from the underlying data model is limited in practice by the capabilities of the EJB product. There is no theoretical reason why a single entity EJB should not model data drawn from two or more database tables, if the product supports it.

- Because remote method calls are associated with substantial overheads, it is customary to expose to clients highly abstract EJBs that encapsulate a significant amount of business logic in each method call. The J2EE jargon for this practice is to 'expose a coarse-grained API.' Decisions about whether to delegate the functionality of these complex objects to a number of simpler objects or to keep it encapsulated in one object, are made on the same grounds as they would be in ordinary programming. However, inter-EJB calls do have higher overheads than intra-EJB calls, even with local interfaces. This favours a smaller number of 'larger' EJBs. Because of the computational cost of remote method calls, it is customary to use 'value objects' (see page 482) to pass large collections of data between the tiers of a multitiered model. These are classes which act as data carriers, and have no application logic of their own.

- There is no reason to expose all entity EJBs to the session EJBs. Some groups of entity EJBs will be, of necessity, tightly coupled, and perhaps only one of the group need be accessible by clients. In situations like this, it may be advisable to use the local client view for inter-EJB calls within the tightly coupled group.

Figure 5.3 and the following subsections describe the EJB design that has been adopted for this example.

5.6.1 'CustomerAgent' EJB

Provides services to create, modify, retrieve, and browse customer details. The implementation of these services will require access to one or more `Customer` EJBs.

5.6.2 'BookingAgent' EJB

This EJB will contain the bulk of the application logic. It provides facilities to create, delete, confirm, browse, and edit bookings for motorcycles. Although it is ultimately individual motorcycles that get loaned out to customers, customers do not place reservations for motorcycles, but for types of motorcycle. Therefore this EJB will make use of the representation of motorcycle types embodied by the `BikeModel` EJB, as well as the booking records modelled by the `Booking` EJB.

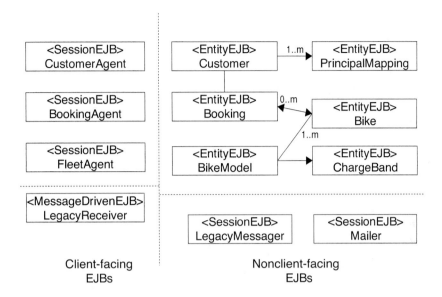

Figure 5.3. Division of the EJB application into specific EJBs. For simplicity, only persistent relationships between EJBs are shown.

5.6.3 'FleetAgent' EJB

This EJB provides services to create, delete, browse, and edit motorcycle and motorcycle type details. It therefore relies most heavily on the `BikeModel` EJB and, through that, the `Bike` EJB.

5.6.4 'EventReceiver' EJB

This message-driven EJB will handle acknowledgements from the legacy financial system, which are generated in response to messages dispatched when the user makes a reservation. This EJB will operate on `Booking` EJBs, changing the status of bookings to reflect the response from the legacy system.

5.6.5 'Customer' EJB

This a straightforward model of a customer, storing persistent details about a specific customer, such as the credit card he or she wishes to use for charging. The customer EJB is supported by a value object, `CustomerData`, which carries the properties of a specific customer between the session and entity tiers of the application and, ultimately, to the Web tier. Each customer object is associated with one or more `PrincipalMapping` EJBs, which contain information about a customer's login ID (see below).

Note that the `Customer` EJB contains a 'customer ID' property, which is simply a number and stands as the primary key for that object in the database. It may be thought—reasonably—that 'primary key' is a database concept, not an object-oriented concept, and that EJBs should not have to be concerned with such matters. However, the entity EJB architecture relies on the use of primary keys to maintain association between clients and EJBs (as we shall see), and so a primary key is necessary. It may not be necessary to expose it to users of the EJB. In some cases, however, it is useful. In this application, customers are told their customer IDs and asked to quote them in correspondence, so the customer ID has to be exposed.

5.6.6 'PrincipalMapping' EJB

The `Customer` EJB contains only properties that are part of the object-oriented model of a customer (plus the primary key property, as discussed above). A user's login ID is a property that is meaningful only to an application, not to the business logic that operates on customers. That is, it is not really part of the `Customer` EJB at all. After all, we may wish to reuse the `Customer` EJB in another application, where authentication is not at the customer level at all. The problem with this is that we need somewhere to store the association between the user's login ID and his customer record. This process is often referred to as 'principal mapping.' The term 'principal' refers to something that identifies a user after authentication (Chapter 16). My preference is to use a separate database table for this. It is debatable whether this table needs to be mapped onto a separate EJB at all, since it could be handled by a straightforward utility class. However, we have made a design decision to use only container-managed persistence for the entity EJBs, and it is inelegant for such an EJB to be doing explicit database operations as well as being managed by the container.

Astute readers may be wondering why we can't use the login ID as the unique primary key for the `Customer` EJB. It is, after all, no less meaningful than an arbitrary customer ID. There are two reasons for using a separate principal mapping relationship. First, an individual user could be able to authenticate in a number of different ways, and receive a different user ID for each method. For example, if the user authenticates by means of his browser supplying a client certificate, he will end up with a different principal than with authentication by user ID and password. Second, principals are not guaranteed to be portable: With container-managed security and authentication at the Web tier, most application servers take the user's login ID as the principal, but this is not mandatory. Using a separate database table makes it easier to accommodate product variations if we have to port the application between platforms.

The relationship between `Customer` and `PrincipalMapping` is therefore one-to-many; this will be a 'container-managed relationship,' as described in Chapter 13.

5.6.7 'Booking' EJB

This EJB models a booking made on a particular motorcycle over a particular range of dates by a particular customer. It is supported by the value object `BookingData`. Because we will only allow a customer to book a single motorcycle at a time, the customer ID and start date properties of the booking will serve as the primary key for this EJB. This means that we don't need to create an arbitrary primary key field, as we did with `Customer`, but we do need to create a separate class (`BookingKey`) to hold the primary key properties on behalf of the container.

5.6.8 'BikeModel' EJB

This EJB represents a particular type of motorcycle, like Harley-Davidson 'Road King.' Each `BikeModel` will be associated with a number of `Bike` EJBs, which model particular motorcycles. Note that clients are more interested in models of motorcycle than in specific motorcycles. This EJB is supported by a value object `BikeModelData`, and has an association with a `ChargeBand` EJB, which describes the charging policy to be applied.

5.6.9 'Bike' EJB

This EJB models a particular motorcycle of a particular type. In this application, the only property that a motorcycle has that is not part of `BikeModel` is its license number. Therefore, it could be argued that specific motorcycles could be represented simply as a `Collection` of `String`s within `BikeModel`. This may be true, but using an EJB allows for some future expansion. `Bike` will provide a local client view to `BikeModel`, to reduce the overhead associated with manipulating a single `String` as an EJB in its own right.

5.6.10 'ChargeBand' EJB

Each type of motorcycle has a charge band from '1' (cheapest) to '5' (most expensive). The `ChargeBand` EJB models the collection of charging properties for each of these charge bands. For example, in each charge band, there are different daily rental charges, according to the overall length of rental.

5.6.11 'LegacyMessager' EJB

This EJB encapsulates the process of dispatching a credit card transaction to the legacy financial system using JMS. The EJB has been designed to be as general as possible, as this is functionality that may be useful in other applications of this sort.

5.6.12 'Mailer' EJB

Like the `LegacyMessager`, this EJB has also been designed to be of general applicability. It encapsulates the process of sending email confirmations to customers using JavaMail.

5.7 Sneak preview

So that it's clear what the *Prestige Bike Hire* application does, let's look at some typical interactions between a user and the system, using the browser-based user interface.

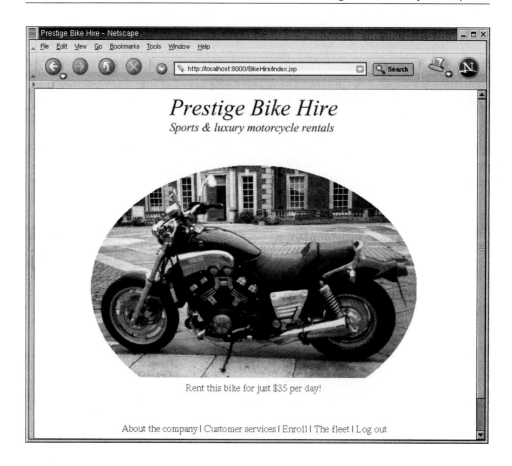

Figure 5.4. The *Prestige Bike Hire* application welcome page, viewed in Netscape Navigator.

On invoking the application as a user, the 'welcome' page (Figure 5.4) is displayed.

Note that the user has not been asked to log in yet. The welcome page, and the other general information pages, have no security restrictions, so the Web container does not need to authenticate the client.

The user may begin making a reservation and browsing the list of motorcycle models available by selecting the link 'The fleet' at the bottom of the page. In a production system, there may be other ways to begin this process—for example by providing links to selected models on other pages. The ability to do this is a matter for the Web-tier developers, rather than part of the EJB tier, and so hasn't been included in the example.

When this link is selected, it causes the browser to make a request on a URL that is subject to a security constraint. Therefore the Web container presents the login page (Figure 5.5).

We rely on the Web container to authenticate the user—that is, to determine whether his credentials are acceptable. If not, the Web container presents an error message and repeats the login process (Figure 5.6). All of this happens outside the EJB tier of the application. When login is successful, the Java code in the Web tier presents the user's security principal (ID) to the EJBs on each method call. The EJB container and the EJBs themselves will then decide whether a particular method call is allowed to that user. In summary, the Web tier will identify the user, and the EJB tier will enforce security based on the credentials presented by the Web tier.

When the login process is successful, the user gets a list of motorcycle models available for rental (Figure 5.7).

Let's make a reservation for a Harley-Davidson 'Road King.' Clicking on the 'Availability and booking' link shows any periods in the near future (30 days, to be exact) when there is likely to be no availability. In this case, there are no such restrictions. We can therefore fill in the required dates and try to make a reservation. The application will check that the date information is meaningful, and that there appears to be a motorcycle of that model available at the requested time (Figure 5.8). Again, in a production application we may wish to make it easier for the customer to select dates for rental using a calendar display, for example, but this is outside the scope of the EJB tier.

If the reservation can be made, the application calculates the total cost of the rental and gives the user the opportunity to confirm the transaction (Figure 5.9).

By accepting the charge, the user commits the booking, and the motorcycle becomes unavailable to other customers (Figure 5.10).

From the 'Customer services' link the user can get a list of bookings currently in effect, as well as bookings made in the past. Figure 5.11 shows that there is now one booking in effect, and that it is 'provisional.' At this stage, the application has dispatched the credit card transaction to the legacy financial system, but has not yet received a response. When it does receive one, the booking will be shown as 'confirmed' or 'rejected,' according to the nature of the response. In either case, the user will have received an email notification.

The user can also edit his or her customer details (Figure 5.12).

What can an administrator (or manager) do that an ordinary user can't do? First, the administrator can view and edit the records of other customers.

The 'Select customer' page allows the administrator to find the requisite customers (Figure 5.13).

The administrator can also change the charging policy for particular motorcycle models, by editing the rental rates for different durations (Figure 5.14).

In addition (not shown), the administrator can browse the fleet and list bookings made for specific motorcycles or to specific customers. He or she can also change the status of bookings (e.g., remove them if payment is not acknowledged in a certain time).

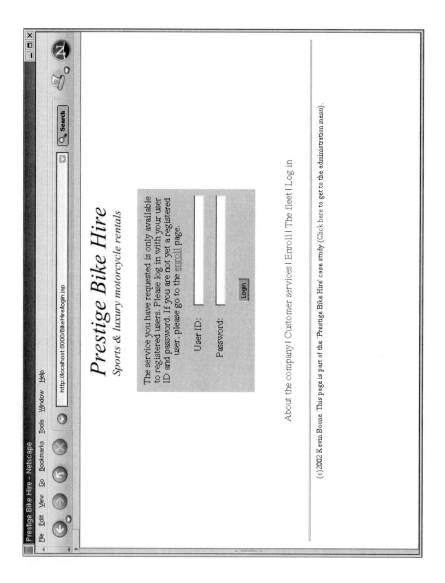

Figure 5.5. The login form.

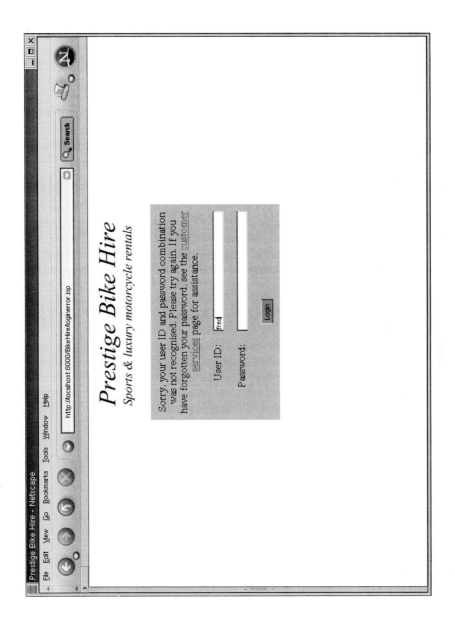

Figure 5.6. It is the job of the Web container, not the EJB application, to prompt users for credentials until they are acceptable.

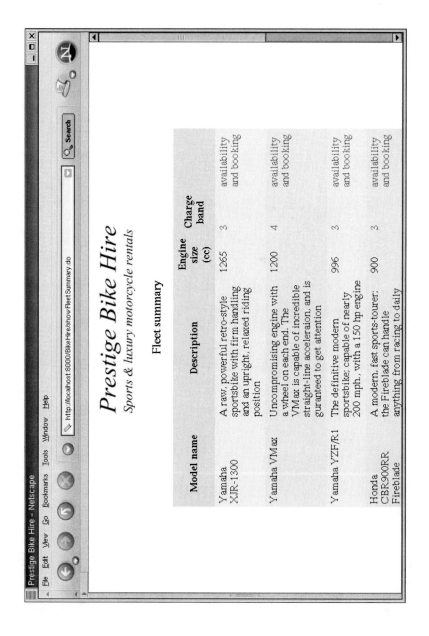

Figure 5.7. Listing the motorcycle models available for rental.

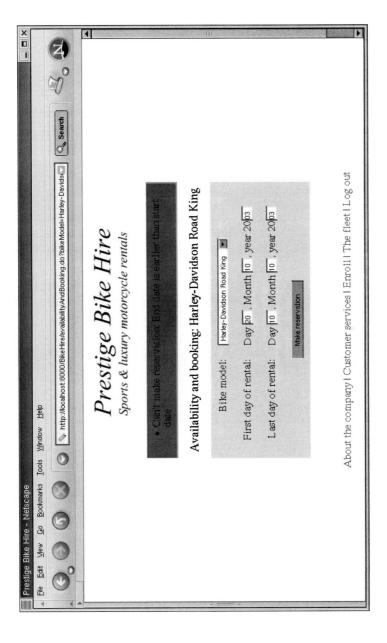

Figure 5.8. Making a reservation for a Road King.

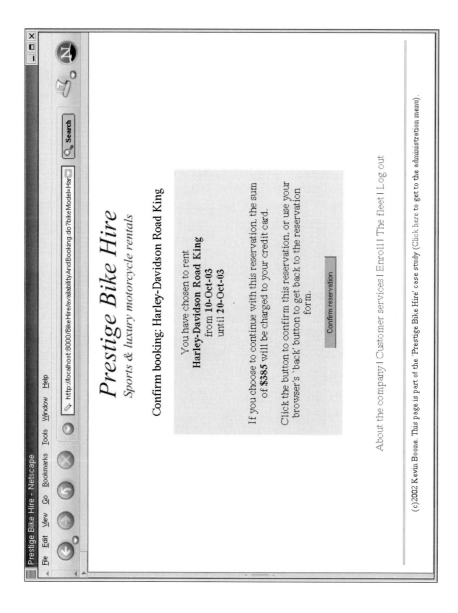

Figure 5.9. The user must specifically accept the charge to confirm the reservation.

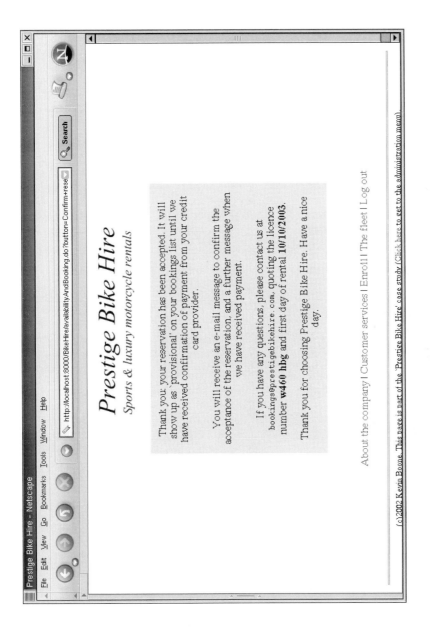

Figure 5.10. The reservation is committed.

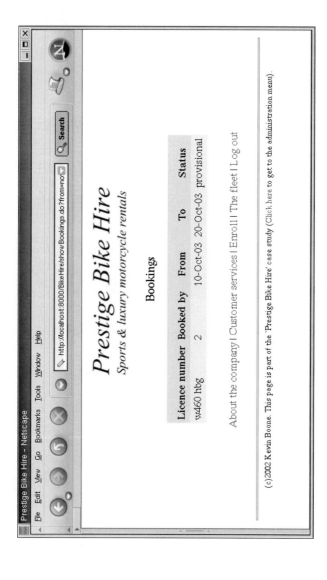

Figure 5.11. The most recent booking is shown as provisional, because the legacy financial system has not yet processed the credit card transaction.

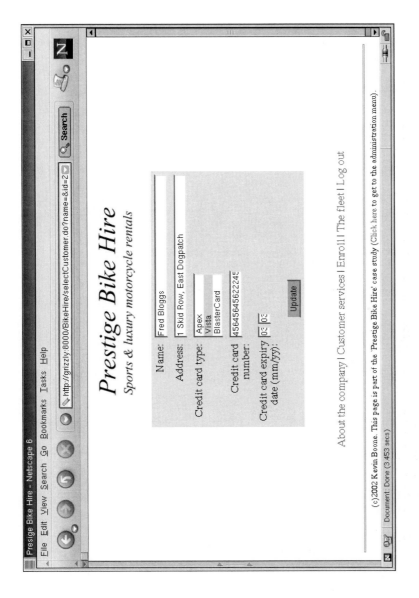

Figure 5.12. Editing customer details.

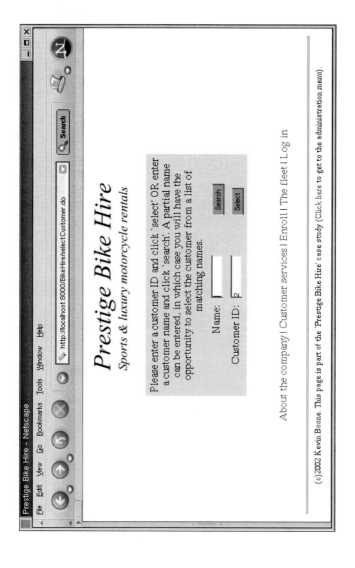

Figure 5.13. The administrator can view and edit customer records, selecting by customer ID or from a list of names.

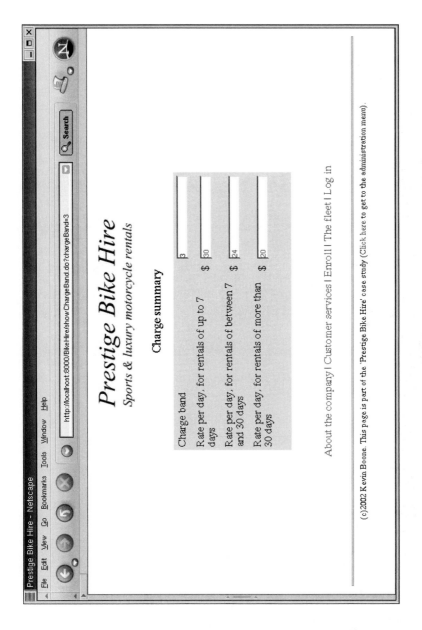

Figure 5.14. Editing the charging policy.

141

5.8   Summary

This chapter introduced the 'Prestige Bike Hire application' case study, which will be used to demonstrate EJB concepts in the rest of this book. The application uses session, entity, and message-driven EJBs, message queues, transaction management, and the EJB security infrastructure. It uses a Web application based on Jakarta *Struts* as the user interface.

Chapter 6

Session EJBs

Overview

We have already discussed the basic principles of session EJBs and seen a very simple example. In this chapter, we will examine the session EJB in much more detail. We start with stateful session EJBs, as their life cycles are conceptually simpler. We will discuss, in particular, issues relating to instance management: activation, passivation, and timeout. We then move on to stateless session EJBs, explaining how the EJB container can optimize performance by pooling instances and the implications that such pooling has for the developer. We will see these principles at work by analyzing the behaviour of the session EJB from Chapter 4 in detail. Finally, we present a more realistic session EJB example and give some practical guidelines on using session beans in applications.

6.1 Types and applications of session EJBs

There are two types of session EJB: *stateful* and *stateless*, distinguished by whether they can usefully store the state of an ongoing conversation with a client. Both can be thought of as models of services provided to clients. They implement the business[1] logic of the application. Both types are created and removed by clients, as required. They are not intended to be persistent, and the server does not have to take precautions to preserve their state in the event of a system crash (although it might).

6.2 What is 'state'?

The issue of 'state' in stateful and stateless EJBs needs some explanation, as do the related terms 'session' and 'session state.'

---
[1] This is a generic term, used even if the EJB is not concerned with 'business' in the dictionary sense.

In object-oriented design, the state of an object is generally taken to mean a snapshot of the data encapsulated within an object at an instant in time. As objects can contain other objects as part of their state, which can in turn contain others, the overall state of an object can be considered as a tree, or hierarchy, of data values. When using Java, state is usually taken to mean the set of values of the instance variables of an object, including the instance variables of instance variables that are themselves objects. Changing an instance variable constitutes changing the state. In session EJBs, the terms 'stateless' and 'stateful' have a slightly narrower meaning than this; they refer to the 'session state.'

If a client establishes a reference to an EJB and then calls multiple methods on it as part of the same conversation, then it is said that a 'session' is in progress. The session state is that part of the EJB's state that is associated with the client and the conversation, rather than with internal functionality of the EJB.

Suppose, for example, that we are developing an online shopping application, and a session EJB is maintaining a 'shopping cart' on behalf of a user. The shopping cart data is associated with the ongoing conversation with the client, and is therefore part of the state of the EJB and, most importantly, part of the *session* state. A client expects to be able to manipulate this data. Whenever a client begins a call on a method of the shopping cart EJB, it expects to see the shopping cart data in the same state as at the end of the previous call.

However, if the EJB looks up the home objects of other EJBs and stores them in instance variables, while this is state in the traditional sense, it is not session state. There is no reason why a stateless EJB should not store instance variables of this type, but it could not meaningfully store instance variables representing a client's shopping cart. For that, we need a stateful session EJB.

This discussion may seem rather academic, but it can be clarified very easily with a simple example. Consider the code fragment below.

```
ejb1.setTaxRate (17.5);
double tr = ejb1.getTaxRate ();
```

If `ejb1` were a reference to a stateful session EJB, we could usefully expect the variable `tr` to take the value '17.5' after execution of the second line, as assigned in the `set` method. If the EJB were stateless, we could not make such an assumption. In fact, the caller could call `getTaxRate()` 10 times and get 10 different values.

Clearly, the stateless programming model is so far from what one expects of object-oriented programming that there must be profound advantages to working this way to compensate for its oddness. And indeed there are.

- If the client does not expect to set or read the object's state, then it *does not matter which instance of a particular EJB's implementation class services a method call.* It does not matter even if two successive method calls from the same client are directed to two different servers. This makes the process of load sharing almost trivial, and stateless session EJBs therefore scale very well.

- With stateless session EJBs, the act of providing load balancing gets us failover in the bargain. This is because if one server in a failover cluster fails, the others have nothing special to do if they want to pick up the load of the dead server. With stateful session EJBs, failover can only be achieved if we have a way to replicate the state of the EJBs across servers, which is no easy job.

- Because instances of the implementation class will not normally be busy all the time, but will have periods of idleness when their clients are busy elsewhere, stateless session EJBs allow more optimal use of server memory resources. This is because we can maintain a pool of instances on the server and share client requests among instances in this pool. Stateful session EJBs cannot be shared among clients, because their instance variables are meaningful to a particular client, so they must be instantiated at the behest of that client.

- It follows from the use of a fixed size pool of implementation instances that we minimize the overheads involved in construction and initialization of the instances themselves.

Therefore, it seems sensible to use stateless session EJBs as much as possible, only resorting to stateful sessions when the application's needs demand it. Table 6.1 shows further points of comparison of the two types. Some of these may not be particularly meaningful until we have considered the session EJB infrastructure in more detail.

6.3   Stateful session EJBs

6.3.1   Overview of operation

Stateful session EJB implementation instances are never pooled; they are instantiated on demand when the client calls `create()` on the EJB's (remote or local) home interface, and removed when the client calls `remove()`. The interaction between the client, container, and implementation instance is shown in simplified form in Figure 6.1 (it is simplified in that the diagram does not show passivation, timeout, or the synchronization during a transaction. These issues are discussed later). The purpose of each of the steps in Figure 6.1 is explained below. Note that the exact ordering may not be maintained by a particular product. The *EJB Specification* sets out where flexibility is allowed and where it is not. For the present, we will not be concerned with the distinction between the local client view and the remote client view. In any event, there is probably little justification for providing a local client view to session EJBs. In the description that follows, the term 'home object' can be taken to include either local or remote home objects. Similarly, the term 'EJB object' can be assumed to include local EJB objects.

1. The client calls a `create(...)` method on the home object. There can be any number of overloaded `create(...)` methods [EJB2.0 6.4.1], whose purpose is to bring about initialization of the EJB in the same way that a constructor would for an ordinary Java class.

Stateless	Stateful
A pool of implementation instances services all clients.	Implementation class is instantiated for each client.
Client calls can be cycled between instances.	Calls from the same client are always directed to the same instance on the server.
Methods cannot set instance variables on a per-client basis, as the client may be allocated a different instance on the next call, perhaps on a different server.	Methods can set instance variables for clients, and they remain valid for the client. If calls are load-balanced between servers, the EJB infrastructure is responsible for synchronizing the states of the stateful session EJBs between calls.
`create()` methods cannot take parameters, as the EJB can't do anything useful with the data supplied.	`create()` methods can take parameters and use them to initialize the instance variables.
Creation and removal is fast for clients, as instances are not actually created or removed, they are simply allocated from a pool.	Creation and removal are slower, as classes have to be instantiated, then freed and garbage-collected.
Easy to load-balance between servers, as instance variables do not reflect client state.	Difficult to load-balance, as instance variables must be synchronized.

Table 6.1. Comparison of stateless and stateful EJBs.

2. The home object or container instantiates the implementation instance.

3. The home object or container creates a `SessionContext` object and passes it to the instance in a `setSessionContext()` call.

4. The home object or container calls an `ejbCreate(...)` method whose arguments match the `create(...)` call on the home object. The EJB's implementation class initializes itself and, after this method call, is assumed to be ready for use.

5. The home object or container instantiates an EJB object for the instance. There is typically a one-to-one relationship between clients, EJB objects, and implementation instances.

6. The client calls whatever business methods it needs on the EJB object.

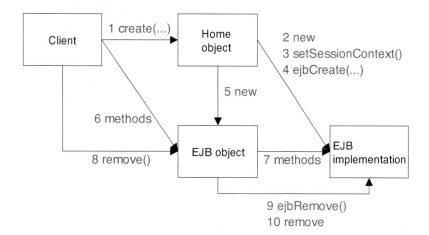

Figure 6.1. Interaction between the client, EJB implementation instance, and container for a stateful session bean (passivation, session synchronization, and timeout not shown).

7. The EJB object passes these calls on to the instance, doing whatever transaction management is required if the EJB is defined to use container-managed transaction demarcation (Chapter 9).

8. The client calls `remove()` on the EJB object.

9. The EJB object or container calls `ejbRemove()` on the instance.

10. The EJB object and container drop their references to the instance, and it becomes eligible for garbage collection. In addition, the container drops its reference to the EJB object, which itself becomes eligible for garbage collection.

We will examine later what happens if the client fails to call `remove()` to clean up properly.

6.3.2   Summary of developer's responsibilities

This section summarises the developer's responsibilities when authoring a stateful session EJB.

Home interface

In the (local or remote) home interface, define `create(...)` methods to allow the client to initialize the EJB for the current session. In the remote home interface, these methods must be defined to throw `java.rmi.RemoteException`, but not in the local home interface. In both local and remote home interfaces, `create(...)` should be defined to throw `javax.ejb.CreateException`. The home interface must extend either `javax.ejb.EJBHome` or `javax.ejb.EJBLocalHome`, directly or indirectly.

Remote or local interface

In the remote or local interface, define methods to match the business methods in the implementation. In the remote interface, these methods must be defined to throw `java.rmi.RemoteException` and any application exceptions that the implementation throws. In the local interface, only application exceptions need be declared (exception handling will be discussed later). The remote interface must extend `javax.ejb.EJBObject`, directly or indirectly, while the local interface extends `javax.ejb.EJBLocalObject`.

Implementation class

The implementation class provides all the functionality that the EJB requires (in collaboration with other classes and EJBs if necessary), and implements the container-callback methods. The minimum required set of methods is listed in Table 6.2. The class must implement, directly or indirectly, the methods in `javax.ejb.SessionBean`.

`ejbCreate(...)`	Implement as many overloaded variants as required (at least one) with appropriate arguments to initialize the instance. In a failure, throw `CreateException`.
`setSessionContext (SessionContext sc)`	At a minimum, store `SessionContext` object in an instance variable for later use. Typically locate data sources and other EJBs using JNDI calls.
`ejbRemove()`	Implement, if desired, to clean up. However, you can't rely on this method ever being called [EJB2.0 7.6.3]. In a failure, throw `RemoveException`.
`ejbActivate()`	Implement, if necessary, to recover from passivation (see below).
`ejbPassivate()`	Implement, if necessary, to prepare for passivation.
Business methods	Implement as required.

Table 6.2. Developer's responsibilities for the EJB implementation class in a stateful session EJB.

> ## Gotcha!
>
> Note that there is a `setSessionContext()` method, but no
> `unsetSessionContext()` method. This is in contrast to the pair-
> ing of `setEntityContext()` and `unsetEntityContext()` meth-
> ods in entity EJBs (Chapter 11). Of course, there is nothing to
> stop you from implementing such a method, but if you are expect-
> ing the container to call it when cleaning up, you will be disap-
> pointed. The reason for this imbalance is this: The *EJB Specifica-
> tion* guarantees that, if a session EJB's implementation instance
> is removed from the pool gracefully, the last method called on it
> will be `ejbRemove()`. On an entity EJB, `remove()` is called by
> the client to delete data, not to end a session, so `ejbRemove()`
> is typically not the last method called by the container. Thus
> `unsetEntityContext()` serves the purpose of being the guaran-
> teed last method called.

6.3.3   Passivation, activation, and timeout

Stateful session EJBs are the only type of EJB that require instances of the implementation class to be created on demand for client and removed afterwards.
Although this allows client state to be held in the instance variables, it does have
the disadvantage that the container must instantiate the implementation class for
every client that is active and, as we shall see, sometimes a fair number of clients
that are inactive.

In a system with many clients, or where clients come and go rapidly, the number
of instances of the implementation can increase beyond the capacity of the server's
virtual memory. Suppose, for example, that the server has allocated 128 megabytes
of memory to store stateful EJB implementation instances (a reasonable position to
adopt), and that each instance has a memory footprint of 10 kilobytes for its state
(not all that unusual). The container can therefore support 128M/10k, or about
13,000 clients. Now 13,000 is a large number of clients to support at any one time,
so we might think that this amount of memory is adequate. There are two quite
common situations where it might not be.

- Some clients hang on to their EJB references longer than they need them.
  This is a particular problem when the clients are servlets or JSPs. Very often,
  each user that interacts with the servlet will get a new instance of the implementation class, which will be saved in the servlet's session (see page 549). If
  end users don't inform the application that they have finished with it (and
  this is usually what happens with browser-based applications), some time can
  elapse between the user leaving the application and the servlet realizing that
  the user has gone away. When this does happen, the servlet can drop its

reference to the EJB, and the garbage collector can finalize it. Then, if the distributed garbage collection is working (and this is a problem in itself), the EJB container can drop its internal reference to the instance of the implementation class, and that can in turn be garbage collected. Putting all these time delays together, one can reasonably assume that there will be a delay of an hour between the user finishing with the servlet and the container's Java engine garbage-collecting the instance. If clients are joining the application and leaving at the rate of, say, 1000 per minute (quite possible on a very busy system), then the EJB container could accumulate 60,000 instances that are waiting to be released. This is well in excess of the 13,000-instance limit we calculated above.

- Clients may fail (e.g., crash) without calling `remove()`. This is a problem because of the lack of robust distributed garbage collection (of which, more later).

The simple solution to these problems, of course, is to increase the amount of memory available to the container; memory is relatively inexpensive, after all. However, we can't increase memory indefinitely, and it is inefficient to have a large amount of memory doing nothing.

The solution provided by the EJB architecture has two aspects: passivation and timeout.

Passivation

To passivate an EJB, the server simply writes its state to disk and releases the instance. It is important to understand that the server *can't* passivate the EJB object that is a proxy for the instance, because it is the EJB object that will have to take charge of reinstating the instance if it is required again.

How is passivation different from standard virtual memory schemes offered by operating systems? Why don't we just increase the amount of swap space that the container has available? After all, passivated instances and swapped-out memory pages are both data on disk. The fact is that on some platforms there may be no obvious benefit to EJB passivation, as the operating system may be able to use paging to handle the available memory to better effect than the EJB container. Nevertheless, systems that do offer passivation can make the following claims in their favour.

- When an instance of the implementation class is passivated, this is done in the expectation that it will probably not be required again. Operating system paging techniques cannot assume that a particular swapped-out block is less likely to be reloaded that any other.

- The granularity of passivation may well be finer than that of paging. Most operating systems like to page in blocks of kilobytes. If pages contain a mixture of redundant EJBs and essential data, then the redundant EJBs will end up being swapped back in because they are part of the same page. Passivation avoids this because it works at the instance level.

On the negative side we could claim the following.

- Operating systems are very good at paging, since their designers have had many years to get it right.

- In practice, passivation schemes are likely to be based on Java-language serialization, which is not conspicuously efficient.

Whether passivation is ultimately more effective than paging is a decision for the system administrator, not the developer. The developer's responsibility is to ensure that if passivation does take place, the EJB is able to handle it. Although this is potentially a problem, in practice the developer does not usually have to do all that much, as we shall see.

The *EJB Specification* does not say *how* passivation is to be achieved, but it does say that the container must call `ejbPassivate()` before passivation can occur. It also says that the container will call `ejbActivate()` after activating the instance again, should it turn out to be needed after all. These two methods between them must manage the passivation process.

> ## Hint
>
> The EJB container will never [EJB2.0 7.3] passivate an EJB in mid-transaction. This is important, because it may be necessary to close resource connections to make passivation possible. Many resource managers will automatically finalize a transaction when a TCP/IP connection is dropped.

In practice, all EJB products use Java-language serialization to passivate EJBs. The Specification says that the container must be able to handle instance variables that are serializable or `null` (of course, the latter is easy). The *EJB Specification* also says that the container must be able to passivate and activate certain types of instance variables, even if they are not naturally serializable [see EJB2.0 7.4.1 for the full (long) list]. These include in particular any resource factories returned from a JNDI lookup. For example, if we look up a data source like this:

```
DataSource ds = context.lookup
  ("java:comp/env/jdbc/orders");
```

then it is guaranteed that we will be able to store the object `ds` in an instance variable and that it will survive passivation. Another thing that the container will always be able to passivate is a reference to the `SessionContext` object. In practice, containers usually implement this functionality simply by ensuring that these objects are, in fact, serializable.

> ## Gotcha!
>
> The *EJB Specification* does say, however, that the EJB cannot rely
> on the container to be able to handle `transient` fields correctly.
> It has long been the practice of developers to use this keyword
> to indicate that an instance variable is volatile and does not need
> to be serialized. Because the container does not have to use Java
> serialization, it does not have to process the `transient` keyword.
> So storing nonserializable references in transient instance variables
> *may* fail with certain containers. The practice is frowned upon in
> the Specification.

If passivation does fail, then the EJB container will discard the instance. This
means that the next client call will result in an exception at the client, as the EJB
object won't be able to find the instance.

One of the major causes of passivation failure is the EJB attempting to keep
a resource *connection* (rather than a resource factory) open during passivation.
Remember that database connections, URL connections, and Java TCP/IP sockets
will most definitely *not* be serializable. Until connection pooling systems became
effective and widespread, it was common practice for a session EJB to open a
database connection in `ejbCreate()` and keep it open until `ejbRemove()`. The
problem with this is that the EJB can't be passivated. If you wish to adopt this
strategy (and there are many good reasons to avoid it), you need to ensure that
the connection is closed in `ejbPassivate()` and reopened in `ejbActivate()`. The
outline of an EJB that works this way might look like this.

```java
public class MyEJBBean
{
// Use instance variables for connection
//   and data source
Connection connection = null;
DataSource dataSource;

public void ejbCreate()
  {
  ds = // look up data source
  // Make connection
  connection = dataSource.getConnection();
  }

public void ejbActivate()
  {
  // Re-establish connection
  connection = dataSource.getConnection();
  }
```

```
public void ejbPassivate ()
  {
  // Close connection
  connection.close ();
  connection = null;  // This is essential!
  }
// Rest of implementation ...
}
```

Note that we don't need to close or null the datasource; this will always be passivated correctly (because the *EJB Specification* mandates that the server vendor provide `datasource` implementations that can be passivated). We do, however, have to close *and* null the connection. Setting it to `null` is the only way that we can be sure the container won't try to passivate it. And, following the Specification, we can't make it `transient` to get this effect, unless we want to sacrifice portability.

> ## Hint
>
> It is usually easier to ensure that all the session EJB's instance variables are serializable than to deal with activation and passivation. With modern database connection pooling schemes, there is no compelling reason to keep an open database connection in an instance variable.

Timeout

We can use passivation to prevent the proliferation of implementation instances, but it does not prevent the proliferation of EJB objects. In practice, with simple EJBs the EJB object is likely to have a larger memory footprint than the implementation itself. In any event, when an instance has been unused for a significant length of time (typically hours), the container can reasonably assume that it is defunct. In this case, the container simply drops the reference to the instance and the EJB object or, if the instance is passivated, deletes the passivated instance from disk.

If the client *were* to try to continue using the EJB again, it would now get an exception from the remote stub, because it wouldn't be able to find the EJB object.

One issue that is sometimes important is that when the container wants to discard an instance of a stateful session EJB, it does *not* have to call `ejbRemove()` on an instance that is passivated, but it *does* on an instance that is active [EJB2.0 7.6.3]. This is logically contradictory, but necessary on efficiency grounds. It would be a waste of CPU resources to deserialize a passivated EJB, only to call `ejbRemove()` on it and then free it again. This does mean, however, that you can't rely on `ejbRemove()` ever being called on a stateful session EJB.

6.3.4   Configuring passivation and timeout durations

The developer, system administrator, and perhaps the customer should ideally work together to determine acceptable values of the passivation timeouts. For best memory utilization, short timeouts are required. However, this may inconvenience the end user, and it does make development more difficult, as more extensive checking must be performed in code. In practice, these figures are difficult to determine in advance, so a common strategy is to set them to be very long (hours) and reduce them if memory limitations become an issue.

Hint

If your application uses stateful session EJBs, and they rely on `ejbPassivate()` and `ejbActivate()` to handle the passivation of instance variables that are not serializable, then it is important that these features be tested thoroughly before entering production. The problem is that they can be quite difficult to test, as by their very nature, they only happen under conditions of high load. A possible strategy is to configure the container to passivate more readily. The Reference Implementation, for example, passivates when a certain memory threshold is reached. The file `default.properties` has an entry of the form `passivation.threshold.memory=...`, which sets the threshold at which a passivation sweep will be initiated. If you set this threshold to, say, 5 kilobytes, you will certainly exercise the passivation and activation procedures, even under light load.

6.4   Stateless session EJBs

6.4.1   Overview of operation

The interactions between client, container, and EJB implementation instance are somewhat different for stateless session EJBs than the interactions we have discussed for stateful session EJBs. This is because the container creates a pool of implementation instances and shares them between clients. Therefore, in the collaboration diagram (Figure 6.2), there are two sets of collaborations. We will begin by considering the interactions that are driven by the client; assume that the pool of instances and EJB objects has already been created. As before, the distinction between local and distributed client views is not important at this stage.

1. The client calls `create()` on the home object. Note that there can only be one `create()` method for stateless session EJBs, and it must take no arguments.

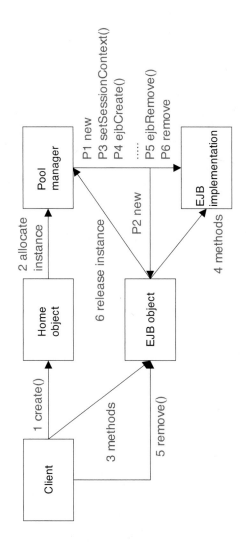

Figure 6.2. Interaction between the client, EJB instance, and container for a stateless session bean.

2. The home object requests an implementation instance from the pool. Because instances can't be entered on multiple threads simultaneously, it may have to wait for an instance to become free. Eventually the instance is allocated to this call. The home object returns to the client a reference to the EJB object.

3. The client calls whatever business methods it needs on the EJB object.

4. The EJB object passes the call on to the instance, after doing whatever transaction management and security authorization checks are required.

5. The client calls `remove()` on the EJB object.

6. The EJB object informs the pool manager that the instance is now available.

The above procedure can only be carried out if there are instances in the pool. So the container will begin by creating and initializing a set of instances in the pool (P1–P4). When the client calls `remove()`, the pool manager will be told that the instance is now free, and it may remove it (P5, P6) if it needs to. However, in practice, these last steps are rarely carried out—when an instance is placed in the pool, it stays there.

6.4.2   Summary of developer's responsibilities

This section summarizes the developer's responsibilities when authoring a stateless session EJB.

Home interface

In the (remote or local) home interface, define exactly one `create()` method (no arguments). In the remote home interface, this method must be defined to throw `java.rmi.RemoteException`, and in all cases should be defined to throw `javax.ejb.CreateException`. The home interface must extend `javax.ejb.EJBHome` or `javax.ejb.EJBLocalHome`, directly or indirectly.

Remote interface and local interface

In these interfaces, define methods to match the business methods in the implementation. In the remote interface, these methods must be defined to throw `java.rmi.RemoteException` and in all cases define any exceptions that the implementation throws. The remote interface must extend `javax.ejb.EJBObejct`, directly or indirectly.

Implementation class

The implementation class provides all the functionality that the EJB requires (in collaboration with other classes and EJBs if necessary), and implements the container-callback methods. The minimum required set of methods is listed in Table 6.3. The class must implement, directly or indirectly, the methods in `javax.ejb.SessionBean`.

`ejbCreate()`	Implement with no arguments to initialize the instance. In a failure, throw `CreateException`.
`setSessionContext (SessionContext sc)`	At a minimum, store `SessionContext` object in an instance variable for later use. Typically, look up data sources and other EJBs.
`ejbRemove()`	Implement, if desired, to clean up. However, you can't rely on this method ever being called. In a failure, throw `RemoveException`.
`ejbActivate()`	Implement as an empty method body (never called).
`ejbPassivate()`	Implement as an empty method body (never called).
Business methods	Implement as required.

Table 6.3. Developer's responsibilities for the EJB implementation class in a stateless session EJB.

Hint

Consider creating a generic base class for your session EJBs that implements all the methods that must exist but don't normally do anything. In the EJB itself, you can override the methods that are really necessary. This technique reduces the amount of redundant code in each EJB implementation, making the EJBs easier to read. This is a similar technique to the one used in Swing programming, where classes like `WindowAdapter` provide empty method bodies for the methods required by the `WindowListener` interface. An example below shows this technique applied to a real system.

6.5   Some notes on the meaning of an 'EJB instance'

When a stateful session EJB is created, there is a fairly clear relationship between the notion of 'creation' on the client, and 'instantiation' on the server. The EJB implementation class is instantiated exactly once for each `create()` call on the client. With stateless session EJBs, however, the relationship is less clear-cut. It is entirely possible that the client's `create()` call does not lead to *any* class being instantiated on the server. If the instance required to satisfy the client's request is taken from the pool for each method call, then the creation and removal operations on the client have no server counterpart. So what is it, exactly, that we create? The answer is that we have created a *conceptual EJB*. The client has every impression that it has brought about the creation of an EJB. It can call methods on it, and ultimately remove it, with no knowledge of the fact that no Java class has been instantiated.

In this book I have tried to be rigorous in my use of the words 'create' and 'instantiate.' Create is a general term for the creation of a conceptual object, which may be linked to one or more instantiations. Instantiate means to create an instance of a specific Java class. To be clear on the distinction, I will avoid the terms 'instantiate an EJB' and 'create an instance': Conceptual EJBs are 'created,' and specific Java platform *classes* are 'instantiated.' Similarly, when discussing instantiation, I try to be very clear about exactly *what* is being instantiated. So although the term 'instantiate the EJB implementation class' is rather long-winded, its meaning is unambiguous, whereas if someone writes 'instantiate the EJB,' it is far from clear what is meant.

When beginning EJB development, failure to understand the notion of the conceptual EJB can lead to confusion and error. For example, developers often complain that 'create' has different meanings for session EJBs, message-driven EJBs, and entity EJBs. For example, when the client calls `create()` on an entity EJB, the EJB is expected to insert data into its underlying database. Is this not a different meaning than creation of a stateless session EJB, which is just a kind of initialization? In fact, no. They are compatible, when one understands the broader meaning of the creation operation. In both cases, a conceptual EJB is brought into existence. In both cases, it is likely that no Java class is instantiated (instances are held in a pool). The situation is perfectly clear if one bears in mind that creation of an entity EJB (in the broad sense) corresponds to creating a database entry: The database entry *is* the EJB in the conceptual sense.

The same applies to passivation and activation. The `ejbPassive()` and `ejb Activate()` methods have very different implementations in session EJBs and entity EJBs (if, that is, they are implemented at all). In entity EJBs, the container calls `ejbActivate()` when it is assigning a new primary key to an instance. In session EJBs, the server calls this method to indicate the the EJB has been read in from disk. Although superficially different, they are compatible in *conceptual* terms. In both cases, the EJB is 'passive' if it is idle and unable to service client requests. In both cases, the container has to activate the EJB to ready it for the client. The difference is that *conceptually* a session EJB is idle when written out to disk, while an entity EJB is idle when not allocated to a primary key.

This is not merely an academic nicety; understanding the notions discussed in this section will make it much more obvious why the EJB API has the form that it does.

6.6 Session EJBs as interfaces to entity EJBs

The EJB developer needs to remember this very important principle: Session EJBs (and message-driven EJBs) are pooled on behalf of clients, while entity EJBs are pooled on behalf of the database. The reason we need a pool of entity EJBs is because the application may need to manipulate large database tables (that is, tables with many rows). The container will not normally increase the pool size to support a larger client load.

It is common design practice to use a session EJB as a facade for a number of entity EJBs, with most of the computational logic encapsulated in the session EJB. There are two main reasons for this:

- to increase concurrency in database access, by reducing the amount of data that is locked in a transaction; and

- to simplify the interface with clients. Clients of an EJB application expect to see services (session EJBs), not data (entity EJBs).

If non-EJB clients communicate directly with entity EJBs, there can be an efficiency bottleneck. Typically every access to an entity EJB will involve a database transaction. If there is significant computation in an entity EJB method, this leaves part of the database locked in a transaction for a significant time. Having the logic in a session EJB *can* reduce the amount of time spent in a transaction (but this requires a lot of design effort to achieve). A more significant efficiency gain is achieved by using session EJBs as a cache of entity EJB data, and this is easier to design for. The problem here is one of ensuring that the data cached remains valid, without locking the database in a transaction. For data that changes only slowly, reading it once per user interaction into a session EJB, rather that frequently from an entity EJB, can be very effective.

6.7 Transaction issues in session EJBs

The *EJB Specification* provides mechanisms to support synchronization of stateful session beans with transactions. This is discussed in detail in Chapter 9. For now, note the following points.

- Session EJBs can participate in database and messaging transactions, either controlled by the EJB itself or by the container. Transactionality is not the exclusive prerogative of entity EJBs.

- Stateful session EJBs can begin transactions in one method and commit them in another. Stateless session EJBs can't do this: A transaction begun in one method must be committed in the same method. The argument for this is subtle, but compelling. The only conceivable reason for beginning a transaction in one method and completing it in another is that the EJB's methods are being called by the same client. It makes little sense for one client to commit a transaction begun by another.[2] But stateless session EJBs don't have an association to a client; they are always pooled. Therefore a stateless session EJB instance should not be involved in repeated calls from the same client. This implies that it is unnecessary for a stateless session EJB to maintain a transaction between methods.

  Whether this argument is convincing or not, it is mandated in the *EJB Specification* [EJB2.0 17.3.3], and EJB servers should reject an attempt by a stateless EJB to leave an uncommitted transaction at the end of a method.

In Chapter 9, we will consider what happens if, for example, a stateful session EJB modifies its internal state during a transaction, and that transaction later fails and has to roll back. This is a particularly tricky aspect of EJB development.

6.8   Analyzing the 'Interest' EJB

In Chapter 4, we implemented a simple session EJB. We are now in position to analyze the behaviour of this EJB, and its interaction with the container, in more detail. In the discussion that follows, I assume that the EJB was deployed to the *J2EE Reference Implementation*; other products will behave similarly, but procedures and naming conventions will be different.

This section is provided for developers who want to know *in great depth* how EJBs work. In practice, you will be able to implement perfectly satisfactory EJBs without knowing this level of detail, but it can be very helpful to understand what's going on 'under the hood' if things aren't working the way you expect.

6.8.1   Recap

The EJB introduced in Chapter 4 is a simple stateless session bean called 'Interest' with two business methods:

```
public double getInterestOnPrincipal
    (double principal , double interestPerTerm , int terms);
public double getTotalRepayment
    (double principal , double interestPerTerm , int terms);
```

The EJB's classes were in the package com.kevinboone.ejb_book.interest: The remote home interface is called InterestHome and the remote interface is Interest. The implementation is in InterestBean.

---

[2]But see [EJB2.0 17.7.1] for a counterexample.

6.8.2   Deployment

During the deployment process, the deployment tool automatically creates supporting classes based on the bean's home interface and remote interface. These classes can be categorized as follows.

- 'Container proxy' classes: These are the actual implementations of the home interface and remote interface. They are created, complied, and instantiated on the server and control access to the instances of the bean class itself.

- 'Skeleton' classes: These classes handle the server side of the client-server communications protocol between the client and the container's proxy classes. They are instantiated on the server.

- 'Stub' classes: These classes handle the client side of the communication. These are downloaded to the client during deployment and instantiated on the client when it executes.

Note that during deployment, the developer's home interface, remote interface, and implementation class must also be copied to the server, as the container will create implementations of the interfaces and instantiate the implementation on demand.

During deployment, the skeleton, stub, and proxy classes will be created as Java source files, compiled and packaged. The intermediate files are then deleted.

The client-side stub classes are packaged into a JAR whose name is chosen by the developer.

For the 'Interest' EJB, the classes created on the server are as follows. Please note that I have not shown the full package name for each class as it would be too long to fit on the line.

`InterestBeanHomeImpl`

This is the home object, which also serves as the EJB container for instances of InterestBean (in the Reference Implementation; other containers don't always combine these roles). This class implements the interface `InterestHome` and extends `com.sun.ejb.containers.EJBHomeImpl`. A simplified version of this class is shown in Listing 6.1 at the end of this section. Note that most of the functionality of the home interface is in the superclass `EJBHomeImpl`; the generated class contains functionality specific to this EJB.

`_InterestBeanHomeImpl_Tie`

This class implements an IIOP skeleton for the home stub. It mediates between the client's home stub (`_InterestHome_Stub`) and the container `InterestBeanHome Impl`. It also implements the server end of the IIOP protocol.

`InterestBean_EJBObjectImpl`

This class implements the EJB object that will act as a proxy for the 'real' bean class, `InterestBean`. It implements the remote interface `Interest` and extends `com.sun.containers.StatelessSessionEJBObjectImpl`. This class will handle sequentialization of access to the bean, creation and completion of transactions, and security validation. A simplified version of this class is shown in Listing 6.2. Again, most of the functionality is in the superclass; the generated class handles only functionality specific to this EJB.

_InterestBean_EJBObjectImpl_Tie

This class implements an IIOP skeleton for the remote stub. It mediates between the client's remote stub (`_Interest_Stub`) and the EJB object `InterestBean_EJB ObjectImpl`. It also implements the server side of the IIOP protocol.

Each of these classes will be described in more detail as we examine the process of running a simple client application.

After deployment, and any time the server is restarted, the deployment information for the EJB is examined, and the JNDI name registered with the naming service. In addition, a home object and home skeleton are instantiated. The home object (of class `InterestBeanHomeImpl`) will manage all requests to create, find, and delete Interest EJBs. Note that `Interest` is a stateless session bean, and the home object will create and delete instances of the bean class as it sees fit. This creation and deletion is not controlled directly by the client.

Listing 6.1: **EJB home implementation (simplified). This class is representative of the home implementation that is generated automatically by the deployment tool when the EJB is deployed. Note that the listing is very short; there is only one method that is specific to the current EJB: create(). All the other work is handled by the superclass `com.sun.ejb.containers.EJBHomeImpl`.**

```
     package com.kevinboone.ejb_book.interest;

     public final class InterestHomeImpl
         extends com.sun.ejb.containers.EJBHomeImpl
   5     implements InterestHome
     {
         public InterestHomeImpl(com.sun.ejb.Container c)
           throws java.rmi.RemoteException
         {
  10     super(c);
         }

     public Interest create()
           throws java.rmi.RemoteException,
  15         javax.ejb.CreateException
         {
           InterestBean_EJBObjectImpl ejbObject =
               (InterestBean_EJBObjectImpl) createEJBObject();
               // method in superclass
```

```
20        return ( Interest ) ejbObject . getStub ( ) ;
      }
```

Listing 6.2: **EJB object implementation (simplified).** This listing is representative of the EJB object class that is generated automatically by the deployment tool when the EJB is deployed. This class handles all requests for business methods sent from the client to the EJB, delegating them where appropriate to the real bean, `InterestBean`. For clarity, I have removed the exception handling code (which is quite extensive) and some other code that isn't particularly relevant.

```
    package com . kevinboone . ejb_book . interest ;
    import java . util .*;

    public final class InterestBean_EJBObjectImpl
5       extends
        com . sun . ejb . containers . StatelessSessionEJBObjectImpl
        implements Interest
    {
    public InterestBean_EJBObjectImpl ( )
10      throws java . rmi . RemoteException { }

    public double getInterestOnPrincipal
        ( double principal , double interestPerTerm , int terms )
          throws java . rmi . RemoteException
15      {
        com . sun . ejb . Invocation i =
          new com . sun . ejb . Invocation ( ) ;
        i . ejbObject = this ;
        i . method =
20          com . kevinboone . ejb_book . interest . Interest . class . getMethod
            ( "getInterestOnPrincipal" , /*...*/ ) ;
        this . getContainer ( ) . preInvoke ( i ) ;
        com . kevinboone . ejb_book . interest . InterestBean ejb =
          ( com . kevinboone . ejb_book . interest . InterestBean ) i . ejb ;
25      double d2 = ejb . getInterestOnPrincipal
          ( principal , interestPerTerm , terms ) ;
        this . getContainer ( ) . postInvoke ( i ) ;
        return s2 ;
      }
30
    // Other methods ...
    }
```

6.8.3 Execution

The EJB's methods are executed in response to method calls on the client. The code in the client that is important from an EJB perspective is quite simple:

```
   InitialContext  ic = new InitialContext();
   Object  lookup = ic.lookup("Interest");
   InterestHome  home = (InterestHome)
       PortableRemoteObject.narrow(lookup, InterestHome.class);
5  Interest  interest = home.create();
   double  r = interest.getInterestOnPrincipal("...");
   first.remove();
```

We will now consider in detail what happens when this client code is executed. For simplicity, we will assume that this is the first time it has been run, and no other client has had occasion to use the 'Interest' EJB.

1. Get the initial naming context. Because we haven't indicated otherwise, there will be no URL or naming context factory associated with this naming context. This means that when the lookup is performed, it will be carried out using the default naming context class `com.sun.jndi.cosnaming.CNCtx` and the default URL `iiop://localhost:1050`. These defaults (which are specific to the Reference Implementation) are appropriate if the client and the EJB server are actually on the same host. If not, we will need to instantiate `InitialContext` with the appropriate environment. The naming context `CNCtx` handles the client side of the CORBA naming service (CoSNaming). When the EJB server started, it obtained name-object mappings from information that was provided (in the deployment descriptor XML) when the EJB was deployed. For more information about JNDI and naming, see Chapter 7.

2. Look up the home interface for the EJB using the CORBA naming service on the specified server. The naming context client essentially maps the information about the EJB known to the naming service on the server into a class that the client can make method calls on. In this case, the object returned by `lookup("Interest")` is an instance of the home stub class `_Interest Home_Stub`. Notice how this name is derived from the name of the home interface `InterestHome`. Where is this stub class? It was generated automatically by the deployment tool when the bean was deployed and returned in the 'Client JAR' file. The home stub class has the following signature:

```
   public class _InterestHome_Stub
           extends javax.rmi.CORBA.Stub
           implements InterestHome
   {
5  public _InterestHome_Stub();

   public Interest  create()
       throws javax.ejb.CreateException,
           java.rmi.RemoteException;
10
   public javax.ejb.EJBMetaData getEJBMetaData()
       throws java.rmi.RemoteException;

   public javax.ejb.HomeHandle getHomeHandle()
15     throws java.rmi.RemoteException;
```

```
public void remove(java.lang.Object)
    throws java.rmi.RemoteException,
        javax.ejb.RemoveException;

public void remove(javax.ejb.Handle)
    throws java.rmi.RemoteException,
        javax.ejb.RemoveException;
}
```

(The Reference Implementation uses class names beginning with an underscore (_) for stubs and skeletons.) Note that this home stub class is a CORBA (IIOP) stub, and implements the bean's home interface, `InterestHome`. It provides implementations of methods like `create()` that are specified in the home interface, but does not implement any 'real' functionality in them. Instead, methods in the home stub will communicate with the 'home skeleton' on the server. This is the class `InterestBeanHomeImpl_Tie`. This will in turn delegate method calls to the home object implementation `InterestHomeImpl` on the server. It is this class that will do the real work.

The home stub also provides implementations of the API methods `getHome Handle()`, etc.

3. The client now calls `PortableRemoteObject.narrow()` to get an RMI-compatible stub that corresponds to the object returned by the lookup operation. In this case, the returned object is already an RMI-compatible stub (we are using a Java implementation of an IIOP client, after all), so we get another instance of class `_InterestHome_Stub`. In other words, `narrow()` has no effect here, and we could have written

```
InterestHome home = (InterestHome)ic.lookup ("Interest");
```

and skipped the narrowing step. However, this may prevent the client from communicating with the EJB using other transport protocols, should we wish to do so in future. With or without the call to `narrow()`, we are doing a *narrowing cast* here—that is, we are casting something that can be any subclass of `java.lang.Object` (the defined return type for `lookup()`) into a `InterestHome`. Some developers use the term 'downcast' for this operation.

4. We call `create()` on the home interface, which has the following effects.

   - The call is actually on `_InterestHome_Stub.create()` (because we cast an object of this class into `InterestHome` in line 3).
   - The `create()` method in the stub communicates with the home object on the server. Specifically, the create call is passed through the stub and skeleton to the `create()` method in the home object `InterestHomeImpl` on the server (see Listing 6.1). This object then instantiates the EJB object (`InterestBean_EJBObjectImpl`) and the communication skeleton (`_InterestBean_EJBObjectImpl_Tie`) (line 17 in Listing 6.1).

- Note that although we now have a home object and a remote object on the server, we don't yet have any actual `InterestBean` instances, and the bean is not ready to do any work. However, since stateless session beans can be pooled, on subsequent invocations of this client there may be existing instances of `InterestBean` in the pool.

- The home object returns to the client, via its skeleton and stub, a reference to the newly created EJB object (line 20 in Listing 6.1). The home stub on the client actually returns to the client an instance of the remote stub; this stub will handle future communication with the EJB object. In this example, the remote stub is an instance of an IIOP stub that implements `Interest`. Its signature is shown below.

```
   public class _Interest_Stub
      extends javax.rmi.CORBA.Stub
      implements com.kevinboone.ejb_book.interest.Interest
      {
5  public _Interest_Stub();

   public javax.ejb.EJBHome getEJBHome()
      throws java.rmi.RemoteException;

10 public javax.ejb.Handle getHandle()
      throws java.rmi.RemoteException;

   public java.lang.Object getPrimaryKey()
      throws java.rmi.RemoteException;
15
   public boolean isIdentical(javax.ejb.EJBObject)
      throws java.rmi.RemoteException;

   public void remove()
20    throws java.rmi.RemoteException,
         javax.ejb.RemoveException;

   public double getInterestOnPrincipal
         (double principal, double interestPerTerm, int terms)
25       throws java.rmi.RemoteException;
   }
```

The client does not have to cast this reference, as it is *defined* to be of the proper type (it was created by a call to `create()` in the home stub, whose return type is `Interest`).

- Note that the remote stub contains implementations of the business method `getInterestOnPrincipal()`. Of course, this stub does not implement the functionality of this method, as that is done by the implementation class `InterestBean` on the server. The stub simply passes method invocations through to the implementation via the remote skeleton and the EJB object.

Note also that the stub provides implementations of the API method `isIdentical()`, although it probably delegates these requests to the container as well.

In summary, the chain of communication between the client and the EJB home object is as shown in Figure 6.3.

5. Now that we have a remote reference to the bean, we can call any of its business methods. In this example, we are calling `getInterestOnPrincipal()`.

- In fact, the client calls this method on the remote stub, which communicates with the remote skeleton (`_EJBObjectImpl_Tie`), which calls the corresponding method `getInterestOnPrincipal()` on the EJB object on the server.

- The EJB object asks the container for an instance of `InterestBean`. It starts this process by creating an instance of `com.sun.ejb.Invocation` and setting its fields to indicate the method that will be invoked and the EJB object (itself) that is requesting it (lines 15–19, Listing 6.2). This object is then passed to the container (line 20), which carries out the following actions.

- The container checks whether the client is authorized to call the requested method. If not, it throws an exception.

- The container checks whether an instance of the bean implementation is available—remember that this is a stateless EJB, and can therefore share instances between clients. In this case, the container will instantiate the implementation class, while in subsequent calls, it will simply return a reference to an existing instance. So the container creates a new instance of `InterestBean`, by calling `newInstance()` on its class. A reference to this new instance is held in a pool for future invocations. Note that calling `newInstance()` causes the bean's no-arg constructor to be called, but does not initialize it in any other way.

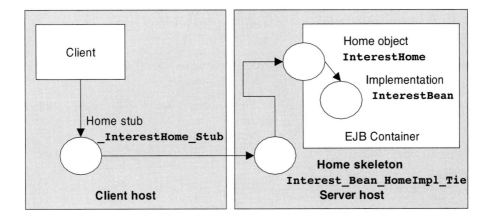

Figure 6.3. The objects that are involved when the client makes a `create()` call on the home interface.

- The container creates a new `SessionContext` object. This object will allow the bean to determine security and transaction attributes, for example. In fact, the container instantiates `com.sun.ejb.containers.SessionContextImpl`, a class which implements the `SessionContext` interface.

- The container calls `setSessionContext()` on the new instance of `InterestBean`, passing in the instance of `com.sun.ejb.containers.SessionContextImpl` created previously. The bean may store this reference or ignore it, at the discretion of the developer. Of course, a good reason for storing it is that its methods can be used to check the security roles of the client.

- The container calls `ejbCreate()` on the implementation instance.

- The container begins a new transaction for the requested method call, if the transaction attributes specify that a transaction is required and no transaction currently exists.

- The container returns the reference to the new bean instance to the remote object. In fact, it simply initializes the `ejb` instance variable in the `Invocation` instance (line 23 in Listing 6.2).

- The remote object calls the business method `getInterestOnPrincipal()` in the bean instance (line 25).

- The bean executes the `getInterestOnPrincipal()` method and returns a `String` value to the EJB object.

- The EJB object signals the container (line 27) that the method call is complete. The container will commit or roll back the transaction if it initiated a transaction for this method call.

- The EJB object returns the output from the business method to the remote skeleton (line 28), which passes it over the network to the remote stub, which unmarshalls the data and passes it back to the client. At this point the method call is complete, and the client can call other methods if it needs to.

6. The client calls `remove()`, which signals to the container that the client has finished with the EJB. The container could, if it wished, free the EJB instance (specifically, it could call `ejbRemove()`) and drop its reference to the instance, making it eligible for garbage collection. In this example, the EJB is stateless, and the container will not do this. Instead, it will keep the instance (and, indeed the skeleton and the EJB object) for the next client.

6.8.4   How would a stateful session EJB behave differently?

One of the most important issues that this example brings out is the total dissociation between the client's calls to `create()` and `remove()`, and the container's actual creation and deletion of instances of the implementation. With a stateless session bean, creation and deletion of instances is simply beyond the control of the client.

Because this is the case, the *J2EE Reference Implementation* uses a 'lazy initialization' strategy for the implementation class. Note that the container did not even attempt to initialize an instance until the client called the method `getInterest OnPrincipal()`. At this point, the container constructed the instance, calling `set SessionContext()`, `ejbCreate()`, and `getInterestOnPrincipal()` in one operation.

This strategy is appropriate when instances are held in a pool, and it is used by many EJB products. An alternative is for the server to create a pool of instances at start-up time, and use the pool to service all requests from clients.

It is straightforward to modify the Interest EJB to be stateful: The change is simply in the deployment tool, and no code needs to be modified. If we do this and execute the test client again, we will notice some differences.

First, the container creates a new instance for each client. It also creates a new EJB object and a new remote skeleton. That is, none of these things are pooled.

Second, this means that the container will have to initialize the instance (calling `setSessionContext()` and `ejbCreate()`) when each client calls `create()`.

Third, the container will delete the instance, EJB object, and skeleton when the client calls `remove()`.

It should be obvious that using stateful EJBs presents a significant overhead to the server; they should only be used where the EJB really does maintain conversational state with the client. Otherwise, stateless EJBs offer significant performance benefits.

6.9   An example

Let's look at a real example.[3] In the *Prestige Bike Hire* application, the EJB `BookingManager` handles all operations involving making, searching, and retrieving motorcycle bookings. Because it is intended to be used by a servlet client, it has only a remote client view (that is, no local interface or local home interface).

So the Java entities to be provided are

Remote home interface	BookingManagerHome
Remote interface	BookingManager
Implementation class	BookingManagerBean

Because many of the container callback methods (`ejbActivate()`, etc.) are either never called by the container or have no effect, I have written this EJB to be an extension of an adaptor class `GenericStatelessSessionBean`. This provides dummy implementations of all the compulsory callback methods. Having all my stateless session EJBs inherit from this base class makes the implementation code much shorter and more more readable. The adaptor class is straightforward, and is shown in full in Listing 6.3.

---

[3]The full source code is too long to list in its entirety in this chapter, and only important features will be highlighted. Full source code can be obtained from `www.kevinboone.com/ejb_book`.

Listing 6.3: **Adaptor class for the stateless session EJBs in the** *Prestige Bike Hire* **application. This provides dummy functionality for methods that are not usually implemented and some debugging support.**

```
      package com.kevinboone.bikehire.ejb;
      import javax.ejb.*;
      import javax.naming.*;

5     /**
      GenericStatelessSessionBean is a general-purpose base
      class for stateless session EJB implementations. It provides
      dummy implementations of the specified methods in
      the SessionBean interface
10    */
      public class GenericStatelessSessionBean implements SessionBean
        {
      protected SessionContext ctx;
      protected boolean debug = true;

15
      /**
      debugOut prints its output to the standard output if
      the 'debug' flag is set. The flag is set from the
      environment variable 'java:comp/env/debug' in
20    setEntityContext()
      */
      protected void debugOut (String s)
        {
        if (debug)
25        System.out.println (this.getClass().toString()
            + ": " + s);
        }

      public void ejbActivate()
30      {
        // Never called
        }

      public void ejbCreate()
35        throws CreateException
        {
        debugOut("Dummy ejbCreate()");
        }

40    public void ejbPassivate()
        {
        // Never called
        }

45    public void ejbRemove()
        {
        debugOut("Dummy ejbRemove()");
        }

50    public void setSessionContext(SessionContext _ctx)
        {
        ctx = _ctx;
        try
          {
```

```
55      Context c = new InitialContext ();
        Boolean temp =
          (Boolean) c.lookup ("java:comp/env/debug");
        if (temp != null)
          debug = temp.booleanValue();
60      }
      catch (NamingException e){}
      debugOut ("setSessionContext()");
      }
    }
```

<hr>

Hint

All the methods in this EJB—real and dummy—make a call to
the method call **debugOut()** to write some debugging data. You
should consider providing your EJBs with a technique for generating debugging output that can easily be switched on and off
without recompilation. Generating copious debugging output can
be a performance bottleneck in a practical system. This issue is
discussed in more detail beginning on page 439. In this example,
we use an EJB environment variable to control whether debugging
information should be displayed or not. This allows debugging levels to be controlled after deployment without modifying any code.

The home interface is unremarkable, containing one no-argument `create()`
method (Listing 6.4).

Listing 6.4: **Home interface for the `BookingManager` EJB.**

```
package com.kevinboone.bikehire.ejb;
import javax.ejb.*;
import java.rmi.*;
import java.util.*;

5
/**
(Remote) home interface for the 'BookingManager' EJB
(c)2002 Kevin Boone
*/
10  public interface BookingManagerHome extends EJBHome
    {
    public BookingManager create ()
      throws CreateException , RemoteException ;
    }
```

The remote interface exposes the business methods of the EJB (Listing 6.5).

Listing 6.5: **Remote interface for the** BookingManager **EJB.**

```
    package com.kevinboone.bikehire.ejb;
    import javax.ejb.*;
    import java.rmi.*;
    import java.util.*;
5

    /**
    (Remote) business method interface for the 'BookingManager'
    EJB
    (c)2002 Kevin Boone
10  */
    public interface BookingManager extends EJBObject
    {
    /**
    Get a Collection of AvailabilityData objects to represent when
15  the selected bike or model is available. Either bikeModel or
    licenseNumber may be supplied, but (presumably) not both. If
    startDate is null, take the current date. If endDate is null,
    take the date on month after the startDate
    */
20  public Collection getAvailability(final String bikeModel,
        final String licenceNumber, final java.util.Date startDate,
        final java.util.Date endDate)
            throws BookingManagerException, RemoteException;

25  /**
    Get a Collection of BookingData objects to represent when the
    selected bike is booked to the selected customer. A null
    license number matches any license number; a customerId of
    Customer.ID_UNKNOWN matches any customer. A customerId of
30  Customer.ID_CURRENT matches the current logged-in user. This
    method should not be directly callable from a non-privileged
    client: call getMyBookings instead
    */
    public Collection getBookings(final String licenceNumber,
35      final int customerId, final java.util.Date startDate,
        final java.util.Date endDate)
            throws BookingManagerException, RemoteException;

    /**
40  Get a Collection of BookingData objects to represent when the
    selected bike is booked to the currently logged in customer.
    A null license number matches any license number.
    */
    public Collection getMyBookings(final String licenceNumber,
45      final java.util.Date startDate,
        final java.util.Date endDate)
            throws BookingManagerException, RemoteException;

    /**
50  Explicitly adds a booking to the booking table. This method is
    intended to be used only be test clients, because it merely
    inserts a value into the table without any sort of checks.
    Real clients should use makeReservation()
    */
55  public void addBooking (final String licenceNumber,
        final int customerId, final int status, final Date startDate,
```

```
        final Date endDate)
           throws BookingManagerException, RemoteException;

60   /**
     Provisionally checks whether a reservation is possible, and
     calculates the cost. This method does not actually make a
     reservation, or alter any data in the database. It is provided
     to allow clients to check whether a booking is likely to
65   success, and how much it will cost. The return value is the
     cost in whatever units are stored in the ChargeBand EJB.
     */
     public int checkReservation (final String bikeModel,
        final Date startDate, final Date endDate)
70         throws BookingManagerException, RemoteException;

     /**
     Make a reservation for a particular model of motorcycle for
     the specified customer ID. Unprivileged users should not be
75   able to call this method (use makeMyReservation instead). This
     method actually makes a provisional reservation, and sends a
     message to the customer's credit card company for confirmation
     of payment.
     */
80   public String makeReservation (final String bikeModel,
           final int id, final Date startDate, final Date endDate)
           throws BookingManagerException, RemoteException;

     /**
85   As makeReservation (), but takes the ID of the user currently
     logged in.
     */
     public String makeMyReservation (final String bikeModel,
           final Date startDate, final Date endDate)
90         throws BookingManagerException, RemoteException;
     }
```

Note that these methods are defined to throw `RemoteException`, as always, and, in addition, a `BookingManagerException`. What is this? It is important to remember that this EJB is client-facing: Everything that goes into it or comes out (including exceptions) must be in a form that is meaningful to the client. In this case, the client will be the Web application that forms the user interface. Let's suppose that a database failure occurs while updating the bookings database (via the `Booking` entity EJB, for example). What kind of exception will be meaningful to the *client*? We don't want to throw `SQLException` or `TransactionRolledBackException` to the client, as these exceptions are meaningful only to the business logic. Instead, the EJB catches low-level exceptions and relays them back to clients in more meaningful terms. This process is illustrated in the following extract from the `makeReservation()` method.

```
try
  {
  Customer customer = customerHome.findByPrimaryKey
    (new Integer(realCustomerId));
  // business logic here...
  return licenceNumber;
  }
catch (FinderException e)
  {
  debugOut ("Caught exception in makeReservation(): " + e);
  ctx.setRollbackOnly ();
  throw new BookingManagerException
    ("Can't get customer details for specified ID");
  }
// Handle other low-level exceptions...
```

A `FinderException` is thrown by an entity EJB to indicate that an attempt to find a specific instance of the EJB failed. In this method, the entity EJB in use is `Customer`. If a `FinderException` is thrown from `findByPrimaryKey()`, it is almost certainly the case that the method was supplied with an invalid customer ID. Now, we could have arranged the session EJB method `makeReservation()` to throw the `FinderException` back to its client, but would this help the client? In the example, the session EJB catches the `FinderException` and throws back to the client a general exception `BookingManagerException` whose message field contains information that may make some sense to an end user.

You may have noticed a reference to a `CustomerHome` object in the example above. How has the `BookingManager` EJB gotten a `CustomerHome` object? In short, it has done this the way any client of the `Customer` EJB would do: It uses a JNDI `lookup()` operation. I have chosen to do this kind of initialization in the `setSessionContext()` method; `ejbCreate()` would also be a sensible choice.

```
protected CustomerHome customerHome;

public void setSessionContext (SessionContext sc)
  {
  super.setSessionContext(sc);
  try
    {
    customerHome = (CustomerHome)BeanLocator.getHome
      ("java:comp/env/ejb/Customer", CustomerHome.class, false);
    //... initialize other EJB home references
    }
  catch (BeanLocatorException e)
    {
    debugOut ("Caught exception in setSessionContext():" + e);
    throw new EJBException (e);
    }
  }
```

Because finding EJB home objects is such a common task, it is common practice to create a helper class to do it. In this example, the `BeanLocator` class carries out this task. If it can't look up the home object, it throws a `BeanLocatorException`. The session EJB catches this exception and throws `EJBException`. This latter exception is a runtime exception, and is used to indicate a catastrophic, nonrecoverable error.

As always, we are using the `java:comp/env` namespace to locate the home object in JNDI; this allows the EJB names to be resolved at deployment time if necessary (Figure 6.4).

6.10 Summary

Session EJBs are models of services provided to clients or encapsulations of business logic. They are not expected to be persistent, although they can interact with databases and other data sources, and can be involved in transactions. Stateful session EJBs model a sequence of interactions between the same client and the service, and can maintain data on behalf of the client. Stateless session EJBs model simple client-server interactions where no data is stored on behalf of the client. Stateless session EJBs are much more efficient to use than the stateful variant, as method calls from any client can be dispatched to any instance.

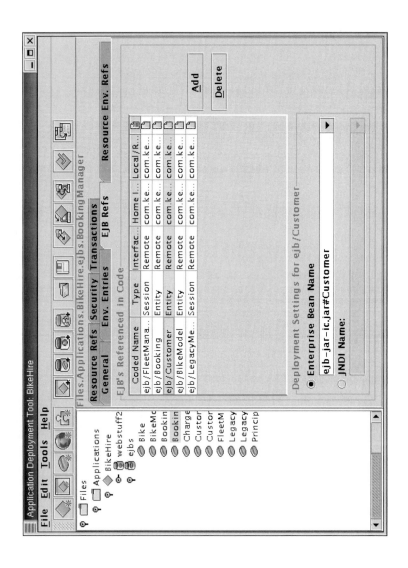

Figure 6.4. Mapping the java:comp/env names of the EJBs references by the BookingManager EJB to the real JNDI names of these EJBs. In this example, because I wrote all the EJBs, I have made the coded names and the JNDI names the same. In a multiteam development exercise, this probably won't be the case.

Chapter 7

Naming and JNDI

Overview

While previous chapters have shown in outline how EJBs and their clients use JNDI to find home interfaces, this chapter describes the JNDI system in more detail. We start with an outline of the JNDI architecture, and describe some of the key terms and concepts used in JNDI programming. This is followed by a description of the use of JNDI by EJBs and their clients, including the distinction between the server-wide namespace and the 'local' namespace provided for each EJB. This will lead to a discussion of the use of the 'java:comp/env' prefix in name lookups; this is an issue about which many developers and, sadly, some container vendors are unclear. Finally, to provide a detailed description of the JNDI architecture, there is a complete implementation of a JNDI interface to a set of objects stored in a file. This is provided for those readers who need a very thorough understanding of JNDI, perhaps to support EJB container extensions.

It is easy for an EJB developer to forget that JNDI was designed not as a support service for EJBs, but to simplify access from Java programs to naming and directory servers (rather as JDBC is used for database access). Much of JNDI is intended to support this more general usage and is not directly used in EJB development. However, EJB developers are increasingly being called on to use the more general features of JNDI in their applications to support such features as user and group management.

7.1 Naming and directory servers

In general, a *name server* is anything that can accept a name and return some related information. There are many different naming services currently in use. Here are some typical examples.

- DNS (domain name service): takes a hostname and provides an IP number. DNS servers are used by almost all computers that have Internet connections, to map hostnames onto IP numbers.

- NIS (Network Information Service): takes the name of a user, group, or server and returns various information. NIS is a proprietary system widely used in Unix environments. An NIS server can supply information about the machines, users, and groups on a particular network.

- LDAP (lightweight directory access protocol): takes a record identifier (technically a *distinguished name*) and returns a set of name-value data elements for that record. LDAP is now very widely used for storing user and group information for security purposes. In such an application, we would supply a distinguished name that identifies the user or group and get access to all the stored information about the user or group. For groups, for example, we would be able to get a list of members. For users we can typically get a user ID, password, email address, and real name.

- COSNamimg (CORBA Object Services Naming): takes the name of an object and supplies a reference to that object, which can be used to make remote method calls on it. COSNaming is a specification for object request brokers (ORBs) to supply objects by name. This type of naming is particularly important here, as many EJB servers will also be CORBA-compliant ORBs. When a client looks up an EJB in the Reference Implementation server, the JNDI service provider actually converts the lookup into a CORBA name lookup on the built-in ORB. While not all EJB1.1 servers support CORBA naming, it is a requirement of EJB 2.0 [EJB2.0 19.7].

Naming and directory servers are usually proprietary, but they have three important factors in common.

First, they operate a one-to-one mapping—that is, one name goes in and one set of related data comes out. Of course, the content and structure of the data will vary according to the name and the purpose of the system. In contrast, most SQL queries will return multiple results.

Second, they tend to follow a hierarchical data model—that is, some names reference collections of other names, and some of these in turn reference other collections. For example, an LDAP directory may be organized into countries, which are divided into organizations, which are divided into departments, which consist of people. To get a particular person's record, I would need to specify the country, organization, department, and personal name. Hierarchical name servers are often called *directory servers*, but this term is also widely (ab)used to mean any kind of name server.[1]

---

[1] I am frequently told off by directory server gurus, who tell me that the X.500 naming convention, which LDAP directories follow, is not really hierarchical at all. The hierarchy, they say, is a construct of the human mind, and the data space is really flat. While this is true, it is also irrelevant as far as most practical directory setups are concerned. JNDI, as we shall see, assumes that directories can be hierarchical.

Third, the server can normally enumerate entries as well as find a particular entry. For example, in the LDAP example above, we would expect to be able to get a list of all the organizations in a particular country or all the people in a particular department.

Because these name servers have these features in common, it was recognized that they could be made accessible to Java programs using a common API; this is where JNDI comes in.

7.2   What is JNDI?

JNDI—Java Naming and Directory Interface—is a specification and API that allows Java programs to get access to information in a variety of different naming services. Whatever the underlying naming service, and independent of the vendor, the JNDI client gets access to data in the same way. Of course, the *kind* of data that is retrieved will depend on the underlying server. Thus, JNDI lookups return Java objects, which will be of classes that are appropriate to model the data returned. The *JNDI Specification* says little about the kinds of objects that can be retrieved from, and stored in, the underlying naming service. The Specification allows clients to write and rename entries, as well as reading them.

Internally, JNDI uses vendor-specific driver classes (called *naming context classes*) to carry out the communication with the name server. These naming contexts are responsible for converting data between the format understood by the name service and the appropriate Java object. In some cases, the JNDI service provider will simply serialize Java objects into strings in the name server and de-serialize them when they are looked up. In other cases, more complex strategies will be necessary. In all cases, the JNDI architecture hides the details from the client. This architecture is shown in outline in Figure 7.1. Naming context classes communicate with the JNDI via the *service provider interface* (SPI).

A key feature of the *JNDI Specification* is its ability to represent *references*. If it is inappropriate or impossible to store a particular object internally, a reference provides a way for the client to get access to the object. The underlying name service stores sufficient information in the reference for the JNDI system to find that particular object and return it to the client. This is the mechanism by which EJB home object references are usually delivered to clients. On the whole, JNDI clients that are looking up objects are not all that concerned about the mechanics of references, since the service provider is responsible for turning the references into real objects.

7.3   JNDI terms and concepts

There is a whole jargon associated with JNDI. Some of the key terms are described in this section.

Name: Anything that identifies an object uniquely on a given server. Names are vendor-specific: Most product vendors use the '/' as a separator between

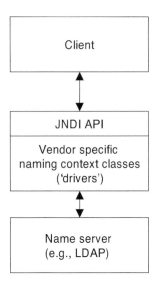

Figure 7.1. Basic architecture of JNDI.

atomic names, where each atomic name indicates a context (part of the hierarchy). In the rest of this chapter, I will assume that the JNDI implementation uses '/' as a separator. JNDI implementation vendors supply classes that convert their particular name format to JNDI's internal representation (described below).

Atomic name: The smallest single units into which a name can be divided. For example, in the name 'jdbc/orders,' 'jdbc' and 'orders' are atomic names.

Compound name: A sequence of atomic names, forming a complete name in a single namespace. For example, 'jdbc/orders' and 'java:comp/env/jdbc/orders' are both compound names.

Composite name: A sequence of compound names, forming a complete name that spans namespaces. Composite names are only indirectly relevant to EJB developers, as they are intended to support distributed namespaces.

Name parser: A piece of software that can convert a name in string format into the representation used by JNDI. Internally, JNDI uses objects of class `javax.naming.Name` to represent names. This internal format is independent of the way in which different vendors specify names. The JNDI implementation vendor must supply a class that can convert from the vendor-specific to the vendor-neutral representation. Normally, this class will make use of the standard `CompoundName` class, which is part of JNDI, as this class can convert many common name formats.

Namespace: The set of all names recognized by a particular name server.

Binding: The association between a name and its object. The types of objects that can be bound depends on the implementation.

Bind: To make a binding—that is, to link an object to a name in a name server.

Rebind: To change a binding—that is, to change the object associated with a name. As an example, overwriting a file on disk with different contents is a type of rebind. This is subtly different from rename.

Rename: To change the name bound to an object. This is in contrast to a rebind, which means changing the object while keeping the name the same. Changing the name of a disk file is a type of rename in this sense.

Context: A set of bindings at the same hierarchical level. Some of the bindings may be to other contexts. For example, in a filesystem, the directories form contexts. Each directory entry may be a file or another directory. Each context is represented by an atomic name. For example, in the name 'jdbc/orders,' 'jdbc' is probably the name of a context, while 'orders' is probably the name of a binding to an object. Contexts are an important part of JNDI, and are discussed in more detail later.

Initial context: The starting point for name lookups. In JNDI, all names are relative to the initial context; there is no concept of an 'absolute' name (as there is in filesystems). The initial context is, of course, logically just another context.

7.4   Using JNDI

In this section we discuss the various services that JNDI provides to its clients.

7.4.1   Basic JNDI lookups

In an EJB client (and, indeed, any JNDI client) the starting point for name resolution is to instantiate an `InitialContext`. This object does not necessarily do any work itself; normally, it delegates to the vendor-specific naming context class via the service-provider interface. This vendor-specific class acts as a driver for the underlying directory server, and will implement the functionality required to communicate with it over a network, if necessary. In many cases, the vendor's class will supply objects directly—without a network operation—but this is transparent to the developer.

Having created an `InitialContext`, we can use its `lookup()` method to find things. For example, an EJB gets access to a database by looking up a `DataSource` object and calling its `getConnection()` method (the full procedure is described on page 217). If the JNDI name of the database is 'orders', this piece of code should do the trick:[2]

---

[2]In a way, this is a bad example. We discourage the use of absolute JNDI names in J2EE components, for reasons that will become clear later.

```
     import javax.naming.*;
     import javax.sql.*;
     try
       {
5      Context c = new InitialContext();
       DataSource ds =
         (DataSource) c.lookup ("orders");
       Connection c = ds.getConnection ();
       }
10   catch (NamingException)
       {
       // handle naming exceptions
       }
     catch (SQLException)
15     {
       // handle connection exceptions
       }
```

> ## Gotcha!
>
> It is a common mistake when starting EJB development to confuse
> 'naming contexts' with 'EJB contexts.' An EJB context is supplied
> by the EJB container to an EJB to allow it to determine security
> and transaction attributes, while a naming context is used to look
> up names on a name server. Apart from having context in the
> name, these entities have *nothing* in common. To make matters
> worse, servlets have a context object as well. Do not assume that
> because J2EE Java constructs have the word 'context' in their
> names that they are similar in any other way.

The `InitialContext` constructor and the `lookup()` method can throw a number of exceptions, all of which are subclasses of `javax.naming.NamingException`.

Note that the example above provided no information about the location or type of the name sever itself. In such cases, JNDI will use defaults. The JNDI vendor is responsible for making sure these defaults are correct when lookups are between different parts of the same application (e.g., from a servlet to an EJB in an application server). When the JNDI client is a standalone program, the client will be expected to tell JNDI where and what the name server is, although this does not have to be done in the code itself. This issue will be examined in more detail later. For the moment, we will assume that the `InitialContext` defaults are adequate.

7.4.2   JNDI contexts

As we have seen, JNDI supports hierarchical name servers. The term used in JNDI for a particular part of the hierarchy is a *context*. An example of a context in a more familiar setting is a directory in a filesystem: Directories can contain a number of files, and also other directories. In other applications, a context might be a group of users in an LDAP directory or a collection of EJBs on an EJB server. In any case, when finding an object that is located below the top-level (initial) context, JNDI (usually) expects the names of the subcontexts to be separated by '/' characters, just as directories are in a URL. For example, if our orders database is in a context called 'jdbc,' we would look it up like this:[3]

```
Context c = InitialContext();
DataSource ds =
   (DataSource) c.lookup ("jdbc/orders");
```

If we specify the name of a context, rather than a data item, the object we get back from JNDI is a `javax.naming.Context`, not a piece of data. This context can in turn be used to carry out another name lookup. So the example above could equally have been written

```
Context c = InitialContext();
Context c2 =
   (Context) c.lookup ("jdbc");
DataSource ds =
   (DataSource) c2.lookup ("orders");
```

We first get a reference to the 'jdbc' context, then we use that context to look for the 'orders' object.

There will be occasions when this second form is more convenient and readable than the first, particularly if the code makes many lookups in the same context.

7.4.3   JNDI enumerations

As well as looking up the object bound to a particular name, the JNDI architecture provides techniques for enumerating (listing) the contents of a particular context. The `InitialContext` class, and all naming context classes derived from it, have the methods `list()` and `listBindings()`. Both these methods return a vendor-specific class that implements the interface `javax.naming.NamingEnumeration` (a subinterface of `Enumeration`) and can be used to iterate through the bindings in the selected part of the namespace.

For example, here is a way to list the contents of the context 'jdbc':

```
Context c = new InitialContext();
Enumeration ne = c.listBindings("jdbc");
while (ne.hasMoreElements())
   {
   Binding b = (Binding) ne.nextElement();
   System.out.println (b);
   }
```

---

[3]Note that, unlike a directory or URL, we don't specify a leading '/' to indicate the top level of the hierarchy. JNDI lookups are always relative to the current context, and never start with '/'.

The difference between `list()` and `listBindings()` is that the former provides more information: It returns an enumeration of `javax.naming.Binding` objects that contain the actual objects bound. `listBindings()` returns an enumeration of `javax.naming.NameClassPair` objects, which provides information only about the class of the object, not the object itself. In many cases, `listBindings()` will be much quicker than `list()`, but of course does not provide the objects themselves.

In EJB development, the list methods are used far less frequently than the lookup methods, but are useful for EJB development and deployment tools that need to get lists of EJBs on a particular server.

7.4.4 Binding

Binding is the process of adding a name-object mapping to the namespace. Once bound, the object can be retrieved by supplying its name to a `lookup()` call. Normally a JNDI client will not bind an object for its own use, but for use by other clients. For example, an EJB server will bind the names of its EJBs so that EJBs can be found by their clients.

Binding is straightforward: The following code fragment shows an object of class `MyDataSource` being bound into the namespace with the name 'orders' in the 'jdbc' context. The 'jdbc' context is assumed to exist.

```
Context c = new InitialContext();
Context jdbc = c.lookup ("jdbc");
jdbc.bind ("orders", new MyDataSource());
```

If the object cannot be stored directly in the name server, it is possible to store a reference to it, as discussed below.

7.4.5 References

A key notion in JNDI is that of a 'reference.' Many name servers are not able to store sufficient information to represent a complete Java object. In addition, the object may change between the time it was bound and the time it is looked up, and we may want to retrieve the later version. Both these problems are solved using references.

To insert a reference, we bind a name to an object of class `javax.lang.Reference`. The reference contains enough information for JNDI to be able to locate and retrieve the object. When initializing the reference, we supply information about the location of the object (one or more URLs, for example) and, crucially, the name of a *class factory* for that object. A class factory is a vendor-specific class that is able to use the information provided in the address to retrieve and construct the object, and return it to the client. It is the decision of the vendor whether to supply a range of different class factories for the objects it supports or use the same class factory for different classes.

When enumerating a JNDI namespace, the enumeration will render references as objects of class `Reference`—that is, it will not attempt to resolve references. However, the `lookup()` methods are expected to be able to resolve references into real objects. Behind the scenes, JNDI finds the class factory from the reference and calls its `getObjectInstance()` method, passing the reference information. The method by which the class factory produces the required object is vendor-specific.

7.5   Examining a typical EJB server namespace

To examine a JNDI namespace, we need a piece of software that can act as a general-purpose JNDI client, displaying all the information in the namespace. A simple utility class for recursively enumerating a JNDI namespace is shown in Listing 7.1. A command-line interface for this class is shown in Listing 7.2.

> Hint
>
> The full source code for this example is in the source code package, in directory `jndidump`.

> Gotcha!
>
> If you run this code against the *J2EE Reference Implementation*, and you have registered JNDI names for the XA-compliant `cloudscape` database driver, you will get a `ClassNotFoundException` unless you ensure that `cloudscape.jar` is on the class search path.

This class uses the `listBindings()` method described above to enumerate each context in the namespace.

Listing 7.1: `JNDIDumper` **class: a utility to enumerate a JNDI namespace.**

```
    package com.kevinboone.ejb_book.jndidump;

    import javax.naming.*;
    import javax.sql.DataSource;
 5  import javax.transaction.UserTransaction;
    import java.util.Hashtable;
    import java.io.PrintStream;
    import java.util.Enumeration;

10  /**
    JNDIDumper is a simple utility that recurses through a
```

```
     JNDI  namespace,  and  dumps  the  details  to  a  print
     stream.  To  use,  simply  construct  an  instance  using
     the  appropriate  constructor,  and  call  the  instance's
15   'dump()'  method.

     (c)2001  Kevin  Boone
     */
     public class JNDIDumper
20   {
     Context  c = null;
     String  contextName = "";

     /**
25   Initializes  the  dumper  with  default  naming  environment
     */
     public JNDIDumper() throws NamingException
        {
        c = new InitialContext();
30      }

     /**
     Initializes  the  dumper  with  default  naming  service  and
     specified  context
35   */
     public JNDIDumper(final String namingContext)
          throws NamingException
        {
        c = (Context)(new InitialContext()).lookup
40        (namingContext);
        }

     /**
     Initializes  the  dumper  with  specific  naming  factory
45   and URL
     */
     public JNDIDumper(final String factory,
          final String url)
        throws NamingException
50      {
        Hashtable env = new Hashtable();
        env.put ("java.naming.factory.initial", factory);
        env.put ("java.naming.provider.url", url);
        c = new InitialContext(env);
55      }

     /**
     Initializes  the  dumper  with  specific  naming  factory
     and URL,  and  specific  context  name
60   */
     public JNDIDumper(final String contextName,
          final String factory,
          final String url)
        throws NamingException
65      {
```

```
         Hashtable env = new Hashtable ();
         env.put ("java.naming.factory.initial", factory);
         env.put ("java.naming.provider.url", url);
         c = (Context)(new InitialContext(env)).lookup
70         (contextName);
         }


     /**
     Begin the dump process, starting at the top of the
75   specified namespace
     */
     public void dump(PrintStream out)
         throws NamingException
         {
80       dump (out, c, 0);
         }


     /**
     Dump the specified context whose depth in the tree
85   is 'level'. This parameter is used only to
     format the output.
     */
     public void dump(PrintStream out, final Context c,
             final int level)
90        throws NamingException
         {
         Enumeration ne = c.listBindings ("");
         if (ne == null)
             {
95           System.err.println ("empty");
             return;
             }
         while (ne.hasMoreElements ())
             {
100          Binding b = (Binding) ne.nextElement ();

             tab (out, level);
             out.print ("'" + b.getName() + "'");
             Object o = b.getObject ();
105          if (o instanceof javax.naming.Context)
                 {
                 out.println (", subcontext");
                 dump (out, (Context)o, level + 1);
                 }
110          else
                 {
                 String s = o.getClass ().toString ();
                 int p = s.lastIndexOf (".");
                 String shortClassName;
115              if (p < 0)
                     shortClassName = s;
                 else
                     shortClassName = s.substring (p + 1);
                 out.println (", " + shortClassName);
```

```
120            }
        }
    }

    /**
125  Output a specified number of spaces; used in
     formatting output
     */
     protected void tab(PrintStream out, final int level)
       {
130      for (int i = 0; i < level; i++)
           out.print("  ");
       }
}
```

Listing 7.2: **Command-line test driver for the** JNDIDumper **class.**

```
     package com.kevinboone.ejb_book.jndidump;

     /**
     Test driver for the JNDIDumper class.
5    Usage:
       java ejbook.jndidump.Main
         context_name class url
       All arguments are optional.
       With no arguments, dumps the top-level context
10       in the default naming service
       With one argument, dumps the specified context
         in the default naming service
       With two arguments, dumps the top-level context
         in the specified naming service
15     With three arguments, dumps the specified context
         in the specified naming service
     */
     public class Main
     {
20   public static void main (String[] args)
       {
       try
         {
         JNDIDumper jndiDumper = null;
25       if (args.length == 0)
             jndiDumper = new JNDIDumper();
         else if (args.length == 1)
             jndiDumper = new JNDIDumper(args[0]);
         else if (args.length == 2)
30           jndiDumper = new JNDIDumper(args[0],
                 args[1]);
         else if (args.length == 3)
             jndiDumper = new JNDIDumper(args[0],
                 args[1], args[2]);
```

```
35        else
          {
            System.err.println ("Argument syntax error");
            System.exit(-1);
          }
40        jndiDumper.dump(System.out);
        }
      catch (javax.naming.NamingException e)
        {
          System.err.println ("Caught exception: " + e);
45      }
      }
    }
```

The command-line interface allows the JNDI dumper to be instantiated in a number of different ways. For example, the command

```
java JNDIDumper jdbc
```

dumps the namespace starting at the context 'jdbc.' Without arguments, the program dumps the namespace from the 'top' (that is, the default initial context). The result of running it against the *J2EE Reference Implementation*, with the *Prestige Bike Hire* application deployed, is shown in Listing 7.3.

Listing 7.3: **Output from** `JNDIDump` **from top-level naming context when executed from the command line; the EJBs installed are from the *Prestige Bike Hire* application.**

```
    'BookingManager', Reference
    'BikeModel', Reference
    'ServerObject', Reference
    'jms', subcontext
5     'financialresponsequeue', QueueImpl
      'TopicConnectionFactory', ConnectionFactoryWrapperStandalone
      'QueueConnectionFactory', ConnectionFactoryWrapperStandalone
      'financialtransactionqueue', QueueImpl
      'Topic', TopicImpl
10    'Queue', QueueImpl
    'TopicConnectionFactory', ConnectionFactoryWrapperStandalone
    'ContainerXAQueueConnectionFactory', JMSXAQueueConnectionFactoryImpl
    'Booking', Reference
    'Customer', Reference
15  'RemoteLogReader', Reference
    'WebInstaller', Reference
    'QueueConnectionFactory', ConnectionFactoryWrapperStandalone
    'JMSXATopicConnectionFactory', JMSXATopicConnectionFactoryImpl
    'JarInstaller', Reference
20  'J2EE_UNIQUE_VALUE_GEN', Reference
    'JMSXAjms', subcontext
      'QueueConnectionFactory', JMSXAQueueConnectionFactoryImpl
      'TopicConnectionFactory', JMSXATopicConnectionFactoryImpl
    'DatabaseInformation', Reference
25  'ServerConfiguration', Reference
    'LegacyMessager', Reference
    'UserTransaction', UserTransactionImpl
```

```
       'jdbc', subcontext
         'XACloudscape_xa', RemoteXaDataSource
30       'EstoreDB', JdbcDataSource
         'InventoryDB', JdbcDataSource
         'XACloudscape', JdbcDataSource
         'DB2_pm', SystemJdbcDataSource
         'DB1_pm', SystemJdbcDataSource
35       'EstoreDB__pm', SystemJdbcDataSource
         'InventoryDB__pm', SystemJdbcDataSource
         'DB2', JdbcDataSource
         'DB1', JdbcDataSource
         'XACloudscape__pm', SystemJdbcDataSource
40       'Cloudscape__pm', SystemJdbcDataSource
         'Cloudscape', JdbcDataSource
       'JMSXAQueueConnectionFactory', JMSXAQueueConnectionFactoryImpl
       'CustomerManager', Reference
       'Realm_Manager', Reference
45     'FleetManager', Reference
       'ContainerXATopicConnectionFactory', JMSXATopicConnectionFactoryImpl
       'ChargeBand', Reference
```

There are a few things to note about this output.

- The *Prestige Bike Hire* application EJB names `Booking`, `FleetManager`, and others are accessible at the top level of the namespace, and their type is `javax.naming.Reference`. These entries correspond to entities that are not strictly 'within' the naming service itself. When a client calls `lookup` to find these objects, the JNDI service provider is responsible for resolving the references and retrieving the objects to which they refer. In the case of EJBs, the JNDI implementation will either produce a stub or a portable object reference (see page 39).

- Some entries are stored in the name service as objects. For example 'jdbc/-Cloudscape' is of class `JdbcDataSource`. This is a vendor-specific implementation of the `javax.sql.DataSource` interface, as will be discussed in Chapter 8. A lookup of this object will be satisfied from within the JVM of the client, perhaps by being deserialized from some persistent store or, more likely, read directly from the JNDI service provider's memory cache.

- There are a number of other bindings of type `Reference` whose purpose is undocumented. These are, presumably, related to the internal operation of the server.

7.6   JNDI and EJB

JNDI is important in EJB technology, because an EJB will use JNDI to look up all its configuration information, get access to resources like databases, and locate other EJBs. EJB clients that are not themselves EJBs also use JNDI to get access to EJBs. EJBs increasingly use JNDI to obtain application data as well.

Why did the EJB designers stipulate the use of JNDI for these purposes? It is possible to envisage other, perhaps more elegant, methods, after all. Essentially,

JNDI already exists, and can do all the things that an EJB name lookup service needs; it seemed unnecessary to implement another naming API just for EJB servers.

The vendor of an EJB product can use whatever naming server it likes to store information that the EJBs will need to look up—including its own memory—but it must be made available by means of JNDI. A popular choice in modern products is to integrate the EJB server with an LDAP directory server. As many applications call for LDAP to be used to authenticate users, it makes some sense to use the LDAP server to store EJB information as well. Whether the EJB server uses LDAP or something else, it must be capable of supporting JNDI lookups. As EJBs will use JNDI frequently, the vendor has the responsibility to ensure that name lookups are fast. Whatever underlying name service is used, it is likely that most or all EJB-specific information present can be cached in Java objects (rather than needing to be fetched from the directory on each occasion). In practice, the EJB server's JNDI service will satisfy frequent lookups directly out of its memory. As always, whether the JNDI interface is doing this or making real name server lookups over a network is not relevant to the client.

7.6.1   What an EJB can look up in the namespace, and what it can't

We have already seen some of the entities that an EJB can retrieve from the naming service by a JNDI lookup. This section summarizes some of the other objects that the container may make available. The EJB container is at liberty to make available any kind of object by a JNDI lookup. In practice, however, containers usually limit themselves to providing things that are required by the *EJB Specification*, particularly the following.

EJB remote home references

We have already seen that EJB servers provide access to the home objects of EJBs by JNDI. When a client attempts to retrieve such an object using a `lookup()` call, the naming provider must resolve the reference and return to the client something that makes that remote reference accessible for method calls. As we have already seen, in the case of EJBs that 'something' is usually a stub that can communicate with the home object. This mechanism for looking up EJBs must be used by all objects that will use the EJB, even other EJBs in the same container. This allows the container to propagate transaction and security contexts between EJBs. An exception in EJB 2.0 is that when container-managed relationships exist between EJBs, the related EJBs can obtain references to one another using abstract `get` methods, without a separate lookup (see Chapter 13).

EJB local home references

In EJB 2.0, a client located in the same JVM as an EJB is able to get a local reference to the EJB's home object. The client uses exactly the same JNDI procedure as described for remote references; however, the client's deployment descriptor must indicate that it requires a local reference. Typically the client will do a lookup in the `java:comp/env` namespace, which is discussed below.

Resources

EJBs are encouraged to get certain resources from their container, rather than in a more direct way. These resources include data sources (usually relational databases), email services, asynchronous message services, and network connections identified by URLs. The reason for this stipulation is simply to increase efficiency. The container can pool these resources and share them among different EJBs, allowing a larger number of clients for the same load. An object that acts as a supplier or creator of resources is commonly called a *resource factory*. The following sections describe the resource factories that are commonly made available.

Data sources

To get access to data sources (typically relational databases), the EJB uses JNDI to retrieve an object that implements the `javax.sql.DataSource` interface. From this object, the EJB can get a database connection by calling its `getConnection()` method. From then, access to the database is largely as for standard JDBC. A more detailed discussion is provided in Chapter 8.

JCA connectors

The Java Connector API allows developers to create connectors to arbitrary external resources, while integrating with the EJB container's security and transaction infrastructures. The starting point for the EJB developer is to use JNDI to obtain a reference to the connector's connection factory. This topic is described in detail in Chapter 18.

Email services

To get access to an email service, the EJB uses JNDI to get an object of class `javax.mail.Session`. From this, we can use the `getTransport()` method to get a connection for a specific address, and with the `Transport` object, we can send a `Message`. Note that this procedure is independent of the email protocol, but most EJB servers only support SMTP. This topic is described in detail on page 584.

Asynchronous message services

To get access to an asynchronous messaging service, the EJB uses JNDI to get access to an instance of something that implements the `javax.jms.QueueConnection Factory` or `javax.jms.TopicConnectionFactory` interface, depending on whether the resource is a queue service or a publish-subscribe service. From the connection factory, the EJB gets an object that represents a connection to the messaging server, and can then post objects of any class to the server or listen for objects posted by other JMS clients.

The EJB will also use JNDI to get access to a specific queue or topic, as will be discussed below.

In EJB 2.0, JMS is used to communicate with message-driven EJBs [EJB2.0 4.2.1]. Clients of such EJBs do not look up the home interface (as they don't have one), but look up the message queue to which the EJB is attached.

Network connections by URL

If a connection to a network server can be identified by a URL (e.g., HTTP or FTP protocols), then the container can provide an object of class `java.net.URL` by which data can be read or written using that protocol.

For example, the following listing shows how to look up a URL called 'UrlName':

```
Context context = new InitialContext();
java.net.URL url =
    (java.net.URL)context.lookup("UrlName");
```

Note that in the deployment descriptor we must provide a mapping from the name 'UrlName' to the real URL (e.g., 'http:...' or 'ftp:...'). The source code above does not depend at all on the type of URL being retrieved.

From the `URL` object we can get an `URLConnection`, and from that an input stream. See page 583 for more details on the use of this technique. Not all containers support this type of resource.

Environment variables

The standard method for supplying site-specific configuration information to EJBs is by means of EJB environment variables. These are not the same as operating system environment variables, but have a similar purpose. When an EJB is created, the developer will insert into the deployment descriptor the names, types, and values of the environment variables. At deployment time, the EJB server will make these variables available to the EJB by a JNDI lookup. Whether the EJB server stores them in an underlying name server, or in its own memory, or somewhere else, is vendor-specific.

Because environment variables are EJB-specific, the EJB looks them up in its local namespace, as described below.

Transaction service

The EJB server's JNDI implementation must provide an object that implements `javax.transaction.UserTransaction` and allows EJB clients to get access to the server's transaction manager. Reasons for doing this are discussed in Chapter 9. Note that this won't normally work with standalone clients, only with servlets and JSPs.

Things that usually can't be looked up in JNDI

Not all resources that we might wish to provide to EJBs can be looked up by JNDI: In some cases, this is because access is forbidden (e.g., files), while in others, it is simply because the container vendor has not implemented it. In the latter case, you will normally be able to get the resource directly. Examples of things that are explicitly forbidden include the following.

- EJB objects and bean implementation classes. Clients are not allowed to call methods on these objects directly, so the container will not provide any mechanisms for getting at them.

- Files, and file URLs. EJBs are not normally allowed to read or write files. See page 584 for a more detailed discussion of this issue. Don't assume that just because you can form your file reference into a URL (e.g., `file:/xxx`) and assign a JNDI name to it, the container will let you use it.

- Stubs. The client should not look up a stub directly. It should look up a home interface and expect JNDI to provide a suitable stub.

The most frequently required of the resources that are not actually forbidden, but not provided by the container, is a network socket connection. In this case, the EJB can normally open a client network socket directly—e.g.,

```
Socket s = new ("hostname", port);
```

However, EJBs are forbidden from opening server sockets (that is, sockets that listen for incoming connections). When using this technique, be aware that network sockets are not normally serializable, and keeping them open in stateless session beans risks a passivation failure.

7.6.2 EJB name resolution and the EJB's local namespace

This subject, and the use of the `java:comp/env` namespace, causes a lot of confusion for many EJB developers; even EJB server vendors don't always handle it correctly. So we will deal with it in some detail.

While EJBs can make lookups in the general JNDI namespace, it is recommended that they don't do this, but make lookups to references in their local namespace. We will examine the mechanism by which one EJB finds the home object for another as an example of why this is necessary.

Suppose I have two EJBs in the same application, called **First** and **Second**. How can **First** get a reference to the home object of **Second** so that it can call methods on it? Well, it could do this, exactly as a standalone client would:

```
Context c = new InitialContext();
Object o = c.lookup ("Second");
// Now convert to home interface type
```

But there is a problem with this approach. The EJB architecture is designed to allow EJBs from different sources to be assembled into a complete application. It is fundamental that each EJB is a 'black box' to all the others: In a collaborative development exercise, we must agree on the home and remote interfaces for each

EJB, but everything else is invisble to everyone except the developer of a particular EJB.

Now, suppose I write an EJB that processes orders, and within that EJB I need to check the validity of a credit card number. I know that someone else is working on a credit card verifier EJB, and I have the home and remote interface for it.

During development, I write a dummy EJB to implement the real home and remote interfaces of the credit card verifier, so that I can test my own code. How does my EJB look up this dummy EJB using JDNI? I could do it like this:

```
Context c = new InitialContext();
Object o = c.lookup ("CreditCardChecker");
// Convert to home interface type...
```

So my ordering EJB could look up the JNDI name 'CreditCardChecker' and get the appropriate home object. Now, my dummy EJB may be called 'CreditCard-Checker' but what reason do I have for thinking that the real credit card checker will be called CreditCardChecker? The fact is that *JNDI names do not exist until deployment time.* In a large collaborative development, it will be almost impossible to agree on all the JNDI names of everything in advance and stick with them right up until completion of the project.

The solution to this problem is—in principle—very simple: Provide some sort of name mapping scheme, where all the names used in the JNDI lookups can be remapped at deployment time. Then, at deployment time we can resolve all the names used in code to their true JNDI names. This mapping has to be per-component, because one EJB may use the name 'Customer,' for example, to reference a database table of customers, while another uses it to reference an EJB called Customer.

Going back to the original example, let's add an EJB reference from EJB First to EJB Second. However, we will not use the name Second, but the 'local' name 'SecondRef.' 'SecondRef' is not a JNDI name; it is an arbitrary name that will be used only by First. We can specify this by adding the appropriate reference to the deployment descriptor, but EJB products typically allow this to be done using software tools. Figure 7.2 shows how this is done using the Reference Implementation's deployment tool.

So we have established a 'virtual name' for the EJB Second within the context of the EJB First. This virtual name is not accessible anywhere else. So, how does First get a reference to Second using this new name? Like this:

```
Context c = new InitialContext();
Object o = c.lookup ("java:comp/env/ejb/SecondRef");
// Convert to {\ tt Second} home interface type
```

So when we specify a name that begins with java:comp/env, the JNDI implementation is being told to make a lookup in the part of the name/directory that is dedicated to that particular EJB. The implementation takes the remainder of the name and uses it for a lookup in the EJB's local namespace. The part of the name after 'java:comp/env' is called the *coded name* in J2EE jargon. In our current

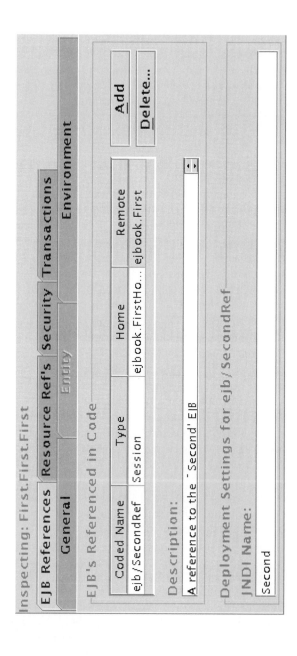

Figure 7.2. Using the Reference Implementation's deployment tool to add an EJB reference from the EJB First to a local name 'SecondRef,' which in turn maps onto the 'real' JNDI name Second.

example, the coded name is ejb/SecondRef, and the JNDI name is `Second`. You should be able to see how these two names are linked using the deployment tool in Figure 7.2. The reason why the local name has the form it does (that is, beginning with `java:`) is discussed below (page 203).

This technique should be used for *all* JNDI lookups from EJBs (and servlets). This allows all names to be remapped at deployment time if necessary.

EJB references are not the only things that can be placed in the EJB-specific namespace. It is common practice to place data source references here as well, for exactly the same reason. Data source references are a specific example of what the *EJB Specification* calls 'resource references,' meaning resources that are made available to EJBs under different names than their JNDI names. Why would we need to use a resource reference? Here is an example.

Suppose that, lacking further information, I write the following piece of code in an EJB to obtain a reference to a database:

```
Context c = new InitialContext();
DataSource ds = c.lookup("jdbc/Bank");
```

This may work on my development system, because I have configured the EJB container to recognize the name 'jdbc/Bank' and relate it to the appropriate database. However, the EJB container used in the *production* environment knows the data source as `BankDB` (for example).

If I had written the code like this:

```
Context c = new InitialContext();
DataSource ds = c.lookup("java:comp/env/jdbc/Bank");
```

the container would look up 'jdbc/Bank' in the EJB's local namespace. Now using a resource reference, we can say that *in this EJB*, the data source known to the container as `BankDB` is referred to locally as `jdbc/Bank`. In this example 'jdbc/Bank' is the 'coded name.' In other words, using resource references allows us to resolve incorrect or unknown resource names at deployment time, without modifying the code.

Of course, there are other ways in which this could have been achieved. The powerful thing about the method used by the EJB architecture is that resolution of references (to EJBs, data sources, or whatever) is done in a uniform way.

Gotcha!

There is no '/' between `java:` and `comp`. If you put one in, it won't work. This is a very common mistake, because people are used to dealing with URLs, and expect the protocol name to be followed by '/something' and not 'something.'

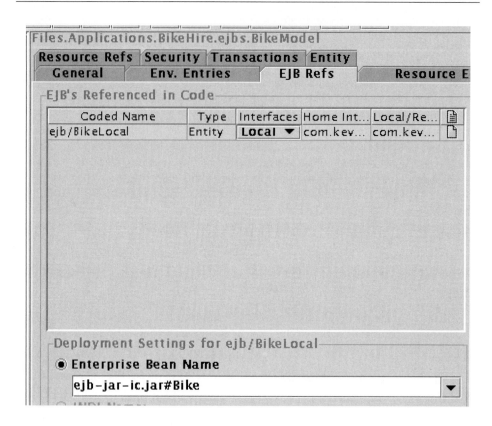

Figure 7.3. Using the Reference Implementation's deployment tool to add a *local* EJB reference from the EJB BikeModel to the EJB Bike, such that the Java code in BikeModel will use the name ejb/BikeLocal to reference it.

A final point to note about looking up EJBs in the local namespace: In EJB 2.0, a client can obtain a reference either to the local view or the distributed view of the EJB. The distinction is made in the deployment descriptor. When we map the coded name of the EJB onto the JNDI name, we also specify whether we want a local reference or a remote reference. Remember that if we get a local reference, we don't need to use the **narrow()** method on it before use.

Taking an example from the *Prestige Bike Hire* application, Figure 7.3 shows the Reference Implementation deployment tool being used to stipulate that the EJB BikeModel has a *local* reference to the EJB Bike.

In this implementation of BikeModel, a reference is obtained to the Bike EJB like this (this code is taken from BikeModelBean.java):

```
public void setEntityContext ( EntityContext ec )
    {
    super.setEntityContext(ec);
    try
```

```
 5        {
          Context  c = new  InitialContext();
          bikeLocalHome  =  (BikeLocalHome)  c.lookup
            ("java:comp/env/ejb/BikeLocal");
          }
10      catch  (NamingException  e)
          {
          debugOut  ("Failed  to  initialize  BikeModel  EJB: "  + e);
          throw new  EJBException  (e);
          }
15      debugOut  ("Leaving  setEntityContext()");
        }
```

Note the correspondence between the deployment tool entries and the source code.

7.6.3   EJB environment variables

The java:comp/env namespace is used not only for looking up objects, but also configuration variables that are EJB-specific. The values of these variables are specified in the deployment descriptor, and can be edited by graphical deployment tools. For example, in GenericStatelessSessionBean.java, we have:

```
       public  void  setSessionContext(SessionContext  _ctx)
         {
         ctx = _ctx;
         try
 5         {
           Context  c = new  InitialContext();
           Boolean  temp =
             (Boolean)  c.lookup  ("java:comp/env/debug");
           if  (temp != null)
10           debug = temp.booleanValue();
           }
         catch  (NamingException  e){}
         debugOut  ("Leaving  setSessionContext()");
         }
```

In this piece of code, we are initializing the value of a boolean instance variable, debug, that indicates whether this EJB should emit debugging information or not. The deployer can change this property at deployment time by changing the value assigned to the variable, as shown in Figure 7.4.

7.6.4   Resource references and the deployment descriptor

Although I promised in the introduction to this book to limit the discussion of the XML deployment descriptor, this is one case where a brief look at the deployment descriptor may be useful. There are some knotty issues with the use of resource references and portability, which can only be understood with reference to the mechanics of deployment.

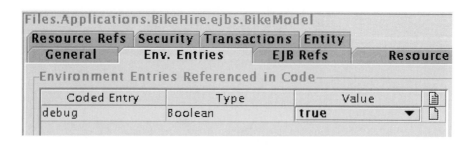

Figure 7.4. Using the Reference Implementation's deployment tool to create and set the value of an environment variable `debug` for the EJB `BikeModel`.

Consider the `LegacyMessager` EJB from the *Prestige Bike Hire* application (which is described in detail in Chapter 10). This EJB gets a reference to a JMS connection factory (a type of resource factory) like this:

```
Context c = new InitialContext();
Object o = c.lookup ("java:comp/env/jms/qcf");
QueueConnectionFactory qcf =
   (QueueConnectionFactory) o;
```

The name `jms/qcf` is mapped to the JNDI name of the connection factory, which is `QueueConnectionFactory` (see Figure 10.8). In other words, the coded name is `jms/qcf`, and the JNDI name is `QueueConnectionFactory`. So far, so good.

Now, if we look at the relevant section of the deployment descriptor for this EJB, we see the following:

```
<resource-ref>
  <res-ref-name>jms/qcf</res-ref-name>
  <res-type>javax.sql.DataSource</res-type>
  <res-auth>Container</res-auth>
  <res-sharing-scope>Shareable</res-sharing-scope>
</resource-ref>
```

The field `res-ref-name` is the coded name of the reference—that is, everything after `java:comp/env`. But where is the real JNDI name? *It is not in the deployment descriptor.* This reinforces the fact that it is not the developer's job to assign JNDI names to things: It is the deployer's job. Typically the real JNDI names are in a *vendor-specific configuration file* packaged into the deployable EAR or JAR file. This important distinction can readily be lost when working with graphical tools like the Reference Implementation's deployment tool. The tool will be manipulating both the J2EE-standard deployment descriptor (`ejb-jar.xml`) and the vendor-specific configuration.

Why is this important?

This is exactly as it should be: It is the deployer's job to assign JNDI names. After all, JNDI names are global; it would not do to have two EJBs in different

> ## Gotcha!
>
> The 'real' JNDI names of EJBs are not specified in a J2EE-compliant way, and are therefore not portable between products.

applications with the same JNDI name. It does make things difficult, however, if the developer wants to build an EAR file that can be deployed on different products. Typically, at deployment time an EJB product will examine the EAR or JAR file for product-specific name mapping information. If it can't find it, the product's deployment tool will present the deployer with a list of un-named EJBs and cross-references to them, and ask for the JNDI names to be filled in.

> ## Hint
>
> Portability note: Many EJB products use sensible defaults for the JNDI names of EJBs if the vendor's configuration file is missing from the EAR file. In almost all cases, the JNDI name is taken to be the same as the EJB internal name. In addition, many products supply default mapping information. For example, the coded name `java:comp/env/ejb/XXX` will be assumed to map onto the EJB with JNDI name `XXX`. Don't rely on this, however; some products will simply leave the missing information blank.

7.6.5   Resource environments

The concept of a 'resource environment' is new in EJB 2.0. It supports the notion that some objects that are the subject of a JNDI lookup are not independent in the way that, say, database connections are, but are subordinate to another resource.

Consider references to messaging services, for example. An EJB will use JNDI to get a reference to a connection factory for the messaging service. This is a reference to an entire service. Within that service, there will be various message queues and topics (for a discussion of these concepts, see Chapter 10). These queues and topics are not independent, but are meaningful only within the scope of the message service.

This issue is not problematic for clients: They do JNDI lookups in both cases. It is an issue, however, in the deployment descriptor. Authentication happens when a connection is established to a resource. For example, when the EJB makes a connection to the messaging service, it will have to be authenticated. The supplied authentication information will then be used to authorize requests for specific resources within that service. This means that authentication data needs to be supplied in respect of a messaging service, but not of a message queue.

In the *EJB Specification*, a reference to a messaging service or a database connection is called a 'resource reference,' while one to a message queue or topic is called a 'resource environment reference.' The defining difference is that resource environment references denote resources that do not require a specific network connection to the resource, and therefore don't need authentication information.

All this means that resource environment references need a different set of properties in the deployment descriptor to resource references, even though both are bound to JNDI names. In practice, we use graphical tools to build the deployment descriptor, so the technicalities are not particularly important, but you may find information about resource environment references and resource references accessible in different places in your assembly tool. This is the case with the *J2EE Reference Implementation*.

7.7   JNDI in more detail

As we have seen, carrying out a JNDI lookup is not difficult. However, in order to understand why JNDI configuration works the way it does, it is helpful to understand in more detail how JNDI works internally. If you only need to know the *how* of JNDI configuration, rather than the *why*, you could usefully skip directly to Section 7.8.

7.7.1   Principle of operation

Figure 7.5 shows the interaction between the various classes that are involved in a typical JNDI lookup. Of course, many more supporting classes may be involved in a practical implementation. The numbers in this section refer to the interaction numbers in the diagram.

When the JNDI client does a JNDI lookup, it first instantiates `InitialContext` (1). The `InitialContext` class will instantiate a vendor-specific *naming context factory*, based on its current configuration information (2). This is a class that is able to instantiate (3) a class that can do lookups within a particular part of the namespace, on a particular kind of server. The naming context factory also receives the URL of the name server, if the client supplies one. It may use this URL to determine the kind of naming context class to instantiate. When the client performs the lookup on the initial context (4), the initial context passes the name to an appropriate naming context instance (5), and it is this that performs the interaction with the server (6).

The naming context class is responsible not only for communicating with the name server using the appropriate protocol, but for converting the data retrieved into appropriate Java objects. For example, suppose the the JNDI name 'jdbc/orders' corresponds to a data source, represented as an instance of `javax.sql.DataSource`. The JNDI client will be expecting to get a `javax.sql.DataSource` instance, which it can use to get a database connection. It does not care whether this instance was stored internally in the name server (perhaps as a serialized object) or is synthe-

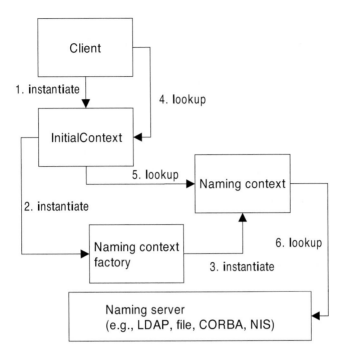

Figure 7.5. Sequence of operations in a simple JNDI lookup. See text for details.

sized by the naming context using configuration data in the name server. A typical approach is to store in the underlying name server the database driver name, URL, user ID, and password. When the client looks up this data source, the naming context class instantiates a `DataSource` based on these parameters. The client does not care how the object is generated, provided that it works.

7.7.2   JNDI names as URLs

By default, a single naming context factory is used to serve all naming requests made on a particular `InitialContext`. Thus, all requests will go to a particular server, using a particular protocol. However, the *JNDI Specification* allows for the name supplied to influence the naming service that is chosen. Specifically, if the name begins with an identifier followed by a colon (e.g., 'java:'), the identifier is used to select a naming context factory to be used to serve that particular lookup. The JNDI documentation refers to names like this as being in 'URL format.' The initial part of the name (before the colon) is called the 'scheme ID.'

When a name in URL format is looked up, JNDI uses the scheme ID to instantiate a particular class. The name of this class is the scheme ID followed by 'URLContextFactory'. This class will be looked for in a number of standard packages (which can be configured by the client). So, for example, when the EJB looks up `java:comp/env/jdbc/orders`, the default naming context provider is overridden, and the class `javaURLContextFactory` used to instantiate a naming context for this lookup. We need to do this because the way in which 'java:comp/env' names are looked up is somewhat different than a lookup in the general namespace.

If the item looked up is a remote reference, then the naming context will attempt to resolve this reference and return to the client a stub that will allow remote access to the object referenced.[4]

Technically the JNDI architecture and Specification consist of two parts: the API and the SPI (service provider interface). Both are vendor-neutral. A JNDI client makes calls on classes in the API, such as `InitialContext`. The SPI mediates between the API classes and the vendor-specific classes. The SPI is largely invisible to JNDI clients.

7.8   JNDI configuration

All the code examples presented so far have assumed that the JNDI lookup was being done using the default configuration. This is appropriate when EJBs are looking up each other, or looking up resources, but won't allow a standalone client to get access to an EJB server. To see how this can be done, we need to know first the general technique for configuring the JNDI system on the client.

The set of configuration information that JNDI requires is called its *environment*. `InitialContext` looks for its environment in three places, in this order:

- in a `Hashtable` passed to its constructor;

- in any file on the CLASSPATH called `jndi.properties`; and

- (in some cases) in the system properties.

Wherever the environment is supplied, the information is in the form of name-value pairs.

With the *J2EE Reference Implementation*, for example, a default `jndi.properties` is located in the archive `j2ee.jar`. This file contains the following two entries:

```
java.naming.factory.initial=\
i   com.sun.enterprise.naming.SerialInitContextFactory
java.naming.factory.url.pkgs=\
    com.sun.enterprise.naming
```

Thus, unless the client specifies otherwise, the class `SerialInitContextFactory` will be used to instantiate naming context classes to do lookups, and the package prefix `com.sun.enterprise.naming` will be used to locate classes that handle JNDI names in 'URL' format.

Note that there is no entry in this file for the location (hostname or port) of the naming service. This is because the `SerialInitContextFactory` class assumes that the naming service is in the JVM as the client, so no URL is necessary.

---

[4]More accurately, it resolves it into something that can be *narrowed* into a stub. See page 39.

In practice, EJB clients will normally have to modify only two of the JNDI configuration settings: `java.naming.factory.initial` and `java.naming.provider.url`.

java.naming.factory.initial

This specifies the naming context factory that will be used when the client instantiates an `InitialContext`, except for name lookups in 'URL' format. This is a class that is specific to a particular naming service (often to a specific vendor), and knows how to do name lookups on that service. The vendor may provide multiple naming context factories. For example, the Reference Implementation provides the `SerialInitContextFactory`, as described above, and a class that can do lookups using the CORBA naming protocols, which is `com.sun.jndi.cosnaming.CNCtxFactory`.[5] It is this latter class that you would need to specify if your client is a standalone program calling an EJB on a different server. In this case, you would also need to specify the provider's URL, as described below.

java.naming.provider.url

This setting indicates the location, protocol, and port number of the naming service. This URL has a format that is specific to the vendor's naming class factory, but is likely to be of the form 'protocol://host:port.' For example, the Reference Implementation's naming service understands IIOP URLs, like this: `iiop://host:port`. To make a connection to a naming service on the local machine, but not necessarily in the same JVM, use `iiop://localhost:1050` (unless you've changed the default port).

7.9   JNDI lookups across servers

We now have the information we need to implement a client that can use JNDI to look up an EJB using a directory on a specified remote server. We simply need to specify an appropriate (vendor-specific) context factory and the URL that references the directory server. It is important to remember that if the name lookup is being done from within an EJB or a servlet, for example, the client should not have to worry about this. The server should initialize the naming system so that its defaults are correct. The issue should only ever arise when a standalone program is calling into an EJB server. In addition, the client is locating the directory, not the EJB. There is no J2EE-compliant way for the client to locate a specific EJB. In practice, the EJB may be served from the same host as the directory but, in a load sharing system, it may just as likely not be.

The following code fragment shows how we could look up an EJB called 'MyEJB' via a host called 'fred,' which implements a CORBA name server listening on port 1050.

---

[5] The Reference Implementation includes a CORBA-compatible name server, which already knows how to do name lookups for objects (that's its job), so the naming context class is simply a wrapper over a CORBA naming client.

```
     import javax.naming.*;
     import javax.sql.*;
     import javax.util.*;
     try
 5     {
       Hashtable env = new Hashtable();
       env.put ("java.naming.factory.initial",
         "com.sun.jndi.cosnaming.CNCtxFactory");
       env.put ("java.naming.provider.url",
10       "iiop://fred:1050");
       Context c = InitialContext();
       Object o =
         c.lookup ("MyEJB");
       // Now cast to home interface type...
15     }
     catch (NamingException)
       {
       // handle naming exception
       }
20   catch (ClassCastException)
       {
       // handle exception resulting from
       //   EJB being of wrong type, or stubs
       //   not available
25     }
```

If we didn't want to hard-code the URL, we could specify it as a system property when running the client—e.g.,

```
java -Djava.naming.provider.url=iiop:fred:1050 ...
```

7.10   Further reading

The JNDI concepts discussed in this chapter are described in detail in the *JNDI API Specification* and the *JNDI SPI Specification*, both available from `http://java.sun.com`. The same site also provides a tutorial on JNDI programming, and a graphical JNDI namespace browser.

Chapter 8

JDBC and databases

Overview

This chapter presents an overview of the JDBC specification, particularly as it applies to EJB development. Readers who are already familiar with JDBC in other environments will find its use within EJBs similar to their previous experience; however, there are some small technical differences that have profound practical consequences, as we shall see. We will discuss how the container provides `DataSource` objects that allow clients to open and close database connections, and how the database connections are, in fact, container-supplied proxies for real connections. This will lead to a discussion of connection management and connection pooling, and how to author EJBs to take advantage of these facilities. Finally, we look at some practical techniques for improving the modularity and manageability of database access procedures in EJBs.

8.1   What is JDBC ?

JDBC is a specification and API that Java applications can use to interact with a relational database or other tabular data source. Using JDBC, Java platform classes can execute queries and examine the results, update data, and control transactions.

The JDBC API, like Microsoft's ODBC, is based on the x/open 'call-level interface' (CLI) for database drivers. Most developers who have used database connectivity libraries will find the principles of JDBC quite familiar.

A key design element of JDBC was that it should be vendor-independent. However, because the starting point for most JDBC operations is the execution of an SQL query, and SQL dialects vary considerably from vendor to vendor, this independence can be difficult to achieve in practice. While the *JDBC Specification* says that it is officially based on the SQL-92 'entry level' standard, JDBC is *not* highly dependent on that variant of SQL. Indeed, JDBC support could readily be provided for any data source that works with tabular data and has a query language of some sort. The mapping to SQL-92 really affects the SQL data types supported, but it does not limit the SQL queries that can be processed.

Before discussing the JDBC API in more detail, the next section presents a brief summary of SQL syntax and a discussion of the limits of vendor independence. Feel free to skip this section if you are already familiar with SQL.

8.2   SQL

8.2.1   Overview

It is not possible, in a book on EJB technology, to provide a detailed description of relational databases and SQL. If you are unfamiliar with database technology, the brief overview that follows may be enough to get you started, but at some point you will almost certainly need to spend some time reading about SQL, particularly if you intend to use entity EJBs with bean-managed persistence (see Chapter 12).

> Hint
>
> The documentation that comes with the *Cloudscape* database—supplied with the *J2EE Reference Implementation*—is a good place to start reading about SQL in more detail, and it's free. Nice one, Informix.

SQL (Structured Query Language) is a language for querying and updating the data on relational database servers. For most relational databases, SQL is the primary, or only, means by which clients can interact with the database. SQL assumes that data is organized into tables, where each table has a fixed number of columns and a variable number of rows. The entries in one column are all of the same specific data type, or may be `null`, if no data is provided. When a table is created, the create operation indicates which columns, if any, are allowed to be `null`. Such columns are said to be 'nullable.' Other than `null`, SQL supports numbers (fixed point, floating point, and integers of various sizes), character strings of fixed or variable length, date, time, and 'large object' data types. The 'binary large object' (BLOB) data type can store an arbitrary sequence of bytes, which can be very useful; however, BLOB support is not universal.

There are many, many variants of SQL, and it can be difficult to identify a common subset of features that all SQL systems implement. The most widely-used version of SQL is usually called 'SQL-92,' but don't let the name fool you into thinking that it hasn't changed since 1992. At the time of writing, the most recent version of SQL-92 is the 1999 version. This is an international standard, defined jointly by the ANSI, ISO, and IEC standards bodies. If you are interested in obtaining the full specification, it is ANSI/ISO/IEC 9075:1999; but be aware that it comes in five parts, the largest of which are over a thousand pages long.

Part 2, which defines the SQL grammar and syntax, is over 1100 pages alone. It would be nice to think that a standard this comprehensive and with this level of international support would be definitive—that is, if a vendor claimed 'SQL-92 compliance,' this would define exactly what features are available. Sadly, this is not the case. The *ANSI Specification* defines three basic levels of SQL support: entry level, intermediate, and full. In addition, there are a large number of optional features that vendors may or may not choose to support. In practice, many database servers don't even support the entry level specification in full, and very few are prepared to claim support above the entry level.

This is less of an issue for EJB developers than for authors of standalone database clients. In an EJB, most of the business logic is likely to be implemented in Java code, not in SQL. For this reason, the more complex features of SQL may not be required. However, complex or extensive queries are usually executed much more efficiently in SQL than as Java code, simply because the database designers have had many years to optimize this type of operation. In summary, on most occasions the basic SQL operations to be described below will serve your purposes, but occasionally you will have to use more sophisticated SQL to improve performance.

In my experience, most database developers don't know (or care) whether the SQL features they employ are generic SQL-92 or specific to products with which they are familiar. If you have the good fortune to be developing an EJB application for a known database platform, and you are sure that portability will never be an issue, then you can freely use whatever features are available on that platform. If, however, you do need to ensure portability, there are two ways to proceed.

First, you can use the very smallest subset of SQL statements, which are guaranteed to be portable. The examples given later in this section, and in the rest of this book, are of that type. Second, you can employ a general SQL-92 compliance checker. Some application servers (*iPlanet*, for example) have such tools built in. The compliance checker intercepts the SQL as it passes through the JDBC drivers, and checks its grammar for compatibility with the selected SQL-92 level.

8.2.2 Basic SQL grammar

SQL queries comprise keywords (SELECT, UPDATE, INSERT, etc.), literals ('hello', 123, etc.) and operators ('=', LIKE, etc.). Most SQL processors are case-insensitive with respect to keywords but, by default, the data in the database is searched with respect to case. Most SQL queries are SELECT, UPDATE, INSERT, or DELETE statements.

In the examples, keywords are shown in capitals for clarity, but they don't need to be capitalized in real queries. In addition, the backslash character is used below to indicate continuation of a line where the line is too long for the page; you don't need to enter this in practice.

The examples below refer to database tables and operations that may be applicable to the *Prestige Bike Hire* application case study used in this book. We will be using container-managed persistence in this application, however, so we won't need to code SQL directly. The examples are therefore for illustration only.

> **Gotcha!**
>
> SQL is not sensitive to carriage-return or line-feed characters, which are treated like any other whitespace. Therefore, most SQL clients allow the user to enter a specific character (usually a semi-colon) to denote the real end of the line. However, the semicolon is not part of the SQL language, and should not be appended to SQL queries passed to JDBC. Some JDBC drivers anticipate this common error, and silently remove the terminating semicolon; however, this is nonportable and should not be relied upon.

SELECT statement

A SELECT statement is used to find rows in a specific table, or set of tables, that match certain criteria. A simple SELECT statement has the following form.

```
SELECT [fields] FROM [tables] WHERE [condition]
```

Here is a simple example, which finds the `startdate` and `enddate` columns from all rows in the `booking` table where the `custid` field has the (integer) value '1'.

```
SELECT startdate,enddate FROM booking \
  WHERE custid=1
```

SELECT statements can span multiple tables. In this example, the table `bike` has a field `modelname`, which corresponds to the field `name` in the table `model`. The example finds the information from both `bike` and `model` tables for the motorcycle whose registration number is x123 xyz. Note that the string literal is enclosed in single quotation marks. The asterisk ('*') indicates that all fields are to be returned.

```
SELECT * FROM bike,model \
  WHERE modelname=name AND regno='x123 xyz'
```

Because the `bike` and `model` tables don't have any field names in common, the query does not have to be told to which tables the specific fields refer. If there are ambiguous field names, use the notation 'table.field'. Note that the model name appears twice in each row output from this query: once as `bike.modelname` and once as `model.name`. However, as `regno` (the vehicle registration number) is the primary key on table `bike`, we can guarantee that only one row is returned.

Other comparison operations are allowed, as well as strict equality. Number and date fields can be compared using '>' (greater, later) and '<' (less, earlier), while character fields can be compared using 'LIKE', where the arguments to LIKE can include wildcard characters. In SQL, the percent character '%' matches anything, while the underscore '_' matches any single character.

The results of executing a SELECT query are called the *result set*. An optional 'ORDER BY [column]' clause can be provided in the SELECT, in which case the results are sorted before being presented to the client.

Non-result-set SELECTs

Many database engines support the use of SELECT to find metadata rather than result sets. For example, we may wish to find the number of rows in a database table or the sum of all the values in an integer column. Now, we can do this by iterating the rows, extracting any relevant values as we go. The problem is that this would generate a huge amount of network activity if the table is large. It is preferable to do this kind of work on the server. For example, suppose I wanted to get a quick count of the number of motorcycles in the *Prestige Bike Hire* rental fleet. We could iterate the table using JDBC, or alternatively, we could execute the following query, which is guaranteed to return exactly one row with exactly one column, which will contain a long integer whose value is the number of `licenceNumber` entries in the `BikeBeanTable`. Because `licenceNumber` is the primary key, this must equate to the number of motorcycles in the fleet.

```
select count ("licenceNumber") from "BikeBeanTable"
```

Note the use of quoted identifiers, as this SQL was automatically generated by the Reference Implementation, as discussed in Chapter 13.

> ### Gotcha!
>
> Expressions like SELECT COUNT and SELECT SUM are of questionable portability, particularly if anything other than the simple syntax shown above is used.

As we shall see, SELECT COUNT and SELECT SUM remain important in EJB development, because the new EJB Query Language (EJB QL) has no built-in support for this functionality.

UPDATE statement

UPDATE modifies one or more fields in one or more tables. Its basic syntax is

```
UPDATE [tables] SET [column=value {,column=value}] \
  WHERE [condition]
```

For example

```
UPDATE customer \
  SET name='Fred Bloggs', email='f.bloggs' \
  WHERE id=20
```

This statement sets the `name` and `email` fields of `customer` to have the specified values in any row where the `id` field is equal to (integer) 20. Any other fields on matching rows retain their previous contents.

INSERT statement

INSERT creates new rows in tables. Either it can set all the column values in a particular row, in which case the columns don't have to be named, or it can set particular values and leave the rest `null`. The two forms are:

```
INSERT INTO [table] ([fields]) VALUES ([values])
```

and

```
INSERT INTO [table] ([values])
```

For example, the following two statements both have the same effect, that of inserting a row in the `bike` table:

```
INSERT INTO bike (regno, modelname, status) \
   VALUES ('abc 123', 'Yamaha YZF-R1', 0)
```

```
INSERT INTO bike
   VALUES ('abc 123', 'Yamaha YZF-R1', 0)
```

The first form can be used to set fewer than the full complement of columns, but this will only be accepted if the columns with no values are nullable. The second form requires all fields to be specified, in the order they appear in the table.

DELETE statement

The DELETE statement removes one or more rows from a table. The basic form is:

```
DELETE FROM [table] WHERE [condition]
```

For example, the following example deletes the customer whose ID is 25 from the `customer` table. This query cannot match more than one row in this example, because `id` is the primary key on the `customer` table, but in general a DELETE can match multiple rows.

```
DELETE FROM customer WHERE id=25
```

In an extreme case, 'DELETE FROM [table]' deletes all rows from the table.

8.2.3   A note on 'quoted identifiers'

This odd quirk of SQL grammar is rarely important, but needs to be mentioned in the context of the *J2EE Reference Implementation*, where it causes some confusion.

The principle is that SQL allows identifiers to be enclosed in double-quote characters, which makes them case sensitive; normally, SQL ignores the case of column, field, and table names. Why is this important? Consider a scheme that generates SQL statements to write the instance variables of a Java class to a relational database. If a particular class is called `Customer`, and has an instance variable `id` of type `int`, we may create a table called 'customer' with an integer column called 'id'. The SQL may then manipulate the instance variables like this:

```
UPDATE customer set id=25...
```

as we have already discussed. However, suppose (for the sake of illustration) that the class also has an instance variable called 'ID' which is a `String`. What will we call the corresponding field in the table? If we call it 'ID,' we will be in trouble, because SQL can't distinguish 'id' from 'ID'. A possible solution is to use quoted identifiers. In this case we may create the table like this:

```
CREATE TABLE "Customer" ("id" integer, "ID" string,...)
```

Now we can frame SQL statements that distinguish columns by case only:

```
SELECT "ID","id" FROM "Customer" WHERE "id"=25
```

> ### Gotcha!
>
> The quoted identifiers are *different identifiers* from unquoted ones. For example, the "Customer" example above could also have an unquoted `id` field in addition to its two quoted ones. A common problem developers experience when investigating at the SQL prompt a table created by the Reference Implementation is to neglect the quotes, thinking that they are only needed to disambiguate mixed-case identifiers. This is not true: *The quotes are part of the name.*

The issue of quoted identifiers rears its ugly head when using the container-managed persistence features of the *J2EE Reference Implementation*. By default, it quotes all identifiers when generating database tables, presumably for the reasons discussed above. You can turn this feature off if it breaks your database or offends your sense of aesthetics, but you may have problems if your EJBs have any properties that are distinguishable only by case.

8.2.4 Primary keys

A primary key is any piece of data that can uniquely and unequivocally identify a particular record out of a set of records. If we know the primary key of a record, we can always find the rest of the data for that record. In a relational database, primary keys typically operate at the row level—that is, the primary key for a row identifies that row uniquely in a table.

The concept of the primary key is absolutely crucial to the entity EJB architecture. Two entity EJBs cannot have the same primary key, any more than two rows in a table can. The container uses the primary key to organize the EJB instances and EJB objects.

Now in many cases, the database table will have a 'natural' primary key. The table that underlies the `Bike` EJB in the *Prestige Bike Hire* application will have a column for the license number, which is an effective natural primary key. No two motorcycles in the UK have the same license number, and if I know the license number, I can find out the rest of the relevant information.

If a database table does not have a 'natural' primary key, we must find a way to generate one. Consider, for example, a table of information about individuals, which has columns `name`, `address`, and `telephone`. None of these columns readily lend themselves to interpretation as a primary key. If we have control over the database schema, we might be able to add a column that provides a unique identifier (a synthetic primary key). It does not matter, in principal, what this identifier is; in many cases, we can use a number that increments for each row that is added (a *sequence number*). The `Customer` EJB has an `id` property that maps onto such a primary key. Customers don't care what their IDs are, so long as each customer has a different one. Many database engines provide built-in techniques for generating sequence numbers. In particular, it is frequently possible to declare an integer column as 'AUTOINCREMENT' or the like, and allow the database to generate a new number on each successive row. The problem with this technique has always been and remains this: How do we determine the generated number in the JDBC client? Many developers use stored procedures for this,[1] and accept the loss of portability. Others adopt a portable approach, like sorting the table on the sequence column, and accept the inefficiency. This problem is fixed in JDBC 3.0 (see below), but remains troublesome at present.

Alternatively, we can use a composite of two or more columns as the primary key (this is a composite primary key or compound primary key).

There are theoretical reasons for asserting that a primary key, once assigned, cannot be changed. In the `Customer` example, this means that although we can change the customer's name, address, and everything, we can't change his ID after assignment. Database developers tend to have strong, polarized opinions on the validity of changing a primary key; suffice it to say here that most database engines allow it, but EJBs don't.

---

[1] Most database implementations allow the stored procedure to return a value, and this value can be extracted using a JDBC call.

8.2.5   Stored procedures

Most database servers support extensions to the SQL language that allow programmatic operations to be expressed. Such operations are typically called *stored procedures*. Some systems support *stored functions* as well, the difference being that functions have a return value.

For example, the listing below is of an Oracle stored procedure that deletes all entries from the database table `booking` for a motorcycle whose registration number is supplied as a parameter. The notation `the_bike IN CHAR` indicates that `the_bike` is a parameter to the procedure, it is an input (and not an output), and it is of type `CHAR` (a character string).

```
CREATE PROCEDURE cancel_booking (the_bike IN CHAR)
AS
BEGIN
DELETE FROM booking WHERE bike=the_bike;
END;
/
```

When this procedure is executed (using the Oracle SQL client and entering a command like `exec cancel_booking('x123 xyz');`) or using a JDBC `Callable Statement` object; see below), the SQL statement `delete from booking...` is executed, with the supplied registration number as the query term.

This example is very simple, but stored procedures can be of arbitrary complexity. They have two important performance benefits.

- They can iterate result sets on the server, rather than the client. This can significantly reduce network traffic with large queries.

- They can be precompiled. If the stored procedure is called repeatedly, time is saved because the SQL does not have to be compiled on each call.

The problem with stored procedures is that they are even less portable than other forms of SQL. While most database servers use similar syntax for stored procedures, there is usually sufficient difference to mean that some human intervention is required when moving from one database server to another. However, although the definition of a stored procedure is vendor-dependent, the *use* in JDBC is not; JDBC provides a standard syntax for calling stored procedures. This means that although portability is an issue, it is not an issue for the EJB designer *per se*. Stored procedures will typically be uploaded from an SQL script, not defined in EJB code.

8.3   The JDBC API

This section describes the JDBC API and the architecture that underlies it.

8.3.1   JDBC architecture

Figure 8.1 shows the basic interaction between a JDBC client, the JDBC API, and the JDBC drivers. The client does not communicate with JDBC drivers; these are

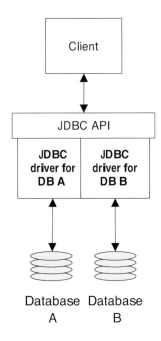

Figure 8.1. Basic JDBC architecture.

concealed within the implementation of the API. Instead it communicates exclusively with the API classes and interfaces in the `java.sql` package. The most important API elements are `Connection`, `Statement` (and its variants), and `ResultSet`, all of which are discussed below. The JDBC API communicates with low-level drivers; the application server will usually expect to be provided with one driver for each database type that is to be supported. Drivers are also discussed below. Note that `Connection`, `Statement`, and `ResultSet` are all interfaces. In practice, when the client calls methods on a JDBC `Connection` object, it is really calling methods on a vendor-supplied object that implements the `Connection` interface. This object will be instantiated by the vendor's JDBC driver. All this is, of course, transparent to clients.

8.3.2   Fundamentals

Listing 8.1 shows the basic sequence of steps in a database query using JDBC. Note that all the classes and interfaces in this listing are in package `java.sql`.

The starting point for clients of a JDBC service (and this includes EJBs, of course) is to obtain a `Connection` for the required database (line 2). This procedure depends on the environment of the client, and is discussed below. From the `Connection` the client obtains a `Statement` object for the type of statement that will be required (line 3). There are `Statement` objects for use with prepared statements, callable procedures, and ordinary statements. The distinction is discussed below. The client then calls one of the execute() methods on the Statement. In this example, we are using executeQuery(), as this is a SELECT operation (line 4).

The client can then iterate through the result set, which may be empty. The client does not know, in general, how long the result set is, except by iterating it. The call ResultSet.next() makes available the next matching row. This call can return false if there are no more rows. The JDBC driver may fetch more than one row at a time from the database and store them in a buffer, for efficiency; there is some limited programmatic control over this.

For each row, the getXXX() methods on ResultSet extract the appropriate field. The method getString() will succeed on a column of any data type, converting to String representation as required. For nontext fields, it may be more convenient to use one of the methods that return data as the matching Java data type. Lines 8 and 9 respectively return fields as an integer and a java.sql.Date object. Of course, these methods may fail if the field cannot be converted to the selected type.

Listing 8.1: **Basic steps in a database query using JDBC. This listing does not show exception handling.**

```
    import java.sql.*;
    Connection c =... // depends on environment
    Statement s = c.createStatement();
    ResultSet rs = s.exectuteQuery
5      ("SELECT * FROM booking");
    while (rs.next())
      {
      int custID = rs.getInt ("custID");
      java.sql.Date startDate = rs.getDate ("startdate");
10      }
    rs.close();
    s.close();
    c.close();
```

If the database operation was not expected to return a result set (for example, if it was an UPDATE query), then we could have used executeUpdate() rather than executeQuery(), which returns an integer count of the affected rows.

8.3.3   Getting a connection

Since JDBC Version 2.0, the preferred way for a JDBC client to get a Connection to a specific database is by a JNDI lookup() call. Prior to this it was normal to use the class DriverManager, which maintained a list of installed drivers and attempted to find one to match a given database URL. DriverManager should not be used by EJBs—even if it works, it will probably give a reference to the driver that bypasses the EJB container's resource manager. Typically a JDBC 2.0 client gets the connection like this:

```
Context  c  =  new  InitialContext ();
javax . sql . DataSource  ds  =
   c.lookup  ("java :comp/env/jdbc /name" );
Connection  c  =  ds . getConnection ();
```

You should remember from Chapter 7 that the `java:comp/env` namespace is specific to the EJB, and names of this form can be remapped in the deployment descriptor. The name that is passed into the `lookup()` call is therefore arbitrary,[2] and will be mapped to real database properties elsewhere. Because all decent EJB servers use connection pooling—as discussed below—the `Connection` object returned may well not represent a real, physical connection to the database, but a shared connection.

8.3.4   Statements

JDBC supports three kinds of statement: an ordinary, uncompiled `Statement`, a partially precompiled `PreparedStatement`, and a fully compiled `Callable Statement`. The latter is intended to be used to execute stored procedures.

The `Statement` interface (or, rather, the vendor-specific class that implements this interface) is used to execute arbitrary queries without precompilation. For example:

```
Statement  s  =  connection. createStatement ();
s.execute
   ("DELETE FROM  booking  WHERE  bike='x123  xyz '");
```

The client creates a blank statement object, then uses it to execute whatever SQL is required. The SQL is supplied as a `String` and must be compiled on each invocation, unless the JDBC driver is smart enough to cache the SQL queries and their compiled equivalents. Even in this case, the query will probably need to be recompiled if any of the literals change (for example, if the query is called once for the string 'x123 xyz' and then again for 'x123 abc').

This form of statement offers best performance when statements are unlikely to be repeated in a single connection, even with different variables.

A `PreparedStatement` is used to provide the JDBC driver and the database an opportunity to use partial precompilation. This statement is created by specifying the SQL with the variables replaced by question marks as placeholders. The client can then execute this statement repeatedly, perhaps replacing the variables with different values on each execution. For example:

```
PreparedStatement s  =  connection. prepareStatement
   ("DELETE FROM  booking  WHERE  bike=?" );
s.setString(1 , "x123  xyz" );
s.execute ();
```

The only parts of the SQL statement that need to be recompiled on each call are the variables. This type of statement offers good performance if similar queries are repeated in the same connection, with different parameters. However, if queries

---

[2]The *JDBC Specification* recommends that the coded name begin with 'jdbc/'.

are not repeated, the additional steps make this statement less efficient than the previous type.

> ## Gotcha!
>
> The parameters in a prepared statement are numbered from *one*, not zero. This is true of most JDBC entities that are numbered, and is at odds with the usual Java convention of using zero-based numbering.

Note that the prepared statement only has the scope and lifetime of a single `Statement` instance. As only one statement can be open at a time on a given connection, it is not practical to prepare a set of statements on initialization of an EJB, and then execute them with different parameters at different points in the life cycle of the EJB. This means that whether prepared statements offer significant performance benefits depends on a complex set of interactions between the application server's connection pool, the database driver, and the database itself. It is therefore difficult to give general guidelines about whether to use prepared statements or not, although it is always possible to find developers with strong opinions on both sides.

A `CallableStatement` is primarily used to call stored procedures. Like a `PreparedStatement` the arguments to the procedure are represented as question marks, then **setXXX** methods are used to supply values to these arguments. JDBC defines its own syntax for calls to stored procedures, and the driver is expected to convert that to the vendor's own syntax. Here is an example that calls the `cancel_booking` procedure listed above:

```
Statement s = connection.prepareCall
  ("{call cancel_booking(?)}");
s.setString(1, "x123 xyz");
s.execute();
```

This example calls the `cancel_booking` procedure defined earlier in this chapter, and sets its one (and only) argument to 'x123 xyz'. We can use both input and output parameters from stored procedures but, with the latter, the client must call `registerOutputParameter()` on the `CallableStatement` to tell JDBC what data type is expected to be returned in an output parameter.

The fundamental method on a `Statement` is execute(). Having called `execute()`, we can call `getUpdateCount()` to determine whether any rows were modified, or `getResultSet()` to determine whether the query matched any rows. `getUpdateCount()` produces a result zero or greater if the query *was of the type that could modify data*. `getUpdateCount()` can return zero if an UPDATE query matches no rows, for example. It will return −1 with a SELECT query.

For convenience, there are two methods derived from `execute()`: execute `Query()`, which returns a `ResultSet`, and `executeUpdate()`, which returns an integer count of the affected rows. Although convenient, these methods should only be used when you know in advance whether the query modifies data or not.

8.3.5 Result sets

SQL SELECT statements will typically produce results in the form of a `ResultSet`. The `ResultSet` object allows clients to fetch the contents of database columns returned by the query. The most reliable, widely supported method to process a result set is to iterate it one row at a time. The `ResultSet.next()` method makes the next row available, returning `true` if a row was retrieved and `false` otherwise. When `next()` returns `false`, this indicates that iteration has reached the end of the result set.

> Gotcha!
>
> The method `ResultSet.next()` should be called *before* reading the first row, not after. That is, after executing the query, `next()` should be called to make the first row available. It is a common mistake to assume that if a query can only ever match exactly one row (e.g., it is done on a primary key), that `next()` is unnecessary.

For each row loaded, the various `getXXX()` methods can be used to retrieve each field. Each has two variants, one taking an index number and one a column name. For example:

```
int getInt (int index);
int getInt (String columnName);
```

The index number is determined by the order of the columns in the SELECT query. For example, with a query like this:

```
SELECT a,b,c FROM table WHERE...
```

index number 1 corresponds to column 'a,' 2 to 'b,' and 3 to 'c.'

> Gotcha!
>
> The variants of `ResultSet.getXXX()` that take an index number as a parameter count from *one*, not zero.

In a query like this:

```
SELECT * FROM table WHERE...
```

the index numbers correspond to the creation order of the columns. The use of index numbers can be error-prone and difficult to read, and should probably be avoided except where the slight efficiency advantage is critical. Using column names is more readable and easier to maintain.

> ### Hint
>
> If `ResultSet.getString()` retrieves a fixed-length character column, it will return a `String` that is followed by enough trailing spaces to make up the fixed length. For example, if `getString()` retrieves a five-letter word from a nine-character column, it will be padded with four spaces. Use `trim()` on the `String` if the padding is not required. This behaviour is defined by the JDBC specification, and applies only to *fixed-length* columns; VARCHAR columns are not padded even if they are of defined upper length.

8.3.6   Scrollable result sets

The most widely supported technique for processing a result set is to iterate it from start to end, but some drivers support the notion of *scrollable* result sets. A scrollable result set allows the client to set the active row in the result set and to iterate it in the reverse direction if required.

The decision whether to use scrollable cursors is made when the `Statement` is created, and is accompanied by a selection of concurrency mode (see next section).

```
Statement s = connection.createStatement
  (TYPE_SCROLL_SENSITIVE, CONCUR_READONLY);
```

There are two scrollable cursor modes: sensitive and insensitive. Creating a sensitive scrollable cursor indicates to the database that you don't want the database data to be locked by reading it. That is, it is 'sensitive' to changes made by other applications. In EJBs, you will probably want database locking issues to be handled by transactions, but the *JDBC Specification* does not indicate how the scrollable result set locking mode interacts with transaction isolation (see Chapter 9).

Not all JDBC drivers support scrollable result sets.

8.3.7   Updateable result sets

After executing a database query, the client can execute an update to modify the data. In some circumstances, it can be more efficient to interleave the modifications with the query. Suppose, for example, the application needs to read a table of financial balances and add interest to each one that meets certain criteria. Obviously we could perform the SELECT and build a Java `Collection` of all the matching rows. Then we could execute an UPDATE for each balance in the `Collection`.

The use of updateable results sets allows just that. After retrieving a row using `ResultSet.next()`, the application can modify specific columns by calling one of the `ResultSet.updateXXX()` methods. Like the `getXXX()` methods, these can be called with a column index number or a column name. For example:

```
updateString ("column_name" , "new_string");
updateString (index , "new_string");
```

The updates are made permanent by calling `ResultSet.updateRow()`. To be able to use this technique, the `Statement` must be created with the appropriate concurrency attributes.

```
Statement s = connection.createStatement
  (TYPE_FORWARD_ONLY, CONCUR_UPDATABLE);
```

Note that not all JDBC drivers support this mode of operation, and in some cases, a query may be issued that cannot be satisfied by an updatable row set, in which case the JDBC driver will return a nonupdateable one, and then the updates will fail.

Gotcha!

Scrollable result sets, updateable result sets, and `RowSets` are all considered optional features in JDBC. If portability is an issue, be careful that the features you use will be supported on all target platforms.

8.3.8   Result set metadata

The `ResultSetMetaData` object can be used to determine information about the columns returned in a SELECT statement. For example, the following gets the name of the first column:

```
ResultSet rs = // do query
ResultSetMetaData rsmd = rs.getMetaData();
String colName = rsmd.getColumnName (1);
```

`ResultSetMetaData` can be very useful for general-purpose data browsing tools, but is not really relevant to EJB development, as the information it returns will usually be known at development time.

8.3.9   Database metadata

The DatabaseMetaData object allows the client to determine information about the features supported by the driver and the database. In principle, the EJB developer should never need to use this, as the properties of the database and driver should be known well in advance. In my experience, however, it is sometimes easier to find out detailed information about capabilities by writing a short program that gets a DatabaseMetaData object, than from the vendor's documentation. For example, the following code fragment will determine whether the JDBC implementation supports 'sensitive' scrollable result sets.

```
Connection c = // open connection
DatabaseMetaData dmd = c.getMetaData();
boolean supports = dmd.supportsResultSetType
    (TYPE_SCROLL_SENSITIVE);
```

8.3.10   RowSets

An implementation of javax.sql.RowSet combines the facilities of a Connection, a Statement, and a ResultSet. RowSets therefore allow database operations to be carried out using a single class. The RowSet API was developed to support database manipulation using JavaBeans design tools, but can be convenient in other applications. The following example uses a RowSet to execute a SELECT query.

```
   RowSet rset = new JDBCRowSet();
   rset.setDataSourceName("jdbc/orders");
   rset.setCommand("SELECT * FROM orders);
   rset.execute();
5  while (rset.next())
     {
     String s = rset.getString ("name");
     //.. process data
     }
10 rset.close();
```

The *EJB Specification* indicates that EJBs must be able to make use of RowSets [EJB2.0 24.1.1]—that is, it is the container vendor's responsibility to provide this support. The Specification does not indicate how this is to be achieved if the JDBC driver does not support RowSets. Typically, a product can achieve compliance by stipulating which JDBC drivers it is prepared to work with. Alternatively, it can provide RowSet support on top of the JDBC API. If you use RowSets, be aware that this feature may not be available if you use a JDBC driver not supported by the EJB server.

8.3.11   Closing resources

Database connections typically involve, at some level, native machine resources (network sockets, memory, etc.). If these resources are not closed explicitly, the garbage collector will eventually release them, but this could take some time. To ensure efficient management of resources, it is important to use the close() methods on JDBC objects to give them a chance to tidy up. The complication is that the `close()` methods are defined to throw `SQLException`, and this exception must be handled. The following section of code, although intuitive, may not be adequate:

```
try
  {
  rs.close();  // close result set
  s.close();   // close statement
  c.close();   // close connection
  }
catch (...)
  {
  // handle
  }
```

This is because, if the `ResultSet.close()` operation fails, the `Connection` will not be closed. Execution will pass directly to the `catch(...)` block. The developer needs to be careful that if one `close()` fails, the others are not bypassed. The example above could be rephrased like this:

```
try { rs.close(); } catch (...) { /* handle */ }
try { s.close(); } catch (...) { /* handle */ }
try { c.close(); } catch (...) { /* handle */ }
```

> ## Gotcha!
>
> `ResultSet` and `Statement` objects depend upon the `Connection` object that created them. Closing the connection invalidates any object derived from it. In theory, this also releases any associated resources. In other words, calling `close()` on a `Connection` should obviate the need to call it on any object derived from that connection. In practice, too many EJB products handle this situation badly for it to be trustworthy in a production system.

8.4   JDBC drivers

At the time of writing, most JDBC driver implementations support Version 2.0 of the *JDBC Specification*. Version 2.0 is divided into two sections: the core API and the 'Standard Extension.' The latter specifies features that are considered optional—a JDBC driver is not required to implement them to be considered JDBC 2.0 compliant. These features include support for connection pooling, distributed transaction management, and rowsets. Be aware when choosing a JDBC driver that it may not support features in the Standard Extension.

8.4.1   Driver suppliers and driver support

JDBC support is available for almost all database servers that are likely to be encountered in practice, although the quality of the drivers varies considerably.

With EJB applications, there is likely to be a choice between drivers supplied by the EJB server vendor, drivers supplied by the database vendor, and drivers from independent suppliers.

EJB server vendors will usually only provide their own drivers for the most popular database servers. Moreover, some EJB servers do not allow the use of drivers other than those supplied with the product—check before you buy, if you want to use an unusual database. This limitation usually arises because the EJB server is using proprietary interfaces for transaction management or connection pooling. Even where EJB products do support the use of other suppliers' JDBC drivers, drivers supplied by the EJB server vendor will usually integrate better into the EJB product than those from elsewhere. This is particularly relevant for applications that rely on distributed transactions. Although JDBC 2.0 does describe an API for communication between drivers and a transaction manager, many EJB products do not use it, relying instead on proprietary support in their own drivers. This is starting to change, as drivers with full JDBC 2.0 support become more widely available.

8.4.2   Driver types

JDBC divides drivers into four types.

Type 1: bridging drivers These act as an interface between JDBC and another general-purpose database API, notably Microsoft's ODBC. These drivers were very important when JDBC was first introduced, as many vendors already had support for ODBC. However, they are less efficient than the other types, as four stages of interaction are required (JDBC-bridge, bridge-ODBC, ODBC-native library, native library-database). These drivers are probably best avoided now, but they can be useful where no other JDBC support exists. At least one JDBC-ODBC bridge is available free of charge, from Sun Microsystems.

Type 2: Java interface to native library These drivers are implemented as a Java interface to a driver that has been compiled to native machine code from some other language (usually C or C++). The native driver is typically supplied by the database vendor, but the JDBC driver often is not. Very often, there are competing JDBC drivers for the same native driver. For example, there are a number of JDBC implementations that use Oracle's OCI client library to interact with Oracle databases. This library is written in C and made available to developers as a dynamically linked library. Because the library itself is well-documented, it is relatively easy to write JDBC drivers for it. In some cases, independently written drivers are superior to those supplied by the database vendor, in that they have better support for JDBC 2.0 features or are more efficient.

At the time of writing, most commercial application servers that supply their own JDBC drivers supply type 2, although there has recently been a rapid proliferation of superior type 4 drivers, and this trend will probably continue.

Type 3: all-Java intermediate network protocol A type 3 driver uses a generic network protocol between the client and the database system. This generic protocol is converted to the database's native protocol on the server. These drivers are effective for providing JDBC support to Java applets, although any kind of 'thick' Java database client will probably benefit. Some EJB servers also support this mode of operation.

Type 3 drivers work because the generic protocol they use normally supports only a subset of the features of the native protocol. This is not usually a problem, because a middleware product will handle the more complex interaction.

Type 4: all-Java native protocol Type 4 drivers are implemented entirely in Java and communicate directly with the database in its native protocol. Type 4 drivers are to be preferred for EJB applications, compared to other types, because they are portable and usually very efficient. Suitable drivers are starting to become available for the major database platforms, although type 2 drivers still predominate. Unlike type 2 drivers, development of type 4 drivers requires a detailed knowledge of the database vendor's protocols, so there is less third-party support.

Ideally, the issues surrounding database driver types should be of no concern to an EJB developer. However, not all features that the developer might wish to use (e.g., scrollable result sets) are supported by all drivers, even where the capabilities exist in the underlying database implementation. At the time of writing, most commercial application servers only have limited support for type 4 drivers—this is because they tend to be supplied with transaction managers that plug into the native-code part of a type 2 driver. The decision to use type 4 drivers may lead to problems at deployment time, so the costs and benefits need careful consideration. I anticipate that these issues will soon be academic, as an increasing number of vendors switch over to type 4 driver support.

8.5   JDBC and JNDI

Any EJB can use JDBC calls to interact with a database, except entity EJBs with container-managed persistence. In that case, the database interaction is implemented by the container. Entity EJBs will almost always require database connectivity, but session and message-driven EJBs will often interact with a database as well.[3]

---

[3]The improvements in the entity EJB architecture introduced with EJB2.0 have reduced the need for session and message-driven EJBs to interact directly with databases.

EJBs obtain a connection to the database using the EJB server's JNDI implementation—that is, they perform a `lookup()` call on the `InitialContext` or one of its subcontexts. The name supplied to the `lookup()` call is arbitrary; it will be mapped to a real database by the administrator, using vendor-supplied tools. In particular, the *EJB Specification* recommends that EJBs use the `java:comp/env` naming domain to look up data sources, so that names can be remapped at deployment time [EJB2.0 20.4.1.1]. This process is described on page 197.

The interaction between JNDI, the EJB 'client' and the application server is shown in Figure 8.2. This diagram does not show the connection pooling components, which are discussed later.

1. The EJB creates a JNDI `InitialContext` and calls `lookup()` with the name of the data source. The EJB server will already have bound the appropriate `DataSource` object in its naming service. It may, in fact, use a vendor-supplied `DataSource` class, but it is the EJB server's naming service that supplies makes it available to EJBs.

2. The EJB calls `getConnection()` on the `DataSource` object.

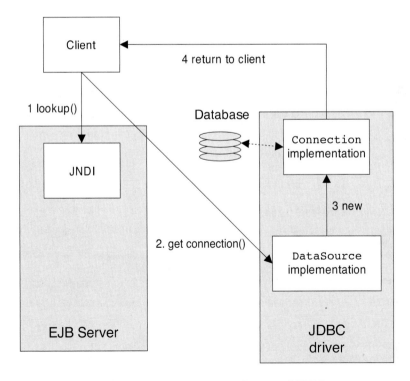

Figure 8.2. Basic JDBC architecture, showing the use of JNDI to get a `DataSource`, and from that a `Connection`.

3. The `DataSource` implementation creates a new `Connection`, which may represent a real, physical connection or some kind of shared resource.

4. The client gets the `Connection` object, which it can then use to create a `Statement`.

Note that there are no connection parameters in the `getConnection()` call; the database server, user ID, and password are all supplied at deployment time, and not specified in code. It is permitted for the EJB to specify a user ID and password for authentication, like this:

```
Connection c = ds.getConnection(username, password);
```

If this is done, the username and password override any settings provided by the container. Such a practice is deprecated, however, as it constrains the user accounts on the database, which won't be appreciated by the database administrator.

8.6 EJB and JDBC example

The `JdbcTest` EJB demonstrates the JDBC API features described in this chapter, and simple usage of JDBC in an EJB. This is a stateful session EJB, exposing two methods to clients: `executeQuery()`, which executes the supplied SQL query and returns the results as a printable text string, and `getMetaData()`, which generates a text string containing some general information about the database. The implementation class is shown in Listing 8.2. Note that the database connection is only opened as required, and closed immediately afterwards, following modern practice (see below). The client creates this EJB by passing the JNDI name of a `DataSource` to the `create()` method on the home interface (Listing 8.3). The remote interface is shown in Listing 8.4. The `executeQuery()` method and the `getMetaData()` methods can trap `SQLException`, and other low-level errors; these are thrown back to the client as a `JdbcTestException`.

The test client (Listing 8.5) for this EJB prompts the user for an SQL query and calls `executeQuery()` on the EJB. The client then simply dumps the return from this method to the console. The test client expects the JNDI name of the `DataSource` to be specified on the command line. A sample of the output from this client is shown in (Listing 8.6).

Listing 8.2: `JdbcTestBean` **is the implementation class for the** `JdbcTest` **EJB.**

```
package com.kevinboone.ejb_book.jdbctest;

import javax.ejb.*;
import javax.naming.*;
import java.sql.*;
import javax.sql.*;

/**
This EJB executes SQL statements supplied by its clients. It
```

```
10  is a stateful session EJB. The client creates the EJB using a
    create() call with the DataSource name as a paramter. The
    client can then call executeQuery() as often as required,
    specifying an SQL query as input. This method returns a
    String which is formatted for display. If the query produces
15  a result set, this is displayed one row at a time. If it
    updates the database, the String contains a message
    indicating the number of rows affected.

    (c) 2001 Kevin Boone
20  */
    public class JdbcTestBean implements SessionBean
    {
    /**
    debug is set to the value of the 'debug' EJB
25  environment variable
    */
    protected boolean debug = true;

    /**
30  Store the SessionContext, by convention, although it
    is not used in this EJB.
    */
    protected SessionContext ctx;

35  /**
    The reference to the DataSource is looked up in
    ejbCreate() and stored for future use.
    */
    protected DataSource ds;
40
    /**
    ejbCreate() finds the DataSource object
    corresponding to the specified data source
    name
45  */
    public void ejbCreate(String datasourceName)
       throws CreateException
    {
    try
50     {
       debugOut("Entering ejbCreate()");
       Context c = new InitialContext();
       ds = (DataSource) c.lookup(datasourceName);
       debugOut("Leaving ejbCreate()");
55     }
     catch (NamingException e)
       {
       String message = "Can't create JdbcTestBean: "
         + e;
60     debugOut(message);
       throw new CreateException(message);
       }
     }

65  /**
    debugOut prints the specified String, if the
    debug flag is set.
    */
    protected void debugOut(String s)
```

```
70      {
        if (debug)
          System.out.println ("JdbcTestBean: " + s);
        }

75    /**
      ejbActivate () has nothing to do in this EJB
      */
      public void ejbActivate()
        {
80      debugOut("Called ejbActivate()");
        }


      /**
      ejbPassivate () has nothing to do in this EJB
85    */
      public void ejbPassivate()
        {
        debugOut("Called ejbPassivate()");
        }
90
      /**
      ejbRemove () has nothing to do in this EJB
      */
      public void ejbRemove()
95      {
        debugOut("Called ejbRemove()");
        }

      // Get the value of the 'debug' environment
100   //   variable, if set
      public void setSessionContext(SessionContext _ctx)
        {
        ctx = _ctx;
        try
105       {
          Context c = new InitialContext();
          Boolean temp =
            (Boolean) c.lookup ("java:comp/env/debug");
          if (temp != null)
110         debug = temp.booleanValue();
          }
        catch (NamingException e){}
        debugOut ("setSessionContext()");
        }
115
      /**
      Format the specified ResultSet for display
      */
      protected String formatResults (ResultSet rs)
120       throws SQLException
        {
        /**
        Use the ResultSetMetaData to get the
        column names for the display
125     */
        ResultSetMetaData rsmd = rs.getMetaData();
        int columnCount = rsmd.getColumnCount();
        String s = "";
        for (int i = 1; i <= columnCount; i++)
```

```
130     {
        s += "column " + i;
        s += ": " + rsmd.getColumnName(i);
        s += ", " + rsmd.getColumnClassName(i) + "\n";
        }
135     s += "\n";
        // Generate display for each row
        while (rs.next())
            {
            for (int i = 1; i <= columnCount; i++)
140             {
                s += rs.getString(i).trim();
                if (i != columnCount) s += ", ";
                }
            s += "\n";
145         }
        return s;
        }


/**
150 Return a String containing information
    about the database. This method demonstrates the
    use of DatabaseMetaData.
    */
    public String getMetaData()
155     throws JdbcTestException
        {
        try
            {
            Connection c = ds.getConnection();
160         DatabaseMetaData md = c.getMetaData();
            String s = "";
            s += "user: " + md.getUserName() + "\n";
            s += "read only: " + md.isReadOnly() + "\n";
            s += "ANSI entry-level SQL: "
165             + md.supportsANSI92EntryLevelSQL() + "\n";
            s += "ANSI intermediate SQL: "
                + md.supportsANSI92IntermediateSQL() + "\n";
            s += "ANSI full SQL: "
                + md.supportsANSI92FullSQL() + "\n";
170         s += "SQL keywords: " + md.getSQLKeywords();
            return s;
            }
        catch (SQLException e)
            {
175         debugOut ("Caught SQLException while creating connection: "
                + e);
            throw new JdbcTestException (e);
            }
        }
180
    /**
    Execute the specified query on a new database connection,
    returning a String formatted for display. Note the rather
    complex exception handling: this is designed to ensure that
185 all open resources are closed, whatever the nature of the
    failure. This method throws JdbcTestException if any
    low-level exception occurs during processing.
    */
    public String executeQuery(String query)
```

```
190       throws JdbcTestException
       {
       debugOut ("Entering executeQuery()");
       debugOut ("Query is: " + query);
       try
195         {
         Connection c = ds.getConnection();
         try
           {
           Statement s = c.createStatement();
200          try
             {
             String ss = "";
             s.execute (query);
             if (s.getUpdateCount() >= 0)
205            ss = "" + s.getUpdateCount()
                 + " row(s) affected\n";
             ResultSet rs = s.getResultSet();
             if (rs != null)
               {
210            ss = formatResults(rs);
               rs.close();
               }
             debugOut ("Leaving executeQuery()");
             return ss;
215            }
           catch (SQLException e)
             {
             s.close();
             c.close();
220            debugOut ("Caught SQLException while querying: "
                 + e);
             throw new JdbcTestException (e);
             }
           }
225        catch (SQLException e)
           {
           c.close();
           debugOut ("Caught SQLException while creating statement: "
               + e);
230          throw new JdbcTestException (e);
           }
         }
       catch (SQLException e)
         {
235      debugOut ("Caught SQLException while opening connection: "
           + e);
         throw new JdbcTestException (e);
         }
       }
240 }
```

Listing 8.3: `JdbcTestHome` **is the home interface for the** `JdbcTest` **EJB.**

```
package com.kevinboone.ejb_book.jdbctest;

import java.rmi.RemoteException;
import javax.ejb.CreateException;
import javax.ejb.EJBHome;

public interface JdbcTestHome extends EJBHome
{
public JdbcTest create(String dataSourceName)
  throws RemoteException, CreateException;
}
```

Listing 8.4: `JdbcTest` **is the remote interface for the** `JdbcTest` **EJB.**

```
package com.kevinboone.ejb_book.jdbctest;

import java.rmi.RemoteException;
import javax.ejb.EJBObject;
import java.sql.SQLException;

public interface JdbcTest extends EJBObject
{
public String executeQuery(String query)
  throws RemoteException, JdbcTestException;

public String getMetaData()
  throws RemoteException, JdbcTestException;
}
```

Listing 8.5: `JdbcTestClient` **is a test client for the** `JdbcTest` **EJB.**

```
package com.kevinboone.ejb_book.jdbctest;
import javax.naming.*;
import javax.rmi.PortableRemoteObject;
import java.io.*;

/**
This simple client tests the 'JdbcTest' Enterprise JavaBean
which is implemented in the package 'ejbook.JdbcTest'.
*/
class JdbcTestClient
{
/**
This method does all the work. It creates an instance
of the JdbcTestBean EJB on the EJB server, and calls its
```

```
15    executeQuery() method whenever the user enters a query
      The command—line is expected to contain the JNDI name
      of the DataSource
      */
      public static void main(String[] args)
20      {
        if (args.length != 1)
          {
          System.err.println
            ("DataSource JNDI name must be specified on command line");
25        System.exit(-1);
          }

        // Enclosing the whole process in a single 'try'
        //   block is not an ideal way to do exception handling, but
30      //   I don't want to clutter the program up
        //   with catch blocks in this simple example
        try
          {
          // Get a naming context
35        Context context = new InitialContext();

          // Get a reference to the Bean
          Object ref  = context.lookup("JdbcTest");

40        // Cast this to the Bean's Home interface
          JdbcTestHome home = (JdbcTestHome)
            PortableRemoteObject.narrow
              (ref, JdbcTestHome.class);

45        // Create a bean object from the Home interface
          JdbcTest jdbcTest = home.create(args[0]);

          // Use a BufferedReader to accept input from the
          //   keyboard, one line at a time
50        BufferedReader br =
            new BufferedReader
              (new InputStreamReader (System.in));

          // Repeat until user enters end—of—transmission
55        //   (Ctrl—D on Unix, Ctrl—Z on Windows).
          String line = null;
          do
            {
            // Show prompt
60          System.out.print ("JdbcTest> ");
            System.out.flush();
            // Get line
            line = br.readLine();
            if (line != null)
65            {
              // If the line is 'metadata', call the
              // getMetaData method on the EJB.
              // If it is 'quit', exit. Otherwise
              // call ExecuteQuery
70            if (line.equalsIgnoreCase ("metadata"))
                {
                System.out.println (jdbcTest.getMetaData());
                }
              else if (line.equalsIgnoreCase ("quit"))
```

```
75              line = null;
              else try
                {
                  String s = jdbcTest.executeQuery(line);
                  System.out.println (s);
80                }
              catch(Exception e)
                {
                  System.out.println(e.toString());
                }
85            }
            } while (line != null);

          jdbcTest.remove();
          System.out.println ("");
90          }
        catch(Exception e)
          {
            System.out.println("JdbcTest: " + e.toString());
            e.printStackTrace(System.err);
95          }
        }
      }
```

Listing 8.6: **Output from the test client when running an SQL query on the "BookingBeanTable" table in the** *Prestige Bike Hire* **application database. This table is automatically generated by the** *Reference Implementation* **persistence manager.**

```
    JdbcTest> select * from "BookingBeanTable"
    column 1: CUSTID, java.lang.Integer
    column 2: STARTDATE, java.sql.Date
    column 3: ENDDATE, java.sql.Date
5   column 4: BIKE, java.lang.String
    column 5: ACTIVE, java.lang.Boolean

    1, 1999−01−14, 1999−01−18, x123 xyz, true
    1, 2000−04−20, 2000−04−25, t487 lfg, true
10  3, 2010−10−20, 2010−10−25, p345 aak, true
    [ ... other rows ommitted ...]
    JdbcTest>
```

Authoring EJBs that make effective use of the database requires an understanding of connection pooling, which is described in the next section. This will be followed by a discussion of practical techniques for using JDBC in EJBs.

8.7 Connection management and pooling

8.7.1 The need for connection management

An enterprise application may employ many EJBs, each supported by many instances of the EJB implementation class. Between them these implementations may open and close connections to external resources very rapidly. This leads to two problems. First, opening and closing database connections is computationally expensive. It typically takes a second or two to establish a new connection to a commercial-grade database server, which gives an idea of the amount of work that's going on behind the scenes. Second, there is often a limitation on the number of database connections that can be open simultaneously, since each consumes significant resources; there may also be software licensing restrictions.

In reality, although many EJB instances will need access to a database, they will probably only need access from time to time, and for short periods. This suggests that some connection management scheme could be implemented that would optimize access to the database. However, the EJB developer should not have to deal with the issues that arise from contention for database access. It is the job of the container to provide the EJBs with timely, efficient access to the database, and to deal with issues of resource contention internally.

Most database connection management schemes are based on the idea of *connection pooling*, although other techniques are also used. The use of connection pooling is shown in Figure 8.3. Each client has its own 'virtual connection' to the database, which it can use as an ordinary connection. There are four 'real' connections in the pool, two connected as 'user 1' and two as 'user 2.' In its current state, a further

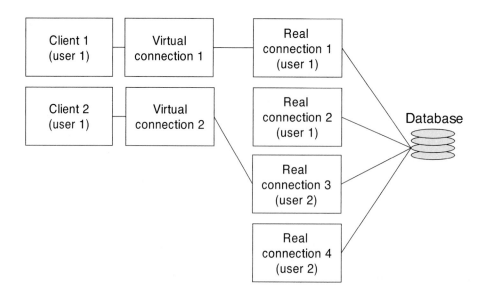

Figure 8.3. Connection pooling and connection sharing.

client could connect as user 1 and another as user 2 before the pool needs to be expanded. When new clients request connections, the pool manager assigns a virtual connection, possibly creating a new real connection at the same time. When the client disconnects, it only closes its virtual connection; the pool manager can keep the real connection open in the pool.

The developer should bear in mind that the EJB container is responsible for supplying viable database connection objects to EJBs. Beyond this, the *EJB Specification* has nothing to say about how the container implements connection management. When the EJB gets a `DataSource` reference from JNDI and calls `get Connection()` on it, the EJB expects to get an object that implements the `java.sql.Connection` interface and behaves like a regular connection. In reality, the connection will be a proxy connection supplied by the EJB server, which will delegate calls onto a real connection. This process must be completely transparent to the EJB, because it reduces portability if the EJB makes assumptions about how connection management is implemented. However, all connection pooling systems have certain features in common, and an understanding of these features will help to maintain good database throughput.

8.7.2   JDBC connection pooling architecture

For the purposes of illustration, we will examine the connection pooling architecture standardized in the JDBC 2.0 Standard Extension; your EJB server may use this technique, but it is equally likely to use a proprietary alternative.

It is often said the JDBC 2.0 supports connection pooling, but this is only true to a degree. JDBC 2.0 defines interfaces that a JDBC driver can implement to allow it to interact with a JDBC 2.0-compliant pooling manager. It has nothing to say about how the pool is managed, how large it is, or how the pool manager determines whether to reuse an idle connection or create a new one. That is, the *pooling algorithm* is not defined by JDBC.

To be able to take part in JDBC 2.0 connection pooling, the JDBC driver must provide implementations of two key interfaces: `ConnectionPoolDataSource` and `PooledConnection`. The former is a factory for the latter—that is, if the EJB server calls `getConnection()` on the driver's `ConnectionPoolDataSource`, it will retrieve an instance of an object that implements `PooledConnection`. This object represents a real, physical connection to the database.

The `PooledConnection` object creates 'virtual' connections to the database when its `getConnection()` method is called. Although the `PooledConnection` can be asked to create any number of virtual connections during its life, it is only expected to be able to manage one active virtual connection at a time. The EJB server is responsible for keeping track of which `PooledConnection` objects currently have an active virtual connection, and which do not.

The interaction between the EJBs, EJB server, and JDBC driver is shown in Figure 8.4. The grouping of components in this diagram represents the responsibilities for their implementation, not necessarily the physical location of the classes.

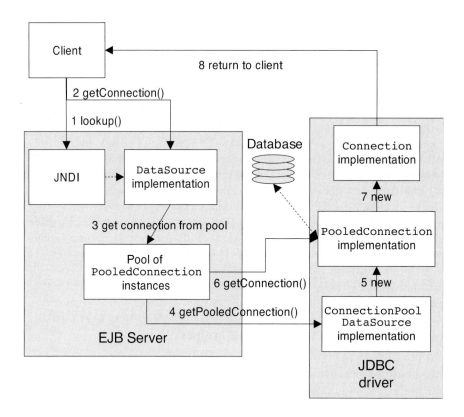

Figure 8.4. JDBC 2.0 connection pooling architecture; see text for details.

1. The client locates the required `DataSource` object by a JNDI `lookup()` call as usual. The EJB server returns its own implementation of `DataSource`, which knows how to interact with its pooling manager.

2. The client calls `getConnection()` on the `DataSource`.

3. The `DataSource` requests a connection to the database from the pool manager.[4]

4. The pool manager inspects its pool for the presence of a `PooledConnection` instance that is idle and has the requested properties, or gets a new `Pooled Connection`. The decision whether to use an idle connection or create a new one is made by a vendor-specific algorithm.

5. If the pool manager elects to create a new pooled connection, it uses a `ConnectionPoolDataSource` from the JDBC driver. Typically, it will use the driver's JNDI interface to locate this object.

---

[4]In some implementations, the `DataSource` implementation may itself be the pool manager; this is, of course, vendor specific.

6. The pool manager uses the `ConnectionPoolDataSource` to create a `Pooled Connection` instance. This is then added to the pool. A new, physical connection is opened at this point.

7. Whether the pool manager added a new `PooledConnection` to the pool or uses an existing one, it now calls `getConnection()` on the selected `Pooled Connection`. Because it implements the `Connection` interface, this proxy is used by the client in exactly the same way as a real connection. The vendor's implementation takes care of serializing access to the database when multiple proxies refer to the same real connection.

8. The driver returns a proxy connection object to the client.

When the client closes its database connection, it is really only signalling a close to the `PooledConnection` object that issues it. The pooled connection is not closed, but the pool manager is notified of the closure of the virtual connection. To do this, the `PooledConnection` object calls the `connectionClosed()` method on the `ConnectionEventListener` registered with the `PooledConnection` by the pool manager. The pool manager can then decide whether to keep this connection in the pool for future clients or to close it fully. In the latter case the physical connection to the database is broken.

8.7.3   The pool manager

JDBC does not define how a pool manager is to be implemented, except insofar as it interacts with the driver's `ConnectionPoolDataSource` and `PooledConnection` implementations. Moreover, it does not define *where* the pool manager is implemented. Some driver vendors include their own pool managers—after all, if the vendor has gone to the length of implementing a poolable connection object, it represents little extra work to implement a simple pool manager as well. This means that a JDBC driver many contain everything necessary to use connection pooling. In practice, an EJB server will probably want to implement its own connection pool manager, rather than relying on the vendor's implementation. This will allow the EJB server's administration tools to configure connection pooling across all supported databases and drivers using a common user interface.

The pool manager is responsible for creating, connecting, and disconnecting pooled connections. When deciding how to handle an incoming client connection request, the pool manager will have to consider various factors.

First, there may be an upper limit on the number of pooled connections; even if there is not, or the pool has spare capacity, a pooled connection is a consumer of resources, and it may not always be to the application's advantage to create a new connection.

Second, if clients make many rapid connection and disconnection requests, the pool manager may prefer to wait for an existing connection to become idle, rather than creating a new connection.

The pool manager cannot allow the connection pool to grow indefinitely, even if no fixed upper limit has been assigned. Periodically, it will need to purge idle connections. Even if the pool is of a fixed size, the pool manager will probably need to close idle connections after a certain period of idleness. This is particularly important if different database user IDs are in use. It will be easier to make a new connection if the pool manager does not have to disconnect an idle connection first.

With these factors in mind, the pool manager will typically follow a procedure similar to the one below when EJBs make connection requests.

- Is there a logged-in connection in the pool that is not assigned to an EJB, but has the same connection attributes as the new request? If so, allocate it to the EJB.

- If there are no unassigned, logged-in connections with the right attributes, but the pool can be expanded, create a new connection for the pool and assign it to the EJB.

- If the pool is at its maximum size and there are no connections with the right attributes unassigned to EJBs, but there are unassigned connections with *different* attributes, log out an unassigned connection and log it in with the new EJB's connection parameters.

- If the pool is at maximum size, and all connections are assigned, queue the connection request.

Typically a connection pool manager will allow the administrator to set properties such as:

- the maximum number of logged-in connections in the pool;

- the number of connections that are allowed to be logged in but not assigned to EJBs;

- the length of time that a connection remains unassigned before being logged out;

- the length of time that a new connection request will be queued rather than creating a new connection, before creating a new connection anyway.

8.7.4   Design implications of connection pooling

Connection pooling reduces the overhead associated with opening and closing database connections. Some implementations may also allow a larger number of active virtual connections than there are real connections, typically by using some form of multiplexing. However, the use of connection pooling has implications for the designer of EJB applications.

- An EJB does not need to keep a database connection open for an extended duration to avoid database connection overheads. There may be other reasons for keeping a connection open, which we will discuss later, but in the absence of other considerations, it is usually more effective to open a database connection for only as long as required to carry out a particular operation.

- Connection pooling cannot work effectively in an environment where clients have different database identities. When developing standalone database clients, it is customary to rely on the database's own security systems to authenticate and authorize clients. With EJBs, a strategy like this would render the connection pooling ineffective. Best results will be achieved when the number of database user IDs is kept low—ideally only one.

  Of course, this strategy defeats database-level security. Typically the designer handles security at the EJB level, using the techniques described in Chapter 16.

A consequence of the transferal of authentication from the database to the EJB server is that database-level auditing is no longer available. Some databases can log the identity of each user that makes a change to the database; with EJB-level security, the end user cannot be determined from the database audit log. If the design calls for user-level auditing, then it will have to be applied at the EJB level. Some EJB servers can do this automatically, but otherwise the EJB developer will have to implement it.

Hint

There are solutions on the horizon for this problem. For example, database vendors are starting to implement facilities by which the effective user of a connection can be changed on the fly. This means that a single set of user credentials can be used to establish the initial connection, and then the application server will supply the database user for subsequent transactions. Such techniques are currently proprietary, and therefore nonportable.

8.8   Transactions

JDBC defines a mechanism for demarcating database transactions, although EJB developers are encouraged to use the technique defined by the EJB API instead. The use of JDBC transactions is described on page 253.

8.9   Practical JDBC usage in EJBs

Two strategies are widely used for handling JDBC connections in EJBs.

Connections are kept open Until very recently, this was the preferred approach: All the required connections are created when the EJB implementation instance is initialized and remain active for the life of the instance. With this strategy, the appropriate places to open and close connections are summarized

Type	Open	Close
Stateless session	`ejbCreate()` or `setSessionContext()`	`ejbRemove()`
Stateful session	`ejbCreate()` or `setSessionContext()` *and* `ejbActivate()`	`ejbRemove()` *and* `ejbPassivate()`
Message-driven	`ejbCreate()` or `setMessageDrivenContext()`	`ejbRemove()`
Entity	`setEntityContext()`	`unsetEntityContext()`

Table 8.1. Suggested methods in which to open and close JDBC connections, if the connection is held open for the life of the instance.

in Table 8.1. This strategy has the advantage that it does not depend on the efficiency of the connection pooling algorithm for its effectiveness. It has two important disadvantages. First, the connection pooling system may not allow an arbitrarily large number of virtual connections. With stateful session EJBs in particular (which are not pooled), the capacity of the connection pool could be exceeded. Second, database connections are not serializable. The developer must take care that if a stateful session EJB stores a `Connection` object in an instance variable, the connection is closed and set to `null` in `ejbPassivate()` and reopened in `ejbActivate()` [EJB2.0 7.4.1]. Some EJB products may not support automatic failover of stateful session EJBs if they contain nonserializable instance variables, as this prevents the instances being replicated across a network.

> ## Gotcha!
>
> It is a common mistake, when beginning EJB development, to attempt to open database connections in `ejbCreate()` in entity EJBs. This usually fails because the first method called on the instance is unlikely to be `ejbCreate()`. In most cases, clients will do a `findXXX()` first. The correct place to open the connection is in `setEntityContext()`. In a session EJB, use `ejbCreate()` or `setSessionContext()` as you prefer.

Connections opened and closed on demand Most authorities recommend this strategy, and it is used in all the examples in the *EJB Specification*. An EJB that executes a database operation should obtain a connection as required, carry out the JDBC operations, then close the connection (and all its associated resources). The connection management system eliminates the connection overhead that this approach would otherwise engender.

Because the connection object does not have to be stored in an instance variable, all the issues relating to serialization are avoided, and it is unlikely that there will be sufficient virtual connections in use to exceed the capacity of the pooling system. This technique is slightly less efficient that the alternative, but the benefits usually outweigh the costs.

These considerations are summarized in Table 8.2.

> ### Hint
>
> Although a `Connection` should usually not be stored in an instance variable, there is no reason to avoid storing the `DataSource` object that will be used to obtain the connection. This gives a small efficiency gain, as it avoids a JNDI `lookup()` before each connection opening.

Using on-demand connection allows all database operations to be encapsulated inside helper classes, which can be instantiated and released only in the methods that require database access. There are many ways to write such helper classes. In J2EE circles, these they are often called data access objects (DAOs), although this is not a term that is used in the *EJB Specification*.

Consideration	Kept open	On demand
Connection set-up overhead?	none	negligible
Constrained by limited virtual connections?	unlikely	possibly
Precompilation benefits of stored procedures?	yes	yes
Serialization issues?	no	yes

Table 8.2. The implications of an EJB opening and closing database connections on demand, compared with those of keeping a connection open over the life of the EJB.

> **Hint**
>
> When writing Java code that emits SQL into a JDBC call, it is very easy to make trivial syntactical errors, such as missing quotes around character literals. It may be helpful to output the query string to the debugging console to make it easier to check if there are problems.

> **Gotcha!**
>
> All JDBC methods can throw an `SQLException`, which must be handled. Ideally, EJBs should not throw an `SQLException` back to the caller, as it is somewhat too low-level for clients to interpret. Instead, the EJB should rethrow the exception as an application-defined exception that makes sense in the context of the application.

> **Hint**
>
> It is much quicker to test SQL queries using an SQL standalone client than by executing them within EJBs. Most database servers are supplied with at least a command-line client, e.g., Oracle's *SQLPlus*. For *Cloudscape*, the command-line client is a program called 'ij,' which is described in the *Cloudscape* documentation.

8.10   What's new in JDBC 3.0?

At present, few EJB products formally support JDBC 3.0. But as the API is now part of JDK 1.4, and some EJB products are designed to run with JDK 1.4 or equivalent, it may be possible to use JDBC 3.0 features, assuming that suitable drivers can be obtained. In any event, the advantages of JDBC 3.0 for application server use are such that vendors are likely to support it quite rapidly. It is therefore worth a brief look at some of these improvements.

Portable retrieval of automatic keys As we discussed above, the ability of database engines to generate sequential primary keys automatically is difficult to exploit, as there is no portable, efficient way to retrieve the generated

key in a JDBC client. JDBC 3.0 adds a method `getGeneratedKeys()` to the
`Statement` interface, which puts the responsibility for retrieving the keys onto
the driver vendor.

Multiple result sets A single `Statement` can now maintain multiple result sets
at the same time.

Tighter integration with connection pooling systems Where an application server makes use of connection pooling infrastructure in the JDBC driver,
there are now standardized properties that can be specified and drivers are
expected to support them. These govern, for example, the maximum and minimum number of physical connections to maintain.

PreparedStatement pooling We discussed earlier how the use of `Prepared`
`Statement` would allow precompilation of SQL, and thereby reduce the load
on the database engine. However, it was uncertain whether this benefit would
be realized because the precompilation was associated with a physical connection, and we could not guarantee that the same physical connection would be
used for success operations on the client's virtual connection. JDBC 3.0 overcomes this problem by specifying the interaction between the connection and
a pool of compiled statements. This operation is transparent to the developer.

'Savepoint' support In JDBC 3.0, a JDBC client can specify multiple operations
and insert 'savepoints' between operations. Then, when an operation fails, the
transaction can be rolled back to the most recent savepoint and retried, rather
than rolled back to the start of the transaction. In theory, this should allow
significant improvements in throughput without compromising data integrity.
However, it remains to be seen how the 'savepoint' model will integrate with
J2EE's 'flat' transaction model.

8.11   Summary

JBBC provides a vendor-independent way for EJBs to interact with relational
databases, but it does not prevent vendor-specific SQL from being used. If portability is required, the developer needs to be careful to use generic SQL statements.
An EJB server will provide a connection pooling system that allows EJBs to open
and close database connections on demand, without incurring connection overheads.
This means that an EJB should not need to keep a database connection open except when it is in use. Opening and closing database connections on demand allows
database operations to be neatly encapsulated in helper classes.

Chapter 9

Transactions

Overview

This chapter explains how to make use of the transaction management features offered by the EJB architecture. It describes the basic principles of transactions and the standard features that are supported by the EJB architecture. We then discuss the appropriate uses of bean-managed and container-managed transactions including the `SessionSynchronization` interface in stateful session EJBs. The concepts of this chapter will be demonstrated using both simple test EJBs and a practical example from the *Prestige Bike Hire* application. Finally, for readers with an interest in the underlying technology, there is a description of the roles of the transaction manager and resource managers, and the protocols by which these components communicate with one another and with the EJB container.

9.1 Introductory note

This chapter is probably the most technically complex in the book, and the subject material the least likely to be familiar. This being the case, I think it is appropriate to begin with a rule-of-thumb that sums up most of what is to follow:

Hint

If in doubt, set all your EJBs to use container-managed transaction demarcation, and set all methods to have the transaction attribute `Required`.

Provided you follow the guidance about exception handling given in Section 15.2, this rule-of-thumb will give acceptable results in most situations. The problem is that it won't give acceptable results in *all* cases, which is why we need a whole chapter.

9.2   Transactions described

Transaction management is described in all decent database management books,[1] so I won't go into much detail here. The following should be considered the minimum you need to know about transaction management to develop transactional EJB applications.

9.2.1   Transaction examples

A transaction is a sequence of operations that are carried out together and form a single unit. The 'textbook' example is that of transferring money between bank accounts. To do this, we must withdraw money from one account (first operation) and deposit it into another (second operation). Between, and in addition to, these major steps may be any number of supporting operations. Now, if both deposit and withdrawal operations succeed, everyone is happy. If both operations fail, then we can at least try again later. However, if one operation fails and the other succeeds, we are likely to be in trouble. This will leave the data in an inconsistent state: Either too little money in one account or too much in another.

The 'bank account' example emphasises the 'atomicity' or 'indivisibility' of a transaction (more later). That is, the most important feature is that both the required operations succeed or fail together. The classic 'airline seats' example emphasises the 'isolation' of transactions—that is, the fact that different transactions are prohibited from interfering with each other's data. In this example, a travel agent checks the number of free seats on a specific airline flight, then makes a reservation for a particular seat. It would be inconvenient if another transaction could reserve the selected seat between checking the availability and placing the reservation.

In the *Prestige Bike Hire* application, the process of making a motorcycle reservation for rental combines elements of both these stereotypical operations. The reservation process itself requires multiple steps (involving different data sources), and this must be preceded by a check for availability.

These issues lead to the well-known standard transaction properties, discussed next.

9.2.2   Transaction properties

There are often said to be four properties of a transaction: *atomicity, consistency, isolation,* and *durability.* These are often collectively known by the acronym ACID. Typically a transaction must also be *recoverable*—that is, it leaves the data in a consistent state even after a system failure.

---

[1] Alternatively, save money and read the documentation that comes with *Cloudscape*, which is free. It includes a number of nice hands-on exercises that demonstrate the principles of transactions and locking.

Atomicity

'Atomicity' means that all the operations of a transaction succeed or fail as a single unit. If we apply a number of operations, and the last one fails, then all the others must be reversed. The term *commit* is normally used for the process of making the changes permanent. The process of reversing operations to get back to the pretransactional state is called *rollback.*[2]

There are numerous examples of atomicity in the *Prestige Bike Hire* application. For example, when we reserve a motorcycle for hire, this consists of two main operations: modifying the `bookings` table to indicate that the booking has been made, and dispatching a message to the legacy ordering system to create a credit card debit. Both must succeed or fail together. If we successfully update the `bookings` table, but fail to dispatch the message, then the booking must be reversed to get back to the original state.

Database engines usually manage atomicity by the use of *transaction logs*. The transaction log records each operation carried out during the transaction, so that the operations can be undone in reverse order if necessary. It goes without saying that the transaction log should be protected against system failure. This is a matter for the database administrator, not the EJB developer.

Consistency

Whether a transaction succeeds or fails, it should leave the data internally consistent. If there are constraints in effect between tables, these constraints should continue to hold, whether the transaction succeeds or fails.

Isolation

Two transactions are isolated if they are applied in such a way that one does not compromise the validity of the other. This sounds simple, but is very difficult to achieve in practice without sacrificing efficiency. EJB developers should take note: *It is your job to set isolation levels correctly!* Moreover, unlike the setting of transaction boundaries (see below), this has to be done in code, not in a deployment descriptor.

Isolation anomalies

Suppose we don't isolate transactions fully: What consequences are there likely to be? There are three main problems: dirty reads, nonrepeatable reads, and phantom reads. These are called *isolation anomalies.*

Dirty reads   A dirty read occurs when one transaction reads data that has been modified by another transaction, but not committed. This is not, in itself, a problem; the issue is that of deciding which transaction has 'correct' data if the first transaction rolls back. Here is an example from the *Prestige Bike Hire*

---

[2]'Rollback' is a noun; the corresponding verb is 'to roll back.' It is bad enough that we have introduced 'rollback' to the English language as a noun; I certainly don't intend to promulgate its use as a verb as well (to rollback).

application. One customer attempts to place a reservation on a motorcycle. This succeeds, but for some reason we can't dispatch the credit card debit, so we have to roll back the reservation. In the meantime, another customer has viewed the reservations for the same vehicle and seen that it is reserved. At the end of the two operations, which customer has the right information about the reservation status? The data in the database is internally consistent, but customer two has received false information.

In this example, the worst that could happen is that we lose a booking, but it is possible to envisage much worse scenarios in other applications.

Nonrepeatable reads Nonrepeatable reads occur when a transaction reads the same data twice, and finds it changed between reads. This is subtly different from the dirty read problem. Nonrepeatable reads don't need a rollback to exert their effect, they simply need one transaction to write while another is reading. Suppose a customer wants to make a booking for a motorcycle, and searches for all vehicles available on a certain date. From the list of vehicles available, he makes a reservation on one of them. During this process, one of the company's staff withdraws the selected vehicle for maintenance. The first transaction has experienced a nonrepeatable read—that is, if the customer were to repeat the search for available bookings, the search would have found different data.

Phantom reads A phantom read occurs when one transaction begins reading data, and another inserts or deletes data from the table being read. This problem is, in a way, a special case of the nonrepeatable read problem, and both are typically handled with the same kind of database locking as we shall see.

How are we to prevent isolation anomalies? Unless we are prepared to design the application around them, there is only one possibility: database locking of some kind.

For example, suppose we wanted to avoid all the problems above. This is simply accomplished by locking all the rows written or read by a transaction until that transaction is committed. Any other transaction that tries to read or write the locked rows will have to wait. There are two problems with this strategy. First, there is the obvious performance bottleneck: The more data that is locked, the less concurrency there can be between operations and the slower the overall response. Second, if the updates are large (involving many rows), then maintaining information about locked rows can be quite memory-intensive and slow in its own right. We can reduce the impact of the second problem at the expense of the first by using table-level locking. This scheme, which is very simple to implement, locks an entire table for the transaction that is updating it. We can get an improvement in performance by recognizing that, although a SELECT statement may ultimately require the locking of many rows, they do not need locking *until an application requests the data*. Typically, an application steps through the results of a SELECT query one row at a time. This avoids the possibility of dirty reads, but does not eliminate nonrepeatable reads.

Level	JDBC name	Anomalies prevented
0	TRANSACTION_READ_UNCOMMITTED	None: all anomalies are possible.
1	TRANSACTION_READ_COMMITTED	Dirty reads.
2	TRANSACTION_REPEATABLE_READ	Dirty reads and nonrepeatable reads.
3	TRANSACTION_SERIALIZABLE	All.

Table 9.1. Isolation levels, their effects, and JDBC names.

Database vendors have standardized the types of isolation that an application is likely to require into four levels. These levels, and the names used for them in the JDBC API, are shown in Table 9.1.

Note that if a database implements locking at the table level, then there is no difference between levels 1 and 2; locking the whole table effectively prevents both nonrepeatable reads and phantom reads. In addition, a competent database will not really serialize database transactions even at isolation level 3—that is, it won't queue transactions and apply them in sequence. It is, in general, safe to allow concurrent reads if no transaction is writing.

Not all databases support all isolation levels. Most will balk at setting level 0 (no protection against isolation anomalies), and many can't distinguish between levels 1 and 2. In practice the choice for the developer often comes down to deciding between level 1/2 or level 3. We will see later how this is implemented in an EJB, and the issues the developer has to be aware of.

Isolation and deadlock

The use of stringent isolation strategies not only decreases the responsiveness of an application, but can lead to *deadlock*. This happens when two or more transactions are waiting on each other to commit. No transaction can commit, because each one is waiting for another transaction to commit and release its locks on the data.

A database is normally able to tell when a deadlock has arisen but, sadly, it can't do much about it. Normally it will have to fail (and therefore roll back at least one pending transaction) to resolve the deadlock.

Hint

An EJB developer may be able to reduce the likelihood of deadlock by using one or more of these strategies.

- Select a lower level of isolation, if the application can tolerate it.

- Set the databases to use row-level locking, rather than table-level locking.

- Where different operations span the same group of tables, arrange them (as far as practicable) to operate on the tables in the same order.

- Although it may seem counterintuitive, it can sometimes be an advantage to *increase* the amount of locking on selected operations. Remember that a transaction can only contribute to a deadlock if it actually starts. A transaction that is waiting to start presents no hazard, because nothing else can be waiting on it. Whether you can use this strategy depends on the type of manual locking that your databases can support. Most offer a 'LOCK TABLE...' or equivalent, but any of these constructs is likely to be nonportable.

Durability

A transaction is durable if, once committed, nothing short of catastrophic failure can prevent the changes from being made permanent. In particular, this means that a transaction must survive a database crash.

Recoverability

A transaction is at its most vulnerable between the database receiving the signal to commit it and the final changes being made that result in its being durable. While the transaction should not fail at this point for logical reasons, it may fail in the case of a system-level fault (e.g., a server crash). A transaction in this state is said to be in doubt, because if the database system were to fail at this point it would not be obvious whether the transaction should be committed or rolled back. Typically a database system will examine its transaction log on startup, to detect whether any transactions are in doubt. Often manual intervention will be required to deal with such transactions.

9.2.3   Types of transaction architecture

The EJB architecture supports all three of the major transactional architectures: *local*, *distributed*, and *global*, although not all EJB *products* can. Distributed and global transactions can be *homogeneous* or *heterogeneous* (encompassing the same type of database or different types). For the EJB developer, the important point to note is that it makes little or no difference to the Java code.

Local transactions

This is the simplest kind of transaction: All operations are carried out on the same database engine. The database will take care of committing and rolling back transactions internally, so no transaction manager is required.

An EJB can enforce local transactionality by demarcating transactions at the JDBC connection level, like this:

```
Connection c = // get JDBC connection
c.setAutoCommit (false);
c.begin();
try
  {
  // JDBC operations
  c.commit();
  }
catch (...)
  {
  c.rollback();
  }
```

Local transactions are faster than distributed transactions, as no synchronization of database servers is required. However, the explicit use of local transactions reduces flexibility, as it prevents the expansion to a distributed model at a later stage. If you do want to use JDBC-level local transactions, be sure to set the EJB to use bean-managed transaction demarcation, and don't mix JDBC transaction methods with EJB transaction methods. For the remainder of this chapter, I assume the use of the EJB transaction model, whether transactions are local or not. Most EJB products can be configured to use local transactions automatically if the database operations are all against the same server. Thus the developer can code for the EJB model and allow the EJB server to use the most effective technology.

Distributed transactions

A distributed transaction is one that includes multiple database servers, which are usually, but not always, deployed on different hosts. Distributed transactions require a *transaction manager* to co-ordinate them; they are usually managed by a *two-phase commit* process. The technicalities of this process are discussed at the end of this chapter.

Global transactions

A global transaction is a distributed transaction that encompasses not only different servers, but different applications. If an EJB-based application is deployed across two different servers (for load balancing, for example), transactions that encompass the two servers are not necessarily global. However, if an EJB application sends messages to a legacy system by some sort of enterprise messaging product, that would constitute a global transaction.

Gotcha!

To the EJB developer it is largely irrelevant whether transactions are local or distributed. The API calls and the transaction attributes are the same in both cases. It is the EJB product that must take care of the low-level details. This is generally a good thing, but there is one problem: EJB products are not *obliged* to support distributed transactions. Even if they do, some configuration may be required. The *J2EE Reference Implementation* is quite good about preventing invalid configurations. For example, as we shall see, it prevents the execution of code that attempts to open multiple database connections on different databases unless the drivers have the requisite distributed transaction support built in. Not all products are so thorough. In short, don't assume that because you can code a distributed transaction, your EJB product is coordinating a distributed transaction. Check the documentation to see what else may be required.

9.2.4   Which operations are transactional?

Most developers are aware that database operations will often need to involve transaction management. However, it is increasingly the case that transactions encompass other types of interaction as well. For example, suppose that an EJB system handles ordering by dispatching orders to an order processing system by a message queue. If an ordering operation is combined with, say, an operation that modifies the stock level of a product, then clearly these two operations constitute a transaction.

Many enterprise messaging products support transactional semantics—that is, they are able to commit and roll back message deliveries. Most EJB products are able to handle transactions that encompass both databases and message queues.

However, it is important to understand that in the JMS architecture, the transactions are between the messaging clients and the messaging provider. Transactions do not (and can not) encompass the producer and consumer of a message. For example, if a transaction encompasses three message deliveries to three different message queues, then the transaction can be committed when the message queues have received the messages. The queued messages do not become available to the consumers until the message transaction is committed.

The issue of transaction management in messaging is discussed in more detail in Chapter 10 on page 296.

There will be occasions when you need to involve in your applications legacy systems that have no notion of transactionality. There is no straightforward way to combine operations on these systems with operations that have implicit transactional semantics. Normally, you will have to work around this as best you can.

9.3   The EJB transaction model

This section discusses the main features of the EJB transaction model. In later sections, we will look in detail at the particular methods that are available to the developer to control transactions.

9.3.1   Fundamental design decisions

The EJB transaction model is based on three fundamental design decisions.

First, transactions are *flat*. This means that for any EJB instance, exactly one transaction can be in effect at a time [EJB2.0 17.1.2]. If an EJB method that is currently running in a transaction calls a method that begins a new transaction, then the first transaction is suspended until the method call is complete. The suspended transaction will not be affected by anything that happens in the method call. This rule is strictly enforced. At no stage will transactions be nested. Although some databases support nested transactions, it was felt that this support was not widespread enough to justify extending the *EJB Specification*.

Second, transaction context is propagated automatically from one method call to another by the container [EJB2.0 17.1.1]. The EJB does not have to include a transaction ID when calling methods on other EJBs. This works because inter-EJB calls are always on the EJB object or local object; with remote method calls, the stub on the caller knows how to get the current transaction context and pass it on to the target, along with the rest of the method-call information.

Third, as a consequence, an EJB's influence over transactions is limited to demarcation—that is, an EJB can begin, commit, or rollback a transaction. The container is responsible for resource enlistment (see below), communicating with the transaction manager, and all the other technicalities.

9.3.2   Transaction boundaries and transaction demarcation

Transaction demarcation can be defined as the specification of *transaction boundaries*. The *EJB Specification* makes frequent mention of transaction boundaries, and it is important to understand what is meant by this term. The execution of a program 'crosses a transactional boundary' whenever there is a change in transaction context. Because the EJB architecture does not support nested transactions, a transaction boundary is crossed every time one of the following happens:

- a new transaction begins, and no transaction was currently in progress;

- a new transaction begins, and an existing one is suspended;

- a transaction is committed or rolled back, leaving no transaction in effect;

- a transaction is committed or rolled back, and a suspended transaction resumed.

Most EJB applications are concerned with *transaction demarcation*, rather than transaction management. Transaction demarcation involves indicating when a transaction begins and ends, and possibly bringing about a rollback. Transaction management, on the other hand, is a much more complex operation. It involves initialization of the transaction manager, determining and initializing the components of the transactional system, and dealing with failure recovery. The EJB architecture, in fact, only allows EJBs to demarcate transactions, not manage them. It is the job of the EJB container to manage transactions on behalf of EJBs. This terminological distinction is not widely maintained, and many books and articles mix them up. The *EJB Specification* is very strict on this point.

In general, a transaction is considered to be in progress between its starting and ending boundaries. This implies that the transaction boundaries dictate the length of time for which database data is likely to be locked. Having widely spaced transaction boundaries (that is, transactions encompassing many method calls) can lead to a loss of database concurrency, which is undesirable, but also to a reduction in entity EJB synchronization overhead, which is a benefit. This issue will be discussed in more detail later.

9.3.3   Transaction demarcation strategies

There are three sources of transaction demarcation control: the EJB itself (*bean-managed demarcation*), the container (*container-managed demarcation*), and the client (*client-managed demarcation*). Each of these will be discussed in detail later. The rest of this section describes the API for transaction demarcation, parts of which apply to all transaction demarcation strategies.

> #### Hint
>
> There are few compelling reasons to use bean-managed transaction demarcation. In most cases, the container can do the job just as well, and this strategy removes some common causes of error. However, container-managed transaction demarcation forces transaction boundaries to align with method-call boundaries. It will be inappropriate if you need multiple transactions in the same method. There are even fewer reasons to use client-managed demarcation.

9.3.4 Transaction demarcation API

This section describes the API provided by the *EJB Specification* to support transaction demarcation. Note that some of these methods are available only when using container-managed transaction demarcation, and some only with bean-managed demarcation.

9.3.5 EJBContext methods

As we have seen already, when the EJB container creates an EJB it calls `setSession Context()`, `setMessageDrivenContext()`, or `setEntityContext()` and passes in an object of class `SessionContext`, `MessageDrivenContext`, or `EntityContext`, respectively. The EJB normally stores this reference in an instance variable to make it available for future use. The context object has the various methods that are relevant to transaction management (Table 9.2).

The `getUserTransaction()` method in `EJBContext` returns an object that implements the `javax.transaction.UserTransaction` interface. This is the EJB's point of access to the container's transaction manager. Table 9.3 describes these methods in outline; a full discussion will be found in the section on container-managed transactions.

9.4 Container-managed transaction demarcation

9.4.1 Fundamentals

With container-managed demarcation, the developer's responsibilities are to

- declare each method's transaction attributes in the deployment descriptor, and

- handle exceptions appropriately, calling `EJBContext.setRollbackOnly()` where necessary.

With container-managed demarcation, the container considers the transactional state at the beginning and end of every method call on an EJB. Based on the current transaction context, and the transaction attributes given in the deployment descriptor, the container can do one of four things before calling the method itself:

- continue the current transaction;

- suspend the current transaction and run the method without a transaction;

- suspend the current transaction and begin a new one; or

- refuse to execute the method at all.

At the end of a method call, the container will attempt to complete any transaction it started (commit or roll back) and resume any transaction it suspended. In general, if the method called `setRollbackOnly()`, or threw an `EJBException`, the

`boolean` `getRollbackOnly()`	An EJB can call this method to determine if it is currently involved in a transaction that has already been set to roll back. It is advisable to call this method before embarking on a lengthy database operation in a method that is called in a transaction. If `getRollbackOnly()` returns `true`, we know that the database operations are going to be rolled back, so there is no point proceeding. This method can only be used if an EJB is using container-managed transaction demarcation. If it is demarcating its own transactions, it will have to provide its own method to determine whether a rollback has to be initiated.
`void` `setRollbackOnly()`	If this method is called, any transaction that is currently in progress will be rolled back, rather than committed. The rollback won't necessarily happen right away, but it will certainly happen eventually. This method is only meaningful in EJBs with container-managed transactions, and it represents the only way that an EJB of this type can initiate a rollback directly (that is, it can't do it by talking to the transaction manager directly).
`UserTransaction` `getUserTransaction()`	Gives an EJB access to the container's transaction manager through the JTA interface. The method returns an object that implements the `javax.transactions.User Transaction` interface. This object will be vendor-specific, but will have functionality defined by the JTA (Java Transaction API). Using this object, an EJB can begin, commit, and roll back transactions. This method can't be used on EJBs that are defined to use container-managed transactions.

Table 9.2. Transaction methods in the `EJBContext` interface.

`void begin()`	Starts a new transaction. All operations on resources controlled by the transaction manager will be part of the same transaction after this.
`void commit()`	Attempts to commit the operations carried out since the last `begin()` operation. This method can fail if the operations cannot be committed.
`int getStatus()`	Returns an integer that indicates the state of the current transaction. See below.
`void rollback()`	Forces the current transaction to roll back.
`void setRollbackOnly()`	Prevents the current transaction from committing, without necessarily starting a rollback at this point.
`void setTransactionTimeout (int)`	Sets the timeout value for the current transaction.

Table 9.3. The `UserTransaction` interface.

transaction is rolled back. Otherwise, it is committed. In more detail, the action taken by the container depends on the transaction attribute of the called method, as follows (in these descriptions, the term 'failure' refers to the method throwing an `EJBException` or calling `setRollbackOnly()`. We will discuss what a failure is, and the effect of exceptions, in more detail later).

For each method, one of the following attributes should be supplied.

NotSupported [EJB2.0 17.6.2.1] When a call is made on a method with this attribute, the container suspends any ongoing transaction and continues without a transaction. The suspended transaction is resumed after the method returns. `NotSupported` is an appropriate attribute for methods that must not cause a rollback in their callers, whatever failures may occur during the method call itself. However, this method is inappropriate for entity EJBs (which should usually use `RequiresNew` to get the same effect) for reasons that will be explained later.

Required [EJB2.0 17.6.2.2] When calling a method with this attribute, the container will ensure that a transaction is always in effect. If the caller was in a transaction, then that transaction is carried on in the called method. In that case, if the method fails, everything done by the method and its caller is rolled back.

If the caller does not have a transaction, then the container begins a new one. In that case, a failure causes the work done in the method to be rolled back, but does not affect the caller.

`Required` should probably be the default for all EJB methods, unless there is a good reason to select something else.

Supports [EJB2.0 17.6.2.3] With this attribute, the called method runs in the transactional context of its caller, if it has one, or runs without a transaction, if it doesn't. If the method fails, the outcome depends on whether the calling method had a transaction. If it did, then the called method and the calling method will be rolled back. If it didn't, nothing is rolled back.

This is a rather dangerous attribute to use, unless you can be sure that your application is completely nontransactional (unlikely). The problem is that whether the *called* method gets rolled back depends on the transactional state of the *caller*, which is usually the exact opposite of what you want.

RequiresNew [EJB2.0 17.6.2.4] A method with this attribute will always run in its own transaction. The container will first suspend any existing transaction, then create a new one for the called method. If the method fails, its work will be rolled back, but it won't otherwise affect the caller. This is the right attribute to use for a method that is transactional, but has to have no effect on its callers. You should use this method in entity EJBs if you want to ensure that their business methods don't cause a rollback in their callers' transactions (not `NotSupported`).

Mandatory [EJB2.0 17.6.2.5] A method with this attribute will never be entered unless the caller is in a transaction. The container will throw a `Transaction RequiredException` to the caller otherwise. If the method fails, it is rolled back along with its caller.

Never [EJB2.0 17.6.2.6] A method with this attribute will never be entered in a transactional context, and the container will reject any call made for which a transaction is currently in progress. Specifically, the caller will receive a `RemoteException`.

9.4.2   Session synchronization

This is one of the least-well understood aspects of EJB development. The key issue underlying `SessionSynchronization` is that while the EJB container always knows how to roll back a database operation (or tell the transaction manager to do so), it *has no idea how to roll back a session EJB's internal state*. This is only ever a problem for stateful session EJBs: Message-driven EJBs and stateless session beans have no state, and entity EJBs can be rolled back by the container calling the `ejbLoad()` method after rolling back the database.

Consider the following scenario. A stateful session EJB is maintaining a 'shopping cart' on behalf of a client. The client, in this case, is a servlet. The shopping cart data is in instance variables of the shopping cart EJB. When the user wants to place a firm order for the items in the shopping cart, the servlet creates a new transaction, calls the method `getCartDetails()` on the shopping cart EJB to get the items requested, transfers them to the ordering service, then calls `clearCart()` to empty the shopping cart. The servlet then commits the transaction.

The client cannot commit the transaction before calling `clearCart()`, because the clear operation needs to be part of the transaction. The problem is that the `clearCart()` method carries out operations that the container can't roll back if the transaction ultimately fails. For all we know, the client may even have called `remove()` on the shopping cart before the transaction commits.

To get around problems like this, the *EJB Specification* defines a technique for synchronizing a stateful session EJBs with transactions whose boundaries are outside the scope of the EJB itself [EJB2.0 7.5.3]. If the EJB class implements the interface `javax.ejb.SessionSynchronization`, the container will call the methods it specifies to indicate the life of a transaction. The methods available are as follows.

afterBegin()

This indicates that the container has started a new transaction, and is about to call a method on this EJB in that transaction. This is a good place for the EJB to get itself into a state to which it can return if the transaction later fails.

beforeCompletion()

This indicates that the container is about to commit a transaction that has involved this EJB at some point. The EJB does not normally have to do any work here, but it can force the transaction to roll back by calling `setRollbackOnly()`.

afterCompletion()

This indicates that the container tried to commit the transaction, and whether it succeeded or failed. The method has one argument, a `boolean` that is set `true` for success and `false` for failure. The EJB should put itself back into the pretransaction state.

> ### Hint
>
> If a stateful session EJB is being used simply to cache database data on behalf of a client, we can handle session synchronization simply by rereading the database if `afterCompletion()` signals a failure. This is because the database will already have been rolled back by the container before it calls `afterCompletion()`.

In the example above, the 'shopping cart' EJB could implement `afterBegin()` to save a copy of the shopping cart and restore the instance variables from that copy if `afterCompletion()` indicates a failure.

Hint

It can be quite tricky to debug EJBs that use `Session Synchronization`, and its use can often be avoided by providing methods that prevent the need for a transaction to span methods in stateful session EJBs. In the 'shopping cart' example, if we had provided a method `placeOrderAndClearCart()` in the stateful EJB, the state of the instance variables could have been handled within the method itself.

Gotcha!

You can't use `SessionSynchronization` to handle a failure in the EJB itself: If a method in a stateful session EJB throws a run-time exception, the container will *not* call `beforeCompletion` or `afterCompletion`, because there won't be anything to call these methods on. The container removes the EJB instance, so it doesn't have any state to synchronize.

9.4.3   Examining container-managed demarcation in detail

To investigate the container's handling of rollback and session synchronization, we will use a simple test system. This system will consist of two session EJBs: `Transtest_A` is stateless (Listing 9.1), while `Transtest_B` (Listing 9.2) is stateful.

   `Transtest_A` has exactly one method, unimaginatively named `method_A()`. Its job is to create a new `Transtest_B` and call its two methods, `method_B1()` and `method_B2()`. So when a client calls `method_A()` on `Transtest_A()`, the sequence of calls looks conceptually like this:

```
client -->
  Transtest_A.method_1() -->
    Transtest_B.method_B1()
    Transtest_B.method_B2()
```

   In reality, of course, the methods would do some useful work. In this example, all they do is output trace messages to the server log, including the value of the 'rollback only' flag.

   Of course, no EJB is ever called directly by a client; all calls go through the container's proxies. So in reality, the call sequence is like this:

```
client -->
  Transtest_A EJB object -->
    Transtest_A.method_1() -->
      Transtest_B EJB object -->
        Transtest_B.method_B1()
      Transtest_B EJB object -->
        Transtest_B.method_B2()
```

This distinction is important, as we shall see, as it is the container proxies that coordinate transactions.

Note that `method_B1()` in `Transtest_B` is defined to be able to throw an `SQL Exception`, for reasons that will become clear later. The home and remote interfaces for these two EJBs are not listed, but you should be able to work them out by now!

> ### Hint
>
> But if not, they are available in the source code package that accompanies this book, in the directory `transtest`.

Listing 9.1: **Implementation class for `Transtest_A`.**

```java
   package com.kevinboone.ejb_book.transtest;
   import java.util.*;
   import javax.ejb.*;
   import javax.naming.*;
 5 import java.rmi.*;
   import javax.rmi.*;
   import java.sql.*;
   import javax.sql.*;

10 public class Transtest_A_Bean extends GenericStatelessSessionBean
   {
   public void method_A()
     {
     debugOut ("Entering method_A");
15   debugOut ("Rollback only flag = " + ctx.getRollbackOnly());

     debugOut ("Creating instance of Transtest_B()");

     try
20     {
       Context context = new InitialContext();
       Object ref    = context.lookup
         ("java:comp/env/ejb/Transtest_B");
       Transtest_B_Home home = (Transtest_B_Home)
25       PortableRemoteObject.narrow
           (ref, Transtest_B_Home.class);
       Transtest_B tt = home.create();
```

```
      debugOut ("Calling Transtest_B.method_B1()");
30    tt.method_B1();
      debugOut ("Called Transtest_B.method_B1()");
      debugOut ("Rollback only flag = " + ctx.getRollbackOnly());

      debugOut ("Calling Transtest_B.method_B2()");
35    tt.method_B2();
      debugOut ("Called Transtest_B.method_B2()");

      debugOut ("Removing Transtest_B");
      try {tt.remove();} catch (Exception e){}
40    }
    catch (SQLException e)
      {
      debugOut ("Caught SQLException in method_A");
      debugOut ("Rollback only flag = " + ctx.getRollbackOnly());
45    throw new EJBException(e);
      }
    catch (RemoteException e)
      {
      debugOut ("Caught RemoteException in method_A");
50    debugOut ("Rollback only flag = " + ctx.getRollbackOnly());
      throw new EJBException(e);
      }
    catch (NamingException e)
      {
55    debugOut ("Caught NamingException in method_A");
      debugOut ("Rollback only flag = " + ctx.getRollbackOnly());
      throw new EJBException(e);
      }
    catch (CreateException e)
60    {
      debugOut ("Caught CreateException in method_A");
      debugOut ("Rollback only flag = " + ctx.getRollbackOnly());
      throw new EJBException(e);
      }
65
    debugOut ("Rollback only flag = " + ctx.getRollbackOnly());
    debugOut ("Leaving method_A");
    }
  }
```

Listing 9.2: **Implementation class for** Transtest_B.

```
    package com.kevinboone.ejb_book.transtest;
    import javax.ejb.*;
    import java.sql.*;

5   public class Transtest_B_Bean
        extends GenericStatefulSessionBean
        implements SessionSynchronization
    {
    public void method_B1()
```

```
10        throws SQLException
        {
        debugOut ("Entering method_B1");
        //throw new EJBException ("This is a mock EJB exception");
        //debugOut ("Leaving method_B1");
15      }
    public void method_B2()
        {
        debugOut ("Entering method_B2");
        debugOut ("Leaving method_B2");
20      }
    public void afterBegin()
        {
        debugOut ("Called afterBegin ()");
        }
25  public void beforeCompletion()
        {
        debugOut ("Called beforeCompletion ()");
        }
    public void afterCompletion(boolean flag)
30      {
        debugOut ("Called afterCompletion()");
        debugOut ("commit flag = " + flag);
        }
    }
```

Let's start with a simple case: All the methods on all the EJBs have transaction attribute `Required`. Listing 9.3 shows the output to the server log when the two EJBs are exactly as listed (i.e., nothing throws an exception) and the client calls `method_A()` in `Transtest_A`.

There are a few important points to note about Listing 9.3.

- `Transtest_B` is a stateful session EJB, so the server must initialize it for each new client call. So we see `setSessionContext()` and `ejbCreate()` called for `Transtest_B` where we don't for `Transtest_A`, which is stateless and therefore drawn from the pool.

- The container starts a new transaction on entry to `Transtest_A.method_A()`. This transaction is carried through to `Transtest_B.method_B1()`. Now, this is the first call on `Transtest_B` in this transaction, so the container must call `afterBegin()`. Only then does `method_B1` get entered.

- The transaction does not get committed until the end of `Transtest_A.method_A()`. This means that the container *cannot call* `Transtest_B.beforeCompletion()` *until after* `Transtest_A` *has removed its instance of* `Transtest_B`. In other words, the container can't respond to the `remove()` call on `Transtest_B` by removing its instance, as it will need to call `beforeCompletion()` and `afterCompletion()` on it later. Note from the listing that there is no log entry to show that `ejbRemove()` is ever called on `Transtest_B`.

Listing 9.3: **Output to the server log from the transaction tester when all methods succeed. See text for details.**

```
   Transtest_A_Bean :  Entering  method_A
   Transtest_A_Bean :  Rollback  only  flag  =  false
   Transtest_A_Bean :  Creating  instance  of  Transtest_B ()
   Transtest_B_Bean :  setSessionContext ()
5  Transtest_B_Bean :  Dummy  ejbCreate ()
   Transtest_A_Bean :  Calling  Transtest_B . method_B1 ()
   Transtest_B_Bean :  Called  afterBegin ()
   Transtest_B_Bean :  Entering  method_B1
   Transtest_B_Bean :  Leaving  method_B1
10 Transtest_A_Bean :  Called  Transtest_B . method_B1 ()
   Transtest_A_Bean :  Rollback  only  flag  =  false
   Transtest_A_Bean :  Calling  Transtest_B . method_B2 ()
   Transtest_B_Bean :  Entering  method_B2
   Transtest_B_Bean :  Leaving  method_B2
15 Transtest_A_Bean :  Called  Transtest_B . method_B2 ()
   Transtest_A_Bean :  Removing  Transtest_B
   Transtest_A_Bean :  Rollback  only  flag  =  false
   Transtest_A_Bean :  Leaving  method_A
   Transtest_B_Bean :  Called  beforeCompletion ()
20 Transtest_B_Bean :  Called  afterCompletion ()
   Transtest_B_Bean :  commit  flag  =  true
```

In Listing 9.3, the value of `getRollbackOnly()` is always `false`, as it should be.

Response to EJBException

Now suppose that `method_B1()` fails dramatically and throws an `EJBException` (or, for that matter, another runtime exception like `NullPointerException`). We can simulate this by modifying `method_B1()` as follows.

```
   public void  method_B1 ()
      throws SQLException
      {
      debugOut ("Entering  method_B1");
5     throw new EJBException ("This  is  a  mock  EJB  exception");
      }
```

If we run the client now, we get the server log shown in Listing 9.4. Please note the following points.

- As the exception is thrown from `method_B1()`, `method_B2()` never gets called, as we expect. The exception is trapped in `method_A()` of `Transtest_A()`, which produces the output shown on line 9 of Listing 9.4. When an EJB throws an `EJBException`, its client gets a `RemoteException`.

- At this point, the container has marked the transaction for rollback, as evidenced in line 10. So at some point the current transaction is going to be rolled back, probably when method_A() finishes.

- There are no calls to beforeCompletion() or afterCompletion(). This may seem odd: Surely the container would want to tell Transtest_B that a transaction failed? The reason it doesn't do so is that it has discarded the instance of Transtest_B, as required by the Specification [EJB2.0 6.6], so there is nothing to call these methods on. In other words, if a stateful session bean throws an EJBException, its beforeCompletion() and afterCompletion() methods are never called. This is sensible behaviour, because these methods are provided to allow the instance to remain in sync with the transaction, and the instance has been removed.

Listing 9.4: **Output to the server log from the transaction tester when Transtest_B.method_B1() throws an EJBException. See text for details.**

```
     Transtest_A_Bean :  Entering  method_A
     Transtest_A_Bean :  Rollback  only  flag = false
     Transtest_A_Bean :  Creating  instance  of  Transtest_B ()
     Transtest_B_Bean :  setSessionContext ()
  5  Transtest_B_Bean :  Dummy ejbCreate ()
     Transtest_A_Bean :  Calling  Transtest_B . method_B1 ()
     Transtest_B_Bean :  Called  afterBegin ()
     Transtest_B_Bean :  Entering  method_B1
     Transtest_A_Bean :  Caught  RemoteException  in  method_A
 10  Transtest_A_Bean :  Rollback  only  flag = true
```

So throwing an EJBException out of a method in an EJB and back to the container causes the transaction, if any, to be marked for rollback. This cannot be reversed by the caller.

EJBException is a subclass of RuntimeException and, in fact, the container will treat any runtime exception the same. This applies, for example, to ClassCast Exception and NullPointerException.

Response to nonruntime exceptions

Now let's make things more interesting. Suppose that something went wrong in Transtest_B and it threw an SQLException (a database server was out of commission, for example). To simulate that effect, we will modify Transtest_B.method_B1() so that it looks like this:

```
public void method_B1 ()
    throws SQLException
  {
  debugOut ("Entering  method_B1");
```

```
5      throw new SQLException ("This is a mock SQL exception");
   }
```

If we run the client now, we get the server log shown in Listing 9.5. Please note the following points.

- As the exception is thrown from `method_B1()`, `method_B2()` never gets called, as we expect. The exception is trapped in `method_A()` of `Transtest_A()`, which produces the output shown on line 9 of Listing 9.5.

- Despite a database operation failing, and an SQL exception being thrown, *the container has not marked the transaction for rollback.* This is evident from line 10, where the value of the 'rollback only' flag is still false.

Listing 9.5: **Output to the server log from the transaction tester when Transtest_B.method_B1() throws an SQLException. See text for details.**

```
    Transtest_A_Bean :   Entering   method_A
    Transtest_A_Bean :   Rollback   only   flag  =  false
    Transtest_A_Bean :   Creating   instance   of   Transtest_B ()
    Transtest_B_Bean :   setSessionContext ()
5   Transtest_B_Bean :   Dummy ejbCreate ()
    Transtest_A_Bean :   Calling   Transtest_B . method_B1 ()
    Transtest_B_Bean :   Called   afterBegin ()
    Transtest_B_Bean :   Entering   method_B1
    Transtest_A_Bean :   Caught   SQLException  in   method_A
10  Transtest_A_Bean :   Rollback   only   flag  =  false
    Transtest_B_Bean :   Called   afterCompletion ()
    Transtest_B_Bean :   commit   flag  =  false
```

The key thing to note about this example is that *throwing a nonruntime exception, even `SQLException`, is not in itself sufficient grounds for the container to roll back a transaction.* To ensure that this error does cause a rollback, the client needs to catch the exception and rethrow it as an `EJBException`. This is what `Transtest_A_Bean` does in line 44. This ensures that the transaction does still get rolled back. But note that it is the responsibility of the caller of the failed method to take action that brings about a rollback, if desired. An alternative approach is to call `setRollbackOnly()` and then throw an application-defined exception.

Response in a suspended transaction

Finally, consider a case where `method_B1()` has the transaction attribute `Not Supported`. Remember that this means that the container must suspend any ongoing transaction for the duration of `method_B1()`. Let's assume that this method throws an `EJBException` for some reason. This produces the output in Listing 9.6. Now the container has removed the instance of `Transtest_B`, as it always will if an EJB throws an `EJBException`. However, line 9 shows the container has not marked

> ## Gotcha!
>
> In the example above, the container did not mark the transaction to roll back. However, if the `SQLException` that was thrown represented a failure at the database level, then there probably would be a rollback as a result of that failure. But it is important to remember that the throwing of a nonruntime exception itself is never sufficient on its own to back out a transaction.[3]

the transaction for rollback. When `method_A()` completes, any transactional operations it carried out can still be committed. In other words, a failure in a method with transaction attribute `NotSupported` does not cause the caller's transaction to roll back. Of course, the caller is catching a `RemoteException` as before, and can then decide to roll back its own transaction if necessary.

Listing 9.6: **Output to the server log from the transaction tester when `Transtest_B.method_B1()` throws an `EJBException`, but has `NotSupported` transaction attribute. See text for details.**

```
    Transtest_A_Bean:  Entering  method_A
    Transtest_A_Bean:  Rollback  only  flag  =  false
    Transtest_A_Bean:  Creating  instance  of  Transtest_B()
    Transtest_B_Bean:  setSessionContext()
5   Transtest_B_Bean:  Dummy  ejbCreate()
    Transtest_A_Bean:  Calling  Transtest_B.method_B1()
    Transtest_B_Bean:  Entering  method_B1
    Transtest_A_Bean:  Caught  RemoteException  in  method_A
    Transtest_A_Bean:  Rollback  only  flag  =  false
```

9.4.4   Summary of attribute selection and exception handling

So what have we learned from all this? The important issue is that when using container-managed transactions, the developer must combine transaction attributes with exception handling to get the desired effect. If a called method throws an `EJBException` or other runtime exception, and it is in a transaction, then the container will roll back the transaction. The calling method—if it is not on a local client—will receive a `RemoteException` or its subclass `java.rmi.Transaction RolledbackException` (note the odd capitalization), and can make its own decision about what to do next. If the called method and the calling method are in the same transaction (e.g., we are using the `Required` attribute), then the caller *can't*

---

[3]But see the note on throwing `RemoteException`.

abort the rollback: Any work it does will be rolled back by the container. If the caller and the called method were in different transactions (e.g., the called method has `RequiresNew` attribute) then the caller can decide whether to roll back its own transaction or not.

Gotcha!

Awkwardly for the *EJB Specification*, `TransactionRolledback` `Exception` is a subclass of `RemoteException`. The introduction of the local client view in EJB 2.0 has caused an inconsistency, because the local home interface and local interface can't be declared to throw this exception. This means that a local client cannot receive a `TransactionRolledbackException`. To get around this problem, the local proxies must now throw `TransactionRolledbackLocalException` to the client. However, this is a subclass of `EJBException` and is therefore an unchecked exception. This means that the client can be coded (intentionally or otherwise) without handling the exception. Because local clients of EJBs will usually themselves be EJBs, if they don't handle the exception it will be caught by the container and used to roll back the client's transaction. Thus, the complication will usually work itself out in a natural way. This issue does mean, however, that exception handling is slightly different between local and distributed clients.

If a method throws an application exception (even `SQLException`), the container does not roll back the transaction, but the method can call `setRollbackOnly()` to get a rollback if it wants. If it does not do this, the calling method will catch the exception and make its own decision about whether to roll back or not.

9.4.5   An example of container-managed demarcation

In this section, we will look at a specific example where transaction control is required. In the *Prestige Bike Hire* application, the process of making a reservation for a motorcycle is handled by the `makeReservation` method in the `BookingManager` EJB. This method interacts both with entity EJBs (`Customer` and `Booking`), which in turn interact with the relational database and with the message queue that communicates with the legacy financial system. Thus, we have a distributed, heterogeneous transaction.

The method can be described in outline as follows.

```
public void makeReservation(...)
    throws BookingManagerException
  {
5    // Determine customer ID from login credentials
```

```
      // Determine  customer  credit  card  details

      try
        {
10    // Check  dates  and  details

      // Get  availability

      // Create  Booking  EJB  to  represent  new  booking
15
      // Dispatch  credit  card  transaction  to  legacy  system

      // Notify  customer  by  e-mail
        }
20    catch ( Exception  e )
        {
      ctx . setRollbackOnly ();
        }
        }
```

Here are a few things to note about this method.

- It is not intended to be called from an EJB. The first point to note about this method is that it is *not* intended to be called from an EJB, but from a servlet. Now, although we can do transaction demarcation in a servlet (see below), it isn't recommended.[4] Because the client isn't starting the transaction, it can't roll it back or commit it. Therefore, the `makeReservation` method can't throw an exception to the client and let it decide whether to roll back or not, as we discussed earlier. Instead, the method must ensure that any internal failure brings about a rollback. However, we want to be able to throw a meaningful exception to the client (the servlet), which it can then use to format an error message for the client. So we can't have `makeReservation()` throw an `EJBException`, although this would have the correct transactional effect. The solution is to catch exceptions arising out of the operation of the method and call `setRollbackOnly()` on the `SessionContext`.

- The operations to determine the user's customer ID from his login credentials, and to determine the customer details (which we get from the corresponding `Customer` entity EJB), have no effect on any transactional data. If these operations fail, we don't need to call `setRollbackOnly()` because there is nothing to roll back. Of course, it wouldn't hurt to call it, but it is redundant.

- The `catch(...)` block catches `Exception`, not the specific exceptions known to be thrown by the code in the method. Why? If something throws, say, a `NullPointerException` and the container catches it, this will cause the transaction to roll back. However, it is unhelpful for the (servlet) client to get a `RemoteException`. The strategy adopted here ensures that the client catches

---

[4]Servlets can control transaction boundaries using JTA calls, but there is no mechanism for declarative transaction control outside of EJBs.

a `BookingManagerException` with a meaningful message, and the transaction is still rolled back.

- Not all the operations in `makeReservation` necessarily need to cause the transaction to back out if they fail. For example, the process of notifying the user by email, it could be argued, should not have this effect. In this case, the method `sendMail()` on the `Mailer` EJB could have attribute `NotSupported`.

- The `makeReservation` method itself needs to be executed in a transaction. Because the intended client is a servlet, and we aren't expecting the servlet to initiate a transaction, then either of the attributes `Required` or `RequiresNew` will have the right effect.

9.4.6 Issues in container-managed demarcation

To wrap up our discussion of container-managed demarcation, here are a few things to watch out for, in no particular order.

- The developer sets transaction attributes on the methods exposed by the factory and business method (remote or local) interfaces, not the implementation class. For session EJBs, all the business methods require a transaction attribute. For entity EJBs, all the business methods, `create(...)` methods, and `findXXX()` methods require a transaction attribute. For message-driven EJBs, only the `onMessage` method needs a transaction attribute.

- There are some circumstances where the container requires a transaction in order to function correctly, particularly with entity beans. Entity beans typically involve database access, which is *always* transactional.

> Gotcha!
>
> When an entity EJB's business methods have transaction attributes that don't specify a transaction (e.g., `NotSupported`), the container may not be able to determine when to call `ejbLoad()` and `ejbStore()` on the instance. The container is allowed [EJB2.0 12.1.6.1] to forego calling these methods in this instance. What this means to the developer is that business methods that don't specify a transaction will almost certainly find the EJB's instance variables incorrect. If you want to ensure that the entity EJB does not cause a transaction rollback in its caller, use `RequiresNew` instead.
>
> Note that the necessity for entity EJB methods to run in some kind of transaction is mandated in Version 2.0 of the *EJB Specification* [EJB2.0 17.4.1], at least where container-managed persistence is used.

- Even when the developer sets a transaction to all methods of an EJB, there are a few cases where some methods have an 'unspecified' transaction context [EJB2.0 17.6.5]. The most relevant of these are the `ejbCreate()` methods of session and message-driven EJBs. Because, in general, the container invokes these methods when filling the instance pool, and not in response to a client request, it is impossible for the container to know what transaction attribute is required. It is simple enough to avoid getting into difficulty with this.

> Hint
>
> Don't put database operations into `ejbCreate()` methods in session and message-driven EJBs, unless they are encapsulated in other EJBs with well-defined transaction state. This restriction does *not* apply to entity EJBs.

- Message-driven EJBs are not called by clients directly, and therefore the notion of inheriting the caller's transaction context is unhelpful. Therefore, the only valid transaction attributes are `Required` and `NotSupported`, meaning 'use a transaction' and 'no transaction,' respectively.

- In Version 1.0 of the *EJB Specification*, EJBs were supposed to throw `Remote Exception` to indicate a system-level error. This had the effect of causing the container to roll back a transaction. Although this use of `RemoteException` is now deprecated, the *EJB Specification* [EJB2.0 18.3.8] stipulates that containers continue to support it. This means that throwing a `RemoteException` acts exactly like throwing `EJBException`, even though the latter is a runtime exception. This should not be a problem for new developments, as the vendor's deployment tools should warn you if you attempt to throw a `RemoteException` out of a method.

9.5   Bean-managed transaction demarcation

This section describes techniques available to the developer who wants to control transaction boundaries more finely than is possible with container-managed demarcation. Variations of this technique can be used by servlets, JSPs, EJBs (except entity EJBs) and CORBA clients, provided that the RMI protocol supports the passing of transaction context between components.

> ## Gotcha!
>
> In general, if servlets and EJBs are deployed as part of the same application (i.e., in the same EAR file), then it should be possible for servlets to initiate transactions that encompass EJBs (although it may not be advisable). If they are deployed as different applications, and particularly if the servlets and EJBs are hosted by different products, then the servlets are essentially 'thick clients' of the EJBs. In such a case, you should pay attention to the section on client-demarcated transactions below.

9.5.1 Fundamentals

If an EJB wants to demarcate its own transactions, it uses the methods of `User Transaction` to do this. This interface is defined in the Java Transaction API, and all EJB 2.0-compliant products are required to support it. To get a `User Transaction` object, it calls `getUserTransaction()` on the `EJBContext` object passed in by the container when the EJB was initialized (e.g., `SessionContext` for session EJBs). It can then use this object to begin a transaction, commit a transaction, or roll back a transaction. It can also find the status of a pending transaction.

> ## Gotcha!
>
> Bean-managed transaction demarcation is not available to entity beans, whatever persistence management scheme they use [EJB2.0 18.3.1]. This is because the relationship between database operations and business methods is largely not under the control of the developer. The container cannot be expected to maintain the relationship between the instance variables and the database if the bean is manipulating the transaction context itself.

9.5.2 Bean-managed transaction demarcation in detail

As we did for container-managed demarcation, we will use a simple test EJB to demonstrate what happens in bean-managed demarcation. Listing 9.7 shows a suitable EJB (only the implementation class is shown). This EJB has two accessible methods. `method_C1()` initiates a transaction, opens two database connections, and carries out an update operation on each of them. It then closes the connections. `method_C2()` then commits the transaction. If a client calls the two methods in sequence, we get the output (to the server log) shown in Listing 9.8. Note that an EJB with bean-managed transactions *cannot* implement `SessionSynchronization`. The container is no longer in control of the transaction boundaries, and cannot notify the EJB about transaction progress. The EJB must therefore inform itself whether a transaction succeeded or failed and maintain its instance variables based on this knowledge.

Listing 9.7: **Implementation class for the bean-managed transaction demonstration. This class has two methods,** `method_C1()` **and** `method_C2()`, **that a client should call in sequence.**

```
   package com.kevinboone.ejb_book.transtest;
   import java.util.*;
   import javax.ejb.*;
   import javax.naming.*;
 5 import java.rmi.*;
   import javax.rmi.*;
   import java.sql.*;
   import javax.sql.*;
   import javax.transaction.*;

10
   /**
   Implementation class for the bean—managed transaction
   demonstration EJB, Transtest_C

15 (c)2001 Kevin Boone
   */
   public class Transtest_C_Bean extends GenericStatelessSessionBean
   {
   /**
20 Print the status of the current transaction
   */
   protected void showStatus ()
     {
     try
25     {
       String s = "?";
       int status = ctx.getUserTransaction().getStatus();
       switch (status)
         {
30       case Status.STATUS_ACTIVE:
           s = "active"; break;
         case Status.STATUS_COMMITTED:
           s = "committed"; break;
         case Status.STATUS_COMMITTING:
35         s = "committing"; break;
         case Status.STATUS_MARKED_ROLLBACK:
           s = "marked for rollback"; break;
         case Status.STATUS_NO_TRANSACTION:
           s = "idle"; break;
40       case Status.STATUS_PREPARED:
           s = "prepared"; break;
         case Status.STATUS_PREPARING:
           s = "preparing"; break;
         case Status.STATUS_ROLLEDBACK:
45         s = "rolled back"; break;
         case Status.STATUS_ROLLING_BACK:
           s = "rolling back"; break;
```

```
              }
            debugOut ("Status = " + s);
50          }
          catch (Exception e){};
          }


        /**
55      This method begins the transaction , and does
        database inserts on two database connections
        */
        public void method_C1()
          {
60        debugOut ("Entering method_C1");
          try
            {
            debugOut ("Getting datasources");
            InitialContext c = new InitialContext();
65          DataSource ds1 = (DataSource)c.lookup
              ("java:comp/env/jdbc/database1");
            DataSource ds2 = (DataSource)c.lookup
              ("java:comp/env/jdbc/database2");
            showStatus();
70
            debugOut ("Opening connections");
            Connection c1 = ds1.getConnection();
            Connection c2 = ds2.getConnection();
            showStatus();
75
            debugOut ("Beginning transaction");
            UserTransaction ut = ctx.getUserTransaction();
            ut.begin();
            showStatus();
80
            debugOut ("Creating statements");
            Statement s1 = c1.createStatement();
            Statement s2 = c2.createStatement();
            showStatus();
85
            debugOut ("Executing updates");
            s1.executeUpdate
              ("insert into booking values "
                 + "(1, '1999-01-14', '1999-01-18', "
90               + "'x123 xyz', true)");
            s2.executeUpdate
              ("insert into booking values "
                 + "(1, '1999-01-14', '1999-01-18', "
                 + "'x123 xyz', true)");
95          showStatus();

            debugOut ("Closing connections");
            c1.close();
            c2.close();
100         showStatus();
            }
          catch (Exception e)
            {
            debugOut (e.toString());
105         throw new EJBException (e);
            }
          debugOut ("Leaving method_C1");
```

```
      }
110 /**
    This method commits any active transaction.
    */
    public void method_C2 ()
       {
115   debugOut ("Entering method_C2");
      showStatus ();

      try
         {
120     debugOut ("Committing");
        UserTransaction ut = ctx.getUserTransaction ();
        ut.commit ();
        showStatus ();
        }
125   catch (Exception e)
         {
        debugOut (e.toString ());
        throw new EJBException (e);
        }
130
      debugOut ("Leaving method_C2");
      }
    }
```

Listing 9.8: **Implementation class for the bean-managed transaction demonstration. This class has two methods, `method_C1()` and `method_C2()`, that a client should call in sequence.**

```
    Transtest_C_Bean : setSessionContext ()
    Transtest_C_Bean : Dummy ejbCreate ()
    Transtest_C_Bean : Entering method_C1
    Transtest_C_Bean : Getting datasources
  5 Transtest_C_Bean : Status = idle
    Transtest_C_Bean : Opening connections
    Transtest_C_Bean : Status = idle
    Transtest_C_Bean : Beginning transaction
    Transtest_C_Bean : Status = active
 10 Transtest_C_Bean : Creating statements
    Transtest_C_Bean : Status = active
    Transtest_C_Bean : Executing updates
    Transtest_C_Bean : Status = active
    Transtest_C_Bean : Closing connections
 15 Transtest_C_Bean : Status = active
    Transtest_C_Bean : Leaving method_C1
    Transtest_C_Bean : Entering method_C2
    Transtest_C_Bean : Status = active
    Transtest_C_Bean : Committing
 20 Transtest_C_Bean : Status = idle
```

```
Transtest_C_Bean:  Leaving  method_C2
Transtest_C_Bean:  Dummy  ejbRemove()
```

Here are some important points to note about the behaviour of this EJB.

- On entry to `method_C1()`, the current transaction state is 'idle,' and it remains idle until the EJB calls `begin()` on the `UserTransaction()`. At this point the transaction becomes 'active.'

- When `method_C1()` exits, even though both database connections have been closed, the transaction remains active. *Nothing* is committed at this point. This means that when `method_C2()` is entered, the transaction state is still 'active.' When this method calls `getUserTransaction()` it is not starting a new transaction, it is merely getting a reference to the ongoing transaction for this thread of execution.

- As soon as the `commit()` method is called, the transaction state goes to 'idle.' At this point, we assume the transaction has been committed.

- In this simple example, we don't see any of the intermediate states between 'active' and 'committed,' because although the EJB opens two different data sources, they are in fact referencing the same database (*Cloudscape*, in this case). Thus the transaction is not distributed, and no resource managers[5] are involved.

> ### Hint
>
> If the method `method_C1()` had been called by an EJB that used container-managed transactions, and a transaction was already active, then the container would have to suspend that transaction before calling `method_C1()`, because only one transaction can be in effect at a time. In other words, when calling a method on a bean-managed-transaction EJB, the container suspends any existing transaction before entering the method.

9.6   Client-demarcated transactions

The *EJB Specification* [EJB2.0 17.2.4] makes provision for transactions to be demarcated by clients of EJBs that are not themselves EJBs. For the developer, the procedure is much the same as for bean-managed demarcation: The client gets a `UserTransaction` object and calls the `begin()`, `commit()`, and `rollback()` methods as required.

---

[5]For a definition of 'resource manager,' see hint on page 279.

The container makes the `UserTransaction` available through a JNDI lookup:[6]

```
Context  c  =  new  InitialContext ();
UserTransaction  ut  =  ( UserTransaction )
    c.lookup ("java :comp/UserTransaction");
```

The *EJB Specification* does not stipulate which kinds of EJB clients can de-marcate transactions. Most containers will only allow this for clients that run in the same application server environment (e.g., servlets, JSPs). Standalone clients using Java will not, in general, be able to manipulate the container's transaction (however, see [EJB2.0 19.6], which describes how CORBA clients can propagate a transaction to EJBs, and vice-versa).

In practice, there is rarely a good reason to use client transaction demarcation. We can usually avoid it by providing 'wrapper' methods in EJBs that encapsu-late the methods that the client wants to call as part of the same transaction. For example, suppose the client wants to call `method_A()` and `method_B()` in one transaction. We can simply provide a method (`method_C()`, for example) in the EJB that calls `method_A()` and `method_B()`. These will automatically be part of the same transaction, because the method calls to `method_A()` and `method_B()` are intra-EJB, not between EJBs. This works with both bean-managed demarcation and container-managed demarcation.

9.7   Handling transaction isolation in EJBs

We have discussed in some detail how the transaction boundaries are demarcated in EJBs. This takes care of the 'atomicity' requirements of transactions. We now have to deal with the 'isolation' requirements.

The important point is that isolation is handled by resource managers, not transaction managers.

Hint

What is a resource manager? Technically it is anything that con-trols the transactional state of a data repository. The term is often used as if it were a separate piece of software (which, of course, it could be), but in most cases, the resource manager is part of the functionality of the data source. Nevertheless, we speak of inter-actions with the 'resource manager' to reinforce the notion that we are carrying out 'metaoperations' on the data source, rather than reading or writing the data itself.

---

[6]This JNDI name is mandated in Version 2.0; prior to this it was at the container's discretion.

It is the job of the resource manager to consider the transactions it is being asked to take part in and isolate them appropriately. Therefore, there is in general no way for the EJB container to set isolation (but see below).

It is the EJB developer's responsibility to set the isolation level of each JDBC connection that it opens, unless the resource manager's default is to be accepted. The default is *usually* `TRANSACTION_READ_COMMITTED`, preventing dirty reads but not nonrepeatable reads or phantom reads. However, as an application developer, you may not know what database engine(s) will ultimately support your application, and in that case it may be safer to set the isolation level explicitly. If you want something other than the default, you will have to set it explicitly.

To set the isolation level, simply call `setTransactionIsolation()` on the database connection, like this:

```
Connection c = dataSource.getConnection();
c.setTransactionIsolation
  (Connection.TRANSACTION_SERIALIZABLE);
```

What could be simpler than this? The problem is—as it always is in EJB technology—a subtle one. When the EJB opens a database connection, it does so from a `DataSource`. It gets the `DataSource` from JNDI. If the application opens more than one connection in the same transaction, it has no way to know whether it is interacting with one resource manager or more: Remember that EJBs get `DataSource` references from a lookup of a `java:comp/env` name, which can be mapped in the deployment descriptor. During the development process, the connections used in the EJB may map onto the same physical host, while in production, multiple connections may target different hosts. So it would be very dangerous to set the isolation levels to be different on different database connections, because they *may* map onto the same physical connection. If they do, this will result in an attempt to change a resource manager's isolation level mid-transaction, which the resource manager will not handle with good grace. How can this happen in practice? Suppose we write an EJB method that carries out some operation on a particular database. It decides it wants level 3 isolation for this operation. This EJB method is called from another method that operates on what it thinks is a different database. The calling method has already set isolation level 1 on its connection. So long as these connections are on different resource managers, there is no difficulty. If, at deployment time, it turns out that the required database tables are actually on the same database, then the deployer will configure both EJBs to map onto the same database. Now we have two EJBs setting different isolation levels on the same resource manager.

In summary, you need to be very careful when setting isolation levels in EJBs. Ensure that all methods that will ever run as part of a single transaction all set the same isolation level.

The one time the container is able to set the isolation level is when using container-managed persistence in entity EJBs. Whether the developer has any control over this is at the discretion of the server vendor.

9.8   Distributed transactions and two-phase commit

In this section, we examine in detail the operation of a typical distributed transaction management system, particularly the 'two-phase commit' process. This information goes beyond what is required for EJB development. In fact, one of the benefits of EJB technology is that the transaction management infrastructure is completely invisible to the developer and can be configured at deployment time. This section is provided simply to demonstrate that there is no black magic in distributed transactions and to assist developers who are called upon to debug their applications in a production environment.

9.8.1   X/Open architecture

Nearly all distributed transaction managers and most database systems support the *X/Open Distributed Transaction Processing* architecture, often (wrongly) called the 'XA protocol.' The X/Open DTP architecture, in its most general form, is shown in Figure 9.1.

In the X/Open scheme, a *resource manager* is anything that is able to control a transactional resource and participate in a two-phase commit operation (see below). A relational database may itself be a resource manager, or, the resource manager may be a separate piece of software that communicates with its controlled resource. Specifically, in X/Open terms, a resource manager is anything that is prepared to implement the *XA interface* and respond to XA commands from the transaction

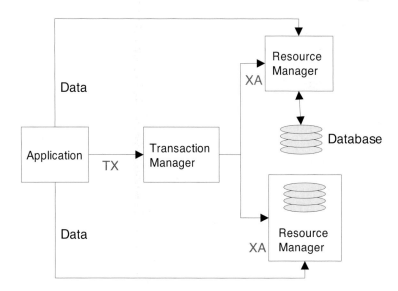

Figure 9.1. The X/Open DTP architecture in its most general form. In very large systems, multiple transaction managers can communicate by means of *communication resource managers* (not shown).

manager. In any event, the resource manager is usually tightly bound to the resource it controls and usually located on the same host system.

As well as receiving XA commands from the transaction manager, the resource manager will interact with the application. Of course, the X/Open architecture has nothing to say about this latter interaction: It depends on the type of resource (database, message queue, etc.) and the nature of the application.

A *transaction manager* is a piece of software or hardware that can co-ordinate the various resource managers. The application communicates with the transaction manager by means of its *TX interface*, described below.

In a very large system, multiple transaction managers can communicate via *communication resource managers*. The X/Open architecture also defines a scheme for interacting with another transaction management architecture, the *OSI Transaction Processing Service*.

9.8.2   X/Open interfaces

In the X/Open architecture, interaction between the resource managers, transaction manager, and applications is defined in terms of 'interfaces.' These interfaces are not Java interfaces, but they have a similar purpose. They are abstract definitions of the actions that one part of the system must be able to carry out on another. These definitions are in terms of function calls with arguments and return values. Obviously, we can't make function calls on relational databases. In most well-established database products, the interfaces are implemented in the form of C-language software libraries. The 'methods' in the TX interface are shown in Table 9.4, and the XA interface in Table 9.5. The way in which the methods in these interfaces are called in a typical transaction is described below. The other interfaces in the architecture will not be described here, as they are very unlikely to be of interest to EJB developers, or even to EJB container developers. These are *XA+*, which defines the interaction between transaction managers and communications resource managers, *CRM-OSI*, which defines the interaction between a communications resource manager and the OSI transaction service, and *TXRPC*, which defines interaction between different applications in the same global transaction.

9.8.3   Two-phase commit

When multiple databases are involved in a single transaction, all have to commit or roll back as a group. To manage this process, most transactional systems use a form of two-phase commit. Both phases are carried out when the application has finished all the transactional operations it intends to carry out, and has told the transaction manager to commit the transaction.

Phase 1

In the first phase, the transaction manager tells the resource managers to *prepare*. Preparation usually means carrying out the operations previously requested by the application, but in a way that could be reversed if necessary. This preparation phase can fail, for a variety of reasons; if it succeeds, we assume that there is no *logical*

tx_open	Initializes the transaction manager and indicates that it should enlist the appropriate resource managers.
tx_begin	Tells the transaction manager to start a new transaction.
tx_commit, tx_commit_return	Tells the transaction manager that it should attempt to commit the current transaction.
tx_rollback	Tells the transaction manager to roll back the current transaction.
tx_set_ transaction_control	Sets the transaction mode (chained, unchained).
tx_set_ transaction_timeout	Sets the time that will be allowed for the transaction to complete.
tx_txinfo	Asks the transaction manager for information about the current transaction.
tx_close	Closes the session with the transaction manager and delists[7] any associated resource managers.

Table 9.4. Methods of the X/Open TX interface.

reason for the changes to the data not to be made permanent. Resource managers communicate to the transaction manager whether the prepare operation succeeded, failed, or succeeded but no data was modified.

Phase 2

If any resource manager indicates that preparation succeeded, and that some data was modified, then the transaction manager will assume that it can now commit. If all resource managers indicate that preparation succeeded, then the transaction manager tells them to commit. This is the second phase. The transaction manager will log the fact that the transaction prepared successfully, in case something drastic happens while attempting the final commit.

If a resource manager indicates that preparation failed, the transaction manager will tell all the resource managers to abandon the current transaction, rolling back any operations carried out so far.

If any resource manager indicates that no data was modified, then the transaction manager does not have to tell that resource manager to commit or roll back.

---

[7]As well as the word 'rollback,' transaction management technology has given the English language the dubious benefit of the word 'delist' as the opposite of 'enlist.'

`xa_open`	Tells the resource manager to initialize itself. This method takes a vendor-specific string parameter (the `xa_open string`; see Section 9.8.4), which should provide all the information that the resource manager needs to initialize itself.
`xa_start`	Indicates that the resource manager should begin a new transaction and associate it with the transaction context supplied.
`xa_end`	Indicates that the specified transaction is complete or suspended, in the sense that any further interaction between the application and the resource manager is not to be considered part of the transaction.
`xa_prepare`	Tells the resource manager to prepare to commit the specified transaction. The resource manager should reply, indicating whether it can commit or not.
`xa_commit`	Tells the resource manager to commit the specified transaction. The transaction manager will not usually send this command unless all resource managers replied affirmatively to the `xa_prepare` command.
`xa_rollback`	Tells the resource manager to roll back the specified transaction.
`xa_close`	Indicates that the transaction manager has finished using the resource manager.
`xa_recover`	Tells the resource manager to return a list of 'in-doubt' transactions. The transaction manager will typically call this when initializing the resource manager, so that it knows whether the previous transactional operation succeeded or not. In normal circumstances, there will be no in-doubt transactions.
`xa_forget`	Tells the resource manager to forget (i.e., ignore) a transaction that was prepared but not committed. This is an alternative to committing or rolling back a transaction, only relevant for in-doubt transactions.

Table 9.5. Methods of the X/Open XA interface.

> ## Gotcha!
>
> Many newcomers to this subject are confused by the word 'prepare' here. This word gives the impression that we are telling the databases to 'prepare to commit,' and that the next stage will be to 'actually commit.' This then leads to the question: What if we successfully 'prepare to commit,' but then can't 'actually commit'? In reality, 'prepare' means 'make all changes permanent, but be prepared to roll back if I tell you to.' In other words, the 'prepare' phase does all the work, and the 'commit' instruction merely signals the data source that it can mark the transaction as complete and release its 'undo' information. This means that the likelihood of a failure between 'prepare' and 'commit' is very small.

Recovery and transaction manager logs

The two-phase commit process described above protects the application from any failure of any resource manager (database) at any point in the process. However, there is still a small period of vulnerability between the 'prepare' and the 'commit' phases. If the transaction manager (which may, as we have said, be part of the application server) fails between the prepare and the commit phases, then eventually the resource managers will time out any transactions that had been prepared. However, this may take several minutes, and in the meantime the transaction manager may have restarted. It will then have to 'recover' the transaction. Typically, a transaction manager will attempt at start-up to determine the list of in-doubt transactions and complete them. Some products give the administrator a way to select whether an in-doubt transaction should be commited or 'forgotten' (not commited).

The *J2EE Reference Implementation* has a fairly rudimentary recovery process, which is not enabled at all by default (see the configuration guide for information about enabling it. It does slow the start-up process considerably). If an in-doubt transaction is detected, then the transaction manager attempts to commit it, if a commit was scheduled, or roll it back, if the resource managers had not agreed to commit.

9.8.4   X/Open two-phase commit process

This section describes how the general two-phase commit process described above is implemented in the X/Open architecture. The operations listed below form a typical sequence, but there is some flexibility in the order in which they are applied. Remember that as far as an EJB system is concerned, the term 'application' here refers the EJB server, not the EJB itself.

- The application calls `tx_open()` on the transaction manager.

- The transaction manager calls `xa_open()` on the resource managers. Information passed in the `xa_open` string allows the resource manager to initialize itself.

- The application calls `tx_begin()` on the transaction manager.

- The transaction manager calls `xa_start()` on the resource managers. Resource managers now know that subsequent operations from the application are to be associated with a transaction. This is called *resource enlistment.*

- The application carries out whatever operations it wants in this transactional context. When all the transactional work has been done...

- The application calls `tx_commit()` on the transaction manager.

- The transaction manager calls `xa_end()` on the resource managers, indicating that any further interaction with the application is outside the scope of the transaction. This process is called *resource delistment* (the opposite of enlistment).

- The transaction manager calls `xa_prepare()` on each resource manager. Resource managers ensure that the operations carried out by the application in the previous transaction can be committed.

- If all resource managers respond to indicate success, then the transaction manager calls `xa_commit()` on each resource manager. Otherwise, it calls `xa_rollback()` on them. Resource managers that indicated that no data was modified are excluded from commit or rollback.

- The application calls `tx_close()` on the transaction manager.

9.8.5   The `xa_open()` string

When the transaction manager calls `xa_open` on the resource manager, it provides a configuration string. The contents of this string are supplied—directly or indirectly—by the application to the transaction manager. This string (often called the 'open string') has a format set by the database vendor, and supplies information relevant to that vendor's product. Typically, you will need to supply some user authentication and timeout information, and you may need to specify explicitly which database will be involved.

There is, in general, no way to guess the correct format of the `xa_open` string, and this operation needs to be carried out in conjunction with the database product documentation and the database administrator. When setting up a database for distributed transactions, the administrator will normally have to create tables to contain details of pending transactions and set the access rights appropriately.

In EJB development, EJBs should never have to supply the `xa_open` string; it is the EJB server that does this. You (or someone else) may have to supply it when configuring the EJB server, but JDBC drivers may supply defaults.

Gotcha!

In previous versions of the *J2EE Reference Implementation*, it was possible to carry out operations against multiple data-sources (which could be heterogenous—e.g., messaging services and databases) without using XA-compliant drivers. It was never clear how this could be done safely, and in the latest version of the Reference Implementation, this 'feature' has been re-moved. Now if you want a transaction to encompass multiple databases you *must* use XA drivers. Failure to do so leads to an `IllegalStateException` when opening the second connection. The `cloudscape` database supplied with the product does have both XA and non-XA drivers. For the *Prestige Bike Hire* applica-tion, it is important that the XA driver is used, as this application uses distributed transactions.

9.8.6   The Java Transaction API

The Java Transaction API (JTA) is a specification for mapping an X/Open-compliant transaction manager into the Java domain. That is, it defines a Java interface corresponding to the X/Open XA interface and a set of interfaces that map to the TX interface. The reason that there is not one single mapping to the TX interface is that JTA recognizes the different roles played in transaction control by an application component (like an EJB) and an application server (like an EJB server).

The XA interface is modelled in JTA as the `javax.transaction.xa.XAResource` interface. Java interfaces to resource managers are responsible for providing an im-plementation of `XAResource`. In JTA terminology, the entity that provides this im-plementation is called the *resource adapter*. Any Java interface to anything can be a resource adapter, provided that it can provide an implementation of `XAResource`. There are at present only two types of resource adapter with specified behaviour in the J2EE API: JDBC database connections and JMS messaging connections that implement the optional XA support.[8]

The TX interface is represented most completely by `javax.transaction.TransactionManager`; however, there are some significant differences. First, JTA uses separate `Transaction` instances to represent the transactions in progress on the transaction manager, rather than numeric IDs. Second, JTA defines a class `UserTransaction` (which we have already seen) that gives an application access to a subset of the transaction manager's facilities. In an application server, it is the server's job to create transactions and enlist resources; all the application can do is begin, commit, or roll back transactions.

---

[8] The J2EE connector API (Chapter 18) specifies a method by which arbitrary resource adapters can be developed and installed.

A complete discussion of JTA is beyond the scope of this book: Full details are provided in the *JTA Specification*, currently Version 1.0.1, available from `java.sun.com/products/jta`

9.8.7 JTA in EJB servers

In the X/Open architecture, the interaction between the 'application' and the transaction manager is relatively complex, as it includes notification of the resources to be enlisted, and the methods require transaction context IDs so that the transaction manager can distinguish requests from different applications.

In an application server-based system, the application server should conceal these details from the applications it serves. In an EJB system, for example, we would not want EJBs to have to manipulate transaction IDs. JTA distinguishes between the access required to the transaction manager from an application server and from a supported application. In addition, it defines an object `Transaction` to encapsulate information about a particular transaction, so neither client has to deal with transaction IDs explicitly.

A JTA-compliant transaction manager implements three important interfaces that allow applications to control and monitor it.

javax.transaction.TransactionManager This interface provides generic access to the transaction manager, and allows new transactions to be created and controlled. This interface is used by the EJB server to create new transactions, using the `begin()` method, which returns a `Transaction` object that represents the new transaction.

javax.transaction.Transaction This interface represents a particular transaction, out of the many that the transaction manager may be handling at any time.

javax.transaction.UserTransaction This interface provides methods that demarcate a transaction (begin, commit, and rollback). The EJB server will make available to each EJB an object that implements this interface. When the EJB calls methods on it, these are typically translated into method calls on the `Transaction` object that represents that EJB's transaction.

In EJB systems, it is the EJB container (or server) that is responsible for managing distributed transactions. The EJB container must make available to the EJBs an object that implements `UserTransaction`. However, the EJB itself sees no other part of the JTA. The EJB server is not required to implement the other JTA interfaces and does not have to use the `XAResource` interface for communicating with resource managers. Many EJB servers provide their own transaction infrastructure with their own database drivers.

One final note: Java developers are often confused about the relationship between the Java Transaction API and the Java Transaction Service (JTS). JTA is simply an API; `javax.transaction` contains no classes. JTS is an interface between

JTA and a transaction service that implements CORBA's *Object Transaction Service* (OTS). An EJB container may use an OTS implementation as part of its internal structure, but it doesn't have to. The *EJB Specification* [EJB2.0 17.1.3] makes it clear that EJB developers should not assume that the container implements JTS.

9.9 Summary

We have seen how important transaction management is to many applications, and how the application, EJB server, and transaction manager work together to co-ordinate complex distributed transactions. For the developer, the important issue is to decide where the transaction boundaries lie, and whether to demarcate these boundaries using API calls or transaction attributes. Both methods have their strengths and weaknesses.

Chapter 10

Messaging and message-driven EJBs

Overview

Message-driven EJBs are new in Version 2.0 of the *EJB Specification*. This chapter begins with a discussion of enterprise messaging in general, with a particular focus on the practical benefits of this technology. We then discuss the JMS specification and the general procedures for sending messages using the JMS API. This leads to a discussion of the problems of asynchronous communicaton in the EJB architecture, which is essentially a request-response system, and how the use of message-driven EJBs can help in development of asynchronous services. We then discuss the development and use of message-driven EJBs themselves, illustrated by examples from the *Prestige Bike Hire* application.

10.1 Overview of enterprise messaging

This section explains the meaning of 'enterprise messaging' and describes typical messaging strategies. We then discuss some essential features of enterprise messaging, like reliability and transaction management.

10.1.1 What is messaging?

The term 'messaging' is used to describe any scheme that allows computer applications to exchange data in a way that is loosely coupled[1] and (usually) asynchronous. The use of messaging has a number of important benefits over other forms of distributed programming, like RMI.

---

[1] 'Loose coupling' is a general software engineering term that describes systems whose components have minimal interdependence.

- Messages are not associated with any particular programming language; if they are in a well-understood format like plain text or XML, even widely different applications can be integrated.

- The asynchronous nature of messaging provides greater overall throughput, because faster parts of the system are not held up in waiting for responses from slower parts. Messaging products buffer messages until they can be processed.

- Many legacy mainframe applications were designed to process data offline in batches. Such systems can readily be adapted to accept data from messaging systems. For example, IBM's *MQSeries* messaging product can be integrated with almost any software on any platform, including most of its mainframe range. Thus IBM mainframe applications can readily be adapted to accept batch jobs from a messaging service.

- As well as supporting batch processing, the asynchronous nature of messaging prevents a distributed system from becoming unavailable merely because one part of it is unavailable.

- The loose coupling leads to easier maintenance, as the interface between any two application components is defined completely in terms of the message format. This makes it more straightforward than would otherwise be the case to change a component of the system without affecting other components.

An 'enterprise' messaging service is one that provides mechanisms for reliable delivery, transaction management, security, scalability, and fault tolerance (of which, more later).

It is only fair to point out that messaging has some disadvantages as well.

- Messaging interactions are typically more difficult to implement than RMI interactions, because of the additional processing involved. Using a messaging format, like XML, for which well-established parsers are available overcomes this problem to an extent, but...

- The use of message formats that appear to be cross-platform does encourage subtle problems in data conversion. For example, if I represent the amount of currency $3.21 as the string of characters '3.21', and this has to be converted to and from each participant system's native floating-point representation, we could end up with subtle differences in each amount.

- Messaging has to be supported by additional server infrastructure.

- Messaging systems do not allow transactional context to be passed from component to component, unlike RMI.

Enterprise messaging is *not* email, even though some vendors of email systems refer to them as messaging services. There is, however, clearly an overlap in the functionality of email systems and messaging systems, and a general purpose messaging product could, no doubt, be used to support an email service. The endpoints of email systems tend to be end-users' mailboxes, whereas the endpoints of enterprise messaging systems are usually applications or application components.

> ## Gotcha!
>
> If you are buying or specifying a messaging product for the type of application described in this chapter, ensure that you are getting something suitable. Vendors do not always name their products in a way that makes them easy to distinguish. For example, in Sun Microsystems's product range there is a 'Sun ONE messaging server'—which is an email product—and a 'Sun ONE message queue'—which is an application messaging product. Similar names do not denote similar products in this case.

Java Message Service (JMS) is a specification for a messaging service to make its service available to Java applications. The JMS API is a set of Java interfaces that the developer can assume have been implemented by the messaging vendor.

10.1.2   Messaging strategies

The simplest messaging strategy—and the most widely used—is the asynchronous queue (Figure 10.1). This is also known as *first in, first out* messaging, because messages are delivered in the order they were sent.[2] Application 1 (the *producer*) delivers a message to a named queue in the messaging service; this is called a *send* or *put* operation. At some later stage, application 2 (the *consumer*) picks up the message (a *receive* or *get* operation). If the messaging strategy allows only one consumer per message, it is usually called a *point-to-point* system.

The point-to-point architecture should be familiar: It underlies many standard computing services, such as printer queuing, email, and input/output buffering. The queue to which the message is sent by the consumer is called the *destination*; it is important to understand that the term 'destination' does *not* refer to the final consumer of the message. A producer produces messages to the *queue*, not to the consumer. This has important implications for transaction management, as we shall see.

In addition to queue-based messaging, many systems support *publish-subscribe* messaging (Figure 10.2), often abbreviated to 'pub-sub' or 'PubSub.'

In this architecture, multiple consumers can retrieve each message. The message destination is typically called a *topic*, rather than a queue, because publish-subscribe systems do not normally allow queuing. Usually, each new message overwrites any existing data in the topic.[3]

---

[2]But see the discussion of priorities below.

[3]But see the discussion of a 'durable subscription' below.

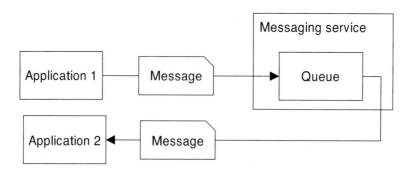

Figure 10.1. The concept of a message queue: Application 1 puts messages into the queue, allowing application 2 to retrieve them. Application 1 and application 2 are asynchronous with respect to one another.

Most messaging services allow the message producer to specify the priority of a particular message. The service will usually attempt to deliver the high-priority messages before the low-priority ones, rather than following a strict first in, first out protocol. Within a particular priority level, however, the messages will still be delivered in order or production.

Although it is possible to envisage other types of messaging, the point-to-point and publish-subscribe architectures are the most widely used, and it is these that are supported by the JMS API.

10.1.3   Reliability and durability

An enterprise messaging system must usually do more than make a 'best effort' at delivery of messages. It should be able to offer some guarantee of successful delivery. As a minimum, it should be able to survive a server crash without losing undelivered messages. A system that offers some guarantee of delivery is referred to as *reliable*; there are, of course, different degrees of reliability.

The most widely used reliability mechanism is to use persistent storage to hold messages until they are successfully delivered. While a messaging service may use any form of persistent storage (a disk file, for example), the majority use tables in a relational database.

The use of persistent storage only guarantees producer-to-service delivery; it does not ensure delivery from the messaging service to the consumer. The only way to achieve this level of reliability is for the consumer to acknowledge receipt of each message, and the service to relay the acknowledgment back to the producer. The developer should bear in mind, however, that insisting on this level of reliability increases the coupling between producer and consumer and reduces the effectiveness of messaging as an asynchronous service.

Most messaging products allow the message producer to stipulate the degree of reliability required, because in general an increase in reliability corresponds to a decrease in throughput. Some applications may require speed in preference to

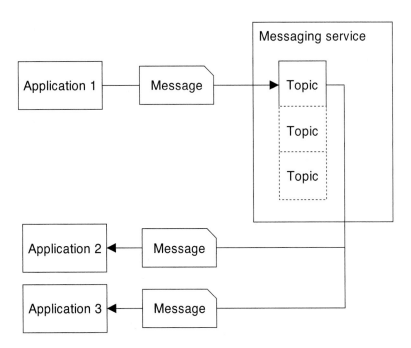

Figure 10.2. The concept of publish-subscribe messaging: Application 1 puts messages into the topic, allowing any number of subscribers to retrieve them. Typically, the subscribers expect to receive notification of new messages from the service, rather than to block until messages arrive. The JMS Specification supports both blocking and nonblocking operations.

reliability. Even if persistent storage is used, a message producer will usually be able to stipulate the length of time for which the service will continue to attempt to deliver the message. After this timeout period has expired, the message will be discarded.

Reliability is easy to define (if not to implement) for queue-based messaging, as there is typically one consumer per message on a given queue. For publish-subscribe messaging, however, the semantics of reliability is much more complex. For example, if the number of consumers is unknown by the producer, how many consumers have to acknowledge receipt of the message for the consumer to be able to assume a successful delivery? Different service vendors will have their own ways of dealing with issues like this. Moreover, the use of transactional messaging tends to prevent acknowledgment being used at all, as will be discussed.

Please note that 'reliable' here does not mean the same as 'robust' or 'fault tolerant.' Of course a messaging service should be robust as well as offering guaranteed delivery, but these are different issues. Fault tolerance is discussed later.

10.1.4   Distributed messaging

In practice, enterprise messaging systems are distributed, in the sense that messages may be produced by one server and consumed at another. The messaging infrastructure provides facilities for forwarding the messages between servers; the usual term for the interqueue communication is a *message channel* (see Figure 10.3).

10.1.5   Transaction support

Messaging services typically allow the sending and receipt of messages to be transactional. However, transaction scope does not usually encompass both sending and receiving in a single transaction, as we shall see.

Transactional production

The messaging service does not necessarily allow the producer's messages to be dispatched to the consumer as soon as they are delivered. In practice, messaging is transactional: The sender can group a series of messages into a transaction and insist that either all messages are enqueued successfully or none are. Typically, when then the producer commits the transaction, the service makes the messages available to consumers. If it can't do this, it will roll back the transaction and remove all messages that were produced in that transaction. In addition, the client can roll back a transaction and cause the messaging service to remove all messages sent until that point.

Transactional consumption

A message consumer can retrieve a number of messages as part of a transaction. If all messages are retrieved successfully, the transaction is considered to be committed. If any retrieval fails, then the messages remain in the queue or topic, and can be retrieved again later. In other words, the message service does not discard messages that are retrieved transactionally until the transaction commits. If the retrieval fails, the application is responsible for discarding the messages it received up until the failure point, as these messages will be retained in the queue or topic.

Transaction scope

It is possible to envisage two levels of transaction scope in a messaging system: client-to-server and client-to-client (Figure 10.4).

Consider a simple example, where the producer dispatches three messages to the service, and these three messages are picked up by the same consumer.

With client-to-server scope (Figure 10.4a), the producer's transaction is complete when it has successfully delivered the three messages to the messaging service. If the service is reliable (in the sense described above), then the producer can reasonably assume that the service will attempt to deliver the messages to the consumer. However, the producer has no way of knowing that the consumer retrieved the messages, or that it was able to process them successfully. For the consumer, its transaction is complete when it has been able to retrieve the three messages

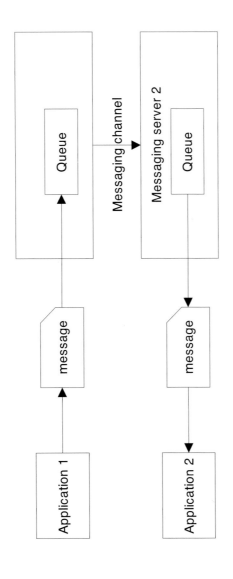

Figure 10.3. Distributed messaging using queues: Application 1 queues messages on messaging server 1, which forwards them to messaging server 2, where they are picked up by application 2.

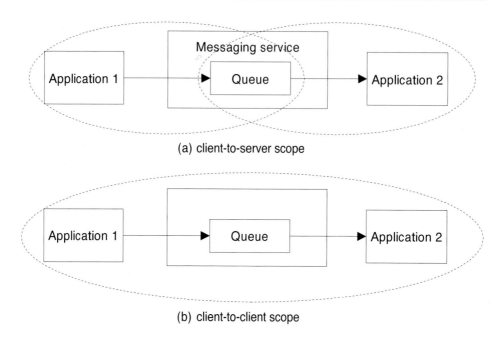

(a) client-to-server scope

(b) client-to-client scope

Figure 10.4. Two levels of transaction scope in a messaging application. (a) A transaction encompasses the interaction between each messaging client (application) and the service. There is loose coupling between applications. (b) The transaction encompasses both applications. They are tightly coupled.

successfully. If the retrieval of, say, the third message failed, then all three messages are retained by the messaging service so that the consumer can retry the retrieval later. Whether the retrieval is successful or not, the consumer has no way to prevent the producer's transaction being committed.

With client-to-client transaction scope (Figure 10.4b), the transaction encompasses both producer and consumer. The producer's transaction cannot be committed until all three messages have been accepted and processed by the consumer, which then acknowledges this fact. The consumer's transaction cannot be committed until the producer has committed, as a rollback on the producer must propagate a rollback to the consumer. It should be obvious that the transactional interactions are likely to be very complex, particularly if the producer's transaction is part of a broader, global transaction. The messaging service cannot adopt the simple strategy of waiting until the producer has committed before releasing messages to the consumer (as most products do), as the consumer would then be *unable* to roll back the producer (it is too late). In any event, having the producer and consumer as tightly coupled as this negates the benefits of asynchronous messaging. For these reasons, client-to-client transaction scope is not widely used, and there is no support for it in the JMS API [JMS1.0.2 8.5].

10.1.6   Security

Clearly, the messaging service must impose some restrictions on which applications are able to send messages to it, particularly if any part of it is accessible to the Internet. Otherwise, there would be nothing to prevent an unauthorized individual from dispatching messages and bypassing the application-level security. This would be exceedingly dangerous in a financial system if messages could bring about, for example, arbitrary funds transfers. Typically, the service will expect its clients to present a signed digital certificate to identify themselves, which has the additional benefit of reducing the likelihood that the message has been tampered with in transit.

In addition, messages may well contain confidential data; the messaging service will probably provide some form of public-key cryptography to prevent unauthorized access to this data.

Currently all messaging vendors implement security differently.

10.1.7   Scalability and fault tolerance

If messaging provides a large part of the infrastructure of an enterprise application, the message volume is likely to be large. When combined with the requirement to use persistent storage, this is likely to lead to a significant load on the server. Ideally, it should be possible to deal with an increasing load simply by adding more servers. Moreover, if a messaging system is central to an enterprise, we probably want to ensure its constant availability. Both requirements can be met by the use of load-sharing schemes, which distribute messages among a number of different servers, so that each receives a portion of the total load. If one server fails, its load can be picked up by the remaining servers, albeit at reduced efficiency. Not all messaging products support load sharing, and those that do use widely different schemes to provide it.

10.2   The JMS API

This section provides an overview of the JMS API. It is impossible to describe the whole API in detail here: A whole book would be required. What follows is the minimum information required to begin writing EJB applications that use messaging services.

The Java Message Service (JMS) API supports the basic features of point-to-point (queue-based) and publish-subscribe (topic-based) messaging. A Java application that uses this API should be able to interact with a messaging service in a vendor-independent manor. The API is defined in a set of Java interfaces; JMS services supply Java platform classes that implement these interfaces and that communicate with their messaging products (Figure 10.5).

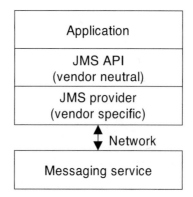

Figure 10.5. Basic architecture of a JMS application.

10.2.1   JMS terminology

Before discussing the API in detail, we need to introduce some terms that are used in the JMS documentation and whose sense may differ from the usual meaning.

Domain The *JMS Specification* uses the term 'domain' to mean the messaging strategy: point-to-point or publish-subscribe. It has no connection with network (e.g., DNS or NIS) domains [JMS1.0.2 1.2.3.3].

Session A session is a set of interactions between the Java application and the messaging service that together constitute a transaction. The `Session` object also acts as a factory for message objects and for producer and consumer objects for a particular transaction (this is illustrated in more detail below).

Connection A logical connection between the application and the messaging service; several sessions (transactions) may occur within one connection.

Administered object, destination Both these terms are used to describe the queues or topics to which messages are dispatched or retrieved. Note that a destination is *not* a consumer. JMS does not define the semantics of client-to-client messaging, only the interaction between the clients and the messaging service.

Produce, send, publish To 'produce' is to place a message into a queue or topic. 'Production' is the general term for any messaging operation that provides new data. Adding new messages to a queue is normally referred to as 'sending,' while for a topic it is 'publishing.'

Consume, receive, subscribe To 'consume' or 'receive' is to remove messages from a queue or topic. To be able to consume from a topic, the client must first 'subscribe.' Subscription may be durable or nondurable, as discussed below.

10.2.2 JMS domains

The *JMS Specification* formally defines two messaging domains: point-to-point and publish-subscribe. However, there are two different types of publish-subscribe: durable and nondurable. These are sufficiently different as to require separate discussions.

JMS point-to-point

In JMS, point-to-point messaging is based on queues; there can be any number of queues, and any client can produce a message to the queue. However, each message can only be consumed by one client. The messages can be persistent or nonpersistent.

JMS publish-subscribe (nondurable)

Nondurable publish-subscribe allows any number of clients (subscribers) to retrieve each message, but messages are available only during the time for which the subscriber is active. If a subscriber is not connected, it will miss any messages supplied in its absence.

JMS publish-subscribe (durable)

With durable publish-subscribe, any number of clients can retrieve each message, and messages are retained on behalf of clients that are not available at the time the message was produced. Thus durable publish-subscribe combines the features of topic-based and queue-based messaging.

Table 10.1 shows a summary of the properties of these three messaging types.

Domain	Point-to-point	Publish-subscribe (durable)	Publish-subscribe (non-durable)
Producer-consumer relationship	one-to-one	one-to-many	one-to-many
May use persistent storage?	yes	yes	yes
May use volatile storage?	yes	yes	yes
Messages retained while consumer inactive?	yes	yes	no

Table 10.1. Comparison of point-to-point, publish-subscribe (nondurable), and publish-subscribe (durable) messaging in JMS.

10.2.3   Using the JMS API

The JMS API is complicated by the fact that there are three complete sets of interfaces: a set for point-to-point messaging, a set for publish-subscribe messaging, and abstract superinterfaces for both these sets. There is almost a one-to-one correspondence between the interfaces in these sets, and the API can be understood by examining just one of them.

Figure 10.6 shows the interactions between the objects that a JMS application uses; this diagram shows the 'abstract' interfaces that apply both to queue-based and topic-based messaging. We will examine a code example later that uses queue-based messaging specifically.

To use the JMS API, an application proceeds as follows (numbers relate to number on the interaction diagram).

1, 2. Use a JNDI lookup to get a reference to the connection factory and the destination (queue or topic). In an EJB, this lookup must be done via the container and be in the `java:comp/env` namespace. A standalone application uses the

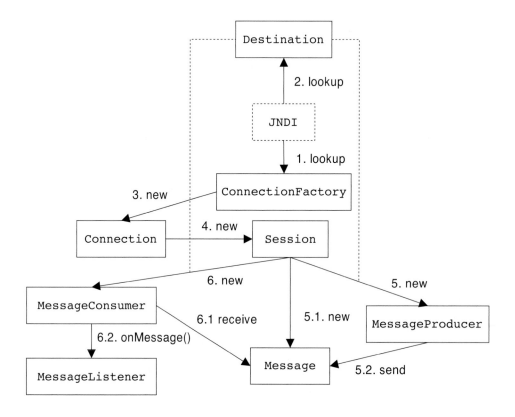

Figure 10.6. Essential interfaces of the JMS API ('JNDI' is shown in dotted lines because it is not part of the JMS API).

real JNDI names, but must be prepared to tell JNDI the location of the naming service.

3. The `ConnectionFactory` creates a new `Connection`. This represents a connection to the messaging service, perhaps across a network.

4. The `Connection` object creates one or more `Session` objects. Each `Session` represents a messaging transaction, and can consist of a number of produce or consume operations.

5. If this application wishes to produce (send) messages, it uses the `Session` object to create a `MessageProducer`, based on the `Destination` retrieved earlier from JNDI.

    5.1. The `Session` object creates one or more messages, whose type and contents are specified by the application.

    5.2. The `MessageProducer` object sends these messages to the messaging service.

6. If this application wishes to consume (receive) messages, it uses the `Session` object to create a `MessageConsumer`, based on the `Destination` retrieved earlier from JNDI. It can then use blocking or nonblocking calls to receive messages.

    6.1. If the application is prepared to wait for a message to become available, it simply calls a `receive` method on the `MessageConsumer`. This call blocks until a message is available.

    6.2. Alternatively, the application can register a `MessageListener`, and the `MessageProducer` will call its `onMessage()` method when each new message arrives.

After completing the messaging operation, the application should close any open sessions and connections.

10.2.4   Reliability and acknowledgment

In JMS, messaging is persistent by default. That is, the messaging service will use persistent storage for messages (if it can). This can be overridden either for a `MessageProducer`—which affects all messages sent with that producer—or at the message level. If persistent storage is used, the JMS client may wish to call the method `MessageProducer.setTimeToLive()` to set the timeout interval. This informs the messaging service that it can destroy the message if it has not been consumed within this time.

JMS supports four types of acknowledgment, one of which can be selected at the session level by setting the appropriate flag in the `QueueConnection.create` `QueueSession()` or `TopicConnection.createTopicSession()` methods.

Acknowledgment by commit This is the only kind of acknowledgment permitted in a transactional messaging session. The message is considered to be acknowledged when the producer's transaction commits. This issue is discussed in more detail below.

Automatic acknowledgment (AUTO_ACKNOWLEDGE) A message is considered to be acknowledged when the consumer has received it (that is, its `Message Consumer.receive()` or `MessageListener.onMessage()` method has returned successfully). No special action is required of the consumer; simply getting the message constitutes an acknowledgment. Note that the messaging service will typically attempt to redeliver a message if it is negatively acknowledged—for example, if `onMessage()` throws a runtime exception.

Client acknowledgment (CLIENT_ACKNOWLEDGE) The client must specifically acknowledge the message by calling the `acknowledge()` method on the `Message` object.

Lazy acknowledgment (DUPS_OK_ACKNOWLEDGE) Essentially the messaging service acknowledges messages as soon as they are made available to consumers. The name reflects the fact that this does not prevent the delivery of duplicate messages if the service fails and restarts.

10.2.5　Message types

In JMS, a `Message` consists of a header and a body. The header is composed of a number of properties (name-value pairs). An application can create a `Message Selector` to filter messages based on the contents of these properties. The API defines subtypes of these messages for different types of body. Of these, the `Text Message` is likely to be the most useful. This can store a plain (Unicode) string, a special case of which is an XML document.

The use of message selectors and headers is outside the scope of this book. See the *JMS Specification* for more details.

10.2.6　Transactions in JMS

JMS-compatible messaging services can participate in both 'local' and 'distributed' transactions, where these terms have essentially the same meaning as they do in JDBC. A transaction is a group of message dispatches or retrievals that must succeed or fail as a unit. Remember that transactions take effect between the application and the messaging service, not between applications.

Local transactions

Local transactions are controlled by the `Session` object (`QueueSession` for queues, `TopicSession` for topics). A transactional session is created by specifying the appropriate flag to the method `QueueConnection.createQueueSession()` or `Topic Connection.createTopicSession()`. If a session is transactional, there is no explicit 'begin' method; a transaction begins when the session is created and extends until it is either committed or rolled back. This automatically starts the next transaction. In effect, therefore, a transactional session is always in some transactional context.

> ## Gotcha!
>
> The use of transactional message production is not compatible with client acknowledgment in JMS applications. This is because the messages do not become available to the client until the producer has committed its transaction. After committal, the transaction cannot roll back (by definition), so it is too late for a consumer's negative acknowledgment to affect the producer's transaction. If the producer asks for a transactional session, the acknowledgment mode is ignored.

Distributed transactions

Distributed transactions will be co-ordinated by a transaction manager. The application will control transactions through JTA methods (page 287), so the use of the methods `Session.commit()` and `Session.rollback()` is forbidden. Messaging operations can be combined with database transactions in a single transaction.

10.2.7   Messaging features not defined in JMS

The following features of messaging products are not defined in the Specification.

Encryption The *JMS Specification* assumes that the messaging service can encrypt messages for security, but this has no implication for applications that use the service. The messaging service is expected to apply or co-ordinate encryption in a way that makes it transparent to the application developer.

Access control The *JMS Specification* considers this to be an administrative issue; the messaging services will undoubtedly provide some form of access control, but this should be transparent to the application developer.

Load sharing There is no provision for controlling this programmatically, but this does not prevent it from being used, of course.

Administration of queues and topics JMS does not define a way for applications to create new named queues or topics, although this feature might be useful. The variety of methods that messaging service vendors use to implement destination management makes it difficult to standardize it in the API.

10.3   JMS and EJBs

An EJB application can interact with a messaging service in either or both of the
following two ways.

- EJBs can send messages to queues or publish to topics in exactly the same
  way as standalone JMS clients. Ideally, the EJB will be able to locate queues
  and connection factories by making JNDI `lookup()` calls on the container's
  default `InitialContext()`. However, at present not all containers support
  JMS directly, and the EJB may need to specify the initial naming factory and
  URL explicitly (as described on page 204).

- Message-driven EJBs can receive messages from queues or topics (since
  EJB2.0). This is the only way that EJBs can receive messages: They can't
  create `MessageConsumer` objects directly.[4] Why is this? The problem is that
  the message consumer must either block until a message arrives or instantiate
  a new thread to monitor message arrival. The first approach is unacceptable
  to clients, and the second is forbidden by the EJB container.

In an EJB application, JMS transactions will be under the control of the container's transaction manager, so both the transaction attribute and acknowledgment
attribute of the `createQueueSession()` and `createTopicSession()` methods will
be ignored.

Before describing messaging in EJB applications in more details, we will elaborate how the *Prestige Bike Hire* application uses messaging to communicate with a
legacy system.

10.4   Interlude: messaging in the *Prestige Bike Hire* application

The *Prestige Bike Hire* application uses messaging to communicate with a financial service. This is a legacy system that maintains customer accounts and does
electronic funds transfers from credit card providers. The details of the this system
are not important to the developers of the application; all we need to know is the
format of the messages it sends and receives (this was described on page 118).

The financial service can only accept new jobs when it is not processing existing
jobs; typically, there is a period of two hours every day when new jobs can be sent.
This means that the application must store charges locally before dispatching them
in batches.

When a customer makes a reservation for a rental vehicle, an instance of the
`Booking` is created to reflect this, and the fact that confirmation is pending. The
application uses the `LegacyMessager` EJB to format a message and dispatch it to a
queue known to the application server as `jms/financialtransactionqueue`. The
legacy system processes the message, and returns an acknowledgement by way of
the queue `jms/financialresponsequeue`. This queue is 'connected' to a message-
driven EJB `LegacyReceiver`, which 'closes the loop.' These interactions are summarized in Figure 10.7.

---

[4]Some containers may allow this, but it will be nonportable.

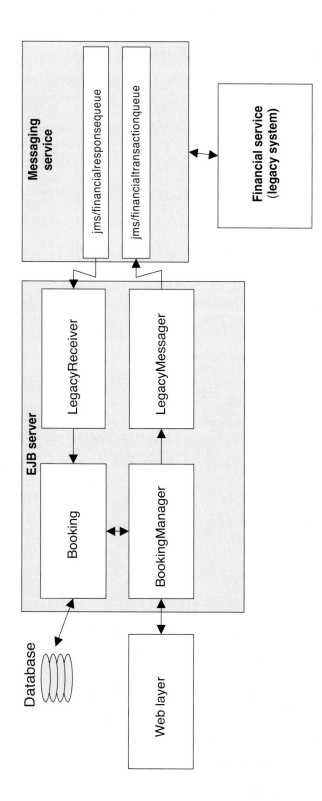

Figure 10.7. Messaging in the *Prestige Bike Hire* application.

10.5   Sending messages from EJBs

The process of sending JMS messages from an EJB will be illustrated using the example of `LegacyMessager` from the *Prestige Bike Hire* application. This EJB has one exposed method: `dispatchToQueue()`, which takes as arguments information about the customer (including credit card details) and the amount of money to be charged. This method is called by `makeReservation()` in the `BookingManager` EJB when the customer makes a reservation. This latter method also creates an instance of `Booking` to represent a new booking.

Note that the update of the database (that is, creating a `Booking` EJB) and the delivery of the message to the queue constitute a transaction. If the message can't be delivered, we want the database to be rolled back to the state it had before the reservation was made. Similarly, if the database can't be updated, we need to withdraw the messaging operation. The client will then have the opportunity to retry the reservation at a later time when—we hope—the problem has been resolved. This situation is handled very simply by ensuring that the `makeReservation()` method has the transaction attribute `Requires`.

This example assumes that the EJB container has built-in support for JMS. All EJB 2.0 containers will have such support, but earlier containers may require that the `InitialContext` for the JNDI lookup be supplied with configuration data that allows the messaging service to be located.

10.5.1   The LegacyMessager EJB

Listing 10.1 shows the implementation class of the `LegacyMessager` EJB. The JMS messaging operations are performed in the `dispatchToQueue()` method. To send a message using JMS from within an EJB, we proceed as follows.

Listing 10.1: **Implementation class of the `ChargeDispatcher` EJB.**

```
     package com.kevinboone.bikehire.ejb;
     import com.kevinboone.bikehire.utils.*;
     import javax.ejb.*;
     import javax.jms.*;
   5 import javax.naming.*;
     import java.rmi.*;
     import java.util.*;

     /**
  10 Implementation class for the 'LegacyMessager' EJB
     (c)2002 Kevin Boone
     */
     public class LegacyMessagerBean
        extends GenericStatelessSessionBean
  15 {
     protected QueueConnectionFactory qcf;
     protected Queue q;

     public void setSessionContext (SessionContext sc)
  20    {
        super.setSessionContext(sc);
```

```
     try
     {
       InitialContext  c = new InitialContext();
25
       // Get a connection factory, but _not_ a connection
       qcf = (QueueConnectionFactory)c.lookup
           ("java:comp/env/jms/qcf");

30     // Get a queue reference
       q = (Queue) c.lookup
           ("java:comp/env/jms/outgoing");

       debugOut ("Initialized QueueConnectionFactory and Queue");
35     }
     catch (NamingException e)
     {
       if (debug)
         debugOut ("Caught exception in setSessionContext():" + e);
40     throw new EJBException (e);
     }
   }


   /**
45 Dispatch a credit card transaction request to the
   off-line system via a message queue. Note that the
   off-line system cares about the customer name and
   customer address, etc., but not about our customer
   ID or start date of rental. These are supplied so
50 that they can be echoed back to the application
   in the acknowledgement.
   */
   public void dispatchToQueue (final int customerId,
       final String customerName,
55     final String address, final String cardNumber,
       final int cardType, final Date startDate, final int cost)
     throws MessagerException
   {
     debugOut ("Entering dispatchToQueue");
60
     // We will build the message in a StringBuffer because
     //   it is less CPU-costly than concatenating Strings
     StringBuffer sb = new StringBuffer();
     sb.append ("our_ref=");
65   sb.append(customerId + "/" + startDate.getTime());
     sb.append("\n");
     sb.append ("name=");
     sb.append(customerName);
     sb.append("\n");
70   sb.append ("address=");
     sb.append(address);
     sb.append("\n");
     sb.append ("card_number=");
     sb.append(cardNumber);
75   sb.append("\n");
     sb.append ("card_type=");
     sb.append(CustomerData.creditCardTypeToString(cardType));
     sb.append("\n");
     sb.append ("cost=");
80   sb.append(cost);
     sb.append("\n");
```

```
       debugOut ("message:");
       String message = new String (sb);
85     debugOut (message);

       try
       {
           // Create a connection to the messaging service
90         debugOut ("Creating queue connection");
           QueueConnection qc = qcf.createQueueConnection();

           // The arguments to createQueueSession are ignored
           // in EJBs; the container manages transactions
95         debugOut ("Creating queue session");
           QueueSession qs = qc.createQueueSession(true, 0);

           // Create a sender from the session
           debugOut ("Creating queue sender");
100        QueueSender qsender = qs.createSender (q);

           // Create a message from the session
           TextMessage tm = qs.createTextMessage (message);

105        // Send the message
           debugOut ("Sending");
           qsender.send(tm);
           debugOut ("Dispatched message");

110        qc.close();

           debugOut ("Leaving dispatchToQueue");
       }
       catch (JMSException e)
115    {
           debugOut ("Caught exception in dispatchToQueue");
           e.printStackTrace();
           throw new MessagerException
               ("Can't dispatch message: " + e.getMessage());
120    }
       }
}
```

- Make two JNDI lookups: The first obtains a reference to the connection factory for queue connections, and the second to a `Queue` object that will be used to identify the queue itself. Note that both these names are arbitrary; they must be mapped at deployment time to the JNDI names of the connection factory and queue. With the *J2EE Reference Implementation*, the default JNDI name of the queue connection factory is simply `QueueConnectionFactory`. The JNDI name of the queue is created when a new queue is installed. This can be done at the command line, like this:

```
j2eeadmin -addJmsDestination\
    jms/financialtransactionqueue queue
```

This command creates a queue whose JNDI name is `jms/financial transactionqueue`. In the EJB, we use the `java:comp/env` namespace to reference the JMS objects, so that they can be remapped at deployment time, if necessary. These mappings will have to be resolved in the deployment descriptor (see below).

- Use the connection factory to get a connection to the messaging service. This connection is represented by a `QueueConnection` object. Notice that we did not do this when initializing the EJB (e.g., in `setSessionContext()`. This is because we expect the application server to pool connections to the messaging service, so there is no need to retain open connections. Note that the `Queue` object does not represent a physical connection to anything; it is simply a descriptor. It is therefore safe to store it at initialization time.

> ## Gotcha!
>
> This operation will fail unless the JDBC drivers and the JMS drivers are compatible with distributed transactions—that is, they have support for the XA interfaces or whatever your product uses. With the *J2EE Reference Implementation*, if you are using the `cloudscape` database, ensure that you have selected the XA-compliant driver. No changes need be made in the Java code.

- From the connection, get a `QueueSession` object. This object controls a single transaction between the client and the messaging service. This transaction can encompass multiple send and receive operations, although there is only one queue operation in the transaction in this case.

- Get a `QueueSender` object from the session object, by supplying the `Queue` whose identity was earlier retrieved by JNDI.

- The session object also supplies `TextMessage` objects to encapsulate individual messages. In this example, we only use one message per session and one session per connection. In a more complex system, there may be many messages sent in a single session.

- Pass the message to the `QueueSender`.

- Close the connection. This closes any associated sessions as well.

10.5.2 Deploying the LegacyMessager EJB

Deploying this EJB is the same as deploying any other session EJB, except that we must resolve the references to the resource factory and to the queue itself.

Figure 10.8 shows the 'Resource refs' page for this EJB in the *J2EE Reference Implementation*. The 'Coded name' entry is jms/qcf, which corresponds to the name java:comp/env/jms/qcf given in the implementation. The JNDI name is QueueConnectionFactory, which is the default provided by the EJB container. The tick in the 'Shareable' box indicates that we are prepared to use a shared virtual connection to the messaging service.

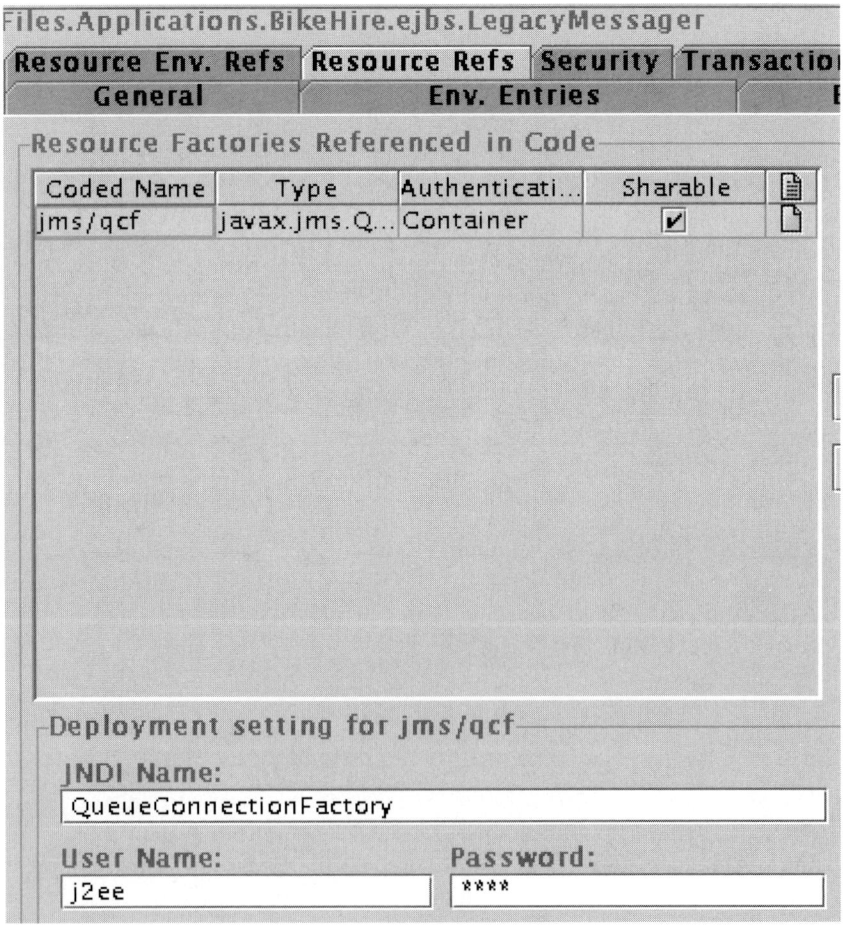

Files.Applications.BikeHire.ejbs.LegacyMessager

Resource Env. Refs	Resource Refs	Security	Transactio
General	Env. Entries		

Resource Factories Referenced in Code

Coded Name	Type	Authenticati...	Sharable	
jms/qcf	javax.jms.Q...	Container	✔	

Deployment setting for jms/qcf

JNDI Name:

QueueConnectionFactory

User Name: Password:

j2ee   ****

Figure 10.8. Entering a reference to the QueueConnectionFactory resource factory. See text for details.

Figure 10.9 shows the 'Resource env refs' page for the EJB. The coded name jms/outgoing corresponds to the name java:comp/env/jms/outgoing used in the implementation, while the JNDI name corresponds to the name given using the j2eeadmin command-line tool as described above.

If your EJB container does not have built-in support for looking up JMS destinations, you will need to use real JNDI names in the code (not java:comp/env references) and configure JNDI to use the JMS vendor's naming classes.

We will discuss the process of testing this EJB using a test client later.

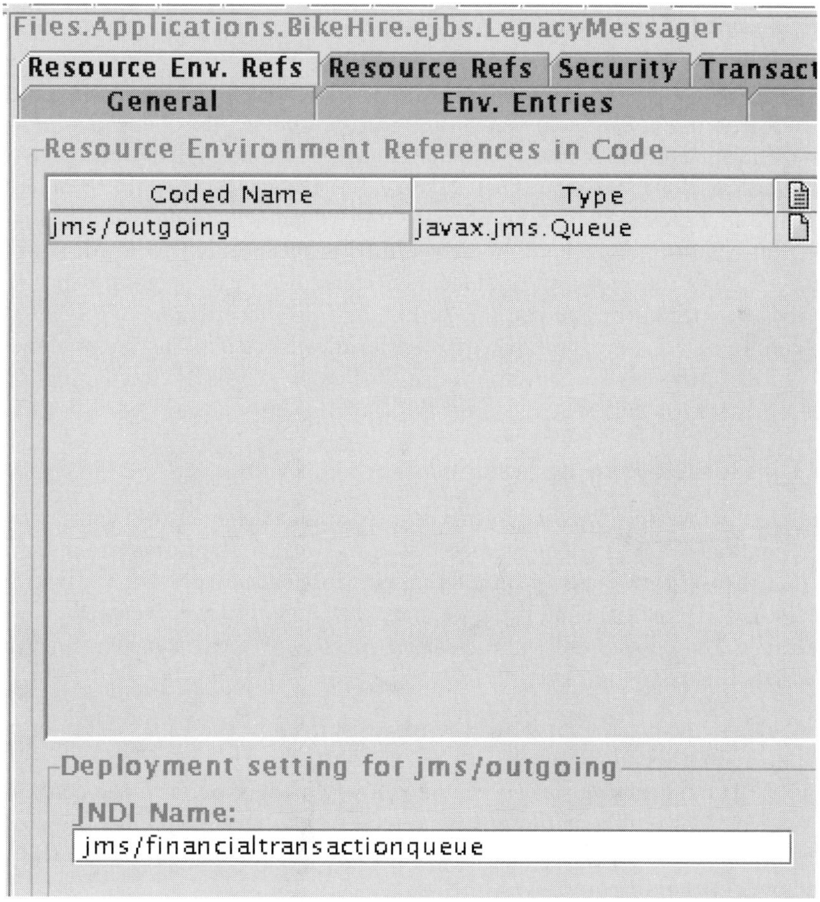

Figure 10.9. Entering a reference to the jms/financialtransactionqueue queue. See text for details.

10.6   Message-driven EJBs

The only portable mechanism by which an EJB can receive JMS messages is through the use of message-driven EJBs. As message-driven EJBs are new in Version 2.0 of the *EJB Specification*, this implies that there is no portable way for a container that supports only earlier versions to receive asynchronous messages.

> ### Hint
>
> It is possible to simulate the functionality of message-driven EJBs in a system that has no support for them by writing a standalone Java program that monitors a message queue for incoming messages and calls a stateless session bean on the receipt of each message. It is an interesting exercise to consider how this differs from what happens in a 'real' message-driven EJB.

A message-driven EJB registers an interest in a particular queue or topic (destination), and the container invokes its onMessage() method when a message arrives on that destination. The container takes care of creating the JMS Connection, Session, and MessageConsumer objects, and of message acknowledgment. This means that constructing a message-driven EJB is very straightforward: Fewer JMS calls are required than for a standalone JMS consumer. A message-driven EJB that subscribes to a topic can use durable or nondurable subscription.

To improve efficiency, the EJB container is allowed to pool instances of message-driven EJBs, although the developer uses the same single-threaded programming model as for session EJBs.

10.6.1   Overview of operation

Figure 10.10 shows, in simplified form, the interactions between the client, messaging service, container, and implementation instance. Because the EJB instances are held in a pool, there are two sets of interactions in the diagram: P1–P5 are interactions between the EJB instance and the pool manager, while 1–6 are interactions between the instance, the client, and the messaging service. We will consider client-driven interactions first.

1. At deployment time, or when the server starts up, the EJB container creates a MessageListener object that listens to the queue or topic registered by the EJB. The messaging service may be closely associated with the container, or even part of it, but it doesn't have to be. Note that in reality the container can pool connections to the messaging service, but for simplicity this is not shown in the diagram.

2. The client produces a message to the destination in which the EJB has registered an interest—that is, it publishes a message to the topic or sends to the queue to which the container is listening on behalf of the EJB.

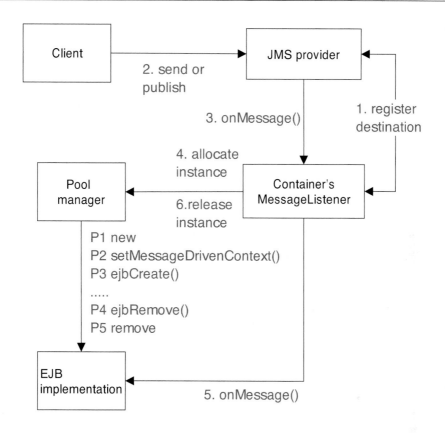

Figure 10.10. Principle of operation of a message-driven EJB. See text for details.

3. The messaging service calls the `onMessage()` method on the container's `MessageListener`.

4. The container allocates an implementation instance from the pool. If there are no free instances, then a wait will have to be imposed.

5. The container delegates the `onMessage()` call to the instance. If the EJB has declared container-managed transaction demarcation, and the transaction attribute for `onMessage()` is `Required`, the container begins a new transaction first. If it is `NotSupported`, then no transaction is created. After the method call, the container commits or rolls back any transaction it started. It will roll back if the `onMessage()` method threw an EJB exception or called `setRollbackOnly()`.

6. The container releases the instance back to the pool.

Because the instances are held in a pool, there is an initialization and finalization sequence for the instance that is independent of the client-driven interaction.

P1. The container's pool manager creates a new instance of the implementation class.

P2. The container calls `setMessageDrivenContext`, passing in a `MessageDriven Context` object. This object can be used to bring about a transaction rollback (with container-managed transaction demarcation) but, unlike in other EJB types, can't be used to find the caller ID (as there is no caller, as such) [EJB2.0 15.5.1].

P3. The container calls `ejbCreate()`. The implementation should do whatever initialization it requires.

P4. When the container has finished with this instance, it calls `ejbRemove()` before removing it. This method can be used to clean up.

P5. The container drops its reference to the instance, allowing it to be garbage-collected.

10.6.2 Summary of developer's responsibilities

Because message-driven EJBs cannot be called directly by clients, they require neither a home interface nor a remote interface. The developer provides only an implementation class. The class implements both the `MessageDrivenBean` and `javax. jms.MessageListener` interfaces. Table 10.2 summarizes the requirements of the methods in this class.

`ejbCreate(...)`	Initialize the EJB. In a failure, throw `CreateException`.
`setMessageDrivenContext (MessageDrivenContext sc)`	At a minimum, store the `Message DrivenContext` object in an instance variable for later use.
`ejbRemove()`	Implement, if desired, to clean up. However, you can't rely on this method ever being called [EJB2.0 15.4.11]. In a failure, throw `RemoveException`.
`onMessage(Message m)`	Do whatever work is required when a message arrives. This message should not throw any application exceptions. [EJB2.0 15.4.10].

Table 10.2. Developer's responsibilities for the EJB implementation class in a message-driven EJB.

Gotcha!

Message-driven EJBs don't have 'callers' in the sense that other
EJBs do. A message does not carry across the ID of the sender
in a way that the EJB container can use. Thus the methods
`getCallerPrincipal()` and `isCallerInRole()` in `EJBContext`
are disallowed.

Hint

Developers frequently wonder why the `onMessage()` method is
left to be specified in the `MessageListener` interface, and not
incorporated in the `MessageDrivenBean` interface. In other words,
why do we need to implement two interfaces, when one would do?
The answer, according to the Specification [EJB2.0 15.4.2] is that
in the future there may be other types of message-driven EJB,
with other types of listener. The approach adopted allows new
types to be added without changing the base API.

10.6.3   Message acknowledgment in message-driven EJBs

The EJB should not attempt to acknowledge receipt of a message (by, for example,
calling `Message.acknowledge()` [EJB2.0 15.4.8]. The container will acknowledge
the receipt of the message in one of three ways.

- If the EJB has been defined to use container-managed transaction demarcation, then the container will create a transactional session with the messaging
  service. Thus acknowledgment will be handled automatically when the transaction commits.

- If the EJB has been defined to use bean-managed transaction demarcation,
  and the deployment descriptor 'acknowledgment mode' flag is set to
  JMS_AUTO_ACKNOWLEDGE, the container acknowledges the message when
  the EJB's `onMessage` method completes successfully.

- If the EJB has been defined to use bean-managed transaction demarcation,
  and the deployment descriptor 'acknowledgment mode' flag is set to
  DUPS_OK_ACKNOWLEDGE, the container acknowledges the message when
  it is consumed by the container's `MessageConsumer`.

> **Hint**
>
> A message-driven EJB should anticipate that the container may call onMessage() repeatedly if this method throws a runtime exception. The *J2EE Reference Implementation*, for example, will call an onMessage() eight times before giving up (this is a default that can be changed in jms_server.properties). The designer should give some thought to whether this behaviour will ever give useful results. If it won't, then consider handling all errors within the onMessage() method and never throwing a runtime exception out to the container. In general, this will only be possible if you are using bean-managed transaction demarcation.

10.6.4   Threading and pooling

Message-driven EJBs are stateless—that is, they carry no client state. The container considers all instances to be identical, so an incoming message can be handled by any free instance. Therefore the container will normally hold a pool of instances and allocate an instance to each incoming message. There is no association between the identity of the message producer and the instance that handles the message. In order to allow message-driven EJBs to run in a single-threaded environment, the container will prevent the onMessage() method from being entered on multiple threads [EJB2.0 15.4.5]. Thus, there must be sufficient instances in the pool to be able to handle the degree of concurrency required.

10.6.5   The LegacyReceiver EJB

In the *Prestige Bike Hire* application, as we have seen, credit card transactions are sent to the legacy financial system via the queue jms/financialtransactionqueue. We can't assume that all these transactions will succeed; a customer's credit card provider may refuse to honor the charge. In this case, we need to notify the customer and give him the opportunity to provide an alternative payment. If the customer cannot do this, we need to release the reservation on the booked motorcycle. These steps will be handled by the administrators; for the application, the important factor is to update the Booking EJB to indicate that the credit card transaction was declined. Therefore the legacy system dispatches an acknowledgement of each order to the queue jms/financialresponsequeue. The EJB LegacyReceiver accepts the incoming messages from this queue and updates the Booking EJB accordingly.

As for session EJBs in the *Prestige Bike Hire* application, I have separated the functionality of the LegacyReceiver EJB into two classes. Those parts that are generic and likely to be common to all message-driven EJBs are in the class GenericMessageDrivenBean (Listing 10.2). The specific functionality of the EJB is implemented in ChargeAcceptorBean.java (Listing 10.3), which has Generic MessageDrivenBean as its base class.

Listing 10.2: **Generic base class for message-driven EJBs. This base class provides dummy implementations for the `MessageDrivenBean` interface methods and debugging methods.**

```
     package com.kevinboone.bikehire.ejb;
     import javax.ejb.*;
     import javax.naming.*;
     import javax.jms.*;
5
     /**
     GenericMessageDrivenBean is a general-purpose base
     class for MessageDriven EJB implementations. It provides
     dummy implementations of the specified methods in
10   the MessageBean interface
     */
     public abstract class GenericMessageDrivenBean
        implements MessageDrivenBean, MessageListener
     {
15   protected MessageDrivenContext ctx;
     protected boolean debug = true;

     /**
     debugOut prints its output to the standard output if
20   the 'debug' flag is set. The flag is set from the
     environment variable 'java:comp/env/debug' in
     setEntityContext()
     */
     protected void debugOut (String s)
25   {
       if (debug)
         System.out.println (this.getClass().toString()
            + ":" + s);
     }
30
     public void ejbCreate()
       {
       debugOut("Dummy ejbCreate()");
       }
35
     public void ejbRemove()
       {
       debugOut("Dummy ejbRemove()");
       }
40
     public void setMessageDrivenContext(MessageDrivenContext _ctx)
       {
       ctx = _ctx;
       try
45       {
         Context c = new InitialContext();
         Boolean temp =
           (Boolean) c.lookup ("java:comp/env/debug");
         if (temp != null)
50         debug = temp.booleanValue();
         }
       catch (NamingException e){}
```

```
      debugOut ("setMessageDrivenContext()");
      }
55  }
```

Listing 10.3: **Implementation class** for the `LegacyReceiver` **EJB.**

```
    package com.kevinboone.bikehire.ejb;
    import com.kevinboone.bikehire.utils.*;
    import javax.ejb.*;
    import javax.jms.*;
5   import javax.naming.*;
    import java.rmi.*;
    import java.util.*;

    /**
10  Implementation  class  for  the  'LegacyReceiver'  EJB
    (c)2002 Kevin Boone
    */
    public class LegacyReceiverBean
      extends GenericMessageDrivenBean
15  {
    /**
    This  method  is  called  by  the  EJB  container  when  a
    message  arrives.  It  parses  the  'your_ref'  field  from  the
    message,  which  should  identify  both  the  customer  ID  and
20  the  start  date  of  the  booking.  These  two  fields  are  used
    to  compose  a  primary  key  for  the  Booking  EJB,  whose
    'status'  property  is  then  updated.
    */
    public void onMessage(Message m)
25    {
      debugOut ("Received message:");
      String text = m.toString();
      debugOut (text);
      int p = text.indexOf ("your_ref");
30    String s = text.substring (p + 8);
      System.out.println ("YR=" + s);
      p = s.indexOf ('/');
      String sCustomerId = s.substring(0, p);
      String sDate = s.substring(p+1);
35    System.out.println ("id=" + sCustomerId + ", date=" + sDate);
      /**
      Update  the  Booking  EJB  instance  whose  customer  ID
      and  start  date  property  correspond  to  the  values
      parsed  out  of  the  supplied  message
40    ...
      ...
      */
      /**
      Notify  the  customer  by  email  of  the  outcome  of  the
45    credit-card  transaction
      */
      }
    }
```

Remember that no home interface or remote interface is required for this EJB.

10.6.6   Deploying the LegacyReceiver EJB

Deploying a message-driven EJB is likely to be similar to deploying other EJBs (although this is vendor-specific), but it will be necessary to enter information specific to message-driven EJBs, such as the topic or queue to register. The procedure that the *J2EE Reference Implementation* uses is to ask for queue and topic details along with the basic EJB information, as shown in Figure 10.11.

Note that this EJB will not have a JNDI name, as it can't be looked up by other beans. Also, we don't need to add resource factory or resource environment references for the message queue, as it is not referred to in the Java code.

10.7   Testing messaging EJBs

Message-driven EJBs need test clients, just as other EJBs do. With message-driven EJBs, the test client will be a program that produces messages to the queue to which

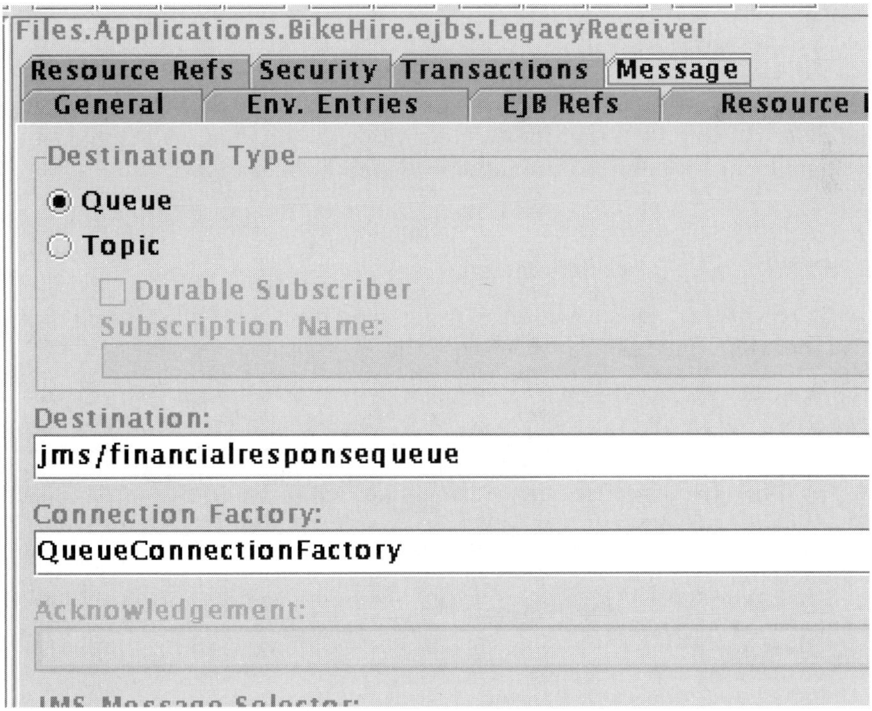

Figure 10.11. Entering basic message-driven EJB properties using the *J2EE Reference Implementation*.

> ### Hint
>
> Because a message-driven EJB does not have a 'caller' in the usual sense, the developer must assign a security role to the onMessage() method, as the container can't determine it from the caller. In practice, you may not be ready to assign security roles when initially testing EJBs. The *J2EE Reference Implementation* server *will* operate a message-driven EJB with an empty security role for its onMessage() method, despite complaints from the verifier.

the EJB is listening. It is not possible for a client to call the EJB's onMessage() method directly.

In this example, the application is intended to communicate with a legacy system, and as we don't have a real legacy system, the need for a test client is even more compelling. Now, it is possible to use separate test clients for the LegacyMessage and LegacyReceiver EJBs, but as these EJBs form a closed loop with the legacy system, it is easier—as well as being more realistic—to write a test client that closes the loop. This means that we need a client that receives the messages from LegacyMessager, and sends simulated acknowledgements back to LegacyReceiver. You will see (Listing 10.4) that the JMS operations required in this standalone Java program are not very different from those used in EJBs except

- the standalone client can't use remappable java:comp/env names, but must use absolute JNDI names, and

- the client can receive messages using the (blocking) call QueueReceiver. receive(), an option not open to EJBs.

Listing 10.4: **Implementation class for the LegacyReceiver EJB.**

```
    package com.kevinboone.bikehire.testclient;
    import com.kevinboone.bikehire.utils.*;
    import com.kevinboone.bikehire.ejb.*;
    import javax.ejb.*;
  5 import javax.naming.*;
    import javax.jms.*;
    import javax.rmi.*;
    import java.rmi.*;
    import java.util.*;
 10
    /**
    Dummy legacy system for handling off−line order transactions
    (c)2002 Kevin Boone
```

```
    */
15  public class LegacyOrderSystem
    {
    public static void main (String[] args)
        throws Exception
        {
20      // Get a naming context
        Context c = new InitialContext ();

        System.out.println ("Getting the connection factory");
            QueueConnectionFactory qcf =
25              (QueueConnectionFactory)c.lookup ("QueueConnectionFactory");

        System.out.println ("Getting the inbound queue");
        Queue qIn = (Queue) c.lookup
            ("jms/financialtransactionqueue");
30
        System.out.println ("Getting the outbound queue");
        Queue qOut = (Queue) c.lookup
            ("jms/financialresponsequeue");

35      System.out.println ("Getting the connection");
        QueueConnection qc = qcf.createQueueConnection ();

        System.out.println ("Getting the session");
        QueueSession qSession = qc.createQueueSession
40          (false , Session.AUTO_ACKNOWLEDGE);

        System.out.println ("Getting the receiver");
        QueueReceiver qReceiver = qSession.createReceiver (qIn);

45      System.out.println ("Getting the sender");
        QueueSender qSender = qSession.createSender (qOut);

        qc.start ();
        do
50          {
            System.out.println ("Waiting for message");
            Message m = qReceiver.receive ();
            System.out.println ("Received message:\n");
            String s = m.toString ();
55          System.out.println (s);

            int p = s.indexOf ('\n');
            String s1 = s.substring (0, p);
            p = s1.indexOf ('=');
60          String yourRef = s1.substring (p+1);

            System.out.println ("Your ref: " + yourRef);

            s = "your_ref=" + yourRef + "\n";
65          s += "response_code=" + "0" + "\n";
            s += "info=" + "OK" + "\n";

            System.out.println ("Sending message:");
            System.out.println (s);
70          m = qSession.createTextMessage (s);
            qSender.send (m);

            } while (true);
```

```
        }
75  }
```

Listing 10.5 shows the console output of this test client when a message is received and acknowledged back to the application.

Listing 10.5: **Output from the LegacyOrderSystem test client.**

```
    Getting the connection factory
    Getting the inbound queue
    Getting the outbound queue
    Getting the connection
5   Java(TM) Message Service 1.0.2 Reference Implementation (build b14)
    Getting the session
    Getting the receiver
    Getting the sender
    Waiting for message
10  Received message:

    ID: _grizzly.bears_1021753429752_13.14.6.6: our_ref=2/1065740400000
    name=Fred Bloggs
    address=1 Skid Row, East Dogpatch
15  card_number=4564564562224562
    card_type=Vista
    cost=385

    Your ref: 2/1065740400000
20  Sending message:
    your_ref=2/1065740400000
    response_code=0
    info=OK

25  Waiting for message
```

10.8   Summary

Messaging is a powerful and versatile technique that allows applications to communicate in a loosely coupled, asynchronous manner. JMS is a tool for mapping into Java the basic functionality of point-to-point and publish-subscribe messaging systems. Any EJB can send JMS messages, but only message-driven EJBs—new in Version 2.0 of the *EJB Specification*—can receive them directly. Enterprise messaging systems provide support for load sharing, fault-tolerance, and transactionality, as well as reliable message delivery. Messaging operations can be combined with database operations in a single transaction, but messaging transactions only control the interaction between a messaging client and the messaging service, as they don't have client-to-client scope.

Chapter 11

Entity EJBs

> ## Overview
>
> This chapter analyzes entity EJBs in more detail. It starts by describing
> the life cycle of an entity EJB and how the container manages the instance
> pool to handle database tables of arbitrary size. This will include a discus-
> sion of the container's manipulation of primary keys, including cases where
> the primary key is not a simple database field and has to be modelled as a
> class. We then discuss methods that the container can use to keep the in-
> stance variables in sync with the database tables, and the implications these
> techniques will have on the efficiency of the EJB. This chapter covers those
> aspects of entity EJB development that are relevant to both bean-managed
> and container-managed persistence. Later chapters will deal with each of
> these techniques in depth.

11.1 What is an entity EJB?

An entity EJB is an object that represents some kind of persistent item in the
application domain. In the *Prestige Bike Hire* application, for example, persistent
objects include the customers, motorcycles, and bookings: These are implemented
as the entity EJBs Customer, Bike, and Booking respectively. All these items have
a 'life' outside the application. When the application or the server shuts down, the
persistent objects continue to 'exist,' and are available the next time the application
starts up.

To make this possible, the state of each entity EJB must be synchronized to
some sort of persistent storage. Typically, we use a relational database for this,
although there are other possibilities. This synchronization does not happen by
magic: Someone has to implement it. Of course, it would be possible to implement
a persistent object by having the client of that object tell the object to load its
state from the storage device before use, then write its state back after use. Such a
strategy, although simple, has a number of problems.

- Forcing the client to take control of the state management of its target is not properly 'object oriented.' The OO philosophy dictates that objects are responsible for managing their own state.

- It does not address the problems that may arise when two or more clients try to get access to the same pieces of data at the same time.

- It compels the client object (or rather its author) to be concerned with setting transaction boundaries, as the persistence-management operation calls are intermingled with business method calls.

The EJB architecture obviates these problems by making persistence management part of the contract between an EJB and its container, and not between an EJB and its clients.

When authoring EJBs, we can choose whether to implement the persistence management operations explicitly in code (which is called *bean-managed persistence*, or BMP), or let the EJB container implement it automatically (*container-managed persistence*, or CMP). When using the latter, the developer needs to specify the mapping between the entity EJB state and the elements of the underlying database, among other things, but does not write any JDBC code if the persistence device is a database.

Clients interact with entity EJBs in much the same way as with session EJBs. The main apparent difference is that the `create()` and `remove()` methods on the home object correspond to the creation and deletion of persistent data;[1] in many cases, a client will use `find()` methods to locate an existing EJB, rather than creating a new one. The EJB can be provided with as many finder methods as required. These methods are defined in the home interface using a name that starts with `find....` With bean-managed persistence the developer provides matching `ejbFind...` methods in the implementation class. With container-managed persistence, the vendor's tools will generate the implementation directly in the home object.

11.2   Principle of operation

11.2.1   Overview

Consider this problem: An entity EJB is required to model an object that is actually represented as rows of a large database table (let's suppose it has a million rows). It would be conceptually simple for the container to instantiate the EJB

---

[1]This is only an apparent difference: In both session and entity EJBs, the `create()` method creates a 'conceptual' EJB, not a Java platform class. In neither case need *any* Java platform class be instantiated. The 'conceptual' EJB in this case is a piece of persistent data, and there the `create()` method is doing exactly as specified. Many developers new to this subject find this point hard to grasp, because they assume that 'create' means the same thing as 'instantiate,' which it doesn't here. 'Create' on an EJB is an abstract operation, not an instantiation. Although this is a rather academic point, if grasped it does allow the developer to understand that the `create()` method on a session EJB and the `create()` method on an entity EJB are doing the same 'conceptual' job.

> ### Hint
>
> The *EJB Specification* does not say that entity EJBs must be synchronized to a database; in fact, it has very little to say about what the persistent storage mechanism should be. However, because the overwhelming majority of EJB applications use relational databases for persistence, I will use the term 'database' rather than 'underlying persistent storage' where it is more convenient. Please don't take this to mean that relational databases are the only thing that entity EJBs can be synchronized to—for example, I developed an EJB application where entities synchronize to timer events controlled by a microcontroller. Using entity EJBs to model data in a legacy application is also fairly common practice.

implementation class for each row in the table. Then there would be a one-to-one mapping between rows and EJB implementation instances. When a client wanted to make use of the EJB that represented a particular element of data, it could just be given a reference to the EJB instance that contained the data itself. This strategy is simple, but inadequate[2] for two main reasons.

First, it is very inefficient in memory usage. Most of these million instances would be idle most of the time, wasting memory. Second, this strategy would only be effective if the whole database table was locked by the EJBs; otherwise, the instance variables of the EJBs could quickly become stale (out of sync with the database). However this problem is to be overcome, it must be transparent to clients. If a client executes a method on a particular EJB, it must be able to assume that its state is correct.

The way this is achieved in practice is to allow the container to pool entity EJB instances, just as it pools stateless session and message-driven instances. Instances are assigned to particular rows (strictly, to particular primary keys) on demand from clients. This has advantages and disadvantages compared to the 'brute force' strategy of one-to-one mapping. Because EJB instances are only allocated to database rows when required by a client, data is locked only when necessary. In addition, it turns out that a relatively small pool can service a large database.

A problem that arises from this pooling strategy is that of ensuring that the instance variables of the pooled instances are in sync with the database when the EJB's business methods are called by a client. After all, the container will be swapping the state of the instances to match client demand for particular EJBs. When container-managed persistence is used, the container will load data from the

---

[2]Although rarely useful in practice, synchronization by exclusive locking of data is explicitly allowed by the *EJB Specification* [EJB2.0 10.5.9].

Gotcha!

The container can only correctly sequence calls to `ejbLoad()`,
`ejbStore()`, and the business methods if it knows the transaction
context of the EJB at all times. This means that bean-managed
transaction demarcation is *not allowed* in entity EJBs, no matter
what persistence management scheme is used. The developer's
responsibilities for transaction demarcation are limited to setting
transaction attributes in the deployment descriptor and calling
`EJBContext.setRollbackOnly()` if necessary to bring about a
rollback.

---

database, and store data to the database, as required. With bean-managed persistence, the EJB's synchronization methods (`ejbLoad()` and `ejbStore()`) are called by the container when it wants the EJB to update its state from the database or write its state out. With container-managed persistence, these methods are still called, but their function is to notify the EJB of the progress of synchronization.

With both BMP and CMP, it is the container's responsibility to synchronize, or to call the synchronization methods, at appropriate points to maintain data integrity. Ideally, the developer should not rely on the container following any particular strategy. However, there are certain places where the container *must* synchronize, and it will attempt to minimize the use of load and store operations other than at these points. Understanding how database operations are synchronized to transaction boundaries will help you to optimize the efficiency of your entity EJBs. Careless design of entity EJBs can be very inefficient, as the container can easily spend more time on synchronizing data than on servicing the application.

11.2.2   Primary keys in entity EJBs

A primary key is any piece of data that can uniquely and unequivocally identify a particular entity. If we know the primary key, we can always find the rest of the data for that entity.

The concept of the primary key is crucial to the entity EJB architecture. Two entity EJBs with the same primary key are considered to be identical. The container uses the primary key to organize the EJB instances and EJB objects. For example, with bean-managed persistence, the EJB will be expected to retrieve its primary key from the container, and then use it to load the rest of its state. This is only possible if the primary key is genuinely unique.

In the entity EJB architecture, a Java class is used to represent the primary key. In many cases, you will be able to use one of the standard classes, like `java.lang.String` or `java.lang.Integer`. If none of these is appropriate (and it won't be if the primary key is composite; see below), then it is possible to define a specific primary key class.

Clients get access to entity EJBs via their home interfaces, just as for session EJBs. The client can choose to create a new EJB or find one or more existing EJBs. We can define any number of create and find methods, to suit the needs of clients. The only method that an entity EJB *must* provide to clients is `findByPrimaryKey()`, which returns the EJB object that corresponds to the specified primary key.

11.2.3   Example of a client-container-EJB interaction

To understand the interaction between the client, container, and EJB implementation we will consider the steps involved when a client calls a single-EJB finder (like `ejbFindByPrimaryKey()`), then calls a number of business methods on the EJB reference returned (Figure 11.1). We will consider more complex scenarios later. For simplicity, we will assume that the methods called are all part of the same transaction (for reasons that will become clear later), and that we are using bean-managed persistence (in fact, it matters little whether we use BMP or CMP as far as the principle of operation is concerned). The client code that brings about this sequence of operations is shown in Listing 11.1.

Because the EJB instances are pooled, there are two sets of interactions: In Figure 11.1 steps 1–12 are interactions driven by the client, while P1–P3 are interactions between the instance and the pooling system, and these are controlled separately. We will consider the client-driven interactions first.

1. The client has found the EJB's home object by a JNDI `lookup()` call in the usual way (lines 1–6 in Listing 11.1).[3] It then calls a `find` method (line 7) (this is shown as as 'findX' in the figure, because 'X' can be any string; in reality, we would use names that are meaningful to the EJB and its clients).

2. The home object finds the primary key of the matching EJB. In BMP, it calls `ejbFindX(...)` on any free EJB instance, which is expected to return a primary key. In CMP, the home object does the appropriate SQL SELECT operations itself, using a query descriptor supplied by the developer (of which, much more later). In either case, the primary key corresponding to the desired EJB is determined.

3. The home object finds, or creates, an EJB object corresponding to the located primary key. The container will normally only allow one instance of the EJB object for each primary key, and will share it among all clients. Note that the lifetime of the EJB object is unspecified.

4. The home object returns to the client a reference to the EJB object. As always, if the client is using the distributed view, what the client really gets is a stub that can communicate with the EJB object.

---

[3]Of course, in practice if this client code were in a J2EE component, we would do a lookup for a name beginning `java:comp/env...`, rather than an absolute JNDI name.

5. The client calls the business methods on the EJB object reference (lines 9 and 10).

6. On receipt of the first business method call, the EJB object gets an inactive instance of the EJB implementation from the pool. If there are a relatively large number of clients, and a relatively small number of instances, then this stage may impose a delay until an instance is available to service requests.

7. The free instance is assigned to the primary key stored in the EJB object. The EJB object calls `ejbActivate()` to inform the instance that this has happened. This process is called *activation*: The EJB charges from the 'passive' to the 'active' state.[4]

8. The EJB object (or some other part of the container) calls `ejbLoad()` on the implementation, to instruct it to make its internal state match the database. The instance knows its primary key (or can find it from the container) and will probably do some kind of SQL SELECT statement. With CMP, the code to do this will be generated automatically by the vendor's tools, while with BMP, the developer will have written the appropriate code in `ejbLoad()`. If the caller did not have an active transaction, and the transaction attributes for the business methods require a transaction, the container will begin a new transaction before calling `ejbLoad()`. Whether the container starts the transaction or continues a transaction from the caller, the container will probably only call `ejbLoad()` at the start of the first business method of a transaction, so in this example it is only called at the start of the first business method, not for the second.

9. The EJB object calls the business methods on the implementation instance.

10. After the last business method, but before committing any active transaction, the container will call `ejbStore()` on the instance, which will write its state to the database. This will probably correspond to an SQL UPDATE statement, either supplied by the developer (BMP) or the vendor's tools (CMP).

11. When the container has finished with the instance, it calls `ejbPassivate()` on it to inform it of this fact. This process is called *passivation*.

12. The container puts the instance back into the pool.

---

[4]Compare this with 'activation' in session EJBs; again the EJB is 'conceptually' activated in that it is made ready for use.

Listing 11.1: **Simple lookup, finder call, and method calls on the** `Customer` **EJB. This code is intended to be read in conjunction with Figure 11.1.**

```
Object ref   = context.lookup("Customer");

CustomerHome home = (CustomerHome)
    PortableRemoteObject.narrow
      (ref, CustomerHome.class);

Customer customer = home.findByPrimaryKey (1);

String name = customer.getName();
String address = customer.getAddress ();
```

The creation and initialization of instances is carried out at the discretion of the container. Some products will create a pool of instances at start-up, while others will create instances on demand until the pool is full. In either case, the sequence of operations is as follows (Figure 11.1).

P1 The container creates a new instance of the implementation class

P2 The container calls `setEntityContext()`, passing in an `EntityContext` object, which the EJB should save for future use.

P3 When the container wants to remove the instance, it calls `unsetEntityContext()` to inform it. It then releases its reference to the EJB, making it eligible for garbage collection. In practice, most containers never call this method.

Note that `ejbCreate()` and `ejbRemove()` are never called as part of this interaction; these are called when the client calls `create()` and `remove()`, as described next.

11.2.4   Creating an entity EJB

The client creates an entity EJB by calling one of the `create()` methods on the home object. This gives the client a reference to the EJB object, as in the simple 'find' example above.

The sequence of interactions is shown in Figure 11.2.

1. The client calls a `create(...)` method on the home object. In contrast to the situation that obtains in session EJBs, `create()` methods in EJBs invariably take arguments. The number and nature of these arguments is discussed later.

2. The home object, or some other part of the container, gets a free instance of the implementation. If the transaction attributes require it, the container may have to begin a new transaction at this point. Otherwise, the operation may continue a transaction created by the caller.

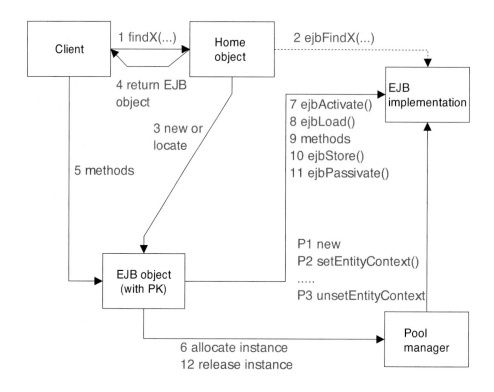

Figure 11.1. Interaction between the client, implementation instance, and container for an entity EJB in response to a client `findX()` method call.

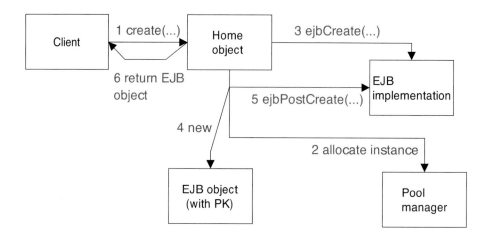

Figure 11.2. Interaction between the client, implementation instance, and container for an entity EJB in response to a client `create` method.

3. The container calls `ejbCreate(...)` on the instance, passing the same arguments as the client passed to `create(...)`. The instance should set its internal state to be appropriate for the arguments passed—for example, it should set its instance variables to correspond to the arguments. In a BMP entity, the instance now creates the data in the database to match its internal state. Most often, an SQL INSERT operation will be performed here. With a CMP scheme, the container will do this itself after calling `ejbCreate()`. With BMP, the `ejbCreate()` method is expected to return a primary key. The container will use this to create the EJB object. With CMP, the EJB must return `null`.

4. The container creates a new EJB object and sets its primary key based on the result of `ejbCreate()` (BMP) or its own notion of what the primary key should be (CMP). Note that an EJB object will probably not exist until this point; a `create` operation can only succeed if it results in a new primary key, and there can only be one EJB object for each primary key.

5. The container calls `ejbPostCreate(...)` on the instance, which does whatever is required in the way of initialization. If the container initiated a new transaction for this sequence of operations, it will attempt to commit it after `ejbPostCreate()` returns.

6. The home object returns a reference to the EJB object to the client, which can then call its business methods.

A note is in order about `ejbPostCreate()`: Many developers are unclear about what this method is for and what it should do. The simple answer is that in most cases it can be empty. To understand why it won't always be empty, we need a short digression to discuss how EJBs pass references to themselves to other EJBs.

In ordinary Java practice, if object `X` wants to create an instance of object `Y`, and pass a reference to itself to `Y`, then `X` could execute code like this:

```
Y myY = new Y( this );
```

There is no equivalent to this in EJBs, for two reasons. First, `this` is a pointer to something that cannot be passed by reference in a distributed method call. Remember that only classes for which stubs exist can be passed by reference; there are stubs for the EJB object and for the home object, but not for the implementation class. This means that, if this method call succeeded at all, it would result in the *value* of the EJB being passed, not a reference to it. Second, EJBs cannot call one another on their implementation classes. To do so would bypass the container's management of the EJB. However, an EJB *might* be able to do something like this:

```
Y myY = Y.create ( ctx.getEJBObject() , ...);
```

where `ctx` is the `EntityContext` object passed by the container to `setEntity Context()`. Giving object `Y` a reference to `X`'s EJB object (or local object) effectively provides a reference to the EJB itself, via the container. It should be remembered that even this approach is potentially unsafe, and the EJB must specifically be marked as 're-entrant' for it to be used (see page 477 for a full discussion).

Anyway, returning to `ejbPostCreate()`: This method is provided so that when the EJB instance is created, it can do initialization that *requires the EJB object to exist*. Remember that, unlike session EJB initialization, the container can't create the EJB object until *after* `ejbCreate()` has returned. This is because it needs the primary key, which is not known until then. If part of the initialization of the EJB involves calling a method on another EJB, and this method requires a reference to the caller (i.e., the EJB currently being created) to be passed as a parameter, then we must pass the EJB object or local object, and this cannot be completed until we have an EJB object or local object (remember that we can't pass `this` to another EJB).

This is a rather subtle technical point, and often isn't important. However, if the entity EJB has associations (see below) to other EJBs, then it often turns out that we can't initialize these associations in `ejbCreate()`. This is because the associated EJB may need to be supplied with a reference to the EJB being created, and that reference will have to be a reference to an EJB object.

Gotcha!

In EJB 2.0, `ejbCreate()` and `ejbPostCreate()` are required to be defined to throw **CreateException** [EJB2.0 10.6.4] when using container-managed persistence, even if the code never throws the exception. The reason for so doing is not intuitively obvious, and it represents a change from previous versions of the *EJB Specification*. The *J2EE Reference Implementation* fails silently at the stub compilation stage if this is incorrect, and its own verifier fails to detect the problem.

After creation, an EJB is considered to be in the 'active' state, because its instance variables match the database. It can then have methods called on it without an intervening call to `ejbLoad()`. Thus, it is very important for `ejbCreate()` to set the instance variables correctly, even with BMP. In practice, however, many EJB containers repool instances after `ejbCreate()` if the transaction has committed.

11.2.5   Removing an entity EJB

When the client calls `remove()` on an entity's EJB object, or `remove(primary_key)` on the home object, the container calls `ejbRemove()` on the EJB instance. Normally, the EJB should update its underlying persistent store in such a way that the data can be considered deleted. This may, or may not, correspond to issuing an SQL DELETE statement. In many cases, the EJB will set a field in the corresponding row to indicate that the row is considered deleted.

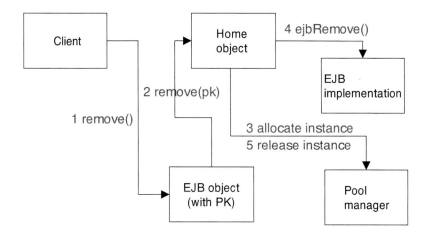

Figure 11.3. Interaction between the client, implementation instance, and container for an entity EJB in response to a client `remove()` call.

The sequence of interactions is shown in Figure 11.3.

1. The client calls `remove()` on the EJB object, or `remove(pk)` on the home object, where 'pk' is the primary key.

2. The EJB object delegates the call to the home object (if the client called the home object directly, this step is not necessary).

3. The home object obtains a free instance of the implementation.

4. The home object calls `ejbRemove()` on the instance. If the EJB uses BMP, then it should perform the delete operation on the database at this point. With CMP, the container *will already have deleted the data* and any dependent objects of the EJB being deleted.

5. The implementation is returned to the pool. It is *not* deleted or garbage collected. The EJB object, however, is now redundant (because the primary key no longer exists) and will eventually be garbage collected or assigned to a new primary key.

Unlike session EJBs, the `ejbRemove()` method is *not* the last method called by the container. `ejbRemove()` indicates the removal of the 'conceptual EJB' (that is, the data in the database), and not the implementation instance.

Gotcha!

With session EJBs, there is a way for a client to tell the EJB container that it has finished with the EJB: It calls `remove()`. This allows the container to remove the implementation instance and the EJB object. This is inappropriate with entity EJBs, as `remove()` removes a persistent data item. There is, in fact, no way for the client to tell the container that it has finished with the EJB. While the container will not instantiate the implementation more often than it needs to fill the pool, the number of instances of the EJB object is only limited by the number of rows of the database table. The developer should take care when using entities that model large tables, because EJB objects tend to proliferate. Such EJBs should perhaps not be provided with unconstrained finder methods. EJB 2.0 encourages the EJB developer to return query results to the client by value, not as EJB references, and provides techniques to support this. Such support was not well developed in EJB 1.1.

11.2.6   Multi-EJB client 'find' operation

We have seen how the container handles `find` operations that can only return one EJB. `ejbFindByPrimaryKey()` is a good example: By definition this method can only return one EJB. In most cases, however, we would like clients to be able to locate multiple matching EJBs. For example, in the *Prestige Bike Hire* application, we want clients to be able to find bookings for vehicles that overlap with a certain range of dates. Clearly, this finder method can return more than one EJB (it may also return none, of course).

The container follows exactly the same sequence of operations for multi-EJB finders as it does for single-EJB finders. The only differences are in the return type for `ejbFindX(...)` and the return type to the client. The `ejbFindX(...)` method returns to the home object a Java `Collection` of primary keys (typically an `ArrayList`). The home object creates or finds an EJB object for *each* of these primary keys, and makes them into a new `Collection`. This is returned to the client. The client can then iterate through the collection and carry out whatever actions are required on each EJB (see Listing 11.2, which is an extract from the implementation of the `BookingManager` EJB).

Clearly, this technique has to be used with care. A method like '`findAll()`'— while intuitively useful—will be very dangerous on an EJB with many instances ('conceptual' instances—that is, database rows). First, the container will have to instantiate an EJB object for every row. Second, the EJB objects will have to be marshalled and unmarshalled over a network connection.

Hint

In EJB 2.0, we can use a 'home method' (see below) to carry
out database SELECT operations and return the results to client
by value or, for example, as a collection of primary keys. This
can significantly increase network efficiency. There is no compara-
ble mechanism in earlier versions, and multi-EJB finder methods
should be used with caution. 2.0-style CMP has built-in support
for passing multiple matches by value, as we shall see.

Listing 11.2: **Client's view of a multi-EJB 'find' operation.**

```
    Object ref  = context.lookup("Booking");

    BookingHome home = (BookingHome)
      PortableRemoteObject.narrow
5       (ref, BookingHome.class);

    Collection c = home.findByDate (/* dates */);
    Iterator i = c.iterator();
    while (i.hasNext())
10      {
      Booking b = (Booking)i.next();
      // process booking
      }
```

11.3   Associations between entities

Although it is quite clear than entity EJBs will have persistent data elements—the
`Customer` EJB has persistent name, address, and credit card details, for example—
closer inspection reveals that it is not only the data that is persistent. The problem
is that entity EJBs have associations with other entity EJBs, and these associations
will themselves be persistent.

   In this section, we discuss associations in general, followed by typical schemes
for implementing them.

11.3.1   What are associations?

The real power of object-oriented development comes from the expressiveness of object interactions. Objects can be associated[5] (related) in a number of ways and interact along those associations. Of course, a particularly important association is that of inheritance, but objects can be associated in many other ways (contain, use, and implement, for example). In this discussion, we will focus on two simple associations in the *Prestige Bike Hire* application (the relationships between the EJBs in this application has already been discussed in Chapter 5; the relevant diagram is reproduced here as Figure 11.4 for convenience).

Following standard UML notation, the *multiplicity* (also called 'cardinality') of an association is labelled at each end; if no label is shown, the multiplicity is 'one.' So (each one) Bike is associated with 0..M (zero to many) instances of Booking, and with exactly one BikeModel. Read in the opposite directions, these relationships indicate that (each one) Booking is associated with (exactly one) Bike, and (each one) BikeModel is associated with 0..M instances of Bike. In English, 'each motorcycle can have any number of bookings, but is of one model only; each booking is associated with one bike; each bike model is associated with any number of bikes.'

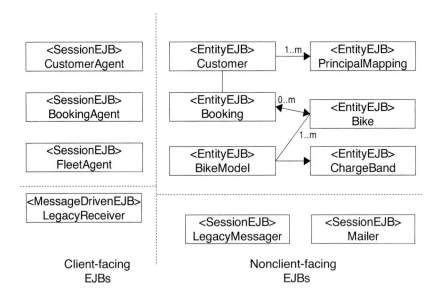

Figure 11.4. The *Prestige Bike Hire* application EJBs, showing associations between the various entities.

---

[5]In this book, I use the term 'association' in preference to 'relationship' because this is the term used in the *UML Specification* and the one that most object-oriented designers and developers are familiar with. However, the *EJB Specification* uses the term 'relationship' more commonly. They mean the same thing.

A related concept is that of *navigability*, which indicates the direction in which the associations can be traversed. In our example, the association between `Customer` and `PrincipalMapping` is unidirectional: A `Customer` EJB can find the security principals (credentials) that a given customer may have, but a `PrincipalMapping` cannot find the customers with which it is associated. Navigability is about the needs of the application, rather than logical necessity. There is no reason in principle why the `PrincipalMapping` should not be able to find its associated `Customers`, but in this particular application, it doesn't need to. Navigability can be bidirectional, and very frequently will be.

Hint

Associations are only an issue at all if we need to be able to navigate from one object to another. A client of `Booking` can find all the bookings for a particular motorcycle using a finder method in its home interface; we don't necessarily need to be able to find this information from a `Bike` EJB, although it is useful. Only implement associations if they improve the design. If there is *no navigability*, then associations are of academic interest only. Having said that, many developers fail to capitalize on the advantages offered by associations, because they don't fully understand how to implement them in EJBs. EJB 2.0 improves matters considerably, by providing built-in support for persistent associations.

11.3.2   Handling associations in Java

Before examining the handling of associations in EJBs, we should first review how it is done in ordinary programming for the Java platform (programmers use associations all the time, but may not think of them in those terms, as we shall see).

The Java programming language has no built-in support for associations. If I wanted to indicate that the class `Bike` is associated with zero-or-more `Bookings` and one `BikeModel`, it would be nice to have a construct like this:

```
public class Bike
  {
  association BikeModel(1 to 1);
  association Booking(1 to 0-many);
  }
```

and some built-in support for finding and managing the associated objects. But there is no such thing. In practice, we frequently use a simple technique that object-oriented designers call 'buried references.'[6] A buried reference is simply an instance variable that stores an association. In the case described we could have:

---

[6]There are other techniques for modelling associations, especially where they are many-to-many, including the use of specific association objects.

```
public class Bike
  {
  protected BikeModel model;
  protected Collection bookings;
5 }
```

We need the `Collection` to model the fact that there are a number of `Booking` objects for each `Bike`. Of course, Java developers use this technique all the time, but may not think of it as implementing an association. If the association is navigable in both directions, we need a buried reference in both associated classes, and some code to ensure that the references remain synchronized.

11.3.3   Dependent and independent associations

The associations between `Bike`, `BikeModel`, and `Booking` shown in Figure 11.4 are *independent*. This means that the creation and deletion of the objects are independently controllable (up to a point), and each object can enter into relationships with other objects outside the scheme shown. However, in many cases, one object is dependent on another. That is, the dependent object is accessible only from its 'owner,' and is created and deleted along with it. An example is the association between `Customer` and `PrincipalMapping`. The application as a whole is uninterested in `PrincipalMapping` EJBs; the only way to find a `PrincipalMapping` is from the `Customer` that 'owns' it.

Of course, whether an object is dependent or not is not always clear-cut: The designer has to weigh the advantages and disadvantages of such a representation in each case. For example, the `Booking` object is *almost* a dependent of `Bike`. In this case, I felt that `Booking` objects were owned as much by `Customer` objects as by `Bike` objects, and therefore not strictly dependent.

Why is this important? The *EJB Specification* (particularly Version 2.0) makes a sharp distinction between handling dependent and independent associations, as we shall see.[7]

11.3.4   Handling associations in entity EJBs

Entity EJBs are persistent objects, and therefore have persistent associations. This means that whenever a client of the EJB makes a method call that refers to an associated entity, that entity must be accessible and correct. Now, although all EJBs of type `Bike` will have associations with a number of `Booking` EJBs, these associations are *different for each EJB*. This means that when an entity implementation instance is activated from the pool, not only must it restore all its persistent instance variables, it *must restore its persistent associations as well*. It also means that if a method modifies an association, the modifications must be written back to

---

[7]In fact, earlier drafts of EJB 2.0 proposed that dependent objects actually be implemented as a separate type of mini-EJB, with its own container contract. This proposal was mercifully killed by the introduction of the local client view; it was accepted by most (but not all) of those involved in the specification process that an entity EJB with a local client view could usefully stand as a dependent object. See page 411 for a more detailed analysis of this decision.

the database at the end of the database transaction (or earlier). Let's see how this might be achieved in practice.

The Bookings EJB has a finder method called findByDate() that finds all the bookings for a particular vehicle over a particular date range. Let's suppose for a moment that we wanted the Bike EJB to have an association with *all* Booking objects for this vehicle, regardless of date. In Bike we can get a Collection of matching Booking EJBs like this:

```
BookingHome home = // get booking home
bookings = home.findByDate
  (null, null, regNo);
```

In this example, regNo is the registration number of this motorcycle. As the registration number is the primary key of the bike table, and of the Bike EJB, the EJB can always find its registration number.

We have also to restore the association with the BikeModel object. The model name is a field in the bike database table, so we can do this at the same time we restore the other instance variables from the database.

In the simplest case, the EJB will need to carry out these operations every time ejbLoad() is called. This can be implemented as shown in the code fragment below.

```
    public class BikeBean implements EntityBean
    {
    protected Collection bookings;
    protected BikeModel model;
 5  protected EntityContext ctx;
    protected String regNo;

    public void ejbLoad ()
      {
10    regNo = (String)ctx.getPrimaryKey();
      BookingHome home = // get Booking home
      bookings = home.findByDate
        (null, null, regNo);
      // Restore persistent instance variables
15    String modelName = // get from table
      model = modelHome.findByPrimaryKey(modelName);
      }
    // Other methods...
    }
```

So we have a method for restoring the persistent associations at the start of a transaction. What about saving them at the end? In the example above, there is no real problem here. First, the association between Bike and BikeModel is read-only once it is created. A motorcycle cannot change its model (a Honda C90 can't become a Harley-Davidson Road King, however much you might want it to), and a model can't be removed as long as there are any motorcycles of that model on the records. So the Model association is no problem, as it won't change during a transaction. Second, even though the Bookings association may change (if we provide a method that can change a booking, or delete it), the change or deletion operation happens

in the `Booking` EJB, which brings about its own database modifications. In the
`Bike` EJB, we simply remove the `Booking` from the `Collection`. So again, there is
no real problem.

In many cases, however, we will need to deal specifically with synchronizing
associated objects when they are changed across the association.

11.3.5 EJB associations, dependent objects, and dependent values

Version 1.1 of the *EJB Specification* distinguished between dependent objects and
EJB associations [EJB1.1 9.1.2]. Consider the case where one object is fully dependent on another (in the sense discussed above). The designer has to make a
choice whether to make the dependent object an EJB or a simple class. This is true
whether or not the dependent has its own database mapping. There are advantages
to each approach.

Dependent as an EJB The advantages of this approach are that the persistence
of the dependent can be managed by the container (rather than by the EJB
developer), the dependent can have its own transactional attributes and security controls, the dependent can be distributed (e.g., for load balancing), and
the dependent is less tightly coupled to its owner, allowing for easier maintenance. The disadvantage is that it can be very inefficient. Calls between the
owner and the dependent would (in EJB 1.1) always be network calls, with the
concomitant overhead of security and transaction management. It was often
argued that since we don't need the benefits of EJBs in a dependent object,
we shouldn't encumber ourselves with the costs.

Dependent as a class With this strategy, we avoid the overhead of EJB security,
transaction management, and network interaction, which gives the benefit of
increased speed. The disadvantage is that the dependent becomes less of a
reusable component, and more of a 'helper' class.

In the *EJB Specification*, Version 1.1, the term 'dependent object class' was used
exclusively to mean a persistent helper class that is managed by an EJB, and not
an EJB itself. That is, dependent objects are never EJBs. Of course, EJBs can have
associations, but not of an owner-dependent nature.

Version 2.0 of the *EJB Specification* [EJB2.0 9.4.3] goes a step further: it divides
dependent objects into two types: *dependent value classes* and *dependent object
classes*. A dependent value class is simply a helper class; it is under the control of the
developer and can be stored as an instance variable of its owner. If it is persistent,
the developer must write code that controls its persistence and synchronizes its
persistence with that of the owner. Thus a dependent value class is just a helper
class in the same sense as in EJB 1.1.

A dependent object class, however, is something rather different: an EJB that
has only a local client view. It thus combines the advantages of an EJB (container-
managed persistence and transactions) with the reduced overheads of simple method

calling. A dependent object class can automatically be put into one-to-one, one-to-many, and many-to-many interactions with its owner. We will have more to say about this later.

11.4 Persistence management

Effective persistence management is the key to efficient use of entity EJBs, but only part of this process is under the control of the developer. Version 1.1 of the *EJB Specification* defined two persistence schemes: bean-managed and container-managed. Version 2.0 extends this to include a new version of container-managed persistence that supports not only persistent instance variables, but persistent associations between EJBs. I will refer to the old scheme as '1.1-style CMP' and the new one as '2.0-style CMP' in the rest of this chapter.

11.4.1 Fundamental principles

Whatever persistence management strategy we use, the interaction between the container and the instance follows exactly the same pattern, which is this: The container will call `ejbLoad()`, `ejbStore()`, and its own internal methods in whatever sequence is necessary to keep the EJB instance state in sync with the database. It's as simple as that. Ideally, the EJB developer should never have to worry about how it does this. However, an understanding of the principles will make it easier to optimize the performance of entity EJBs.

Consider the situation shown below, where one client (`client1`) is modifying a database row (`RowXXX`) by an EJB (`ejb1`), while another client is reading and writing that row directly.

```
client1-->
    ejb1.methodA() <--> RowXXX     client2 <--> RowXXX
    ejb1.methodB() <--> RowXXX
```

`client1` makes a business method call, `ejb1.methodA()`, on the EJB object that holds the primary key for `RowXXX`. Assume that the client does not have a transactional context, so the container will have to create one. No instance is associated with this EJB object, so the container needs to get one from the pool, calling `ejbActivate()` as it does so. The container then needs to make the instance variables correct before the business method starts. It can do this either internally (with CMP) or by calling `ejbLoad()` (with BMP). By starting a new transaction before calling `ejbLoad()`, transaction isolation will prevent the row from being modified by a different EJB or client. When `client2` tries to modify the row, it won't be able to, because it will be locked by the `ejb1` transaction.

When the business method is complete, the container can call `ejbStore()`, then commit the transaction. Data integrity is guaranteed, because the data is locked while in use by the EJB.

Now the container has a choice: It can call `ejbPassivate()` and return the instance to the free pool or leave it associated with the same primary key, in antic-

ipation of a subsequent method call. In the *EJB Specification*, the first strategy—
returning to the pool—is called *commit option C*. The second—retaining the association with the EJB object—is called *commit option B* [EJB2.0 10.5.9].

Now the client calls another business method. Does the container have to call
`ejbActivate()` and `ejbLoad()` again? With commit option C, both are required,
because no EJB instance is associated with the EJB object. With commit option B, the container doesn't have to call `ejbActivate()`, but it does have to
call `ejbLoad()`, because the data in the database may have changed since the last
call on the instance.

So using commit option B is slightly faster, because it avoids the process of
activating and deactivating instances in the pool. However, performance gains are
likely to be small, as the demanding operations—`ejbLoad()` and `ejbStore()`—are
still required at the beginning and end of every business method.

The *EJB Specification* recognizes another procedure, called *commit option A*,
where the data in the database table is locked by the EJB container *between* transactions. While this limits the need for repeated load and store operations, it is
difficult to implement in practice, and can lead to a loss of database concurrency.
For these reasons, this option is rarely used.

Now consider the situation shown below, where the client is calling `methodC()`
in `ejb2`, which in turn calls `methodA()` and `methodB()` in `ejb1`. `ejb2` is a session
bean.

```
client-->
  ejb2.methodC() -->
    ejb1.methodA()  <--> RowXXX    client2 <--> rowXXX
    ejb1.methodB()  <--> RowXXX
```

Assume that `ejb2.methodC()` has transaction attribute `Required`, so the container begins a new transaction before calling the method. When `ejb2` calls `ejb1`.
`methodA()`, a transaction is already in progress, so the container doesn't have
to start a new one. The container has to call `ejbActivate()` and `ejbLoad()` as
usual, but when `methodA()` finishes, the container does *not* commit the transaction and does *not* call `ejbStore()` or `ejbPassivate()`. When `methodB()` is called,
the container does not have to call `ejbLoad()`, because the data is locked by the
transaction: `client2` cannot modify `RowXXX` until this transaction commits. Finally,
`methodB` completes, and `ejb2.methodC()` completes. The container now has to call
`ejbStore()` so that the data in the database is correct, and then commit the transaction.

So this strategy—using one EJB to make two successive calls on another—
halves the number of `ejbLoad()` and `ejbStore()` calls required. As the number
of method calls encompassed by the transaction increases, the number of load and
store operations decreases.

Of course, this increase in load and store efficiency is not without a price. First,
we may need `methodA()` and `methodB()` to run in separate transactions for functional or logical reasons. Second, there is a loss of database concurrency because
the database is locked in a transaction for longer. Normally, this loss is offset by

the gains, and isn't a problem. But the developer needs to think about the scope of transactions quite carefully in a system that has a lot of entity EJB activity.

One final note: The container must be smart enough interpret the change in transactional context correctly, and call `ejbLoad()` and `ejbStore()` appropriately. Not all containers are this smart at present: Many call `ejbLoad()` and `ejbStore()` more frequently than they need to.

> ### Hint
>
> If the EJB server supports commit option B, it will probably handle EJB synchronization *slightly* faster than commit option C, with no compensating disadvantages. However, the improvement is unlikely to be significant enough to base a purchasing decision on. Much greater performance gains can be achieved by controlling transaction boundaries appropriately and (as will be described) eliminating unnecessary database operations.

11.4.2   Bean-managed persistence

With bean-managed persistence (BMP), the developer is responsible for maintaining the state of the instance variables in sync with the database, by handling the container's calls on `ejbCreate()`, `ejbRemove()`, `ejbLoad()`, and `ejbStore()`. The developer is also responsible for implementing the `ejbFindXXX()` and `ejbSelectXXX()` methods with (usually) JDBC operations.

The advantage of BMP is flexibility: The mapping between the EJB instance and the underlying data store can be as complex as required, limited only by the developer's skill and patience. In addition, you will be able to synchronize to stores other than relational databases, such as legacy systems, hardware, or files (through a connector in this last case, because direct file access is not allowed). CMP schemes generally support only relational databases.

The disadvantage of BMP is the amount of work required. The developer is responsible for implementing all the synchronization operations. If you want persistent associations as well as persistent instance variables, you will have to code this, either in `ejbLoad()` and `ejbStore()`, or in the business methods.

We will discuss the developer's responsibilities for BMP in more detail later (Chapter 12).

11.4.3   Container-managed persistence

Container-manager persistence (CMP) is the area of the *EJB Specification* that has undergone the most revision since Version 1.1 of the Specification. The new version actually has very little in common with the earlier version. According to Version 2.0, a compliant EJB container is required to support Version 1.1 techniques as well, but the developer must specify at deployment time which type to use. Version 2.0

of the *EJB Specification* has separate chapters for 1.1-style CMP (Chapters 12 and 13) and 2.0-style (Chapters 9–11) CMP. One of these chapters (Chapter 11) is given over to the new 'EJB Query Language.' Because many readers will still be working with code that was developed for EJB 1.1 products, this book can't ignore 1.1-style CMP, tempting as it might be. In any case, it aids comprehension of EJB 2.0 CMP to understand the scheme it seeks to improve upon. In this chapter, therefore, we will follow a strategy similar to the *EJB Specification*, but in reverse—that is, we will deal with Version 1.1-style CMP first, then 2.0-style CMP. Only an overview is given in this section; details of the developer's responsibilities are provided later (Chapter 13).

1.1-style CMP

In 1.1-style CMP, the developer codes the EJB exactly as for BMP, but the synchronization methods (`ejbLoad()` etc.) are empty. `ejbCreate()`, provided by the developer, sets the instance variables, but does not insert any data. The persistent instance variables have to be `public`, as they are read and written by the container,[8] as do the instance variables of the primary key class if there is a composite primary key. At deployment time, the vendor's tools provide the implementations of all the synchronization methods, usually directly into the home object and EJB object. The vendor provides the tools that map the persistent instance variables onto database tables and fields. The usefulness of this scheme depends on the flexibility of the vendor's mapping tools; most vendors can map an EJB onto a single database table, but such a scheme is trivial to implement in BMP. For this reason, CMP has not been widely used in practice. The limitations of this scheme (discussed in Section 13.3) have led to an entirely new CMP strategy for Version 2.0 of the *EJB Specification*.

2.0-style CMP

The new persistence management strategy does not use instance variables to store persistent data; instead the developer supplies abstract `getXXX` and `setXXX` methods for the EJB's properties, and these are implemented by the container's tools. This allows the container to optimize the loading and storing of data. In addition, a new query language—EJB QL—is specified for specifying the logic of operations on the persistent store, as distinct from the mechanics of mapping object data to database data. The new CMP scheme is much more sophisticated than the old one, and is discussed in detail in Section 13.3.2.

11.5   Developer's responsibilities in general

This section describes in general what the developer must do in order to create an entity EJB. It covers issues that are independent of the particular persistence

---

[8]The *EJB Specification* offers no satisfactory answer to the question, 'Why could the instance variables not have been associated with matching `get` and `set` methods rather than being `public`?' In practice, the use of public variables is not a violation of the principles of encapsulation, as EJBs are encapsulated by their containers.

> **Gotcha!**
>
> What is a 'property'? Many developers use the term 'property' as a synonym for 'instance variable.' In fact, the JavaBeans (not *Enterprise* JavaBeans) Specification defines a property as follows: If a class has a method `getAbc()` and a method `setAbc()` with compatible return types and arguments, then it has a property `abc`. This is true whether or not there is a real instance variable called 'abc' or not. In EJB 2.0, CMP entity EJBs have properties in the JavaBeans sense, and may have no instance variables at all. This will be described in more detail later.

management strategy. In later chapters, we will discuss the particular requirements of BMP, 1.1-CMP, and 2.0-CMP in more detail.

In summary, the developer must provide either or both of a remote client view (remote interface and home interface) or a local client view (local interface and local home interface), and the EJB implementation class.

11.5.1 Home interface (local or remote)

The home interface must declare the `create(...)` and `findXXX(...)` methods of the EJB. It can also declare 'home methods.' Home interfaces must extend `javax.ejb.EJBHome` directly or indirectly. The only compulsory method is `findByPrimaryKey()`, which should take a primary key argument and return the remote or local interface type.

There can be any number of other `findXXX()` methods. If they find a single EJB, they should return the remote or local interface type, while if they find multiple EJBs they should be defined to return `java.util.Collection`.[9]

There can be any number of `create(...)` methods, provided they have different arguments. All must return the primary key type.

With a remote client view, `create` methods should be defined to throw `Create Exception` and `RemoteException`, and finder methods should be defined to throw `FinderException` and `RemoteException`. Home methods should throw `Remote Exception` in addition to any application-defined exception. With a local client view, `RemoteException` is not required.

Listing 11.3 shows a typical home interface; this example has one `create` method, one single-EJB finder method (`findByPrimaryKey()`), and three multi-EJB finder methods (`findByName()`, `findAll()`, and `findByPrincipal()`).

---

[9]The *EJB Specification* recognizes other acceptable return types, but `Collection` is the most common.

11.5.2   Remote interface and local interface

The remote or local interface has exactly the same structure in an entity EJB as it does in a session EJB. It exposes the business methods to clients. The remote interface must extend `javax.ejb.EJBObject`, directly or indirectly. With a distributed client view, all methods must be defined to throw `RemoteException` in addition to any application-defined exceptions.

Listing 11.4 shows a typical remote interface. This example has three 'types' of business methods.

Methods that manipulate properties In the example, we have `getId()`, `get Address()`, `setAddress()`, etc. These methods generally have trivial implementations (if any; with EJB 2.0 CMP these methods have no implementation provided by the developer!).

Methods that manipulate associations In this example, `addPrincipal` supplies a new security principal ID, which is turned into a `Principal` EJB inside the implementation and added to the collection of associated `Principals` (remember that each customer can have multiple security principals, if he or she has multiple methods of authentication to the application).

Methods that manipulate properties through value objects This EJB has methods that get and set properties through the value object, as well as individual `get` and `set` methods. This is to reduce the number of method calls required to initialize the EJB or extract its data. Remember that if we are using the distributed client view, there are significant overheads in each distributed method call, so reducing the number of method calls is to be recommended. In many cases, we will see methods that return collections of value objects, as well as individual value objects. For example, the `BikeModel` EJB is associated with zero-to-many `Bike` EJBs. From an instance of `BikeModel`, we can get all the instances of `Bike` of that model. This could be done by providing a method to get a collection of `Bike` EJBs or a collection of `BikeData` value objects. If the caller does not need to modify the properties of the `Bike` EJBs, it is much more efficient to get a collection of value objects. As it happens, this functionality has been implemented in a method that returns a collection of `Strings` containing the license numbers of individual motorcycles, which is quicker even than using a value object.

Listing 11.3: **An example of an entity home interface:** `CustomerHome` **from the *Prestige Bike Hire* application.**

```
package com.kevinboone.bikehire.ejb;
import javax.ejb.*;
import java.rmi.*;
import java.util.*;

/**
```

```
      (Remote) home interface for the 'Customer' EJB
      (c)2002 Kevin Boone
      */
10    public interface CustomerHome extends EJBHome
      {
      public Customer findByPrimaryKey (final Integer id)
        throws FinderException, RemoteException;
      public Collection findByName (final String name)
15      throws FinderException, RemoteException;
      public Collection findAll ()
        throws FinderException, RemoteException;
      public Customer findByPrincipal(final String principal)
        throws FinderException, RemoteException;
20    public Customer create (final int id, final String name,
          final String address, final int creditCardType,
          final int creditCardExpiryMonth,
          final int creditCardExpiryYear, final String creditCardNumber)
        throws CreateException, RemoteException;
25    }
```

Listing 11.4: **An example of an entity remote interface:** Customer **from the** *Prestige Bike Hire* **application. Note that the rules are exactly as for a session EJB remote interface.**

```
      package com.kevinboone.bikehire.ejb;
      import javax.ejb.*;
      import java.rmi.*;
      import java.util.*;
5
      /**
      (Remote) business method interface for the 'Customer' EJB
      (c)2002 Kevin Boone
      */
10    public interface Customer extends EJBObject
      {
      // Status of customer. A 'defunct' customer
      //  is one that has withdrawn from the service
      //  but still has a record for the time being
15    public static final int STATUS_UNKNOWN = -1;
      public static final int STATUS_ACTIVE = 0;
      public static final int STATUS_DEFUNCT = 1;

      // Constants to define credit card types
20    public static final int CARD_UNKNOWN = -1;
      public static final int CARD_APEX = 0;
      public static final int CARD_BLASTERCARD = 1;
      public static final int CARD_VISTA = 2;

25    // These constants are used by classes throughout
      //  the application that take a customer ID as input
      //  or output. All 'real' customer IDs are > 0; these
```

```
     // special values indicate 'virtual' customers
     public static final int ID_CURRENT=0;
30   public static final int ID_UNKNOWN=-1;
     public static final int ID_INTERNAL=-2;

     // Business methods that simply get and set properties
     // Note no setId()! Primary key is immutable in EJBs
35   public Integer getId()
         throws RemoteException;
     public void setName(final String name)
         throws RemoteException;
     public String getName() throws RemoteException;
40   public void setAddress(final String address)
         throws RemoteException;
     public String getAddress() throws RemoteException;
     public void setStatus(final int status)
         throws RemoteException;
45   public int getStatus() throws RemoteException;
     public int getCreditCardExpiryMonth()
         throws RemoteException;
     public int getCreditCardExpiryYear()
         throws RemoteException;
50   public int getCreditCardType()
         throws RemoteException;
     public String getCreditCardNumber()
         throws RemoteException;
     public void setCreditCardType(final int creditCardType)
55       throws RemoteException;
     public void setCreditCardExpiryMonth
       (final int creditCardExpiryMonth)
         throws RemoteException;
     public void setCreditCardExpiryYear
60     (final int creditCardExpiryYear)
         throws RemoteException;
     public void setCreditCardNumber
       (final String creditCardNumber)
         throws RemoteException;
65   public Collection getPrincipals()
       throws RemoteException;

     // Business methods that manipulate associations
     public void addPrincipal(final String principal)
70     throws RemoteException, CustomerManagerException;

     // Business methods that manipulate value objects
     public CustomerData getCustomerData()
         throws RemoteException;
75   public void setCustomerData(final CustomerData cd)
         throws RemoteException;
     }
```

11.5.3   Implementation

The implementation class provides implementations of the business methods, in addition to the methods specified by the `javax.ejb.EntityBean` interface, which it should implement. The business methods have the same structure and purpose no matter what type of persistence management is used, but they may well be implemented differently internally.

11.5.4   Home methods

Home methods are new in Version 2.0 of the *EJB Specification* [EJB2.0 9.5.4]. This version allows methods to be specified in the home interface, in addition to `create` and `findXXX`, which are implemented in the implementation class as methods whose names begin with `ejbHome`. Home methods are conceptually similar to `static` methods when programming for the Java platform, in that they aren't associated with a specific instance of the EJB.

Why do we need home methods, and why aren't they available in session EJBs? Consider the case where the client wants to call a method on an entity EJB that does not relate to a specific instance. A good example would be a method that returns a count of the number of instances in the database. Such a method would not be associated with any particular instance of the EJB. In EJB 1.1, there were two ways to implement this.

- Use a 'dummy' entity instance that did not map to the database. The client could get this by calling, for example, `findByPrimaryKey("")`. The EJB would know that if its primary key was the empty string, it should not synchronize to the database. This proved to be a bit tricky to implement in practice, requiring technical tricks that were developed by each individual developer and not easy to communicate to others.

- Use a session EJB to carry out the operation, rather than the entity EJB.

Neither method is very elegant. In EJB 2.0, we can provide a home method called, for example, `getCount()` that does this job. When the client calls `getCount()` on the home object, the container calls `getCount()` on a *pooled instance* of the EJB implementation class. No synchronization to the database is involved.

Home methods aren't required in session EJBs because the client can create and remove instances as required; these instances do not have to be synchronized to the database and, with stateless EJBs, little overhead is involved.

The only limitation on home methods is that their names must not start with 'create' or 'find,' for reasons that should be obvious. Home methods may be provided on both the local and remote home interfaces and, if both local and remote interfaces are provided, the methods may have the same names. In that case, both delegate to the same method in the EJB implementation class.

Exception	Usage
CreateException	Throw from ejbCreate() or ejbPost Create() to indicate that creation failed.
DuplicateKeyException	Subclass of CreateException. Throw from ejbCreate() to indicate the client is trying to create an EJB with a primary key that is not unique.
FinderException	Throw from any find() method to indicate a general failure.
ObjectNotFoundException	Subclass of FinderException. Throw from any single-EJB find method to indicate that the EJB could not be found. This is particularly important in ejbFindByPrimaryKey().
RemoveException	Counterpart of CreateException. Throw from ejbRemove() if removal fails.

Table 11.1. Summary of exceptions thrown by entity EJBs.

11.5.5   Exception handling

Exception handling is slightly more complex for entity EJBs than for session EJBs. Table 11.1 briefly describes the exceptions that should be thrown by entity EJB methods. For full details refer to the Specification [EJB2.0 12.1.8].

The EJB should usually throw an EJBException to indicate a catastrophic failure that requires a transaction rollback; none of the exceptions listed in Table 11.1 will by itself cause the container to roll back a transaction.

A more detailed discussion of exception handling in EJBs is provided in Chapter 15 (page 464).

11.6   Handling data sets with no natural primary key

This section is included here because it related equally to both container-managed and bean-managed persistence. However, the issues described are rather subtle, and you may prefer to come back to this section after reading about BMP and CMP (and/or writing some code!).

We have already discussed the importance of the notion of a 'primary key' to the entity EJB architecture. We must now examine ways to handle situations in which the data set has no 'natural' primary key—that is, for example, where no single column uniquely identifies a particular row in a database table.

If a database table does not have a natural primary key, we must find a way to generate one. Consider, for example, a table of information about individuals, which has columns `name`, `address`, and `telephone`. None of these columns readily lends itself to interpretation as a primary key: Any two people could have the same name, or the same address, or the same telephone number.

If we have control over the database schema, we might be able to add a column that provides a unique identifier. It does not matter, in principal, what this identifier is: In many cases, we can use a number that increments for each row that is added (a *sequence number*). Alternatively, we can use a composite of two or more columns as the primary key. Whatever method is chosen, the use of entity EJBs demands a robust primary key.

11.6.1   Composite primary keys

As discussed above, in some cases we won't be able to identify a specific column of a database to use as a primary key—for example, there may be no column that can be guaranteed to be unique. Entity EJBs *must* be associated with a unique primary key. In some cases, we will be able to use a sequence number[10] as a primary key where no other exists, but in many cases we will have to use a *composite primary key* (the term 'compound' is often used in place of 'composite'; the meaning is the same). A composite primary key is a set of field values that together identify the item uniquely. A composite key can consist of any two or more fields; in some cases, four or more fields may be required.

Principle of operation

The primary key for an entity EJB is always represented as a Java platform class. With bean-managed persistence, there are few restrictions on this class, while things are a bit more complicated with container-managed persistence, as we shall see.

With BMP, the container does not operate directly on a primary key class, except in a very limited way. When the client does a `findByPrimaryKey()`, the container needs to find the EJB object that contains the specified primary key (if any). To do this, it needs only to be able to tell whether two primary keys are equal. If it can do this, it can iterate through the set of EJB object instances until it either finds one that matches or gets to the end of the list without finding a match. In the latter case, it can create an new EJB object and pass it the primary key. Similar considerations apply to multi-EJB finders. When the client calls a `create()` method, the `ejbCreate()` method returns a primary key, and the container creates an EJB object for that primary key. The container does not need to know anything about the primary key class itself.

So, in fact, all the container needs to do with a primary key (in BMP) is to be able to compare it to another primary key. To do this, it expects the primary key class to implement the following two methods:

---

[10] A sequence number is an integer that is incremented as each new row is entered in a database table. The relationship between the number and the rest of the data is arbitrary, but the number is guaranteed to be unique.

```
public int hashCode();
public boolean equals(Object o);
```

All the standard Java low-level platform classes (e.g., `Integer`, `String`, `Date`) implement these methods correctly, and can be used directly as primary keys.

Hint

The standard Java API provides two date classes: `java.util.Date` and its subclass `javax.sql.Date`. The SQL variant can parse and emit dates in SQL format, which is extremely useful when generating queries involving dates. In most other senses, the two classes are equivalent.

Gotcha!

It is a very common mistake to implement the `equals` method to take a primary key as a parameter, not an `Object`—for example, `public boolean equals (MyPrimaryKey pk)`. This *won't work*. The container will never call this method, because all classes are implicit subclasses of `java.lang.Object`, and the Java system will always find a match for `equals (Object o)` in `java.lang.Object` before it finds the real method. This is one of the few common errors that the verification tool in the *J2EE Reference Implementation* does not spot.

Hint

The `hashCode()` method does not have to be definitive. Ideally, it should be fast. If two primary keys have the same hash codes, then the container will call `equals()` to determine if they are really the same. So `equals()` should be definitive. There is nothing to be gained by implementing complex hash code algorithms in your primary key classes. It is valid, but slow, to implement `hashCode()` simply to return 0.

Of course, for `hashCode()` and `equals()` to give sensible results, the primary key class must store sufficient data. With BMP, it is irrelevant to the container *how* it does this, as the only code that will set and get this data is provided by the developer (in `ejbCreate()`, for example).

Example

The *Prestige Bike Hire* application manipulates a table of motorcycle bookings. Each time a customer reserves a motorcycle, we create a new entry in this table. The booking information required includes the customer ID (which is the sequential integer primary key described above), the start and end dates, and the vehicle.

None of the properties described so far are unique, so none of them will serve as a primary key. We could, of course, create a sequence number and use it as the primary key, as we did for the `Customer` EJB, but we could also use a composite primary key here. Because we only allow a customer to hold one booking for a given time, a primary key can be formed from the composite of the customer ID and start date fields.[11] The database schema for the booking table *might* be defined by the following SQL statement:

```
    CREATE TABLE booking (
        customerId INTEGER not null,
        startDate DATE not null,
        endDate DATE not null,
5       status INTEGER not null,
        licenceNumber char(9) not null,
        CONSTRAINT c3 FOREIGN KEY (customerId)
            REFERENCES customer (id),
        CONSTRAINT c4 FOREIGN KEY (licenceNumber)
10          REFERENCES bike (licenceNumber))
```

Note that the `licenceNumber` field references the `licenceNumber` (registration number) field of the `bike` table, and the `customerId` field references the `customer` table. This allows the database engine to ensure that only valid values for the customer ID and registration number are inserted into the database. This prevents us, for example, from making a booking for a nonexistent vehicle.[12]

So how do we implement this in an EJB? We can't use any of the standard Java platform classes (`String`, `Integer`, etc) as the primary key, as we need two distinct values in each primary key. We will have to use a `primary key class`. With bean-managed persistence, the *EJB Specification* allows any class to be used as a primary key, provided that it is serializable and overrides the methods `hashCode()` and `equals()` in `java.lang.Object` (with container-managed persistence there are some additional restrictions).

Listing 11.5 shows the primary key class for `Booking` EJB. Here are a few points to note about this class.

- Its instance variables store enough information to identify a booking uniquely (customer ID and start date).

- It is serializable, because it will be passed as a parameter to the home object over the network.

---

[11] I have given the `Booking` EJB the form it has to demonstrate the use of a composite primary key in an EJB. I would not necessarily do this in practice if I had control over the database schema.

[12] The *J2EE Reference Implementation* does not allow us direct control of the database schema when CMP is used. Therefore in practice the table will be like the one shown here, but not identical.

- The `hashCode()` method does not have to be definitive, as the container will go on to call `equals()` on two primary keys that have the same hash code. As comparing whether primary keys are identical is a frequent operation, it is probably better that the `hashCode()` method be fast, rather than definitive. In the example shown, the likelihood is that most of the `Booking` EJB objects instantiated will correspond to different customers, rather than multiple bookings for the same customer, so using the customer ID value as the hash code will be almost definitive, and very fast. If two customer IDs are equal, the container must then go on to compare the two start dates. This is likely to be quite slow, so there is nothing to be gained by doing this as part of the hash code operation.

- The `equals()` method will be called by the container not on an object of class `BookingKey`, but on a variable of type `java.lang.Object`. The container has to be able to handle all types of primary key. Thus your `equals()` method must override the `equals(Object)` method in `Object`. If you write:

```
public boolean equals (BookingKey pk) {....
```

this will compile perfectly well, and will probably get past the verification tool, but it won't work. This is because the method never gets called. The container will be calling the `equals()` method in `Object`, which only returns **true** when the two objects are actually the same instance. *If you get this wrong on the* J2EE Reference Implementation, *the EJB container goes into an infinite recursion and crashes!*

- The container will not attempt to manipulate the instance variables in the primary key class (in bean-managed persistence); it only calls the methods `hashCode()` and `equals()`. It is up to the developer to decide what the access modifiers should be for the instance variables in the primary key class. In general, the primary key will only be manipulated by objects in the same package (not by, for example, clients), so there do not necessarily need to be `get()` and `set()` methods for the instance variables. As we will be using container-managed persistence for this example, the instance variables must be public, and must have names that match the properties of the `Booking` EJB.

Listing 11.5: **A suitable primary key class for the** Booking **EJB.**

```
package com.kevinboone.bikehire.ejb;
import javax.ejb.*;
import java.rmi.*;
import java.util.*;

/**
Primary key class for the Booking EJB.
(c)2002 Kevin Boone.
*/
```

```
10   public class BookingKey implements java.io.Serializable
     {
     // The primary key is formed from the customer ID and
     //    the start date of the booking.
     public Integer customerId;
15   public long startDate;

     public BookingKey()
       {
       this.customerId = new Integer(-1);
20     this.startDate = 0;
       }
     public BookingKey(int customerId, long startDate)
       {
       this.customerId = new Integer(customerId);
25     this.startDate = startDate;
       }

     /**
     equals() method _must_ take Object as a parameter, _not_
30   the tyep of this class!
     */
     public boolean equals (Object _other)
       {
       if (!(_other instanceof BookingKey)) return false;
35     BookingKey other = (BookingKey)_other;
       if (other.customerId.equals(customerId) && other.startDate == startDate)
         {
         return true;
         }
40     return false;
       }

     /**
     hashCode() method does not have to be definitive
45   */
     public int hashCode ()
       {
       return customerId.hashCode();
       }
50   }
```

Gotcha!

Don't forget that you can't compare two dates (or **Strings** or **Integers**, for that matter) for equality in any meaningful way using the '==' operator. If we write if (**date1 == date2**), this is only true if **date1** and **date2** are the same instance. Usually what we want is equality if they refer to the same calendar date. Most objects that are likely to be used as components of a composite primary key provide an **equals()** method that returns **true** in a more useful definition of equality. For example, **String.equals(String)** compares two **Strings** for textual equivalence.

> ## Gotcha!
>
> Don't assume that the object passed by the container into your `equals(Object o)` method will be of the same type as your primary key class. Nothing in the *EJB Specification* says that the container is obliged to make your life easy in this way. If the object passed is not of a type that can be compared for equality, then then `equals` should return false.

> ## Hint
>
> The JDBC API provides a date class, `java.sql.Date`, which is very useful when working with date fields. The `toString()` method writes out the date in a format that can be used in an SQL statement, and the `valueOf(String)` method can parse a date from a `String`. This is much more convenient than using `java.util.Date` (which is the base class for `javax.sql.Date`) with custom formatting.

Using a composite primary key does not necessitate dramatic changes to the EJB implementation class, particularly with container-managed persistence. With bean-managed persistence, the following may need to be taken into account.

- When we check that the primary key supplied corresponds to a real entry in the table, we need to check all components of the primary key in any SQL WHERE clause.

- In multirow finders, the instances added to the `Collection` are instances of the primary key class, initialized with the correct values.

- `ejbCreate()` returns a primary key instance, derived from the arguments supplied.

- In `ejbLoad()`, the row we select from the database table is chosen by matching all parts of the primary key.

11.6.2 Sequential primary keys

It is very often the case that an EJB models some business entity that does not have a 'natural' primary key. Remember that the primary key should uniquely and efficiently identify each row of the table. Consider, for example, the `Customer` EJB in the *Prestige Bike Hire* application. Information we need to store about the customer includes name, address, email address, and telephone number. None of these appears to be a 'natural' primary key. Probably the email address satisfies the uniqueness requirement, but it fails on philosophical grounds. The problem is that customers are cross-referenced from a number of other EJBs, and a customer may want to change his or her email address from time to time. We don't really want a piece of information that is volatile being used as a foreign key between database tables, because changing it may result in an enormous database update.

Of course we could find something that is unique and permanent about the customer, like the National Insurance number in the U.K., or Social Security number in the U.S., for example. This would work here, but we don't necessarily want to introduce superfluous data into the database if we can help it. In any case, there will be occasions when we won't be able to do this.

It is quite common to use a generated field as the primary key when

- there is no other stable, unique primary key available, and

- the table is cross-referenced from other tables.

If the table is not the subject of cross-references, then we can use composite primary keys instead, as described below.

In many cases, the generated field will simply be an integer; each new row gets the next available integer. This is typically called a *sequence number* field or, sometimes, an *auto-increment* field.

It is important to realize that an entity EJB normally only creates database table entries in its `ejbCreate()` method. This method is called, as we have discussed already, when the EJB's client calls `create()`. Because the `create()` method must cause the EJB to initialize its database entry, this method will nearly always take some arguments. Which arguments should it take? It is a common misconception that the client must pass a primary key to the EJB's `create()` method. In fact, there is no need to do this, and it is often a practice to be discouraged. Why? The simple answer is that 'primary key' is a database concept, not an object-oriented programming concept. Clients of EJBs should only rarely have to deal directly with primary keys. Of course, in many cases the primary key will be a meaningful property of the EJB, as well as being the primary key. Consider the `Bike` and `Customer` EJBs, for example. The primary key for `Bike` is the `licenceNumber` property; this is a meaningful piece of data that the EJB's clients will need to be aware of. Users of the application will need to know the license number so that they can find a particular motorcycle among others of the same model. The `Customer` EJB, however, has `customerID` as the primary key. A `customerID` may well be meaningless outside the EJB and its immediate clients. In this case, we could argue that `customerID` should not be passed as a parameter to `create()`.

The rest of this section describes some possible approaches to generating and using sequential primary keys.

Using container-managed persistence with sequential primary keys

Some container-managed persistence schemes are smart enough to be able to handle sequential primary keys automatically. Typically, these rely on the database engine being able to support an 'auto-increment' or 'sequence number' column, which not all databases do. Even where the database provides this support, many CMP schemes are unable to capitalize on it. Remember that with CMP the container inserts a database record itself after calling `ejbCreate()`. If the CMP system does not support sequence numbers, there is nothing that the developer can do in `ejbCreate()` that will help. Instead, you will have to pass a sequence number to `create()`, after generating it elsewhere in the application.

Generating a sequential primary key by sorting the table

If you are using bean-managed persistence, then you have more freedom in how you create the primary key, but you will have to code the operation yourself using JDBC. Typically, you will need to code the `ejbCreate()` method so that it generates or determines the sequential value and returns it to the container. One of the 'classical' methods for generating a sequence number is to sort the database table in descending order of sequence number, select the first row, extract the sequence number column, increment it, and insert the new row with the generated sequence number. All these operations must take place in the same transaction, to avoid attempts by concurrent clients to insert the same sequence number. This makes the operation somewhat inefficient. Careful indexing of the table can reduce the time taken for the sort operation, thereby improving efficiency.

Generating a sequential primary key using a counter table

This is the technique recommended by the suppliers of the *Cloudscape* database engine. Here we use a table that has one row for each table in the database that requires a sequence number. Each row has two fields: the table name and the current largest sequence number for that table. The `ejbCreate()` method will do something like this.

- Do a SELECT on the sequence number to get the current maximum integer from the counter table.

- Add 1 to get the next ID in the sequence.

- Insert the new database row, using the new ID as the primary key.

- Increment the ID in the counter table.

It is important that these four steps be executed as part of a single database transaction. Otherwise, if something goes wrong in the middle of the sequence, we could end up with the counter being out of step with the database table it controls. However, the advantage of this approach over sorting the database table is that the main table (not the counter table) will only be locked for the length of time it takes to do the insert, not for the whole operation. This procedure is therefore probably somewhat faster than sorting the table. It is, however, awkward to code in such a way that modularity is maintained. By its very nature, each insert operation will require the support of two related database tables, and one of these tables (the counter table) will be the target of a dependency for many different EJBs. Of course, the dependencies can be managed by using a different counter table for each EJB.

Generating a sequential primary key using a sequence cache

This is a popular technique with EJB developers, and can be used with both BMP and CMP. It is an extension of the 'counter table' technique described above. In this approach, we use an entity EJB to represent the counter table, and a session EJB to provide a wrapper around it. When we need to create an EJB that requires a sequence number, we call a method on the *session* EJB to get the next sequence number. The session EJB maintains the sequence number *in an instance variable*, not the counter table. It only synchronizes with the entity EJB, and therefore the database, at preset intervals. For example, we may set the session EJB to update the entity EJB once in every eight calls. This reduces the load on the counter table, and reduces its tendency to become a bottleneck.

Popular as this technique is, it has a number of intricacies that merit some consideration. Not least among these is the fact that it requires that we store something akin to 'state' in a stateless session EJB. If the EJB container pools instances of the session EJB, what prevents the different instances from attempting to serve the same sequence numbers from their caches? In practice, some kind of retry logic has to be built into the system to cater for occasions where this happens. Anyone planning to use this strategy could do worse that to read the debate about it on the various EJB discussion lists.

Using built-in sequence number fields

Many database engines support sequence numbers in 'auto-increment' fields. When an INSERT operation is performed, the sequence number field is left unspecified, and the database fills it in automatically. The operation is robust, fast, and requires no specific coding. What could possibly be wrong with that?

What's wrong is that the EJB container needs to *know* the primary key for a newly inserted row. The fact that there is a valid primary key is, in itself, of no help. So how do we get the new sequence number into the EJB? Well, we sort the database table in descending order of sequence number, select the first row... Sound familiar? The fact is that autoincrement functionality is currently only useful if you are prepared to use stored procedures (page 215) to manipulate the database. With a stored procedure, you can use the database's own method for extracting a new sequence number, and return it to Java as an 'OUT' parameter.

If you require database platform portability, then the forgoing is clearly unacceptable. At present there is no portable solution to this problem. JDBC 3.0 (page 244) will introduce a new API call for extracting automatically generated fields, which should improve matters considerably.

11.7   Summary

Entity EJBs model persistent objects in the application domain. They are synchronized to a persistent store—usually a database—under the control of the EJB container. The container uses transaction boundaries to determine the correct places to synchronize the EJB and the database. The developer has to pay some attention to transaction attributes, and the way entity EJBs are called from session EJBs, for entity EJBs to perform effectively in practice.

With bean-managed persistence, the EJB's persistent state is managed by code written by the developer, which will typically consist of JDBC calls to the database. With EJB 1.1-style container-managed persistence, the persistence manager reads and writes the instance variables using JDBC calls generated by the vendor's tools. These tools also provide JDBC implementations of the finder methods, which are unsatisfactory because they do not allow application logic to be distinguished from schema mapping. 2.0-style CMP uses a query language to specify the application logic, but schema mapping is still done at deployment time. 2.0-style CMP also obviates a number of other limitations of the earlier CMP scheme, by providing abstract persistent properties, association support, and dependent objects.

Chapter 12

Bean-managed persistence

Overview

When using bean-managed persistence, the developer writes the Java code that synchronizes the EJB's internal state with the underlying database. This chapter describes in detail how to accomplish this. We begin by summarizing the developer's responsibilities, then describe step-by-step how to code, compile, assemble, deploy, and test a fully featured entity EJB, which supports reads, writes, insertions, and deletions, single-object finders, multiobject finders, and home methods. The example also presents the use of data access objects (DAOs) to decouple the EJB implementation from the data store. Finally, the chapter provides some advice on how more complex constructs like persistent associations can be handled using bean-managed persistence.

12.1 Developer's responsibilities

Chapter 11 described the fundamental principles of operation of an entity EJB. In this chapter, we discuss what the developer must do to make use of bean-managed persistence. This initial description will be quite brief, as there is a fairly detailed example later in the section that demonstrates the essential characteristics more clearly. In the discussion that follows, we will refer to the persistent data storage device as a 'database' for brevity, even though it need not be a relational database in practice.

12.1.1 Interfaces

The developer should provide local and/or remote home interfaces, and remote and/or local interfaces. These interfaces were described in detail on page 347, and don't need further discussion. The client's view of an entity EJB, whether local or distributed, is independent of the type of persistence management in use.

363

12.1.2   Implementation class

The implementation class should implement (directly or indirectly) `javax.ejb.EntityBean`. The class can contain any instance variables and associations required, whether persistent or nonpersistent; there are no special requirements for these. However, the management of the persistent instance variables and the persistent associations is entirely the job of the developer. Typically nonpersistent instance variables will be used to store things like resource factory references and the home objects of other EJBs.

Table 12.1 summarizes the developer's responsibilities in creating this class.

The EJB should throw an `EJBException` to indicate a catastrophic failure that requires a transaction rollback; none of the exceptions listed in Table 11.1 will cause the container to roll back a transaction.

create(), ejbCreate(), and ejbPostCreate() methods

An entity EJB's home interface can have as many `create(...)` methods as required, with any arguments (subject to the usual rules about argument types) [EJB2.0 9.5.1]. Each must be implemented as a corresponding `ejbCreate()` in the implementation class—that is, with the same number and type of arguments. However, the `ejbCreate()` methods to which they correspond are expected to return a primary key to the container, so the arguments must be adequate for a primary key to be determined. In many cases, the primary key will be one of the arguments, but it need not be. In the example later in the chapter, we will see how `ejbCreate()` can determine a primary key internally, so clients need not refer to primary keys themselves.

> ### Hint
>
> Your `ejbCreate()` methods don't have to write all the values into the persistent store that the EJB requires; if some database fields are nullable, for example, then `ejbCreate()` only has to set the non-nullable fields. Of course, if `ejbCreate()` does not set all the fields, some other method must be provided, such as other `setXXX(...)` methods.

In some cases, the primary key will be generated internally within `ejbCreate()` (e.g., a sequence number). Chapter 11 (page 358) provides some ideas for handling this situation.

Strictly speaking, `ejbCreate()` methods should throw `DuplicateKeyException` in the event that the client tries to create an EJB with a primary key that already exists, and `CreateException` for any other kind of failure. `DuplicateKeyException` is a subclass of `CreateException` so these exceptions don't have to be declared separately in the `throws` clause. In practice, it can be quite difficult to distinguish between a failure in a JDBC call that results from a duplicate primary key, and

Method	Usage
setEntityContext (EntityContext ec)	First method called by container; saves reference to context in an instance variable. This is a good place to look up resource factories (e.g., DataSource objects, and the home objects of other EJBs).
unsetEntityContext (EntityContext ec)	Last method called by the container; usually empty but can be used to clean up resource allocation done in setEntityContext().
ejbCreate (...)	Called by the container when the client calls a create(...) on the home object. Implement to correspond to create(...) methods in home interface; arguments must match. This method should create persistent data in the database, set the instance variables and associations, and return the primary key.
ejbPostCreate (...)	Called by the container after creation of the EJB object. Implement to correspond to each ejbCreate(..) method. Usually empty.
ejbLoad ()	Called by the container when the EJB should set its internal state to match the underlying database. Must be implemented.
ejbStore ()	Called by the container when the EJB is about to commit a transaction with which this EJB was involved. EJB should write its internal state to the database *if necessary*. This method can be empty if the database is read-only.
ejbActivate ()	Called by the container to indicate that the EJB is being readied. The method EntityContext.getPrimaryKey() will return a valid primary key. This method may be empty, but some developers like to retrieve the primary key here and save it in an instance variable.
ejbPassivate ()	Called by the container to indicate that the EJB is being returned to the pool. Usually empty.
ejbRemove ()	Called by the container when the client calls remove() on the EJB object or remove(primary_key) on the home. Implement to delete the underlying data, or flag it as deleted, unless the database is read-only or the client does not have delete authority.
Business methods	Implement to match declarations in the remote interface.

Table 12.1. Developer responsibilities for the implementation class in a BMP entity EJB.

other kinds of failure (JDBC will throw an `SQLException` in both cases). Many developers do not strive for strict compliance with the Specification in this case. If you do wish to ensure that the correct exception is thrown, it may be necessary to do a database lookup first to check whether the expected primary key already exists. This will slow things down a little, but will help the client (this is the approach taken in the example later).

Hint

If the entity models read-only data, or if you don't want to allow clients the opportunity to create new EJBs, there is no obligation to provide any `create()` methods at all.

Gotcha!

An entity EJB's `ejbCreate(...)` methods are required to fail if the entry can't be created. If the reason for failure is that there is an existing entry with the same primary key, then it should throw a `DuplicateKeyException`. In no event should `ejbCreate()` attempt to return the value of an existing entry in such circumstances. When a client calls `create(...)`, it needs to be sure that the lack of an exception signifies the creation of new data.

Gotcha!

The corollary to this, of course, is that the author of the client of an entity EJB can't assume that `create()` will return an existing EJB, rather than creating a new one, if the entity being created already exists. This isn't always what you want: What about a method `createOrFind(...)` that returns a particular EJB or creates it if it doesn't exist? If you want this behavior, you will have to code it (perhaps as a home method). Overriding the specified behavior of `ejbCreate()` will lead to a nonportable EJB.

Finder methods

The developer can provide any number of finder methods, by which clients can locate existing EJBs. These are declared in the home interface with names beginning `find`, and implemented as corresponding `ejbFind()` methods. For example, the method declared as findByCustomerName(String s) would be implemented as ejbFindByCustomerName(String s) [EJB2.0 9.5.2]. Finders can return a single EJB or a collection of EJBs. In both cases, the client gets references to EJB objects, not primary keys or implementation classes.

The only finder method that is compulsory is findByPrimaryKey(...), which *must* be declared in the home interface [EJB2.0 9.5.2]. This method always takes a single argument, which is of the primary key type. It always (by definition) returns the same argument to the caller. So why does it need to exist at all? Many developers misunderstand the purpose of this method: findByPrimaryKey() determines whether the underlying data for the specified primary key actually exists. If it does, the method simply returns the argument passed. If it doesn't, then it throws ObjectNotFoundException. This method must *never* return null to indicate a failure.

Gotcha!

It is perfectly reasonable for a client to call findByPrimaryKey() to determine whether or not the object with a specified primary key exists. The ejbFindByPrimaryKey() method should distinguish between a nonexistent primary key and a more serious database error. For example, it is probably acceptable to throw an EJBException if an SQL error occurs in ejbFindByPrimaryKey(); this will be treated by the container as a drastic failure, and it will roll back any ongoing transaction. However, it would be an error to throw an EJBException simply because the primary key could not be found.

Hint

Finder methods return their results by reference. In EJB 1.1, there was no straightforward way to return a collection of EJBs by value. EJB 2.0 provides for 'home methods,' which can call finders, extract the state of each returned EJB, and return the states as a collection of value objects. This is much more efficient, but clients should be aware that what they are getting is a 'snapshot' of the database state at a given instance. If transaction attributes are not set correctly, the data held by the client could become stale with respect to the database. This technique is illustrated in the example later in this chapter.

ejbRemove()

When the client calls `remove()` on the EJB object, or `remove(primary_key)` on the home object, the container calls `ejbRemove()` on the EJB instance. Normally, the EJB should update its underlying persistent store in such a way that the data can be considered deleted. This may correspond to issuing an SQL DELETE statement, but in many cases the EJB will instead set a field in the database table row to indicate that the row is considered deleted.

> ### Hint
>
> The EJB can't prevent the client calling `remove()` on the home object or EJB object, but it doesn't have to do anything in `ejbRemove()` if the data store is read-only. It may be helpful to clients if the EJB throws a `RemoveException` in such a case, to indicate that the remove was not permitted.

> ### Hint
>
> Although poorly understood, the EJB container must call `ejbRemove()` on an EJB in the 'ready' state—that is, one that is synchronized to the data. It is not called on a pooled instance. Why? The reason is that EJB may have associations with other EJBs, and those associations will need to be deleted before the EJB's data representation is deleted. If associations are stored in a database table, for example, the rows reflecting associations with the EJB being removed must themselves be deleted.

Business methods

These should be implemented to correspond to the declarations in the remote interface, as usual. Don't forget that any application-defined exceptions thrown by the business methods must be declared in the remote interface.

12.1.3   Primary key class

The primary key class can be any class that implements `hashCode()` and `equals (Object)` as discussed above. The container will never attempt to call methods other than these, and will never create new primary key objects itself. Thus the developer is free to use any class that can contain sufficient information to represent the underlying primary key. More details of the requirements for primary key classes may be found on page 353.

12.2 Optimizing database access

When using BMP, it is the developer's responsibility to ensure that the EJB is efficient in its access to the database. In general, the container is unable to determine whether a call to `ejbLoad()` or `ejbStore()` is really necessary; it will always call `ejbLoad()` at the start of a transaction and `ejbStore()` before committing the transaction, but it may call either of these methods at other times if it thinks it might be necessary. Note that it is permissible for the container to passivate an EJB mid-transaction [EJB2.0 10.5.1], which would involve another pair of calls to `ejbStore()` and `ejbLoad()`. The entity EJBs described in most textbooks use a naive approach to loading and storing, for reasons of clarity. In a production system, this may not give adequate performance. For example, it may be unacceptable to handle `ejbStore()` by writing instance variables to the database without checking whether this is really necessary.

Developers frequently misunderstand this aspect of EJB programming. There is a myth in circulation that an EJB server 'knows,' for example, only to call `ejbStore()` when the internal state of the EJB has changed. But how can it possibly know this? Consider the case where there are two business methods—`getName()` and `setName()`—called in two different transactions. It may be reasonable to expect a person to understand that `setName()` has changed the internal state, while `getName()` has not, but how should the EJB container figure this out? Moreover, how should it figure it out in a way that is efficient and robust? The fact is that the EJB container *can't* figure this out. Therefore it calls `ejbStore()` before committing a transaction, even though that transaction contained only one method call, and even though `getName()` has done nothing to require a database update.

In summary, the purpose of the container's calling `ejbStore()` is *not* to tell the EJB to write to the database (despite what you will see in textbooks), it is to give the EJB an *opportunity* to write to the database. It doesn't have to take that opportunity if it doesn't need to.

Hint

If an entity bean maps to a read-only database table, `ejbStore()`, `ejbCreate()`, and `ejbRemove()` can be empty, and the issues to be discussed in this section will be less relevant. You can force a JDBC connection to be treated as read-only, whatever the database connection parameters, using the method `setReadOnly()` on `javax.sql.Connection`. To determine at runtime whether a connection is read-only, use the method `isReadOnly()` on the `DatabaseMetaData` object, obtained by calling `getMetaData` on the `Connection`.

So for optimal performance, a BMP entity should only load and store when really necessary. There are numerous strategies by which this may be accomplished. The example presented later in this chapter attempts to minimize data store updates by the simple expedient of maintaining its own internal flag to indicate whether the instance variables have changed since the last read or write.

12.3   Example: a directory-server mapping EJB

In keeping with the spirit of EJB 2.0, which says that entity EJBs that map to databases are best handled by CMP, this article demonstrates the use of an entity EJB to represent personal data in a directory server. It's a serious example, with about 1,200 lines of code, only snippets of which will be presented here. Full source code is available, as always, on the book Web site `www.kevinboone.com/ejb_book`.

This example demonstrates the following features of entity EJB design.

- The use of 'home methods' to handle 'class level' entity operations (i.e., operations carried out on no particular instance).

- The use of a DAO with an abstract method schema to decouple EJB operations from the data store.

- Implementation of single-object and multiobject finder methods.

- Simple techniques for minimizing unnecessary data store synchronization.

- The use of EJB environment variables to configure the EJB at deployment time.

- The confinement of the primary key to within the EJB (that is, the client does not have to manipulate primary keys).

Gotcha!

Directory servers are, in general, not transactional and therefore cannot be rolled back in a failure. It therefore makes little sense to set the transaction attributes of the EJB to 'Required,' which is the usual default for EJBs mapped to relational databases. The container *must* resynchronize on each business method, because data cannot be locked. Happily, directory reads are usually fast.

12.3.1   Background information

This example presents an entity EJB, called `Person`, that models some basic personal data. Specifically, a `Person` has the following properties: a given name and a family name, a full name (which may be formed from the given name and family name, but need not be), an address, a telephone number, and an email address. Of course, we could add as many properties as the application demands, but these six will be enough for the example.

Following modern practice, the personal data will be stored in an LDAP[1] directory server. There are many such directories currently available, but the set-up instructions provided with the source code concentrate on the use of OpenLDAP, which is a free, open-source directory implementation, available for a number of different platforms.

Directories can be structured in various different ways, but on the whole they tend to be set up with a 'shallow hierarchy.' What is this? Modern practice tends to favor the location of all personal data in the same node of the directory tree, rather than building a 'tree' of people based on the structure of the organization. Ten years ago, the usual practice was to create a node for the organization, then subnodes for departments, then more subnodes under the departments for teams, then personal entries for the teams. The modern practice is to have a single node called 'People' and have all the personal data in that node. Other nodes are then used to model the organizational structure.[2]

Each node in the structure is identified by a set of name-value pairs, where the names are constrained by the directory schema (in the same way that contents of the database fields are constrained by the database schema). Although a particular node can be modelled by more than one name-value pair, in the example I have assumed that this is not the case (Figure 12.1). A set of name-value pairs that uniquely identifies a particular entry is called a *distinguished name*. Within a particular entry are a number of attributes, each of which have a name and a value. So the

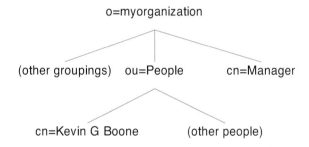

Figure 12.1. The directory structure assumed by the example in this chapter. In fact, this is easy enough to change to match a different structure, by modifying the EJB environment variables as will be explained. A detailed description of directory server terminology is beyond the scope of this book; for now note that 'o' stands for 'organization,' 'ou' for 'organization unit,' and 'cn' for 'common name.'

---

[1] Lightweight directory access protocol.

[2] Strictly speaking, an LDAP directory does not implement a 'tree' structure at all. In a real tree structure, a particular node contains a pointer to its parent, so any node can identify all the other parent nodes right to the top of the tree. There is no equivalent to this concept in LDAP. Viewing an LDAP directory as a tree structure is a convenient fiction, widely promoted in the industry, and one which I intend to continue for simplicity. LDAP purists can grit their teeth or skip ahead to the next section.

distinguished name will usually have a component that is one of the attributes of the entry itself (see below for an example if this is not clear).

The directory server administrator has, in theory, a free hand to choose which attributes must be included in each entry, and which may be included but are not compulsory. In practice, there are well-defined attributes that directories of personal data nearly always include. For this example, I have picked six attributes that nearly all directories will use. The way the EJB properties are mapped onto directory attributes is shown in Table 12.2.

Now, you may be wondering why I didn't just use EJB attributes that map directly onto the directory attributes. That is, why don't we have an EJB property called l, for 'locality'? The reason is that part of the job of an entity EJB is to decouple the business logic from the representation of the data. 'Locality' is a directory server term (strictly, it's an X.500 term). 'Address' will probably be more useful to the client of the EJB. Moreover, we may wish to change the underlying data representation at some point in the future, and this will be easier if the EJB is not tightly mapped to a particular directory server. Later on, we will discuss the 'abstract DAO' pattern for supporting this flexibility.

So, my directory entry may have the following attributes:

```
givenname: Kevin
sn: Boone
cn: Kevin G Boone
l: London
mail: kb@kevinboone.com
telephoneNumber: 1234 5678
```

How do I reference this within the directory? I need a distinguished name (DN). To get a DN I pick an attribute in my entry that will be unique in my node of the directory, and append it to the distinguished name of that node. In the example, I

EJB property	Attribute name	Conventional meaning
givenName	givenname	given name
familyName	sn	surname
fullName	cn	common name
address	l	locality
telephoneNumber	telephoneNumber	guess what?
email	mail	email address

Table 12.2. EJB properties mapped onto directory attributes.

assumed the that full name (`cn`) attribute is unique. As the personal data is all in the node `ou=People,o=myorganization`, I can write my DN like this:

```
cn=Kevin G Boone,ou=People,o=myorganization
```

If you're more familiar with filesystem hierarchies, you may be surprised to see that DNs are written in the opposite order, with the 'top' node on the right, not the left.

Because the DN is (by definition) unique in the directory, this can stand as the primary key for the EJB. However, DNs are unwieldy, and they are written in directory-server notation; EJB clients shouldn't have to be concerned with such matters. We will see later how the details of the DN can be hidden inside a DAO, so neither the client nor even the EJB needs to be aware of it.

There is one other important 'person' in the directory, and that is the directory manager. This is not (necessarily) the manager of the organization that owns the directory, but the manager of the directory itself. The directory manager is therefore identified by a DN, like any other user. In the example of Figure 12.1, the directory manager's DN is

```
cn=Manager,o=myorganization
```

This is important because the EJB will need to be able to modify personal data in the directory when its client modifies its properties. For example, when a client calls `setAddress()` on the EJB, the EJB will need to update the `l` (locality) attribute for that user in the directory. To do this it will need to log in[3] to the directory server as a user that has rights to do this update. The 'directory manager' user will have such rights, or you could choose another sufficiently privileged account instead. In any event, the EJB will need to be told which user credentials to supply when it connects to the directory, and we'll see how this is done later.

12.3.2   Design overview

So, we have a directory structure and an idea of how the EJB should behave. Now we have to decide on a design outline for the EJB. What the design has to accomplish is to make the EJB largely unaware of the details of the directory server. This would make it a relatively straightforward job to change the underlying data representation without changing the EJB. The ideal might be to design in such a way that the data store could be changed, for example, to a relational database, without changing the EJB at all.

To accomplish this, we will use a design pattern called the 'abstract data access object.' A data access object is simply a helper class that encapsulates the data store access. In the abstract DAO pattern, the EJB interacts with the data access object through the medium of its abstract base class. The EJB contains only one reference to the DAO itself, and that is the line of code that instantiates it. All other method calls are on the abstract base class.

---

[3]Directory server technologists use the term 'bind' rather than 'log in.'

The purpose of this pattern is to decouple the EJB from a specific DAO. The abstract DAO contains logic that is common to all likely 'concrete' DAO implementations, plus abstract methods that form the specification of the contract between the EJB and the DAO (Figure 12.2).

For example, `PersonDAO` has a method, `store()`, which causes the DAO to write its contents to the directory. The EJB needs to know that the method exists, and that it has this specific function, but it does not need to know how it is implemented or even in what class. `LDAPPersonDAO` has another method, `store()`, which contains an implementation that is specific to a directory server. Another DAO could implement this method to write to a database.

It is customary to provide an entity EJB with a *value object* class, which is a helper class for transferring data in bulk between the EJB and its clients. Because the value object for the `Person` has to have the properties `givenName`, `address`, and so on, it is convenient to make the DAO a subclass of the value object, which has the effect of avoiding a large amount of repetition of code.

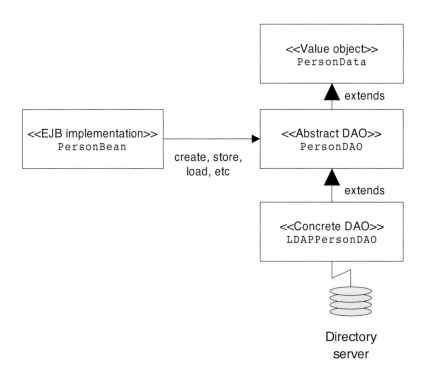

Figure 12.2. Design overview for the `Person` EJB. The EJB instantiates an `LDAPPersonDAO` to communicate with the directory server, but refers to this object only via is base class `PersonDAO`.

12.3.3   Implementation

> ### Hint
>
> Space precludes a full listing of all the classes used in this example. Complete source code can be found in the accompanying source code package, in directory `bmp`.

Value object

The value object `PersonData` is the simplest part of the implementation. It contains instance variables to contain each EJB property, and corresponding `get` and `set` methods. In outline, it looks like this:

```
   public class PersonData
   {
   String id, fullName, address, ....

5  public String getFullName { return fullName; }
   public void setFullName (String fullName)
     {
     this.fullName = fullName;
     }
10 // etc...
   }
```

The 'id' field will contain the primary key for the `Person`. With a directory server, as we have discussed, this will be a distinguished name. I have used the name `id` in preference to, for example, `distinguishedName` because the EJB is decoupled from its data store: Other DAO implementations would use different kinds of primary key.

Abstract and concrete data access objects

The abstract DAO contains logic that all DAOs that work with this EJB would be expected to implement. It also contains abstract methods for the functionality that will be available in each specific subclass. It is important that the DAO is fully documented, as this documentation is what will be available to a person who has to modify the data store representation and create a new DAO for it. The abstract DAO is shown in full in Listing 12.1. Note that this class is a subclass of `PersonData`, so it inherits the instance variables `address`, `fullName`, etc. This is simply to avoid the need to implement these instance variables, and their `get` and `set` methods in this class, as well as in `PersonData`.

For a DAO to be of use, it needs to be sufficiently comprehensive that an EJB can do *all* its data store manipulation through the DAO, without referring to the data store itself. This means that the DAO will need methods to read and write its data in the data store (`load()` and `store()` in this example), insert new data (`create()`) and remove data (`remove()`). In addition, to be of use the DAO must contain methods for searching the data store, which EJB will use to implement its finder methods.

Listing 12.1: **Abstract DAO class `PersonDAO` contains the specifications of the methods that the EJB will use to read and write the data store. Specific DAOs will implement these methods to support different data stores.**

```
     package com.kevinboone.ejb_book.person;

     import javax.ejb.*;
     import java.rmi.*;
   5 import java.util.*;
     import javax.naming.*;

     /**
      Abstract DAO class for the 'Person' EJB; DAOs for specific
  10 datasources override the abstract methods.
      (c)2002 Kevin Boone
      */
     public abstract class PersonDAO extends PersonData
     {
  15 /**
      Set the ID property of the object; this must be done before
      calling load(), store(), or remove(); create() assumes that
      id is null, and must be set internally.
      */
  20 public void setId(String id) { this.id = id; }

     /**
      Initialize the DAO by preparing resource connections, etc.
      connectionData is a String containing additional connection
  25 parameters that may be of interest to a specific subclass,
      e.g., database table, directory base DN
      */
     public abstract void init
         (String host, int port, String userId, String password,
  30         String connectionData)
       throws PersonDAOException;

     /**
      Tidy up; close connections, etc. This method must succeed, or
  35 throw a runtime error to indicate a catastrophic failure. No
      application-defined exceptions are permitted
      */
     public abstract void uninit();

  40 /**
      Synchronize all the properties of the object from the data
      store entry specified by the 'id' property; all properties
      are overwritten. If the 'id' property references an entry
```

```
     that  does  not  exist  in  the  data  store,  throw  a
 45  NoSuchPersonException.  In  all  other  failures  throw
     PersonDAOException
     */
     public abstract void load ()
        throws PersonDAOException , NoSuchPersonException ;
 50

     /**
     Synchronize  the  data  store  entry  specified  by  'id'  to  the
     properties  of  this  DAO.  All  properties  retain  their  values.
     If  the  'id'  field  specifies  a  person  for  whom  there  is  no
 55  entry,  throw  a  NoSuchPersonException.  In  all  other  failures,
     throw  PersonDAOException
     */
     public abstract void store ()
          throws PersonDAOException , NoSuchPersonException ;
 60

     /**
     Create  a  new  entry  using  the  properties  of  this  object.  The
     id  property  is  assumed  to  be  null,  and  is  set  in  this  method
     to  indicate  the  new  primary  key.  The  primary  key  may  be
 65  derived  from  the  properties  themselves,  or  generated  by  the
     DAO  in  another  way.   If  the  person  cannot  be  created  because
     there  is  already  an  entry  with  the  same  primary  key,  and  it
     is  not  appropriate  to  choose  a  new  primary  key,  then  throw
     DuplicatePersonException.  In  all  other  failures  throw
 70  PersonDAOException
     */
     public abstract void create ()
          throws DuplicatePersonException , PersonDAOException ;

 75  /**
     Remove  the  person  entry  specified  by  the  ID  property;  all
     other  properties  are  ignored.  If  there  is  no  entry  in  the
     data  store  with  the  specified  id,  throw
     NoSuchPersonException.  In  all  other  failures  throw
 80  PersonDAOException.
     */
     public abstract void remove()
          throws NoSuchPersonException , PersonDAOException ;

 85  /**
     Returns  the  number  of  person  entries  in  the  data  store.  All
     properties  are  ignored.  Throws  PersonDAOException  in  the
     event  of  any  failure
     */
 90  public abstract int getCount ()
          throws PersonDAOException ;

     /**
     Returns  a  Collection  of  Strings,  where  each  String  is  the
 95  primary  key  of  an  entry  in  the  data  store.  Entries  are
     selected  on  the  basis  of  a  matching  (case−insensitive)
     address  value.  This  method  should  leave  the  properties  in  the
```

```
      same  state  as  it  finds  them.  Throws  PersonDAOException  in  the
      event of any failure
100   */
      public abstract Collection getIdsByAddress(String address)
          throws PersonDAOException;


      /**
105   Returns  a  Collection  of  PersonData  objects,  selected  on  the
      basis  of  a  matching  (case-insensitive)  address  value.  This
      method  should  leave  the  properties  in  the  same  state  as  it
      finds  them.  Throws  PersonDAOException  in  the  event  of  any
      failure
110   */
      public abstract Collection getValuesByAddress(String address)
          throws PersonDAOException;
      }
```

In this example, the only search functionality is on the basis of 'address,' so the EJB will only be able to provide a `findByAddress()`. This is adequate for the example, as the other search functionality will be implemented in a similar way. You may have noticed that the DAO provides two ways to search the data store by address: `getValuesByAddress()` and `getIdsByAddress()`. The significance of this provision will be explained later.

To communicate with the directory server, we need a concrete implementation of `PersonDAO`, which is, in this case, provided by the class `LDAPPersonDAO`. The power of the abstract DAO pattern should now become apparent: *We don't need to describe this class.* The EJB developer does not need to know how LDAP operations are coded in the DAO. All he needs to know is the specification embodied in the abstract DAO. Provided the concrete DAO implements the specification correctly, its contents are irrelevant to the developer.

There is one small exception to this statement. DAOs will need to be supplied with some configuration data, and that data will vary from one data store (and therefore DAO) to another. Thus, you'll see that the `init()` method in `PersonDAO` has a parameter `connectiondata` in addition to the expected parameters for host name, user ID, password, and so on. `conntectiondata` is a string that is passed through to the concrete DAO for the purposes of supplying DAO-specific configuration. The EJB does not need to know anything about this data: It simply reads it from its environment as will be discussed later. In this example, `LDAPPersonDAO` expects this argument to contain the DN of the node in the directory that contains the person data entries, which is `ou=People,o=myorganization`.

As a result of all this, we don't need to list any of `LDAPPersonDAO` in this chapter. You may wish to see it if you are interested in writing Java code that reads and writes an LDAP directory, in which case you'll find the source code in the usual place.

Implementation class

With the data access logic safely tucked away in the DAOs, the EJB developer can concentrate on matters concerned with the EJB architecture. In particular, the implementation class must handle the following.

- Initialize the DAO from the EJB environment.

- Implement the methods `ejbCreate()`, `ejbRemove()`, `ejbLoad()`, `ejbStore()`, and `ejbFindXXX()` (the finders) to make the appropriate calls on the DAO *where required*.

- 'Convert' DAO exceptions into EJB exceptions (such as `DuplicateKey Exception`).

- Implement the business methods.

To initialize the DAO, the EJB reads data from its environment using JNDI. A good place to do this is in `setEntityContext()`, because we are guaranteed that this will be the first method called by the EJB container. The relevant code looks like this:

```
     Context  c = new  InitialContext ();
     host  = (String)c.lookup
             ("java:comp/env/host");
     port  = ((Integer)c.lookup
 5           ("java:comp/env/port")).intValue ();
     userid  =   (String)c.lookup
             ("java:comp/env/userid");
     password  = (String)c.lookup
             ("java:comp/env/password");
10   connectiondata = (String)c.lookup
             ("java:comp/env/connectiondata");
```

Notice that these environment variables are all of `String` type, apart from the port number, which is an integer.

The values of these environment variables are set in the deployment descriptor. With the *J2EE Reference Implementation*, we use the 'Environment' tab to do this (Figure 12.3).

The `ejbCreate()` method (see below) takes personal data as its parameters and creates a new entry in the directory. Notice that this method does *not* have a parameter for the distinguished name, or any other form of primary key. In fact, the DAO generates the primary key itself, and stores it in its `id` property. `ejbCreate()` simply returns this value, where it is picked up by the container and used to initialize the EJB object. Note also that, whatever exceptions the DAO throws, the `ejbCreate()` must throw `CreateException`.

Because the DAO is held as an instance variable of the EJB implementation class, setting its properties is tantamount to setting the properties of the EJB. This means that, at the end of the `ejbCreate()` method, the instance variables are ready

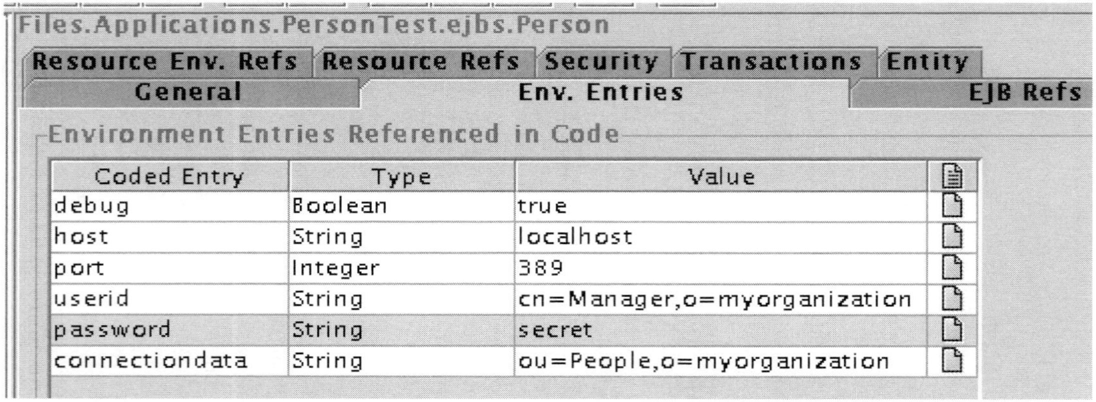

380

Figure 12.3. Setting the EJB's environment: It will use these variables to initialize the DAO for communication with the directory server.

for a client to call a business method. Moreover, because we know that the instance variables now match the data in the directory, we can set the `needWrite` flag to false, indicating that we don't need to write to the directory when given the next opportunity to do so.

```
public String ejbCreate (String givenName,
    String familyName, String fullName, String telephoneNumber,
    String address, String email)
      throws CreateException
  {
    try
      {
      dao.setGivenName(givenName);
      dao.setFamilyName(familyName);
      dao.setFullName(fullName);
      dao.setTelephoneNumber(telephoneNumber);
      dao.setEmail(email);
      dao.setAddress(address);
      // DAO must create a new primary key if
      //   PersonData.id is null
      dao.setId(null);
      dao.create();
      needWrite = false;
      }
    catch (DuplicatePersonException e)
      {
      debugOut ("abandonning ejbCreate(): " + e);
      throw new DuplicateKeyException();
      }
    catch (PersonDAOException e)
      {
      debugOut ("abandonning ejbcreate(): " + e);
      throw new CreateException(e.toString());
      }

    // Return the primary key generated by the DAO
    return dao.getId();
    }
```

`ejbLoad()` is straightforward to implement: We just call `load()` on the DAO. We also set `needWrite` to false because, as was the case for `ejbCreate()`, if the method succeeds, we know that the EJB state is in sync with the directory. Even if the method *fails*, we don't want to write to the directory (what would be the point of writing uncertain data?) so the method clears the `needWrite` flag at the very beginning. The method is shown below (with some of the debugging code removed for clarity).

If the required person cannot be found in the directory, then the DAO throws a `NoSuchPersonException`. This exception is part of the DAO design, not the EJB model. The *EJB Specification* says that we should throw a `NoSuchEntityException` in this situation. In the event of any other kind of failure, we throw `EJBException`. Note that we can't throw anything else: The method `ejbLoad()` is precluded from throwing any checked exception, with only run-time exceptions permissible. In all cases, the container will trash the instance so it can't do any further damage. It will also try to roll back the transaction but, as already discussed, directory servers are usually not transactional.

```
public void ejbLoad ()
    {
    needWrite = false;
    try
        {
        dao.load ();
        }
    catch (NoSuchPersonException e)
        {
        throw new NoSuchEntityException
            ("no such person: " + dao.getId ());
        }
    catch (PersonDAOException e)
        {
        throw new EJBException (e.toString ());
        }
    }
```

How does the DAO know which person's data to load? It knows because we initialized it in `ejbActivate()`, as described next.

`ejbActivate()` is called whenever the EJB is mapped to a new EJB object— that is, whenever it is associated with a new primary key. We know from the *EJB Specification* that the container won't call `ejbLoad()` or `ejbStore()` without first calling `ejbActivate()`, unless the primary key remains the same. So this method is a good place to get the primary key and store it for later use. The place we store the primary key in this example is in the DAO's `id` property.

```
public void ejbActivate ()
    {
    String id = (String)ec.getPrimaryKey ();
    dao.setId (id);
    }
```

Here `ec` is the `EntityContext` object that was passed to the EJB when it was initialized.

`ejbStore` is called when a transaction is about to be commited. In this example, the directory server is not transactional, and I recommended earlier that the transaction attributes all be set to `RequiresNew`. Thus `ejbStore()` will be called upon exit from **all** business methods. It is therefore even more important than usual to ensure that this method does not update the data store if it doesn't need to. If the `needWrite` flag is set, this indicates that it does need to. As we have seen, this flag is reset by methods that synchronize to the directory; as we will later see, it is set by methods that modify the EJB's state without updating the directory.

Because the DAO does most of the work, `ejbStore()` is quite simple. If `needWrite` is set, `ejbStore()` calls `store()` on the DAO, then sets `needWrite` to `false`.

```
   public void ejbStore ()
     {
     try
       {
 5     if ( needWrite )
         {
         debugOut ("data has changed: will store");
         dao.store ();
         needWrite = false;
10       }
       else
         {
         debugOut ("data is clean: won't store");
         }
15     }
     catch ( NoSuchPersonException e )
       {
       throw new NoSuchEntityException
         ("no such person: " + dao.getId ());
20     }
     catch ( PersonDAOException e )
       {
       throw new EJBException (e.toString ());
       }
25   }
```

Business methods are implemented to do whatever is required, with the additional requirement that any method that changes the state of the EJB, but does not write to the directory, sets the `needWrite` flag to `true`. This ensures that the directory is really updated on the next call to `ejbStore`. As an example, here is the implementation of `setAddress()`.

```
   public void setAddress (String s)
     {
     debugOut ("setAddress ()");
     needWrite = true;
 5   dao.setAddress (s);
     }
```

Because calling `setAddress()` on the DAO only changes its state, and does not cause a directory write, we must set `needWrite` to ensure that a write does happen on the next opportunity.

The method `ejbFindByPrimaryKey()` simply tests whether the data identified by the primary key really exists. If it does, we return the primary key itself, and if it doesn't, we throw a `NoSuchObjectException`. If something else goes wrong, we throw a `FinderException` with an appropriate message, as required by the Specification.

This method is implemented simply by setting the DAO's `id` field, and then calling `load()` on it. Although this does change the state of the DAO, and therefore of the EJB, this does not give rise to a need to resynchronize the directory to the EJB. Why not? The Specification says that finder methods are only called on pooled instances, never on active instances, so the instance variables of the EJB and the DAO are irrelevant.

Strictly speaking, we should provide the DAO with a 'check' method rather than asking it to do a load, as checking the primary key may be a faster operation that loading the data itself. With a directory server, it doesn't make that much difference.

```
public String ejbFindByPrimaryKey(String id)
    throws FinderException
    {
    try
5       {
        dao.setId(id);
        dao.load();
        return id;
        }
10  catch (NoSuchPersonException e)
        {
        throw new ObjectNotFoundException
            ("no such id: " + id);
        }
15  catch (PersonDAOException e)
        {
        throw new FinderException (e.toString());
        }
    }
```

Apart from `findByPrimayKey()`, the `Person` EJB should expose whatever other finder methods are of value to its clients. In this example, I have implemented only one other finder method, `findByAddress()`, although others could be provided using the same pattern. In fact, *two* implementations of this functionality are provided: One, `findByAddress()`, is a 'traditional' finder method, that returns to the EJB's clients a `Collection` of EJB references. For comparison, I have also provided a `getByAddress()`, which is a home method. The difference is that `getByAddress()` returns to its clients a `Collection` of `PersonData` value objects, as we shall see.

Let's consider `findByAddress()` first. It is declared in the home interface as

```
public Collection findByAddress(String address)
    throws FinderException , RemoteException ;
```

and the corresponding implementation is as follows. Note that it is really the DAO that does all the work; the EJB simply delegates the call and handles any resulting exceptions.

```
public Collection ejbFindByAddress (String address)
    throws FinderException
    {
    try
5       {
        Collection c = dao.getIdsByAddress(address);
        return c;
```

```
        }
    catch ( PersonDAOException  e )
        {
        throw new  FinderException  (e.toString ());
        }
    }
```

The method calls `getIdsByAddress()` on the DAO, which is defined to return the primary keys of all the entries that match the specified address. The home object in the EJB container will iterate this `Collection` and return to the client a different `Collection` of EJB references. It is sometimes a source of confusion that the method declaration in the home interface and the corresponding implementation both return a `Collection`. This does not indicate that they return the same `Collection`: The home object (governed by the home interface) returns a `Collection` of EJB references, while the implementation returns a `Collection` of primary keys. In this example, the primary key type is simply `String`.

As we shall see, providing EJB references to the client does allow the client to interact with the EJB in a natural way, but imposes certain overheads.

Turning to `getByAddress()`: This is a home method, the principles of which were described on page 351. The method is declared on the home interface as

```
public Collection getByAddress ()
    throws FinderException , RemoteException ;
```

There is no reason why this method should necessarily throw `FinderException` in the event of failure, but it is simpler for the client if its exception handling is the same as for the finder method `findByAddress()`, which *must* by defined to throw `FinderException`.

The corresponding implementation is shown below, and, again, it is the DAO that does most of the work.

```
public Collection ejbHomeGetByAddress ( String  address)
        throws  FinderException
    {
    try
        {
        Collection c = dao.getValuesByAddress(address);
        return c;
        }
    catch ( PersonDAOException  e )
        {
        throw new  FinderException  (e.toString ());
        }
    }
```

The relevant DAO method here is `getValuesByAddress()`, which is defined to return a `Collection` of value objects. Alternatively, the method could have called `getIdsByAddress()` and then called `PersonDAO.load()` to retrieve each person's data. This would move some of the logic from the DAO to the EJB, but otherwise would be similar. Because, in this example, it is as easy for the directory server to retrieve all the person's data as it is to extract the ID of a matching user, but doing the work in the DAO is slightly more efficient.

So we have provided two methods by which a client can find personal records that match a specified address: a home method and a traditional finder. These techniques appear similar to clients, but have significant differences in efficiency and practicality.

- The finder returns EJB references, while the home method returns value objects. The clear advantage of giving the client EJB references is that the client can then call methods on the EJBs, which may, perhaps, modify their state. This is not possible with a value object, as it represents a 'snapshot' of the data at the time the method call was made.

- If the client merely wants to query a person's data (rather than update it, which is most likely with a directory server as the data source), then using the home method is considerably faster. This is because the client needs to call no further business methods on the EJB, and therefore the overhead of synchronizing to the data store is eliminated.

- The home method returns data that is only guaranteed to match the underlying data store so long as a transaction is locking the data. As soon as the transaction is committed, the data can become stale, and the client cannot rely on it. If the client gets live EJB references from finder methods, it can guarantee that any data it subsequently extracts from the EJB is valid with respect to the data store.

The `Person` EJB also provides another home method: `getCount()`. This method returns to the client an integer representing the number of person entries currently in the directory. This method *must* be implemented as a home method: We have no discretion here. This is because the client can only call methods on the home object or the EJB object, and if the current count value happens to be zero, then there are no EJB objects on which to make the call. In any event, it is inefficient to have the client locate an arbitrary EJB just to call a method on it, even if it could guaranteed that an EJB instance exists.

Strange as it may seem, this functionality was notably absent in EJB 1.1. To get a count of the number of EJBs of a particular type we had to implement this in a session EJB. This broke the clean separation between the session tier and the entity tier. Even stranger, the functionality remains absent from container-managed persistence, even in EJB 2.0. There are proposals to rectify this in EJB 2.1, currently in early draft.

The final method to consider is `ejbRemove()`. This one is trivial to implement: It simply calls `remove()` on the DAO.

The `Person` EJB implements a simple method of reducing data store synchronization overheads, by eliminating unnecessary writes in `ejbStore()`. There are a few other things to note about this approach to optimizing database access.

- Finder methods need no extra code to support the technique; finders are called on an EJB in the 'passive' state, and changes to instance variables are of no consequence. Notice that, in the `Person` example, `ejbFindByPrimaryKey()` and `ejbLoad()` both read from the database. It may be thought that `ejb FindByPrimaryKey()` could set the instance variables in the DAO, so that `ejbLoad()` does not have to. With BMP, this won't work, because we can't guarantee that the container will call these two methods on the same instance. CMP schemes may be able to optimize this.

- `ejbCreate()` writes directly to the database and sets `needWrite` to `false`. Small efficiency gains are available if we defer the row insertion until `ejb Passivate()` or `ejbStore()` because a client might have called `remove()`, making the creation unnecessary. In my opinion, however, the increase in the complexity of the logic outweighs the nugatory efficiency gain.

- `ejbRemove()` does not need any extra logic. The container has to call `ejb Activate()` before any operations on instance variables, and this resets the EJB to its 'start of transaction' state.

The developer needs to exercise self-discipline when using the approach described above, and others like it. In particular, business methods should not read and write instance variables directly, but must use the corresponding `getXXX` and `setXXX` methods. We will see that the CMP scheme in EJB 2.0 enforces the use of `getXXX` and `setXXX` to read and write instance variables, as the instance variables themselves are usually hidden inside a container-generated class.

> ### Hint
>
> There is little to be gained by minimizing the *amount* of data exchanged with the database in a load or store operation. For example, if an EJB has 10 persistent instance variables, synchronizing them to the database individually is likely to worsen performance rather than to improve it. On some occasions, we may save a bit of time by writing only one or two columns in an UPDATE statement, but unless the developer is very careful, the EJB will end up carrying out more individual database operations than we really need. Real efficiency gains come from reducing the *number* of database operations.

12.3.4 Deployment

Deployment of the `Person` EJB should present no particular challenges by now. You will need to ensure that the 'primary key type' is set to `java.lang.String`, that transaction attributes are all `RequiresNew`, and that the environment is set up as described above.

> ## Gotcha!
>
> A `String` primary key type should be entered as `java.lang.String`, and not just `String`. The EJB server has no reason to think that `String` is a special case that should be expanded to a fully qualified name using 'java.lang.' as the package. Java compilers do make this assumption, but other software doesn't have to.

12.3.5   Testing and analysis

To understand fully the interaction between the client, the EJB, and the container, we must examine the sequence of operations line-by-line. It's a bit tedious, but essential for a detailed comprehension.

To follow this explanation, you will need to refer to the test client (Listing 12.2) and the output from the EJB server (Listing 12.3). The client is quite long, because it exercises all the functionality of the EJB: creation, deletion, getting and setting properties, the home methods, and the finders.

Listing 12.2: **Test client for the `Person` EJB. This code is examined step by step in the text.**

```
    package com.kevinboone.ejb_book.person;
    import javax.naming.*;
    import javax.rmi.PortableRemoteObject;
    import java.util.*;
5
    /**
    This simple client tests the 'person'
    Enterprise JavaBean
    */
10  public class PersonTestClient
    {
    public static void main(String[] args)
       throws Exception
       {
15     long t1, t2; // millisecond timing counters
       Context context = new InitialContext();
       Object ref = context.lookup("Person");
       PersonHome home = (PersonHome)
          PortableRemoteObject.narrow
20           (ref, PersonHome.class);
       System.out.println ("Finding user Eric");
       Person eric = home.findByPrimaryKey
         ("cn=Eric Cartman,ou=People,o=myorganization");
       PersonData personData = eric.getPersonData();
25     System.out.println
```

```
              ("person data: " + personData);
      System.out.println ("Changing Eric's telephone number");
      eric.setTelephoneNumber ("123");
      System.out.println
30      ("new telephone number: "
            + eric.getTelephoneNumber ());
      Person stan = null;
      try
         {
35      System.out.println
            ("There are currently " + home.getCount ()
                + " person entries");
         System.out.println
            ("Creating user Stan");
40      stan = home.create ("Stan", "Marsh", "Stan Marsh",
            "0121342", "South Park", "stan@southpark.colorado");
         System.out.println
            ("There are now " + home.getCount ()
                + " person entries");
45      System.out.println ("Deleting user Stan");
         stan.remove ();
         System.out.println
            ("There are now " + home.getCount ()
                + " person entries");
50      }
      catch (Exception e)
         {
         System.out.println ("Can't add person: " + e);
         System.out.flush ();
55      }


      System.out.println
         ("Finding EJBs with 'South Park' address");
      t1 = System.currentTimeMillis ();
60   Collection c = home.findByAddress ("South Park");
      Iterator it = c.iterator ();
      while (it.hasNext ())
         {
         Person person = (Person) it.next ();
65      System.out.println (person.getFullName ());
         }
      t2 = System.currentTimeMillis ();
      System.out.println ("Took " + (t2 - t1) + " msec");

70   System.out.println
         ("Finding value objects with 'South Park' address");
      t1 = System.currentTimeMillis ();
      c = home.getByAddress ("South Park");
      it = c.iterator ();
75   while (it.hasNext ())
         {
         PersonData person = (PersonData) it.next ();
         System.out.println (personData.getFullName ());
         }
```

```
80      t2 = System.currentTimeMillis();
        System.out.println ("Took " + (t2 - t1) + " msec");
        }
    }
```

Listing 12.3: **The output from the EJB to the server log when the test client is executed. I have annotated it with the line executed by the client just before each section of output is generated. This annotation is for clarity of explanation and is, of course, not part of the output of the EJB.**

```
    //client: findByPrimaryKey("cn=Eric Cartman...")
    PersonBean: entering ejbFindByPrimaryKey()
    PersonBean: leaving ejbFindByPrimaryKey()

5   //client: getPersonData()
    PersonBean: entering ejbLoad()
    PersonBean: leaving ejbLoad()
    PersonBean: entering getPersonData()
    PersonBean: leaving getPersonData()
10  PersonBean: entering ejbStore()
    PersonBean: dn is: cn=Eric Cartman,ou=People,o=myorganization
    PersonBean: data is clean: won't store
    PersonBean: leaving ejbStore()

15  //client: setTelephoneNumber()
    PersonBean: entering ejbLoad()
    PersonBean: leaving ejbLoad()
    PersonBean: setTelephoneNumber()
    PersonBean: entering ejbStore()
20  PersonBean: dn is: cn=Eric Cartman,ou=People,o=myorganization
    PersonBean: data has changed: will store
    PersonBean: leaving ejbStore()

    //client: getTelephoneNumber()
25  PersonBean: entering ejbLoad()
    PersonBean: leaving ejbLoad()
    PersonBean: getTelephoneNumber()
    PersonBean: entering ejbStore()
    PersonBean: dn is: cn=Eric Cartman,ou=People,o=myorganization
30  PersonBean: data is clean: won't store
    PersonBean: leaving ejbStore()

    //client: create()
    PersonBean: entering ejbCreate()
35  PersonBean: leaving ejbCreate()
    PersonBean: entering ejbStore()
    PersonBean: dn is: cn=Stan Marsh, ou=people,o=myorganization
    PersonBean: data is clean: won't store
    PersonBean: leaving ejbStore()
40
    //client: remove()
    PersonBean: entering ejbLoad()
    PersonBean: leaving ejbLoad()
```

```
   PersonBean:  entering ejbRemove()
45 PersonBean:  leaving ejbRemove()

   //client: findByAddress()
   PersonBean:  entering ejbFindByAddress()
   PersonBean:  leaving ejbFindByAddress()
50
   //client: getFullName()
   PersonBean:  entering ejbLoad()
   PersonBean:  leaving ejbLoad()
   PersonBean:  getFullName()
55 PersonBean:  entering ejbStore()
   PersonBean:  dn is: cn=Eric Cartman, ou=people,o=myorganization
   PersonBean:  data is clean: won't store
   PersonBean:  leaving ejbStore()

60 //client: getFullName()
   PersonBean:  entering ejbLoad()
   PersonBean:  leaving ejbLoad()
   PersonBean:  getFullName()
   PersonBean:  entering ejbStore()
65 PersonBean:  dn is: cn=Kyle Broslowski, ou=people,o=myorganization
   PersonBean:  data is clean: won't store
   PersonBean:  leaving ejbStore()

   //client: getByAddress()
70 PersonBean:  entering ejbHomeGetByAddress()
   PersonBean:  leaving ejbHomeGetByAddress()
```

Client uses `findByPrimaryKey()` to locate a specific EJB This results in the EJB container calling `ejbFindByPrimaryKey()` on the server.

Client calls `getPersonData()` The container first has to call `ejbLoad()` on the EJB, then `getPersonData()`, then `ejbStore()`. Because the `needWrite` flag has not been set, `ejbStore()` does nothing.

Client calls `setTelephoneNumber()` The container calls `ejbLoad()`, `setTelephoneNumber()`, and `ejbStore()`. This time, the `setTelephoneNumber()` method has set the `needWrite` flag, so the `ejbStore()` method knows to write to the directory.

Client calls `getTelephoneNumber()` The container calls `ejbLoad()`, `getTelephoneNumber()`, and `ejbStore()`. Because `ejbLoad()` set `needWrite` to `false`, `ejbStore()` does nothing. Notice, however, that we have now read the directory even though the instance variables are, in fact, in sync with the directory. This was necessary, because the container has no way of knowing that the directory has not been modified outside of the EJB since the last `ejbLoad()`.

Client calls `create(...)` The EJB server calls `ejbCreate()`, `ejbPostCreate()` (which is empty in this example), and then `ejbStore()`. The `ejbStore()` method does not write to the directory, because `needWrite` is `false`.

Client calls `remove()` Notice that the container calls `ejbLoad()` before calling
`ejbRemove()`. This is because the EJB *may* need to be synchronized to the
data store before it can remove itself. In this example, it doesn't, but the
container does not know that.

Client calls `findByAddress()` The EJB server calls `ejbFindByAddress()`, and
the client gets a `Collection` of EJB references that it then iterates.

Client calls `getFullName()` **on the two EJBs that were returned by the
finder** For each iteration, we have a complete set of calls on `ejbLoad()`,
the business method, and `ejbStore()`. Because we are calling a `getXXX()`
method, `needWrite` is not set, and the directory is not updated.

Client calls `getByAddress()` The EJB returns a `Collection` of value objects, so
the client does not need to call any further methods on the EJB. Thus the EJB
container does not interact with the EJB while the `Collection` is iterated.

There is one final point to note about the execution of the test client, which
should be clear from an examination of Listing 12.4. This listing shows the elapsed
times for the two 'find by address' operations made by the client. In this run of the
client, getting the list of names that match the specified address took 118 msec using
the finder method, but only 44 msec using the home method. That's a reduction by
about a factor of three in time for the home method. Moreover, the home method
returns to the client all the personal data, not just the full name of the person.
It should be obvious that using a home method to return a `Collection` of value
objects from a search operation is much, much faster than using a finder and then
iterating the results. This is to be expected, as there is no synchronization on the
server after the home method has completed. However, efficient though it may be,
we have only a limited confidence that the data in the value object actually matches
the database, once the transaction has committed. Moreover, the client only has a
representation of the EJB's data, not a reference to the EJB itself, so it can't act
on the EJB without going through the home object and getting new references. In
summary, using home objects to handle search functionality is usually faster than
using finders, but only appropriate if a snapshot of the data is required.

Listing 12.4: **The output from the test client to the console when it is
executed. Note the difference in timings for the two different implementations of the 'find by address' functionality.**

```
    Finding  user  Eric
    person  data:  id=cn=Eric  Cartman,ou=People,o=myorganization
    givenname=Eric
    familyname=Cartman
5   fullname=Eric  Cartman
    telephone=123
    email=eric.cartman@southpark.colorado
    address=South  Park
```

```
10   Changing Eric's telephone number
     new telephone number: 123
     There are currently 4 person entries
     Creating user Stan
     There are now 5 person entries
15   Deleting user Stan
     There are now 4 person entries
     Finding EJBs with 'South Park' address
     Eric Cartman
     Kyle Broslowski
20   Took 118 msec
     Finding value objects with 'South Park' address
     Eric Cartman
     Eric Cartman
     Took 44 msec
```

12.4 Entity EJBs and nonflat data structures

A 'flat' data structure is one in which the all the relevant entities are collated into one searchable unit, such as a single database table or a single directory suffix. In many applications, the underlying data structure is not flat; it may be that a given EJB models data in different database tables, or even in different data sources.

When using bean-managed persistence, there is no reason why an entity EJB's data should not be drawn from a number of different database tables. Indeed, a prominent advantage of entity EJBs is that they can provide a simple, object-oriented view of a complex underlying data model. All that is necessary is that the developer have a sufficiently good grasp of SQL to be able to code the appropriate queries and updates, and that the joined tables honor a unique primary key. However, it will sometimes be more flexible to define an EJB for each table and implement persistent associations between the EJBs. Clients can then navigate to the data they require by following the associations. It is not always straightforward to choose between these strategies.

Many developers favor the 'normalization' of EJBs to database schemas. This involves the creation of an EJB for each database table, such that each row of the database table corresponds to a conceptual instance of an EJB. Such a scheme is straightforward to implement—indeed, it is possible to get tools that will generate all the EJB code automatically from a database schema. However, it does not necessarily help the *client* to see data modeled in this way. Remember that one of the principal goals of the entity EJB architecture is to provide an object-oriented view of the underlying data store; it is not to provide a 'thin layer' of Java on top of the database.

12.5   Many-valued associations in BMP

Consider the relationship between the EJBs `Bike` and `Booking` that was described
on page 338. At any given time, a motorcycle will be subject to a number of bookings. This association is one-to-many in the direction `Bike-Booking`. Clients are
going to want to be able to ask the `Bike` EJB what bookings it is subject to. We
will either provide this data by value (e.g., a `Collection` of `BookingData` objects)
or by reference (e.g., a `Collection` of `Booking` EJB references). In either case,
the EJB developer is going to have to implement the data synchronization logic to
support it.

A straightforward approach is to implement `ejbLoad()` to populate a `Collection`
of `Booking` primary keys. Then, when clients request the collection of bookings we
can generate either `BookingData` or `Booking` instances from the primary keys.

The performance of this system can be improved considerably by using lazy
loading, but this requires delivering to the client proxies that are capable of telling
the `Bike` EJB to load on demand. EJB 2.0 handles this sort of thing automatically,
and a discussion of the issues can be found in Chapter 13. With BMP, the developer
has to exercise some ingenuity.

12.6   Summary

Bean-managed persistence requires the developer to code the synchronization of
the EJB's properties and associations with the database. This means extra work
for the developer (compared with container-managed persistence), but does allow
synchronization with nonstandard data sources. At present (that is, with EJB 1.1-
compliant products), many developers achieve better performance with BMP than
can be achieved with CMP. It is likely that with increased availability of EJB 2.0
products, this will no longer be possible, and CMP will offer the advantages of
convenience *and* efficiency. Undoubtedly EJB 2.0 shifts the emphasis onto CMP.

Chapter 13

Container-managed persistence

Overview

Container-managed persistence (CMP) is a technique for allowing the EJB container to handle all the synchronization between the entity EJB and the underlying persistent storage device, usually a relational database. This chapter describes how to make use of CMP in both the EJB 1.1 and EJB 2.0 models. The chapter starts with a description of some of the issues that any persistence management scheme must address. It then describes how these issues were tackled in the EJB 1.1 scheme. Examination of some of the problems with the EJB 1.1 model allows an insight into the way in which the EJB 2.0 CMP model, although complex, solves many of the problems that prevented a wide uptake of CMP in EJB 1.1. We finish with a description of some practical examples from the *Prestige Bike Hire* application.

13.1 Persistence management overview

Container-managed persistence has the potential to be of great help to the developer, as well as offering a number of efficiency advantages. The *EJB Specification* defines a philosophy of persistence management in which the EJB devolves *all* its persistence management to the container. The container's job is therefore a significant one.

We have already seen (Chapter 11) that the EJB container can determine when the EJB must be given a chance to read its persistent state from the database, and when it must be given the chance to write it. In summary, the container knows that state is likely to be stale at the start of a transaction, and may well need to be written out just before a transaction commits. With bean-managed persistence, the container calls the methods `ejbLoad()` and `ejbStore()` at these points, and code supplied by the EJB developer carries out the actual synchronization. The container also knows when new data must be created in the database (the client calls a `create()` method on the home object), and when data must be deleted

395

(client calls `remove`). Again, with BMP the container simply calls `ejbCreate()` and `ejbRemove()` and the developer's code supplies the functionality.

With container-managed persistence, all the functionality—loading, storing, creating, and deleting—must be implemented internally by the container. Moreover, we need a way to implement finder methods so that clients can locate specific EJBs. These also must be provided by the container.

Let's begin by considering a very simple case. An entity EJB has three persistent instance variables: `A`, `B`, and `C`. These are accessible to clients via the business methods `getA()`, `getB()`, and `getC()`. We will examine the various challenges posed by persistence management using this example, and others, and examine some possible responses to these challenges. My intention is to show that the CMP schemes adopted by EJB 1.1 and EJB 2.0 (which are different) are simply possible approaches to solving a general problem.

13.1.1 Providing access to persistent properties

The first question we need to answer is this: How can the container get the values of the instance variables from the instance, so that it can write them to the database or set the values from the database? A number of alternatives suggest themselves.

- Method 1: The container could manipulate the instance variables through the `getXXX()` and `setXXX()` methods, just as a client would. That is, it could call `getA()`, `setB()`, etc.

- Method 2: The instance variables could be declared as `public`, so that classes outside the implementation class package can read them directly.

- Method 3: The implementation class could provide `getXXX()` and `setXXX()` methods to be called by the container; these may, or equally may not, match the `getXXX()` and `setXXX()` methods provided to support clients.

- Method 4: The instances variables could actually be stored in some part of the container, rather than in the implementation class itself, with transparent access provided by the container to the implementation class.

Of these techniques, method 1 is likely to be the least effective. If the container can only get access to the EJB state the same way as a client, then we can't persist anything in a form that is different than that in which it is offered to clients. In many cases, that would be fine, but it isn't very flexible.

Methods 2 and 3 are essentially the same: Using `getXXX()` and `setXXX()` methods rather than public instance variables is more elegant, but using public instance variables simplifies the container's job a little.

Method 4, while initially seeming unappealing, merits closer attention. Obviously, if the EJB implementation class stored its persistent data directly in the EJB container somewhere, this would simplify things considerably. It would also offer some important efficiency gains, as we shall see. The trick is to find a way to do this such that it is transparent to clients. While it is technically feasible to ask an EJB to get and set its properties by means of calls on, say, the `EntityContext` object, this would probably be objectionable to developers.

In fact, EJB 1.1 adopts the use of method 2—public instance variables written and read directly by the container. This leads to a number of problems, which were never adequately addressed, as we shall see. EJB 2.0 adopts method 4, with an ingenious strategy for concealing the implementation from developers—more later.

13.1.2   Specifying which properties are persistent

Whether the container interacts with the EJB implementation through public instance variables or through method calls, we next need some way for the container to determine which variables or which method calls correspond to persistent data and which do not. Again, several possibilities present themselves.

- Method 1: The EJB container could use reflection (see Appendix D) to obtain a list of instance variables or methods from the EJB implementation, and select for persistence those that follow some naming convention. For example, all persistent variables or persistence methods could be required to have names beginning with `persistent`.

- Method 2: The EJB could register its persistent properties by means of method calls on the container when it is initialized.

- Method 3: The EJB developer could specify persistence properties in the deployment descriptor.

Both EJB 1.1 and EJB 2.0 settle on the third approach, the use of the deployment descriptor. In truth, there is little to choose between the various approaches, but we have to use the deployment descriptor for configuration of everything else, so we may as well use it for this as well.

13.1.3   Creating new persistent data in the store

So we have a number of possible techniques that allow the container to get access to the EJB implementation's persistent data, and to tell it which data is persistent and which is not. Next, we need to think about what happens when the client calls `create(...)`. The container will need to insert some data in the database in response to this call, but how does it know what to insert? Here are some possible approaches.

- Method 1: The arguments to `create()` must mirror the set of persistent properties. In the simple example we described above, where the EJB had three persistent instance variables, `A`, `B` and `C`, we could stipulate that `create(...)` took three arguments, corresponding to the values of these three properties.

- Method 2: The container could delegate the method call onto `ejbCreate()`, as usual. `ejbCreate()` would then call a method on the container specifying what data to insert.

- Method 3: The container could delegate the method call onto `ejbCreate()`, as usual. `ejbCreate()` would prepare the implementation to be persisted by the container using the same technique it would ordinarily use before committing a transaction.

The first method is inflexible: We don't always want the client to have to initialize the EJB in the same way. As a matter of convention, we can supply multiple `create(...)` methods, each with different arguments, but method 1 would break that convention because only one form of `create(...)` would work.

Method 2 would be practical and not offend against convention, but method 3 is simpler, because it makes use of functionality that is already provided by the container. So, in summary, both EJB 1.1 and EJB 2.0 assume that the job of `ejbCreate()` is to *get the implementation ready to be persisted*. Now, a consequence of this is that the database cannot be updated until `ejbCreate()` returns. This means that if the primary key cannot be derived from the instance variables (e.g., it is a sequence number), then `ejbCreate()` does not know the current primary key. It also means that we can't generate a sequence number or other artificial primary key *within* `ejbCreate()`, as we can with BMP. This means that whether we can make use of auto-increment database columns and the like rather depends on the capabilities of the EJB server, not the EJB developer. In practice, if we want to use artificial primary keys with CMP, we typically implement the primary key generation as part of the business logic, using EJBs dedicated to the purpose. This is an unsatisfactory, but inevitable, consequence of automated persistence management.

13.1.4   Deleting persistent data from the store

So we have a way to identify and manipulate the persistent data, and a way to create new data in the database. Removal of an EJB's data from the database is straightforward, because the EJB container always knows the primary key for an EJB that its client has asked to be deleted. EJB 2.0, but not EJB 1.1, supports the notion of 'cascaded delete' as well. With this technique, when an EJB is deleted, the container can also delete all EJBs that are associated with it. Of course, this won't always be appropriate,[1] and the developer must specifically enable this functionality if it is required (Figure 13.6).

13.1.5   Implementing finder methods

What else must the persistence management scheme deal with? We know that clients can make `findXXX()` calls to locate certain EJBs. With BMP, these methods are delegated onto `ejbFindXXX()` calls that do the real work, while the container is just an intermediary. With CMP this won't do at all: The developer should not have to code JDBC operations to satisfy finder methods, when the container does this for everything else. So, what possibilities are there?

---

[1]If we have an EJB `Book` that is associated with a number of `Chapter` EJBs and a `Publisher` EJB, then deleting a `Book` may require that we delete the associated `Chapter` entities, but not the `Publisher`. The EJB container can't figure this out: It is an OO modelling issue.

- Method 1: When the client calls a finder method, the EJB container delegates to the corresponding `ejbFindXXX()`, as usual. This method then calls a method on the container, passing some sort of description of the search to be carried out (note that we *can't* do this in SQL, as this would defeat one of the primary purposes of CMP, which is to decouple the EJB from database logic).

- Method 2: The developer specifies how the container should implement each finder method using some notational convention in the deployment descriptor.

- Method 3: The whole job is left to the deployer, using tools provided by the server vendor.

Notice that methods 2 and 3 relieve the developer of the need to code any `ejbFindXXX()` methods at all; when the client calls a finder, the call is 'absorbed' by the EJB container, which handles it internally, as specified by the developer outside of the code. In methods 1 and 2, we need to find some way to describe a database search without using SQL. Possibilities include an abstract (non-SQL) query language that is data-store independent or a mathematical expression of some sort.

EJB 1.1 adopts method 3—everything is vendor specific, as we shall see. We will also see that this approach was highly unsatisfactory, as it had the effect of rendering EJB applications nonportable, quite against the ethos of EJB. EJB 2.0 applies method 2, and requires the developer to specify the search semantics in a new object-oriented query language called EJB QL.[2]

13.1.6   Handling associations

The next issue to consider is that of handling associations (the *EJB Specification* uses the term 'relationships,' but I believe that 'associations' is more generally used). The logical aspects of association management were discussed on Section 11.3.1; here we must turn to practicalities. Because we are bound by the constraints of the Java programming language—which has no syntactic support for associations as independent elements—associations will have to be modelled by storing references in each EJB's instance variables to its associated EJBs. These references will be persistent, but not in the sense that properties will be persistent. This is a crucial point in the understanding of EJB 2.0 CMP, and merits some discussion.

Suppose we have a financial application that uses an entity EJB called `Currency` that models some properties of a particular monetary currency. One of these properties is a list of symbols that may be used to represent the currency in printed output (for example, twenty U.S. dollars may be written 'US$20', or 'USD20', or '20$US'). Let's suppose further that we represent this property as a `Collection` of `Strings`. In the EJB's implementation class, the property may be declared like this:

---

[2]I can almost hear the groans. Does the world really need a new query language? I hope to show that this decision was the best compromise available and that, in fact, EJB QL is sufficiently close to SQL to look familiar to most developers.

public Collection currencySymbols;

Now, in the same EJB we have an association with EJBs of type `Broker`, modelling the currency brokers that are prepared to trade that particular currency. How do we declare this in the implementation class? Because the association is many-valued, we need another `Collection`:

public Collection brokers;

Here is the crucial point: Both these `Collections` are persistent, but *in totally different ways*. The container could, for example, persist the `currencySymbols` property simply by serializing the whole `Collection` into the same column of a database table. Alternatively, it could iterate the `Collection` and persist each element separately as a `String`. In fact, it isn't that important, because the container is not concerned what the contents of the `Collection` actually are.

Now, how do we persist the `brokers Collection`? Do we even know what it is a `Collection` of? With BMP, the developer would very likely implement it to be a `Collection` of primary keys of the associated objects. With CMP, however it is implemented, the difference between this `Collection` and the `Collection` of currency symbols is that the container does have an interest in the contents. If the whole `Collection` is stored by serialization in a database column—as would work perfectly well for the currency symbols—a number of situations could arise where the stored data fails to accurately reflect the true data model. For example, suppose another EJB deletes an instance of the `Broker` EJB with which our `Currency` EJB has an association. This changes the nature of the `Collection` of `Broker` objects: One element must be deleted from the `Collection`. It isn't important for the purposes of this discussion to consider how the container might manage processes like this: My purpose here is to show that associations and properties have superficial similarities, both being implemented as instance variables, but the persistence management implications are rather different.

So far as the EJB architecture, the choices open to the designers of the Specification were quite straightforward:

- Do something: put in place a strategy for container management of associations, including a persistence scheme, or

- Do nothing: let the developer handle associations using ordinary Java techniques.

EJB 1.1 simply failed to address the issue at all: It was left to the developer, perhaps with support from tools provided by the server vendor, to deal with the matter as circumstances dictated. EJB 2.0, on the other hand, puts in place an elaborate scheme for handling persistent associations.

13.1.7   Schema mapping

One final problem remains: How do we map the EJB properties (whether they are represented as instance variables, EJB1.1, or `get/set` methods, EJB2.0) onto things that make sense to a relational database? The way in which the EJB's state is represented may well not match the representation in the underlying database. There is no particular reason to think, for example, that instance variable names will match column names or that EJB names will match table names. In fact, there is no reason to be sure that the EJB's state can be drawn from the same database table, or even the same database.

We have reached a point beyond which the *EJB Specification* cannot venture without laying down rules about how data storage is to be implemented. While most EJB systems are using relational databases as their storage, the Specification cannot mandate this. Therefore the procedure for mapping properties from the EJB to the data store will always be product-specific. Some products provide graphical tools for mapping, while others require textual descriptions. Rather unfortunately, commercial products vary in the sophistication of the mapping schemes they support. Some, for example, allow an EJB to be mapped onto multiple database tables, while others don't.

13.2   CMP in EJB 1.1

Although EJB 2.0 defines a new persistence management scheme, a compliant product must continue to support the EJB 1.1 scheme. Although it is not widely used, an understanding of this scheme is helpful in seeing why the EJB 2.0 scheme has the form that it does.

EJB 1.1 defines a CMP scheme based on *persistent public instance variables.* It assumes that all the EJB's properties are represented by values of its instance variables. Of course the implementation class can include both persistent and non-persistent instance variables. Those that are intended to be persistent must be public (yes, public) and serializable [EJB1.1 9.4.1]. The necessity for these variables to be public is to allow them to be read and written by the container. Although this does not really compromise encapsulation (EJBs are encapsulated by the container), many developers were unhappy about this. Happily, public instance variables are not a requirement of EJB 2.0-style CMP (although they still have to be public in the primary key class). The deployment descriptor lists those instance variables that have to be persistent and defines which of them represents the primary key. All other instance variables are assumed to be volatile.

In EJB 1.1, the developer provides the same methods as for bean-managed persistence: `ejbLoad()`, `ejbStore()`, and so on. The container does call these methods, but they will mostly be empty. This is because the container will be doing the database operations behind the scenes, and calling these methods to indicate that it has done so. The implementation class should be a subclass (direct or indirect) of `javax.ejb.EntityBean`. Table 13.1 summarizes the developer's responsibilities in creating this class, with EJB 1.1 CMP.

Note that there are no `ejbFindXXX()` methods in the table. Does this mean that EJB 1.1 does not support finder methods? Not at all: The developer declares them in the home interface, and the container implements them itself. Typically, the implementation will be placed into the home object or one of its supporting classes.

Method	Usage
setEntityContext (EntityContext ec)	First method called by container; saves reference to context in an instance variable.
unsetEntityContext (EntityContext ec)	Last method called by the container; usually empty but can be used to clean up resource allocation done in setEntityContext().
ejbCreate (...)	Called by the container when the client calls a create on the home object. Implement to correspond to create(..) methods in home interface; arguments must match. This method should set the instance variables, because the container will write them to the database immediately after the method returns. Although declared to return the primary key type, ejbCreate() must return null. The container generates the primary key.
ejbPostCreate (...)	Called by the container after creation of the EJB object. Implement to correspond to each ejbCreate(..) method. Usually empty.
ejbLoad ()	Called by the container when the EJB's instance variables *have been read* from the database. Often empty, but this is a good time to restore persistent associations if there are any. You can assume that the persistent instance variables are correct when this method is called.
ejbStore ()	Called by the container just before it writes the instance variables to the database. Usually empty.
ejbActivate ()	Called by the container to indicate that the EJB is being readied. Usually empty.
ejbPassivate ()	Called by the container to indicate that the EJB is being returned to the pool. Usually empty.
ejbRemove ()	Called by the container when the client calls remove() on the EJB object or remove(primary_key) on the home. This method is usually empty, but it is a good place to delete dependent objects if necessary.
Business methods	Implement to match declarations in the remote interface.

Table 13.1. Developer responsibilities for the implementation class in an EJB 1.1 CMP entity EJB. Most of these methods retain the same purpose in EJB 2.0.

The *EJB 1.1 Specification* has nothing to say about how this implementation is managed; everything is left to the vendor. This is a serious flaw in the architecture, which is substantially remedied in EJB 2.0.

13.3   The EJB 2.0 CMP philosophy

Before discussing the development of 2.0-compliant entity EJBs, we need to spend a little time examining what is wrong with the 1.1 scheme. At first glance, EJB 2.0 CMP appears extremely complex. Understanding the limitations of the 1.1 scheme should make it easier to see why this complexity is necessary, and why it might ultimately be to the advantage of the developer to come to grips with it.

13.3.1   Issues with 1.1-style CMP

Issue 1: application logic and schema mapping are entangled

A 1.1-style entity EJB will often contain very little code (less than 20 lines in some cases). All the work (synchronizing to the database) gets done in vendor-supplied classes, usually generated at deployment time. This is where the problems start.

Suppose we are developing an EJB application to handle stock control in a book warehouse. The EJB `Book` models a book, and has six persistent fields: `ISBNnumber` (primary key), `location`, `price`, `author`, `title`, and `publisher`, for example. This EJB maps onto two database tables, the first of which contains information about physical stock items. This is called `BookStock`. This table contains information about the location and price of the book in our stock, and has the ISBN number as the primary key. The second table contains general information about books, and also has the ISBN number as the primary key. This table is called `BookData`. The organization of the tables and persistent fields is shown in Figure 13.1. Note that there is no consistency of names between the EJB instance variables and the names of the table columns; with legacy databases this situation is far from uncommon.

When synchronizing the EJB from the database in readiness for a business method, the EJB will have to draw the values from the two tables, probably using an SQL statement like this:

```
SELECT isbn , loc , unitprice , author , title , publisher \
  FROM BookStock , BookData \
  WHERE ( BookStock . ISBN = BookData . ISBN_No ) AND\
    ( BookStock . ISBN = ? )
```

where the question mark is a placeholder for the primary key of the EJB, as retrieved by calling `EJBContext.getPrimaryKey()`.

Then it will have to store the results of the SELECT in the appropriate instance variables (some of which don't have the same names as the database columns they model). How does the container know how to do this? There is no information about the relationship between the instance variables and the database in the code or in the deployment descriptor.

Here is another issue: Suppose the `Book` EJB is to have a finder method called `findInPriceRange(min, max)` that takes two arguments, both `double`. The method

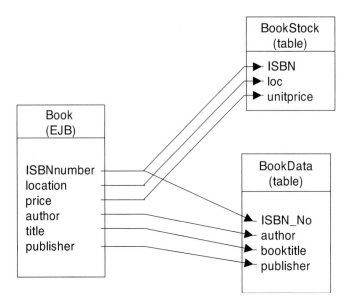

Figure 13.1. Relationship between the `Book` EJB and the tables it maps to, in the hypothetical 'book stock control' example.

is supposed to return all EJBs that correspond to books whose prices lie in the specified range. The corresponding SQL will probably look something like this:

```
SELECT isbn from BookStock
  WHERE unitprice >= ? AND unitprice <= ?
```

where the two question marks substitute for the lower and upper prices respectively. How does the container know how to make this SQL from the method name `findInPriceRange(min, max)`?

The answer, in both cases, is that the container doesn't know. The developer or the deployer has to tell it. The *EJB Specification* gives no guidance about how this should be carried out. It is all left to the vendor. This means, in practice, that whether an EJB will be able to draw data from two different tables, or perform a search for prices within a range, depends on how flexible the vendor's CMP tool is. Clearly this is a limitation of portability, and has deterred uptake of CMP by developers.

In fact, the problem is more subtle than it appears. A close examination of the two queries above—the `ejbLoad()` query and the finder—should reveal that they are not merely different, but different *in kind*.

The first simply handles the problem of mapping programmatic entities (the EJB properties) to the correct physical disposition of data (the tables). We will call this *schema mapping*, as it is a mapping from the EJB's persistence schema to the database schema. In a sense, this is a trivial problem: Provided that the two tables and the EJB are logically compatible (they all share a primary key, for example, and the two tables actually contain the data required by the EJB), then it is straightforward at deployment time to make the appropriate mappings. Clearly, if an EJB is to be portable, and capable of adaptation to change, it has to be possible to modify these mappings at deployment time, rather than in code.

The finder query, however, is rather different. This query *is* concerned with physical disposition of data (it has table and field names) but—much more importantly—it contains *application logic*. It is this fact—that the ability to code the correct program logic depends on the capabilities of the vendor's tools—that most developers find objectionable. No one objects to the deployment-time mapping of EJB properties to a database schema; indeed, this is a necessary step. The deferral of application logic to deployment time, however, is not appreciated, particularly because *there is no standard place to specify what the logic should be, either in code or in the deployment descriptor.*

There is no compelling reason why the *logic* of the query should not be separated from the *schema mapping*. The logic can be expressed quite succinctly in terms of operations on EJB properties, and is completely independent of the database schema mapping. The logic of `findInPriceRange(min, max)`, for example, could be expressed simply as the condition

```
price >= ?1 and price <= ?2
```

where '?1' is the first argument to the finder method (`min`, in this case) and '?2' is the second argument (`max`). `price` is the EJB property that contains the price of a given book. At the schema mapping stage, we specify that the property `price` corresponds to the column `unitprice` in the table `BookStock`, but this is totally independent of the application logic.

Let's consider one final example, to make the distinction totally clear.

Suppose that the `Book` EJB has an association with a `Publisher` EJB, not merely the name of a publisher. The association is navigable from `Book` to `Publisher`; in other words, given a reference to a `Book` the application can determine the properties of the book's publisher (name, address, speciality, etc). The database schema is illustrated in Figure 13.2.

Now, when loading `Book` we must obtain not only the persistent fields, but the persistent association with the `Publisher` object. As a book (let us assume) has only one publisher, this association can be modeled as a reference within `Book` to the appropriate `Publisher` object (strictly, to an EJB object for `Publisher`). Now, if `Publisher` has the `name` field as the primary key, then the `Book` EJB can get the publisher `name` from the `BookData` table, then call `findByPrimaryKey()` on `Publisher` to find the appropriate `Publisher` object.

But consider the problem of writing a finder method in `Book` that is based on publisher information. Suppose, for example, I want a method called `findBySpeciality(String)` that returns all `Book` EJBs for books that are published by a publisher with a particular speciality book (for example, I want to retrieve all books published by specialist computing publishers). The information the EJB needs to complete this request is not local to the `Book` EJB, it is a property of `Publisher`,

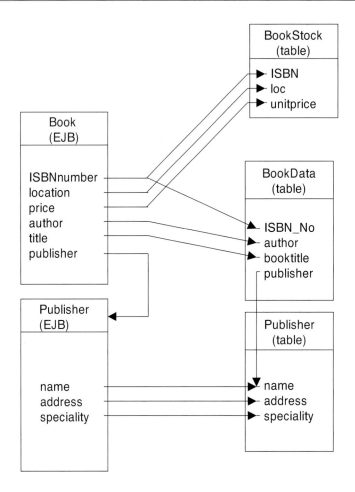

Figure 13.2. Relationship between the `Book` and `Publisher` EJBs, and the tables they map to, in the hypothetical 'book stock control' example.

which is linked to `Book` by an association. Again, the *logic* of this query is separate from the *schema mapping*. It is possible to express the logic purely in terms of associations and properties. What we need is a query that can select all `Book` EJBs where the following condition is true:

```
publisher.speciality = ?1
```

This means 'find all EJBs where the `speciality` attribute of the associated `Publisher` object is equal to the parameter passed to the finder method' (i.e., the speciality). This query could be expressed in SQL in a statement like this:

```
SELECT isbn FROM BookData,Publisher
  WHERE (BookData.publisher = Publisher.name) AND
  (Publisher.speciality = ?)
```

However, I hope it is clear that the schema-independent query is much clearer to read, as well as being independent of the database schema. Of course, we haven't avoided the problem of schema mapping, we've simply separated it from the application logic. As well as avoiding the problems described above, the maintenance of the application would be much easier.

Issue 2: inefficiencies in using instance variables

The use of instance variables to store persistent data, while intuitive, is very inefficient. This is because the container doesn't have any straightforward way to determine which instance variables will be read and written by business methods in any one transaction. It *can* determine which variables *were* written during the transaction, and can optimize by only writing these out to the database, but at the start of the transaction, it has to read all the instance variables *and* persistent associations into their respective variables.

Ideally, the EJB's persistent properties should not be stored in instance variables. Suppose, for example, that rather than loading the instance variable `author` in the `book` EJB at the start of every transaction, the container provides an implementation of a method `getAuthor()` that returns the author. The container does not have to read the `author` field from the `BookData` table until something calls `getAuthor()`. If the author is never required in a particular transaction, then it never needs to be read. This is called 'lazy loading,' and we have already discussed how such a scheme can be implemented. It is only possible if access to the properties of the EJB is obtained through `getXXX()` and `setXXX()` methods, even in the EJB itself. If we do this, we can also benefit from 'selective writing,' where only changed properties are written to the database at commit time.

Lazy loading and selective writing will give some performance benefit with persistent instance variables, but enormous benefits are to be had with persistent one-to-many associations, as we shall see.

Issue 3: tight coupling of the client view of persistence with the EJB view

The purpose of finder methods is to allow clients to locate entity EJBs of a particular type. With CMP, as we have seen, the implementation of finders is provided by the container, using vendor-supplied tools. However, suppose the EJB itself wants to use a finder method as part of its internal operation. Of course, it has access to the same finder methods as a client, but there is no way to distinguish finders that can be called by clients from finders that are internal to the EJB. Thus the client's view of persistence is essentially the same as the EJB's.

This is particularly problematic in the management of one-to-many associations. It would be nice for the EJB to locate persistent associations using a finder method, but we don't really want to expose the persistent associations directly to clients.

Ideally, we would like to decouple the client's view of persistence from that of the EJB's, so the finders presented to clients provide facilities that are meaningful to clients, while internal finder methods are accessible only to the EJB itself.

Issue 4: no control over granularity of client-EJB interaction

In the EJB 1.1 CMP scheme, all persistent objects are EJBs, unless the developer wants to use helper classes and manage the persistence in code. We have already discussed the limitations of this scheme. If one object is dependent on another, it does not need to be an EJB, as it does not need to be exposed to clients. The overhead of EJB access has no compensating benefits.

13.3.2   The solution: EJB 2.0-style CMP

The EJB 2.0 CMP scheme is intended to solve all the problems described above, and represents a radical revision of the fundamental philosophy behind CMP technology.

EJB QL: decoupling logic from schema mapping

In 2.0-style CMP, there is a clear distinction between the logic of access to the persistent storage and the disposition of data in the persistent store (schema mapping). The logic is specified in terms of a new query language called EJB QL. Although EJB QL is new in Version 2.0 of the *EJB Specification*, object query languages are not new in concept. Other EJB products already have query languages for specifying finder methods—for example, BEA *WebLogic* has WLQL. However, imposing a query language in the Specification is a step forward in terms of portability.

Let's see how the finder methods described above could be specified in EJB-2.0 CMP, using EJB QL.

The first example was to implement a finder method for the `Book` EJB that could find all books whose prices were in a specified range. We would declare the finder in the home interface in the usual way, like this:

```
public Collection findInPriceRange
    (double min, double max)
  throws FinderException , RemoteException ;
```

where the `Collection` returned to the client would be of `Book` EJB objects.

The logical implementation of this query is placed in the deployment descriptor as an EJB QL query:

```
SELECT OBJECT (b) FROM book b
  WHERE b.price >= ?1 AND b.price <= ?2
```

The syntax of this query is not very different from SQL, so developers familiar with SQL should have little trouble adapting to the new language. There *are* significant differences, however, so don't be lulled into a false sense of security. The FROM clause specifies the source for the query and the identifier it will have in the query. Strictly, the name following FROM ('book' in this case) is not the name of an EJB, but of an *abstract persistence schema*. The distinction will be discussed later—for now, assume it denotes an EJB. The WHERE clause specifies a condition that must be true for the object to be matched by the finder. Mathematical operators like '$>=$' and logical operators like 'AND' have the same meanings as they do in SQL. The tokens '?1' and '?2' refer to the two arguments to the finder, `double min` and `double max` respectively.

In the queries above, 'price' is *not* an instance variable in the implementation class, but a *property* of the EJB. 2.0-style EJBs don't use instance variables to store persistent data, as will be explained, but have 'abstract properties.'

The second example was a finder that could locate all books whose publishers had a given speciality. In the home interface we have

```
public Collection findBySpeciality
    (String speciality)
  throws FinderException, RemoteException;
```

The query that would be appropriate is

```
SELECT OBJECT (b) FROM book b
  WHERE b.publisher.speciality = ?1
```

Again, the token '?1' denotes the first (and only) argument to the finder (`String speciality`).

Note that these queries are expressed entirely in terms of entity EJB properties, and have nothing to say about how the persistent data is organized in whatever persistent store is used. It is still necessary to specify the mapping between the EJB properties and the database, but this process is now independent of application logic. Typically, a product will generate SQL statements from the EJB QL queries and some other description of the object-database mapping. This part of the process is necessarily database-dependent.

EJB QL is described in detail in Chapter 11 of the *EJB Specification*, Version 2.0.

Abstract properties

With EJB-1.1 CMP, I would have started the implementation of `BikeModelBean` like this:

```
public class BikeModelBean implements EntityBean
{
public String name;
public String description;
5 public int chargeBand;
public int engineSize;
//...
}
```

With 2.0-style CMP, we don't use instance variables to store persistent data. Instead, we define *abstract persistence methods*. This makes the class itself `abstract`.

```
public abstract class BikeModelBean
  implements EntityBean
{
public abstract String getName();
public abstract void setName(String s);

public abstract String getDescription();
public abstract void setDescription(String s);

public abstract int getChargeBand();
public abstract void setChargeBand(int n);
//...
}
```

This set of methods represents the definitions of some *abstract persistent properties*. For a given EJB, its total set of abstract persistent properties is called the *abstract persistence schema*. These methods are abstract because, for example, the client can call `getDescription()` to retrieve the value of the property `description`, but the physical representation of `description` does not lie in the class itself. The implementation class is `abstract`, and must be subclassed by a container-generated class. This subclass will provide the implementations of the methods like `getDescription()` and *may* store the 'real' status in an instance variable, but need not. This strategy gives the container the flexibility to optimize the loading and storing of persistent properties. In 1.1-style CMP, the container must load all the instance variables at the start of each transaction, because it can't determine which will actually be required. With 2.0-style CMP, the container knows when the value of `description` is required, because something has called `getStatus()`. Similarly, it knows when the value of `description` needs to be written back to the database, because something has called `setDescription()`. This can lead to significant efficiency gains, by allowing the container to use 'lazy loading' strategies (where the database is read on demand, rather than in advance). In addition, if a client or a business method does not call any `setXXX()` method during a transaction, then *nothing* needs to be written back to the database at commit time.

Abstract relationships

EJB 2.0 also provides a scheme for handling persistent associations, as well as persistent data. All that is necessary from a development perspective is to declare the association as an abstract property, in a similar way to that used with persistent properties. For example, the `BikeModel` EJB has a one-to-many association with `Bike` EJBs. This can be implemented as an abstract `Collection`.

```
public abstract Collection getBikes();
public abstract void setBikes(Collection bikes);
```

Of course, we have to tell the EJB container that this is a relationship, not a collection-valued property. This information is declared in the deployment descriptor, constructed in the usual way. With the *J2EE Reference Implementation*, for example, we could use the deployment tool or create the deployment descriptor as an XML file.

There is another important point to note about the example above. The remote interface for the `BikeModel` EJB may expose to clients the persistent properties `description`, `chargeBand`, etc. That is, the remote interface exposes `getDescription()`, `getChargeBand()`, etc., as appropriate. But it *must* not [EJB2.0 10.3.1] expose the container-managed association `getBikes()`. This is because the container should be free to optimize the delivery of the elements of the collection to the EJB (using lazy loading, for example). If it is passed directly out to clients, then the opportunities for optimization are restricted. Some developers like to use a naming convention in their EJBs to reflect this. For example, we could declare `getBikesInternal()` in the EJB implementation class as a reminder. So how does a client get access to the collection of `Bikes` associated with this EJB? We provide business methods that return information about the associated classes *by value*. The example at the end of the chapter demonstrates this in practice.

Client-view and EJB-view finders

2.0-style CMP distinguishes client-view finders from EJB-view finders. Client-view finders are defined in the home interface, as usual, and specified in the deployment descriptor in terms of EJB QL queries. Because finders always return a collection of references to remote objects, the type of object returned does not have to be specified in the EJB QL query.

EJB-view finders are rather different. These are finder methods that are only used internally. Their purpose is to support the business methods, home methods, and `ejbCreate()` methods where they require EJB QL queries. EJB-view finders are not exposed to clients. They are defined in the implementation class as abstract methods, like this:

```
public abstract Collection ejbSelectBookings(String regNo)
   throws FinderException, RemoteException;
public abstract Collection ejbSelectBookingsInEntity()
   throws FinderException, RemoteException;
```

These methods are implemented automatically by the container's subclass of the implementation class, based on a specification in EJB QL by the developer in EJB QL. Select methods don't have to return the same data type as the EJB that calls them.

The distinction between client-view and EJB-view finders allows the EJB to 'decouple' the client's view of the object from its representation in the persistent store. Typically an EJB will use `ejbSelectXXX()` methods to assist in satisfying the business methods.

Support for dependent persistent objects

One of the problems identified in EJB 1.1 was the inability of the persistence manager to handle persistent dependent objects efficiently. Typically, a dependent object will be tightly coupled to its owner, which will make many short method calls upon it. This type of interaction shows the EJB RMI system at its worst: RMI works best when making small numbers of complex method calls.

An earlier draft of EJB 2.0 suggested explicit container support for persistent dependent objects. These were to be structured like CMP entity EJBs, but without the container callback methods for life cycle management. Like EJBs, they were to have had an abstract persistence schema—that is, a set of abstract methods that get and set properties and associations. Unlike EJBs, they could only be created by their owners. In addition, the developer could specify that the container delete them automatically when the owner is deleted ('cascaded delete').

The introduction of persistent dependent objects added significant complexity to the Specification, and led to a number of irreconcilable logical irregularities. Moreover, it was clear that the construct would be largely unnecessary if RMI did not have such significant overheads. Thus it was decided to provide a scheme by which RMI could be bypassed for tightly coupled dependent objects. A dependent object is now simply an ordinary entity EJB with a local client view.

13.4   Developer responsibilities with EJB 2.0 CMP

This section describes in more detail what the developer must do to author an entity EJB using 2.0 CMP.

13.4.1   Implementation class

The implementation class must be defined as `abstract` and must implement `javax.ejb.EntityBean`. The developer's responsibilities are summarized in Table 13.2.

13.4.2   Interfaces

The local home, remote home, local, and remote interfaces are exactly as for bean-managed persistence. These interfaces were described in detail on page 347, and don't need further discussion. The client's view of an entity EJB, whether local or distributed, is independent of the type of persistence management in use.

13.4.3   Primary key class

The requirements for the primary key class are exactly the same as for 1.1-style CMP [EJB2.0 10.6.13]—that is, you can use a standard class (`String`, `Integer`) or an application-defined primary key class. The latter, if used, must have public instance variables whose names are a subset of the names of the abstract persistent fields of the EJB [EJB2.0 10.8.2].

13.4.4   Object-database mapping

The use of EJB QL to specify query logic does not prevent the need to specify the mapping between persistent properties in the EJBs and database. This job should be relatively straightforward. Nevertheless, it remains to be seen how vendors will deal with cases such as a single EJB having properties based on a JOIN between

Method	Usage
`setEntityContext (EntityContext ec)`	First method called by container; saves reference to context in an instance variable This is a good place to look up resource factories (e.g., `DataSource` objects) and the home objects of other EJBs. However, the EJB won't need a `DataSource` for its own database; it is the job of the container to synchronize this EJB with the database.
`unsetEntityContext (EntityContext ec)`	Last method called by the container; usually empty but can be used to clean up resource allocation done in `setEntityContext()`.
`ejbCreate (...)`	Called by the container when the client calls a `create` on the home object. Implement to correspond to `create(..)` methods in home interface; arguments must match. When this method returns, the container will write the persistent state to the database, so the method should use its arguments to call whatever abstract `setXXX()` methods are required to initialize the state. Although declared to return the primary key type, `ejbCreate()` must return `null`. The container generates the primary key.
`ejbPostCreate (...)`	Called by the container after creation of the EJB object. Implement to correspond to each `ejbCreate(..)` method. Usually empty.
`ejbLoad ()`	Called by the container when the EJB's persistent state has been read from the database. If the EJB uses persistent instance variables (not recommended), this is the place to initialize them.
`ejbStore ()`	Called by the container just before it writes the persistent state to the database. Usually empty.
`ejbActivate ()`	Called by the container to indicate that the EJB is being readied. Usually empty.
`ejbPassivate ()`	Called by the container to indicate that the EJB is being returned to the pool. Usually empty.
`ejbRemove ()`	Called by the container when the client calls `remove()` on the EJB object or `remove(primary_key)` on the home. This method is usually empty.
`ejbHomeXXX ()`	Implement to match the home methods defined in the home interface. Return and argument types must match.
`ejbSelectXXX ()`	Implement as appropriate to support the business methods and home methods. These methods must be `abstract`; they will be implemented as EJB QL queries in the deployment descriptor.
Abstract persistence methods	Define the abstract `getXXX()` and `setXXX()` to match the EJB's persistent properties.
Business methods	Implement to match declarations in the remote interface. In particular, where we have one-to-many relationships that cannot be exposed directly to clients ([EJB2.0 10.3.1]), we need business methods to extract data from these relationships on behalf of clients.

Table 13.2. Developer responsibilities for the implementation class in a 2.0-style CMP entity EJB.

two tables, for example. The *J2EE Reference Implementation*, Version 1.3, uses the EJB QL to generate SQL, which the deployer can then edit to provide the correct table and column names in the database. While this is fine for a proof-of-concept, commercial products will probably have to provide more sophisticated tools. It remains to be seen how they will rise to this challenge.

13.5   EJB QL overview

EJB QL is defined in detail in the *EJB Specification* [EJB2.0 11], which includes some relatively helpful examples, so only a basic introduction will be given here. Some practical examples from the *Prestige Bike Hire* application are described later in the chapter.

13.5.1   Structure of an EJB QL query

EJB QL is superficially similar to SQL, for obvious reasons, but has only 'SE-LECT' functionality. There are no 'UPDATE', 'INSERT', or 'DELETE' operations in EJB QL. In fact, EJB QL reflects the smallest common subset of common SQL SELECT operations. All relational databases will offer functionality that is inexpressible in EJB QL; this issue is an important one, and we will return to it later.

EJB QL queries all have the following structure:

```
SELECT {something} FROM {something} WHERE {expression}
```

In this chapter, EJB QL keywords will be given in uppercase to distinguish them from identifiers. In reality, EJB QL is not case-sensitive in keywords. It is, of course, case-sensitive in *identifiers*, as these match the properties of EJBs, and Java is a case-sensitive language.

The SELECT and FROM clauses are compulsory: It follows that all queries will begin with the word 'SELECT' and contain the word 'FROM' somewhere. The WHERE clause is optional, but usually present. As in SQL, if there is no WHERE expression, the query selects all entities that are within the scope of the FROM clause.

13.5.2   SELECT clause

The SELECT clause denotes the return type of the expression. Formally, the return value of an EJB QL expression is single-valued, but the 'single value' may be a `Collection`, so a query can select multiple EJBs.

If the query is supporting a finder method, then the return type must be a `Collection` of EJBs of the same type as the EJB that is being implemented (this is not a restriction: If a client calls `findBySomething()` on EJB `Customer`, it expects to get a `Collection` of `Customer` EJBs, rather than a `Collection` of something else).

In this case, the SELECT clause is conventionally written

```
SELECT OBJECT (o)
```

Here o is an *identification variable*; it will be used in the FROM clause to determine which of the entities referred to is the one that is being selected for return (see below).

If the query is to support an `ejbSelectXXXX()` method, then it need not return an EJB of the same type as the one issuing the query; it is for the business logic to interpret the resulting `Collection` of EJBs, not the client. In such cases, we can still use the 'SELECT OBJECT' form of the expression, or the more flexible

```
SELECT path_expression
```

where a *path expression* denotes a particular property of an EJB that will be specified in the following FROM clause (see below). As in SQL, SELECT can be qualified by DISTINCT, which has the effect of removing any duplicates from the results.

13.5.3   FROM clause

The FROM clause denotes the entities over which the query ranges. A following WHERE can be used, and usually is used, to restrict the matches to a particular subset. FROM can be extended by the 'collection operator' IN. The use of FROM can be illustrated by extending the previous examples.

```
SELECT OBJECT (o) FROM book o
```

denotes a query that ranges over an *abstract schema* book. In practice, the abstract schema probably denotes a specific EJB, so this query can be interpreted as ranging over EJBs of a specific type. In this query, the identification variable o serves as a placeholder to indicate that it is results of type `book` that are to be returned. I could just have correctly have written

```
SELECT OBJECT (sillyname) FROM book sillyname
```

When the EJB QL query is not supporting a finder method, then we can be more free with the return type.

```
SELECT m.title FROM book b, IN (b.chapters) m
```

This example ranges over all the `chapters` in all `books`, assuming `chapter` is a many-valued association of `book`. The clause 'IN (b.chapters)' extends the range of the query to all `chapters` that are reachable from each `b`. It results in a collection of `title` EJBs, one for each `chapter` in each `book`. Notice that although the query has 'FROM book b', we do not return EJBs of type `book`, but of type `title`; this is the purpose of the SELECT clause and the use of identification variables.

13.5.4   WHERE clause

The WHERE clause introduces an expression that restricts the EJBs that are selected. The simplest form of WHERE is probably one that operates on a single property of the selected EJB. For example:

```
SELECT OBJECT(o) from book o
   WHERE o.price < 20
```

This selects all books for which the value of the price property is less than
'20'. Expressions can be constructed using the usual operators: AND, OR, NOT,
LIKE, and so on, which have the same meanings as they have in SQL. In addition,
expressions can be based on functions, so

```
SELECT OBJECT(o) from book o
   WHERE length(o.title) < 10
```

selects all books whose title property has less than 10 characters. A full description
of all the functions and operators available is beyond the scope of this book. See
[EJB2.0 11.2.7] for a full list.

13.5.5   Input parameters

EJB QL expressions can be built from constants, as the previous examples were, but
it will often be more useful to execute queries based on the values of the arguments
to finder methods. Suppose we want to implement a finder for the Book EJB, which
selects all EJBs whose price property is in a certain range. For example:

```
public Collection findByPrice (int min, int max);
```

We could assign to this finder an EJB QL expression like this:

```
SELECT OBJECT(o) from book o
   WHERE o.price < ?1 and o.price > ?2
```

Here ?1 denotes the first argument to the finder (that is, min) and ?2 the second (max).

13.5.6   EJB QL limitations

EJB QL abstracts the smallest common subset of search functionality that viable
data stores are likely to offer. The advantage of this design decision is that it should
be relatively easy for a server vendor to map EJB QL to data stores other than
relational databases.[3] The disadvantage is that it fails to offer functionality that
most SQL programmers take for granted. This section describes this and other
obvious limitations of the EJB 2.0 CMP system as it currently stands.

- Queries over associations only work when the associated EJBs also use CMP.

  To see why this is the case, consider a query for locating all books that were
  published by a publisher with a particular speciality:

  ```
  SELECT OBJECT(o) from book o
     WHERE o.publisher.speciality = ?1
  ```

---

[3]In practice, it will probably be data store vendors who do this, rather than EJB server vendors. EJB 2.0 defines more precisely the interface between the EJB container and the persistence
manager, so it should be possible for data store vendors to implement plug-in persistence managers
for their products.

For this query to work, the EJB QL processor needs to be able to find which publishers have a particular speciality. Now the publisher information is not in the `Book` EJB, but in the `Publisher` EJB, which is an association of the `Book` EJB. Because `Book` is container-managed, the persistence manager knows whether it has an association called 'publisher' or not (because it is managing it). But if `Publisher` is bean-managed, the container simply doesn't have information about its persistent properties. It has no way of knowing how to extract the `speciality` property, or even if there is such a thing.

In previous drafts of EJB 2.0, a work-around was proposed for this limitation, in which a query could be directed through an EJB's exposed finder methods, rather than through its abstract persistence schema. To see how this was supposed to work, let's assume that the `Publisher` EJB uses bean-managed persistence and has a finder method `findBySpeciality(String speciality)`. We would have been able to write EJB QL queries that make finder calls; here is something that should have worked:

```
SELECT OBJECT(b)
   FROM book b
   WHERE b=>publisher  IN
      (publisher >> findBySpeciality(?1))
```

The expression `Publisher >> findBySpeciality(?1)` would have represented a call on the finder method `findBySpeciality()` in the `Publisher` EJB, returning a collection of all the matching EJB objects from this finder. The IN condition determined whether one item is in a collection. So the WHERE term would have evaluated to 'true' for every `Book` EJB where the `Publisher` reference is in the list of references returned by the finder method.

The problem with this approach is that it is impossible to translate the EJB QL to plain SQL; the implementation is technically feasible (an early beta of the *J2EE Reference Implementation* supported it, and it did work), but would require a mixture of Java and SQL. It was felt that no realistic implementation could have offered tolerable efficiency.

- Although bidirectional associations are supported, they are only supported between EJBs that have container-managed persistence and share a persistence manager. The reasons are the same as discussed above. In practice, this means that they have to be deployed in the same JAR file. This may be no limitation in practice; tightly coupled EJBs are likely to be packaged together anyway.

- The EJB QL language is less feature-rich than SQL, even SQL-92 'entry level.' For example, EJB QL does not support date or time fields. This means, in effect, that the EJB can't have `java.util.Date` properties that can be used in queries.[4] EJB QL does not support fixed-precision decimals. EJB QL is much more restrictive in the syntactic ordering of expression terms.

---

[4]See below for a work-around.

- The return value from an EJB QL query can only be an EJB. There is no provision to return, say, an integer. This means that, even if the language supported operations like 'SELECT COUNT'—common in SQL—there would be no way to return the result. The absence of an efficient way to count the number of entities of a given type is a major headache for the developer. Happily, the draft version of EJB 2.1 proposes an extension to EJB QL to support such operations. We should see implementations of SELECT MIN and SELECT MAX as well.[5]

- There is no equivalent of SQL's 'ORDER BY' term. This means that it is difficult to process the results of an EJB QL query in a particular order. End-users of an application may well want to see results ordered (names in alphabetical order, for example). At present, there is no viable solution to this problem; all the proposed work-arounds are either ugly, inefficient, or both. This, also, is to be fixed in EJB 2.1.

- There are a number of logical inconsistencies in the grammar, for which no rational explanation has ever been offered. Some are particularly problematic. For example, we can compare properties for equality with constants like this:

      ... WHERE name='fred'

  or with arguments to finders like this:

      ... WHERE name=?1

  We can compare properties with constants using 'LIKE':

      ... WHERE name LIKE 'fred'

  but there is no equivalent for arguments. That is, the following is invalid:

      ... WHERE name LIKE ?1

  What this means is that it is impossible to implement a finder that selects EJBs by matching a property using a wildcard search whose search term is entered by the user (or, at least, it's prohibitively inefficient in practice).

Many of these problems should be resolved in products that implement EJB 2.1, but at the time of writing it was in early draft (for a brief overview, see Appendix A).

---

[5] Logically SELECT COUNT, etc., can be implemented by doing a `findAll()` and then getting the size of the resulting `Collection`. This won't be very efficient.

Hint

Don't forget that the identifiers in EJB QL queries are *not* database columns, they are abstract EJB properties. One of the main purposes of EJB QL is to allow application logic to be specified in a database-independent fashion.

13.6   Example: the `BikeModel` **EJB**

13.6.1   Overview

`BikeModel` is an EJB that represents a particular model of motorcycle. It stores persistent information about the type, engine size, cost, and a general description. The name of the model is the primary key for this EJB.

The `Bike` EJB models an individual motorcycle of a particular model. In the case study, `Bike` has only one property: `licenceNumber`, that is, its license plate number ('registration number'). In reality, of course, we may need to store more than this.

The relationship between `BikeModel` and `Bike` is one-to-many, navigable in the direction `BikeModel` to `Bike` (Figure 13.3).

In the design adopted, `Bike` is a dependent object of `BikeModel`. That is, it will never be manipulated as an EJB in its own right. Only the `BikeModel` EJB will interact directly with `Bikes`. This is because a license number is sufficient to identify a particular motorcycle, so other EJBs will manipulate license numbers for efficiency. As a result, we only provide `Bike` with a local client view. `BikeModel` will have a remote client view, to avoid the necessity for the EJB server to locate it in the same JVM with the session EJBs that use it.

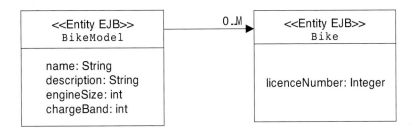

Figure 13.3. `BikeModel` and `Bike`, and the relationship between them.

13.6.2   Interfaces

The home interface (Listing 13.1) for `BikeModel` exposes a `create()` method and a `findAll()` method, as well as the compulsory `findByPrimaryKey()`. We will see that the finder methods have no implementation in Java at all; instead, they are implemented in EJB QL.

Listing 13.1: **Home interface for the** `BikeModel` **EJB.**

```
     package com.kevinboone.bikehire.ejb;
     import javax.ejb.*;
     import java.rmi.*;
     import java.util.*;
 5
     /**
     (Remote) home interface for the 'BikeModel' EJB
     (c)2002 Kevin Boone
     */
10   public interface BikeModelHome extends EJBHome
     {
     public BikeModel findByPrimaryKey (final String name)
       throws FinderException , RemoteException;

15   public Collection findAll ()
       throws FinderException , RemoteException;

     public BikeModel create (final String name, final String description,
         final int engineSize ,
20       final int chargeBand)
       throws CreateException , RemoteException;
     }
```

A `findAll()` method is frequently not to be recommended. However, in this case, it is unlikely that the business will stock more that a few dozen *models* of motorcycle, even if the overall fleet is much bigger than this. So this is a safe operation here.

The remote interface (Listing 13.2) for `BikeModel` exposes the usual `get` and `set` methods for the EJB's properties, and some additional methods that operate *via* the BikeModel on its associated Bike EJBs. These methods are

getBikeLicenceNumbers() This method retrieves a `Collection` of `Strings` representing the license numbers of the `Bike` EJBs of this model. In a more complex example, we may provide methods to return `Collections` of value objects for the dependent EJBs, but in this case, we don't return a value object for `Bike`, as it only has one property, and that can conveniently be represented as a `String`.

addBike(String licenceNumber) This method adds a `Bike` EJB by specifying a license number. Again, in a more complex example, we may want to pass a number of arguments, or a value object, to effect this addition.

So, in summary, we have methods to add motorcycles of a particular model to the fleet and to obtain lists of motorcycles of a particular model. In practice, we will probably need to provide methods to remove motorcycles from the fleet as well.

Listing 13.2: **Remote interface for the** BikeModel **EJB.**

```
package com.kevinboone.bikehire.ejb;
import javax.ejb.*;
import java.rmi.*;
import java.util.*;

5

/**
(Remote) business method interface for the 'BikeModel' EJB,
(c)2002 Kevin Boone
*/
10  public interface BikeModel extends EJBObject
{
public String getName()
  throws RemoteException;
public String getDescription()
15    throws RemoteException;
public int getChargeBand()
  throws RemoteException;
public int getEngineSize()
  throws RemoteException;
20  public void setDescription (final String description)
  throws RemoteException;
public void setChargeBand (final int chargeBand)
  throws RemoteException;
public void setEngineSize (final int engineSize)
25    throws RemoteException;
public BikeModelData getBikeModelData()
  throws RemoteException;

/**
30  Returns a collection of strings representing the
license numbers of bikes of this model
*/
public Collection getBikeLicenceNumbers()
  throws RemoteException;

35

/**
Adds a new bike of this model to the stock list
*/
public void addBike (final String licenceNumber)
40    throws RemoteException, FleetManagerException;
}
```

13.6.3 Implementation class

As this is CMP, the implementation class is very short, and we will present it section-by-section.

The declaration of the class should be relatively familiar, but notice that it is `abstract`. As in the other examples in this book, the implementation class extends `GenericCMPEntityBean`, which hides EJB methods that must be implemented, but are usually empty.

```
public abstract class BikeModelBean
  extends GenericCMPEntityBean
{
```

Now we declare the abstract methods that allow access to the various properties of the EJB, which correspond to the `get` and `set` methods on the remote interface.

```
    public abstract String getName();

5
    public abstract void setDescription(final String address);
    public abstract String getDescription();

    public abstract void setEngineSize(final int engineSize);
10  public abstract int getEngineSize();

    public abstract void setChargeBand(final int chargeBand);
    public abstract int getChargeBand();
```

However, there are other abstract methods that must be defined, which *don't* correspond to methods exposed in the remote interface:

```
    public abstract void setName(final String name);

15
    public abstract Collection getBikes();
    public abstract void setBikes (Collection bikes);
```

Why aren't these methods exposed in the remote interface? `setName()` manipulates the primary key property, and we aren't going to give clients a way to do that. However, the EJB itself will need to store its own primary key, as we shall see. `getBikes()` and `setBikes()` do not manipulate properties at all: They manipulate persistent relationships. Remember that each `BikeModel` is associated with zero or more `Bike` EJBs. We are providing clients with a means to manipulate the `Bike` EJBs known to the `BikeModel`, but not by exposing the `Collection` directly.

More important, perhaps, than describing what is included in the implementation class is pointing out what isn't. Notice that there are *no* instance variables corresponding to the methods `getDescription`, etc. That is, there is no `description` instance variable for `getDescription` to get. In fact, the local storage of these properties is simply not defined in this class at all. So where are they defined? The simple answer is that we just don't care. The EJB implementation class is not allowed to interact with the representations of the persistent properties in any way other than through the abstract `get` and `set` methods. In practice, instance variables corre-

sponding to the abstract properties will be created in the vendor-specific subclass
of the EJB implementation class.

Because we will be using `Bike` EJBs within the `BikeModel` EJB, we need to store
the home object of `Bike` in an instance variable. In particular, because `BikeModel`
uses the local client view of `Bike`, we need to store a reference to the local home
object:

```
protected BikeLocalHome bikeLocalHome;
```

The `setEntityContext` method initializes the `Bike` home object (the debugging
code is not shown here, for brevity):

```
     public void setEntityContext (EntityContext ec)
20   {
     super.setEntityContext(ec);
     try
       {
       Context c = new InitialContext();
25     bikeLocalHome = (BikeLocalHome) c.lookup
         ("java:comp/env/ejb/BikeLocal");
       }
     catch (NamingException e)
       {
30     throw new EJBException (e);
       }
     }
```

Notice that we don't do a `narrow()` operation on the result of the `lookup()`
call. Because we are using the local client view, we are going to get an object in
the same JVM, not a remote reference. Nothing in the Java code above serves to
make the EJB container deliver a local reference to the `Bike` EJB: The `lookup()`
method works on a `java:comp/env/...` name in the usual way. This is specified
to be a local reference in the deployment descriptor when declaring the mapping of
the coded name `ejb/BikeLocal` onto a real name (Figure 13.4).

The `ejbCreate()` method initializes the values of the abstract properties, but
does not create any data in the database, nor does it return a primary key to the
container. The container will create the data in the database after this method
returns.

```
     public String ejbCreate (final String name,
         final String description,
35       final int engineSize, final int chargeBand)
         throws CreateException
       {
     setName (name);
     setDescription (description);
40   setEngineSize (engineSize);
     setChargeBand (chargeBand);
     return null;
       }
```

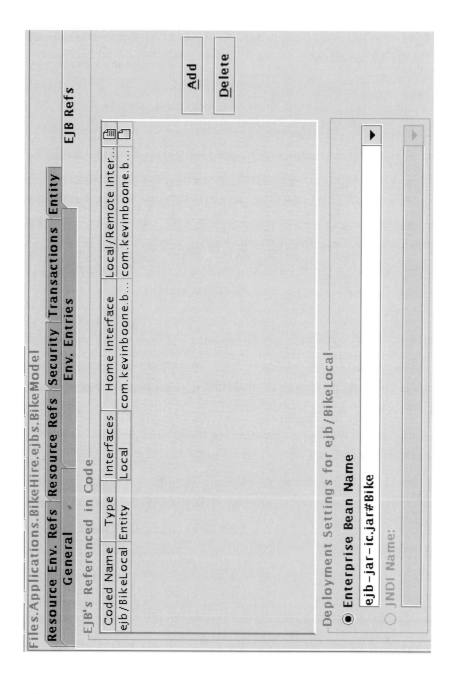

Figure 13.4. Mapping the reference to the Bike EJB used in the BikeHire EJB (i.e., ejb/BikeLocal) onto the real Bike EJB, via a local client view.

424

This code snippet demonstrates why the EJB needs to have a `setName()` method, even though it can't be called by clients: The EJB itself can only set its `name` property through the `setName()` method. There are no instance variables to set directly.

> ## Gotcha!
>
> The `ejbCreate()` method must be declared to throw `CreateException`, whether it really throws it or not [EJB2.0 10.6.4]. No reason for this is given in the Specification, and there seems to be no logical explanation. However, the *J2EE Reference Implementation* won't deploy an EJB that does not comply with this rule.

The `ejbPostCreate()` method does nothing in this method, but it will be called by the container anyway. If it were necessary to create associated EJBs and pass them a reference to the current EJB's object, `ejbPostCreate()` would be a good place to do this. Remember that in `ejbCreate()` the EJB does not yet have an EJB object—the container creates it after `ejbCreate()` returns—so a call to `getEJBObject()` will fail.

```
    public void ejbPostCreate (final String name,
45        final String description ,
          final int engineSize , final int chargeBand)
            throws CreateException
        {
        }
```

Clients can interact with the `BikeModel` EJB through the abstract property methods (`setDescription()`, etc.), but this is not necessarily the most efficient method. So we also want to provide a method by which the client can get a value object (`BikeModelData`, in this case).

```
50  public BikeModelData getBikeModelData ()
        {
        return new BikeModelData (getName(),
          getDescription () , getEngineSize () , getChargeBand ());
        }
```

Now, let's see how a client can interact with the `Bike` EJBs that are dependent on `BikeModel`. First, we need a way to add a new motorcycle. All the client needs to supply is a license number.

```
55  public void addBike (final String licenceNumber)
        throws FleetManagerException
        {
        try
            {
```

```
60        BikeLocal bike = bikeLocalHome.create
            (licenceNumber, getName());
          getBikes().add(bike);
          }
        catch (CreateException e)
65        {
          throw new FleetManagerException
            ("Can't create new bike record");
          }
        }
```

This method takes a license number and uses it to create a new `Bike` EJB (by calling `create(...)` on `bikeLocalHome`). It then adds the new EJB to the collection of `Bike` EJBs known to `BikeModel`. Notice that we get to this `Collection` by calling `getBikes()`: There is no access to the actual object that implements the `Collection`. In fact, we don't even know what kind of object we get when we call `getBikes()`; we know only that it implements the `Collection` interface. In fact, it is unlikely that this object will be a generic `Collection` implementation like `ArrayList` or `Vector`. It will be a specific implementation provided by the EJB container.

As well as being able to create `Bike` objects by specifying a license number, clients can also get a list of license numbers of motorcycles of the specified model.

```
70  public Collection getBikeLicenceNumbers()
        {
        ArrayList al = new ArrayList();
        Iterator it = getBikes().iterator();
        while (it.hasNext())
75        al.add(((BikeLocal)(it.next())).getLicenceNumber());
        return al;
        }
```

Here the EJB calls `getBikes()` to get a `Collection` of `Bike` objects associated with the `BikeModel`. It then iterates this `Collection` and, for each EJB extracted, calls `getLicenceNumber()`. It then adds the license number to a *new* `Collection` of `String` objects, which gets returned to the client.

This example demonstrates the importance of providing a local client view of the `Bike` EJB. Without this, there would be considerable overhead in the distributed method calls on the `Bike` EJBs. However, using a local client view does not eliminate the need for `Bike` EJB instances to be synchronized to the database, so this remains an overhead. As we iterate the `Collection` and call `getLicenceNumber()`, the EJB container will have to prepare an instance of the `Bike` implementation class by loading data from the database. But—and this is important—the container *can* optimize this process by fetching a block of `Bike` data from the database and caching it for the duration of the current transaction. Not all containers will do this, but the important fact is that the architecture makes it possible to do it.

13.6.4   Configuration and deployment

You'll notice, of course, that there is no database logic or SQL in the EJB implementation class. The EJB container needs more information before it is able to construct the final implementation of the EJB. In particular it needs to be told the following:

- which of the EJB's properties correspond to persistent data items;

- which properties represent persistent associations (relationships);

- how to determine which EJBs of other types are associated with a particular instance of this one;

- which EJBs are to be selected by the `findAll()` method, and other finder methods that might be provided;

- how the persistent data properties map onto database tables and columns.

All this information is supplied either in the deployment descriptor, or by tools supplied by the vendor. In some cases, the vendor's tools will do both vendor-specific and J2EE-compliant operations with the same tool. This is the case for the *J2EE Reference Implementation*, and it can be quite important to understand when it is doing something proprietary and when it is doing something defined by the *EJB Specification*.

Specifying persistent data items

With the *J2EE Reference Implementation*, this operation can be carried out with the deployment tool, using the 'Entity' tab of the specific EJB's properties (Figure 13.5). This page also allows the specification of the primary key class, `java.lang.String` in this case, and primary key property (`name` here).

The information provided by this process ends up in the deployment descriptor `ejb-jar.xml`—that is, it is vendor-neutral.

Specifying persistent relationships

Relationships between EJBs are set up at the JAR-file level, not at the EJB level. With the *J2EE Reference Implementation* deployment tool, select the JAR file, then select the 'Relationships' tab. This displays a list of known relationships. The 'Add...' button allows a new relationship to be defined. Figure 13.6 is what you get when you click 'Add ... '.

Information about relationships is also vendor-neutral, and is generated into `ejb-jar.xml`.

Specifying finder methods

Finders must be specified in EJB QL. Although there are two finder methods, `findAll()` and `findByPrimaryKey()`, only `findAll()` needs an EJB QL statement.

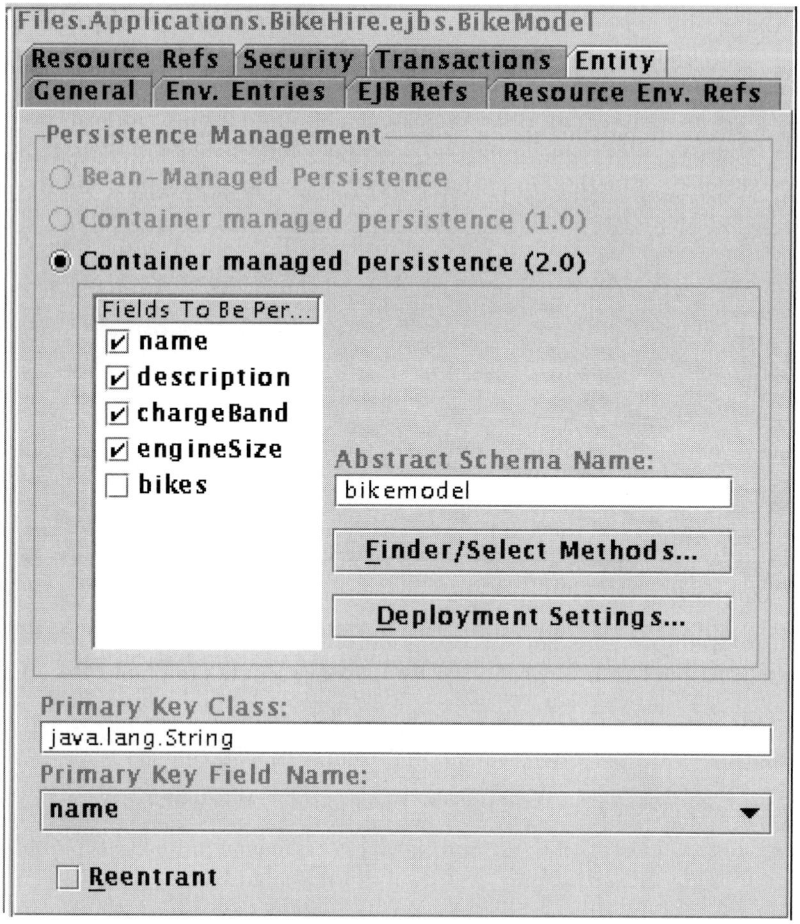

Figure 13.5. Selecting the persistent properties of the `BikeModel` EJB. Notice that `bikes` is *not* a persistent property. There is a `getBikes()` method, but it is linked to a persistent association with the `Bike` EJB, not to a property. The deployment tool has no way to know that a method called—e.g., `getAbc()`—does *not* correspond to a property `abc`. You must tell it.

This is because the EJB container always knows every EJB's primary key property.[6] With the RI's deployment tool, select the 'Entity' tab and then click 'Finder/Select' methods (Figure 13.7).

The EJB QL for `findAll()` is trivial:

```
select object(b) from bikemodel b
```

---

[6]You will still need to tell the container how the EJB's primary key property maps onto something in the database; this will be part of the general process of mapping EJB properties to database attributes, described later.

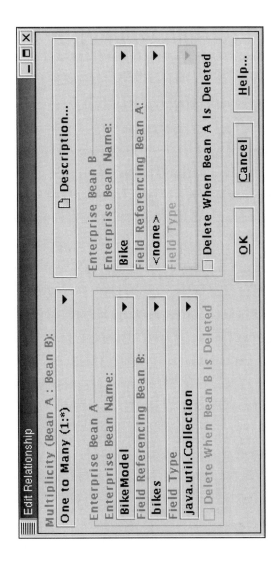

Figure 13.6. Creating the relationship between BikeModel and Bike. The relationship is unidirectional: BikeModel has a property, bikes, which maps onto the associated bike EJB, but the opposite is not the case. Note that 'cascaded delete' is not enabled in this example.

429

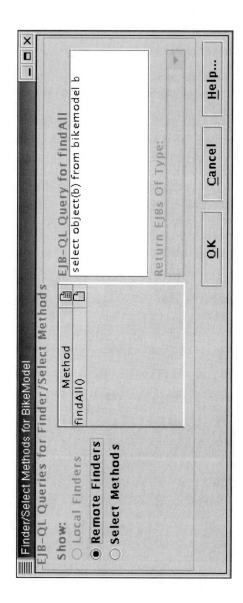

Figure 13.7. Entering an EJB QL SELECT statement for the findAll() method.

> ## Gotcha!
>
> Although I've said this before in this chapter, it's important
> enough to bear repeating: There is a world of difference between
> a container-managed field and a container-managed relationship.
> If the deployment tool inspects the EJB's set of `getXXX` methods
> to determine candidate properties for persistence management,
> and it encounters a `getXXX` with return type `Collection`, is this
> a field or a relationship? Only you know. If you tell the deploy-
> ment tool that it is a field, then it will generate code that persists
> the contents of the collection by serializing them to the database.
> That is, it will make a copy of everything in the `Collection` and
> put it into a database field. If the `Collection` is a `Collection` of
> EJBs, that probably isn't what you want: The EJBs are usually
> targets of an association, and should be managed by the container
> as relationships, not data.

There is no WHERE clause, so all `BikeModel` EJBs are selected. What is
'`bikemodel`' in this statement? It is *not* the EJB name with the case shown incorrectly; it is the name of the 'abstract persistence schema'—that is, the set of
specific persistent properties and relationships defined for this EJB. This was entered in the 'Entity' tab as shown in Figure 13.5.

Of course, the relational database won't support EJB QL directly, so in the next
step, we will tell the RI how to convert from EJB QL to SQL.

Specifying database mappings

This part of the process is vendor-specific, and is likely to remain that way in
the future. The *EJB Specification* does not mandate any particular form of data
storage device for persistence management, and therefore cannot lay down rules
about how database mapping is to be performed. In fact, as we shall see, the process
is very straightforward with the RI, because it is so inflexible. From the 'Entity'
tab, click the 'Deployment settings...' button. Click 'Generate default SQL.' The
tool will generate SQL statements that mirror your EJB QL. It will also generate
SQL statements to support operations that are not specified in EJB QL, such as
synchronizing the EJB properties to the database. All these generated statements
will contain default table names and column names. Now you *can* modify the table
and column names to be appropriate for a different database schema, if you are
diligent. The problem is that you will need to do this every time you need to click the
'Generate default SQL' button, which means every time you add or modify a finder
method. In practice, it is much easier when using this tool to allow it to do all the
database management itself. In that case, the 'default' SQL it generates is invariably

correct and should not need any manual modification. Of course, this may well not be appropriate in a real deployment, and it is envisaged that commercial products will provide more flexible methods for mapping EJB to database properties.

It is only at this stage that you will find out whether your EJB QL statements are valid or not. Until now the EJB QL could be syntactically incorrect, or the statement could refer to nonexistent properties: These problems only come to light at translation time.

From Figure 13.8, you will see that the SQL code generated for the `findAll()` method is

```
SELECT "b"."name" FROM "BikeModelBeanTable" "b"
```

Although the double-quotes in the identifiers do serve to make the identifiers case-sensitive—to aid mapping to Java identifiers—bear in mind that the double-quotes are essentially a part of the identifier name; they are not just punctuation. This is important if it becomes necessary to inspect the database using an SQL prompt. For a more detailed discussion of this issue, see page 213.

13.7   EJB QL examples

findByPrincipal() in Customer EJB

This example demonstrates how EJB QL can be used to select EJBs based on the properties of their associated EJBs, rather than their own properties.

Each `Customer` EJB is associated with one or more `Principal` EJBs: The principal denotes a credential that can serve to identify a particular customer from his or her login ID. This relationship was described in more detail on page 128.

When a session EJB needs to find the `Customer` EJB that represents the customer who is currently logged in, it gets the security principal from the container, then calls `findByPrincipal(String)` on the `Customer` EJB. This returns the (single) customer that has a principal corresponding to the supplied `String` argument.

How do we express `findByPrincipal()`? The `Customer` EJB has a property, `principals`, that represents a `Collection` of `PrincipalMapping` EJBs. Each `PrincipalMapping` EJB has a property, `principal`, that stores the principal in `String` format. Thus we can express the operation in EJB QL like this:

```
SELECT DISTINCT OBJECT(c) FROM customer c,
   IN (c.principals) p
   WHERE p.principal=?1
```

This can be read as 'find `Customers` by examining the `PrincipalMapping` EJBs referenced in the `principals` association and selecting those `Customer` EJBs for which any `PrincipalMapping` EJB has a `principal` property the same as the supplied argument.'

More technically, the clause 'IN (c.principals) p' sets the search to range over the `PrincipalMappings` EJBs defined by the property `principals`, and to give the selected `PrincipalMapping` the identifier 'p' at each iteration. The WHERE

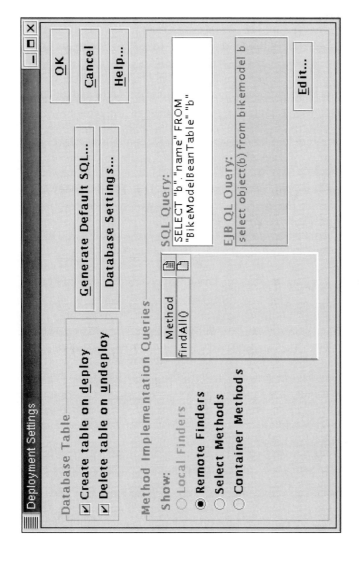

Figure 13.8. Generating an SQL statement for the `findAll()` method. The database synchronization process will also be driven by SQL code generated by this tool.

clause tests the `principal` property of the current `PrincipalMapping` (that is, `p.principal`) against the argument supplied (?1).

findByDate() in Booking EJB

This example demonstrates more complex EJB QL expressions.

The `BookingManager` EJB needs to be able to select `Booking` EJBs that lie within a specific data range. `Booking` has properties `startDate` and `endDate` that represent the (inclusive) start dates and end dates of the booking. The first complication we encounter is that EJB QL, as it currently stands, has no built-in support for date calculations. Instead, we have to represent the date numerically. The properties `startDate` and `endDate` cannot, therefore, usefully be `java.lang.Date` objects, but must be numerical. Because the JVM has built-in methods for converting times and dates into millisecond values, I have chosen to define the `startDate` and `endDate` properties as type `long`, to accommodate the large numbers that are required. We could use, say, an `int` if we implement methods for converting a date in day-month-year format into an `int`, but Java provides no support for this.

So, `startDate` and `endDate` are of type `long`, and the finder method signature is defined thus:

```
public Collection findByDate (long startDate , long endDate);
```

These arguments are derived by using standard Java techniques to convert the required date into milliseconds.

When we have dates in milliseconds, we can compare then using standard EJB QL operators like '<' (less than) and '>' (greater than). Where the numbers represent dates, these operators correspond to 'earlier than' and 'later than.'

When a customer wishes to rent a motorcycle, we need to determine whether it is booked at the time requested. But it is important to consider that a motorcycle is unavailable if it is reserved for a customer on any day requested by the potential hirer. Naively, we may try to express the `findByDate()` operation as

```
SELECT OBJECT(b) FROM booking b
   WHERE (b.startDate > ?1 AND
     b.endDate < ?2
```

but this won't work; it will only select bookings whose start and end date lie entirely within the requested period. We need to select bookings that overlap with the requested period at either end, as well as being encompassed. The necessary expression, in fact, is

```
SELECT OBJECT(b) FROM booking b
   WHERE
     (b.startDate <= ?1 AND b.endDate > ?1) OR
     (b.startDate < ?2 AND b.endDate >= ?2) OR
     (b.startDate >= ?1 AND b.endDate <= ?2)
```

Gotcha!

An EJB can have a property of type `java.lang.Date`, and it can be synchronized to the container automatically, but it can't be manipulated in EJB QL as a date. It can still be manipulated in Java as a date. This works because the persistence manager can store any instance variable in the database if it is serializable: It just serializes it and stores the serialized form. However, a serialized Java object is not something on which calculations can be carried out. In short, at present date properties that need to be compared in EJB QL must be represented as integers or long integers.

13.8   Persistence strategies compared

We round off this discussion of CMP with a discussion of the relative merits of the different methods of persistence management that are available. With an EJB 2.0-compliant product, three methods are available: bean-manager persistence, EJB 1.1 CMP, and EJB 2.0 CMP. The developer can choose which one to use, even at the level of the individual EJB.

Bean-managed persistence is still the most flexible system, and will be the only choice when the persistent store is something other than a relational database.[7] Simple implementations of BMP can be very inefficient in their use of the database; at a minimum the developer has to ensure that database updates aren't carried out if the persistent data has not changed during a transaction. There are tools available that can generate the BMP logic automatically to match a particular database scheme. *CocoBase* from Thought, Inc. is a popular example. However, with such tools, you are using container-managed persistence in all but name.

In hindsight, it is clear that EJB 1.1 had a rather naive approach to container-managed persistence, which led to the untenable situation that the usefulness of the system depended entirely on the flexibility of the server vendor's tools. Most commercial EJB 1.1 servers implemented CMP schemes that were less efficient than BMP, and far less flexible. However, some EJB servers could be integrated with proprietary object-relational mapping tools, which improved the situation somewhat. These tools often included object-based query languages, making the CMP scheme much closer to that of EJB 2.0. It seems fair to say now, however, that EJB 1.1 CMP is obsolete, and there is little reason to use it.

EJB 2.0-style CMP is a different matter entirely. It is a far more sophisticated scheme, which should lead to more efficient, portable EJBs. More importantly, it

---

[7]This isn't quite true: An alternative approach is to implement a JDBC driver for your non-standard persistent store. This will allow it be used with CMP implementations. This will only be possible if the persistent store is database-like.

removes the need to use vendors' tools to implement application logic. It is as yet too early to say whether EJB 2.0 CMP will enjoy a better uptake than its predecessor, but there are good reasons to expect that it will. It is important to understand that a CMP implementation is *theoretically* more efficient that even the most carefully implemented BMP scheme. This is because the EJB container has control of the instance pooling scheme and the transaction context, and can make calls in such a way that database overheads are minimized. The container does not expose this functionality to the EJB, so a BMP implementation cannot take advantage of it. Here is a simple example that should make this clear.

Suppose that the client of a BMP entity EJB calls `findByPrimaryKey()` to locate an EJB by its primary key. The method `ejbFindByPrimaryKey()` reads from the database to ensure that the requested EJB exists as a table row. As part of this process, it obtains the relevant table row in a JDBC `ResultSet`. Now, the implementation can't store this information for future use. There is a reasonable chance that the EJB may subsequently have to satisfy a business method call for the same EJB—that is, the same primary key. If the `ejbFindByPrimaryKey()` method *could* store the data it retrieved, then the `ejbLoad()` method could use the cached data in the instance variables, rather than reading from the database again. But it can't. The reason the EJB can't store the data in `ejbFindByPrimaryKey()` is because it can't be sure that the next business method call for that EJB goes to the same implementation instance. The container has a pool of instances available, and can select any one of them. Moreover, the EJB itself has no way of knowing whether the `ejbFindByPrimaryKey()` and the following `ejbLoad()` will be called in the same transaction context. If they are not, the data stored during `ejbFindByPrimaryKey()` can become stale by the time `ejbLoad()` is called.

Now, the container *does* know whether `ejbLoad()` is being called in the same transaction as the most recent `ejbFindByPrimaryKey()`. It can also ensure that the client's calls are directed to the same instance, so as to take advantage of the cached database data. With BMP, this level of control is not possible.

In summary, the EJB container's integration with the instance pool and the transaction manager allows it, in principle, to achieve a far higher level of database access optimization than is possible even with the best BMP implementation.

However, EJB 2.0 is not perfect. There are, as we have seen, a number of limitations to the CMP scheme, some of which are essential consequences of the way the system works, while others may well be overcome in later releases of the Specification.

13.9   Summary

Container-managed persistence removes the need for the developer to code the synchronization of an entity EJB with its persistent store. This work is done by code generated automatically by the container. EJB 1.1 implemented a simplistic scheme for persistence management that was not widely adopted. EJB 2.0 introduces a much more sophisticated scheme that is much more portable and allows a greater degree of optimization. As part of this scheme, a new query language—EJB QL—

> Hint
>
> It's probably obvious by now, but worth stressing, that EJB 2.0
> CMP is only effective if embraced wholeheartedly. An application
> that has a mixture of BMP and CMP is likely to be quite difficult
> to manage. In particular, one of the major strengths of 2.0 CMP
> is its support for container-managed relationships, while such re-
> lationships are not supported where one of the participants uses
> BMP.

abstracts the database query operations so that they become vendor-neutral and
independent of the data store. EJB QL has a small number of striking limitations,
some of which are addressed in the new EJB 2.1 draft specification.

Chapter 14

Practicalities of EJB development

> **Overview**
>
> This chapter discusses some practical matters that may be of interest to the EJB developer, such as the use of remote debugging tools, IDE capabilities, problems with EJB server configuration, and portability.

14.1 Debugging hints

Debugging EJBs presents particular challenges, as they operate in a distributed environment. The fact that they are called by the container and never directly by clients also introduces complications. This section describes some basic approaches to debugging EJBs.

14.1.1 Test clients

I recommend creating standalone test clients for all EJBs in the application, even where the EJBs will never be called from an end-user client. Even entity EJBs that are only ever called by session EJBs need their own test clients. The more versatile the test client, the more useful it will be. Ideally, a test client will be able to exercise all the methods on the EJB, passing different parameters.

Test clients for EJBs can be standalone programs for the Java 2 platform, JSP pages, or servlets. In my view, standalone command-line programs make the best test clients, and can often be generated automatically from the home and remote interfaces using test harness generators. Some IDE tools include facilities for generating test applications. For example, Sun Microsystems's *SunONE Studio* will generate a Web application with a graphical user interface to test any set of EJBs. Using such clients allows each EJB to be tested completely independently of any other components.

If an EJB is to be provided only with a local client view, then it will, of course, not be testable by standalone test clients. In such cases, the EJB is likely to be tightly coupled to another EJB, which will be making use of the client view, and the EJBs may have to be tested as an assembly. Alternatively you may be able to use a servlet-based test client, as many application servers can be configured to locate EJBs and their servlet clients in the same JVM.

14.1.2 Logging debug output

Although it is possible to use debugging tools with EJBs, as we shall see, many problems can be detected simply by generating copious debugging output in all EJBs. Techniques for logging debugging information vary from implementation to implementation. All EJB servers should allow the use of `System.out.println(...)` to generate a debug message, but don't assume your server puts this output on the console. In most cases, it will end up in a log file on the server. The *J2EE Reference Implementation* takes this approach unless it is started with the `-verbose` switch, in which case it does write to the console.

Copious logging is very useful during debugging, but is a performance penalty in a production system. In C and C++ development, it is possible to use preprocessor directives to control whether debugging instructions should be included in the compiled output or not. When the system is compiled for nondebugging use, the fact that debugging instructions appear in the source code has no performance penalty at all, as their representations do not appear in the binaries. There is no equivalent system for Java—at least none that is standardized. This means that the debugging code must remain in the compiled classes. Ideally, therefore, you should provide a system for controlling the level of debugging an application will use. My preferred approach is to provide an environment variable for each EJB, which determines what level of debugging to use. In simple applications, 'on' and 'off' settings are fine, while in more complex projects, an integer representing the amount of debugging may be more appropriate. In either case, the EJB makes a JNDI `lookup()` call to find the value of this variable at initialization time, and records it in an instance variable. All debugging output is generated by calling a single method in the EJB, which determines whether to produce the output by inspecting the variable (and, perhaps, the priority of the message).

Some developers use more sophisticated systems in which the level of debugging can be changed at runtime. Typically, all debug output is routed through an EJB—usually a stateless session EJB—provided for that purpose. This EJB maintains a list of the application EJBs that have debugging enabled. This list can be updated at runtime using a client. Although techniques like this are very flexible, they inevitably incur a performance penalty, even when debugging is turned off. This is because all intra-EJB calls have a certain call-setup overhead, even in the same JVM. This is not an issue with calls to a debugging method in the same class. There are an increasing number of tools designed to simplify the logging process without incurring significant performance penalties. Probably the best known is *log4j*, which is now part of the Apache-Jakarta project. This tool allows logging output to be collected and dispatched to a remote server, put in a message queue, or simply written to standard output. This is not rocket science, but does relieve the developer of a mundane task that might otherwise not get done.

14.1.3   Using interactive debugging tools

Many commercial EJB products come with built-in debugging tools, which are sometimes quite sophisticated. However, if your EJB server is based on a JVM that supports the Java VM Debugging Interface (JVMDI), and most are, then you can debug EJBs using any JVMDI-compliant debugging tool. In a pinch, you could probably use the `jdb` command-line debugger that is supplied with the Sun JDK. With some debugging tools, you may be able to use remote debugging (debugger runs in a separate process to the EJB server), which allows an EJB server to be debugged over a network. In all cases, you should be able to use in-process debugging. Whatever technique you use, remember that you will be running the debugger on the JVM hosting the EJB server, not on the EJB clients. This means that you will need to develop sufficient familiarity with your EJB server to distinguish its own classes from those that make up your application. In addition, if you want to debug at the source code level, you will need to ensure that your source code is visible to the debugger hosting the EJB server, in addition to the compiled classes. This is not usually a problem when running the EJB server on the same host as the development tools, but may be a problem when using simple in-process debugging on a remote server. The solution is usually simply to copy the source code onto the remote machine and tell the debugger where it is (see below).

> **Hint**
>
> Whatever debugging tools you use, to get access to the local variables in Java platform classes requires that they be compiled with full debugging information. With Sun JDK, use the '-g' switch to `javac`.

Enabling in-process debugging using jdb

`jdb` is a simple command-line debugging client that is supplied with all modern Sun Microsystems JVM versions. If you are running a local instance of the EJB server— that is, the server is running on your development system—this is probably the simplest way to debug. Your Java development tools may provide more sophisticated in-process debuggers than `jdb`, but remember that it is the EJB *server* that you must run under the debugger, not the EJB's clients. So for this process to work, you must have at least command-line access to the EJB server. In this section, I will assume that your EJB server uses the JDK `java` command, launched from a batch file or shell script. Before following the procedure described here, see if your EJB product has a built-in way to achieve the same effect.

To run the EJB server under jdb, simply modify the command line that launches the EJB server's JVM to use jdb instead of java. As jdb and java use essentially the same command line, this should be a simple operation. For example, to run the *J2EE Reference Implementation* under jdb, simply find the j2ee shell script or batch file, and modify the line that starts the JVM to start jdb instead. In the Unix versions, the shell script j2ee ends with

```
$JAVACMD $SAX_PROPS $PROPS -classpath "$CPATH" \
  com.sun.enterprise.server.J2EEServer "$@
```

and we just modify it to

```
jdb $SAX_PROPS $PROPS -classpath "$CPATH" \
  com.sun.enterprise.server.J2EEServer "$@
```

On Windows versions, the corresponding file is j2ee.bat, but the command line is essentially the same. The rest of the command line should not need to be changed,[1] unless you want to debug at the source code level. In this case, you could use jdb's '-sourcepath' switch to tell it where the source code is installed. In practice, it may be easier to do this at the debugger prompt itself, as described below.

Once the EJB server is running under the debugger, you can set breakpoints, examine threads, single step, etc. Some examples of this usage are given below.

Enabling remote debugging

To enable remote debugging, you need to run the EJB server in a JVM that supports the JPDA remote debugging protocol. JPDA support is included as standard in all Sun JDK versions from 1.3, and can be added to earlier versions by downloading and installing the appropriate software support from the JavaSoft Web site. To enable remote debugging support, you need to find the Java command line and modify it to enable the appropriate support. For Sun JDK Version 1.3, simply add the following switches to the command that starts the EJB server (in the Unix versions, this is in the script j2ee, for Windows, in j2ee.bat):

```
java -Xdebug \
  -Xrunjdwp:transport=dt_socket,server=y,address=12345 \
  ... rest of command
```

The arguments to runjdwp specify the use of TCP/IP for the protocol (other protocols may be available), that the process should act as a server (listening for connections from a debugging client), and that it should bind to port 12345. You may also want to add suspend=n to tell the JVM to start the process without waiting for a client to connect. With previous Sun JDK versions, you may also need to include the switch -Xnoagent to prevent the loading of the default user client.

---

[1]On some systems, some of the '-Dx=y'-type arguments in $PROPS confuse the debugger's command-line parser, and you may need to delete some of these properties while debugging.

Some JVMs emit a password at start-up time, which the debugging client must use to connect to the process; check your JVM documentation for full details.

To use `jdb` as a remote debugging client, it needs to be launched like this:

```
jdb -attach myserver:12345
```

This tells it to run against an existing process, listening on port 12345 on the server 'myserver.' If you are running the debugger and the EJB server on the same server, 'myserver' can usually be `localhost`. From this point on, the debugging process is the same as when using `jdb` as an in-process debugger. Most remote debugging clients can be used with JDPA, and are usually much more user friendly than `jdb`.

jdb examples

Later we will consider the use of graphical source-level debuggers, which make remote debugging rather more user-friendly. However, the *facilities* these tools offer are constrained by the debugging architecture in use (JDPA, etc.), rather than by the tools themselves. This means that a simple command-line debugger like `jdb` will allow exactly the same kind of debugging as sophisticated graphical tools, even though it is provided with the JDK. Moreover, an understanding of the interaction between the debugger client and the target JVM is easier to gain by examining how `jdb` works.

Whether you are using `jdb` as a remote debugger or an in-process debugger, the user interface is the same. It is entirely command-line based. The following example describes in outline how to debug the `Interest` EJB described in Chapter 4. The test will execute the method `getInterestOnPrincipal()`, and we want to trace the execution of this method. The implementation class is `InterestBean`.[2]

A detailed discussion of the `jdb` debugger is outside the scope of this book. For more information see the documentation that comes with the JDK.

Assume that the EJB server is running under `jdb`, either in-process or remote, as described. When running it in-process, you will need to issue the command

```
> run
```

to get the server started.

To get a list of threads currently executing, enter

```
> threads
```

To set a breakpoint in method `getInterestOnPrincipal()` in the implementation class of the `Interest` EJB, for example, enter

```
> stop in InterestBean.getInterestOnPrincipal
```

---

[2]In this section, for brevity I have ommitted the full package names or classes, both in the command lines supplied and the output from the debugger. In practice, of course, you must supply fully-qualified class names.

which should generate the response

```
Set breakpoint InterestBean.getInterestOnPrincipal
```

> ## Gotcha!
>
> You can't set a breakpoint in an interface! Remember that in this example, although the client calls `Interest.getInterestOn Principal`, this itself is not a method that can have a breakpoint, as it is merely an interface.

Now run the test client on the EJB. If you are using `Ant`, for example:

```
ant run
```

As soon as the EJB container delegates a call to the `getInterestOnPrincipal()` method in the implementation, the breakpoint will trigger, and suspend implementation just before the first line in the method. You will see a message similar to this:

```
> Breakpoint hit: thread="RequestProcessor[1]",
  InterestBean.getInterestOnPrincipal(),
  line=24, bci=0
```

where 'line=24' is the line in the source at which execution is suspended. The command `list` issued at this point will display the source code around this line, with the current line highlighted, like this:

```
20 */
21 public double getInterestOnPrincipal
22     (double principal, double interestPerTerm, int terms)
23   {
24   => log ("Called getInterestOnPrincipal");
25   return principal * Math.pow
26     ((1 + interestPerTerm / 100.0), terms) - principal;
27   }
28
29 /**
```

> ## Hint
>
> If this doesn't work, check whether `jdb` knows where the source code is located. Use the `sourcepath` command to tell it the top of the source tree. *Don't* specify the actual directories that contain the classes; `jdb` uses the same rules (package hierarchy = directory hierarchy) for source code as the JVM does for bytecode.

Let's see what the arguments to this method are at this point. For example:

```
> print principal
principal=10000.0
```

You can then step through the code one line at a time by entering **next**, displaying the new current line using **list** if necessary. Note that if you trace past the end of the method, you will follow the execution into the EJB container. While this can be interesting for figuring out how the container works, it probably doesn't help in understanding why your EJB doesn't work.

That's all there is space for here; more information about **jdb** can be found on the JavaSoft Web site.

Remote debugging using an IDE

Most integrated development environment (IDE) tools provide a JVMDI client, which provides a nicer user interface than **jdb**. In particular, you should be able to view code and set breakpoints using a source code display, rather than a command line. JVMDI support is only really helpful if you run the whole EJB server under the IDE. Some IDE tools support JPDA, and can provide a user interface for debugging on a remote JVM. This is far more likely to be useful, as you probably want to keep the EJB server away from the IDE. A few EJB products have proprietary debugging interfaces that are used by the vendor's own debugging tools. These will often be much more effective than the generic JVM debugging tools, but try before you buy.

By way of illustration, we will carry out the same debugging exercise as shown above, but using the integrated source-level debugger in Sun's *SunONE Studio* IDE.[3] There isn't space to describe the operation of this IDE, or any IDE, in detail in this book, so I assume that you have a basic understanding of the operations an IDE is likely to support.

The first step is to ensure that the EJB server's JVM is running in remote debugging mode, using the **-Xdebug -Xrunjdwp** switches as described above. The EJB server should 'freeze,' pending the attachment of the debugger client. After starting the IDE, we need to carry out this attachment. With *SunONE Studio*, simply select 'Attach' from the 'Debug' menu. This allows the developer to determine which remote JVM to attach to (Figure 14.1).

To set the breakpoint we need to open the source code editor for the affected class. Figure 14.2 shows the package hierarchy viewer ('Explorer') on the left and the **InterestBean** source on the right. To add a breakpoint, just highlight the required line and select 'Add breakpoint' from the context menu. This brings up a dialog box, which allows the breakpoint properties to be refined (Figure 14.3).

Raising the debugger window confirms that this breakpoint is set, and allows its properties to be edited if necessary (Figure 14.4).

Now when we run the test client, and it calls the method **getInterestOn Principal()**, the breakpoint will be triggered (Figure 14.5). From here we can

---

[3]Formerly Forte for Java. In this example, I am using version 3.0 of the 'community edition,' which is available free of charge. At the time of writing, version 4.0 had just gone into beta testing.

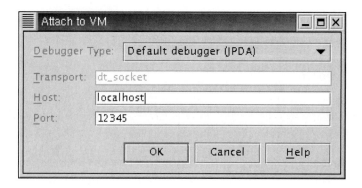

Figure 14.1. Attaching the integrated debugger to a running JVM. Note that the EJB server's JVM need not be running on the same host as the debugger, although in this example it is. For the integrated debugger to work in this mode, the EJB server's JVM must have been invoked with remote debugging enabled.

single-step through the method, examine the call stack, and view the values of variables (Figure 14.6).

> Gotcha!
>
> It's worth remembering, whether you are using command-line or graphical debugging techniques, that the EJB server will undoubtedly be multithreaded. The fact that one thread is suspended at a breakpoint does not mean that other threads are inactive. There may be some rather complex timing issues to contend with in this kind of debugging.

In summary, if you like working with IDE tools, you'll probably want to become familiar with their remote debugging features. If you don't, you'll find that simple command-line tools offer exactly the same features. We will have more to say about the use of IDE tools in EJB development below.

14.2   Packaging and assembly of applications

Developing EJB applications presents particular practical challenges that may not be present in other forms of development, as well as technical challenges. This is because EJB applications must be supplied to the EJB server in a particular form, with configuration files of a specific type and structure. In general, experienced EJB developers tend to follow one of three general strategies, although there are, of course, substantial variations in individual practice.

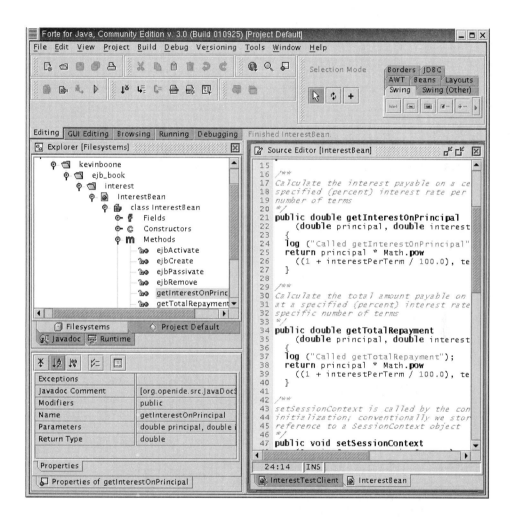

Figure 14.2. The *SunONE* IDE showing a view of the `InterestBean` implementation class. From this view, we can insert a breakpoint simply by right-clicking the appropriate line of code and selecting 'Add breakpoint' from the menu.

448

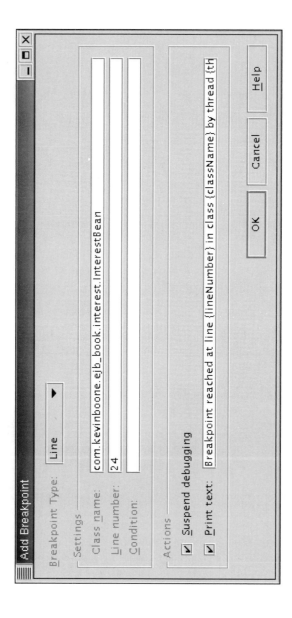

Figure 14.3. The IDE asks what we want to do when the breakpoint is hit. In this case, we want an unconditional stop. In more complex cases, the breakpoint may be triggered only if a specified expression evaluates a certain way.

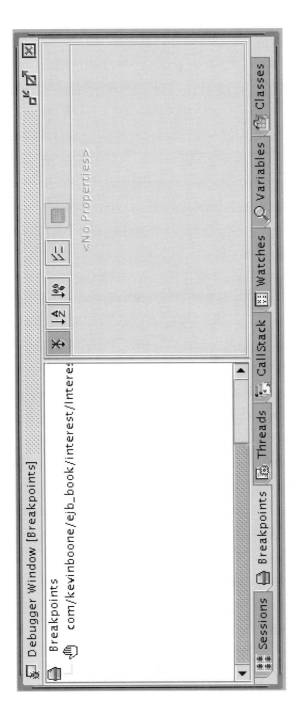

Figure 14.4. After inserting the breakpoint, the debugger window confirms that one breakpoint is now in effect.

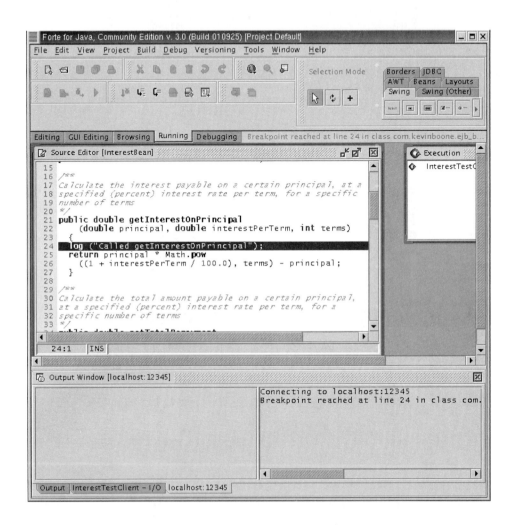

Figure 14.5. The breakpoint has been triggered. The 'Execution' window shows that
`InterestTestClient` is running in the IDE, and that the remote JVM (i.e., the EJB
server) has stopped on line 24 of `InterestBean`. We can now single-step using the buttons
on the toolbar.

450

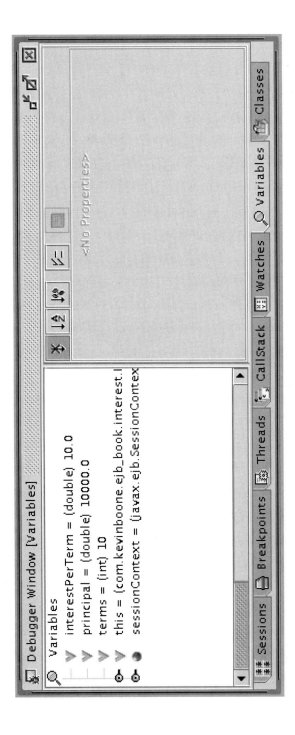

Figure 14.6. The debugger window shows all the variables that are currently in scope at the point of execution.

- Use of an IDE tool for all stages of development: creating, compilation, assembly and packaging, deployment, and testing. While adherents of this approach stress its productivity, there is no doubt that a tool that offers this level of sophistication takes some time to master and demands an initial commitment which is only repaid after extensive use.

- Development and compilation using standard Java techniques (IDEs, editors, etc), followed by assembly and packaging using a specialized assembly tool. This is the approach followed by the examples in this book: Java platform classes are compiled in the usual way and assembled using the `deploytool` application that is supplied with the *J2EE Reference Implementation*. The advantage of this approach for the relative novice is that it avoids the requirement to understand the particulars of the packaging structure and deployment descriptor, while allowing relatively simple tools to be used. This in turn allows the novice EJB developer to concentrate on the technology, rather than mastering complex tools. This method is rather limited in practice, however.

- Development and compilation using standard Java techniques followed by assembly and packaging using command-line utilities controlled by scripts, batch files, or `Ant` build files. This technique is fast and flexible, but requires extensive knowledge of packaging and deployment descriptors. Although the XML deployment descriptors can be assembled by hand using a text editor, many developers who favor this approach prefer to use specialized XML editors (of which, more later).

In my experience, most developers start off with the 'middle' approach (a mixture of standard Java techniques and specialist assembly tools) and then migrate either to a fully automated or fully manual system of development. Each, of course, has its advantages and disadvantages, and the choice often reflects the personality of the developer more than anything else. I have twenty years of experience using text editors and command-line tools for software development, so I have never really mastered IDE tools—although I often feel guilty for not trying harder. There is no doubt that modern IDEs offer some very nice features for the EJB developer.

14.2.1   IDE tools

Traditionally Interactive Development Environments (IDEs) have offered the ability to edit, compile, run, and debug programs all in the same working environment. These capabilities are well-understood, and I won't discuss them further here. What is more interesting is the range of EJB-specific features that may be offered. Some examples include the following.

EJB construction from templates These facilities remove some of the drudgery from the process of constructing EJBs. For example, the tool may automatically create the home interface, remote interface, and implementation class outlines, given the name and type of the EJB. Smarter tools offer the ability to keep the templates in sync after generation. For example, if I choose to add a business method with a particular signature to an EJB, the tool can add the method's outline to the implementation class, remote interface, and local interface in one operation. Even smarter tools will detect changes in the method signature in any of these places and update the others to maintain consistency.

Integrated packaging tools   The IDE may include facilities to assemble and package JAR and EAR files, and create the XML deployment descriptors, based on a graphical representation of the EJB's properties manipulated by the developer.

Multivendor targeting   Some EJB servers allow (or indeed insist upon) vendor-specific configuration information to be supplied in the EAR and JAR files (the implications of this policy for portability are discussed below). Some IDE products are able to incorporate this vendor-specific information into EAR and JAR files for a range of different products. This job is *much* more difficult than it first appears. For example, the SunONE application servers expect to authenticate users against the groups defined in an LDAP directory server. This means that the IDE tool must have directory integration, so that the developer can pick the correct group information to put into the vendor-specific deployment descriptor for this product. Another vendor's product may do authentication in a completely different way, requiring additional support in the IDE.

Database integration   Many commercial IDEs contain a relational database engine, allowing data access functionality to be exercised from within the IDE. This removes the need for the developer to be concerned with configuring database drivers and provides for rapid debugging of problems related to SQL operations.

Automatic test client generation   For example, the *SunONE* Studio IDE can generate a Web-based test client for any package of EJBs.

Support for design patterns   As we shall see, there are a number of standard design patterns widely used by EJB developers. The *Prestige Bike Hire* application, for example, makes extensive use of the 'value object' pattern. Some IDE tools can generate the classes required to implement certain patterns automatically.

Integrated verification   As you will have already discovered, a Java compiler cannot test whether the classes and interfaces that comprise an EJB are correctly integrated. A compiler operates on one class at a time. A verification tool can check that the EJB classes and interfaces are consistent—for example, it will ensure that business methods exposed in the remote interface have corresponding implementations in the implementation class. The *J2EE Reference Implementation* has a standalone verification tool, but a case can be made for claiming that it is more productive to integrate the verifier into the IDE.

It's also worth pointing out that, as many EJB applications are developed along-side Web-based user interfaces, an IDE that can automate the development of servlet/JSP applications is likely to be particularly appealing.

Clearly, a tool that can offer all these features, in addition to standard IDE operations, is likely to be quite complex, and take some time to come to grips with.

14.2.2   Command-line tools

It is important to realize that the capabilities of an EJB application are set by the *EJB Specification*, not the software tools used to create EJBs. Although IDEs and other tools may simplify the development process, there is nothing that they can do that will increase the functionality available to the application. It is entirely possible to carry out all the operations required to compile, assemble, and deploy EJB applications using only command-line tools. Of course, the sensible developer will automate these command-line operations using scripts or build files. The Ant build utility is becoming increasingly popular for this, as it allows operations like Java compilation and JAR file assembly to be specified in a platform-independent way. Thus is not true of, for example, the standard Unix make utilities. Developers should bear in mind that EAR files, WAR files, and EJB-JAR files are nothing more than standard Java JAR files, and they can be created using the jar utility supplied with all JVMs. JAR file assembly is particularly easy to do using the Ant tool, as it has built-in support for this operation.

What this all means, in practice, is that if the developer creates a suitable Ant build file, then it should be possible to compile, package, and deploy an application simply by typing ant on the command line. When set up properly, this is *much* faster than any IDE tool. Of course, it does take a while to become sufficiently familiar with Ant and the command-line tools to achieve this degree of automation.

14.2.3   XML editors

Developers that eschew the use of IDEs and specialized packaging tools are faced with the problem of creating the XML deployment descriptors manually. As will be discussed below, in most cases the developer will have to provide ejb-jar.xml *and* a vendor-specific XML file with each JAR file.

Creating an EJB deployment descriptor from scratch using a text editor is not a job for the faint-hearted. The deployment descriptor for the *Prestige Bike Hire* application contains about 4,000 lines of XML. Undoubtedly a strong knowledge of the structure of the deployment descriptor is required before attempting such a job.

However, there is a compromise position between using integrated tools and doing everything manually, which is to use a specialist XML editor to support the creation of the deployment descriptor, while using command-line tools to insert the XML file into the JAR file along with the appropriate Java platform classes. An XML editor won't build the deployment descriptor for you, but it will prevent you from making structural errors in the XML. There are an increasing number of these tools available, some at low cost (or no cost). All work along the same lines. An XML file has a structure that is rigidly specified in a *document type descriptor*

(DTD). The DTD specifies which elements are valid at which places in the XML document, which elements are compulsory, and whether elements can be repeated and/or nested. The XML editor reads the DTD and constrains the XML author to build a document that compiles with the DTD. An XML editor won't prevent the developer from entering meaningless information in the XML—it can't tell, for example, if a class name that you enter is correct or not—but it will provide guidance by presenting a 'palette' of allowable XML elements at each point in the document.

Figure 14.7 shows IBM's *Xeena* XML editor in use on the deployment descriptor for the *Prestige Bike Hire* application EJB JAR. The right-hand pane shows a tree view of the XML document structure, while the left-hand pane shows the elements that can validly be inserted at the point selected.

Hint

DTDs for the EJB-JAR deployment descriptor, and indeed all the other J2EE XML files, are supplied with the *J2EE Reference Implementation* in directory `lib/dtds`. You can use an XML editor without a DTD, but the functionality is much reduced.

14.3   Portability and interoperability

An issue that is frequently of burning importance to EJB developers is that of code portability. Developers want to know if they can develop and test applications on one platform, with a view to deploying them eventually on another platform. Why should we want to do this? The problem is that many real-world EJB applications end up being deployed on heavy-duty, commercial-grade application servers. These products are optimized for high throughput and reliability and, on the whole, do not make good development platforms. Developers frequently complain about this, but it has never been clear to me why one should expect the same product to offer good development facilities *and* commercial-strength throughput and reliability. This is rather like a pilot complaining that a passenger airliner is harder to fly than a single-engine trainer. Of *course* it is: No one expects anything else.

Nevertheless, the expectation among server suppliers that integrating development tools into a production platform will increase sales has led to its own demand. Now all the major application server vendors supply development, assembly, and packaging tools with their servers. Very frequently, developers are tempted to use these tools, and to develop against a platform that is totally unsuited to the task. This leads to frustration with the product and disenchantment with the technology as a whole.

More sophisticated developers realize that one of the philosophical foundations of J2EE is that J2EE applications should run on any compliant product, so it should

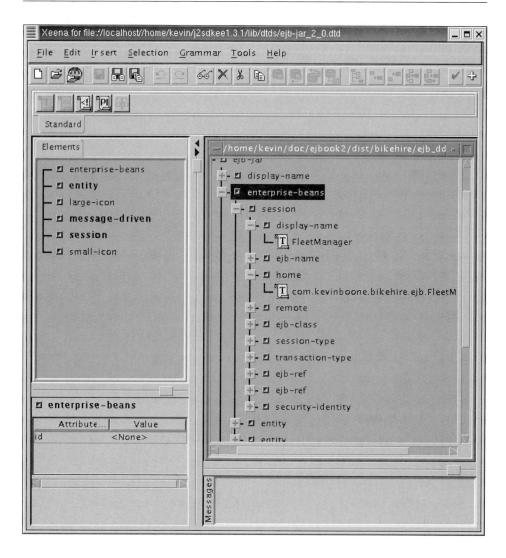

Figure 14.7. Using an XML editor to assist in the construction of the deployment descriptor. See text for details.

be possible to develop on one platform and run on another. However, they don't know what problems they are likely to encounter in doing so, and are deterred from making the attempt.

In general, J2EE applications are very portable, so there should be few problems with developing on one platform and running on another. However, anyone who plans to do this should pay attention to the following points.

- Portability depends absolutely on following the J2EE rules. The following widespread practices will lead to problems: implementing your own authentication procedures (rather than using container security); interacting with JDBC at the `DriverManager` level; writing to files from EJBs; optimizing entity EJBs by making assumptions about the container's synchronization strategy; and using proprietary container APIs.

- The *EJB Specification* does not prohibit server vendors from requiring vendor-specific configuration files in the EJB JARs. In practice, all EJB products expect to see vendor-specific XML files in addition to the standard `ejb-jar.xml`. These files will contain information about, for example, the mapping of JNDI names onto physical resources, load balancing properties, and session management settings. While the container may be able to supply defaults for some of these, it can't usually provide JNDI names for resources.[4]

  The implication of this is that you will need to provide vendor-specific XML files as required by the target platform. XML editors can be useful here; the vendor will probably supply a DTD for the XML that it expects, and this can be used to assist in the construction of a valid XML file. This is one area where developers who adopt a 'manual' approach to application assembly—using command-line utilities and scripts—hold a distinct advantage. These developers are familiar with the process of creating XML deployment descriptors and packaging them appropriately in the JAR files, so they have little extra to do. If you have become dependent on, for example, the packaging tool supplied with the *J2EE Reference Implementation*, you will have a bit of extra work in this respect.

  In practice, the creation of vendor-specific XML files is a job you'll only have to do once for each project, when porting the application to the new platform, and it should not be seen as a deterrent to working on multiple platforms. In any event, many IDE tools are now able to generate deployment descriptors to suit a range of different target servers.

- There are particular portability problems with EJB 1.1-compliant container-managed persistence. Porting an application that uses this persistence management strategy is not a trivial undertaking. EJB 2.0 CMP does not have this problem to anything like the same extent. Nevertheless, not all EJB 2.0 products support the mapping of entity EJBs onto multiple overlapping database tables, for example.

At the time of writing, Sun Microsystems had just launched a pilot program to evaluate a new product called the 'J2EE Application Verification Kit'. This is a set of software tools for verifying that the developer's code uses the J2EE APIs in a way that is 'correct,'—that is, likely to be portable. At present, it is nececssary to

---

[4]This isn't strictly true. The product can provide defaults, but there is no guarantee that they are meaningful. For example, if you don't explicitly provide JNDI names for EJBs, many products assume that the JNDI name should be the same as the internal name of the EJB. This will work in some situations, but not in all.

enroll in the pilot program to use this software, but it may be in more widespread release by the time you read this.

14.4   Utility classes and the server CLASSPATH

Consider the following section of code, which is in a method in an EJB implementation.

```
utils.JDBCHelper helper = new utils.JDBCHelper();
helper.executeQuery ("UPDATE....");
```

Assume that the class `JDBCHelper` contains general-purpose methods for simplifying database access. The code will compile if the compiler can find the class `utils.JDBCHelper` at compile time. At runtime, the situation is more complicated. What has to be true for the operation `new utils.JDBCHelper()` to succeed?

- The container must allow the operation.

- The container's JVM must be able to load the class.

There are a number of reasons why the operation may not be allowed. According to the *J2EE Specification*, the fundamental unit of deployment is the *application*; an application is a set of classes and supporting files packaged into an EAR file. It is the vendor's responsibility to ensure that the classes deployed in an EAR file are visible to one another, within the constraints of the architecture, and not visible to other components. This makes perfect sense when one understands the philosophy: Expecting an EJB server to make classes from one EAR file available to those in another EAR file is like expecting an operating system to allow applications to read each other's program code from memory.

The developer should not assume that because the container uses the same JVM for all EJBs, their classes are accessible to one another. The container may well use separate class loaders for each application, or even for each EJB. The class loaders will implement the container's policy with respect to loading classes across applications.

What this all means is that if you want to be certain that shared utility classes are available to all components in an application, the only way to do this that is fully portable is to *deploy the utility classes along with each set of J2EE components*. That is, replicate them in each JAR and WAR file. This applies even to classes that are to be loaded by the container as a result of an operation on a home object or remote object. The client may carry out a successful JNDI `lookup()` operation to find the home object, then be unable to use it because the JVM won't allow the home interface to be loaded. This behavior seems strange when it is first encountered, but it is entirely in keeping with the J2EE philosophy: An EAR file is an application, and applications are independent of one another.

The need to replicate helper classes in multiple EAR and JAR files can be inconvenient, and most containers support (vendor-specific) methods to get around it. In particular, it is usually possible to deploy system-wide helper classes. Typically, classes that are accessible by the EJB container's own CLASSPATH can be loaded by any component. Many containers have a designated directory into which system-wide classes can be installed. With the *J2EE Reference Implementation*, this is the directory `$J2EE_HOME/classes`. Similar arrangements exist for most products. Otherwise, it is usually possible to extend the container's CLASSPATH to encompass additional directories or JAR files.

> ## Gotcha!
>
> Don't assume that you will always be able to force the EJB server to find shared classes by modifying the JVM CLASSPATH. Most products use custom classloaders to keep applications separate, and it is a decision of the server vendor whether the custom class-loader honors the system CLASSPATH or not. Some do, some don't.

14.5 Summary

This chapter discussed some of the practical issues associated with EJB development, and provided some general techniques to handle a number of common problems.

Chapter 15

Design, patterns, and good practice

Overview

This chapter discusses higher-level design issues in the EJB architecture and provides general guidance on building efficient, maintainable EJB applications. Some of the matters it describes are fairly technical, such as the effect on the application when exceptions are thrown from one EJB to another, while others are more pragmatic, like the use of design patterns.

15.1 Architectural and structural issues

So far in this book we have considered the various types of EJB in isolation. It is important to have a detailed understanding of the way the various types work, but it is also important to realize that in practice an application may well make use of all three types. This section provides some general guidelines on structuring and architecting an EJB application that consists of multiple EJBs of different types.

15.1.1 The EJB architecture is designed for tiered applications

The *EJB Specification* says relatively little about the intended applications of each of the EJB types. It is possible, and may be sensible, to build an application entirely of session EJBs, for example. However, the properties of the EJB types themselves strongly favor a 'tiered' application model, where entity EJBs separate the session EJBs from the data sources (see Figure 15.1). In such a model, entity EJBs act primarily to provide an object-oriented view of the data, to simplify the development of the session EJBs, which will then contain the bulk of the application's business logic.

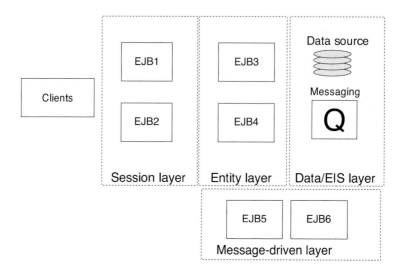

Figure 15.1. The *EJB Specification* does not mandate the use of a 'tiered' development model, but the characteristics of the various EJBs strongly favors such a model. Typically, the application would be divided into a session tier and an entity tier. See text for details.

This model has a number of advantages, which are briefly summarized below.

- Instances of the implementation classes of both session EJBs and entity EJBs are held in a pool by the server, but for different reasons. Session EJBs are pooled to support large client loads, while entity EJBs are pooled to support large databases.

- Session EJBs interact with the database through an object-oriented representation provided by entity EJBs. This makes the session EJBs easier to implement and manage, and decouples the business logic from the database model.

- It simplifies the transaction management model. Because session EJB methods can encompass multiple method calls on multiple entity EJBs, the transaction boundaries can be defined to be equivalent to session EJB method call boundaries. The EJB architecture has built-in support for this notion of transaction management. We will have much more to say about this subject later.

The most important factor in the use of tiered models is sound design of the points where the tiers interact. Careful attention to these interactions will allow for a design with low cohesion—that is, minimal cross-tier dependencies.

At the boundary between the entity tier and the session tier, it is generally felt that optimal design views the entity tier as an object-oriented view of the persistent data in the application domain. The choice of entity EJBs should not—it is argued—be made on the basis of an existing database schema. Instead, the architect should be seeking to provide an entity model that maximally decouples the business logic from the data model. This may be achieved by drawing up a pure object-oriented model of the application's persistent elements, and then trying to design an entity tier that forms the bridge between this model and the underlying data stores, in whatever form they happen to take. In practice, this level of abstraction may not be possible and, even if it is, may require the implementation of an excessively large number of entity EJBs. All the same, it is a worthwhile exercise, and helps to focus the entity design on the needs of the business logic, not the database.

At the boundary between the session tier and the clients, most authorities recommend that a small number of session EJBs form the 'API' to the application. That is, we first identify the services that the client will need of the application, then allocate these services to a small number of session EJBs. Some designers like to work with a use-case model, creating initially one session EJB for each use case. The session tier can then be expanded with additional session EJBs to provide the supporting logic for the use cases. In general, the API presented to the clients should be as 'coarse grained' as possible, to minimize the overheads associated with multiple small interactions, particularly where these are distributed.

It can be argued that an ideal design is one in which the underlying data store can be completely replaced without making a single change to the session tier, and an entirely new client can be added without changing the entity tier.

> ## Hint
>
> Many of these architectural issues are demonstrated in the archetypal *Java Pet Store* application, which is widely available.

15.1.2   Use design patterns

EJB developers don't have to work in a vacuum; there are now enough people doing EJB development that a number of popular design patterns have been established. Some of these have already been discussed in this book. The 'abstract DAO' pattern was introduced in Chapter 12; the 'value object' pattern has been mentioned and is discussed further later in this chapter. The following is a brief description of some other patterns that have found favor with EJB developers. It is only a small selection of the large set of patterns that have been documented. For more information, fire up your Web browser!

'Service locator' pattern This pattern concentrates the JNDI `lookup()` operations for a range of different services into the same class. The service locator class is then used for all lookup operations, whether they are for EJB home objects, datasources, connectors, or message queues. A simple example is the

BeanLocator class used in the *Prestige Bike Hire* application. This class has methods that return narrowed EJB references for a specified JNDI name. More complex locators can cache references, so that if a lookup has already been performed, the reference is returned from the cache. This improves efficiency, as well as reducing code duplication.

'Business delegate' pattern (This pattern is also known as the 'EJB proxy' or 'EJB adaptor.') In this pattern, clients of an EJB are provided with a client-side proxy for the EJB. This proxy encapsulates all the EJB access logic, while looking to the client like an ordinary class. It may help to think of this as a 'smart' value object: Like a value object, it encapsulates the EJB's state, but unlike a value object, it can respond to clients changing its state, by communicating these state changes back to the EJB itself.

'Message facade' pattern This pattern seeks to allow an EJB to carry out a number of operations in the same transaction without blocking while the transaction commits. The EJB that wants to carry out the asynchronous operation posts a message into a message queue using JMS; this message is picked up by a message-driven EJB, which then carries out a number of operations in the the same transaction context.

15.1.3 Use OO concepts

EJB designers have often been reluctant to use proper object-oriented modelling as part of an EJB design. This is largely a result of the poor support for concepts like associations in earlier versions of the *EJB Specification*. EJB 2.0 has built-in support for one-to-one, one-to-many, and many-to-many associations, so now there's no excuse.

Moreover, there is now a specification for mapping UML models onto EJBs; this is being developed as part of the Java Community Process (JCP). This specification should allow UML designers and EJB developers to work together more closely, and for EJB designs to be documented and shared through the medium of UML. This specification is available from the JCP Web site www.jcp.org, under reference JSR0026.

15.2 Exception handling: philosophy and practice

Exception handling is always important in Java development, and particularly so with EJBs. The *EJB Specification* devotes a whole chapter [EJB2.0 18] to this topic. This section describes some of the general issues concerning exception handling in EJBs, the more specific issue of the interaction between exception handling and transaction management is covered in Chapter 9.

15.2.1 Review of Java exceptions

In Java, exceptional circumstances are indicated by generating an object of a class that inherits from java.lang.Throwable, and using the throw keyword to pass it out of the method to the caller. The caller can use `catch` to trap the thrown object, or allow it to be thrown out to its own caller. Ultimately the thrown object, if not handled, will be caught by the JVM and handled in a default manner.

There are three fundamental classes that derive from `Throwable` (Figure 15.2).

- The `Error` class is intended to indicate serious system-level errors that the developer is not expected to handle. In some cases, these are errors that would not even be possible to handle usefully, like `OutOfMemoryError`. (What would you do?) The Java code does not have to declare that it handles or throws `Error` or its subclasses.

- The `Exception` class is the base for all exceptions that the developer may want to handle. If such an exception is thrown, then the Java code must declare that this is the case, except for `RuntimeException` and its subclasses, as described below. Nearly all exceptions handled by the developer will be of this type. Exceptions that must be declared and handled in the Java code are usually called *checked exceptions*.

- Runtime exceptions indicate system-level, or low-level, errors that the developer may not always want to handle. This is in contrast to `Error` and its subclasses, which should never normally be handled, and other `Exception` subclasses, which will always be handled. Although `RuntimeException` is a subclass of `Exception`, it is treated differently by the compiler. This exception and its subclasses do not require explicit declaration in the code, and are therefore called *unchecked exceptions*.

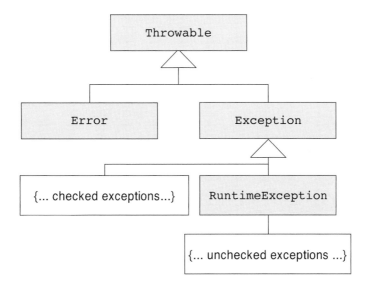

Figure 15.2. Standard Java exception hierarchy.

We will not discuss `Errors` further, as you should never have to throw or catch these in EJB code.

Philosophically the difference between checked exceptions and unchecked exceptions is that the former represent conditions that the developer should anticipate and that the program may be able to recover from. Unchecked exceptions, however, tend to represent system-level failures that are difficult to deal with.

Very often the distinction is clear-cut. For example, `java.io.FileNotFound Exception` represents a very common condition: that of trying to open a nonexistent file. This exception can arise directly from incorrect operation of the software by an end-user, and all reasonable applications should handle it. This is therefore a checked exception. At the other extreme, `java.lang.ClassCastException` can normally only arise directly as a result of developer error. A properly tested application should never throw it, and it is reasonable not to handle it. This is an unchecked exception.

However, things aren't always this straightforward. For example, the method `Integer.parseInt()`, which converts a `String` representing an integer to an `int` primitive, can be thrown because of a developer oversight, a system-level failure, or because the end-user entered incorrect data. The problem is that this method throws `NumberFormatException`, which is an unchecked, runtime exception, and the developer is not required to handle it. This is probably incorrect: The exception arises far more frequently from user error than from system failure or developer error.

In EJB development, a particularly contentious example is `java.rmi.Remote Exception`. This is not defined as a runtime exception, but resembles one in many respects. Typically, a `RemoteException` indicates a problem in communication between client and server, rarely results from anything that a user would do, and is quite beyond the control of the developer. However, anything that calls a remote method on an EJB must be prepared to catch a `RemoteException` because it is a checked exception. To add to the uncertainty, the EJB server is required to treat a `RemoteException` as if it were a `RuntimeException`!

> ## Gotcha!
>
> For backward compatibility with Version 1.0 of the *EJB Specification*, EJB servers should treat `RemoteException` like a runtime exception [EJB2.0 18.3.8]. In particular, the container should roll back a transaction it began, if it catches a `RemoteException` from a business method. See page 273 for more details.

`Throwable` objects can store a stack trace, indicating the state of the call stack at the point at which the exception occurred. The stack trace can provide information that is very useful for debugging, and the application should attempt to preserve stack traces when exceptions are handled, as far as is practical. Examples of correct and incorrect usage in this regard are provided later.

A point that is often not appreciated by developers is the relationship between exceptions declared in an interface and those in classes that implement that interface. Consider the following interface:

```
public interface Test
{
public void test() throws SQLException;
}
```

This interface specifies one method called `test()`, and indicates that the implementation of the method may throw `SQLException`. Now, if a class implements this interface, the implementation of `test()` can be declared to throw `SQLException`, and subclasses of `SQLException`, but no other exceptions. If this were not the case, and the implementation could throw arbitrary exceptions, it would be impossible for the compiler to determine whether the caller of the `test()` method was handling the right exceptions. In any case, the interface represents the contract between the class and its caller, and allowing the implementer to throw other exceptions breaks that contract.

Now, this restriction does not apply to unchecked (runtime) exceptions, as they are not checked by the compiler and represent conditions that the developer may not even be able to anticipate. Therefore the implementation class of an EJB may throw, for example, `NullPointerException` from a business method without declaring it anywhere.

In EJB development, the implementation class is an implementation of `Session Bean`, `EntityBean`, or `MessageDrivenBean`. Its container callback methods are dictated by their definitions in these interfaces. For example, `ejbLoad()` and `ejbStore()` are declared in `EntityBean` to throw no exceptions.[1] This means that these methods in the implementation can *only* throw runtime exceptions. This issue is discussed in more detail later.

15.2.2   EJB exception philosophy

The EJB architecture attempts to make the handling of exceptions in EJBs as close as possible to the handling of exceptions in ordinary Java development. However, the EJB container may be managing transactions, so exception handling and transaction management are related.

Business methods can be declared to throw exceptions, and these exceptions must be caught and handled by the caller using standard Java techniques. The EJB architecture delivers checked exceptions to the caller intact, even though the call may be across a network. The communications protocol takes care of marshalling and unmarshalling the exception at the server and client, respectively.

Runtime exceptions indicate a more severe failure, and are handled in a more radical way. Typically, the EJB container will discard any EJB instance that throws

---

[1] This isn't strictly true. For backward compatibility with EJB 1.0 exception handling, they are declared to be able to throw `RemoteException` and `EJBException`, but this is not relevant any more.

a runtime exception out of *any* method. It will also roll back any active transaction that it started. Therefore, an EJB method should not deliberately throw a runtime exception unless this response is the only way to ensure database integrity. Some EJB methods can *only* throw runtime exceptions; typically these are methods—like ejbLoad() and ejbStore()—that will always require a transaction rollback if they fail.

By the same token, an EJB should not be written in such a way that a runtime exception is prevented from being caught by the container, unless the EJB itself intends to deal with the consequences of the exception. For example, saying catch (Exception e)... is likely to lead to problems, unless the developer fully understands the implications, as described below.

If the EJB needs to throw a runtime exception, it should throw EJBException or one of its subclasses.

15.2.3 Exception handling details

Business methods

An EJB's business methods should be declared to throw whatever exceptions are required by the needs of the application. These exceptions should also be declared in the factory or business method interfaces, as appropriate. The caller of the EJB method catches the exception and handles it in the same way it would if it were an ordinary method call.

In my view, EJB methods should not normally throw low-level exceptions like SQLException or NamingException to clients. Fundamentally, the EJB exists to conceal low-level implementation details from the client. Ideally, the client should not even know that the EJB is using SQL or JNDI. In these cases, the developer should probably create an application-specific exception to indicate to the client what the problem was, in a way that makes sense in the context of the application itself. It may be useful to wrap the original low-level exception inside the application exception, so that clients that require additional information can get it.

ejbCreate()

In general, these methods should throw a CreateException to indicate any failure to initialize the EJB. An entity EJB should attempt to bring about a transaction rollback if it is the only way to ensure data integrity; it will have to call setRollbackOnly() to accomplish this, as ejbCreate() is not supposed to throw a runtime exception. Session and message-driven EJBs should not really be interacting with a database in ejbCreate(), as the transaction context is undefined.

ejbRemove()

In general, ejbRemove should throw a RemoveException to indicate that the EJB could not be removed. An entity EJB should attempt to bring about a transaction rollback if it is the only way to ensure data integrity; it will have to call setRollbackOnly() to accomplish this, as ejbRemove() is not supposed to throw a runtime exception. Session and message-driven EJBs should not really be interacting with a database in `ejbRemove()`, as the transaction context is undefined.

Finders

Finders usually do EJB QL or SQL SELECT queries, and don't update the database. This means that they should not deliberately throw runtime exceptions or signal a transaction rollback. Instead, they should throw `FinderException` or one of its subclasses. If the caller of the finder wants to roll back a transaction, it can, but the finder should not pre-empt this decision.

A special case is the failure of a single-EJB finder—usually `ejbFindByPrimary Key()`—to locate the specified entity in the database. In such an event, the finder should throw `ObjectNotFoundException` [EJB2.0 10.5.8.4].

Container callback methods

Many developers find it difficult to decide how to handle exceptions in container callback methods. Problems typically arise in methods that are subject to low-level failures beyond the control of the developer, such as `ejbLoad()` and `ejbStore()`. If an EJB is using `setEntityContext()` or `setSessionContext()` to locate references to other EJBs, or to data sources, the exceptions arising from these operations must also be handled.

In general, a failure in one of these methods must either be handled internally, in a way that leaves the database consistent, or signalled by throwing `EJBException` or one of its subclasses. The latter will bring about the rollback of any transaction started by the container, and the disposal of the instance. A special case is the inability to locate the primary key in the database in `ejbLoad()`; this should be signalled by throwing `NoSuchEntityException`, which is a subclass of `EJBException` [EJB2.0 18.2.2.1].

The code fragment below indicates the *wrong* way to handle exceptions in `ejbLoad()`.

```
    public void ejbLoad ()
    {
    try
      {
5     // JDBC code for database access...
      }
    catch ( Exception e )
      {
      System.out.println ("Caught exception: " + e );
10    }
    }
```

There are six related problems in this example.

- The `catch` block simply 'squashes' the exception (catches and discards it). Although it outputs a message, that message is not visible to clients. A client can continue to use this EJB, totally unaware that its state may not correspond to the data in the database.

- Catching `Exception` will catch not only checked exceptions, but runtime exceptions as well. Although the EJB may be able to handle `SQLException` sensibly, it should probably not attempt to handle, for example, `NullPointer Exception`. These exceptions are best handled by the container, as they would otherwise leave the EJB instance in an undefined state.

- The failure of the JDBC operations probably indicates that a database transaction should be marked for rollback. The EJB should either throw an `EJB Exception` (or `NoSuchEntityException`) to signal this, or call `set Rollback Only()` on the `EntityContext` object.

- The stack trace information in the exception is lost. Even if the exception is detected, the amount of information provided by the message is not as likely to be as helpful as if a full stack trace were provided.

- The debug message does not indicate what threw the exception, making it harder to locate the problem when debugging.

- It is not clear from the code whether error conditions that *don't* result in an exception from an API call are being handled correctly. The most common oversight on the part of developers is failing to deal with the case where `ejbLoad()` attempts to synchronize the instance variables to a row of a table that has been deleted by another instance. If the method does a SELECT operation, and there are no matching rows, this is *not* an exception at the JDBC level. It is a valid query that happens to return no data. In such cases, the EJB implementation is responsible for throwing `NoSuchEntityException` so that the container, and therefore the client, knows what the problem is.

Here is the same code rewritten to avoid these problems.

```
public void ejbLoad ()
{
try
  {
5   // JDBC code for database access...
  ResultSet rs = ...
  if (rs.next())
    {
    // process results
10    }
  else
    {
    System.out.println
      ("Primary key not found in ejbLoad ()");
15    throw new NoSuchEntityException ();
    }
  }
catch (SQLException e)
```

```
     {
20   System.out.println
        ("Caught exception in ejbLoad (): " + e);
     e.printStackTrace ();
     throw new (EJBException (e));
     }
25 }
```

This code is an improvement over the previous version for a number of reasons.

- The exception is not squashed: It is rethrown to the container as an EJB Exception. The container knows that the operation failed and may be able to communicate this to the client. It will certainly roll back any active transaction that it started.

- The catch block only traps specific exceptions. Unchecked exceptions will be handled by the container. This allows the container to discard the EJB instance in the case of, for example, NullPointerException.

- If an SQLException is caught, it is rethrown as an EJBException, allowing the container to roll back any transaction that it started.

- If the database query completes successfully, but no records are found, this indicates that the database row containing the data for this EJB's primary key has been deleted by another application. The correct response in this case is to throw a NoSuchEntityException.

- The debug message contains a full stack trace.

- The original SQLException is wrapped inside the EJBException. This allows the container, and perhaps the client, to get at the real exception that caused the method to fail.

Notice that a debug message is output whether the method fails internally (that is, catches an SQLException), or fails to satisfy the container's request because the data is not available.

Handling exceptions in intra-EJB calls: distributed view

When one EJB makes a method call on another, it is, by definition, a client of that EJB. The issues relating to throwing exceptions from EJB methods to clients apply equally whether the client is another EJB, or something else. Consider, for example, a session EJB that calls a method on an entity EJB:

```
   public void sessionMethod ()
     {
     EntityHome h = //... find home
     Entity e = h.findByPrimaryKey (...)
5    e.doSomething ();
     }
```

The session EJB should handle application-defined exceptions in exactly the same way as in any other intraobject call. Complications arise from the handling of EJB-specific exceptions. The process of finding the home object can throw a `NamingException`, and `findByPrimaryKey()` can throw a `FinderException`. If the caller is using the EJB's distributed view, rather than its local view, all methods can, as usual, throw `RemoteException`. The correct response to all these exceptions depends on the needs of the application; however, it will almost certainly not be appropriate to propagate these exceptions back to the client of the session EJB, like this:

```
  public void sessionMethod ()
      throws FinderException ,
      NamingException ,
      RemoteException
5     {
      EntityHome h = //... find home
      Entity e = h.findByPrimaryKey (...)
      e.doSomething ();
      }
```

There are two reasons why this is inappropriate. First, `FinderException` and `NamingException` relate to low-level, implementation-specific problems in the entity EJB. The client will almost certainly not be able to recover from these errors, and probably won't want to take different courses of action that depend on which of these exceptions is received. Second, `RemoteException` cannot be thrown from an EJB method while maintaining compliance with the *EJB Specification*. The reason for this is that throwing a `RemoteException` is treated as a system-level failure by the container (for backward compatibility with Version 1.0 of the *EJB Specification*). This will cause a transaction rollback, whether it is required or not.

If the session EJB catches `FinderException` or `NamingException`, it can be sure, if the entity EJB is itself handling exceptions appropriately, that one or the other of the following will be true. Either (i) the entity EJB has ensured that data integrity has not been compromised or (ii) the entity EJB has called `setRollbackOnly()` to bring about a rollback. The session EJB should therefore not try to bring about a rollback unless its own database operations are likely to be compromised. If the session EJB can recover from the entity's exception, then it should do so; otherwise, it should throw a checked exception out to its own client. This exception should be something that makes sense in the context of the application, and may have to be defined specifically for this purpose.

The issue of handling `RemoteException` is more complex and somewhat contentious. All remote method calls on EJBs can, in principle, throw a `Remote Exception`. So the method `doSomething()` can throw `RemoteException` in addition to any application-defined exceptions that may be declared. How is this exception to be handled? The session bean will usually receive a `RemoteException` from the entity EJB in one of three circumstances:

- the business method in the entity EJB throws a runtime exception, typically `EJBException`;

- a container callback method in the entity EJB throws a runtime exception, typically `EJBException` or `NoSuchEntityException`, while the container is servicing the business method;

- the communication between the session and the entity EJB fails at the system level.

In the first two of these three cases, the container will already have marked its transaction for rollback. In the last case, the client will in general have no way to determine whether the method on the entity EJB succeeded or failed, and should probably assume the worst. As has already been discussed, what the EJB can't do (and still remain compliant with the *EJB Specification*) is to throw the `RemoteException` back to its own client. The session bean can catch the `RemoteException` and throw it again as an `EJBException`, if it wants to be sure that a container transaction is rolled back. Alternatively, it can handle it the same way as `NamingException` and `FinderException`, and throw it back to the client as a checked exception. This is appropriate if we think that database integrity has been maintained, or the transaction has already been marked for rollback. With this approach, the exception handling for the example under consideration looks like this:

```
     public void sessionMethod ()
        throws MyGeneralException
     {
     try
 5      {
        EntityHome  h  =  // ... find home
        Entity  e  =  h . findByPrimaryKey ( ... )
        e . doSomething ();
        }
10   catch ( NamingException e )
        {
        MyGeneralException  e2 =
         new MyGeneralException
          ("caught NamingException in sessionMethod ()");
15      e2 . setRootCause ( e );
        throw e2;
        }
     catch ( FinderException e )
        {
20      MyGeneralException  e2 =
         new MyGeneralException
          ("specified data could not be found");
        e2 . setRootCause ( e );
        throw e2;
25      }
     catch ( RemoteException e )
        {
        MyGeneralException  e2 =
```

```
            new MyGeneralException
30             ("caught RemoteException in sessionMethod ()");
            e2.setRootCause(e);
            throw e2;
            }
        }
```

The general exception has been supplied with a method `setRootCause()` so that if a low-level exception is the cause of the general failure, a client can, if it wishes, extract the details of the original exception.

In the *Prestige Bike Hire* application, the `BookingManager` EJB uses a general exception called `BookingManagerException` to wrap low-level failures that occur when it makes intra-EJB calls. This exception class is shown in Listing 15.1. The other session EJBs adopt a similar strategy.

Listing 15.1: **The `BookingManagerException` class, used to wrap a low-level exception thrown when the `BookingManager` EJB makes calls on other EJBs.**

```
    package com.kevinboone.bikehire.ejb;

    import javax.ejb.*;
    import java.rmi.*;
5   import java.util.*;

    /**
    This exception is thrown by BookingManager in response to
    an error that does not have a specific exception.
10  (c)2002 Kevin Boone
    */
    public class BookingManagerException extends Exception
    {
    protected Exception rootCause;
15  protected String name;

    public BookingManagerException (final String message,
        final Exception rootCause)
        {
20      super(message);
        this.rootCause = rootCause;
        }

    public BookingManagerException (final String message)
25      {
        super(message);
        this.rootCause = null;
        }

30  public String getFullMessage ()
        {
        StringBuffer sb = new StringBuffer ();
```

```
        sb.append (getMessage());
        sb.append (name);
35      if (rootCause != null)
          {
          sb.append (" '; root cause: ");
          sb.append (rootCause.toString ());
          }
40      return new String(sb);
        }


    }
```

Handling exceptions in intra-EJB calls: local view

Exception handling is different (and may be simpler) when intra-EJB calls are made using the local client view.

The most obvious difference is that—as the target EJB is not remote from the caller—it cannot throw `RemoteException`. Therefore the caller does not need to trap this exception and handle it internally. However, even when an EJB makes a call on the local interface, it is not really calling the implementation class of the target EJB, but the container's local object proxy. This proxy is subject to failure. For example, suppose that it tries to commit a transaction at the end of a method call and fails. How is this signalled to the client?

The short answer is that the local object throws `TransactionRolledBackLocal Exception`. This is a subclass of `EJBException` and is therefore *unchecked*. The caller therefore does not need to handle this exception explicitly. From the discussion above, you may assume that this is dangerous, and that the caller may be left in an undefined state. This certainly may be true if the local view is used inappropriately. But remember that the local view is intended to support the tight coupling of entity EJBs and their dependents. If an entity EJB makes a local call on another entity EJB, then a failure in the target almost always means that the caller will be in an undefined state. If the caller does not catch `EJBException` (and it shouldn't), then the container will catch it and roll back work done in both the caller and the target. This is exactly appropriate behavior in these circumstances.

In short, then, EJBs that call other EJBs using the local client view will not need to take any special action to handle low-level exceptions, which can simply be propagated back to the container.

If a session EJB calls another session EJB through a local client view, it will be easy for the developer of the calling EJB to overlook the handling of the unchecked exceptions thrown by the local object. If this happens, the exception will eventually be picked up by the container. Unlike entity EJBs, the container does not really know how to handle an unchecked exception from a session EJB, and therefore this situation should be avoided.

15.3   The 'this' reference and loop-back calls

In object-oriented programming it is often necessary for an object to pass a reference to itself to another object. In ordinary programming for the Java platform, we could do this:

```
someObject . someMethod( this );
```

The 'this' reference denotes the calling object, and is passed by reference, subject to the usual method call semantics.

An EJB can (cautiously) pass a reference to itself to another EJB, but it should not normally pass `this`. The usual reason for passing a self-reference is so that the target can call back on the caller. In the *EJB Specification*, this is called a *loop-back call*. Such a call won't be possible in EJBs if we pass `this`: It is serializable and passed by value. The equivalent in an EJB depends on whether it wants to pass a reference to its local client view or its distributed client view. Of course, local client views are only available since EJB 2.0, so users of earlier products don't have to make a choice. With the distributed view, the equivalent of passing `this` is

```
someObject . someMethod( context . getEJBObject ());
\end{verbatim}
```

where `context` is the `EJBContext` object passed by the container when the object was created. What the object is doing here is passing a reference to its own EJB object, which is passed by *reference*; this is a departure from the usual method call semantics of the distributed view.

With the local view, we need something like this:

```
someObject.someMethod(context.getEJBLocalObject());
```

Of course, we can only pass a reference to the local or distributed client view if the EJB developer has provided these views.

Even if we do as suggested, and pass a reference to the EJB object or local object, the target object will still not normally be able to call back on the caller. The problem is that the EJB object is supposed to prevent loop-back calls because it can't distinguish them from concurrent calls with the same transaction context. A loop-back call is probably safe, but a concurrent call isn't, so the container bans both. In fact, loop-back calls are only allowed on entity EJBs that have specifically been denoted 're-entrant.' This is discussed in more detail below.

15.4   Thread management

In short, don't do it. It is the job of the EJB container to ensure that your EJB instance is entered on only one thread at a time, unless the container knows that it is safe to relax this restriction. You should write code as if the EJB were running in a single-threaded environment. The mechanism that the container uses to achieve this illusion of single-threaded operation while maintaining adequate responsiveness is at the discretion of the container vendor. Typically, it will use multiple instances of EJBs with one thread assigned per instance. If there are not enough instances available, then the container will queue method invocations until one becomes available.

Because entity EJB instances and EJB objects are shared between clients, enforcing a strict serialization of client calls would lead to significant performance penalties, or to a proliferation of instances. Therefore the container is allowed to permit re-entrant calls on these instances, so long as they are in different transactional contexts. It relies on the underlying database or transaction manager to perform the appropriate locking that will prevent concurrent calls from interfering with one another. You may well have to be careful if you are writing an entity EJB that encapsulates access to something that does not have transactional semantics and cannot lock data to prevent corruption by concurrent client calls.

It is possible to relax the single-thread model somewhat with entity beans, and denote them as 're-entrant' [EJB2.0 10.5.11]. This will permit the container to enter them on multiple threads, even in the same transactional context. The Specification allows this primarily to support the use of loop-back calls, not to allow concurrent access from different clients. However, the container won't be able to tell the difference between a concurrent call in the same transaction context (bad) and a loop-back call (probably OK), so the developer needs to be exceptionally careful when using this technique.

Note that the *EJB Specification* is quite specific about what is, and isn't, allowed by way of thread synchronization. Specifically, an EJB should not use thread synchronization techniques to 'synchronize execution of multiple instances' of the same EJB implementation [EJB2.0 24.1.2]. However, many of the classes in the standard Java 2 platform API, which *must* be supported to comply with the Specification, implicitly use synchronization primitives to make them easier to use in a multithreaded environment. For example, the classes `Vector`, `Hashtable`, `Stack`, and `TimeZone` in `java.util` have some of their methods defined as `synchronized`. While it could be argued that the use of these classes is not strictly in compliance with the letter of the Specification, they are widely used and don't seem to cause serious problems.

> ## Hint
>
> The Java API provides a nonsynchronized version of `Vector` called `ArrayList`, which has the same functionality.

One aspect of thread management that is frequently misunderstood is the distinction between *concurrent client calls on the EJB object or home object* and *concurrent invocation of the methods on the EJB implementation*.

Suppose, for example, that a client finds the home object for a session EJB, and calls `create()` on it. It then passes the EJB object thus created to a number of different concurrently executing threads, such that there is a high probability of method calls being made concurrently. Is this a problem or not?

The confusion is that, although the container must prevent concurrent access to EJB methods, this does not imply that it must prevent concurrent client calls on the EJB object. The *EJB Specification* is very clear about the container's responsibility in this regard. Specifically, the Specification [EJB2.0 7.11.8] states that the container must prevent multiple threads executing within a given instance of the EJB at the same time (except in the cases discussed above). It does *not* say that the container must prevent multiple client threads being serviced at the same time. When clients make concurrent calls on the EJB object of a stateless session bean, the container can readily create new instances of the implementation class to service those clients. Even if the number of instances in the pool is as large as the server can accept, then it can simply queue method calls until there is an instance free to handle them.

However, with a stateful session EJB, once the client has called `create()` on the home object, the instance created is 'attached' to that specific client. The EJB container cannot meaningfully duplicate instances of this EJB to support concurrent requests, as the one-to-one relationship between client and EJB would be broken. Therefore the EJB object for a stateful session EJB will detect attempts to enter the EJB on multiple threads, and throw `RemoteException` when this happens. With the *J2EE Reference Implementation*, the exception message looks like this:

```
java.rmi.ServerException: RemoteException occurred in server
   thread; nested exception is: java.rmi.RemoteException:
   SessionBean is executing another request
```

Entity EJBs can service multiple client requests on the same EJB object, provided that they are in different transactions. As transactions are associated with threads, this means that concurrent client requests are, by definition, in different transactions.

In summary, the EJB object of a stateless session EJB can service requests from clients on different threads, as can the EJB object of an entity EJB. A stateful session EJB does not allow this, and an exception will result if a client tries to enter the EJB object on more than one thread.

This is an issue of particular importance when EJBs are to be used with servlets or JSPs, as these components are assumed to be thread-safe by default. This is discussed in more detail on page 557.

15.5   Garbage collection issues

It is the EJB container's responsibility to handle garbage collection, or at least to ensure that unused objects are made available for garbage collection. In an ideal world, at no point should the developer have to be concerned about garbage collection, or explicitly free allocated resources. In fact—so the story goes—garbage collection is so much a nonissue for the developer that the *EJB Specification* does not mention the subject even once.

In reality, the EJB architecture has some characteristics that support and assist the use of garbage collection, and some that mitigate against it. The main factor in

its favor is that there is, in most cases, no direct relationship between the number
of clients and the number of instances of anything. All EJBs except stateful session
beans can be pooled, and a small pool (perhaps 20 instances) can support several
thousand clients. It is also often possible to pool EJB objects, local objects, and
RMI skeletons, if desired.

There are two significant issues on the negative side. First, most EJB containers
are programs for the Java 2 platform, and run in an ordinary, general-purpose JVM.
The garbage collection strategy may not meet the needs of the kind of application
that an EJB container supports. Second, the garbage collection system has to support the needs of a distributed application; distributed garbage collection is widely
acknowledged to be a 'hard problem.' Let's consider these two issues in turn.

15.5.1   Problems with inadequate garbage collection performance

EJB applications place particular demands on the garbage collection system. Let's
assume for the moment that we have a perfect method for determining when distributed objects are eligible for garbage collection (which we haven't). Even in this
case, EJB applications may still defeat the garbage collector. In general, these applications will have large numbers of clients, each making very frequent, short requests.
Each request may result in the creation of a number of objects of various classes.
While the garbage collector will eventually remove these objects, it may not do so
frequently enough to keep sufficient free memory.

EJB developers have come up with a number of strategies for dealing with this,
some more sensible than others. The first point to note is that garbage collection may
occur more rapidly if the EJB specifically drops its references to unused instances.
The easiest way to do this is to set such references to `null`. An object's going out
of scope is a less effective way of alerting the garbage collector that the object is no
longer referenced. So for example, in this piece of code:

```
{
Connection c = dataSource.getConnection ();
// Do database work
}
```

the instance c is less easily detected to be eligible for garbage collection than in this
case:

```
{
Connection c = dataSource.getConnection ();
// Do database work
c = null;
}
```

The instance c will no doubt have its own instance variables, which may, or may
not, be eligible for garbage collection when c itself is. Furthermore, c may be holding
an indirect reference to operating-system resources (e.g., a network connection)
that cannot be released simply by setting something to null. For that reason, if an
instance has a method that explicitly frees it, then the EJB should be sure to call

that method. The method may simply set instance variables to null, or it may do something at the operating system level; the distinction is not important to the caller. Thus:

```
{
Connection c = dataSource.getConnection();
// Do database work
c.close();
c = null;
}
```

Setting c to null after the `close()` call offers little extra benefit in this case, because we assume that the c instance is no longer holding any significant references. However, it may be necessary to null the reference to prevent the container from attempting to serialize it, but that's a different matter altogether.

You will frequently see EJB code where instance variables are set to `null` explicitly in a number of places. Typical cases are in `ejbRemove()`, `ejbPassivate()` (in entity EJBs), and `unsetEntityContext()`. Whether these measures have any benefit depends to a large extent on the specific behavior of the container, but it's fair to say they are unlikely to do any harm.

15.5.2 Problems with distributed garbage collection

When an instance holds a reference to another in the same JVM, it is relatively straightforward for the garbage collector to determine when that reference is dropped (at least in theory). The same is not true for remote references, as it isn't well-defined what constitutes an active reference. If one object is holding the JNDI name of another because it intends to make calls on it, does this constitute a reference? What about RMI references that don't require a network socket connection to be held open: How long does the client have to be idle before it is assumed to have dropped its reference? The behavior of a distributed garbage collector is not easy even to define, let alone implement.

For example, in a session EJB there is a method, `remove()`, that specifically releases the EJB—that is, it tells the container that the client no longer needs the EJB. When the client calls this method, the container can free the EJB, the skeleton, and the EJB object (or return them to a pool). But what happens if a client simply drops its reference to the bean (or crashes, or simply exits without calling `remove()`)? Whether the container will be able to detect this condition depends on the specific communications protocol that is supporting the RMI between client and server. With IIOP as the protocol, in general the server cannot tell that a client has dropped its reference. Therefore, failing to call a method that indicates that the client has finished using the EJB can prevent garbage collection.

With the *J2EE Reference Implementation* in the listing below, if 'Oops' is a stateful session EJB, the code will eventually overwhelm the EJB container, although it will create a great many EJBs first.

```
while(true)
  {
  Oops oops = oopsHome.create();
  //oops.remove();
  oops=null;
  System.gc();
  }
```

You can verify this by taking the simple EJB from Chapter 4, changing it to stateful, setting the server JVM's heap size to, say, 5 Mb, and running a client like the listing above. On my system, it crashes after about 1,200 iterations. Naturally a healthier heap size will support more iterations, but not an unlimited number. However, with the line `oops.remove()` reinstated, it will operate indefinitely.

Although the developer isn't going to write code that creates thousands of EJBs without releasing them, similar situations can arise inadvertently. There are two main application areas where this behavior leads to problems for the developer: stateful session EJBs referenced from a servlet and entity EJBs that model large database tables.

Stateful EJBs and servlets

Suppose a servlet creates an a stateful session bean to store information relevant to each specific user (quite common behavior), and stores it in its `HttpSession` instance.[2] The end-user interacts with the servlet through a Web browser. Although a servlet can invalidate its session (if the user explicitly chooses to log out, for example), in practice most users will simply go to a different Web site or close the browser when they have finished with a Web application. Thus the session never gets invalidated, and it cannot drop its references to instances stored in it. If the stateful session bean is stored this way, the servlet will probably never get the opportunity to call `remove()`. Even if the session times out and drops its reference to the EJB's stub, the EJB container may have no way to determine that the client has finished with the EJB (this depends on the communications protocol). The implication is that the number of instances (and EJB objects) will only be limited by the server's timeout interval for stateful EJBs. If the rate of instance creation exceeds the rate at which they are timed out, then the container will eventually crash (although this may take days).

If the number or frequency of client interactions cannot be controlled (and it usually can't), then there are two techniques for dealing with this problem. First, limit the amount of instance data in stateful EJBs that will be referenced by servlets. Second, use a shorter timeout interval.

Entity EJBs and large data sets

Suppose that a client creates a reference to an entity EJB (that is, it calls `find ByPrimaryKey()` on the home). The container must instantiate (or locate) an EJB

---

[2] `HttpSession` is the place where a servlet (which is pooled) stores data related to a specific client.

object and, perhaps, an instance of the EJB implementation. Now suppose that the client drops its reference to the EJB object. Remember that `remove()` on an entity EJBs actually deletes data, it doesn't merely signal the client's loss of interest in the EJB. At what point does the container detect that the implementation instance and/or EJB object can be garbage collected? In practice, it may never do so: These instances may remain active indefinitely. While this is not a problem on relatively small data sets, keep in mind that the number of EJB object instances may become very large as the number of data items increases. Whether this is a problem or not depends on the size of the memory footprint for the EJB object, and this is vendor-specific. EJB server vendors can usually uphold their end of the J2EE 'contract' with a single phrase: Memory is cheap. They will argue that if you have huge database tables for customer records, then you can probably afford a few extra RAM sticks for your servers. Whether this argument is convincing depends on the application.

In EJB 2.0 this problem can be overcome—to a degree—by the use of *home methods* (see Section 11.5.4). Home methods are called on the home object of an entity EJB and can carry out arbitrary database queries, returning the results by value. This reduces the need to create EJB object instances.

15.6 Using value objects with EJBs

Although the entity EJB developer can provide business methods to get and set all the persistent instance variables of the entity EJB, in many cases a client will want to get or set all these attributes in one operation. Because all method calls between EJBs can involve a network operation (except with a local client view—see below), it is becoming standard practice to provide methods that pass all the instance variables in one operation, wrapped inside a utility class. The utility class is usually called a *value object*,[3] but the term *data model class* is also sometimes used.

For example, the `Customer` EJB in the *Prestige Bike Hire* application has a number of persistent instance variables. Rather than providing only single-valued `get` and `set` methods (getName(), getAddress(), getEmail()...), we can implement a utility class (e.g., `CustomerData`) whose instance variables contain copies of all the persistent data of the EJB. A suitable value object for the `Customer` EJB is shown in Listing 15.2, and for the `Booking` EJB in Listing 15.3.

In the Customer EJB we provide methods

```
public CustomerData getCustomerData();
public void setCustomerData(CustomerData);
```

to get and set the instance variables using the `CustomerData` value object.

If you are going to use value objects, I recommend that you consider the following points.

---

[3]The term 'value object' is—rather confusingly—used in the *EJB Specification* to mean something slightly different: any object that is passed by value. The terms are clearly related, but not the same thing. The use of the term 'value object' with the meaning it has in this chapter has come from the *J2EE Blueprint*, not the *EJB Specification*.

- It is largely irrelevant how the users of a value object get access to its instance variables. There is no compelling reason why the instance variables should not be `public` if it is more convenient. The value object is only used as a carrier for data, and it has no logic or functionality of its own.

- The names of the instances variables in the value object should probably match the names of the instance variables in the EJB it serves. It can be very confusing—and a source of error—to have two classes with similar names that use different instance variables to mean the same thing.

- It is a short step from naming the instance variables identically in the EJB and the value object to *using* the value object as a attribute of the EJB. With this strategy, *all* the persistent data of an EJB is in its embedded value object. This makes the implementation much simpler. This is the approach I have followed in the entity EJB examples in this book that use value objects.

- There is little to be gained by using a value object for an EJB that has only one or two instance variables.

- The use of the local client view eliminates at least part of the overhead involved in EJB method calls, so a fine-grained client API (lots of small method calls) is less of a problem on the local view (EJB 2.0 only).

Listing 15.2: **A value object for the** `Customer` **EJB.**

```
     package com.kevinboone.bikehire.ejb;
     import javax.ejb.*;
     import java.rmi.*;

5    /**
     Value object for the Customer EJB
     (c)2002 Kevin Boone
     */
     public class CustomerData implements java.io.Serializable
10   {
     protected String name;
     protected String address;
     protected int id;
     protected int status;
15   protected int creditCardExpiryMonth;
     protected int creditCardExpiryYear;
     protected String creditCardNumber;
     protected int creditCardType;

20   public CustomerData
       (final int id, final String name, final String address,
          final int status, final int creditCardType,
          final int creditCardExpiryMonth,
          final int creditCardExpiryYear,
25        final String creditCardNumber)
       {
       this.id = id;
```

```
         this.name = name;
         this.address = address;
30       this.status = status;
         this.creditCardType = creditCardType;
         this.creditCardExpiryMonth = creditCardExpiryMonth;
         this.creditCardExpiryYear = creditCardExpiryYear;
         this.creditCardNumber = creditCardNumber;
35       }

     public CustomerData ()
         {
         this.name = "";
40       this.address = "";
         this.id = -1;
         this.status = Customer.STATUS_UNKNOWN;
         this.creditCardType = Customer.CARD_UNKNOWN;
         this.creditCardExpiryMonth = -1;
45       this.creditCardExpiryYear = -1;
         this.creditCardNumber = "";
         }

     public String toString()
50       {
         StringBuffer sb = new StringBuffer();
         sb.append("id=");
         sb.append(id);
         sb.append(", name=");
55       sb.append(name);
         sb.append(", address=");
         sb.append(address);
         sb.append(", status=");
         sb.append(status);
60       return new String (sb);
         }

     public String getName()
         { return name; }
65   public String getAddress()
         { return address; }
     public int getId ()
         { return id; }
     public int getStatus()
70       { return status; }
     public int getCreditCardExpiryMonth()
         { return creditCardExpiryMonth; }
     public int getCreditCardExpiryYear()
         { return creditCardExpiryYear; }
75   public int getCreditCardType ()
         { return creditCardType; }
     public String getCreditCardNumber()
         { return creditCardNumber; }

80   public void setStatus (final int status)
         { this.status = status; }
     public void setAddress (final String address)
         { this.address = address; }
     public void setName (final String name)
85       { this.name = name; }
     public void setId (final int id)
         { this.id = id; }
```

```
      public void setCreditCardType (final int creditCardType)
        { this.creditCardType = creditCardType; }
90    public void setCreditCardExpiryMonth
          (final int creditCardExpiryMonth)
        { this.creditCardExpiryMonth = creditCardExpiryMonth; }
      public void setCreditCardExpiryYear
          (final int creditCardExpiryYear)
95      { this.creditCardExpiryYear = creditCardExpiryYear; }
      public void setCreditCardNumber (final String creditCardNumber)
        { this.creditCardNumber = creditCardNumber; }

      public static String creditCardTypeToString (final int type)
100     {
        switch (type)
          {
          case Customer.CARD_APEX: return "Apex";
          case Customer.CARD_VISTA: return "Vista";
105       case Customer.CARD_BLASTERCARD: return "BlasterCard";
          }
        return "Unknown";
        }
      }
```

Listing 15.3: **A value object for the** Booking **EJB.**

```
      package com.kevinboone.bikehire.ejb;
      import javax.ejb.*;
      import java.rmi.*;
      import java.util.*;
5
      /**
      Value object that represents a bike booking.
      (c)2002 Kevin Boone
      */
10    public class BookingData implements java.io.Serializable
      {
      protected String licenceNumber;
      protected int customerId;
      protected int status;
15    protected Date startDate;
      protected Date endDate;

      public BookingData (final String licenceNumber,
          final int customerId, final int status, final Date startDate,
20        final Date endDate)
        {
        this.licenceNumber = licenceNumber;
        this.customerId = customerId;
        this.status = status;
25      this.startDate = startDate;
        this.endDate = endDate;
        }

      public BookingData ()
30      {
```

```
            this.licenceNumber = "";
            this.customerId = -1;
            this.status = -1;
            this.startDate = null;
35          this.endDate = null;
          }

      public String getLicenceNumber() { return licenceNumber; }
      public int getCustomerId() { return customerId; }
40    public int getStatus() { return status; }
      public Date getStartDate() { return startDate; }
      public Date getEndDate() { return endDate; }
      public void setLicenceNumber(final String licenceNumber)
          { this.licenceNumber = licenceNumber; }
45    public void setStartDate(final Date startDate)
          { this.startDate = startDate; }
      public void setEndDate(final Date endDate)
          { this.endDate = endDate; }
      public void setStatus(final int status)
50        { this.status = status; }
      public void setCustomerId(final int customerId)
          { this.customerId = customerId; }


55    public static String statusToString(final int status)
        {
        switch (status)
          {
          case Booking.STATUS_PROVISIONAL: return "provisional";
60        case Booking.STATUS_CONFIRMED: return "confirmed";
          case Booking.STATUS_REJECTED: return "rejected";
          }
        return "unknown"; // Should never happen!
        }
65
      }
```

> **Gotcha!**
>
> Value objects must be serializable, by definition (as they are
> passed by value). This implies that all the instance variables they
> contain are also serializable.

15.7   Handles

A *handle* is a serializable object that uniquely identifies a particular remote object
(EJB object or home object) on a server. Of course, this is true of the stub held by
the client as well, but a stub is not guaranteed to be serializable. In practice, for

reasons that will be discussed, stubs *are* serializable, which means that the use of handles may be considered an unnecessary overhead. However, for strict compliance, they must be used in certain places, as will be discussed.

Why do we need a serializable EJB reference? There are two main reasons: to enable an EJB reference to be stored in an object that is replicated across a network, or to allow a session EJB to have a lifetime longer than its client's process. We will discuss both issues later, but first, let's see how handles are retrieved and used.

15.7.1   Using handles

Handles can be retrieved for entity and session EJBs but are most useful for stateful session EJBs. Stateless session EJBs don't have identity, and therefore don't need handles, and entity EJBs can often by retrieved more conveniently by a finder.

To get a handle, simply use `getHandle()` and `getHomeHandle()` on the EJB object or home object respectively, as in the following example.

```
MyEJBHome home = // get home in the usual way
MyEJB myEJB = home.create();
Handle h = myEJB.getHandle();
HomeHandle hh = home.getHomeHandle();
```

The handles can then be serialized, saved on disk, or passed over a network as required.

To re-establish a connection to the remote object, use the `getEJBObject()` and `getEJBHome()` methods on the handles (see examples below). These methods throw a `RemoteException` if the connection cannot be re-established. This will happen if, for example, the EJB has timed out.

15.7.2   Handles in a servlet session

When using EJBs with an user interface based on servlets or JSPs, it is often necessary to maintain a client's reference to a stateful EJB across multiple requests on the Web server. A servlet or JSP can readily create a stateful EJB; the problem is locating the right instance on subsequent requests from the same client.

To maintain the client state on the server, a servlet will typically get a reference to the client-specific `HttpSession` object, and store client state in that object (this technique is discussed in detail in Chapter 17). Now, suppose the servlet is replicated on two different servers, for load-sharing purposes. When the servlet modifies the contents of the `HttpSession`, the modifications must be made accessible to both collaborating systems. Typically, the server will serialize the `HttpSession` periodically and pass it over the network between the collaborating servers, which will deserialize it in place. Naturally, this process will only work if the contents of the `HttpSession` are serializable. EJB references are not guaranteed to be serializable, but handles are. Therefore, it is common practice for a servlet to store a handle to a stateful session EJB in the `HttpSession` object for each client.

Full details of this technique are given on page 563.

15.7.3   Handles for supporting transient clients

On occasion, the client of a stateful session EJB may interact with the same EJB over a number of invocations of the client process. For example, the 'session' may last several days, and persist through numerous shutdowns of the client. This is likely to be an issue with portable equipment in particular. Because a handle is serializable, it can be written out to disk using the standard techniques (which are summarized in Appendix E). When the client restarts, it recovers the serialized handles from disk and reconnects them.

15.7.4   Issues with handles

Developers that plan to use handles should be aware of the following issues.

You don't need to use handles to support passivation In stateful session EJBs, any instance variable that is to survive passivation must be serializable, with a few exceptions (see discussion on page 149). Among the exceptions are remote home object and EJB object references (stubs). That is, we can freely save these references in instance variables without worrying about the effect that passivation will have on them. There is no compelling reason to store handles instead.

Stubs are usually serializable The *EJB Specification* does not dictate how the container ensures that EJB object and home object references survive passivation. There is, of course, a very straightforward method: Make the stubs serializable. In practice, all EJB products use serializable stubs. Thus it is often argued that stubs are an extravagance having no practical benefits. Many developers prefer to use stubs as if they were handles, passing them over a network or saving them to disk. While there is a small efficiency savings to be had from doing this, be aware that it could be nonportable.

Reconnecting a handle can fail The `getEJBObject()` and `getEJBHome()` throw a `RemoteException` if the reconnection fails. This may happen for a number of reasons, particularly if the EJB itself has timed out, as discussed below.

Holding a handle does not prevent timeout A client can use the handle to re-establish connection some time after the handle was obtained. If this is to be useful, the EJB must not time out in the meantime. The existence of a handle has no impact on the timeout of the EJB; to prevent timeout the client must call methods on the EJB.

A handle does not represent a security capability Despite a common misconception, passing a handle between clients does not necessarily represent a security weakness. The handle should not contain anything that allows the originator's security to be compromised. In particular, it will not contain the client identity. When a handle is reconnected, the identity seen by the server is the identity of the reconnecting client, not that of the client that retrieved the handle. The usual security mechanisms (Chapter 16) are still enforced.

However, a handle may give a client access to an EJB that would otherwise not be able to create an instance at all (if, for example, it didn't have authority to execute the `create()` method on the home). This will only be a security weakness if the developer relies on the security of the `create()` method to restrict access to EJBs.

15.8   Summary

This chapter has presented a variety of techniques for improving the manageability, reliability, and efficiency of EJB applications.

Chapter 16

Security

Overview

This chapter describes how to secure EJB applications, and the implications that EJB technology has for enterprise-level security. It explains how to make use of the security features offered by the EJB server and how EJB security is integrated with authentication features offered by Web-based applications and application containers. We start by describing the philosophy behind the J2EE security architecture and the EJB security model. We then discuss the use of declarative security, which allows security policies to be implemented in the deployment descriptor without coding. Declarative security will not always be sufficient on its own, and the developer will have to put some security procedures into code. We discuss the benefits and implications of doing this. As an illustration of these concepts, we will see how different types of authentication and encryption can be applied to a simple EJB application. Finally, there is a discussion of how EJB security fits into the wider scope of enterprise security and of recent developments in secure, interoperable RMI protocols.

16.1 Security concepts

This section describes some fundamental principles of application security; the discussion is from the standpoint of J2EE and EJB, but most of these issues apply with equal force to any enterprise application. In this chapter, I assume that reader has a basic familiarity with the concepts of public-key cryptography. If this is not the case, then you may wish to review the subject in Appendix G. I would strongly recommend this course of action for readers who are unfamiliar with the concepts of digital certificates and encryption.

16.1.1   Security requirements

A security architecture has to address a number of related, but different, security needs, including the following.

- When a client attempts to interact with the application, something must verify that the client really is who he (or she, or it) claims to be and is permitted to effect that particular interaction. These are the standard issues of *authentication* and *authorization*, which are well-understood in the security field.

- The data passed between the client and the application may need to be protected from eavesdropping, and the container must be allowed to detect if the data has been tampered with. In security terminology, these issues are known as *confidentiality* and *integrity*, respectively.

- An additional requirement in an application server is that the server must protect the internal integrity of its applications and their data. In particular, it must prevent components in different applications from interacting with one another adversely, and prevent badly written components from damaging the container. This is, of course, a different matter than communications integrity.

- A further issue with which the developer may be involved—although not strictly an EJB matter—is the use of firewalls to protect an enterprise's internal resources from the Internet, while still allowing limited access to certain parts of the system. The reason that this may involve the EJB developer is that firewalls limit the types of client-EJB communication that can be used. We will discuss this issue at the end of this chapter.

16.1.2   Authentication

Authentication is any process by which one party in an interaction determines the identity of the other. In an EJB application, clients of EJBs may be user interface components, other EJBs, or other distributed software components. The EJB server will need to determine the identity of all these types of client so that it can determine what level of access to grant. At the same time, the client may want to authenticate the server, to ensure that it really is what it appears to be.[1]

The most well-known form of authentication is the *password challenge*: The client is asked to provide its identity (e.g., a user ID) and a password that is known to the client and the server and (it is hoped) no one else. There are a huge number of variations of this scheme, with different methods for encrypting, hashing, and transmitting the password.

---

[1]In many applications, authentication of the server by the client is at least as important as authentication of the client by the server. If the method call we are about to execute requires the passage of confidential data from the client to the server, we will need to be sure that the server really is what it claims to be.

While passwords are a straightforward way for end-users to identify themselves to an application, and are widely used with browser-based user interfaces, they are less useful when both parties in the communication are distributed software components. Partly, this is a result of the complexity of managing the large number of different credential sets that would be required, and partly because a user ID/password combination does not always provide sufficient information to identify the parties to one another.

For these reasons, the J2EE architecture supports authentication by *certificate*.[2] Certificates may identify end-users, or they may identify servers or software components. In any case, it is the responsibility of the administrators of the clients and the servers to decide which certificates are accepted. The standard format for the representation of certificates is ITU-T X.509; however, this standard does not dictate how or when certificates are exchanged. The SSL (secure sockets layer) protocol, however, defines a mechanism for certificate exchange. The use of SSL, particularly with EJBs, will be discussed in more detail later.[3]

Certificate-based authentication can be *server only*, *client only*, or *mutual*, depending on the needs of the application. With wide-area EJB applications, it is likely that mutual authentication will be required—that is, both the client and the server will need to be confident of each other's identity.

When EJBs are used with a Web-based user interface, the Web browser will provide the first point of access to the application. If the Web server authenticates the user, then that user identity has to be propagated to the EJBs.

16.1.3   Authorization

Having established the identity of the client, the application must then determine what resources it has access to; note that this *authorization* is quite a different matter from authentication. In EJB applications, authorization is handled declaratively (through the deployment descriptor), in preference to programatically, and is based on the notion of *roles*, as will be discussed below.

16.1.4   Integrity and confidentiality

'Integrity' in this context implies that the application can be sure that any data supplied by its clients has not been altered in transit, and the client can be offered the same guarantee concerning data supplied by the application.

'Confidentiality' implies that the data in transit is not easily read by someone who is not a party to the client-application interaction (i.e., an eavesdropper).

For example, when an EJB client calls a method on an EJB, it may be necessary to protect the method call data (arguments and return values) from unauthorized eavesdropping. This will be particularly important if method calls are passing confidential information about users of the application (credit card details, for example).

---

[2]For more details of certificates, and their generation and use, see Section G.4.1.

[3]The term 'SSL' is technically obsolete, since the protocol has been taken over by the IETF and is now called 'TLS' (transport layer security). Despite this, 'SSL' is still widely used in the industry.

This situation is typically handled by encryption, usually with a public key strategy. This protection will usually be in addition to the encryption of data between a Web browser and the Web server, if the client is a browser. Although the use of SSL to carry HTTP messages between browser and server is well established, using SSL to carry EJB method call protocols is a relatively recent innovation.

16.2   J2EE/EJB security architecture

This section describes how the J2EE/EJB security model realizes the security features discussed above. Because the EJB security model is a subset of the J2EE model, it seems sensible to consider the basic principles of both together. EJB-specific matters are described in detail in a later section.

16.2.1   Overview

For the purposes of this chapter, I have divided the security model into three 'layers' (Figure 16.1).

EJB/Web tier security models

As we shall see, the EJB developer expresses the security needs of the application in terms of role permissions—that is, statements of which EJB methods are accessible to users in which roles. In the Web application, a similar approach is adopted, but

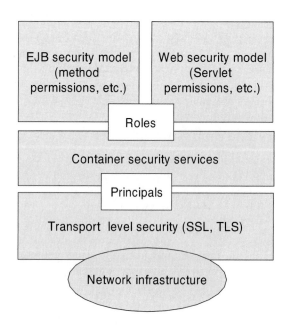

Figure 16.1. A simplified view of the J2EE security architecture. See text for details.

in terms of URL patterns rather than method calls. These matters will be discussed in much more detail later.

Container security services

In an EJB application, the EJB container implements the application's security policy, making use of transport-level security as appropriate. In practice, security policies are enforced by the EJB container in the EJB proxies (home object, EJB object, etc), and by the Web tier in the request handler. These objects will compare the security information propagated in the communications protocols with the security policy set up by the developer, and allow or deny requests as appropriate.

The container's responsibilities do not end here, however; it must protect the JVM and the host machine from unauthorized access by EJBs, and it must protect EJB applications from unauthorized access by other applications. The implications for the EJB developer are set out in the Specification [EJB2.0 24.1.2], and the most relevant ones are discussed in Chapter 14. The *EJB Specification* does not dictate how these security restrictions are to be implemented. In most cases, the container implements a security manager and allows the JVM to deal with these low-level security issues. Very often a custom class loader will be instantiated for each deployed application. Some EJB products provide an additional layer of application protection by using a separate JVM for each application.

Transport-layer security

Many applications require the communication between EJBs, or between EJBs and their clients, to have defined levels of integrity and confidentiality. It is entirely possible for the required encryption and decryption to be implemented by the developer. For example, the client could encrypt the data that will be supplied as arguments to EJB method calls, and the EJB could decrypt those arguments when called. The algorithms to be used would be entirely under the control of the developer.

There are two fundamental problems with this approach. First, it is thoroughly nonportable. It would be impossible to assemble an application from EJBs from different authors without an in-depth knowledge of the encryption technique used. Second, it is inefficient, as it operates on small blocks of data. In practice, all EJB products use transport-layer security (TLS).

Whatever the data passed from the EJB client to the EJB, ultimately it results from a socket connection made between a stub and a skeleton. Having made this connection, data is streamed between the client and server. Transport-layer security operates at this level, encrypting and decrypting the data stream passed over a TCP/IP connection. It does not matter what the structure of the data is, or how it is to be used—to a transport-layer security system it is simply a stream of bytes.

There are already well-established transport-layer security schemes, the most widely used of which are SSL, originally developed by Netscape Corporation, and TLS, a variant of SSL standardized by the Internet Engineering Task Force. These protocols are firmly based on the principles of public-key cryptography, which need to be thoroughly understood by developers who will be working with them. A brief overview is presented in Appendix G. The most widely known use of SSL is for encryption of communication between a Web browser and a Web server; this technology is well-documented elsewhere, and I won't describe it here. In this chapter, we will be concerned with the use of transport-layer security for EJB-EJB, and CORBA-EJB communication.

Although many EJB products support the use of SSL for EJB-to-EJB communication, there was no standard for this in Version 1.1 of the *EJB Specification*. This made it difficult to implement secure communication between products from different vendors. Version 2 rectifies this problem by mandating support not only for IIOP, but for *Common Secure IIOP* (CSI) Version 2. The Specification even goes as far as specifying the encryption algorithms that must be supported by a compliant product [EJB2.0 19.8.2.1]. For example, the container must support RSA/RC4 with 128-bit key and MD5 signatures. CSI is a standard promoted by the OMG, and is designed to be platform- and language-independent. EJB 2.0 specifies that an EJB product must support 'conformance level 0' of this Specification. The main implication for EJB developers of this level of conformance is that the server product is not required to be able to propagate the principal of a caller in calls that it makes itself. Thus, the developer will have to make a decision about the principal to use in delegated calls (of which, more later).

16.2.2   J2EE security is an abstraction

It is crucial for a full understanding of J2EE security to realize that it is based on an abstraction of real security implementations. For example, many commercial application servers use LDAP directory servers to store user security rights and credentials. The *J2EE Reference Implementation* uses a text file. The J2EE model must accommodate this diversity of infrastructure in a fully portable way.

To make this possible, the J2EE security specification is expressed in terms not of users, groups, and access rights, but of *principals*, *roles*, and *role mappings*.

16.2.3   J2EE security authenticates to principals

We have already seen that 'authentication' is the process of determining that a user really is who he (or she, or it) claims to be. Because security in the J2EE model is an abstraction of the real security infrastructure, authentication in this model does not resolve into a user ID or a login ID, but into a *principal*, and this distinction is quite important.

A principal is an *abstract user identity*—that is, the logical name by which a particular user is identified in an application. This is generally *not* guaranteed to be a login username, although some systems use a login name as the principal. The reason that the *Specification* cannot insist on a direct correspondence between username and principal, although this would often be convenient, is that some forms of authentication don't have usernames (e.g., those based on client certificates; see below). Another definition of a principal is an entity that is *capable of authentication*.

Ideally the J2EE developer should not normally have to work with principals at all, but with roles (see below). Principals are only used where roles do not allow a particular user to be identified with sufficient precision. In the *Prestige Bike Hire* application, customers can use the `customerManager` EJB to modify their personal details. Since this operation is carried out at the level of the individual customer, it follows that we must be able to identify the customer with precision, and that knowing the user's role membership won't be sufficient for this operation.

16.2.4   J2EE authorization is expressed in terms of 'roles'

Most security schemes allow users to be placed into groups for ease of management. Although it sounds straightforward, the user-group security model is not very portable. For example, some systems allow users to inhabit multiple groups, while some don't. Some systems assume that groups form a hierarchy, with users in the subordinate groups getting a subset of the access rights of users in the superordinate groups, while others assume a totally 'flat' model. Some systems allow groups to include other groups, while others assume that only users can be members of groups. And so on. The J2EE model abstracts the user-group relationship into the concept of a *role*.

A role is easy to recognize, but difficult to define. A starting point may be to say that a role is a particular way that a user may interact with an application; it defines the access rights that the user must have to perform this interaction. For example, in the *Prestige Bike Hire* application three roles were identified (page 119): `manager`, `administrator`, and `customer`. Each role is associated with a particular set of permissions. Logically, users in the `administrator` role are able to carry out certain operations that are denied to users in the `customer` role, such as making reservations on behalf of other users. Roles are conceptually similar to 'actors' in a use-case model.

To make effective use of EJB security, it is crucial that you understand that J2EE roles are *abstract security roles*. That is, they define the logical structure of access rights in the application. Roles have no direct correspondence with the techniques that are used to enforce security at the EJB container level. When developing an EJB application, it should be possible to define the security with no reference at all to the operating environment. Ultimately, it will be necessary to make mappings between abstract security roles and real individuals, but this *role mapping* is a deployer responsibility, not part of software development.

Individual clients (whether they are human or machine) can be assigned to any number of roles. When a client attempts to carry out a particular operation, access is granted if *any* of the assigned roles is allowed.

16.2.5   J2EE security is implemented by containers,

not by components

Because the J2EE model is an abstraction of the real security infrastructure, it is impossible for the developer to interact directly with that infrastructure; to do so would be to render the application nonportable.[4]

This means that if the developer ever has a need to write code like this:

```
if (user == null)
  {
  user = authenticateUser();
  }
Group[] groups = getGroups(user);
//...
```

then something has gone wrong. The sequence of steps needed to authenticate a user, verify his role membership, and determine whether the role is accepted for the current operation, is entirely under the control of the container. It is essentially an error (or, at least, bad manners) for the EJB developer to usurp this responsibility.

If the developer cannot control the authentication process, then how can we ensure that authentication happens at the right place? The answer is that we specify which parts of the application are subject to security restrictions, and the containers authenticate the user as and when required.

The process of container authentication is simpler when the user interface is a Web browser, because the Web container knows exactly what to do to make the browser display, for example, a login page. Where the application is a standalone program for the Java 2 platform things are more complicated, as the EJB container knows nothing of the user's application and has no way to compel it to interact with the user in a particular way. We get around this problem by the user of *client containers*.

A client container is a piece of software generated by the EJB server's tools, which mediates between the standalone application and the EJB server. The client container usually authenticates the user before transferring control to the application. It may provide a graphical display by which the user can enter his credentials. Alternatively, the client container may supply a digital certificate to the server. In any event, the significant point is that the client container authenticates the user before the 'real' client is invoked. Client containers vary in their sophistication: Some integrate into the application developer's code to allow a seamless authentication process for the end-user, while other just pop up a crude dialog box for the user ID and password. The *J2EE Reference Implementation* supports both the approaches, and we will use the simpler one later in this chapter.

---

[4]There is, in fact, one small but significant exception to this principal: dynamically assigning users to roles. This is discussed in more detail below.

16.2.6   J2EE security is end-to-end

In many applications, EJBs will form the business logic behind a Web-based user interface. The Web application may well be based on servlets or JSPs. Now, the J2EE model states that authentication and authorization are the responsibilities of the containers, not the application code. In such a situation, we can envisage at least two methods by which authentication and authorization could be shared between the Web container and the EJB container.

- The Web server or container collects information about the user (user ID, password, certificate), and forwards them for authentication to the EJB container.

- The Web server or container collects information about the user, authenticates the user against the server's security infrastructure, and forwards the identity of the user to the EJB tier.

In practice, it is the second of these schemes that is used: The user's credentials are inspected by the Web container and only the principal is forwarded to the EJB container. This allows the Web application to benefit from the same role-based security as the EJB application, and for both tiers to share roles.

16.2.7   J2EE security is standards-based

None of the security techniques mandated by J2EE were developed specifically for the J2EE model: All are widely used standards in their own right. In particular, J2EE insists on support for SSL/TLS, X.509, IIOP, CSIv2 (of which, more later), and HTTPS, among others. This has both advantages and disadvantages. Interoperability is improved, making it more likely that systems can be built from components from different vendors. At the same time, many of the standards are exceptionally complex, as they were designed to support a wide range of different applications.

16.2.8   Limitations of the J2EE security model

The J2EE/EJB security model is very simple and places minimal constraints on the server implementation. The *EJB Specification* categorically states [EJB2.0 21.4.2] that its scope does not include defining the EJB container's security infrastructure, as to do so would limit the applicability of EJB technology. As a result, the following three particular challenges face the EJB developer in almost all EJB projects.

- The principal cannot be used on its own to determine the login ID of a user; indeed, certificate-based authentication may not even use login IDs. This issue is discussed in detail in the section on 'principal mapping' below.

- There is no vendor-independent way to add users to a role (dynamic user registration).

- There is no support for Web-based authentication other than password challenge or client certificates.

No dynamic user registration

Neither the *J2EE Specification* nor the *EJB Specification* defines how to add users to an application dynamically (strictly speaking, we would be adding principals to a role). Typically, the developer has to write code that manipulates the security infrastructure directly. For example, if the role `customer` corresponds to a particular group in a LDAP directory, then the developer must write code that manipulates the membership of that group directly. This is typically an issue with large Web-based applications where users can enroll themselves using their Web browsers. Normally, some parts of the application will be denied to users until they have enrolled. If the enrollment is done programatically, then some platform-specific code must be used.

At present, this is recognized as a weakness in the J2EE security model, and a number of solutions have been proposed. The process of adopting a solution is complicated by the fact that it must be independent of any vendor's security infrastructure. One proposal is for a form-based registration procedure. In the same way that Web container vendors are obliged to provide a component that responds to the URL 'j_security_check' for authenticating users, the proposal defines a URL 'j_add_user'. When a form is submitted with this action, the application server would add a new user to a particular role, using its own security infrastructure. The problem with this proposal is that there is no general agreement on the information that needs to be submitted with the form. Clearly a user ID and password are required, and possibly an email address, but other fields are less obvious. Despite these problems, there is an enormous demand for this facility, and undoubtedly it will be standardized at some point. At the moment, the developer must use the server vendor's proprietary extensions.

Oversimplified Web-tier authentication

In many applications, a user/password challenge represents an adequate degree of authentication. However, applications that demand very rigorous access control may well need a multistep approach to authentication. Consider, for example, the various 'token card' authentication schemes, such as the *SafeWord* system from Secure Computing Corporation. With this scheme, the user is first asked to identify himself to the system (user ID, no password). Then the system offers a pseudorandom 'challenge' number, which the user must enter into a hand-held password generator (usually a device about the size of a credit card with a numeric keypad). The password generator emits a number, which the user then supplies to the application. The application then confirms that the number supplied is compatible with the user ID and the supplied challenge.

Schemes of this sort are often preferred by security managers, because the authentication data supplied by the user to the application is different every time. This makes it harder to snoop, and prevents the use of 'weak passwords' (e.g., dictionary words). The problem is that multipage Web authentication like this is incompatible with J2EE form-based login procedures. As we shall see, Web-container authentication makes provision only for a single user ID and a single password, collected from a single page. Although the developer can define the appearance and layout of the page, there is no provision for defining the sequence of steps used in the login procedure. Although there are ways to incorporate multipage authentication into J2EE applications, none of them are very elegant. Again, there is every likelihood that this problem will be addressed in a future version of the J2EE specification.

16.3   The EJB security API

The EJB security model is a subset of the J2EE security model, which also includes support for Web components (JSPs and servlets). It is technically an *authorization model*, since it is concerned with the granting or denial of access to clients that have already been authenticated by the container; authentication is assumed to have happened before any substantive interaction with the system has occurred. This model is intended to isolate the application developer from the technicalities of transport layer security and authentication, allowing better attention to the needs of the application. To recap, the EJB security model, as part of the J2EE model, has the following main features.

- It centers on the concept of *roles*.

- Individual users are specified and identified by *principals*, which can be propagated between containers using transport-layer security (in a way that is invisible to the developer).

- It is predominantly *declarative*—based on a specification of roles and their permissions—although limited programmatic control is allowed where the declarative model is not sufficiently fine-grained.

- It is the job of the container, not the EJB developer, to enforce the security policy at runtime.

- It is the job of the container, not the EJB developer, to provide mechanisms by which the user can be authenticated.

Note that the security model assumes that the identity of the caller can be propagated in calls between different EJB containers (perhaps on different servers), but it does not state how this is to be carried out in practice: This is the job of the RMI protocol.

16.3.1   Declarative security

Developers are encouraged to use *declarative* security wherever possible. This means that the security permissions granted to each role are declared in the deployment descriptor and not coded in the EJB itself. In EJBs, each method that is exposed to clients can be allowed or denied for each role. So defining a security policy for an EJB application consists largely of defining which methods can be executed by which roles.

Most EJB products provide a tool for editing these method-role assignments in the deployment descriptor. In the *J2EE Reference Implementation*, and in most

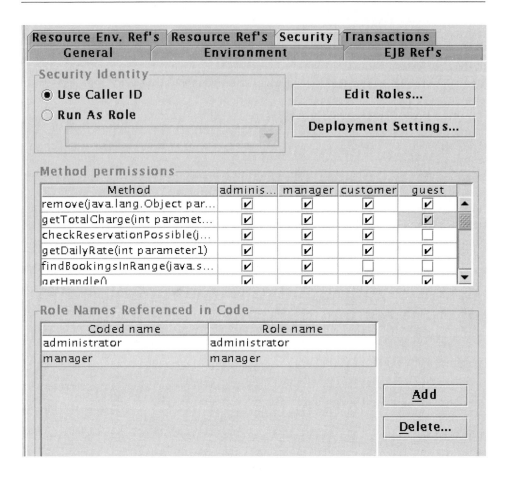

Figure 16.2. Editing the EJB method permissions in the *Prestige Bike Hire* application. The deployment tool provides a helpful 'grid' view of the assignments.

other products, this is integrated into an application assembly/deployment tool. Typically, the developer will be presented with a grid where the rows correspond to method names, and the columns to roles, and the permission for a role to execute a method is indicated by checking a box in the corresponding grid cell (Figure 16.2).

Declarative security is not defined for principals, only roles. This means that any operations involving explicit principals have to be implemented in code.

Declarative security works in a similar way for JSP pages and servlets; however, these have, in effect, only one exposed method (the `service()` method), so roles are allowed at the servlet or JSP level, not at the method level.[5]

---

[5]Strictly speaking, Web-tier security is enforced at the level of URL patterns, not servlets or JSPs. It is possible for the same servlet or JSP to be invoked using different URLs.

16.3.2   Programmatic security

The *EJB Specification* provides only two API calls for managing security at the programmatic level: `EJBContext.isCallerInRole()` and `EJBContext.getCaller` `Principal()`. These are both called on the context object passed into the EJB at initialization time (through the methods `setSessionContext()` or `setEntity` `Context`. Message-driven EJBs don't have callers in the conventional sense, and therefore these methods can't be used).

isCallerInRole

This method returns `true` if the current caller has been mapped to the specified role; it takes one `String` argument, which is not, strictly speaking, a role name, but a role *reference*. Role references are mapped to real roles as described below.

   `isCallerInRole()` is useful if the application requires control over security that is more fine-grained than can be accomplished at the method level. Suppose, for example, that a method can be called by different clients, but the data it returns depends on the security authority of the caller. This cannot easily be accomplished by declarative techniques alone (although some possible approaches are discussed below).

getCallerPrincipal

This method returns a `Principal` object that contains the name of the principal making the method call. The only thing that the *EJB Specification* guarantees about the principal is that, for a given session with a given client, the principal remains the same. Of course, a sensible implementation ought to ensure that a given user retains the same principal over time, but this is not a Specification matter. The *EJB Specification* has nothing to say about the relationship between the name, or user ID, of the user and the principal name. In particular, you *can't* assume that the principal name will be a user's login ID. If, for example, authentication is by certificate, then the principal will often be the X.500 name of the owner of the certificate (an example of this is shown below). There is no general way to derive a login ID from this data. Even if the application uses a user ID/password scheme to authenticate, we can't guarantee that the user ID is propagated to the principal name. We will have more to say about this issue later. For the moment, the notable point is that the developer has to be quite careful when using a mixture of different authentication strategies in the same application.

16.3.3   Declarative versus programmatic security

It is generally a good idea to use as little programmatic security as possible. Overuse of programmatic security makes the application harder to maintain and less portable. However, there will be times when the EJB security model is not sufficiently fine-grained to give effect to the application's requirements, and the developer has to decide between exposing a simpler EJB to clients—at the expense of incorporating some programmatic security—or using purely declarative security with a slightly more complex client interface.

Here is an example. In the *Prestige Bike Hire* application, the `CustomerManager`
EJB can be used to modify the customer's details (name, address, etc). Administrators need to be able to modify the details of any customer (if a customer telephones
to report a change of address, for example), but customers need to be able to modify
their own details. We could either provide the EJB with a single method, called by
both administrators and customers, with some security logic built in, or provide
two different methods, which allows fully declarative control.

Here is a code outline for the first strategy. The method `setCustomerDetails()`
has method permissions such that it can be executed by a user in any role. It assumes
that we have a method `getCurrentCustomerId()` that can return the customer ID
of the current user, based on the user's principal. It also assumes that the client
already knows its own customer ID and can make the call properly.

```
   public void setCustomerDetails
        (int custId, CustomerDetails cd)
     {
     if ((isCalledInRole ("Administrator")
5       || isCallerInRole ("Manager"))
        || (isCallerInRole("Customer")
          && custId == getCurrentCustomerId()))
        {
        // Do the modification
10      }
     else
        {
        throw new AccessDeniedException ();
        }
15   }
```

The logic expressed here is that the client supplies the ID for which the modification is required, and the EJB rejects the call if the ID does not match the user's
customer ID, unless the user is in one of the roles `Administrator` or `Manager`.

Gotcha!

Remember that the argument to `isCallerInRole` is not, strictly
speaking, a role name, but a *role reference*. Role references are
mapped onto real role names at deployment time, as described
below.

Although the security logic is encoded in the method, it is still role-based and
perfectly in keeping with the spirit of the *J2EE Specification*. This technique simplifies the API that clients see, as there is only one method to call to modify customer
details. Any client can call it, safe in the knowledge that the EJB will prevent
unauthorized modifications to the customer data. However, the security logic is
predominantly programmatic.

Here is the second strategy, which uses different method permissions for different roles.

```
// Permissions: Administrator, Manager
public void setCustomerDetails
      (int custId, CustomerDetails cd)
   {
5  _modifyDetails (custId, cd);
   }

// Permissions: Customer only
public void setMyCustomerDetails (CustomerData cd)
10   {
   _modifyDetails (getCurrentCustomerId(), cd);
   }

protected void _modifyDetails
      (int custId, CustomerData cd)
15   {
   // Do the modification
   }
```

With this strategy, a client can call `setCustomerDetails()` to modify a specified customer, or `setMyCustomerDetails()` to modify the details of the logged-in user. The second form does not require a customer ID to be passed as an argument, as this is determined from the principal. The advantage of this second approach is that there is no security logic explicitly coded in the EJB methods. The process of deciding whether a particular client can carry out a particular application is being evaluated in the container. Of course, the developer must ensure that the correct method permissions are assigned in the deployment descriptor.

The choice of which of these strategies to use will be a matter of personal preference, based on knowledge of how the methods are to be used by clients.

16.3.4 Role mapping

There are two aspects to role mapping of which the developer must be aware: mapping of roles onto 'real' users and groups at the deployment site and mapping of roles named used in EJB code to application role names. These requirements add slightly to the complexity of application development, but are necessary for flexibility.

User and group mapping

The mapping from J2EE role names—which are abstract and platform independent—to 'real' users and groups is always platform-dependent. With the *J2EE Reference Implementation*, roles are mapped onto users and groups defined using the deployment tool; the users and groups themselves are created using the `realmtool` command line tool. We will see how to do this in practice later. With other products, the mapping may be to LDAP groups, Windows NT Directory groups, or even operating system users and groups.

It is somewhat inflexible if the assignments from users and groups to roles can only be made in the deployment descriptor. In the worst case, this would make it necessary to redeploy the application whenever access were to be granted to an additional user. At the same time, the *EJB Specification* cannot mandate a particular method for implementing end-user authentication at a particular site. In practice, most EJB server products have (vendor specific) techniques for managing these mappings at runtime as well.

Role names and role references

It is a design feature of the *EJB Specification* that an application can be assembled from EJBs from different suppliers. The problem with this, as far as security is concerned, is that a component developer may have no clear idea of the security needs of a complete application. So, if the component developer assigns method permissions on an EJB, it will be in a generic way. The component developer may use role names like `canPlaceOrders` or `canViewOrders` to indicate the kinds of responsibilities that are required to execute certain methods. This is not a problem when declarative security is used, because these roles are enumerated in the deployment descriptor and are therefore visible to the application assembler and deployer. These roles can be matched up to real users and groups using the vendor's tools, or simply altered to match a role naming convention applied across the application. So the application assembler may identify `canPlaceOrders` as being equivalent to the `customer` role already defined, and simply change the deployment descriptor accordingly.

This deals with declarative security, but the situation is more complicated for programmatic security. Suppose, for example, that the EJB contains code like this:

```
if (context.isCallerInRole("canPlaceOrders"))
{
//...
}
```

If we simply change the role names in the deployment descriptor, this code will no longer make sense: The role `canPlaceOrders` no longer exists. The *EJB Specification* solves this problem by treating 'coded' role names—`canPlaceOrders` in the example—as *role references*, not real roles. In the deployment descriptor we map these references onto the real application roles.

The issues discussed above are illustrated in Figure 16.3. User1 and User2 are members of group 'Group,' while User3 is not a member of any group. These users and this group are platform-specific; they may be operating system users and groups, or LDAP entries, or something else. The three users are each mapped to principals; the correspondence between the user's login ID, or certificate name, and the principal is, again, vendor dependent.

Role1 comprises User1 and User2, by virtue of their membership in Group. Role2 comprises User2 and User3, by an explicit mapping from principals to roles. Again, the mechanism for making this mapping is vendor-specific.

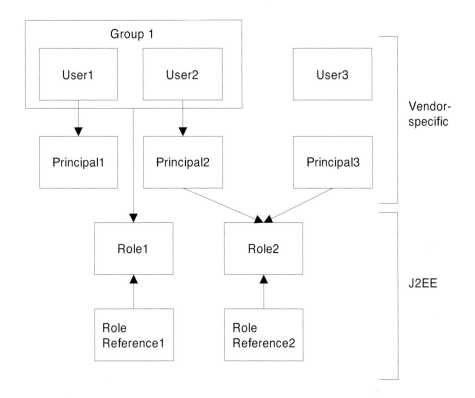

Figure 16.3. Vendor-specific and J2EE aspects of role mapping. See text for details.

Within the application itself, permissions are assigned declaratively to Role1 and Role2. In code, the application will refer to RoleReference1 and RoleReference2, which are mapped to Role1 and Role2 in the deployment descriptor.

The process of mapping names supplied in Java code to other names in a deployment descriptor should not be unfamiliar by now: It is exactly the same process we use when coding an EJB to get access to a JDBC connection, for example. In such cases, the EJB is coded to do a JNDI lookup on `java:comp/env/xxx` and the 'coded name' `xxx` is mapped onto the real JNDI name in the deployment descriptor.

16.3.5   Principal mapping

Many applications maintain information about their users. For example, an online banking application will need to be able to allow a customer to log in, and then retrieve data (account balances, etc.) specific to that user.

Suppose, for example, that the application's legacy database uses a customer ID as the primary key on the table of customer records. If we develop the application so that the internal customer ID is also the user's login ID, then it might be assumed that locating user-specific information is very straightforward: We just use the login ID in a search on the customer records table.

In practice, things are rarely this simple. Suppose, for instance, that the customer ID is a 30-digit number. Do we really want users to log in using this number? In reality, many such applications do work this way, and are well-tolerated by customers, but it is far from ideal. A better approach would be to a assign each customer a simple login ID (the customer's name, for example). This login ID must then be mapped onto the internal customer ID.

Even if we are happy to make the user's login ID the same as the internal customer ID, our problems are not over. An EJB determines the identity of its caller by calling `getCallerPrincipal()`. However, as discussed above, the principal may well not be the user's login ID.

In addition, if the same user may authenticate to an application in a number of different ways, it is very likely that the user would have a different principal depending on the authentication method (see an example of this below). All of a user's principals must be mapped onto the same internal ID. There is no standard name for this process, but I use the term *principal mapping* in this book. It is important to remember that principal mapping is an issue in EJB development in three circumstances:

- We need the application to be portable across servers (the problem is that users will want to keep the same user ID even if the server is changed, but principals may change with the server);

- The application supports multiple authentication mechanisms for the same user (because the same user will have different principals);

- Internal user IDs are defined by a legacy database or application, and cannot themselves be used for authentication.

A simple technique to overcome these problems is to maintain a database table with two columns and an arbitrary number of rows. In each row of the table, one field contains the principal and the other the internal identifier of that user (e.g., the customer ID). EJBs that retrieve user-specific data find the current principal by using `getCallerPrincipal()`, find the internal user ID from the principal mapping table, and then use the internal ID for subsequent operations. This technique allows multiple principals to identify the same user, as each user can have multiple rows in the principal mapping table. In addition, if the application is moved to a different server that uses different principal conventions, all the required modifications are in one database table.

In the *Prestige Bike Hire* application, because we have committed ourselves to using container-managed persistence throughout, we can't use a database table for principal mapping, but must use an entity EJB (`PrincipalMapping`). Each `Customer` EJB is associated with one or more `PrincipalMapping` EJBs, one for each authentication technique supported.

16.3.6   Principal delegation in EJBs

When a client calls a method on an EJB with a particular security principal, the EJB container can determine from the principal—and its role assignments—whether the

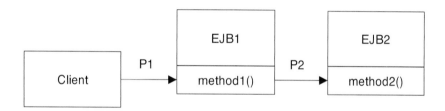

Figure 16.4. A client calls method `EJB1.method1()` as principal `P1`. What dictates the principal `P2` that is propagated to `EJB2`? See text for discussion.

method can be called or not. If it can be called, then the principal remains constant for that method call. If the EJB calls `getCallerPrincipal()`, then the result is Fell-defined. Now consider the situation shown in Figure 16.4.

The client calls method `method1()` on `EJB1` as principal `P1`. `method1()` then calls `method2()` on `EJB2`. What principal is used for this second call? Common sense would suggest that the principal from the client should be propagated to `EJB2`—that is, `method2()` should run as `P1`. This is the default set out in the Specification [EJB2.0 21.4.3]. However, although this approach is sensible if `EJB2` is seen as providing a service to the client, an alternative view is that `EJB2` is providing a service to `EJB1`, not to the client, and the call should use a principal that reflects this distinction. This process is called *principal delegation*.

Version 1.1 of the *EJB Specification* went on to say that the application assembler should specify to the deployer (perhaps using a description field in the deployment descriptor) if a delegated principal is to be used; the deployer would then use whatever proprietary features were available in the product to give effect to the needs of the application. This situation is far from satisfactory, and Version 2.0 provides specific support for principal delegation. In particular, the deployment descriptor now allows each EJB to be assigned a 'run-as' role and principal. This means that when a call is made on the EJB, the caller's principal is used to determine whether the call is allowed. Thereafter, the EJB method runs with the identity defined in the deployment descriptor, not necessarily that of the caller. If the EJB then makes a call on another EJB, it is the defined principal that is passed to the called EJB's container, not the original caller's ID. This mechanism is analogous to the 'suid' mechanism used in Unix. For example, if a user logs in and executes the `ls` command to get a list of files, the `ls` program runs with the identity of that user. However, if the user executes the `passwd` program to change his or her password, that program runs with `root` (system manager) identity, which allows the user to change the system password file—this would ordinarily not be allowed. Of course, the author of the `passwd` program needs to be exceptionally careful to ensure that users cannot abuse the extended access that it allows. Similar issues will almost certainly apply to the use of 'run-as' identity in EJBs, although this facility has not been available for long enough for firm guidelines to be established.

16.4   Security concepts example

This section uses a simple EJB 'PrincipalTest' to demonstrate some of the concepts of EJB security. PrincipalTest (Listing 16.1) has only one method, get Principal(), which gets the current caller's principal and returns it as a String to the client. The client (Listing 16.2) is also very simple: It just writes to the console the String returned by the EJB. The home and remote interfaces are not shown (they are only a few lines each); the home should expose a single create() method, while the remote exposes getPrincipal().

Later in this section we will see the effect of using a servlet to call the EJB, rather than a standalone program.

Hint

There is nothing in this section that won't work, in principle, on other EJB products than the *J2EE Reference Implementation*, but the process of mapping J2EE roles onto real users and groups is platform-specific. With the *SunONE* application server, for example, you will need to create users and groups in a directory server; there is no equivalent of the realmtool program supplied with the RI.

Hint

If you are using the RI, consider checking whether you have the most up-to-date version. Earlier versions used inconvenient defaults for security properties. The effect of these defaults was to make it difficult for the client to choose whether to authenticate or not.

Listing 16.1: **Implementation class for the** PrincipalTest **EJB.**

```
   package com.kevinboone.ejb_book.principaltest;
   import java.util.*;
   import javax.ejb.*;
   import javax.naming.*;
 5 import java.rmi.*;
   import javax.rmi.*;
   import java.sql.*;
   import javax.sql.*;

10 public class PrincipalTestBean
```

```
     extends GenericStatelessSessionBean
     {
     public String getPrincipal()
        {
15     debugOut ("Entering getPrincipal");
       return ctx.getCallerPrincipal().toString();
        }
     }
```

Listing 16.2: **Test client for the PrincipalTest EJB.**

```
     package com.kevinboone.ejb_book.principaltest;
     import javax.naming.*;
     import javax.rmi.PortableRemoteObject;

5    /**
     This simple client tests the 'PrincipalTest'
     Enterprise JavaBean
     */
     public class PrincipalTestClient
10   {
     public static void main(String[] args)
        throws Exception
        {
        Context context = new InitialContext();
15      Object ref  = context.lookup("PrincipalTest");
        PrincipalTestHome home = (PrincipalTestHome)
           PortableRemoteObject.narrow
             (ref, PrincipalTestHome.class);
        PrincipalTest principalTest = home.create ();
20      System.out.println
          ("Principal=" + principalTest.getPrincipal());
        principalTest.remove();
        }
     }
```

Hint

The source code for this example can be found in the source code package that accompanies this book, in the directory **principaltest**. You will also find a ready-to-deploy EAR file containing the EJB and the servlet used later in this section. However, if you want to follow the examples below, you will need to open the EAR file with the deployment tool to set the security properties as specified.

16.4.1   No authentication, authorization, or encryption

Assume for the moment that the EJB has been packaged using default security properties. The default access control, specified by the *EJB Specification*, is that no restrictions are applied to any method. As far as authentication is concerned, it is for the product to choose appropriate defaults. The *J2EE Reference Implementation* defaults to allowing the client to decide whether to attempt to authenticate or not.[6] With these settings, if we run the test client from the command line, perhaps by executing

```
ant run
```

then it will produce the output

```
Principal=guest
```

The principal 'guest' is reserved for an unauthenticated user. This output simply indicates that the client did not supply authentication data that the EJB container was prepared to trust (in fact, it didn't supply any authentication data at all, because we didn't ask it to). If the EJB imposed any security constraints at all on the method `getPrincipal()`, the client would not be able to execute this method, as it cannot be authenticated.

Gotcha!

With the *J2EE Reference Implementation*, if you denote that an EJB requires authentication, then an unauthenticated client will not be able to run *any* method on the EJB. Some developers find this inconvenient, but it favors safety rather than convenience. To allow the client to decide whether to authenticate or not, you need to set the authentication requirement to 'Support client choice,' which is the default.

16.4.2   Authentication by password, authorization,
but no encryption

Now we will see how to apply a simple security constraint. In the first instance, the client will fail because it can't be authenticated, but then we will add a server-generated authentication wrapper to it and show that it can now be authenticated.

Step 1: defining a new abstract role

We begin by defining a role which has exclusive access to the `getPrincipal()` method. From the EJB's 'Security' tab, click the button 'Edit roles.' Then add a new

---

[6]This was not the case with earlier versions of the RI. See note above.

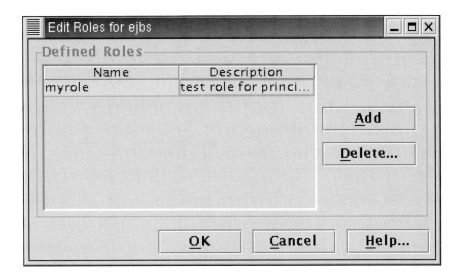

Figure 16.5. Creating a new role called `myrole`.

role (Figure 16.5). In this example, I have called the role `myrole`. The 'description' field is important in a real application, because it gives guidance to the application assembler about the way the role should be assigned to real users and groups.

Step 2: limiting access to the EJB

We now set the `getPrincipal()` method to be exclusively accessible by users in the `myrole` role (Figure 16.6).

Step 3: role mapping

Before we can deploy the EJB with its simple security policy, we must assign the role `myrole` to one or more 'real' users. To make things more realistic, we will make the mapping to a group of users, not just to a single user.

The *J2EE Reference Implementation* is provided with a command-line utility ('`realmtool`') for managing users and groups. Note that we are operating *outside* the J2EE security model in using this utility: J2EE only extends to the definitions of the roles and their permissions; it does not stipulate methods for mapping these roles onto real people. In a production environment, you may need to map roles onto groups in a directory server, for example.

With the *J2EE Reference Implementation*, we will create a group called `PrincipalTestUsers` as follows:[7]

---

[7]With later versions of the RI, the graphical deployment tool can be used to manage users and groups as well as the command-line utility, which you may find more convenient.

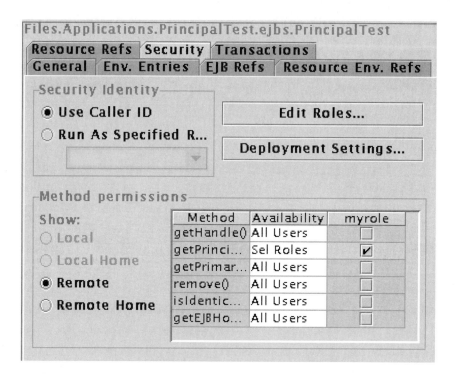

Figure 16.6. Allowing access to getPrincipal() only to myrole; note that the other methods are assigned to 'all roles' and are therefore unrestricted.

```
realmtool -addGroup PrincipalTestUsers
```

Next we must put at least one user in this group. In this case, I will add user 'kevin':

```
realmtool -add kevin secret PrincipalTestUsers
```

'secret' is the password I will be required to specify when using user ID/password authentication.

Back in the deployment tool, we can now map the new group onto the abstract role myrole. To do this, we need the 'Security' tab of the *application*, not the EJB. From this screen, click 'Add' and select the group PrincipalTestUsers from the list provided. The mapping should now be displayed as in Figure 16.7.

The application can then be deployed in the usual way.

Step 4: proving that unauthenticated clients are now denied access

If we now run the client without authentication, the EJB container will block the call to getPrincipal(); in fact, it throws an exception, which should be output from the client like this:

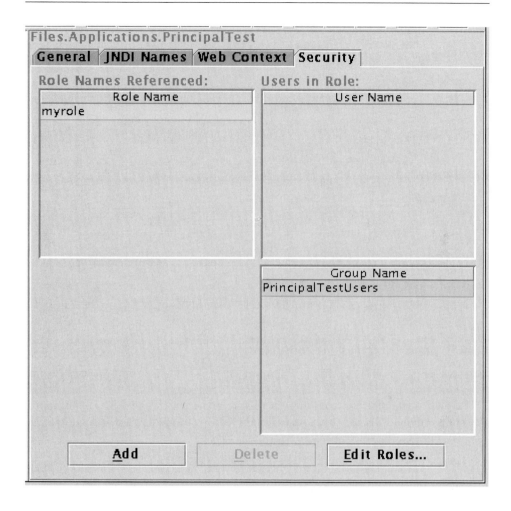

Figure 16.7. The role `myrole` mapped onto the group 'PrincipalTestUsers.'

```
Exception in thread "main" java.rmi.AccessException:
  CORBA NO_PERMISSION 0 No; nested exception is:
    org.omg.CORBA.NO_PERMISSION:  minor code: 0  completed: No
```

So, we have prevented unauthenticated clients from getting access to the protected method. Now, how do we authenticate clients?

Step 5: setting the authentication method

First, we set the EJB to require password-based authentication (Figure 16.8). With the *J2EE Reference Implementation*, this means that unauthenticated clients will not be allowed *any* access to the EJB.

Now we redeploy the application.

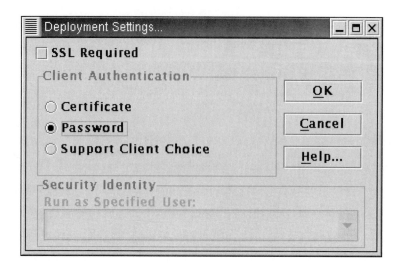

Figure 16.8. Setting the EJB to use password authentication, but no encryption.

Step 6: generating a client container

We have set up the EJB so that it will reject clients that can't supply a user ID and password, but so far we don't have a way for the client to supply these credentials.

Remember that authentication is the job of the container, not the EJB developer. We must tell the EJB server to generate a 'client container,' which is essentially a security wrapper around the client.

We begin the process by selecting 'File-New application client' in the deployment tool. In a real application client (for distribution to end users), we might want to package all the client-side classes into one distributable file; however, for this test client we only need the main class—that is, the one with the `main()` method (`PrincipalTestClient` in this case, Figure 16.9)—and any EJB interfaces it may require.

> Hint
>
> The `runclient` program (see below) does not take a '-classpath' argument on the command line. You should probably ensure that all the classes your client will need are either packaged into the client container or accessible some other way. In fact, it is possible to supply a CLASSPATH, or any other JVM arguments, by setting the environment variable `VMARGS` before executing `runclient`, as described below.

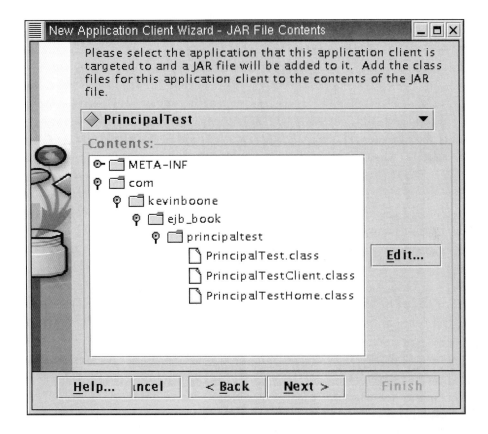

Figure 16.9. Starting the construction of the application client container. Into the package we put the test client itself, and the home and remote interfaces of the EJB it refers to.

The next step asks for the name of the 'main' class in the application (Figure 16.10).

`PrincipalTestClient` refers to the `PrincipalTest` EJB directly, by its JNDI name, rather than by a `java:comp/env` name, so we don't need to add any EJB references. There are no datasource references or environment entries. This means that the rest of the dialog's 'New application client' dialog boxes can be skipped (click on 'Finish').

After this process, the deployment tool shows the new client container as part of the application (Figure 16.11).

We can now deploy the application, ensuring that the option to 'return client JAR' is selected as usual.

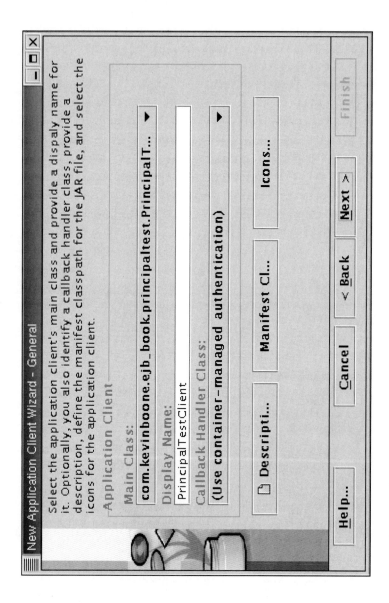

Figure 16.10. Specifying the main class.

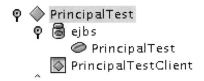

Figure 16.11. The appearance of the application after adding the client container.

Step 7: run the client in its container

To run the client container, use the `runclient` program, which is supplied with the *J2EE Reference Implementation*. In this example, we would invoke it like this:

```
runclient -client PrincipalTestClient.jar \
  -name PrincipalTestClient
```

When `runclient` is executed, it attempts to assign a principal to the user. It typically does this by popping up a login dialog box (Figure 16.12) and passing the username and password to the server to be validated. If the authentication succeeds, `runclient` calls the `main()` method of the specified main class. From this point, the developer's code is in control, but the user has a principal known to the application.

Whether the test client succeeds or not depends on whether the username and password supplied correspond to someone in the role `myrole`. If they do, then the output should be something like this:

```
Principal=kevin
```

that is, the principal returned is the login ID I supplied to the `runclient` program's authentication prompt.

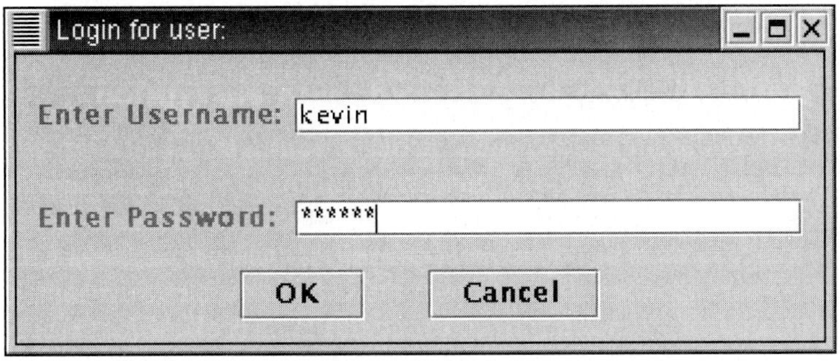

Login for user:	_ □ ×
Enter Username:	kevin
Enter Password:	******
	OK Cancel

Figure 16.12. *J2EE Reference Implementation* 'login' dialog box, produced by the client container.

Hint

`runclient` can be supplied with an argument `-textauth`, which forces it to query the user at the prompt, not in a graphical display. This is somewhat faster. In addition, there are system properties (*not* command-line arguments) that can bypass the prompt altogether. See the *J2EE Reference Implementation* documentation for more details.

Gotcha!

If you see the exception `IllegalAccessException` while testing a secure application, you may be tempted to think that the message is related to a problem with authentication or access control. *It probably isn't.* This exception is thrown when Java code tries to instantiate a class to which it does not have access at the JVM level. A common problem is trying to instantiate a class that does not have the `public` modifier, when the caller is not in the same package.

It is important to remember that supplying a user ID and password with this technique is inherently unsafe, as the *login ID and password are sent in the clear* (unencrypted). In fact, all the data is sent in the clear. Anyone who has access to any part of the network between the client and the EJB server, and who has network sniffing tools like 'snoop' or 'tcpdump,' can readily eavesdrop on the conversation.

16.4.3   Authentication by password, with encryption

To get the benefits of secure communication, all we need do is to check the 'SSL required' button in the dialog box shown in Figure 16.8. The client is invoked in exactly the same way. You will notice a longer delay when starting up, as the SSL handshake is not a particularly fast process. With this technique, all communication between the client and the EJB server is encrypted.

You may be wondering what key is used for the encryption. The client, after all, cannot supply its user ID and password until a secure channel is established, so clearly neither of these form any part of the key. The answer is that the the server's default certificate is used to construct the key. This certificate will contain the server's public key.

> ## Gotcha!
>
> It is a very common misconception that it is necessary to install a certificate at both ends of an SSL connection to encrypt data in both directions. This erroneous belief has been spread, at least in part, by its finding its way into certain popular textbooks. In fact, a certificate (strictly a public key) at either end of the channel will be adequate to establish encryption in both directions. This is because the public key is not used to encrypt the data at all: It is used to encrypt a random number, which is then used by both parties to encrypt the data. This process is explained in detail in Appendix G, at page 675.

What all this means is that to get secure two-way communication, you *don't* need to install any certificate on the client. The reason for installing certificates on the client is to allow the server to authenticate the client by certificate, rather than by password. This is important because there are standards for passing certificates in RMI/IIOP, but no general standards for the use of passwords.

16.4.4 Authentication by certificate and encryption

The use of CSI allows certificate-based authentication as well as encrypted communication between the client and the EJB. While Version 2 of the *EJB Specification* requires that EJB products support CSI transport, the techniques used to configure it (for example, the location and installation of the certificates) will necessarily be vendor-specific. Using a simple example, this section describes how to use CSI with the *J2EE Reference Implementation*. Please note that this feature was newly introduced in Version 1.3 of the product; it changed significantly between beta versions of the RI, and may well have changed again by the time you read this. There is some documentation on configuration supplied with the RI, which is very terse but should be comprehensible if you understand the principles.

Step 1: generating a client certificate

The EJB server will use the client certificate to authenticate the client, while the client will use the server certificate to authenticate the server. A default server certificate is installed along with the Reference Implementation, but a new certificate must be generated for the client.

Remember that certificates are authenticated by tracing back up a chain of signers, until we find a signer we are prepared to trust (this process is explained in detail in Appendix G, at page 682). This means that there are two ways to generate a trustable client certificate.

- Use a certificate signed by one of the certificate authorities (CA) acceptable to the EJB server by default. Most VeriSign and Thawte certificates, for example, will be fine.

- Use a self-signed certificate, or a certificate from another CA, and import the signer's certificate into the trusted certificates keystore.

I will assume for the moment that we are using the first strategy, but there are some brief guidelines for the second at the end of this section.

For this example, I will use my VeriSign personal certificate, which I have exported from Netscape Navigator into the file `kevin.p12`. A complication with this approach is that the certificate is stored in PKCS12 format (along with its private key). The SSL implementation supplied with the RI expects to find this information in a 'Java KeyStore' (JKS) file. We can use the `keytool` program supplied with the RI to convert PKCS12 to JKS format[8] as follows:

```
/usr/j2sdkee1.3/keytool -pkcs12 \
  -pkcsFile kevin.p12 \
  -pkcsKeyStorePass ***** \
  -pkcsKeyPass ***** \
  -jksFile kevin.jks \
  -jksKeyStorePass secret
```

Don't forget that this command is one long line. As always, Windows users will need backslashes rather than forward slashes, but otherwise the command is the same. In this example, I have used the full path to `keytool` to ensure that the RI version is executed, and not the standard JDK version. The asterisks represent the keystore and key passwords assigned to the PKCS12 file, which I don't plan to share. The switch `-jksKeyStorePass` sets the password that will protect the JKS file that the utility generates. In this case, I have used the key 'secret' for simplicity; of course, we wouldn't do this in practice.

The effect of this command is to generate a file `kevin.jks` that contains the same key information as the PKCS12 file, but in Java KeyStore format. I can inspect this file with `keytool` like this:

```
/usr/j2sdkee1.3/bin/keytool -list \
  -keystore /home/kevin/kevin.jks
Enter keystore password:  secret

Keystore type: jks
Keystore provider: SUN

Your keystore contains 1 entry:
```

---

[8]At the time of writing, the `keytool` utility supplied with the Java JDK does not support this feature, so be sure to use the version supplied with the RI.

```
kevin boone's verisign, inc. id, Wed Apr 18 ...
Certificate fingerprint (MD5): D3:C9:07:52:4B: ...
```

Note that there is exactly one certificate in the file. There is also a copy of my private key, which I don't want to export to the server (see below).

Step 2: installing the client certificate on the server

Strictly speaking, the client certificate does not need to leave the client. We only need to provide it to the server if the server needs to trust it implicitly (that is, we abandon the convention of authentication via trusted third parties). However, the *J2EE Reference Implementation* needs to map the certificate ID onto the group `PrincipalTestUsers` in a similar manner to that which we used to map the login ID in the previous example. It is much easier to configure the RI to do this if the certificate itself is made available on the server. However, the keystore file I created in the previous step contains my private key, and I don't plan to pass that over any kind of network (especially since I've chosen the password 'secret' to protect the keystore!). So there are two steps to getting the client certificate to the server: extracting the certificate from the client keystore and importing it into the server's keystore. To export:

```
/usr/j2sdkee1.3/bin/keytool -export \
  -file kevin.cer
  -keystore kevin.jks
  -alias "kevin boone's verisign, inc. id"
Enter keystore password:  secret
Certificate stored in file <kevin.cer>
```

The `-alias` switch selects the certificate to be exported. There is only one certificate in the keystore in this example, but the `keytool` utility won't guess that this is the one I want. The `-file` argument selects the name of the file to be created, while `-keystore` selects the keystore file to be read. The program prompts for the keystore password, which is the one assigned when creating the JKS file in the previous step.

This procedure does not export the private key, which of course, remains on the client. It merely exports the certificate into a file, `kevin.cer`, which we can then *import* into realmtool's certificate database like this:

```
/usr/j2sdkee1.3/bin/realmtool \
  -import kevin.cer
```

Having done this, we will now be able to select the holder of this certificate as an authorized member of the `myrole` role, and therefore someone allowed to execute the method `getPrincipal()`.

Step 3: configuring the EJB

Assembly of the EJB using the deployment tool is as usual, except that the EJB must be configured to use SSL and certificate-based authentication. In the 'Security'

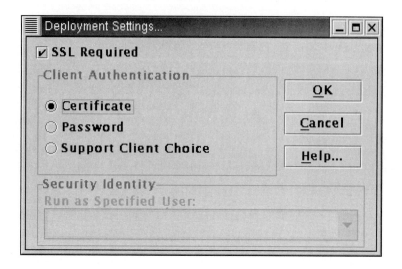

Figure 16.13. Setting the EJB to use certificate-based authentication and SSL.

tab, click the button 'Deployment settings,' which will bring up the dialog box shown in Figure 16.13.

Now we must extend the role `myrole` to include the certificate imported earlier. The procedure is the same as adding a user or group that was set up with `realmtool`, except that we see a certificate ID in the list rather than a login ID (Figure 16.14).

Step 4: running the client

To run the client, the `runclient` program needs to be informed of the location of the keystore containing the client's certificate (this is done using the system property `com.sun.enterprise.keyStore`), and a key that can decrypt the keystore. This is so that the client can supply its certificate to the server and be authenticated. Finally, we need to tell the `runclient` program to use SSL authentication, not passwords; this is done with the system property `com.sun.enterprise.loginMech`. `runclient` does not allow these settings to be given on the command line: It needs them to be set into an environment variable `VMARGS`. To set this environment variable, you will need a command of this form

```
export "VMARGS=...."
```

on UNIX systems, or

```
set VMARGS=....
```

on Windows.

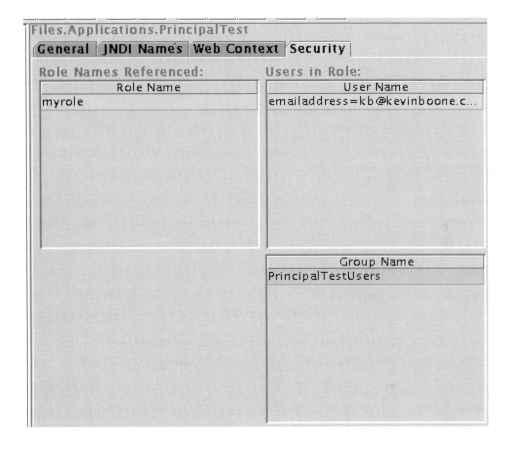

Figure 16.14. The server is now configured such that the role `myrole` is accessible to anyone who can offer the certificate whose ID is `email=kb@kevinboone.com...` (provided that it is validly signed, etc.).

So, to run the test client from the command line, we need a command like this:

```
export "VMARGS=\
-Dcom.sun.enterprise.keyStore=kevin.jks\
 -Dcom.sun.enterprise.keyStorePass=secret\
 -Dcom.sun.enterprise.loginMech=ssl"
runclient -client PrincipalTestClient.jar \
  -name PrincipalTestClient
```

(using `set` rather that `export` on Windows systems, and adjusting the pathnames of the various files to be correct on your system).

When this command is run, the `runclient` script will prompt for a password to decrypt the client-side keystore (`kevin.jks`) in this case. It will then present a list of the certificates in the keystore, so that you can select the one to be supplied to the server. In this example, there is only one certificate in the keystore, but `runclient` won't use it by default.

This produces the following output (which is specific to my certificate, of course):

```
My principal is: EmailAddress=kb@kevinboone.com,
   CN=Kevin Boone, OU=Digital ID Class 1 -
   Netscape Full Service, OU=Persona Not
   Validated, OU="www.verisign.com/repository/RPA
   Incorp. by Ref.,LIAB.LTD(c)98", OU=VeriSign
   Trust Network, O="VeriSign, Inc."
```

Note that the principal in this case is not a login ID, it is a certificate ID. This illustrates why it may be a mistake for the developer to assume that the result of a call on `getCallerPrincipal()` will be a login ID.

Using nondefault CAs

The EJB server maintains its list of trusted CAs in the file `cacerts.jks`, as discussed previously. In order to use certificates that are not signed by one of these CAs, the signer's certificate must be imported into `cacerts.jks`. For example, suppose I generate a self-signed certificate. To have this certificate accepted by the server, I must import the certificate itself into `cacerts.jks` using, for example, `keytool -import`.

More commonly, certificates will be signed by the organization's own CA. In this case, the CA's certificate must be imported into the database of trusted CAs, both on the client and the server.

16.4.5   Using Web-tier authentication

Where the EJB application is accessible through a Web application, the Web tier can be asked to authenticate the user. We may wish to encrypt communication between the Web browser and the Web server, but unless the Web server and the EJB server are physically remote from one another, we probably don't want to encrypt between the Web server and the EJB server. If we do want to do this, then we must proceed as described above, using SSL to support the communication; the process is independent of browser-server communication.

If the Web server and the EJB server are part of the same application, then the EJB server will probably be configured to trust the Web server implicitly. Thus any user authenticated by the Web tier will be acceptable to the EJB tier.

As an illustration, let's see how authentication can be propagated to the simple EJB used above from a servlet.

Step 1: coding and packaging the servlet

A detailed description of the authoring and packaging of servlets is beyond the scope of this book, but a brief overview is provided on page 547.

Listing 16.3 shows a very simple servlet that can call the method `getPrincipal` on the `PrincipalTest` EJB. Note that the way that the servlet interacts with the EJB is almost identical to the standalone test client.[9]

Listing 16.3: **A servlet test client for the `PrincipalTest` EJB.**

```
package com.kevinboone.ejb_book.principaltest;
import java.io.*;
import javax.servlet.*;
import javax.servlet.http.*;
import javax.ejb.*;
import javax.naming.*;
import javax.rmi.*;

public class PrincipalTestServlet extends HttpServlet
{
public void doGet(HttpServletRequest req,
  HttpServletResponse resp)
    throws IOException, ServletException
  {
  resp.setContentType("text/plain");
  PrintWriter out = resp.getWriter();

  try
    {
    Context context = new InitialContext();
    Object ref  = context.lookup("PrincipalTest");
    PrincipalTestHome home = (PrincipalTestHome)
        PortableRemoteObject.narrow
          (ref, PrincipalTestHome.class);
    PrincipalTest principalTest = home.create();
    String p = principalTest.getPrincipal();
    out.println("Principal is: " + p);
    principalTest.remove();
    }
  catch (Exception e)
    {
    out.println (e.toString());
    }
  out.close();
  }
}
```

We have not discussed the process of packaging servlets using the *J2EE Reference Implementation*, but if you try it you'll see that the procedure is very similar to packaging EJBs: Select 'File-New Web component' and the deployment tool follows a step-by-step procedure as for EJBs. Space precludes a detailed discussion of here.

[9]In practice we would initialize the home reference in the servlet's initialization, not the `goGet()` method.

> Gotcha!
>
> The *J2EE Reference Implementation* does not allow servlets to authenticate themselves to EJBs using passwords *or* certificates. Instead, authentication information is supplied directly in the RMI protocol. Therefore you must set the authentication mode of the EJBs to 'Supports client choice' if their clients are likely to be servlets.

Step 2: verifying that access is denied to an unauthenticated servlet

If the servlet is deployed with no authentication configured, then when it is executed from a Web browser, it reports a security exception (Figure 16.15), exactly as expected. Note that the URL required to invoke the servlet is set up in the deployment descriptor when packaging it.

Step 3: configuring servlet authentication

We've seen that a user that does not authenticate at the Web tier remains unauthenticated at the EJB tier. Now we will see how authentication can be achieved at the servlet tier and propagated to the EJB. First, we must configure the Web application to challenge the user for credentials.

Web-tier security is expressed in terms of 'security constraints.' A security constraint is a mapping between one or more URL patterns and one or more roles. To be able to make a successful request on any of the specific URLs, the user must be in one of the specified roles. If the user is not yet authenticated, the Web container must initiate an authentication attempt before allowing access to the requested URL.

The simplest security constraint is shown in Figure 16.16, which is a display of the properties of the WAR file containing our test servlet in the *J2EE Reference Implementation*. Notice that the selected security role is `myrole`, to match the EJB's expectation, and the selected URL is /*—that is, match any URL. If the application is deployed with this configuration, the Web container will challenge the user the first time any request is made for any URL. If the user can be authenticated and is allowed the role `myrole`, then the request will be accepted and the servlet executed.

Notice that there is no part for the developer to play in any of this: The collection, verification, and examination of the user's credentials is entirely the job of the Web container. The Web container can effect this process—according to the J2EE Specification—in one of three ways, while the developer's responsibilities are limited to selecting the method to use and providing any configuration files required.

Client certificate We have discussed the use of client certificates in the context of EJB clients, and the process is similar here. In this case, a certificate is presented by the Web browser to the Web server, in addition to the client getting

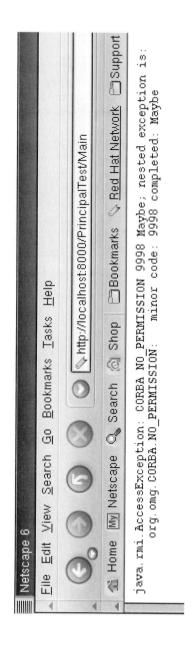

Figure 16.15. What happens when an unauthenticated servlet tries to run a method on an EJB that is only allowed for certain roles.

a certificate from the server. If the client's certificate is valid, the certificate ID is propagated to the EJB tier when servlets make calls on EJBs.[10]

HTTP 'basic' authentication With this form of authentication, when the browser requests a protected URL, the Web server sends back a status code that indicates that the browser should retry the operation after gathering credentials. The browser will typically pop up a dialog box to collect a user ID and password (see below). The browser collects these credentials and resubmits the request. The Web server then collects the credentials and validates them against the application's security configuration.

HTTP 'form based' authentication When the user requests a protected URL, the Web server presents a login page instead of accepting the request. Note that this is different from 'basic' authentication in the sense that the browser is now no longer part of the authentication scheme: As far as the browser is concerned, it issued a request and got a response. The user then fills in the user ID and password fields, and submits the form. The Web server extracts the credentials and validates them in the usual way. If the validation is successful, the original request is reissued automatically. If not, the server presents an error page. The developer can supply the pages that the server presents to the browser.

Each of these techniques has advantages and disadvantages, but space does not allow for a full analysis here. In short, the advantage of form based authentication over basic authentication is that it cuts the browser out of the authentication process. This means that the browser cannot easily cache user credentials and resubmit them without prompting the user. In addition, form based authentication is generally more aesthetically satisfactory, as the authentication pages can be made to integrate with the rest of the application.

Of these types, 'basic' is the easiest to configure, so it has been selected for this simple example (Figure 16.16).

Step 4: testing servlet authentication

After deploying the application, we can retry the request on the servlet with a browser. We should get the basic login dialog box (Figure 16.17). If the correct credentials are entered, then the servlet should invoke the EJB and display the user's principal as before (Figure 16.18).

The key point to note in all this is that the Web container has authenticated the user and determined that he or she is in the correct role `myrole`. It has then propagated the user credentials to the EJB, which is able to determine that the user is in this role, and also to obtain the same principal that was known to the Web tier.

---

[10]Strictly speaking, this is only a default. The developer can configure principal delegation so that the servlet presents its own credentials to the EJB, rather than the user's, if this better suits the needs of the application.

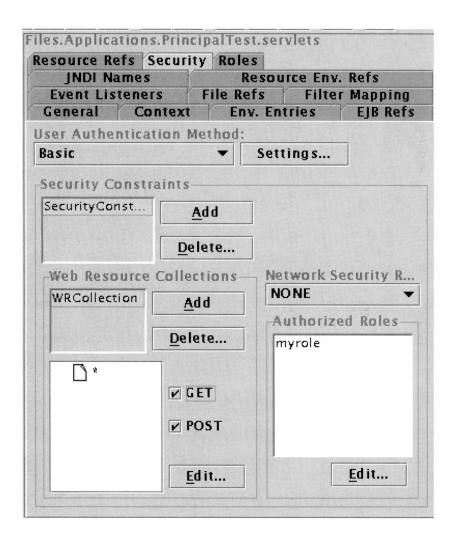

Figure 16.16. Configuring the Web tier to apply a security challenge for any URL requested by the browser.

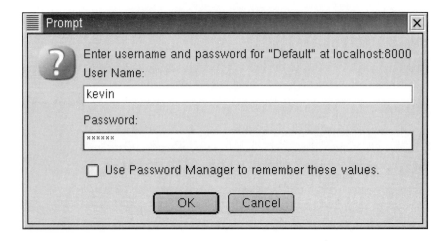

Figure 16.17. The familiar 'HTTP basic' authentication dialog box, shown here presented by Netscape Navigator.

Gotcha!

You will notice that there is no way to *log out*. Once you are authenticated, you remain authenticated forever. This is a limitation of the 'basic' authentication scheme. If you want to try logging in as, say, a different user, you will need to close the browser application and start it up again. Although a servlet can 'log out' a user (strictly, invalidate the session), the browser remembers the credentials and logs right back in again. Using form-based authentication overcomes this problem, because the browser is not part of the system. Note that this is not a weakness in any product; this behaviour is in accordance with the specification for basic authentication.

16.5   EJB security in the enterprise

This section describes the problems that EJB-to-EJB interactions cause for enterprise-level security. It is important to keep in mind that the problems discussed in this section apply mostly to wide-area EJB-to-EJB method calls, which are mostly likely to be significant in business-to-business applications. The more common, Web-based model of application provision does not suffer from the same limitations. We begin with a discussion of the use of firewalls, and the problems that EJB protocols impose on their use. Then we will consider various solutions to

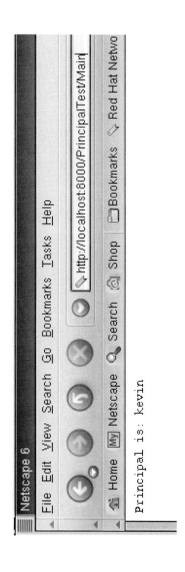

Figure 16.18. The servlet running the getPrincipal() method on the PrincipalTest EJB, after authentication.

these problems, including the use of HTTP-based communications protocols as an alternative to IIOP.

16.5.1   The problem

The Internet is a very useful medium for communication between businesses, or between businesses and their customers. However, communication via the Internet, in any form, means that something in your enterprise is exposed to the Internet. There is no regulation of who is allowed to connect to the Internet, or for what purpose. This means that businesses have to be very careful to limit the amount of the enterprise that is exposed.

Consider the problem shown in Figure 16.19. The organization has two Web servers that are available to service customer requests. These Web servers make use of data on the corporate database. For the Web servers to communicate with the database, they must have a network connection to it. However, the topology shown exposes the corporate database to the Internet: rarely a sound practice. Some improvement can be gained by isolating the internal network from the Internet using Web servers with multiple network interfaces (Figure 16.20). Using these *multi-homed* servers is only helpful if the administrator takes some trouble to 'harden' them. Among other things, this hardening involves limiting the number of IP ports exposing services. Many standard Unix processes, such as `sendmail` (port 25) and `rshd` (port 512) have well-documented security weaknesses. If an unauthorized person can use these services to obtain a login session on the Web server, then the organization is in the same position as when its corporate database was exposed to the Internet. When suitably hardened, the multihomed servers are examples of what are usually called *bastions*.

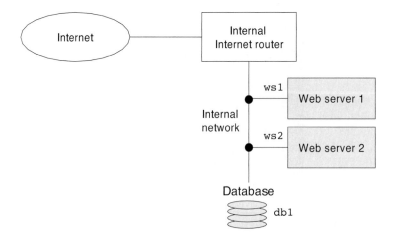

Figure 16.19. An enterprise network in need of attention. The problem: How do we allow customers access to the Web servers but restrict access to the database and other internal services?

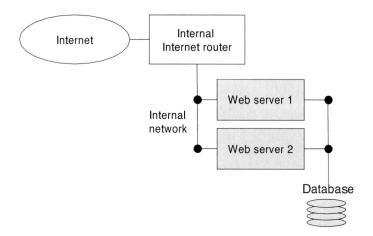

Figure 16.20. Using *multihomed bastions* to isolate the internal network from the Internet. The Web servers use one network interface to connect to the Internet and another for Internal communication.

Another simple—but effective—solution is to install some sort of packet filtering between the Internet and the internal network. This facility is often built into Internet routers, but more sophisticated set-ups may require a separate firewall product. The packet filter knows which services are to be exposed by which hosts, and will reject attempts to open connections to any other host-port combination (Figure 16.21).

A packet filter at the router level may also perform *network address translation* (NAT). This allows the hosts inside the firewall to use private IP addresses, and be exposed to the Internet using different, public addresses. This provides an additional safeguard against penetration of the internal services.

This single-firewall strategy will prevent a direct security attack on the database, but it won't prevent an attack via the Web server itself. Because Web servers are well-understood—and therefore have well-understood security flaws—many administrators prefer to include an additional firewall between the Web server and the database (Figure 16.22). This has the effect of preventing the Web server from getting at the corporate data via services other than the database engine itself. Because the Web servers are in a network which is neither in the 'hostile' Internet, nor the 'friendly' internal network, it has become customary to refer to this area as a 'demilitarized zone' (DMZ).

The use of packet-filtering firewalls is effective with protocols like HTTP for two main reasons.

- The client has a fixed hostname with which it communicates across the firewall. Although we may be using network address translation or round-robin request dispatch inside the enterprise, this does not affect the client. The firewall can reject requests for all but one hostname.

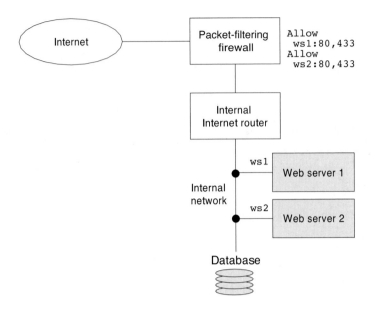

Figure 16.21. Using packet filtering to isolate the internal network from the Internet.

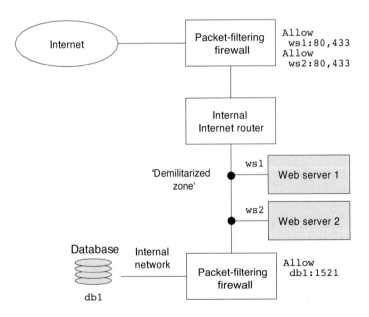

Figure 16.22. Using two packet-filtering firewalls to protect the corporate database from an attack via the Web server.

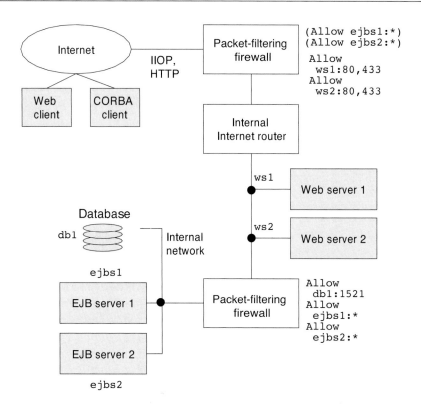

Figure 16.23. Effect on packet filtering when IIOP is used. If IIOP clients are used, as well as Web clients, then both firewalls need to admit a wide range of ports. Even with Web clients, the second firewall will need to accept a wide range of ports. The '*' does not necessarily indicate that all ports have to be admitted, only that there is a wide range.

- All requests from clients are made on the same port, or on the same small range of ports. Typically, the packet filter will need to admit requests on port 80 for HTTP and port 433 for HTTPS. The firewall can usefully block all other ports.

Now, consider the effect of introducing EJB servers into the enterprise (Figure 16.23), assuming that the standard IIOP protocol is used.

To understand why there is a problem, it may be helpful to review the processes by which object references are passed in IIOP.

When the client does a name lookup, it passes the name of the object, and gets back an IOR (interoperable object reference). The IOR contains the host and port details of the ORB that can satisfy method execution requests for that object. Typically the ORB will be listening on one IP socket for each object that is instantiated. In EJB terms, this means one network socket for each home object and EJB object.

This design strategy leads to two significant problems for an enterprise that is protected by firewalls.

- In order to allow access to the EJBs, the firewall must accept connection requests for a wide range of ports, on all EJB servers. This is because it is difficult—if not impossible—to predict in advance the port range that the EJB server will require. The EJB server will have to use port numbers that don't conflict with other sockets that may be allocated by other software, so the ports may vary from time to time. In addition, the number of ports that are in use will increase with the number of clients.

- If network address translation is in use, the host address passed from the naming server to the client in the IOR may not allow the client to connect to the EJB server. This is because the EJB server's view of the network will be based on internal network addresses, and the address in the IOR will be relative to the internal network. However, the firewall will not allow clients on the Internet to connect to servers by these addresses (these are confidential). Moreover, the IOR 'leaks' confidential addressing information about the internal network to the Internet.

If the enterprise supports IIOP clients, as well as Web (HTTP) clients, the problem is particularly acute. This is because a wide range of ports has to be opened on *both* firewalls, with the same port numbers. Many EJB products require all ports in the range 1000–1500 to be open; this range may overlap with a number of other services that should not really be exposed to the Internet, including a number of database products. If IIOP is used only within the organization (all Internet clients are Web clients interacting with servlets, for example) the problem is significantly reduced, although not eliminated.

For these reasons, most authorities suggest that the use of *IIOP is not compatible with packet-filtering firewalls*. If the firewall configuration is relaxed enough to allow IIOP to work, then the enterprise is not adequately protected.

16.5.2   IIOP-aware firewalls

Traditional packet-filtering firewalls make decisions about which traffic to accept based on the server and port addresses in the destination and, sometimes, the source fields of the IP packet. More sophisticated products can interpret higher-level protocols and make decisions based on the semantics of the data itself. For example, HTTP-aware firewalls can make decisions based on the contents of the request header from the browser.

The increased use of IIOP has led to the introduction of firewall products that are specifically designed to protect an organization in which IIOP is used. A notable example is Xtradyne's *Domain Boundary Controller*

At a minimum, a firewall that is compatible with IIOP needs to be able to recognize that a TCP/IP message contains an IIOP request, and allow it to pass even if the port number is in a range that would not normally be allowed. More sophisticated products may also be able to offer discrimination on the basis of the object that is being called, and on the identity of the caller.

Despite the increased availability of IIOP-aware firewalls, many system administrators are reluctant to use them, and the use of IIOP remains a headache for enterprise security administrators.

16.5.3   HTTP tunnelling

Because the HTTP protocol has been around for a long time, there is no difficulty obtaining HTTP-aware firewalls, and they are generally well accepted. The problem with such firewalls is, of course, that they can only correctly deal with HTTP messages. If other protocols can be wrapped up inside an HTTP message, then this suggests a way in which they can cross the firewall without compromising security (Figure 16.24).

The process of using HTTP as a carrier for other protocols is called *HTTP tunnelling*. This technique is not new to IIOP, but has been used for some years to support the use of protocols like FTP and `telnet` across firewalls.

At the time of writing, their are relatively few commercial implementations of stand-alone HTTP/IIOP tunnelling products (Iona's *WonderWall* is an example) although some ORB vendors include support for this feature in their products (e.g., Visigenic's *VisiBroker*). Moreover, a number of authorities believe that the use of HTTP tunnelling is contrary to the spirit of firewall technology. Their concern is that, philosophically, control of access to the corporate network should be regulated by the configuration of the firewall itself. HTTP tunnelling makes it impossible for

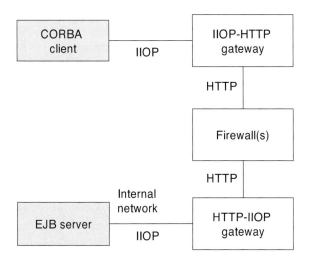

Figure 16.24. The principle of HTTP tunnelling. Incoming IIOP requests are marshalled into HTTP messages and can cross HTTP-aware firewalls. On the friendly side of the firewall, they are unmarshalled into IIOP requests.

the firewall to discriminate between legitimate and illegitimate requests, leaving this job to the tunnelling product.

16.5.4 Alternatives to IIOP

The problems discussed above result from the use of IIOP, although other RMI schemes are not necessarily immune. For the developer, it is often tempting to avoid the use of IIOP and related techniques completely. If interoperability is not an issue (for example, the clients are developed in association with the EJB services and are tightly coupled to them), then the use of custom Web-tier proxies may be worth considering. However, the use of wide-area distributed objects is now sufficiently important that a lot of development effort is currently being put into defining standards for interoperable RMI-over-HTTP protocols.

Custom Web tier proxies

The problems discussed above are particularly troublesome when the enterprise requires Internet access to EJBs; using IIOP internally does not have the same implications. But why would we want to make intra-EJB calls across the Internet anyway? In some, predominantly business-to-business, applications, this may unavoidable. However, if the EJBs are being used to support thick end-user clients, then the use of IIOP can often be avoided altogether.

The main reason for using thick clients, rather than thin (Web browser) clients, is that it allows additional functionality that is not available to a browser. While a thick client can be developed to make direct IIOP calls on EJBs, the developer can implement a client that communicates with a servlet (using HTTP or HTTPS), and the servlet in turn calls the requisite EJBs (Figure 16.25).

In this strategy, the data exchanged is HTTP; no IIOP access is required across the firewall. Of course, some extra effort is required of the developer. It will be necessary to add functionality to the thick client to convert its EJB calls to HTTP messages, and to implement the proxy servlet so that it receives the request, calls the EJB, formats the results, and sends then back to the client.

Since this is a custom proxy, it is at the developer's discretion how to format the data exchanged between the proxy servlet and the client. The client-to-servlet data needs to be in a format suitable for passing in an HTTP GET or POST request, while the servlet-to-client data can be anything that can be put into an HTTP response (that is, anything to which a MIME type can be assigned). In practice, most developers use XML for communication in both directions, because there is widespread parser support for it.

Let's see how this might work in practice. Suppose a thick client for the *Prestige Bike Hire* application wants to display the bookings for a particular motorcycle in a particular date range. This operation is handled by the `BookingAgent` EJB. The client may send a message like this to the proxy servlet for this EJB, inside a POST request:

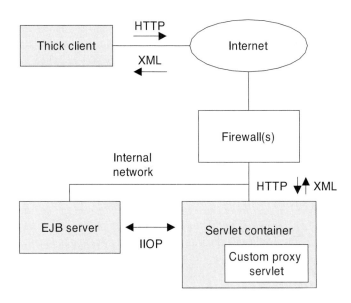

Figure 16.25. Using a servlet as a custom proxy for an EJB. The client and the servlet pass data in HTTP messages, and the servlet calls the EJB on behalf of the client. In this example, the method call data is represented as XML, although of course the developer could use any format that can be wrapped up in an HTTP request and response.

```
<booking-agent-request>
  <get-bookings regno="x123 xyz" start="2002-10-2" end="2002-11-2"/>
</booking-agent-request>
```

The proxy servlet uses `request.getParameter()` to extract this XML message from the request, parses it, creates a `BookingAgent` EJB, calls `BookingAgent.find BookingsInRange()` with the arguments supplied by the client, and then generates a response to be sent back to the client. The response in this case may be something like this:

```
<booking-agent-response>
  <booking start="2002-10-2" end="2002-10-5" custid="1234"/>
  <booking start="2002-10-7" end="2002-10-15" custid="4567"/>
</booking-agent-response>
```

The client parses the XML, extracts the booking information, and does whatever is required with it.

You probably won't be surprised to find that some complexities have been skimmed over in this discussion. For example, in a practical application we would need to deal with the problems of authenticating clients, encryption, and session management (suppose that the EJB were stateful, and that subsequent requests from the same client should be delivered to the same EJB instance). In addition, some mechanism must be provided to enable the client to receive notification of failures on the server. The problems of authentication and encryption can both be dealt with by using HTTPS as the carrier, rather than HTTP. The SSL session ID could also be used to locate the stateful session EJB for a particular client. Failures can be handled simply by defining a message format for encoding exceptions. So these problems are soluble.

In practice, the problem with the scheme described above is this: If the application is complex, and there are many different method calls on many different EJBs, then by the time development is finished, you will have developed your own RMI protocol. It's probably fair to say that the world does not need any more RMI protocols. For this reason, there is currently a lot of interest in standardizing protocols for doing RMI over HTTP/S.

Interoperable RMI/HTTPS protocols

Ideally, an RMI scheme should be interoperable, allow the data to be encrypted, allow the caller to be authenticated, and be acceptable to firewalls. We have seen that there is already a transport protocol that supports all these features: HTTP over SSL (HTTPS). So the question that naturally arises is 'can we do RMI using HTTPS as a transport'? What would be required in order for this to work?

- First, we need a system for encoding the arguments to methods (which may be objects) and their return values into an HTTPS request and response. We have already seen a technique that can do this: SOAP/HTTP (page 42).

- Then we need something on the server that can take the SOAP document (strictly, the *SOAP envelope*) from the HTTP request and demarshall it into a method call on an EJB, and then marshall the return value into a new SOAP response. The Apache SOAP implementation already supports these operations, implemented as servlets. The servlets are installed on a Web server that has access to the EJB container. This Web server's HTTP(S) port must be open on the firewall, but this is the only port that needs to be open.

- Finally we need something that can use the home and remote interface of an EJB to generate client-side stubs that are compatible with SOAP/HTTP.

Does any of this sound familiar? It should: The process of doing RMI over HTTP using XML as the data format was described in detail right back in Chapter 2 (page 41). The ability to expose EJB functionality via HTTP is at the heart of the 'Web services' model, which has shown such an explosive growth of interest in the last year or so. In fact, the draft EJB 2.1 specification proposes a new scheme by which EJBs will offer 'Web service client view' to accompany the existing distributed and local client views.

16.6   Summary

We have seen that the security of an EJB-based application is controlled by policies set up by the developer and implemented by the EJB container and by the transport protocol it uses. Although the security architecture is complex, most of the complexity is concealed from the EJB developer. The developer's roles are to define the application roles and assign method permissions to those roles. Optionally, programmatic techniques can be used to supplement this 'declarative' security model. In an enterprise application, securing the method invocations on EJBs will not offer protection against eavesdropping and impersonation, and certificate-based encryption techniques may be used on the intercontainer protocol itself. The certificates can also be used as part of an authentication process. Although IIOP traffic can be encrypted, IIOP may not be compatible with maintaining a high level of enterprise security, and there is considerable interest at the moment in developing strategies that allow intercontainer calls to be made over HTTPS.

Chapter 17

EJBs and the Web tier

Overview

This chapter describes in outline how to implement a Web-based user interface to an EJB application, focusing specifically on the issues of integrating EJBs to servlets and JSP pages. The chapter begins with a brief overview of the techniques that are available for server-side generation of dynamic content, particularly servlets and JSPs. It then describes how servlets and JSPs can initialize, locate, and use EJBs. Where stateful session EJBs are used, this requires synchronizing EJB instances to the servlet session; this technique is described in detail. Finally, we discuss the additional complexities involved in building an application in which the Web components are not hosted in a application server, but in a standalone JSP/servlet engine.

Many EJB-based applications require a graphical user interface to be implemented in a Web browser. Often this is to support Internet access, but increasingly Web browsers are used for intranet applications because the user interface is so familiar. In addition, the HTTP protocol is well-tolerated by firewalls, so the use of Web clients makes security management easier.

It is also increasingly common to support business-to-business applications using Web services. These use technology similar to Web-based user interfaces, although of course the client is not a Web browser and the data exchanged is not HTML.

Most Web servers do not have any built-in ability to interact with EJBs (although nothing prevents this, in principle). This means that the user interface must be provided using server-side Web programming techniques. JSPs and servlets are particularly relevant here, as they integrate naturally with Java components, but we will consider other possibilities as well.

17.1   Web technology and application servers

The term 'Web server' usually refers to a product that can provide access to static HTML pages using the HTTP protocol, although increasingly Web servers are providing built-in support for dynamic page generation. On its own, a static HTML page cannot contain dynamic information derived from method calls on EJBs; to do this we require some programmatic way of generating Web content. There are many such techniques in widespread use, including JSP pages or servlets (which are functionally equivalent, as we shall see), CGI scripting, and Microsoft's *Active server pages* (ASP) technology. All can be used to provide a user interface to an EJB application. Other techniques are available, but are less widely used with EJBs.

JSPs and servlets *Java server pages* (JSPs) and servlets are essentially Java platform classes that extend the functionality of a Web server, by allowing it to respond to requests by the invocation of program code. The difference between the two is that while a servlet is a standard Java platform class, and must be compiled before being deployed, a JSP is an HTML page with programmatic content, which can be translated into a servlet on demand. We will have more to say about these technologies later. At present, the use of JSP and servlets is rapidly becoming the industry standard for server-side dynamic content generation, and is likely to eclipse the alternatives (CGI and Web server modules, for example).

To use servlets requires software that can load and invoke the appropriate Java platform classes as requested by the browser. JSPs additionally require software that can translate the page into a servlet, and then compile it. These two pieces of software are nearly always combined into a single product, which I shall refer to in this chapter as a 'JSP/servlet engine.'

Because JSPs and servlets are ultimately Java platform classes, they can readily be integrated with EJBs using similar techniques to those we have already seen for standalone clients implemented in the Java programming language.

Active server pages 'Active server pages' (ASP) is a proprietary system developed by Microsoft. It allows Web server functionality to be extended using programmatic content, usually implemented in C or C++. ASP pages can readily be extended to make use of distributed components based on Microsoft's *DCOM* (distributed component object model). In principle, therefore, EJB access via a DCOM-CORBA bridge should be possible (see page 9). The use of ASP is beyond the scope of this book.

CGI scripting CGI ('common gateway interface') scripting is one of the earliest techniques for generating dynamic Web content. Despite the term 'scripting,' a CGI program need not be implemented in a scripting language (like Perl), but can be a native-code executable written, for example, in C or C++. Java is *not* a good choice for CGI, for reasons that will become obvious later.

When the Web server receives a request from the browser that corresponds to a CGI script, it runs the script in a separate operating system process and pipes the output back to the browser. The script must parse the HTTP request and generate HTML as part of its execution.

A CGI script is an independent operating system process, and if it interacts with EJBs, it does so exactly as would a standalone IIOP client. There are no established techniques for implementing CGI-EJB connectivity, so it is difficult to give general advice. In any event, such matters are beyond the scope of this book. The fact that each CGI invocation is a separate operating system process is one of its most important disadvantages. In most operating systems, process set-up overheads are considerable. If Java were used, there would be the additional overhead of initializing a JVM for invocation.

Web server modules Although CGI allows the use of native machine code for generating dynamic Web content, with the performance and flexibility that this entails, CGI is not practical for systems with a heavy client load, as we have seen. If you really must use native code, and want to avoid CGI overheads, most Web servers allow third-party code to be integrated directly into the Web server infrastructure. The code is typically supplied as dynamically linkable libraries (Windows) or shared objects (Unix), and made known to the Web server through a configuration file. These libraries are known variously as 'plug-ins,' 'modules,' or 'connectors,' depending on the product. The APIs needed to use this technique are usually well-documented, as many products use it as the core of their own functionality.

Web server modules can, in principle, interact with EJBs in the same way as a standalone CORBA client, provided that the EJB server supports IIOP, and you have a suitable ORB library for the programming language you intend to use (usually C++).

Of all the techniques currently available for dynamic content generation, Web-server modules almost certainly offer the best speed and flexibility. However, this technology has all the pragmatic disadvantages of CGI: The developer must do a great deal of work, including parsing requests and managing client sessions. Added to this are the specific disadvantages of this technique: It is entirely vendor-specific and not portable, and faulty code can disrupt the other operations of the Web server as well as the module itself.

17.1.1 Servlets

A full description of servlet development is beyond the scope of this chapter,[1] which attempts to deal primarily with the integration of servlets with EJBs. The following brief overview may be considered the bare minimum of information needed to begin this type of development.

A servlet is a Java program class that has a well-defined interface to a Web server. Like stateless session EJBs, servlets are always pooled, and a small number of servlet instances may support a large number of clients. Unlike EJBs, servlets are multithreaded by default, and should be designed with this in mind.

---

[1] A good book on this subject is Hunter *et al.*, *Java Servlet Programming* (1998) (full details in bibliography).

A servlet must implement the `javax.servlet.Servlet` interface, directly or indirectly. This interface has two methods that are particularly important: `service()` and `init()`. The container will call the `init()` method exactly once, to allow the servlet to initialize itself. Thereafter it will call `service()` whenever a request is delivered from a Web browser. The `service()` method must handle the request completely, parsing the request data and generating output for the browser. In practice, most developers don't write classes that implement `Servlet` directly. Instead, they extend the functionality of `javax.servlet.http.HttpServlet`. This class already has the functionality to parse an HTTP request and to generate an HTTP response header. The default behaviour of the `service()` method of the `HttpServlet` class is to call a specific method according to the type of the request from the browser: `doGet()` for a GET request and `doPost` for a POST request, for example. So typically the implementation of a servlet consists of writing a class that extends `HttpServlet` and overrides the `doGet()` and `doPost()` methods. In general, these two methods will produce the same output, so typically they will be implemented to dispatch to a common method.

A simple, but complete, example is shown in Listing 17.1.

Listing 17.1: **A minimal servlet; this one simply displays a title and the current date and time.**

```
    package simpleservlets;
    import javax.servlet.*;
    import javax.servlet.http.*;
    import java.io.PrintWriter;
5   import java.util.Date;

    public class SimpleServlet1 extends HttpServlet
    {
    public void doGet(HttpServletRequest request,
10      HttpServletResponse response)
            throws ServletException, java.io.IOException
        {
        processRequest(request, response);
        }
15
    public void doPost(HttpServletRequest request,
        HttpServletResponse response)
            throws ServletException, java.io.IOException
        {
20      processRequest(request, response);
        }

    protected void processRequest (HttpServletRequest request,
        HttpServletResponse response)
25          throws ServletException, java.io.IOException
        {
        System.out.println
            ("Entering SimpleServlet1.processRequest()");
```

```
30      PrintWriter  out  =  response.getWriter ();
        response.setContentType (" text/html" );
        out.println ("<h1>Simple  servlet  1</h1>" );
        out.println ("Today's  date  is:  "  + new  Date ());
        out.close ();
35
        System.out.println
           ("Leaving  SimpleServlet1.processRequest ()" );
        }

40   public void  init ()
        {
        System.out.println
           ("Servlet  initialization  goes  here!");
        }
45   }
```

The use of a single servlet instance, or a small pool, has important performance
benefits, but it is not without problems. Particularly significant is providing a place
to store data that is specific to a particular client's conversation with the server. For
example, consider an online shopping application: The end-user browses the product
catalogue, and adds selected products to a 'shopping cart.' This shopping cart has
to be maintained on the server, but it can't be stored in the instance variables of a
servlet, as these instance variables are shared by all clients (this is a very common
mistake by developers who are new to this technology).

Instead, the servlet container maintains a list of `HttpSession` objects and keys
them to clients. To get the session object for the current client, a servlet makes a call
on the `HttpRequest` object passed into the `service()` method by the container,
like this:

```
HttpSession  session  =  request.getSession (true );
```

The argument `true` in the example above instructs the container to create a
new session for this client, if one does not already exist.

The session object behaves like a hash table, in that the servlet can insert any
name-value mappings it likes into the session. The container ensures that the servlet
is always presented with the correct session object for the client currently being
serviced. The techniques it uses to do this are (mostly) invisible to the developer;
typically, it will send a cookie to the browser containing a number that identifies the
session. The browser will present this cookie in each subsequent request, allowing
the container to locate the correct session object.

Almost all Web-based applications will require some form of session management, even if only to maintain the user's login ID across servlet invocations. This
has implications for the EJB developer, as both stateful session beans and servlet
session objects can be used to store client state data, and it will be necessary to
determine an optimal distribution of client state data between these two locations.
This issue will be discussed later.

Because the HTTP protocol is stateless (that is, it uses transient connections between browser and server), it is difficult for the servlet container to determine when the user has finished using the application. Although the application developer will usually provide the user interface with some kind of 'log out' facility, we can't rely on users to use it. They are equally likely just to close the Web browser or switch the workstation off. For this reason, servlet sessions usually persist in the container's memory until timed out. The fact that the session object may outlive the client's interaction has important security implications, as we shall see.

17.1.2   Java server pages

One of the significant problems with servlets is that even simple, static HTML has to be generated programmatically. So it is common to see a mixture of Java code and HTML, often on the same line. While this does not cause a problem in a technical sense, it does cause problems with development and maintenance. To develop and maintain good servlets requires a good deal of skill working with both Java and HTML. While there are some people that excel in both these areas, they are rare, and it would be a very optimistic enterprise that relied for its success on obtaining a good supply of such people.

A full description of JSP technology is beyond the scope of this book,[2] and only a very brief overview is presented here.

JSP technology reverses the roles of presentation and code in a servlet. The content of a JSP is assumed to be HTML unless indicated otherwise. Programmatic content is denoted by JSP-specific tags, of which there are a large number. In practice, a JSP is translated into a servlet, so the capabilities of both these technologies are very similar. However, because the translation is usually done at request time, no particular software development skills are required for the creation and management of JSPs. This makes it feasible for this task to be undertaken by an HTML author, rather than a programmer.

The example in Listing 17.2 shows a JSP that is equivalent in function to the servlet in Listing 17.1. The tag

```
<%@ page import="java.util.Date" %>
```

is an instruction to include an **import** statement in the generated Java servlet. This is required for the **Date()** class to be accessible. The section

```
<%!
public void jspInit()
  // ...
%>
```

results in the declaration of the method **jspInit()**, which contains purely Java code. This method is called by the JSP engine to initialize the JSP, and is equivalent

---

[2]A good book is Fields and Kolb, *Web Programming with Java Server Pages* (2000) (full details in bibliography).

to `init()` in a servlet. Most JSP pages do not require a specific initialization block, but it is useful for initializing EJB references, as we shall see.

Listing 17.2: **A JSP page with equivalent functionality to that of the servlet shown above. Note that there is a somewhat better demarcation between HTML and programmatic content.**

```
<%@ page import="java.util.Date" %>
<h1>Simple servlet 1</h1>
Today's date is <%= new Date() %>

<%!
public void jspInit()
  {
    System.out.println ("JSP initialization goes here!");
  }
%>
```

17.1.3   JSP/Servlet engines

In practice, JSP pages are translated into servlets, and can thereafter be handled by the same software as servlets. As a result, servlet and JSP engines are usually combined into a single piece of software, which I shall refer to in this chapter as a 'JSP/servlet engine.' This engine is responsible for managing the pools of servlet instances, initializing servlets on creation, dispatching requests to and between servlets, buffering output to be returned to the client, and translating JSPs to servlets when requested by a browser.

An JSP/servlet engine can be integrated into a Web server in a number of different ways (Figure 17.1).

Gotcha!

Using a dedicated Web server to handle static Web content is very effective at improving the overall performance of an application server. This is because Web servers are highly optimized for handling HTML pages, while JSP/servlet engines are not. However, it takes considerable expertise to take advantage of this architecture and it does lead to additional complexities in development.

17.1.4   Servlets and JSPs in the J2EE model

Not all JSP/servlet engines are J2EE-compliant, but where they are, we can make certain assumptions about their operation.

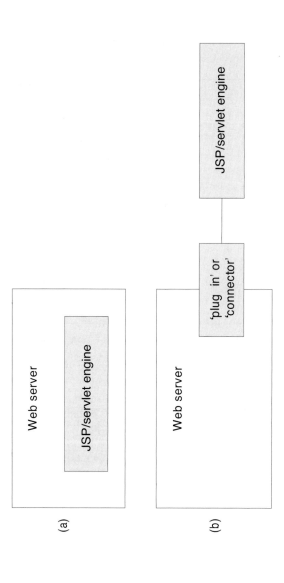

Figure 17.1. Common configurations for integrating a Web server with a JSP/servlet engine. (a) The JSP/servlet engine is an integral part of the Web server; this is the approach taken by some Java-based Web servers (e.g., *Tomcat* in standalone mode). (b) The Web server communicates with the JSP/servlet engine via a Web-server 'plug-in' or 'connector'; that is, the JSP/servlet engine extends the Web server using a proprietary API. For example, we can use *Tomcat* to provide JSP and servlet functionality to the Apache Web server this way. The Web server and the JSP/servlet engine may be part of the same operating system process, different processes on the same host, or on different hosts.

- Servlets and JSPs are packaged and deployed in a *WAR* ('Web archive') file. This is a standard Java JAR archive, with a particular layout. The WAR file can contain static Web content (HTML, images, etc.), as well as JSPs and servlets. It will also contain a deployment descriptor, `web.xml`. As with EJBs, the file and the deployment descriptor are usually assembled using development tools, and won't be discussed further here.

- The deployment descriptor can contain configuration information, such as EJB name mappings, environment variables, and security information.

- The servlet container supports the same role-based security model as the EJB container (see Chapter 16 for a more detailed discussion).

17.1.5   Application servers

The term 'application server' is not a precise one and, contrary to common belief, was in widespread use before the introduction of Java. So to say that an application server is something that supports Java components in not strictly true. For example, iPlanet Application Server (Versions 6.0, 6.5) supports component-based Web programming in C and C++ (iPlanet calls these components 'AppLogics').

In modern usage, however, the term is normally used to denote a *J2EE compliant* application server. Such a product typically consists of an integrated Web server, JSP/servlet engine, and EJB server, often with a built-in transaction manager or database. In some products (iPlanet Application Server is an example), the Web server and JSP/servlet engine are separate processes and may be located on different hosts, but in most cases, they are part of the same process. Similarly, the EJB engine and the JSP/servlet engine may be separate processes, or they may not. All this should not be of concern to the developer; so long as the product is J2EE-compliant, it should be able to deploy a standard EAR file, and no code changes should be necessary.

17.2   JSP/Servlet-EJB connectivity

A JSP or servlet can locate and call methods on an EJB in a very similar manner to that used by a standalone client. However, there are a few subtleties of which the developer should be aware. In general, the implementation of the servlet or JSP will depend to a certain extent on whether the Web container and the EJB container are part of an integrated J2EE-compliant application server, or essentially separate systems. This distinction can lead to a slight loss of portability, which the developer may want to deal with. In this section, we will discuss connectivity only within the confines of a single application server environment, while the issues of integrating disparate products will be dealt with later in the chapter.

17.2.1   Basic principles

A J2EE-compliant application server will usually support EJBs, servlets, and JSPs, deployed via a standard EAR file. Because the application server is J2EE-compliant,

the developer can make certain simplifying assumptions about its support of for
JSP/Servlet-EJB connectivity, including the following:

- The servlet or JSP can use `java:comp/env` names to locate an EJB home
  object if desired.

- The developer should not have to supply JNDI configuration data to `Initial
  Context`.

- The deployment process will install RMI stubs, where needed, automatically.

However, these assumptions can only be applied to application components deployed as part of a single application. A product is not required, for example, to
allow a JSP page to use a `java:comp/env` name to refer to an EJB in a *different
application,* and in some cases this may not even be allowed.

> ## Hint
>
> The standard unit of deployment to a J2EE-compliant application
> server is the EAR file. Many products allow WAR and JAR files
> to be deployed separately, without encapsulating them in an EAR
> file. However, the server has no way to know when these compo-
> nents form parts of the same application and when they don't. Its
> built-in security manager may act to prevent servlets and JSPs
> from loading classes such as the EJB's home and remote inter-
> faces, which will prevent the application from working. Although
> many developers prefer to work this way—without packing an
> EAR file—it may be necessary to tweak the server's configuration
> or CLASSPATH to get this to work.

Looking up the home object

With a J2EE-compliant application server, servlets and JSPs get access to EJBs
by looking up their home objects, just like a standalone client. However, because
servlets and JSPs are considered to be 'J2EE components,' they can—and should—
use `java:comp/env` name lookups, just like an EJB would if it wanted to locate
another EJB. So with this strategy, a servlet can locate the `BookingManager` EJB
like this:

```
InitialContext ic = new InitialContext();
bookingManagerHome = (BookingManagerHome)
  PortableRemoteObject.narrow
    (ic.lookup("java:comp/env/ejb/MyBookingManager"),
      BookingAgentHome.class);
```

(we will discuss where and when this lookup should occur later). As `ejb/MyBooking` `Manager` is not the JNDI name of an EJB, we must map the name in the `lookup()` call to the real JNDI name. With the *J2EE Reference Implementation*, this process is carried out using the 'EJB Refs' tab of the WAR file page, as shown in Figure 17.2.

The advantage of using `java:comp/env` names here is exactly the same as for EJBs: Names can be resolved across servlets and EJBs from different developers, without code changes.

Hint

This chapter generally assumes that a servlet will retrieve a remote reference to an EJB, not a local reference. However, in EJB 2.0, it is theoretically possible for a servlet to retrieve a local reference and make intra-JVM calls on the EJB. As well as being somewhat faster, the call-by-reference semantics should allow us to solve one of the most troublesome problems in servlet-EJB interaction: the inability of the EJB to stream data back to the servlet. The servlet engine will be able to stream data back to the browser, and there-fore show progress to the user, provided that it is able to generate the data quickly enough. However, the synchronous nature of EJB interactions has made this technique somewhat difficult to apply when the servlet relies heavily on EJBs as its source of data. We can't pass an output stream from a servlet to a remote EJB and have it stream data back, because streams aren't serializable. With local references, we now have the possibility for a servlet to pass a stream to an EJB. However, whether this is a good idea or not requires some thought. The J2EE Reference Implementation, and the iPlanet application server, locate the servlet engine and the EJB server in the same JVM. This allows local calling to be used. But if a product uses different JVMs, we could have a problem. In short, using local calling semantics between servlets and EJBs may not be portable, and requires caution.

Default InitialContext

In the previous example, the `InitialContext` object was created by calling the default constructor:

```
InitialContext ic = new InitialContext();
```

that is, the default JNDI configuration is to be used for subsequent `lookup()` op-erations. You may remember that the *J2EE Reference Implementation* makes the

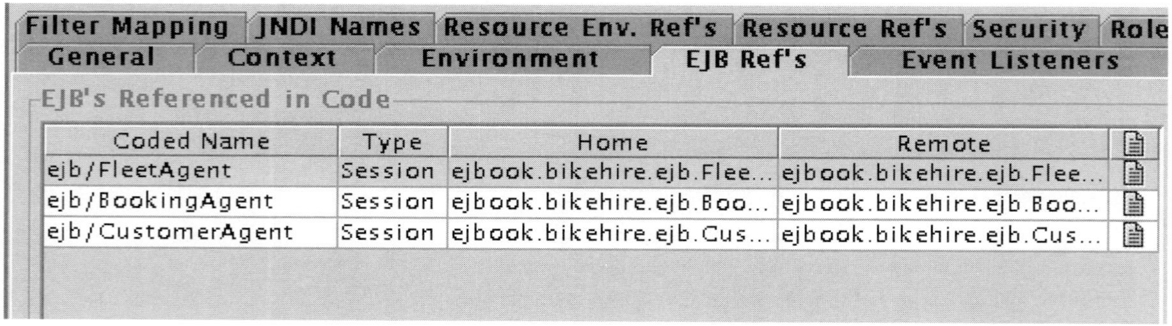

Figure 17.2. Mapping the java:comp/env names of the EJBs onto their JNDI names in the *Prestige Bike Hire* application.

assumption that the name server is on the same host as the EJB client. When using an application server, this may be true—the servlet engine and the EJB server may be colocated—but in a system with load balancing, it equally may not be. In either case, it is the *responsibility of the application server* to ensure that the `InitialContext` defaults are correct. The developer should not have to specify JNDI properties to `InitialContext` to enable the servlet to locate an EJB that is part of the same application. Of course, if the servlet needs to locate an EJB in a different application, on a different server, then we are bypassing the *J2EE Specification*; you will have to proceed as described below for non-J2EE compliant servers. If the developer attempts to code the network location of an EJB, it may well break the application server's load balancing system, as it won't be able to divert EJB requests to different hosts.

Installation of stubs

When an EJB client makes a remote call on an EJB, it will do so through a stub. To run a standalone client in the Java programming language you will have had to ensure that the stubs—usually generated dynamically at deployment time—are available on the client's CLASSPATH. There have been numerous examples of this so far in this book. When deploying on an application server, it is the server's responsibility to ensure that stubs are installed in the correct place: Neither the developer nor the installer should not have to configure this.

17.2.2   Practicalities of JSP/servlet-EJB connectivity

As we have seen, servlets and JSPs can make calls on EJBs in much the same way as standalone clients. However, there are a number of issues to be aware of, and this section discusses some of the most important ones.

Threading issues

By default, servlets and JSPs are assumed by the container to be thread-safe; this is the opposite of the default for EJBs, which run in a single-threaded environment. The developer needs to take a bit of trouble to ensure that there is no conflict between these modes of operation. In particular, when coding a servlet or JSP that makes method calls on an EJB, the developer has to take care to ensure that the `service()` method does not make illegal concurrent calls on the EJB object of an EJB. How might this arise in practice?

Suppose that a servlet's `init()` method locates a stateful session EJB, calls `create()` on it, and stores the resulting reference in an instance variable. When clients make requests, the servlet's `doGet()` method calls a method on this stored reference. Because the servlet is assumed to be thread-safe, the `doGet()` method may be entered on multiple threads, causing the EJB object to be entered concurrently. This is illegal for stateful session EJBs, for reasons discussed in Section 15.4, but is acceptable for stateless session EJBs.

Note that it *is* acceptable to store a reference to the home object, whatever the type of the EJB, and make `create()` calls on it, even if they are concurrent. The reason is that while concurrent calls on `create()` may result in concurrent calls on the home object, they *don't* result in concurrent calls in the implementation instance, even with stateful EJBs. This is because the container will have instantiated a new instance of the implementation before calling any methods on it. Each separate concurrent thread is thus assumed to be a new client of the EJB, and each has its own EJB object.

Although it is not usual for servlets or JSPs to make direct method calls on an entity EJB, if this is done, it is safe to make multithreaded calls on the the EJB object (for the same reasons as for stateless session EJBs).

Hint

You can force the servlet engine to treat a servlet as single-threaded simply by adding `implements SingleThreadModel` to the servlet's class definition. This interface specifies no methods: Its presence simply alerts the container that the servlet is not thread-safe. J2EE-compliant JSP/servlet engines are required to support this functionality, but ...

Gotcha!

they aren't required to support it efficiently. At least one commercial product deals with `SingleThreadModel` by making all calls on the affected servlet in a `synchronized` block. It should be obvious that this will impose a significant throughput bottleneck. In theory, a JSP/servlet engine can handle single-threaded servlets in the same way as stateless session EJBs: by creating a pool of instances and run one thread in each. Most products now work this way.

Locating and using EJBs

As there is only one instance of the home object for any given EJB, a servlet or JSP can usefully locate the home object at initialization time and store it in an instance variable. The request-handling methods can then use the stored home object to create or lookup EJBs as required. This technique is illustrated in Listing 17.3 (this example uses the `PrincipalTest` EJB which is described in more detail in Chapter 16. Here it is used simply for convenience, but elsewhere it will be used to demonstrate Web-tier authentication).

Listing 17.3: **A servlet that uses the** `PrincipalTest` **EJB to display the user's security principal.**

```
package ejbook.simpleservlets;
import java.io.PrintWriter;
import javax.servlet.*;
import javax.servlet.http.*;
import javax.rmi.*;
import javax.naming.*;
import javax.ejb.*;
import java.util.Date;
import com.kevinboone.ejb_book.principaltest.*;

public class SimpleServlet2 extends HttpServlet
{
// Store a reference to the home object
protected PrincipalTestHome principalTestHome = null;

// initOK is set to true if the EJB reference can
// be initialized
protected boolean initOK = false;

public void doGet(HttpServletRequest request,
    HttpServletResponse response)
        throws ServletException, java.io.IOException
    {
    processRequest(request, response);
    }

public void doPost(HttpServletRequest request,
    HttpServletResponse response)
        throws ServletException, java.io.IOException
    {
    processRequest(request, response);
    }

protected void processRequest (HttpServletRequest request,
    HttpServletResponse response)
        throws ServletException, java.io.IOException
    {
    System.out.println
        ("Entering SimpleServlet2.processRequest()");

    PrintWriter out = response.getWriter();
    response.setContentType("text/html");
    out.println("<h1>Simple servlet 2</h1>");
    if (initOK)
        {
        try
            {
            PrincipalTest principalTest
                = principalTestHome.create();
            out.println ("My principal is: "
                + principalTest.getPrincipal());
            principalTest.remove();
            }
        catch (CreateException e)
            {
```

```
            out.println
               ("Sorry, something went wrong while creating the EJB");
            }
         catch (RemoveException e)
60          {
            out.println
               ("Sorry, something went wrong while removing the EJB");
            }
         }
65    else
      {
      out.println
         ("Sorry, this servlet did not initialize correctly.");
      }
70    out.close();

      System.out.println
         ("Leaving SimpleServlet2.processRequest()");
      }
75
   public void init ()
      {
      try
         {
80       System.out.println("Entering SimpleServlet2.init()");
         InitialContext c = new InitialContext();
         principalTestHome = (PrincipalTestHome)
            PortableRemoteObject.narrow
               (c.lookup ("java:comp/env/ejb/PrincipalTest"),
85                PrincipalTestHome.class);
         System.out.println("Leaving SimpleServlet2.init()");
         initOK = true;
         }
      catch (Exception e)
90          {
         e.printStackTrace();
         initOK = false;
         }
      }
   }
95  }
```

By locating the EJB at initialization time, the overhead of a JNDI lookup for
each use of the home object is avoided. In practice, it may lead to more readable
and reusable code if the location of session EJBs is encapsulated in a helper class.
Such classes have a variety of nicknames, of which *locator bean* is probably the most
widespread. The use of the term 'bean' rather than 'class' here *is* significant, as we
shall see.

Using the `init()` method in a servlet to locate a home object is perfectly standard practice; however, the technique does not extend very well to JSPs. While it
is possible to use the `jspInit()` method for this purpose, it does not sit comfort-
ably with the design philosophy that underlies JSP, notably that JSP pages should
remain free of explicit Java code, as far as possible.

Happily, the JSP architecture provides a mechanism for access to arbitrary Java platform classes that requires the embedding of little or no explicit Java. This is provided via the `jsp:useBean` tag. The (simplified) syntax of this tag is as follows:

```
<jsp:useBean id=[instanceName]
  class=[className]
  scope=[scopeId]
/>
```

It is important for the EJB developer to appreciate that the 'Bean' in 'useBean' is *not* an Enterprise JavaBean, but a 'standard' JavaBean (we will discuss ways to fix this later). A JavaBean—as far as JSP is concerned—is simply a Java platform class that has been written according to certain rules about method names. Following these rules allows the JSP engine to pass form data into a helper class in a very elegant, transparent way. As far as EJBs are concerned, we will be making use of the `useBean` technique simply to control the instantiation of helper classes; the more sophisticated form-handling issues are beyond the scope of this book.

The following example of the **useBean** tag *might* be appropriate[3] for initializing a helper class in a JSP:

```
<jsp:useBean id="pageHelper"
  scope="page"
  class="com.kevinboone.bikehire.web.PageHelper"
/>
```

This tag causes the construction of one instance of `PageHelper` at the start of the JSP's `service` method. The JSP will be able to refer to this instance as `pageHelper`.

If the interface between JSP and the EJB application is simple, it might be sufficient to provide one helper class for getting access to all the EJBs accessible to the JSPs. When the JSP page wants to call a method on, say, the `BookingManager` EJB, it might use the `PageHelper` object like this:

```
<%
BookingAgent bookingAgent =
  pageHelper.createBookingAgent();
Collection c =
  bookingAgent.findBookingsInRange(...);
%>
```

The JSP can then proceed to format the `Collection` of bookings returned by the EJB. The `createBookingAgent()` method does whatever is required to bring about the creation of the EJB, including finding the home object and calling `create()` on it. In other words, most of the logic of EJB access is encapsulated in the locator bean (so strictly it's a 'locator/creator bean').

---

[3]As we shall see, the *Prestige Bike Hire* application does not allow EJB access from JSPs, but uses a servlet to coordinate EJB access.

A locator bean for use with JSPs needs to be designed carefully to minimize the amount of Java code that leaks out into the JSP itself. In particular, methods on these beans need to be able to carry out initialization internally, so that JSPs don't have to.

The simplicity of the user interface in the *Prestige Bike Hire* application may make it practicable to use a JSP-only Web tier, but in practice it would probably be unmaintainable. Many developers argue that JSP should contain no Java at all, which requires the use either of combined JSP/servlet interfaces or custom tag libraries. We will examine these techniques later.

Hint

Although JSP pages can make direct reference to EJBs, it is not considered good practice to use JSPs to carry out request processing and data manipulation. Modern Web application design favors using a small number of servlets (possibly only one) to handle all incoming requests, generate an object containing results, and forward that object to a JSP for display. This technique is discussed briefly later.

17.2.3 Session management issues

Consider a Web-based application that asks the user a series of questions (a 'customer satisfaction' survey, for example). Some responses may lead to different sets of questions being presented subsequently. The responses to these questions are stored and, at the end of the session, an analysis of the responses is emailed to an administrator for perusal (or stored in a database, or whatever). The key issue here is that there is a conversational state involving the client and the server: Each stage in the conversation depends on the results of previous steps. Another example is the popular 'shopping cart' application, where the application has to maintain the contents of the shopping cart over an extended period of time.

In applications of this sort, as we have already discussed, the data representing the conversational state is usually stored on the server, not the client. Typically, a servlet-based application can use the `HttpSession` object for this purpose. However, when EJBs are involved, there is another possible storage location: the instance variables of stateful session EJBs. In the 'survey' example given, the servlet could create a stateful session EJB for each client and record the client's responses to questions by calling methods on that EJB. The EJB's instance variables would maintain the data supplied by the client, and another method could generate the summary at the end.

All this is fine, but how does the servlet locate the correct EJB for each client? When the servlet is invoked the first time for a given client, we want to call `create(...)` on the home object to create the EJB. Thereafter, we need to locate and use the previously created instance.

The solution is for the servlet to create the EJB and store a reference to its EJB object in the session object for that client. On each request, the servlet gets the current session and retrieves the EJB reference from it. In fact, we should store a handle to the EJB, not the reference—as described on page 487—as handles are serializable.

Code similar to the following may be used in the servlet's `doGet()` or `doPost()` methods.

```
   Session  session = request.getSession(true);
   Handle h = (Handle)session.getAttribute("ejb");
   if (h == null)
     {
5    myEJB = ... // create EJB
     session.setAttribute("ejb", myEJB.getHandle());
     }
   else
     myEJB = (MyEJB)PortableRemoteObject.narrow
10     (h.getEJBObject(), MyEJB.class);
```

This code checks whether an EJB has already been created and stored for this client[4] (line 3). If it has not, the servlet creates the EJB and stores its handle in the session (lines 5–7). If the EJB already exists, the servlet gets the EJB object from the stored handle (lines 9 and 10). Notice that, strictly speaking, the client should use `narrow()` on the return from `getEJBObject()`, just as it should on a JNDI `lookup()`.

When using this technique, we would ideally not store any other data in the session itself. Since the EJB can store whatever is required. So the developer is faced with a choice whether to use a stateful session EJB or a servlet session to store conversational data; it is probably not advisable to use both in the same application. The relative merits of the two as regards ease of use, maintenance, and portability have been widely argued, and there does not appear to be a consensus in favor of either. However, the developer will need to be aware of some subtle technical distinctions, which are not widely discussed.

Load balancing places constraints on sessional data In a load-balancing environment, the server's infrastructure can direct requests to different instances of the same component. If the component is associated with a client session, then that session needs to be made available to whichever component is handling the request. So, for example, when a servlet gets the session object and calls `getAttribute()` or `setAttribute()` on it, it is probably not interacting with an object in the same JVM but, effectively, with some networked data repository. Similarly, when an EJB method refers to its own instance variables, these may have to be synchronized with another instance across a network. It follows that, in both cases, the data that is being manipulated must be (i) serializable and (ii) small. If it is not serializable, it may be impossible to

---

[4]This code only works if the EJB is always created at the same time as the session. If not, it should check the return from `getAttribute()` as well.

transfer across the network, and if it is too large, then the overhead of session synchronization may overwhelm the system.

It is impossible to derive general guidelines from this issue; specific products vary greatly in the techniques used to achieve session synchronization. However, because servlet sessions are used only for storing client conversational data, it will likely be easier to accept the limitations on these objects imposed by the use of load sharing than it will for EJBs. In many systems, the restrictions that session sharing places on stateful EJBs makes them unsuitable for use in this environment.

Servlet session failover is well-developed Most commercial application servers handle servlet session failover very effectively. If one server fails, the load on the servlets it was hosting can be transferred automatically to a different server, and the servlets will continue to pick up their session data from the same central store. On a well-developed system, this should work seamlessly, without inconveniencing clients. This failover works because servlets interact with their sessions in a very simple way: They get an `HttpSession` object from the servlet container and call one of a small number of methods to insert and retrieve data. These methods can readily be implemented by the product vendor as networked interactions on a central session store.

It should be clear that stateful session EJB failover is considerably more difficult to implement. The 'state' of a stateful EJB is simply the values of all its instance variables. Some of these will be relevant to specific clients, while some will not. The EJB's methods do not normally interact with instance variables in the simple, stereotypical way that servlets interact with an `HttpSession`. This means that the EJB container will usually have to serialize the complete EJB instance, transfer its state over the network, and reconstruct an identical copy on a backup server. This process is slow and involves large network overheads. Few EJB products as yet have a viable scheme that works without placing severe limitations on the way the EJBs are coded.

It follows, I think, that if session failover is an important feature of a system, then the use of servlet sessions is more likely to be effective, at least with the current state of technology.

Neither technique protects against browser failure Typically, the JSP/servlet engine uses cookies to key the session objects to their respective browsers. Cookies may be volatile (stored in the browser's memory) or persistent (stored on disk). The application server *may* allow the administrator to choose which of these to use for session keying, but it would be a brave administrator that allowed persistent cookies in an application where user security was a prime concern. This is because such cookies will contain a session ID, and a knowledgeable person may be able to use this to take over another user's session.

Here's how it might work. Fred and Susan share a PC in an office. Fred starts a Web browser and logs in to an online banking application. He does some work, then closes the browser and logs out at the operating system level. Susan decides that she can't make ends meet on her salary, and determines to supplement it from Fred's bank accounts. She goes to the shared PC, logs in, and starts a Web browser. Because the PC operating system does not protect files on its hard disk, it is relatively straightforward for Susan to find Fred's cookies on the disk and copy the most recent one from the online banking application to her browser's cookie store. When she connects to the application, her browser dispatches Fred's cookie to the site, and Fred's session is resumed. Susan can now instruct the bank to transfer Fred's money wherever she likes.

To limit the risk of problems like this, most application servers do not use persistent cookies for session management. A volatile cookie is lost whenever the browser exits, and does not get stored on disk where it could be copied, so this is much safer. However, the implication is that *neither stateful session EJBs nor servlet sessions survive a browser crash*. In fact, both of these kinds of object may continue to exist in the container's JVM, but without the correct cookie, the client cannot get access to them. So, in effect, a browser crash loses the session.

Hint

Few EJB servers support session EJB failover, so those that do tend to flaunt it. However, its use often presents a headache for the developer and a significant performance penalty. As it does not protect the end user from the inconvenience of a browser crash, you have to think quite hard about the costs and benefits of adopting it. Generally if it is used, it will be for legal, rather than practical reasons. I have come across online banking applications whose designers have insisted on session EJB failover because they couldn't allow a session loss to be *their* fault. If a Web browser fails, that—they argue—is the customer's fault and therefore someone else's problem.

As a result, developers are increasingly avoiding the use of both stateful session EJBs and servlet sessions to store the data managed by the server on behalf of the client. Increasingly relational databases are being used for this; after all, the application most likely interacts with a database anyway, so we may as well use it for client state as well. If the application requires the user to log in, then we can key the session data to the login ID, rather than to a cookie. As the user probably only has one such ID in a given application, this allows a unique mapping between users and state. It also allows the user to move from one browser to another in the course of an extended interaction.

Ultimately neither servlet session nor stateful session EJB provides a satisfactory technique for storing long-term conversational data.

> Hint
>
> Servlet sessions can time out, if the browser has been inactive for
> a long period of time. It's worth checking for this at the top of
> each JSP page or the beginning of the request-handling methods
> in a servlet, and taking appropriate action (returning the user to
> a login page for example). The server won't do this automatically,
> and very odd errors can result from using a timed-out session.

17.2.4   JSP/servlet/EJB architecture issues

If almost all of an application's functionality is expressed in EJBs, and the user
interface is very simple, it may be possible to use a JSP-only Web tier, with a single
helper class to provide the interface between the JSPs and the EJBs.

Such a solution may not be appropriate for a more complex application. Objec-
tions that might be raised include the following.

- Although each JSP includes only a small amount of Java code concerned
  with EJB access, ideally there should be none at all. The maintainer of a
  JSP interface is likely to be a layout and presentation specialist, not a Java
  developer.

- The flow of control through the various JSP pages is not clear, nor easy to
  document. An *ad-hoc* system works for small projects because a single person
  can maintain an accurate mental model of the flow of control across the whole
  application, but this is less likely to be the case in a system with, say, 500
  JSP pages rather than 50.

Whether these arguments are compelling or not has been the subject of much—
often fierce—debate, and I don't propose to add to it. I will simply describe two
additional techniques for management of the interaction between EJBs and Web
components: servlet dispatch models and the use of custom tags, which may be
used in combination if desired.

Servlet dispatch models

In a servlet dispatch model, a JSP never interacts directly with EJBs. Instead,
incoming browser requests are always directed to a servlet, which formulates a
response and dispatches data to a JSP for display. There are a number of configurations for this model. Figure 17.3 shows the use of servlet/JSP pairs. In this
architecture, all requests are made on servlets, which can interact with EJBs as
required, using standard Java techniques. The servlets form the results into dedicated Java objects, which are then passed to JSPs to display. In this architecture,
JSPs are written such that whenever the browser makes a request, it makes it on

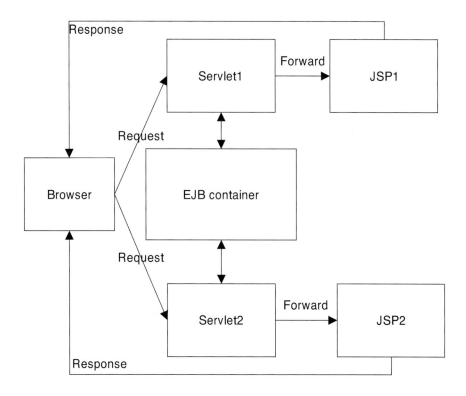

Figure 17.3. The use of servlet/JSP pairs for handling Web-EJB interaction.

a servlet, not on a JSP page. The JSPs and the servlets are tightly coupled and created in pairs.

The servlet dispatch model is taken to its logical conclusion in Figure 17.4. In this model, a single 'controller' servlet receives *all* incoming requests, processes them in conjunction with EJBs, forms the results into a Java object, and dispatches this to the appropriate JSP. In the JSPs, all form actions, links, and other user interface gestures are directed at the controller servlet, with request parameters indicating the action to be carried out.

In this model, only the controller servlet (and its supporting classes) make method calls on EJBs, so the issue of where and how to coordinate EJBs with Web components never even arises.

This centralized architecture has a lot in common with the 'model-view-controller' (MVC) pattern that was very prominent in the early days of object orientation. In this pattern, the 'view' (user interface) can view data represented by the 'model,' but can't modify it. The 'controller' accepts events from the view, and updates the model accordingly.

In the last year, MVC-type Web programming architectures have gained almost universal acceptance. The most common is known colloquially as 'model 2' (this

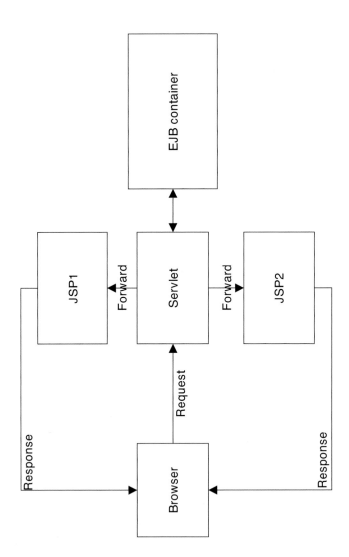

Figure 17.4. Using a single servlet to process requests and dispatch to a set of EJBs.

is not a J2EE term, it is a piece of jargon). In model 2 architecture, the 'view' is comprised of JSPs, servlets, or XSLT stylesheets, which have *no* application logic. All incoming requests are made on the controller (a servlet), which parses the requests, examines the state, and communicates with the 'model'—Java platform classes, DAOs, or EJBs. The controller then forms a value object and passes it to the appropriate view component for formatting. The central feature of this architecture is not that it uses servlets as the controller and JSP as the view—although this statement is commonly heard—but the all incoming requests go to the same component.

When model 2 design is used for mixed Web/EJB applications, it usually has the following features.

- The 'view' is usually comprised of JSPs (not servlets).

- The controller servlet (and possibly its supporting classes) is the only part of the Web tier that communicates with EJBs or carries out any business logic. The view servlets never interact with EJBs, even indirectly.

Because this architecture is so common, a number of frameworks have been developed to simplify its use. Of these, probably the most common is *Struts*, which is now part of the Jakarta project. The Web tier of the *Prestige Bike Hire* application was developed using *Struts*.

A *Struts* application has the following characteristics.

- The 'controller' servlet is, in fact, a generic request processor. The application developer does not write it, but specifies its behaviour in the form of an XML file. In this file, we provide mappings between the events that will be generated by the Web browser and the Java platform classes that will be provided to support them.

- A *Struts* application is provided mainly in the form of two kinds of specialized Java components: 'form beans' and 'action beans.' Form beans are JavaBeans whose properties model the data entered by the user on a Web form. Transferring the data between the Web page and the form bean is the job of the *Struts* framework. An action bean is a Java platform class that is invoked when the user clicks a link or submits a form. The framework automatically invokes the appropriate action bean based on the URL supplied by the browser and the state of the application.

- The *Struts* framework provides a set of general-purpose custom tag libraries (see below) for expressing programmatic operations (loops, branches, conditionals, etc.) without using any Java code. For example, the *Struts* `<logic: iterator>` tag is a substitute for coding operations on `Collections` in the JSP text.

- The *Struts* framework simplifies session management, by allowing form beans to be transparently synchronized to the `HttpSession`.

In a *Struts* application, EJB access will typically be carried out from within the action beans (which are considered to be part of the 'controller' part of the MVC architecture), while form beans are usually considered to be part of the view.

Custom tags

The use of servlet-centered (e.g., model 2) architectures for the Web tier reduces the amount of programmatic material required in JSP pages, but does not eliminate it altogether. Consider, for example, an example in which a servlet carries out a query operation on a product catalogue EJB and forwards to a JSP page a `Vector` of `Product` value objects to display. This product list may be empty, in which case the JSP should display a message to that effect; otherwise, it should formulate an HTML table where each row consists of one product, and there are columns for product code, name, and price. Assuming that the vector is passed in the `request` object, we could formulate this in JSP like this.

```
<%
Vector v = (Vector)
  request.getAttribute("products");
if (v.size() == 0)
  {
%>
  No products selected
<%
  }
else
  {
%>
  <table>
<%
  for (int i = 0; i < v.size(); i++)
    {
    Product product = (Product)v.elementAt(i);
%>
    <tr>
      <td>
        <%= product.getCode() %>
      </td>
      <td>
        <%= product.getName() %>
      </td>
      <td>
        <%= product.getPrice() %>
      </td>
    </tr>
<%
```

```
    }
%>
  </table>
<%
  }
%>
```

Now, while this is considerably less ugly that either of the alternatives we have considered so far (producing all the output with a servlet or carrying out the query operation in JSP), it is still not ideal. It is quite difficult to disentangle the use of indentation to indicate flow control from that used to indicate the structure of the HTML table. With more than two levels of nesting, this type of JSP becomes very difficult to understand and maintain.

It would be much nicer if we could, perhaps, express the same logic in JSP like this:

```
<%
Vector v = (Vector)request.getAttribute("products");
%>
<if test="empty" collection="v">
  No products selected
<else>
  <table>
  <iterate collection="v" class="Product" id="p">
    <tr>
      <td>
        <%= p.getCode() %>
      </td>
      <td>
        <%= p.getName() %>
      </td>
      <td>
        <%= p.getPrice() %>
      </td>
    </tr>
  </iterate>
  </table>
</endif>
```

JSP does not include tags for iterating over `Collections`, or for conditional inclusion, but the use of custom tag libraries allows us to implement them in Java— or at least to come very close. Using custom tag libraries, the example above might be expressed as follows.

```
<%@ taglib uri="conditional.tld" prefix="cond" %>
<%@ taglib uri="iterate.tld" prefix="iter" %>
```

```
<%
Vector v = (Vector)request.getAttribute("products");
%>
<cond:if test="empty" collection="v">
  No products selected
</cond:if>
<cond:else>
  <table>
  <iter:iterate collection="v" class="Product" id="p">
    <tr>
      <td>
        <%= p.getCode() %>
      </td>
      <td>
        <%= p.getName() %>
      </td>
      <td>
        <%= p.getPrice() %>
      </td>
    </tr>
  </iter:iterate>
  </table>
</cond:else>
```

The JSP translator recognizes the prefixes `cond` and `iter` as referring to the *tag library descriptors* `conditional.tld` and `iterate.tld`. These are XML files that provide mappings between the tag names and the Java platform classes that implement the tag's functionality. The JSP translator generates method calls on these classes.

The tag library architecture allows a tag method to determine the flow of 'execution' of a JSP page, so it is straightforward to implement conditional and loop tags.

The *Struts* framework goes a step further than this: It provides tags for iteration and conditional operations that interact directly with the session and request. What this means is that common methods of passing objects between components can be supported with *no* Java code at all.

So what has all this to do with EJBs? Two things.

First, we can use tag libraries to encapsulate EJB calls just like helper beans. The advantage of using custom tags over helper classes is that the method calls can be expressed in HTML syntax rather than Java syntax.

The second reason to use tag libraries is to implement a general-purpose EJB interface, similar in functionality to `jsp:useBean`, but for EJBs. A number of tag libraries of this type are already in circulation. As an example, the JSP code below uses the Orion `ejbtags` library to call the method `getDaily()` on the Charge Band EJB.

```
<%@ taglib uri="ejbtags" prefix="ejb" %>

<ejb:useHome id="cbHome"
   type="ChargeBandHome"
   location="java:comp/env/ejb/ChargeBand"
/>

<ejb:useBean
  id="chargeBand" type="ChargeBand" scope="page"
   <ejb:createBeanInstance instance=<%=cbHome.create()%>
/>

<%= chargeBand.getDaily() %>
```

This code finds the home object with the specified parameters, calls `create()`
on it, and assigns the result to `chargeBand`. We can then use `chargeCalc` exactly
as if it were a standard Java platform class created with `jsp:useBean`. In addition,
the tag library supports session scoping of EJB references, so we can lock an EJB
to a client session without extra coding.

17.3   Using separate JSP/servlet engine and EJB servers

A J2EE-compliant application server *may* consist of separate servers for EJBs and
Web components. If so, it is the vendor's responsibility to see that a standard
EAR file can be deployed, and that the components end up in the right places. If
this involves deployment across a number of networked servers, it is the vendor's
responsibility to implement this. In this section, we will be considering the situation
where the JSP/servlet engine and the EJB server are not part of a J2EE product
or are parts of two different J2EE products. In this case, we will have to deploy
separately on each server, and configure them to be able to communicate. The
techniques to be used for this are vendor-specific.

17.3.1   Protocol issues

It doesn't really matter what protocol is used to communicate with the JSP/servlet
engine and the EJB container, provided that we can generate suitable stubs and
skeletons. Since the stub and the skeleton between them encapsulate the protocol
completely, the servlet and EJB code is protocol-independent.

The problem is that in the EJB container, the skeletons are normally generated
using the container vendor's tools. This means that protocol support is usually
limited to the provision of the EJB server vendor. The JSP/servlet engine is not
usually a limitation, as it does not accept method calls *from* EJBs, and therefore
doesn't need skeletons of its own.

It is not practical for stubs to encapsulate a complete implementation of the
protocol they support (as there would be an enormous amount of duplication of
classes). So the EJB container normally generates stubs that contain only code

that is different for different EJBs. Code that the stubs have in common is normally supplied in a library. It is the container vendor's responsibility to provide this library, along with instructions how to install it on the client.

The *J2EE Specification* requires that products be able to communicate using the IIOP protocol. However, you don't have to use this protocol if your product supports alternatives. When using IIOP, you have a choice whether to install on the JSP/servlet engine the EJB-container-generated stubs and a supporting class library, or to generate stubs on the client using a general-purpose IIOP library. As recent versions of Java JDK are supplied with a full IIOP implementation, the latter course is often more practical.

So in summary, you can implement JSP/servet/EJB connectivity in a heterogeneous environment in one of three ways:

- Generate stubs and skeletons on the EJB server for a vendor-specific protocol, and copy to the client the stubs and supporting class libraries.

- Generate IIOP stubs and skeletons on the EJB server, and copy to the client the stubs and supporting class libraries.

- Generate only IIOP skeletons on the EJB server; generate stubs from the home and remote interfaces on the client using a general-purpose IIOP ORB and supporting tools.

The last of these approaches is the most difficult to come to grips with, but will work in almost all situations; its use is demonstrated in the example below.

Gotcha!

Some application server vendors claim IIOP compliance, but in fact require the client to use supporting classes provided by the vendor. This is *not* IIOP. IIOP is vendor-independent and language independent. If intraoperability is important in your application, ask the vendor if the product supports IIOP method calls from native-code ORBs. If it does, it has a full IIOP implementation. If it doesn't, you may be restricted in the languages and products you can include in the system.

17.3.2 Security issues

In a J2EE-compliant application server, security is end-to-end, and authentication at the Web tier is propagated to the EJB container. If the JSP/servlet engine is not part of an application server, then it probably won't be able to do this unless a protocol is used that supports principal propagation. If the JSP/servlet engine and the EJB container are from the same vendor, then there is a reasonable chance that this can be made to work (if they support IIOP/SSL, for example). In most cases, however, the EJB container will treat the JSP/servlet engine as an unauthenticated client, and must be programmed accordingly. This means, in effect, that the EJB server is unable to impose any security restrictions of its own, which is an argument for putting it behind a sound firewall. This problem should improve when more products support CSI (page 496).

17.3.3   Example

As an illustration I will demonstrate how a JSP running in the *Tomcat* (Version 3.2.1) JSP/servlet engine can make method calls on an EJB hosted by a *J2EE Reference Implementation* server running on a different host. These products are both J2EE-compliant in their own right, but as they do not comprise a single application server in this configuration, the JSP and the EJB must be deployed separately, and the products configured appropriately. This example uses the `PrincipalTest` EJB described in Chapter 16. Because most products do not support encryption for IIOP, I suggest that better results will be obtained if this EJB is deployed with SSL disabled (this is the default, but you may have enabled SSL if you read Chapter 16 before this one). This EJB is used for no other reason that its simplicity.

To make this demonstration as realistic as possible, I assume that *Tomcat* and the J2EE RI are on different hosts, and that nothing application-specific, or generated on the EJB server, can be copied from the EJB host except the EJB home and remote interfaces.

Assuming that the EJB has been deployed, and the EJB server running, the steps required are as follows; each is discussed in detail below.

- Check *Tomcat* configuration.

- Deploy the JSP page on *Tomcat*.

- Install and compile the home and remote interface for the `PrincipalTest` EJB, and locate the classes in *Tomcat*'s CLASSPATH.

- Generate IIOP stubs from the interfaces, and locate the classes in *Tomcat*'s CLASSPATH.

- Test the installation.

Check *Tomcat* configuration

Even though we won't be running EJBs on the JSP container, we will still need access to the interfaces in `javax.ejb`, as these will be used by the JVM when it loads the home and remote interface for the EJB. I will assume that the RI library `j2ee.jar` is available on the same host as *Tomcat*, and installed in directory `/usr/j2sdkee1.3/lib`. *Tomcat* will read the system CLASSPATH variable when it starts up, so the simplest way to ensure that it can locate the `javax.jar` classes is to ensure that `j2ee.jar` is in the system CLASSPATH environment variable.

As we will be using IIOP for JSP-EJB communication, we will need an RMI/I-IOP implementation on the JSP/servlet engine. The Sun RMI/IIOP classes are bundled with Java JDK Version 1.3 and with the *J2EE Reference Implementation*, so if you have either of these on the JSP host, that should be adequate. For earlier JDK versions, the IIOP implementation is available as an add-on, and can be obtained from `java.sun.com/products/rmi-iiop`.

Deploy the JSP page

Although *Tomcat* supports a J2EE-compliant deployment mechanism, in this simple example, we can deploy by simply copying the JSP page to *Tomcat*'s JSP root. Listing 17.4 shows a simple JSP page that calls the `getPrincipal()` method on the `PrincipalTest` EJB.

If this page is copied to the directory `[tomcat_root]/webapps/ROOT`, it can be viewed with a Web browser by pointing it at the URL `[server]:8080/test.jsp`.

This JSP page looks up the home object of the EJB by supplying the JNDI system with a naming factory class, and a URL that will enable that class to find the naming server, as described on page 205. Hard-coding the naming factory class and URL in the JSP page like this is not very portable; in a real system you may prefer to supply JNDI configuration using one of the other techniques described in Chapter 7, such as using a `jndi.properties` file or using system properties. If you do this, bear in mind that the configuration must be applied to the JVM running the JSP/servlet engine, and may affect other JNDI operations in that JVM. Alternatively, the relevant information can be supplied in environment variables in the XML deployment descriptor for the JSP or servlet (if used).

Listing 17.4: **JSP page for testing connectivity to the `PrincipalTest` EJB. Note that the IP number and port of the EJB server are hard-coded: If you want to try this make sure that you reference the right host.**

```
     <%@ page
        import=
           "javax.naming.*,javax.rmi.*,java.util.*"
     %>
  5  <%@ page
        import=
           "com.kevinboone.ejb_book.principaltest.*"
     %>
     This is a test of the 'PrincipalTest' EJB,
 10  running on a remote EJB server
     <p>
     <%
     // Insert correct host and port for EJB server here
     String ejbHost = "192.168.1.20";
 15  String iiopPort = 1050;

     Hashtable ht = new Hashtable();
     ht.put ("java.naming.factory.initial",
```

```
       "com.sun.jndi.cosnaming.CNCtxFactory");
20  ht.put ("java.naming.provider.url",
       "iiop://" + ejbHost + ":" + iiopPort);
    Context  c = new  InitialContext(ht);
    out.println ("initial  context = " + c + "<p>\n");
    out.flush();
25  Object  o = c.lookup ("PrincipalTest");
    out.println ("home  stub = " + o + "<p>\n");
    out.flush();
    PrincipalTestHome  h = (PrincipalTestHome)
      PortableRemoteObject.narrow
30     (o,  PrincipalTestHome.class);
    out.println ("narrowed  home  stub = " + h + "<p>\n");
    out.flush();
    PrincipalTest  principalTest = h.create ();
    out.println ("EJBObject = " + principalTest + "<p>\n");
35  out.flush();
    String  myPrincipal = principalTest.getPrincipal();
    %>

    <b>My principal  is: <%= myPrincipal %></b>
```

Install and compile the interfaces

The JSP engine will need to be able to load the home and remote interfaces for the EJB, and the IIOP stubs derived from them. A simple way to achieve this is to install these classes in a directory that is inherently in the JSP engine's CLASSPATH. For the present example, a suitable directory is [tomcat_root]/webapps/ROOT/WEB-INF/classes. We will need to create the directory com/kevinboone/ejb_book/principaltest under this directory and install the interfaces PrincipalTestHome.java and PrincipalTest.java.

Provided that the system CLASSPATH is set appropriately (that is, includes j2ee.jar or equivalent), we can compile the interfaces from the command line by changing to the directory [tomcat_root]/webapps/ROOT/WEB-INF/classes and running

```
javac com/kevinboone/ejb_book/principaltest/*.java
```

This will leave the classes in the directory [tomcat_root]/webapps/ROOT/WEB-INF/classes/ejbook/principaltest, where they will be locatable by *Tomcat*.

Generate and compile the stubs

When the EJB was deployed, the deployment tool will have offered the opportunity to generate stubs to be used on the client. If the client and the server are both using the same ORB, we can simply copy the stubs from the EJB server to the JSP/servlet engine. In the current example, this technique will work if we are using the Sun RMI-IIOP implementation on the Web container, as this implementation is used by the EJB engine as well. However, to be complete, I will describe how to proceed if the Web container and EJB container are using different ORBs.

IIOP stubs can be generated directly from the home and remote interfaces, so these are the only things that need to be available on the client. The client does not need access to the EJB implementation class, nor to the home object or EJB object implementations.

After compiling the interfaces as described above, we can generate the stubs using the Sun RMI tools by running the following command in the directory `[tomcat_root]/webapps/ROOT/WEB-INF/classes:`[5]

```
java -classpath [classpath1] \
  sun.rmi.rmic.Main \
  -nolocalstubs
  -iiop
  -classpath [classpath2] \
  com.kevinboone.ejb_book.principaltest.PrincipalTestHome
```

Note that there are two `-classpath` switches on this command line. The first, 'classpath1,' should reference the JAR containing the EJB classes (e.g., `j2ee.jar`), and the Sun tools library `tools.jar` (this is part of the Java JDK, not the Reference Implementation). The second, 'classpath2,' is an argument to the stub compiler utility, not the JVM. This should refer to `j2ee.jar` and the current directory. So, for example, on my system, I would execute:

```
java \
  -classpath
    /usr/java/jdk1.3/lib/tools.jar:/usr/j2sdkee1.3/lib/j2ee.jar \
  sun.rmi.rmic.Main \
  -nolocalstubs \
  -iiop \
  -classpath /usr/j2sdkee1.3/lib/j2ee.jar:.
  com.kevinboone.ejb_book.principaltest.PrincipalTestHome
```

The switch `-nolocalstubs` tells the stub compiler to generate stubs optimized for network communication, not for local communication when the client and server are on the same host.

Testing the implementation

Test the installation by pointing a Web browser at the URL `[server]:8080/test.jsp`. It should produce output similar to Figure 17.5.

---

[5] At the time of writing, a limitation in the `rmic` executable prevented this operation from being carried out simply by executing `rmic --iiop` on some platforms.

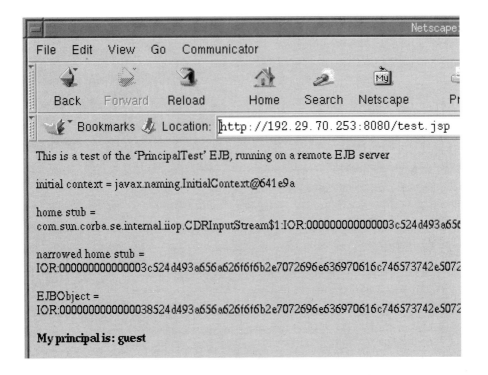

Figure 17.5. Testing the JSP-EJB connectivity using a Web browser.

17.4   Summary

The use of servlets and JSPs is a well-established technique for providing a user interface to an EJB application. It is not, however, the only solution: CGI, ASP, and Web server modules may all be useful in certain applications.

Servlets and—after translation—JSPs are simple Java platform classes, and can implement whatever functionality is accessible to the Java programming language. These classes make calls on EJBs in much the same way as any other client. Where Web components and EJBs are deployed to an application server, as part of a standard EAR file, then some of the complexities of standalone clients are avoided. However, using separate JSP/servlet engines and EJB servers is not normally a significant headache, so long as they have a protocol (e.g., IIOP) in common.

Chapter 18

Connectors
and resource adapters

Overview

This chapter provides a brief introduction to resource adapters and the J2EE connector architecture (JCA). This architecture allows the developer to integrate support for arbitrary external resources into the EJB container. We begin with an example of an application that would benefit from the use of a connector. We then describe the JCA API in outline. Most of this chapter is concerned with the implementation and analysis of a specific resource adapter, which provides EJBs with access to a stock quote server; the API is described in detail with reference to this example. We then move on to a discussion of the proposed 'common client interface.' Finally, there is a brief explanation of the principles of transaction management and security management within resource adapters.

18.1 The need for connectivity

To understand why we need connectors, consider the simple application shown in outline in Figure 18.1. This EJB application uses a 'stock quote server' to retrieve current prices of a range of traded stocks. The quote server implements a custom protocol carried over TCP/IP, where clients connect, authenticate themselves, retrieve whatever quotes they require, and then disconnect.

Of course this is just one example: EJB applications frequently need to communicate with legacy systems, nonstandard data sources, and hardware devices, among other things. As time goes by, standard APIs are being introduced to cover connectivity to more and more back-end systems. In addition, it is increasingly likely that our stock quote server would expose its functionality via a Web service—allowing EJBs to interact with it via XML-based RPC, for example. However, there will always remain a residue of systems that are not sufficiently widespread to justify

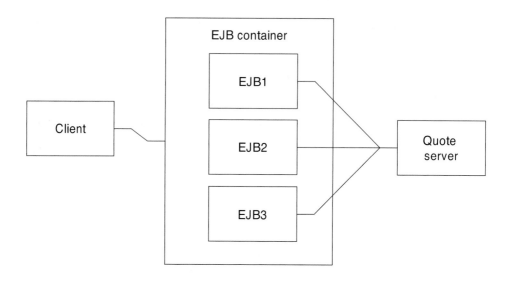

Figure 18.1. An EJB application that makes use of a custom quote server. EJBs open network connections as required, download prices, then disconnect.

developing whole new integration techniques for them; the developer will then have to fall back on his own resources to implement connectivity.

There is nothing built into the EJB architecture that supports such operations, so we will generally have to implement the connectivity ourselves. There are a number of simple, well-established techniques for doing this, and we will discuss these first. We will then examine the latent complications inherent in these simple techniques, which leads on to a discussion of JCA–J2EE connector architecture, which is a general framework for the implementation of sophisticated connectivity strategies.

18.2   Simple connectivity techniques

18.2.1   The Socket API

There is no reason in theory why communication with our quote server should not be implemented directly by an EJB using Java sockets. This technique is specifically allowed for in the *EJB Specification* [EJB2.0 24.2.1]. If the designer encapsulates the communication inside a dedicated class or EJB, the code will not be particularly objectionable.

In practice, the EJB can execute code something like this:

```
Socket s = new Socket ('someserver', somePort);
//... read and write socket
s.close();
```

The container has to support this, because method calls between EJBs can be network calls.

The problems with this strategy should be fairly obvious.

- The developer has to do all the work: The `Socket` connection bypasses the EJB server and operates directly on the JVM. This means that if we want connection pooling, etc., we have to implement it in code.

- Network sockets are not serializable; if this technique is used, for example, in a stateful session EJB, it will be necessary to open and close the connection to handle passivation.

- It can be difficult to co-ordinate a transaction on the remote system (if it is transactional) because the EJB holding the `socket` may be destroyed by the container in the event of certain low-level EJB errors. This prevents the EJB from issuing the appropriate instruction to the remote system to roll back. This is a much more significant problem than it may first seem. In general, the container keeps track of the state of an ongoing transaction, not the EJBs.

18.2.2   The URL API

A more elegant way to read from a network connection—and perhaps to write to it—is to use a URL resource obtained from the container. Although we will still ultimately be using a socket, this technique gives the container the ability to share sockets among different clients.[1] This technique is particularly useful when the remote server uses a well-known protocol for communication (FTP, HTTP) because URL handlers for such protocols are supplied with the JVM.

The code fragment below shows how to use a URL connection to read data from a remote server line-by-line:

```
Context  context  =  new  InitialContext ();
URL  url  =  (URL) context . lookup ("java : comp/env/ url /MyURL" );
URLConnection  connection  =
  ( URLConnection ) url . openConnection ();
InputStream  is  =  connection . getInputStream ();
BufferedReader  br  =  new  BufferedReader
  (new  InputStreamReader  ( is ));
System . out . println  (" line  =  "  +  br . readLine ());
```

Note that this code does not specify the *type* of URL that we are connecting to: It might be a Web server, an FTP server, or anything else that can be represented by a URL. In the deployment descriptor, you should specify the real URL that `java:comp/env/url/MyURL` maps onto.

Most EJB containers support this technique for reading from an HTTP or FTP server, and some support it for reading files, as described below.

---

[1]Nothing in the *EJB Specification* obliges a container to be able to do this; some do, some don't.

Another advantage of the use of URLs is that there are no hard-coded references to network addresses. Of course, we could avoid this problem in the previous example by using EJB environment variables, but using URLs unifies the configuration of the deployed application (as all remote services are located by means of resource references).

Developers often think that this technique can be used to get around the container's prohibition on local file access, but this probably won't work—see below.

18.2.3 'Connectivity' to files

The *EJB Specification* forbids the use of 'classes in the `java.io` package' for reading or writing files [EJB2.0 24.1.2]. It does this because this is not 'an appropriate way to read and write data in an enterprise application.' Many EJB servers allow this restriction to be relaxed, because file access can be useful from time to time. Before embarking on such a course of action, bear in mind the following issues.

- The application may be nonportable; some servers simply don't allow file access.

- In a load-sharing environment, there may be instances of the EJB implementation on multiple servers. If the EJBs read from files, then the files must be accessible, and identical, on all collaborating servers. This may not be difficult to achieve if only reading is allowed, but will be a significant problem if the files are to be written to by EJBs as well.

- Relational databases are optimized for concurrent access, while file systems often are not.

- Unless you are running a transactional file system, and your EJB product knows how to support it, it will be difficult to roll back a filesystem write if some other part of a transaction fails.

If the container enforces the prohibition on file access, it will probably do it using a security manager at the JVM level. This means that we can't get around the problem by using the URL technique described above with a `file:/xxx` URL. The container still knows that this is a local file access.

18.2.4 Email

A question that people frequently ask about EJB development is how to send email messages from EJBs, which is a simple form of connectivity. You'll typically need to do this to send confirmations of orders to customers or dispatch messages for logging and audit purposes, but it may be a useful approach for getting data to a legacy system that supports nothing more sophisticated than a mail daemon.

Hint

You can use email to dispatch logging messages from an EJB server to another system. You might want to do this so that you have a separate log of operations in case the EJB server fails catastrophically and cannot be recovered. However, this technique is not especially fast, and you may get better performance by using JMS and a messaging product for this job.

EJB containers are obliged to support those parts of the JavaMail API that are concerned with sending (but not receiving) email. Typically it will use SMTP (Simple Mail Transport Protocol) to do this, although the details of the protocol are concealed from the application developer. To be able to send an email using this protocol, we need the following minimum set of information:

- the email address of the sender (the 'From:' address);

- the email address of at least one recipient ('To:' address);

- the server hostname or IP number;

- the message itself.

We may also supply a subject for the message, date information, and multiple recipients, among other things, but these are optional.

Other protocols may require other information, such as a user ID and password, to allow access to the service. The basic SMTP protocol does not support authentication.

Gotcha!

EJB containers are not obliged to provide any mechanism by which an EJB can *receive* email, and most don't, so check with your vendor before committing yourself to a design.

Listing 18.1 shows the implementation class of the `Mailer` EJB, which is part of the *Prestige Bike Hire* application. Its one method, `send()`, can dispatch an email message with the specified subject to the specified reciepients. The 'From:' address in this example is picked up from the environment using JNDI. To use this EJB, we must do three things:

- set the environment variable 'fromaddress' to required 'From:' address;

- declare the resource reference `java:comp/env/mail/sender` in the deployment descriptor;

- map the resource reference onto a real mail service, supplying whatever configuration information is necessary.

Listing 18.1: **The implementation class of the** `Mailer` **EJB used in the** *Prestige Bike Hire* **application. It has one method:** `send()` **which dispatches an email message.**

```
package com.kevinboone.bikehire.ejb;
import com.kevinboone.bikehire.utils.*;
import javax.ejb.*;
import javax.mail.*;
import javax.mail.internet.*;
import javax.naming.*;
import java.rmi.*;
import java.util.*;

/**
Implementation class for the 'Mailer' EJB
(c)2002 Kevin Boone
*/
public class MailerBean extends GenericStatelessSessionBean
{
/**
Sends a message with a specified subject
and text to the specified recipients.
The 'from' address is taken from an environment
variable, as this will not change from message
to message.
*/
public void send (String to, String subject, String text)
    throws MessagingException
  {
  debugOut ("Entering send");

  try
    {
    // Get the 'from' address and the mail session
    //   resource from the container by JNDI. The
    //   'from' address is in the EJB environment, while
    //   the session is a resource reference of
    //   type 'java.Mail.Session'.
    Context c = new InitialContext();
    String fromAddress = (String)c.lookup
      ("java:comp/env/fromaddress");
    Session session = (Session)
      c.lookup("java:comp/env/mail/sender");

    // Create a new message object for the current session
    Message msg = new MimeMessage(session);

    // Set the properties of the message
```

```
45      // ... who it's from
        msg.setFrom(new InternetAddress(fromAddress));

        // ... who it's to
        msg.setRecipients(Message.RecipientType.TO,
50          InternetAddress.parse(to, false));

        // ... what it's about
        msg.setSubject(subject);

55      // ... when it was sent (i.e., now)
        msg.setText(text);

        // ... and its contents
        msg.setSentDate(new Date());
60
        // This is where the real work gets done. The Transport
        // class extracts all the information supplied in
        // the message, establishes a session on the mail
        // server, and sends the message
65      Transport.send(msg);

        debugOut("Leaving send");
        }
    catch(NamingException e)
70      {
        debugOut("Caught NamingException in send(): " + e);
        throw new MessagingException
            ("Mail session name lookup failed in send()");
        }
75  }
}
```

The last step, mapping the resource reference to a real service, is vendor-specific. With the *J2EE Reference Implementation* this is carried out in combination with declaring the resource, as shown in Figure 18.2.

There are a few things to note about this configuration.

- The JNDI name of the mail service is largely arbitrary; it will probably only be accessible to EJBs, and they will use it by looking up in the `java:comp/env` namespace anyway.

- In this example, I am using an SMTP server; SMTP does not support authentication of the sender, so it doesn't matter what the authentication settings say. I don't need to supply a username. This may be different for other protocols.

- The 'From:' field in the dialog box is also ignored with this implementation, since the API expects the 'From:' address to be set in code:

```
msg.setFrom(new InternetAddress(fromAddress));
```

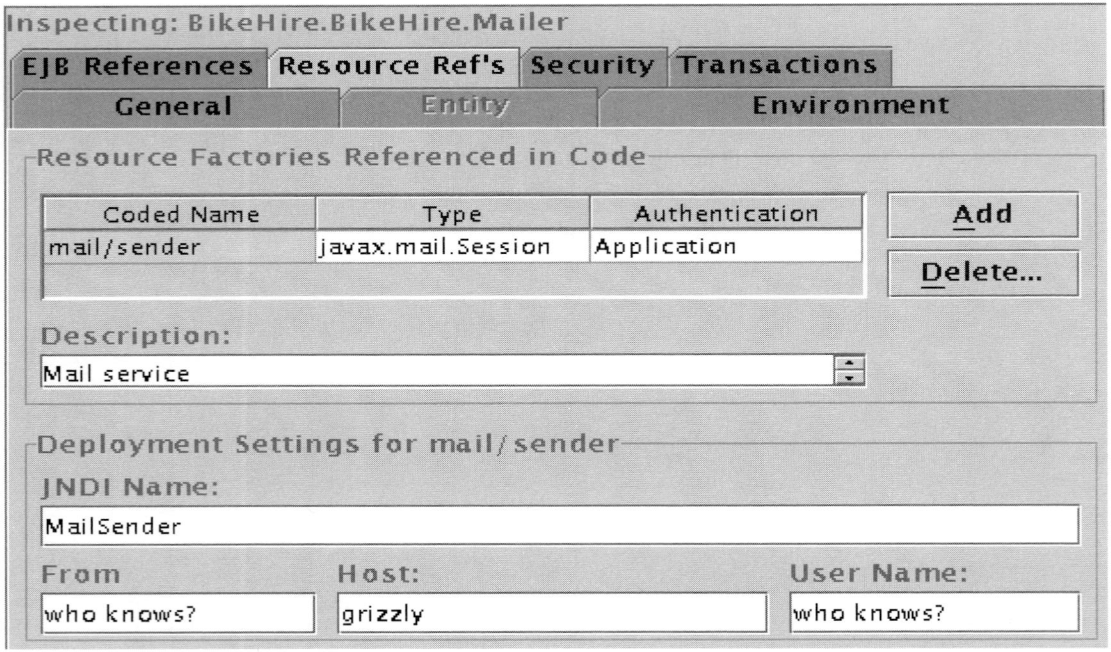

Figure 18.2. Declaring a mail resource and associating it with a real service using the J2EE RI. See text for details.

In this example, the 'From:' address is extracted from an environment variable called `fromaddress`. This arrangement assumes that that all emails sent from the application will appear to come from the same user, but that the user may need to be altered from time to time (so we don't want to hard-code it).

Gotcha!

Some EJB containers allow access only to email services on the same host. This is not usually a limitation, as it isn't difficult to configure a local email server to relay to the real mail server. However, such issues are beyond the scope of this book.

Hint

Because JavaMail sessions are 'resource factories' within the scope of the *EJB Specification*, you can store them in the instance variables of a stateful session bean without worrying that they will interfere with passivation. This is true whether they are serializable or not (of course, server vendors will typically make them serializable to support this functionality). Because JavaMail `Sessions` are not significant consumers of resources, it is reasonable for a session EJB to do the JNDI lookup for the `session` in `ejbCreate()` and store it in an instance variable for future use. This may give a slight efficiency advantage where large numbers of messages are being sent.

18.3   JCA resource adapters: rationale and principles

Using EJBs to interact with external resources via socket connections and the like has a number of complications.

- The external resource may be limited in the number of clients it can support, for technical or pragmatic reasons. In this example, the quote server may be a subscription service, charged per concurrent connection. Concurrent access to the server may be required by many instances of a number of different EJBs. Some legacy systems may even be single-threaded and support only one connection at a time.

- Even if connection concurrency is not, in itself, a problem, setting up the socket connection is a costly operation, particularly if the external resource is not part of the same network as the EJB server, or if there is a significant handshaking overhead. If there are many EJBs that all make short-lived connections, this will be inefficient.

- Although the *EJB Specification* allows EJBs to open client sockets, it forbids the use of server (listening) sockets. This makes perfect sense: If the EJB opens a socket for listening, it must either block a method call until data arrives (which is inconvenient for clients) or create a separate thread to listen to the socket. The creation of threads by EJBs is banned (page 476) because it disturbs that container's attempt to give the illusion of a single-threaded environment.

- Even if the developer takes some care to encapsulate the access to the external resource in a dedicated class, that class will have an API that is very specific to the system it serves and to the individual developer's view of it. The success of technologies like JDBC illustrates very well the benefit of standardizing on an API.

- Socket connections are not serializable. This is an issue if the connection is to be maintained by a stateful session EJB, as the container may attempt to passivate the instance. If this happens, the instance will need to close the connection in `ejbPassivate()` and reopen it in `ejbActivate()`. This opening and closing is an overhead on the system.

- As mentioned above, EJBs are not necessarily kept informed about the overall state of a transaction; in particular, if an EJB is the *source* of a transaction then the container may simply discard it, preventing it from interacting further with its external resources.

These complications become much more significant when the external resource is not a simple data source, as in our simple example, but a complex enterprise information system (EIS).[2] Suppose we want entity EJBs to use this EIS as their persistent store (a reasonable enough requirement). This leads to some additional problems.

- It is one thing to write Java sockets code that sends and receives data from an external resource; it is quite another to do this in a way that allows this resource to participate in distributed transactions with other data sources. The EJB container already has a transaction management strategy; what we need is some way to integrate with it.

- The external resource may have its own authentication mechanism. Ideally, we should use the same (declarative) mechanisms for securing it that we use for database connections and other container-managed resources.

---

[2]The term 'EIS' is frequently used in the *J2EE Connector Specification*. It refers to any enterprise data source, typically with a notion of transactional semantics and of multiclient access. However, the term is not usually used to refer to relational databases.

- Access to the external resource may not be via a straightforward network pipe. It may need native code libraries and other potential security hazards that are normally denied to EJBs.

In summary, we need a scheme for providing EJBs with an interface to external resources that integrates with the container's existing security, transaction, and resource pooling framework. JCA, the 'J2EE connector architecture,' provides such a scheme. Figure 18.3 shows the stock quote application reorganized to make use of the connector architecture. The connector is considered part of the EJB container and, in conjunction with the container, it manages access to the external server. The EJBs don't communicate directly with the external server, but with interfaces in the connector.

Properly speaking, there is no such thing as 'a connector' in the *JCA Specification*: The piece of software that implements the connectivity is called a *resource adapter*, and 'connector' applies to the overall architecture. However, the *J2EE Connector Specification* itself does not distinguish sharply between the two terms, and this chapter will not either.

Gotcha!

The *JCA Specification* was in draft for a long time, and the first public release was issued just after the first draft of this book was completed. Therefore the description that follows, and the source code examples, are based on this version: final release 1.0. Already there is a Version 1.5 in draft, so by the time you read this, you may find that some details have changed.

There is nothing strikingly new about resource adapters: All J2EE-compliant EJB containers support resource adapters for relational databases (via JDBC) and asynchronous messaging services (via JMS). The problem is that until recently there has been no standard technique for implementing connectors for arbitrary resources. Most of the commercial EJB products have their own, vendor-specific techniques for doing this. The *J2EE Connector Specification* is an attempt to provide a platform-independent, vendor-neutral API for connectors to external resources (this is referred to as the 'J2EE Connector API' or simply the 'Connector API'). A resource adapter that is authored to comply with this Specification should be portable to any EJB product. However, the Specification goes further than this, as we shall see, to encourage consistency in the APIs offered by resource adapters to their clients (i.g., to EJBs).

This section describes the *J2EE Connector Specification* and the basic components of a resource adapter. In the next section, we will examine these concepts in more detail with reference to a concrete example.

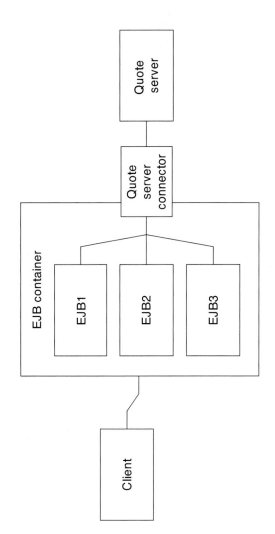

Figure 18.3. The same application as Figure 18.1, but restructured to use a connector.

18.3.1   The *J2EE Connector Specification*

I should point out from the outset that the *J2EE Connector Specification* does not apply exclusively to EJB servers, but to any J2EE-compliant container. In principle, a servlet ought to be able to use a connector to get access to an external resource. In practice, this sort of capability is more likely to be of interest to EJB developers. In what follows, I shall assume that the connector is to be integrated into an EJB container.

The *J2EE Connector Specification* defines contracts between the resource adapter, its clients (EJBs), and the EJB server, as summarized in Figure 18.4. Some of these contracts are compulsory and some optional.

- The compulsory part of the Specification defines the interaction between the clients (EJBs, in this case), the EJB container, and the external resource. The Specification does this by defining certain Java interfaces that the re-

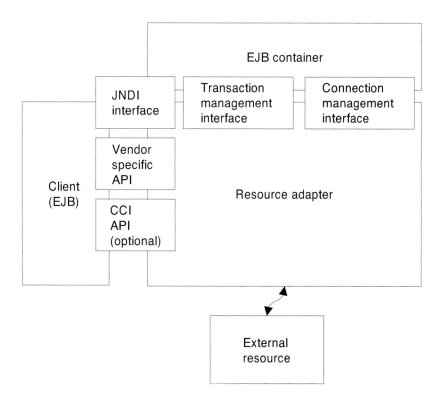

Figure 18.4. The *J2EE Connector Specification* seen as a set of contracts between different software subsystems. Note that the JNDI interface is shown as encompassing the client and the application server; the client will make JNDI calls on the container to locate the resource adapter, while the container will use the resource adapter's JNDI support to instantiate the appropriate classes.

source adapter must implement. This part of the Specification is compulsory, in that it must be implemented by any resource adapter that claims to be compliant. However, the interface seen by the client is allowed to be specific to the resource adapter, with certain stipulations. The Specification also stipulates an interface with clients that are *not* part of an EJB container or application server. Resource adapters have to support this as well.

- The *JCA Specification* also sets out a *common client interface* (CCI). Support for this is optional: If the resource adapter supports it, then the API exposed to clients is based on interfaces defined by the Specification, not by the developer.

When implementing a resource adapter, a decision has to be made whether to implement CCI support or not. It won't always be possible to support the CCI, as it was designed to provide typical operations on typical external resources. These operations all focus on data management, and it would not be appropriate to use the CCI for providing access to a power control system, for example. Where it is possible, the developer probably should support CCI, because it then becomes possible to *change the external resource without changing the EJBs* that use it. It also makes it much easier to use resource adapters created by other developers, as the client view of the resource adapter will always be the same.

We will have more to say about the CCI later, but we will first consider the components that a resource adapter developer must implement.

18.3.2   Components of a resource adapter

An understanding of the *J2EE Connector Specification* is not helped by the fact that four of its six most important interfaces have similar, undistinguished names. We will begin the discussion of the resource adapter API by considering each of these interfaces in turn. Note that, unless we are supporting the CCI, the `Connection` and `ConnectionFactory` can be developer-supplied interfaces and are not controlled by the Specification. It is these two interfaces that form the contract between the resource adapter and its clients.

Connection

A 'connection' is the object that a client will ultimately use to carry out real work on the server. In JDBC, for example, this object is an implementation of `java.sql.Connection`. If the design calls for the use of CCI, then a resource adapter connection must implement `javax.resource.cci.Connection`. If it doesn't, then the connection can be any suitable object, with an interface defined by the connector developer. The connection is typically *not* a real, physical connection to the resource, as closing the connection does not result in a real connection being closed or resources being deallocated. For this reason, this object is often referred to as a 'virtual' connection. Real connections are modeled by the 'managed connection.' Although the details of the specific `Connection` are left to the discretion of the developer, we are encouraged to provide a `close()` method, for obvious reasons.

Managed connection

In connector jargon, a 'managed connection' is the real, physical connection to the external resource. In practice, this is the object that will create instances of `java.net.Socket` or whatever low-level resource is required. A single managed connection can support numerous virtual connections, perhaps concurrently. Clients never interact directly with this object; it is part of the contract between the resource adapter and the EJB container. This object must implement the interface `javax.resource.spi.ManagedConnection`.

Connection factory

A connection factory is an object that will be used by the client to create new (virtual) connections. In JDBC, the connection factory is an implementation of `javax.sql.DataSource`. If the resource adapter supports CCI, it must implement `javax.resource.cci.ConnectionFactory`. Otherwise, it can be any class, with an interface provided by the developer. Typically, this class will have a `getConnection()` method that clients call to create new connections. Clients get a connection factory by means of a JNDI lookup, exactly as we have seen numerous times for JDBC `DataSource`s. Although the connection factory is primarily a contract between the client and the resource adapter, it must implement interfaces that allow the EJB server to store a reference to it in the JNDI namespace. Specifically, it must implement `javax.resource.Referenceable` (see below).

Managed connection factory

The term 'managed connection factory' reflects the fact that this object can create new managed connections; however, it must also be able to create new connection factories as well. The managed connection factory is the main point of contact between the EJB server and the resource adapter. The server calls its methods to create new connection factories to make available to clients by JNDI, and to create new physical connections (and the virtual connections derived from them). This class must implement the interface `javax.resource.spi.ManagedConnectionFactory`. We will discuss the role of this class in much more detail later.

Managed connection metadata

The EJB server uses metadata about the physical connections to optimize its resource allocation. The resource adapter provides a class that implements the interface `javax.resource.spi.ManagedConnectionMetaData`.

Connection manager

A connection manager is something that can allocate new virtual connections on request from clients, perhaps creating new physical connections at the same time. In an EJB application, this activity is coordinated by the EJB container, which will implement its own connection manager. However, the resource adapter is required to implement at least a rudimentary connection manager so that it can be used outside the EJB server if required. This class must implement `javax.resource.spi.ConnectionManager`.

> ## Gotcha!
>
> Don't spend too long on the implementation of the connection manager if you are working with EJBs: The EJB server will almost certainly not use it, preferring its own connection pooling scheme.

Deployment descriptor

Like all other J2EE components, configuration information about the resource adapter is supplied in an XML deployment descriptor.

18.3.3   Capabilities of a resource adapter

Resource adapters are intended to be able to communicate with external systems, and these systems won't always be accessible by a straightforward TCP/IP call. In some cases, it will even be necessary to use native method calls to get access to the external resource.

A resource adapter operates in a runtime environment with its own security framework, set by the container. However, the developer should understand that the *default* security policy is essentially the same as for for EJBs—very restrictive. If the resource adapter requires additional security privileges, then the developer must declare this in the deployment descriptor. The deployer can then examine the security requirements to ensure that they are acceptable on the target system.

Some of the extended security rights that a resource adapter may wish to make use of include the ability to

- load and use native-code libraries;

- open network sockets that listen for connections;

- read and write local files;

- create new threads.

This last point, the creation of new threads, is sufficiently important that consideration is currently being given to including a separate API for it in the *J2EE Connector Specification*.

18.3.4   Packaging a resource adapter

Resource adapters are packaged into RAR ('resource archive') files, which can be installed in an EAR file along with an application, or deployed separately. In either case, the *J2EE Connector Specification* sets out the same structure for the RAR module (Figure 18.5).

In particular, the RAR contains at a minimum the XML deployment descriptor and a separate JAR file containing the classes that make up the resource adapter.

> ## Gotcha!
>
> The classes that form the implementation of the resource adapter *must* be supplied in a separate JAR file, which is inserted into the resource adapter RAR file. Packaging 'loose' classes into a RAR file won't work, at least in the current version of the Specification. This is important to note because the RI's deployment tool will not prevent you from placing loose classes into the RAR file: It just won't work when you deploy it.

The deployment descriptor specifies the names of the Java interfaces that form the client interface to the resource adapter, and their corresponding implementations, and the name of the implementation of `ManagedConnectionFactory` that the container will interact with. It also describes the additional security permissions that the adapter needs.

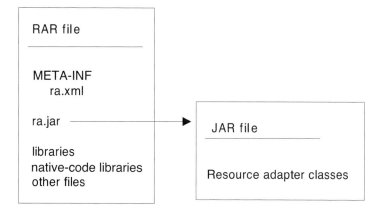

Figure 18.5. A resource adapter is packaged in a RAR file, which is in fact just a standard Java JAR archive. In the RAR file, there must be a deployment descriptor `ra.xml`, and a JAR file containing the resource adapter's classes.

Rather than describing the resource adapter API in detail, we will examine a simple example and later describe its integration with the container and the client step by step.

18.4   A simple resource adapter

In this section, we will describe the implementation and testing of a simple, but complete, resource adapter. This will provide EJBs with access to a stock quote server, as described at the start of this chapter. This is a 'real' resource adapter in that it does communicate with an external resource using a custom protocol; it is not just 'Hello World' in a connector. To test the resource adapter, we will need to implement an EJB that uses it, and a test client for the EJB. For the purposes of testing, we will also use a 'dummy' quote server that runs on the local machine. Because the example is already complicated enough, this simulated server won't do authentication. Figure 18.6 summarizes the software components that will be involved in this example, and the Java platform classes of which they are comprised (the diagram omits package names for brevity).

Hint

As always, full source code is available on the supporting Web site, in directory `quote` in the source package.

This example will not use the common client interface (CCI). We will discuss later how it could be adapted to provide this support if desired.

Gotcha!

Developing a resource adapter is not for the faint-hearted. The example that will be described in this chapter—which is really only one step beyond 'Hello world'—requires six Java platform classes and two interfaces, totaling about 1,000 lines of code, and that's without any security or transaction management.

Hint

Despite the complexity of a resource adapter, a lot of the code is "boilerplate" and will be very similar in all resource adapters. After writing the first one, writing others is much more straightforward.

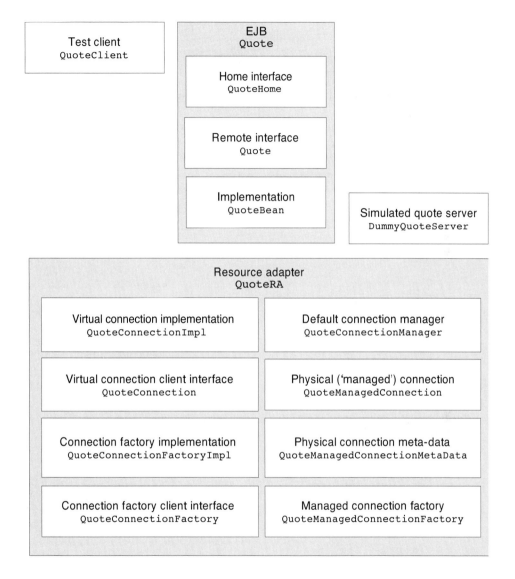

Figure 18.6. The software components involved in implementing and testing a resource adapter.

18.4.1   The 'dummy' quote server

Because we don't necessarily have access to a real quote server, and we don't want to get involved with authentication and protocol complexities in this simple example, we will use a 'simulated' quote server, implemented in Java. To prove that the connection pooling strategy works, this server will be single-threaded and accept only one connection at a time. It is hard-coded to listen for connections on port 30055 (change this if it clashes with something on your system).

The source code for the server is shown in Listing 18.2. This server supports a very simple protocol: The client provides a stock ticker symbol, and the server responds with its price in dollars. Actually, it responds with a random number, which at the time of writing, was a fairly good simulation of stock values, particularly in the computing industry. When the quote server is running, it should be possible to test it using **telnet** (this should work on both Unix and Windows systems):

```
telnet localhost 30055
```

The listing below shows a typical session with the simulated quote server: The client's input is in italic text and output is in typewriter text. The first two lines of the listing are not part of the client-server conversation, they are the output from the Unix **telnet** client when it starts up.

```
Trying 127.0.0.1...
Connected to localhost.
```
MSFT
```
83
```
SUNW
```
92
```
ORCL
```
92
```
...

The protocol is line based: The client sends one line of data, and the server responds with one line. It is fairly straightforward to code the client part of this communication in the resource adapter.

Listing 18.2: **Dummy quote server against which we can test the quote server resource adapter.**

```
    package com.kevinboone.ejb_book.quote;
    import java.net.*;
    import java.io.*;

5   /**
    This is the simulated quote server for use with the Quote resource
    adapter example. A client can connect and enter a stock ticker
    symbol. The server then produces a random number which simulates a
    fluctating stock price.

10  (c)2002 Kevin Boone
    */
    public class DummyQuoteServer
    {
15  public static void main(String[] args)
      {
```

```
        try
          {
          System.out.println ("Startup");
20        // Listen on a socket
          ServerSocket s = new ServerSocket (30055);
          // Handle client requests indefinitely
          while (true)
            {
25          System.out.println ("Waiting for connection");
            Socket s2 = s.accept();
            // Get buffered versions of the input and output
            //   stream to the client
            System.out.println ("Got connection");
30          BufferedReader in = new BufferedReader
                (new InputStreamReader (s2.getInputStream()));
            PrintStream out = new PrintStream(s2.getOutputStream());
            String line;
            // So long as the client keeps the connection open,
35          //   get a line form the client and return a random number
            do
              {
              System.out.println ("Waiting for input");
              line = in.readLine();
40            System.out.println ("Got input: " + line);
              if (line != null)
                {
                out.println ("" + (50 + (int)(Math.random() * 50.0)));
                }
45            } while (line != null);
            System.out.println ("Connection closed");
            s2.close();
            }
          }
50      catch(Exception e)
          {
          e.printStackTrace(System.err);
          }
        }
55  }
```

18.4.2   Designing the client interface

Clients should not manipulate the resource adapter's connection and connection
factory classes directly. Instead, the client should manipulate a pair of interfaces
that expose the methods in these classes to which clients require access. Because we
are not using the CCI, we have some freedom in the choice of the client interface;
however, we must not lose sight of the basic principle of the connector architecture:
The client must do a JNDI lookup to get a connection factory, then get a connection from it, then do the work, then close the connection. The *J2EE Connector
Specification* dictates that the 'close' method must be defined thus:

```
public void close();
```

and that the method that gets a new connection from the connection factory should be called `getConnection()` and should, if possible, take no arguments. Just as with database resource factories, we should set the user credentials and server properties at deployment time, not in code.

The quote server can do exactly one thing: return a stock price for a given stock symbol. So the client interface will provide one method, `getPrice()`, that does exactly that. In the resource adapter itself, all clients will share the same physical connection to the quote server, so the `getQuote()` method will be multiplexed onto that connection internally. However, this is not a concern of the client.

With these facts in mind, we define the client's interface to the connection factory—`QuoteConnectionFactory`—as shown in Listing 18.3, and the interface to the connection—`QuoteConnection`—in Listing 18.4. Notice how simple these interfaces are, as befits a very simple server protocol. The resource adapter implementation is far less simple, as we shall see.

Listing 18.3: **Client interface to the connection factory for the resource adapter.**

```
package com.kevinboone.ejb_book.quote.resourceadapter;
import javax.resource.*;


/**
5  This interface exposes the factory method of the resource adapter
   to clients. Clients find a QuoteConnectionFactory using JNDI, then
   call getConnection to get a QueueConnection object
   */
   public interface QuoteConnectionFactory
10 {
   public QuoteConnection getConnection()
     throws ResourceException;
   }
```

Listing 18.4: **Client interface to the connection derived from the connection factory.**

```
package com.kevinboone.ejb_book.quote.resourceadapter;
import javax.resource.*;
import javax.resource.spi.*;
import javax.security.auth.*;
5  import java.util.*;
   import java.io.*;


/**
   This is the client interface to the Quote server resource adapter.
10 This interface is very simple, and server-specific. It is
   implemented in the class QuoteConnectionImpl
   */
```

```
     public interface QuoteConnection
     {
15   // Close the connection
     public void close();
     // Get a stock price
     public double getPrice(String tickerSymbol)
       throws ResourceException;
20   }
```

18.4.3   Coding the resource adapter

Now it's time to see what's hidden behind the client's view of the resource adapter.

The managed connection factory

This class—QuoteManagedConnectionFactory (Listing 18.5)—is an implementation of ManagedConnectionFactory and is the main interface between the EJB container and the resource adapter. This class creates instances of two other classes: connection factories (QuoteConnectionFactoryImpl) and managed (physical) connections (QuoteManagedConnection).

The first methods that are called on this class by the EJB server (apart from the constructor) are setServerName() and setPortNumber(). These are not part of the connector API, so how does the container know to call them? It knows because the configuration properties required by the resource adapter are specified in its deployment descriptor (described in more detail below). In the deployment descriptor ra.xml are the following lines:

```
<config-property>
  <config-property-name>
    ServerName
  </config-property-name>
  <config-property-type>
    java.lang.String
  </config-property-type>
  <config-property-value>
    localhost
  </config-property-value>
</config-property>
<config-property>
  <config-property-name>
    PortNumber
  </config-property-name>
  <config-property-type>
    java.lang.Integer
  </config-property-type>
  <config-property-value>
```

```
   30055
 </config-property-value>
</config-property>
```

This specifies that this resource adapter has two configurable properties: `Server Name` (a `String`) and `PortNumber` (an integer). It also provides default values for these properties if the deployer does not set them.

Following JavaBeans conventions, the EJB server calls `setServerName()` to set the property `ServerName`, and `setPortNumber()` to set the property `PortNumber`. We will see later how values of these properties are supplied.

Having set the server and port, the EJB server calls `createConnection Factory()`, passing in *its own connection manager* as an argument. In response, the connector creates a new instance of `QuoteConnectionFactoryImpl`, providing it with a reference to the connection manager:

```
public Object createConnectionFactory
    (ConnectionManager connectionManager)
  {
  QuoteConnectionFactoryImpl qcf =
5   new QuoteConnectionFactoryImpl (this, connectionManager);
  return qcf;
  }
```

This connection factory is made available to clients by a JNDI lookup.

When a client gets this connection factory, and calls `getConnection()` in it, this (as we shall see) is delegated to the connection manager—that is, to the EJB server. If this is the first such call, then the EJB server knows that no physical connections have been made to the server, so it calls `createManagedConnection()`. In this method, we create a new physical connection (an instance of `QuoteManaged Connection`) and tell it to open a real network connection to the server. We will see later what the `QuoteManagedConnection` class does here.

```
public ManagedConnection createManagedConnection
    (Subject subject, ConnectionRequestInfo cri)
    throws ResourceException
  {
5 QuoteManagedConnection qmc =
    new QuoteManagedConnection(this);
  qmc.openSocket (serverName, portNumber);
  return qmc;
  }
```

The EJB server passes a `Subject` object, which identifies the client for authentication, and an implementation of `ConnectionRequestInfo`, which contains other (vendor-specific) connection parameters. Neither of these are used in this example.

On subsequent requests for connections, the EJB server's connection manager will not necessarily call `createManagedConnection()` directly; instead it will ask the resource adapter whether the request can be met by an existing `Managed Connection` instance. It does this by calling `matchManagedConnections()`, which must return a suitable `ManagedConnection` or `null` to indicate that no connections are available.

In our example, the quote server only accepts one connection at a time, so we *must* return an existing physical connection from this method, if there is already a connection open to the specified server and port. So our implementation of `matchManagedConnections()` iterates the open connections, checking their host and port settings, and returns the `QuoteManagedConnection` that corresponds to any connection with the requested host and port.

Listing 18.5: **Implementation of the managed connection factory.**

```
    package com.kevinboone.ejb_book.quote.resourceadapter;
    import javax.resource.*;
    import javax.resource.spi.*;
    import javax.security.auth.*;
 5  import java.util.*;
    import java.io.*;
    import java.net.*;

    /**
10  This EJB implements the ManagedConnectionFactory for the Quote
    resource adapter. This class is the central point for creation
    of ConnectionFactories and ManagedConnections

    (c)2001 Kevin Boone
15  */
    public class QuoteManagedConnectionFactory
          implements ManagedConnectionFactory, Serializable
    {
    /**
20  This is the first class that the application server will
    instantiate. In addition to its ordinary duties, it will act as
    the co-ordinator for logging.

    All the other classes in the RA are instantiated, directly or
25  indirectly, by this one. This class therefore calls setLogWriter()
    on each of them, passing its own log writer as an argument. This
    sets all instances of all classes to use the same output stream
    for logging. By default we will point this at System.out; the
    application server may change this.
30  */
    protected PrintWriter out = new PrintWriter(System.out);

    /**
    portNumber is a temporary property, set by the application
35  server before a call to createConnectionFactory
    */
    protected int portNumber;

    /**
40  serverName is a temporary property, set by the application
    server before a call to createConnectionFactory
    */
    protected String serverName;
```

```
45   /**
     Constructor doesn't do anything, but implement it to print a
     debug message so we can track what's going on in the log
     */
     public QuoteManagedConnectionFactory()
50     {
       debugOut ("Called constructor");
     }


     /**
55   The application server calls this method to create a new
     QuoteConnectionFactory, if the application server is supplying its
     own connection pool manager for connection management calls to be
     delegated to
     */
60   public Object createConnectionFactory
            (ConnectionManager connectionManager)
     {
       debugOut ("Called createConnectionFactory(cm)");
       QuoteConnectionFactoryImpl qcf =
65       new QuoteConnectionFactoryImpl (this, connectionManager);
       qcf.setLogWriter(out);
       return qcf;
     }


70   /**
     The application server or a standalone client calls this method
     to create a new QuoteConnectionFactory, and to tell it to use its
     own internal connection manager
     */
75   public Object createConnectionFactory()
     {
       debugOut ("Called createConnectionFactory()");
       QuoteConnectionFactoryImpl qcf =
         new QuoteConnectionFactoryImpl (this, null);
80     qcf.setLogWriter(out);
       return qcf;
     }


     /**
85   This method gets called by the application server to create a new
     physical connection to the server
     */
     public ManagedConnection createManagedConnection
            (Subject subject, ConnectionRequestInfo cri)
90       throws ResourceException
     {
       debugOut ("Called createManagedConnection()");
       QuoteManagedConnection qmc = new QuoteManagedConnection(this);
       qmc.setLogWriter(out);
95     try
         {
         qmc.openSocket (serverName, portNumber);
         return qmc;
         }
100  catch (IOException e)
         {
         throw new ResourceException (e.toString());
         }
```

```
105      }

      /**
      This method is called by the application server when the client
      asks for a new connection. The application server passes in a Set
      of all the active virtual connections, and this object must pick
110   one that is currently handling a physical connection that can be
      shared to support the new client request. Typically this sharing
      will be allowed if the security attributes and host properties of
      the new request match an existing physical connection.

115   If nothing is available, the method must return null, so that the
      application server knows it has to create a new physical
      connection

      To ensure that this method is implemented correctly, the dummy
120   server that accompanies this example only allows one connection at
      a time. So if this method does not locate and return the correct
      ManagedConnection instance, the whole system will fail
      */
      public ManagedConnection matchManagedConnections
125      (Set connections, Subject subject, ConnectionRequestInfo cri)
        {
        debugOut ("Called matchManagedConnection()");
        Iterator it = connections.iterator();
        while (it.hasNext())
130        {
          Object obj = it.next();
          debugOut ("Considering object " + obj);
          if (obj instanceof QuoteManagedConnection)
            {
135          debugOut ("Object is a QuoteManagedConnection");
            QuoteManagedConnection qmc = (QuoteManagedConnection) obj;
            QuoteManagedConnectionFactory qmcf = qmc.getFactory();
            if (qmcf.equals(this))
              {
140            debugOut ("Object has matching Factory: hit");
              return qmc;
              }
            }
          }
145      debugOut ("No object has matching Factory: miss");
        return null;
        }

      public void setLogWriter(java.io.PrintWriter _out)
150      {
        out = _out;
        }

      public PrintWriter getLogWriter()
155      {
        return out;
        }

      /**
160   set/get methods for server and port number are called by the
      application server to set appropriate values for the host and port
      before it goes on to call createManagedConnection(). This allows
      createManagedConnection() to return a connection on a specific
```

```
     host and port
165  */
     public void setServerName (String _serverName)
       {
       debugOut ("Called setServerName(), server="
         + _serverName);
170    serverName = _serverName;
       }

     public String getServerName ()
       {
175    debugOut ("Called getServerName()");
       return serverName;
       }

     public void setPortNumber (Integer _portNumber)
180    {
       debugOut ("Called setPortNumber(), port="
         + _portNumber);
       portNumber = _portNumber.intValue();
       }
185
     public Integer getPortNumber ()
       {
       debugOut ("Called getPortNumber()");
       return new Integer(portNumber);
190    }

     /**
     hashCode and equals are used to determine whether two instances of
     this class are set with the same configuration properties. There
195  are two properties: the server name and IP port number. If they
     are both equal, the two instances are considered to be equal
     */
     public int hashCode()
       {
200    debugOut ("Called hashCode()");
       if (serverName == null) return 0;
       return serverName.hashCode();
       }

205  public boolean equals(Object o)
       {
       debugOut ("Called equals");
       if (o == null) return false;
       if (!(o instanceof QuoteManagedConnectionFactory))
210      return false;
       QuoteManagedConnectionFactory other =
         (QuoteManagedConnectionFactory)o;
       if (serverName.equalsIgnoreCase(other.serverName) &&
         portNumber == other.portNumber) return true;
215    return false;
       }

     protected void debugOut (String s)
       {
220    if (out != null)
         {
         out.println ("QuoteManagedConnectionFactory: " + s);
         out.flush();
```

```
          }
225     }
      }
```

In a practical implementation, we would usually check that the existing connections have properties that are suitable for the new request. For example, if there is an open connection authenticated as user 'bill' (on the external resource), we would not want to use this connection to satisfy a request for a connection as user 'fred'.

The connection factory

The connection factory is used by clients to get connections to the external resource, in the same way as `javax.sql.DataSource` is used to get connections to a relational database.

If we are not using the CCI, then the connection factory is designed to suit the needs of the client, and implements the client interface. So in this example, the connection factory implementation—`QuoteConnectionFactoryImpl` (Listing 18.6)—implements the client interface `QuoteConnectionFactory`. The client will call the `getConnection()` method on this class, and expect to get back an object that implements the client interface `QuoteConnection`. If this happens, then the connector's obligations to the client are satisfied. In practice, this method is usually implemented as a call on the connection manager, which is, in reality, a call on the EJB server's connection pooling mechanism.

```
public QuoteConnection getConnection ()
    throws ResourceException
  {
  return ( QuoteConnection )
5     connectionManager. allocateConnection  (manager , null );
  }
```

Although the connection factory is provided for the benefit of clients, the client does not instantiate it; instead the client gets an instance of the connection factory by a JNDI lookup. This means that the EJB container must know the name of this class and be able to store it in its JNDI implementation. To this end, the Specification dictates that the connection factory implement both the **Serializable** and **Referenceable**[3] interfaces, to suit JNDI implementations that use serialization and those that use a referencing mechanism to locate objects (as described on page 184). In practice, no great effort is required to support the **Referenceable** interface: We simply save and recover the stored reference like this:

```
public void setReference ( Reference _reference )
  {
  reference = _reference ;
```

---

[3]Connection factories implement `javax.resource.Referenceable`, which is a subinterface of `javax.naming.Referenceable` that provides an additional method `setReference()`. This is called by the EJB server to initialize the reference.

```
5
      }

   public Reference getReference ()
   {
   return reference;
   }
```

Listing 18.6: **Implementation of the connection factory.**

```
   package com.kevinboone.ejb_book.quote.resourceadapter;
   import javax.resource.*;
   import javax.resource.spi.*;
   import javax.naming.*;
5  import java.util.*;
   import java.io.*;

   /**
   This class implements the ConnectionFactory for the Quote resource
10 adapter.  Clients get an instance of this class by doing a JNDI
   lookup. Note that this class implements QuoteConnectionFactory;
   this interface exposes the getConnection () method to clients.
   */
   public class QuoteConnectionFactoryImpl
15     implements QuoteConnectionFactory, Serializable,
          javax.resource.Referenceable
   {
   protected  Reference reference;
   protected  ManagedConnectionFactory manager;
20 protected  ConnectionManager connectionManager;
   protected  PrintWriter out;

   /**
   Constructor is called when the QuoteManagedConnectionFactory
25 instantiates this object. It passes in a reference to itself and
   to the connection manager. The connection manager will, in
   practice, be a class passed into the resource adapter by the
   application server. We simple save it in an instance variable, and
   delegate getConnection () calls to it.
30 */
   public QuoteConnectionFactoryImpl (ManagedConnectionFactory _manager,
      ConnectionManager _connectionManager )
      {
      debugOut ("Called constructor");
35    manager = _manager;
      if (_connectionManager == null)
         {
         connectionManager = new QuoteConnectionManager();
         ((QuoteConnectionManager)connectionManager).setLogWriter (out);
40       }
      else
         {
         connectionManager = _connectionManager;
         }
45    }

   /**
   This is the method that application clients will call when they've
   got a reference to the factory object by JNDI. We get a new
50 QuoteConnection object by delegating the whole job to the
   ConnectionManager. If we are running within an application server,
   then the server will want to use its own connection manager, and
   will have specified it when it created the
   QuoteManagedConnectionFactory. So this call actually delegates
```

```
55    back to the application server. The server will in turn call one
      of the methods on QuoteManagedConnection to get a virtual
      connection for the client. If we are not running in an application
      server, this call will be handled by the default connection
      manager which is in this package. It simply creates a new physical
60    connection and then a new virtual connection from it.
      */
      public QuoteConnection getConnection() throws ResourceException
        {
        debugOut ("Called getConnection");
65      return (QuoteConnection)
          connectionManager.allocateConnection (manager, null);
        }

      /**
70    setReference and getReference have to be implemented so that the
      application server can save references to this object in its JNDI
      store, rather than serializing the object itself. The spec
      requires both reference and serialization methods to be supported.
      Of course, the serialization method is automatic; we just say
75    'implements serializable'. Note that setReference is called by
      the application server, not by any part of the resource adapter;
      we don't know (or care) what it passes as an argument, so long
      as we can retrieve it again on demand.
      */
80    public void setReference (Reference _reference)
        {
        debugOut ("Called setReference");
        reference = _reference;
        }
85
      public Reference getReference ()
        {
        debugOut ("Called getReference");
        return reference;
90      }

      public void setLogWriter(java.io.PrintWriter _out)
        {
        out = _out;
95      }

      public PrintWriter getLogWriter ()
        {
        return out;
100     }

      protected void debugOut (String s)
        {
        if (out != null)
105       {
          out.println ("QuoteConnectionFactoryImpl: " + s);
          out.flush ();
          }
        }
110   }
```

The managed (physical) connection

In this example, the physical connection is implemented in the class `QuoteManaged Connection`, shown in Listing 18.7.

Clients never interact directly with the physical connection. When the client requests a connection from the `QuoteConnectionFactory`, it gets a virtual connection in the form of a `QuoteConnectionImpl` object. This object's `getPrice()` method delegates to the corresponding method in this class, which is where all the real communication with the server gets done:

```
public synchronized double getPrice(String tickerSymbol)
    throws ResourceException
{
serverPrintStream.println(tickerSymbol);
String line = serverBufferedReader.readLine();
return Double.parseDouble(line);
}
```

Because the protocol is line-based, we interact with the server via two line-based representations of the network socket: a `BufferedReader` for input and a `PrintStream` for output. These were set up when the network socket was opened:

```
public void openSocket(String serverName, int portNumber)
    throws UnknownHostException, IOException
{
socket = new Socket(serverName, portNumber);
serverPrintStream =
    new PrintStream(socket.getOutputStream());
serverBufferedReader = new BufferedReader
    (new InputStreamReader(socket.getInputStream()));
}
```

If a physical connection can support any number of virtual connections (as is the case in this example), then the developer has to ensure that the shared methods in the physical connection object are thread-safe or appropriately synchronized. In this case, the `getPrice()` method can be entered on any number of threads. I have used the **synchronized** attribute to cause the socket send and receive operations to be executed without interruption from another thread.

The `QuoteManagedConnection` object is notified by its virtual connections (by calls to `removeConnection()` and `sendClosedEvent()`) when a client closes the virtual connection (that is, calls `QuoteConnection.close()`). When this happens, we pass the close notification on to any event listeners that were registered. In practice, the application server will register an event listener after creating each new physical connection. Although the Specification defines other events besides closing a connection, these are mostly concerned with transaction management, so aren't implemented here.

To facilitate connection sharing, the EJB server is allowed to 'move' virtual connections from one physical connection to another. It will call `associateConnection()` on the *new* owner of the virtual connection to do this. Our implementation of this method (shown in simplified form below) gets the `QuoteManagedConnection` object that currently owns the virtual connection specified by the EJB server, calls `removeConnection()` on it, then calls `addConnection()` to add it to our list of virtual connections.

```
   public void associateConnection(Object _connection)
      throws ResourceException
      {
      QuoteConnectionImpl connection =
5        (QuoteConnectionImpl)_connection;

      QuoteManagedConnection qmc = connection.getManager();
      qmc.removeConnection(connection);
      addConnection(connection);
10    connection.setManager (this);
      }
```

Listing 18.7: Implementation of the managed (physical) connection.

```
      package com.kevinboone.ejb_book.quote.resourceadapter;
      import javax.resource.*;
      import javax.resource.spi.*;
      import javax.security.auth.*;
5    import java.util.*;
      import java.io.*;
      import java.net.*;
      import javax.transaction.xa.*;

10   /**
      This EJB implements the ManagedConnection for the Quote resource
      adapter. This is a representation of a real, physical connection
      to the server, so it has a Socket instance variable which remains
      allocated to a server for the life of this object. This class is
15   responsible for creating virtual connections, of class
      QuoteConnection, when the application server calls getConnection()
      */
      public class QuoteManagedConnection implements ManagedConnection
      {
20   /**
      destroyed is set in the destroy() method, so that other methods
      can check it before attempting any operations that require an
      active connection
      */
25   protected boolean destroyed;

      /**
      The output writer used for debug logging
      */
30   protected PrintWriter out;

      /**
      connections is the set of Connection instances that this
      ManagedConnection is looking after
35   */
      protected Set connections = new HashSet();

      /**
      connectionListeners is the list of connection listeners registered
40   for this instance
      */
      protected Set connectionListeners = new HashSet();

      /**
45   This network Socket instance is the shared, real connection
      to the server. All virtual connections created by this
      QuotemanagedConnection object will use this single
```

```
     socket.
     */
50   protected Socket socket;

     /**
     This PrintStream is derived from the physical socket connection
     to the server immediately after opening it.
55   */
     protected PrintStream serverPrintStream;

     /**
     This BufferedReader is derived from the physical socket connection
60   to the server immediately after opening it.
     */
     protected BufferedReader serverBufferedReader;

     /**
65   Store a reference to the factory that created this
     ManagedConnection.  We will need this later to determine whether a
     ManagedConnection can be reused to support a new client request.
     */
     QuoteManagedConnectionFactory factory;

70
     /**
     Constructor stores a reference to the ManagedConnectionFactory
     that created this instance
     */
75   public QuoteManagedConnection(QuoteManagedConnectionFactory _factory)
       {
       debugOut("Called constructor");
       factory = _factory;
       }

80
     public QuoteManagedConnectionFactory getFactory() { return factory; }

     /**
     Create a virtual connection (a QuoteConnection object)
85   and add it to the list of managed instances before
     returning it to the client.
     */
     public Object getConnection(Subject subject,
          ConnectionRequestInfo cxRequestInfo)
90      {
       debugOut("Called getConnection()");
       QuoteConnectionImpl connection = new QuoteConnectionImpl();
       connection.setManager(this);
       connection.setLogWriter(out);
95      addConnection(connection);
       return connection;
       }

     /**
100  This method is called by the application server when it wants to
     remove this resource adapter completely. This method may, in fact,
     never get called. It should do the same stuff as the cleanup()
     method but, in addition, it must free any physical resources. So
     this is where we will shut down the real connection to the quote
105  server
     */
     public void destroy()
       {
       debugOut("Called destroy()");
110    if (destroyed) return; // Don't desctroy twice
       // Invalidate all my virtual connections
       Iterator it = connections.iterator();
       while (it.hasNext())
         {
```

```
115        QuoteConnectionImpl qc = (QuoteConnectionImpl) it.next();
           qc.invalidate();
           }
       connections.clear();
       debugOut ("Closing  network  socket()");
120    if (socket != null)
           try {socket.close();} catch (Exception e){}
       destroyed = true;
       }


125    /**
       This method is called by the application server to inform this
       QuoteManagedConnection that it is about to be repooled. It won't
       do this while it has active virtual connections, but it may do it
       at any other time. We must indicate that our virtual connections
130    are defunct.
       */
       public void cleanup()
           throws ResourceException
           {
135    debugOut ("Called  cleanup()");
       throwIfDestroyed();
       Iterator it = connections.iterator();
       while (it.hasNext())
           {
140        QuoteConnectionImpl qc = (QuoteConnectionImpl) it.next();
           qc.invalidate();
           }
       connections.clear();
       }

145    /**
       This method is called by the EJB container to move a virtual
       connection from the management of a different ManagedConnection to
       the control of this one. In this method we simply call
150    changedManager() on the connection itself
       */
       public void associateConnection(Object _connection)
           throws ResourceException
           {
155    debugOut ("Called  associateConnection()");
       throwIfDestroyed();
       if (_connection instanceof QuoteConnection)
           {
           QuoteConnectionImpl connection =
160          (QuoteConnectionImpl)_connection;

           QuoteManagedConnection qmc = connection.getManager();
           if (qmc == this) return;
           qmc.removeConnection(connection);
165        addConnection(connection);
           connection.setManager (this);
           }
       else
           {
170        throw new javax.resource.spi.IllegalStateException
               ("Invalid  connection  object: " + _connection );
           }
       }

175    /**
       This method is called by the application server to register
       interest in connection events.
       */
       public void addConnectionEventListener(ConnectionEventListener l)
180        {
           debugOut ("Called  addConnectionEventListener()");
```

```
          connectionListeners.add(l);
          }

185  /**
     This method is called by the application server when it has
     finished monitoring connection events. In practice this method is
     never called.
     */
190  public void removeConnectionEventListener(ConnectionEventListener l)
          {
          debugOut ("Called removeConnectionEventListener()");
          connectionListeners.remove(l);
          }
195
     /**
     This resource adapter does not support transactions: throw an
     exception
     */
200  public XAResource getXAResource()
          throws ResourceException
          {
          debugOut ("Called getXAResource()");
          throw new NotSupportedException
205          ("Distributed transaction not supported");
          }


     /**
     This resource adapter does not support transactions: throw an
210  exception
     */
     public LocalTransaction getLocalTransaction()
          throws ResourceException
          {
215       debugOut ("Called getLocalTransaction()");
          throw new NotSupportedException ("Local transaction not supported");
          }

     /**
220  getMetaData must return a ManagedConnectionMetaData object that
     provides information about the resource to which this object is
     connected. It is intended to be used by the application for
     optimizing its resource allocation strategy, but there is no
     guarantee that it will ever be called. The J2EE RI, for example,
225  does not use this technique
     */
     public ManagedConnectionMetaData getMetaData()
          {
          debugOut ("Called getMetaData()");
230       return new QuoteManagedConnectionMetaData(this);
          }

     public void setLogWriter(PrintWriter _out)
          {
235       out = _out;
          }

     public PrintWriter getLogWriter()
          {
240       return out;
          }

     /**
     Indicates whether the physical connection has been destroyed. In
245  this implementation all we have to do is return the 'destroyed'
     flag
     */
     public boolean isDestroyed()
```

```
        {
250     return destroyed;
        }


        /**
        This is a convenience method called at the start of each method
255     that requires the physical connection to the server to be present.
        If it is not, it throws an exception
        */
        protected void throwIfDestroyed()
            throws javax.resource.spi.IllegalStateException
260     {
        if (destroyed)
            throw new javax.resource.spi.IllegalStateException
            ("QuoteManagedConnection is destroyed");
        }
265
        /**
        Add a Connection instance to the list of Connections that this
        object is looking after
        */
270     protected void addConnection(QuoteConnection connection)
            {
            debugOut ("Called addConnection()");
            connections.add(connection);
            }
275
        /**
        Remove a Connection instance from the list of Connections that this
        object is looking after
        */
280     protected void removeConnection(QuoteConnection connection)
            {
            debugOut ("Called removeConnection()");
            connections.remove(connection);
            }
285
        /**
        When a virtual connection (an object of class QuoteConnection) is
        closed by its client, the QuoteConnection calls this method on the
        QuoteManagedConnection that owns it. This in turn passes the event
290     on to anything that has registered as a listener for connection
        events. Typically this will be application server's connection
        pool manager.
        */
        void sendClosedEvent ()
295         {
            debugOut ("Called sendClosedEvent");
            Iterator it = connectionListeners.iterator ();
            while (it.hasNext())
                {
300         ConnectionEventListener listener =
                (ConnectionEventListener) it.next ();
            listener.connectionClosed
                (new ConnectionEvent(this, ConnectionEvent.CONNECTION_CLOSED));
                }
305     }


        /**
        Provide a getUserName() method to be used when a client
        interrogates the metadata for this managed connection. In fact we
310     don't support authentication at all, so just return 'guest'
        */
        public String getUserName ()
            {
            debugOut ("Called getUserName()");
315     return "guest";
```

```
           }

     protected void debugOut (String s)
       {
320    if (out != null)
         {
           out.println ("QuoteManagedConnection: " + s);
           out.flush ();
         }
325    }

     /**
      openSocket initiates the physical connection to the server. This
      method is called by QuoteManagedConnectionFactory immediately
330   after creating the instance of this class
      */
     public void openSocket (String serverName, int portNumber)
         throws UnknownHostException, IOException
         {
335    debugOut ("Called openSocket; opening on " +
           serverName + ":" + portNumber);
         socket = new Socket (serverName, portNumber);
         serverPrintStream = new PrintStream (socket.getOutputStream());
         serverBufferedReader = new BufferedReader
340        (new InputStreamReader (socket.getInputStream ()));
         }

     /**
      When clients call getPrice() on the virtual connections they hold,
345   these connections all delegate to the real connection represented
      by this class. Here we do the actual communication with the
      server.
      */
     public synchronized double getPrice (String tickerSymbol)
350      throws ResourceException
         {
         debugOut ("Called getPrice (), tickerSymbol=" + tickerSymbol);
         serverPrintStream.println (tickerSymbol);
         try
355        {
           String line = serverBufferedReader.readLine ();
           return Double.parseDouble (line);
           }
         catch (Exception e)
360        {
           // We may get NumberFormatException here, among other things
           throw new ResourceException
             ("Caught exception in getPrice (): " + e.toString ());
           }
365    }
     }
```

The (virtual) connection

The virtual connection—QuoteConnectionImpl—implements the client interface QuoteConnection. Specifically, it implements the methods getPrice() and close(). If you examine the source code (Listing 18.8) you will see that this class delegates all its functionality to the QuoteManagedConnection (physical connection) that owns it. This owner is stored in the instance variable manager when the object is created.

Thus a call to `getPrice()` is simply delegated to `QuoteManagedConnection.get`
`Price()`:

```
public double getPrice(String tickerSymbol)
    throws ResourceException
    {
    return manager.getPrice(tickerSymbol);
    }
```

A call to `close()` simply informs the physical connection that this virtual connection is now defunct; the physical connection is also asked to propagate this
information to the EJB server:

```
public void close()
    {
    manager.removeConnection(this);
    manager.sendClosedEvent();
    manager = null;
    }
```

The class also has an `invalidate()` method, which can be called to indicate that
the connection has been invalidated at the request of the EJB server, for whatever
reason.

Listing 18.8: **Implementation of the virtual connection to the resource.**

```
package com.kevinboone.ejb_book.quote.resourceadapter;
import javax.resource.*;
import javax.resource.spi.*;
import javax.security.auth.*;
import java.util.*;
import java.io.*;

/**
This class models a virtual connection to the Quote server.
Clients get an instance of this class when they call
getConnection() on QuoteConnectionFactory, but it doesn't happen
directly, but under the control of the application server's pool
manager
*/
public class QuoteConnectionImpl implements QuoteConnection
    {
    /**
    The output writer used for debug logging
    */
    protected PrintWriter out;

    /**
    The ManagedConnection instance that controls this virtual
    connection. This will get set to null when this instance is
    closed, so that we can't try to close it twice
    */
    protected QuoteManagedConnection manager;

    /**
```

```
30   Clients call this to indicate that they have finished with a
     connection. Of course, we aren't really going to close anything,
     we will simply indicate to the manager of this virtual connection
     that it is now defunct.
     */
35   public void close()
        {
        debugOut ("Called close()");
        if (manager == null) return;   // already closed or invalidated
        manager.removeConnection(this);
40      manager.sendClosedEvent ();
        manager = null;
        }


     /**
45   getManager is called by the QuoteManagedConnection when the
     application server wants to reassociate a virtual connection with
     a new manager.
     */
     public QuoteManagedConnection getManager()
50      {
        debugOut ("Called getManager()");
        return manager;
        }


55   /**
     setManager is called by the QuoteManagedConnection when the
     application server wants to reassociate a virtual connection with
     a new manager.
     */
60   public void setManager (QuoteManagedConnection _manager)
        {
        debugOut ("Called setManager()");
        manager = _manager;
        }
65
     /**
     invalidate is called by the QuoteManagedConnection object that
     owns this virtual connection, to indicate that it is defunct. It
     only does this at the request of the application server. In this
70   implementation we indicate defunct status by setting the 'manager'
     instance variable to null
     */
     public void invalidate ()
        {
75      debugOut ("Called invalidate()");
        manager = null;
        }


     /**
80   This method is called by the client to get a stock price. Because
     this is only a virtual connection, we delegate the work to the
     QuoteManagedConnection object that holds the real connection.
     */
     public double getPrice(String tickerSymbol)
85      throws ResourceException
        {
        debugOut ("Called getPrice(), tickerSymbol=" + tickerSymbol);
        return manager.getPrice (tickerSymbol);
        }
```

```
90   public void setLogWriter(PrintWriter _out)
       {
       out = _out;
       }
95   public PrintWriter getLogWriter()
       {
       return out;
       }
100  protected void debugOut (String s)
       {
       if (out != null)
         {
105    out.println ("QuoteConnectionImpl: " + s);
       out.flush ();
         }
       }
     }
```

The managed connection metadata

The Specification requires the provision of a class that implements the `Managed ConnectionMetaData` interface. The EJB server can use the methods on this class to optimize its resource allocation strategy, but is not obliged to. If it does, it will probably call the method `getMaxConnections()` to determine the number of concurrent physical connections that can be made to the server. In our example, this is '1'. `QuoteManagedConnectionMetaData` is shown in Listing 18.9.

Listing 18.9: **Implementation of the managed connection metadata.**

```
     package com.kevinboone.ejb_book.quote.resourceadapter;
     import javax.resource.*;
     import javax.resource.spi.*;
     import javax.security.auth.*;
5    import java.util.*;
     import java.io.*;
     import javax.transaction.xa.*;

     /**
10   This is the implementation of the metadata for the Quote resource
     adapter.

     (c)2001 Kevin Boone
     */
15   public class QuoteManagedConnectionMetaData
       implements ManagedConnectionMetaData
     {
     /**
     Store a reference to the QuoteManagedConnection object from which
20   this metadata is derived
```

```
    */
    protected QuoteManagedConnection qmc;

    public QuoteManagedConnectionMetaData (QuoteManagedConnection _qmc)
25    {
      qmc = _qmc;
    }

    public String getEISProductName ()
30    {
      return "Kevin's quote server";
    }

    public String getEISProductVersion ()
35    {
      return "Version 1.0";
    }

    public int getMaxConnections ()
40    {
      // We support only one connection
      return 1;
    }

45  /**
    Get this from the QuoteManagedConnection object as we would in a
    real implementation, even though our dummy server does not support
    authentication
    */
50  public String getUserName ()
    {
      return qmc.getUserName ();
    }
  }
```

The connection manager

The Specification requires that each resource adapter implement its own connection manager. A connection manager is responsible for creating new virtual and physical connections on behalf of clients. However, in an EJB server environment, the EJB server will take on this role itself, by interacting with the `ManagedConnection` `Factory` implementation. The built-in connection manager will only be used when the resource adapter is used in a standalone application or, perhaps, an applet.

The connection manager can take on its own connection pooling, but it is not required to. In this simple example, the connection manager—`QuoteConnection` `Manager` (Listing 18.10)—simply creates a new physical connection and derives a new virtual connection from it. There is no connection pooling. I do want to stress that in EJB applications, this class *will never be used.*

Listing 18.10: **The simple, default connection manager. This class is never used in EJB applications.**

```
     package com.kevinboone.ejb_book.quote.resourceadapter;
     import javax.resource.*;
     import javax.resource.spi.*;
     import javax.security.auth.*;
5    import java.util.*;
     import java.io.*;
     import javax.transaction.xa.*;

     /**
10   This class implements a default connection manager for the Quote
     resource adapter. This class is only used when the resource
     adapter is applied outside the context of an application server.
     When an application server is used, it will undoubtedly want to
     take control of connection management itself. To that end it will
15   pass its own ConnectionManager implementation as an argument to
     the createConnectionFactory method.

     As this class will not be used in earnest, I have not bothered to
     make it very sophisticated.
20
     (c)2001 Kevin Boone
     */
     public class QuoteConnectionManager
        implements ConnectionManager, Serializable
25   {
     protected PrintWriter out;

     public void setLogWriter(java.io.PrintWriter _out)
        {
30      out = _out;
        }

     protected void debugOut (String s)
        {
35      if (out != null)
           {
           out.println ("QuoteConnectionFactory: " + s);
           out.flush ();
           }
40      }

     /**
     This is the compulsory method that generates a new (virtual)
     connection for clients. We could implement connection sharing
45   in here if we wished.
     */
     public Object allocateConnection (ManagedConnectionFactory mcf,
                                       ConnectionRequestInfo info)
             throws ResourceException
50      {
        debugOut ("Called allocateConnection()");
        ManagedConnection mc =
           mcf.createManagedConnection(null, info);
```

```
      return mc.getConnection(null, info);
55    }
    }
```

18.4.4   Assembling, deploying, and configuring the resource adapter

Although it is possible to package a resource adapter in an application, it is usually easier to use a separate RAR file. At the time of writing, the deployment tool of the *J2EE Reference Implementation* does offer support for constructing RAR files, but it is not very highly developed. It is, in fact, not very difficult to do this job manually at the command line, which is the procedure described here. In practice, these commands would be automated in a makefile or `Ant` build file.

> ### Hint
>
> If you have the source code for this example, and are using `Ant`, you can compile and assemble the resource adapter RAR file by doing `ant assembleresourceadapter`, which automates the steps described below.

First, we must create a deployment descriptor that describes the roles played by the various classes in the package, and specifies the configuration variables. A suitable XML file is shown in Listing 18.11; it needs to go into a directory called `META-INF`.

Listing 18.11: **The deployment descriptor for the resource adapter; please note that the package names have been replaced with '....' so that the listing fits on the page.**

```
    <connector>
      <display-name>QuoteRA</display-name>
      <vendor-name></vendor-name>
      <spec-version></spec-version>
5     <eis-type></eis-type>
      <version></version>
      <resourceadapter>
        <managedconnectionfactory-class>
          .... resourceadapter.QuoteManagedConnectionFactory
10      </managedconnectionfactory-class>
        <connectionfactory-interface>
          .... resourceadapter.QuoteConnectionFactory
        </connectionfactory-interface>
        <connectionfactory-impl-class>
15        .... resourceadapter.QuoteConnectionFactoryImpl
        </connectionfactory-impl-class>
        <connection-interface>
          .... resourceadapter.QuoteConnection
        </connection-interface>
```

```
20        <connection−impl−class>
            .... resourceadapter . QuoteConnectionImpl
          </connection−impl−class>
          <transaction −support >NoTransaction</transaction −support >
          <config −property >
25          <config −property −name>ServerName</config −property −name>
            <config −property −type>java . lang . String </config −property −type>
            <config −property −value >localhost </config −property −value >
          </config −property >
          <config −property >
30          <config −property −name>PortNumber</config −property −name>
            <config −property −type>java . lang . Integer </config −property −type>
            <config −property −value >30055</config −property −value >
          </config −property >
          <reauthentication −support >false </reauthentication −support >
35    </resourceadapter>
    </connector>
```

Having compiled the resource adapter classes, we package them into a JAR as follows:

```
jar cvf QuoteRA.jar [package_directory]/*.class
```

where [package_directory] denotes the path to the directory containing the compiled classes

Then we package this JAR with the deployment descriptor like this

```
jar cvf QuoteRA.rar QuoteRA.jar META-INF/ra.xml
```

The resulting `QuoteRA.rar` is the resource adapter module, and this is what we will deploy.

The previous steps were platform-independent; however, the deployment into the EJB container will depend on the container. The process to be described works for the *J2EE Reference Implementation*. There are two steps: the physical deployment and the assignment of a JNDI name.

To deploy, use the `deploytool` utility at the command line:

```
deploytool -deployConnector QuoteRA.rar localhost
```

> **Hint**
>
> If you recompile any of the classes in the resource adapter (and of course you will, in a real development exercise), you will need to undeploy the resource adapter before redeploying it. Use the `-undeployConnector` switch in `deploytool`. You may need to restart the J2EE server after doing this. You can also undeploy using the graphical deployment tool.

Now bind a JNDI name to this resource adapter; the name will be needed later when deploying the EJB that uses it.

```
j2eeadmin -addConnectorFactory \
  eis/QuoteRA QuoteRA.rar \
  -props ServerName=localhost PortNumber=30055
```

Here `eis/QuoteRA` is the JNDI name that will be used by the EJB. The names of
the properties in the `-props` option must match the names in the XML deployment
descriptor and should have values that make sense on your system. For example, if
you are not running the quote server on the same host as the J2EE server, you will
need to replace 'localhost' with the appropriate hostname.

If the deployment and JNDI registration is successful, you should be able to
query the server for information about installed connectors, like this:

```
deploytool -listConnectors localhost

Installed connector(s):
        Connector Name: QuoteRA.rar

Installed connection factories:
        Connection Factory JNDI Name: eis/QuoteRA
```

We are now ready to implement an EJB that uses this connector.

18.4.5   Implementing the EJB and test client

We have already defined the interface that the resource adapter will present to the
client; writing a test EJB isn't terribly difficult. Listing 18.12 shows the implementation class for a suitable EJB. This will be a stateless session EJB, so most of the
callback methods can be empty. The only business method—`getQuote()`—takes
a stock ticker symbol as an argument, and returns the stock prices as a `double`.
The home and remote interfaces aren't shown in the text, as they should be fairly
obvious by now.[4]

Listing 18.12: **Implementation class for an EJB that will test the quote
server resource adapter. This will be a stateless session EJB that provides
one method**—getQuote(String)—**to its clients.**

```
    package com.kevinboone.ejb_book.quote;

    // This package contains the interface
    //    classes for the Quote resource adapter
  5 import com.kevinboone.ejb_book.quote.resourceadapter.*;

    // We need the following package for resource manager
    // exceptions
    import javax.resource.*;
 10
    // And all the usual stuff
```

---
[4]As always, the full source is available from `www.kevinboone.com/ejb_book`.

```
   import javax.ejb.*;
   import javax.naming.*;

15 /**
   This EJB exercises the Quote resource adapter module. Its single
   method getQuote() gets a stock quote from the server using
   the resource adapter

20 (c)2001 Kevin Boone
   */
   public class QuoteBean implements SessionBean
   {
   /* Don't implement these methods
25    in this simple example */
   public void ejbActivate() { }
   public void ejbCreate() { }
   public void ejbPassivate() { }
   public void ejbRemove() { }
30 public void setSessionContext(SessionContext ctx) { }

   /**
   getQuote() uses JNDI to locate the resource adapter,
   calls getConnection() on it, then calls getPrice()
35 on the connection.
   */
   public double getQuote(String tickerSymbol)
       throws QuoteException
     {
40   try
       {
       Context c = new InitialContext();
       // use c.lookup ("QuoteRA") if the line below does
       //   not work with the RI...
45     Object o = c.lookup ("java:comp/env/eis/Quote");
       debugOut ("Resource factory object is " + o);
       QuoteConnectionFactory qcf = (QuoteConnectionFactory)o;
       debugOut ("Calling getConnection() on the resource factory");
       QuoteConnection qc = qcf.getConnection();
50     debugOut ("Resource connection object is " + qc);
       debugOut ("About to call getPrice()");
       double price = qc.getPrice (tickerSymbol);
       debugOut ("Closing connection object");
       qc.close();
55     return price;
       }
     catch (NamingException e)
       {
       e.printStackTrace(System.err);
60     throw new QuoteException
         ("Name lookup failed in getQuote(): " + e);
       }
     catch (ResourceException e)
       {
65     e.printStackTrace(System.err);
       throw new QuoteException
         ("Caught resource exception in getQuote(): " + e);
       }
     }

70
   protected void debugOut (String s)
```

```
      {
75     System.err.println ("QuoteBean: " + s);
      }

  }
```

The significant part of Listing 18.12 is, in fact, just these few lines:

```
  Context c = new InitialContext();
  Object o = c.lookup ("java:comp/env/eis/Quote");
  QuoteConnectionFactory qcf = (QuoteConnectionFactory)o;
  QuoteConnection qc = qcf.getConnection();
5 double price = qc.getPrice (tickerSymbol);
  qc.close();
```

Here we get the connection factory (`QuoteConnectionFactory`) from JNDI, use it to get a connection object (`QuoteConnection`), and call `getPrice()` on that connection. Note that we should, as always, call `close()` on the connection after use.

The EJB looks up the resource adapter in the same way that it looks up any other external resource: by a JNDI lookup on the `java:comp/env` namespace. At deployment time, this must be mapped onto the real JNDI name of the resource adapter, which is `eis/QuoteRA`. With the *J2EE Reference Implementation* deployment tool this is done through the 'References' tab in exactly the same way as for a database resource factory (Figure 18.7). You will notice that the deployment tool does not provide a resource class 'other' or 'unspecified,' so we have to select `javax.resource.cci.ConnectionFactory`, which is the interface for CCI-compliant connection factories. This does not usually cause any problems, but if it does, we can code the EJB to look up the JNDI name directly instead.

Other than this, assembly and deployment of the EJB is as it usually is and won't be described in detail here.

Listing 18.13 shows the test client; this calls the `getQuote()` method on the `Quote` EJB, passing the ticker symbol "SUNW", and displays the corresponding stock price.

Listing 18.13: **Test client for the `Quote` EJB.**

```
  package com.kevinboone.ejb_book.quote;
  import javax.naming.*;
  import javax.rmi.*;

5 /**
  This is a simple test client for the Quote EJB. The client locates
  the EJB, and calls its 'getQuote()' method, passing the ticker
  symbol 'SUNW'.

10 (c)2001 Kevin Boone
  */
```

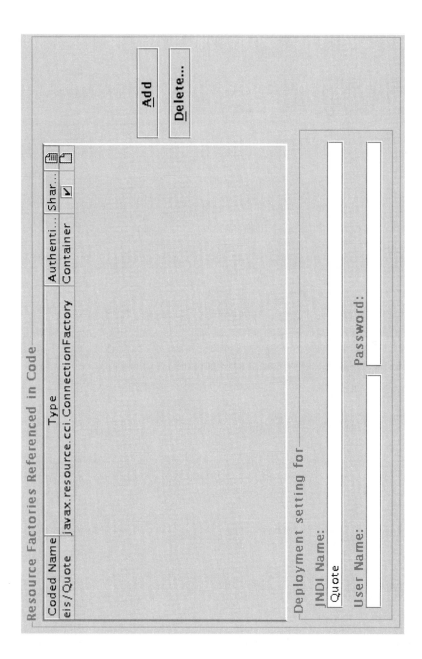

Figure 18.7. Mapping the `java:comp/env` name used by the EJB onto the JNDI name of the resource adapter.

```
     public class QuoteClient
     {
     public static void main(String[] args)
15   {
       try
         {
         Context context = new InitialContext();
         Object ref  = context.lookup("Quote");
20
         QuoteHome home = (QuoteHome)
           PortableRemoteObject.narrow
             (ref, QuoteHome.class);
         Quote q = home.create();
25
         double quote = q.getQuote("SUNW");
         System.out.println ("Quote is: " + quote);
         q.remove();
         }
30   catch(Exception e)
       {
       System.out.println("Test failed: " + e.toString());
       e.printStackTrace(System.err);
       }
35   }
     }
```

18.4.6   Testing the resource adapter

Before running the test client, ensure that the dummy server is running; test by making a `telnet` connection to it if necessary. Don't forget to disconnect, however, as this server only accepts one connection at a time.

If you are using `Ant`, do this:

```
ant rundummyquoteserver
```

It is probably a good idea to run this in a separate console, otherwise it will be in the way.

If everything succeeds, the output from the test client should be something like this:

```
Quote is: 77
```

You should get a different value on subsequent runs. The output to the server log, however, is much more extensive, and we will examine it in detail next.

18.4.7   Analyzing the simple resource adapter

Let's examine how the connector architecture works by examining step-by-step what happens when a client uses the resource adapter. To follow this section you will need to refer to the source code and to the server output log (Listing 18.14). This log was generated by running the test client twice; we will discuss why the response of the resource adapter is different for the second run.

Client does a JNDI lookup for `eis/QuoteRA` (Line 47 of `QuoteBean`). The EJB server does not initialize a connection factory until a client requests it. At this point, it instantiates `QuoteManagedConnectionFactory`, and calls `setServer Name()` and `setPortNumber()` on the new instance (lines 1–3 of Listing 18.14).

EJB server initializes a connection factory The server calls `create ConnectionFactory()` on `QuoteManagedConnectionFactory` (line 60), passing in its own connection manager (line 4 of Listing 18.14). `QuoteManaged ConnectionFactory` instantiates (lines 64–65) a `QuoteConnectionFactory Impl`, passing the connection manager supplied by the container. `Quote ConnectionFactoryImpl` stores (line 43) this reference in an instance variable for later use. The new connection factory is returned to the container, and from there...

Connection factory is returned to the EJB The EJB gets the newly created connection factory instance (lines 5–6 of Listing 18.14). Note that the client does not have to know the class of this instance, as it manipulates it through the interface `QuoteConnectionFactory`.

Client calls `getConnection()` on the factory (lines 7–8 of Listing 18.14, line 50 of `QuoteBean`). `QuoteConnectionFactoryImpl` simply delegates this call (lines 65–66) to the connection manager it stored earlier. The EJB server's connection manager knows that no physical connections yet exist, so...

EJB server asks the adapter to create an new physical connection The EJB server calls `createManagedConnection()` on `QuoteManagedFactory Object` (line 9 of Listing 18.14). The `QuoteManagedFactoryObject` instantiates (line 93) a `QuoteManagedConnection`, the class that models the physical connection to the server. It then (line 97) tells it to open the network socket, using the server name and port number that were supplied earlier by the EJB server. (line 10 of Listing 18.14).

EJB server installs a connection listener on the new connection The server calls `addConnectionListner()` on the new `QuoteManagedConnection` (line 179). This object then adds the server's listener to its set of registered listeners (line 11 of Listing 18.14).

EJB server calls `getConnection()` on the physical connection   The get `Connection()` method in `QuoteManagedConnection` instantiates (line 92) a new `QuoteConnectionImpl` (virtual connection), and adds it (line 95) to the list of active virtual connections (lines 12–13 of Listing 18.14). The object returned to the EJB server is an active, initialized virtual connection to the server, which the server then returns, via the connection factory, to the EJB (lines 14–15 of Listing 18.14).

Client calls `getPrice()` on the connection The `QuoteConnectionImpl` is only a virtual connection: It does not talk to the quote server directly. Instead it (line 88) calls `getPrice()` in `QuoteManagedConnection` (line 349). This in turn sends the ticker symbol to the server, and parses the response (lines 353–357). This sequence appears in the server log as lines 16–18 of Listing 18.14.

Client closes the connection As it has finished with the connection, the client calls `close()` on its instance of `QuoteConnectionImpl`. This does not actually close the physical connection; instead, `QuoteConnectionImpl` (lines 39–41) informs the `QuoteManagedConnection` that the virtual connection is defunct. `QuoteManagedConnection` removes the virtual connection from its list of active `QuoteConnectionImpl` instances (line 283), and sends the 'closed' event to all registered event listeners (lines 297–303). This sequence appears in the server log as lines 19–22 of Listing 18.14.

EJB server tells the physical connection that it is about to be pooled The EJB server calls `cleanup()` in `QuoteManagedConnection` (lines 137–143), which invalidates any open virtual connections. Of course, there should not be any open connections at this point, as `cleanup()` was called in response to the only open connection being closed. (line 23 of Listing 18.14).

At this point, the client call has finished and there are no open virtual connections, but the server is holding one instance of `QuoteManagedConnection` (a physical connection) in its pool.

The next time the client does a JNDI lookup, the sequence above is repeated (lines 24–29 of Listing 18.14) as far as the point where the client calls `get Connection()` on the connection factory. As before, this call goes to the EJB server's connection manager. The server knows that it has one open physical connection in its pool. What it *doesn't* know is whether the resource adapter will allow that to be used to support the new client request. So it calls `matchManagedConnections()` on the `QuoteManagedConnectionFactory()`, which must reply with an instance of `ManagedConnection`, or null. In our implementation, `QuoteManagedConnection Factory` returns the instance of `QuoteManagedConnection` that has matching server name and port number properties. It does this by calling `equals` on each putative `QuoteManagedConnection`; this method returns `true` if two instances have the same server/port properties (lines 30–37 of Listing 18.14). The server than proceeds as before, getting a virtual connection from the physical connection and returning it to the client (lines 38–41 of Listing 18.14). The client then calls `get Price()` on the virtual connection, which delegates to `getPrice()` on the physical connection, exactly as before (lines 42–45 of Listing 18.14). The close and cleanup sequence is also as before, with the `QuoteManagedConnection` remaining in the pool.

Listing 18.14: **Output in the server log when the test client is executed twice. See text for full explanation.**

```
QuoteManagedConnectionFactory:  Called  constructor
QuoteManagedConnectionFactory:  Called  setServerName(),  server=localhost
QuoteManagedConnectionFactory:  Called  setPortNumber(),  port=30055
QuoteManagedConnectionFactory:  Called  createConnectionFactory(cm)
```

```
 5   QuoteBean: Resource factory object is
         ejbook.quote.resourceadapter.QuoteConnectionFactoryImpl@3945e2
     QuoteBean: Calling getConnection() on the resource factory
     QuoteConnectionFactoryImpl: Called getConnection
     QuoteManagedConnectionFactory: Called createManagedConnection()
10   QuoteManagedConnection: Called openSocket; opening on localhost:30055
     QuoteManagedConnection: Called addConnectionEventListener()
     QuoteManagedConnection: Called getConnection()
     QuoteManagedConnection: Called addConnection()
     QuoteBean: Resource connection object is
15       ejbook.quote.resourceadapter.QuoteConnectionImpl@2271f5
     QuoteBean: About to call getPrice()
     QuoteConnectionImpl: Called getPrice(), tickerSymbol=SUNW
     QuoteManagedConnection: Called getPrice(), tickerSymbol=SUNW
     QuoteBean: Closing connection object
20   QuoteConnectionImpl: Called close()
     QuoteManagedConnection: Called removeConnection()
     QuoteManagedConnection: Called sendClosedEvent
     QuoteManagedConnection: Called cleanup()
     QuoteManagedConnectionFactory: Called constructor
25   QuoteManagedConnectionFactory: Called setServerName(), server=localhost
     QuoteManagedConnectionFactory: Called setPortNumber(), port=30055
     QuoteManagedConnectionFactory: Called createConnectionFactory(cm)
     QuoteBean: Resource factory object is
         ejbook.quote.resourceadapter.QuoteConnectionFactoryImpl@40cb76
30   QuoteBean: Calling getConnection() on the resource factory
     QuoteConnectionFactoryImpl: Called getConnection
     QuoteManagedConnectionFactory: Called matchManagedConnection()
     QuoteManagedConnectionFactory: Considering object
         ejbook.quote.resourceadapter.QuoteManagedConnection@6dd8e1
35   QuoteManagedConnectionFactory: Object is a QuoteManagedConnection
     QuoteManagedConnectionFactory: Called equals
     QuoteManagedConnectionFactory: Object has matching Factory: hit
     QuoteManagedConnection: Called getConnection()
     QuoteManagedConnection: Called addConnection()
40   QuoteBean: Resource connection object is
         ejbook.quote.resourceadapter.QuoteConnectionImpl@39da92
     QuoteBean: About to call getPrice()
     QuoteConnectionImpl: Called getPrice(), tickerSymbol=SUNW
     QuoteManagedConnection: Called getPrice(), tickerSymbol=SUNW
45   QuoteBean: Closing connection object
     QuoteConnectionImpl: Called close()
     QuoteManagedConnection: Called removeConnection()
     QuoteManagedConnection: Called sendClosedEvent
     QuoteManagedConnection: Called cleanup()
```

18.5   Common client interface (CCI)

This section describes the common client interface (CCI), support for which is optional in a resource adapter.

18.5.1   CCI rationale

If you followed the description of the resource adapter for the stock quote server, you will remember that the two interfaces presented to the client (`QuoteConnection Factory` and `QuoteConnection`) were not controlled by the Specification, and therefore neither were the classes that implemented them. To be sure, there were some restrictions on these interfaces. We had to provide a `close()` method, for example, on the connection interface, and a `getConnection()` on the connection factory; in addition, the connection factory had to be compatible with storing in a JNDI namespace. Apart from these minor restrictions, we had a free hand to define the client interface.

Now this is entirely appropriate for a resource adapter like the one we have been considering. The external server is very simple, and clients can only do one thing: get a stock price for a given stock symbol. So providing the client interface with a single method `getPrice()` seems very straightforward.

The *J2EE Connector Specification* is intended to support simple external resources like our simulated stock quote server, but it is also intended for complex enterprise information systems. Although these systems are all different, it is possible to identify common functionality in a range of popular systems.

- The conversation between the client and the EIS is connection-based—that is, the client establishes a connection, carries out some operations, and closes the connection. The EIS does not normally 'push' data to clients.

- There is usually a request-response model of interaction, where the client provides some data and a specification of the operations to be carried out on that data, and the EIS returns some data. The parallel in JDBC is the `Connection.execute()` method, which takes an SQL statement and produces a `ResultSet`.

- The data produced by an interaction with the EIS is often representable in one of a number of simple formats—for example, tabular or name-value pairs. The data set produced by an interaction may be large, and the client may want to control the manner in which it is retrieved from the server.

- The EIS usually has transactional semantics but, in the absence of any overt transactional control, defaults to committing changes at the end of each client-server interaction.

The CCI is an attempt to provide a general interface to EIS systems of this sort. A CCI-compliant resource adapter does not use developer-specified interfaces for client-adapter interaction. Instead, the connection factory must be an implementation of `javax.resource.cci.ConnectionFactory`, while the (virtual) connection is an implementation of `javax.resource.cci.Connection`. Let's examine these interfaces—and the other important ones—in turn.

18.5.2   The ConnectionFactory interface

When the client does a JNDI lookup for a resource connection factory that supports CCI, it doesn't get a vendor-specific class; instead, it is guaranteed to get an instance of something that implements `ConnectionFactory`. This interface is very simple: Its most important method is `getConnection()`, which has a similar function to `getConnection()` in the `QuoteConnectionFactory` discussed above. However, in contrast to the quote server example, the result from `getConnection()` is not a class that implements a developer-specified interface, but is guaranteed to be a class that implements `Connection`.

18.5.3   The Connection interface

`Connection` represents a specific (virtual) connection to the EIS. It has, of course, a `close()` method, but other than this, its important method is `getInteraction()`. Clients call `getInteraction()` to retrieve an object that can drive an interaction with the server. The equivalent in JDBC is the `Statement` object.

18.5.4   The Interaction and InteractionSpec interfaces

Clients get an `Interaction` object (a system-specific implementation of this interface) by calling `getInteraction()` on an open CCI connection. The most significant methods on this interface are the various `execute()` methods, which carry out some work on the EIS. These methods all take as input some collection of data (modelled by a `Record` object), and a specification of the action to be carried out; they produce a new `Record` object as output. `Record` is a generic set of data; the CCI defines various subtypes, of which `ResultSet` is one (equivalent to the JDBC result set). The nature of the interaction is specified by an object that implements the `InteractionSpec` interface, which specifies no methods, because it is impossible to stipulate what operations can be carried out by the EIS. However, the Specification does recommend that it be implemented in the form of a JavaBean, with `getXXX()` and `setXXX()` methods for each of its internal properties. It also recommends a set of standard properties that implementations are encouraged to support (e.g, `FunctionName`). It is envisaged that clients will obtain an `InteractionSpec` object from a JDNI lookup or using a `static` method on a vendor-specific class.

18.5.5   CCI client example

The code fragment below shows in outline how a client interacts with a resource adapter that supports the CCI.

```
     // Find the connection factory
     InitialContext ic = new InitialContext();
     ConnectionFactory ccicf =
          (ConnectionFactory) ic.lookup("eis/something");
 5   // Create a connection
     Connection ccic = ccicf.getConnection();
     // Get an Interaction
     Interaction i = ccic.createInteraction();
     // get an Interaction
10   InteractionSpec is = //... vendor specific
     // Execute the interaction
     ResultSet rs = (ResultSet)i.execute(is, null);
     // Process results, just like JDBC
     while (rs.next()) { .... }
```

The important point to note about this example is that, apart from the configuration of the `InteractionSpec` object, the rest of the code is independent of the EIS and the resource adapter.

18.5.6   CCI: costs and benefits

Anyone who is embarking on the development of a resource adapter should bear in mind that CCI support is not mandatory. It should only be used where there are clear benefits that outweigh the costs. The costs are obvious: The developer has to implement another half-dozen or so interfaces. The benefits are likely to be increased portability and decoupling of the EJB code from the external resource. The CCI was designed with a certain class of systems in mind, and the costs of using it certainly won't outweigh the benefits if the external resource is very different from the CCI view (as our 'quote server' is).

18.6   Transaction management

The quote server resource manager presented above has no transactional semantics; it is meaningless to talk of 'rolling back' this server. In practice, many EIS implementations that will be supported by resource adapters will be transactional. A client will be able to carry out operations grouped into a single transaction, such that if one operation fails, the earlier operations can be rolled back.

If the resource adapter is integrated into an EJB container, and the container is managing transactions, then the container needs to get access to the transaction infrastructure of the external resource.

Consider the case where an entity EJB is using a resource adapter for access to its persistent storage. In its `ejbStore()` operation, the EJB opens a connection to the resource and writes its persistent state to it. Later, another EJB operation in the same transaction fails. Now the container has to roll back the work done on the resource adapter.

The container knows *when* it has to roll back, because the *EJB Specification* defines exactly what events should lead to a rollback. The problem is that it does not know *how* to roll back an external resource. The resource adapter developer can choose to support the container's management of its transactions by providing—among other things—implementations of either of two interfaces: `javax.resource.spi.LocalTransaction`, if only local transactions are to be supported, or `javax.transaction.xa.XAResource`, if the resource adapter is prepared to collaborate in distributed transactions. The developer must also specify in the deployment descriptor which of these two interfaces is supported, if either.

18.6.1   Local transaction support

To support local transactions, the developer provides an implementation of `javax.resource.spi.LocalTransaction` and makes it available to the container on a call to `getLocalTransaction()` on the physical connection object (the implementation of `ManagedConnection`). The connector must also be prepared to notify any event listeners of changes in the transactional state. So, for example, if we roll back a transaction internally, we need to arrange for a LOCAL_TRANSACTION_ ROLLEDBACK event to be sent to any registered event listener. In practice, the application server will use this event to detect illegal transaction operations (such as beginning a transaction before completing a previous one).

The *J2EE Connector Specification* has a great deal to say about local transaction support (about 10 pages, in fact), but most of this is for the benefit of container designers; implementation in a resource adapter is conceptually straightforward (of course, it may be *practically* very difficult, especially if the transactional state is being maintained by the resource adapter code itself).

18.6.2   Distributed transaction support

It is quite likely that where EIS implementations are transactional, they will be required to collaborate in a distributed transaction. For example, suppose two entity EJBs are updated in one transaction: The first is storing data in a relational database, and the second in an EIS via a resource adapter. This situation, simple as it seems, calls for a distributed transaction and two-phase commit support. If the database operation fails after a successful EIS operation, then we have to roll back the EIS operation via the resource adapter.

The Specification requires resource adapters that support two-phase commit to do so via an implementation of `XAResource`. The EJB container will get this implementation by a call on `getXAResource()`, and will call its methods as it goes through the transaction co-ordination process. The `XAResource` implementation must respond by carrying out the appropriate transactional operations on the external resource (or managing them internally). The `XAResource` object is a mapping of the X/Open XA interface; the operations in that interface, and therefore the functions of the methods in `XAResource`, were discussed in detail in Section 9.8.2, and won't be reiterated here.

18.7   Security management

The stock quote server example discussed above is not representative of many practical applications, in that it required no authentication. Anyone who knows the hostname and port number can connect and get stock quotes. Practical EISs will require some form of authentication and, very possibly, other security measures as well. These measures may include guarantees of privacy and confidentiality, as discussed in Chapter 16.

This issue is complicated by the fact that there are a great many systems for which we may wish to provide resource adapters, and it would be impossible to set down details of the sign-on procedure in the *J2EE Connector Specification*. However, just as with JDBC, the Specification recognizes two basic procedures: application-managed sign-on and container-managed sign-on.

18.7.1   Application-managed sign-on

You may remember (page 228) that an EJB can get access to a database using credentials supplied by the container, or using its own user ID and password. So, having got a `DataSource` object (call it `ds`), we create a `Connection` like this:

```
Connection c = ds.getConnection("user", "pass");
```

You may remember from the discussion above that we can either use the common client interface (CCI) specification for the client interface to a resource adapter or use a developer-supplied interface. If we are using the latter option, then we could define the `getConnection()` method exactly as for JDBC, so that it takes a user ID and password. It would be up to the resource adapter to decide how to deal with those parameters (in a way that will be discussed below). If we are using CCI, then we are limited to two variants of `getConnection()`:

```
public Connection getConnection();
public Connection getConnection(ConnectionSpec cs);
```

`ConnectionSpec` is an interface that does not specify any methods: It exists just to provide a common way of calling `getConnection()` with some data. The resource adapter vendor must provide an implementation of `ConnectionSpec` that clients fill in with the appropriate data (user ID, password, encryption type, and so on).

So, whether we are using CCI or not, the client calls `getConnection()` and supplies some kind of sign-on data. What does the resource adapter do with this data? You may remember that `getConnection()` in `QuoteConnectionFactoryImpl` was defined like this:

```
public QuoteConnection getConnection()
    throws ResourceException
{
    return (QuoteConnection)
        connectionManager.allocateConnection (manager, null);
}
```

That is, the connection request is delegated to the default connection manager. And the default connection manager is, in all likelihood, part of the EJB server. The *J2EE Connector Specification* defines an interface `ConnectionRequestInfo`, which is the second argument to `allocateConnection` (this was `null` in the example above, because we were not supporting authentication). `ConnectionRequestInfo` is another interface with no methods. The developer's job is to implement it using a class that can contain sufficient information to allow a client to sign in. So the `getConnection()` method may look something like this:

```
public QuoteConnection getConnection(String user, String password)
    throws ResourceException
{
    ConnectionRequestInfo cri = new QuoteCRI(user, password);
    return (QuoteConnection)
```

```
connectionManager.allocateConnection (manager, cri);
}
```

All we have done here is convey the information about the client's credentials to the default `allocateConnection()` method. This, in itself, is not sufficient, as this method is in the EJB container's connection pooling system, and
the EJB server does not know how to make connections to the resource or authenticate users. Instead, it passes the `ConnectionRequestInfo` exactly as supplied
into the methods `createManagedConnection` and `matchManagedConnection` in the
`ManagedConnectionFactory`. It is this class that will use the `ConnectionRequest
Info` to sign on clients.

We could now rewrite `createManagedConnection()` like this (the role of the
`Subject` parameter is discussed below):

```
   public ManagedConnection createManagedConnection
       (Subject subject, ConnectionRequestInfo cri)
       throws ResourceException
       {
5      QuoteManagedConnection qmc = new QuoteManagedConnection (this);
       if (Subject == null)
          {
          qmc.openSocket (serverName, portNumber,
            cri.getUser(), cri.getPassword());
10         }
       else
          // See below...
       return qmc;
       }
```

This assumes, of course, that our implementation of `ConnectionRequestInfo` has
`getUser()` and `getPassword()` methods. Now we must use the user ID and password
in a new implementation of the `openSocket` method in `QuoteManagedConnection`.

This procedure seems very complicated, but it is necessary to allow the resource
adapter to be integrated with the container's connection management system.

18.7.2   Container-managed sign-on

With container-managed sign-on, the EJB code does not pass connection properties to the `getConnection()` method. Instead, the EJB server calls `createManaged
Connection()` with a non-null value of the `Subject` parameter. This argument car-
ries information about the person or entity requesting the information, and may include not only simple username/password credentials, but cryptographic certificates
for certificate-based authentication. If the `Subject` argument is non-null, the `create
ManagedConnection()` method should extract the authentication data from the
`Subject`, and use that to sign on the user.

`Subject` is a class defined in the *Java authentication and authorization service*
(JAAS) *Specification*, and represents a very flexible way to specify user authentication parameters. JAAS is outside the scope of this book (see `http://java.`

`sun.com/products/jaas`), but in outline the `Subject` object will be used by the `createManagedConnection()` method like this:[5]

```
      public ManagedConnection createManagedConnection
          (Subject subject , ConnectionRequestInfo cri )
        throws ResourceException
        {
5       QuoteManagedConnection qmc = new QuoteManagedConnection (this );
        if (Subject == null)
          {
          qmc.openSocket (serverName, portNumber,
            cri.getUser (), cri.getPassword ());
10        }
        else
          {
          Set s = cri.getPrivateCredentials
            ("javax.resource.spi.security.PasswordCredential");
15        Object [] a = s.toArray ();
          PasswordCredential pc = (PasswordCredential)a [0];
          String user = pc.getUserName ();
          String password = pc.getPassword ();
          qmc.openSocket (serverName, portNumber,
20          user, password );
          }
        return qmc;
        }
```

How does the EJB container know what credentials to pass in the `Subject` instance? This is vendor-specific: Typically, this information will be supplied at deployment time, exactly as was the case for JDBC connections. With the *J2EE Reference Implementation*, the information is supplied in the same dialog box as is used to make a mapping to the JNDI name of the resource adapter (Figure 18.7).

18.8 Summary

The *J2EE Connector Specification* defines the interaction between a resource adapter, its clients, and an application server. If a resource adapter is built according to this Specification, then it should be platform-independent and vendor-neutral. That is, the resource adapter itself should be portable between application servers.

Under this specification, the interface presented by the resource adapter to its clients (the EJBs) may be vendor-specific or follow the provisions of the CCI (common client interface). There are advantages and disadvantages to both approaches. In either case, the Specification allows for the external resource to have transactional semantics and to be integrated with the EJB container's transaction manager. It also provides a mechanism for both EJBs and the EJB container to provide authentication information to the external resource.

---

[5]This example uses simple user/password authentication, with the user ID and password encapsulated in a `Subject` instance. JAAS provides more sophisticated authentication mechanisms than these.

Appendix A

New features in EJB 2.1

Overview

This appendix discusses in outline the features that have been proposed for version 2.1 of the *EJB Specification*.

A.1 Overview

At the time of writing, the first public draft of EJB 2.1 had just been made available. It addresses many of the problems that have been discussed in this book and extends functionality in some fairly radical ways. However, it is important to understand that this is an early draft, and there is no indication when it will be fully ratified, or when products will start to become available that support the new features.

The main developments in EJB 2.1 can be grouped into the following categories: improvements to the EJB QL query language, support for the Web services model, extension of the message-driven EJB API to support arbitrary messaging services and deployment-time message-flow modelling, and timer services.

A.2 EJB QL enhancements

The EJB QL language was discussed in Chapter 13. In that chapter, it was suggested that the language had a number of weaknesses that needed to be addressed. EJB 2.1 addresses some of these weaknesses, but not all.

EJB QL enhancements include the following.

Support for sorting It is now possible to include an ORDER BY clause in the query. For example:

```
SELECT OBJECT(o) from book o
   WHERE o.publisher = ?1
   ORDER BY o.title
```

This results in a `Collection` of book EJBs sorted in ascending alphabetical order of `title`.

Support for aggregate functions There will be support for SELECT COUNT, etc. So we can get the number of book EJBs like this:

```
SELECT COUNT(o) from book o
```

There is also proposed support for average (AVG), minimum (MIN), maximum (MAX), and SUM.

New functions Some new functions are proposed for use in WHERE expressions.

The following EJB QL limitations are, at present, *not* addressed.

There remains no support for date properties. You may remember that in the *Prestige Bike Hire* application, we had to represent dates as long integers in order to compare them in EJB QL expressions. We badly need date fields and date comparisons in the CMP scheme.

Although some logical inconsistencies in the grammar have been tidied up, not all have.

A.3   Web services integration

The Web services application model (see page 43) sees application components being exposed by means of XML data interchange over HTTP. The benefits of such a model include a high level of interoperability and avoidance of some of the security problems associated with RMI/IIOP over a wide-area network.

EJB 2.1 radically extends the way in which EJBs provide their functionality to clients. Both stateless session EJBs and message-driven EJBs can be exposed as Web services. The *EJB Specification* defines a new client view for stateless session EJBs: As well as a local client view and a distributed (remote) client view, we now have a 'Web service view.' The developer will simply code another interface, and deploy it with the EJB. The container will read the interface and create an endpoint for an XML-RPC channel. This is all that will be necessary to expose session EJBs as Web services.

Message-driven EJBs will be accessible via XML messaging.

These improvements significantly extend the interoperability of EJB applications, as there is universal industry support for the Web services model.

A.4   Messaging enhancements

In EJB 2.0, message-driven EJBs are associated with JMS message queues and topics. EJB 2.1 extends the API to make it possible for products to support non-JMS messages, such as SMTP email receipts. This scheme is made vendor-neutral by being based on the J2EE Connector Architecture (JCA).

It will also be possible to create 'chains' of message-driven EJBs, and couple them together at deployment time.

A.5   Timer services

The proposed timer service is simple, but likely to be very useful. Any EJB can register itself with the container's timer service, provided it implements the `TimedObject` interface. This interface exposes one method: `ejbTimeout`. When the timer reaches its set time or interval, the container calls this method; the EJB can do then do whatever it needs.

A.6   What's missing

The proposed EJB 2.1 still does not specify how the EJB container should support automatically generated primary keys. For example, it should be possible to stipulate in the deployment descriptor that a sequence number should be used as the primary key and the container should do the rest. It remains necessary for the developer to handle primary key generation in the EJB logic.

Appendix B

Overview of the EJB deployment descriptor

Overview

This appendix provides a very brief introduction to the format and content of the XML deployment descriptor used for configuring EJB applications. It is not intended to be exhaustive; rather it is a guide to interpretation of the detailed description in Chapter 21 of the *EJB Specification*. If you are using graphical tools to package EJB applications, the contents of this appendix may be of no interest to you at all. However, there are just a few technical points that can only be properly understood by reference to the deployment descriptor.

B.1 Vendor-independent and vendor-specific deployment descriptors

The *EJB Specification* stipulates that each EJB-JAR file must contain at least one deployment descriptor, that it must be called `ejb-jar.xml`, that it must have a specified structure, and that it must be packaged into a directory called `META-INF`. However, the Specification does not *limit* the number of deployment descriptors to this one. In fact, server vendors are permitted to require the JAR files they deploy to contain any number of additional deployment descriptors, and there are no requirements as to structure, name, or even content of these files.

There are two reasons for this state of affairs, which seems at first to be in opposition to the major portability goal of J2EE.

First, the *EJB Specification* leaves unspecified a large number of features that a commercial server must have: load balancing, failover, resource pooling, and so on. These things have to be configured *somewhere*, and this can't be in `ejb-jar.xml`, because this file has a structure and content defined by the Specification.

Second, the *EJB Specification* is silent on the configuration of properties that are set 'at deployment time.' This is a philosophical standpoint adopted by the Specification designers. As an example, consider the provision of JNDI names for EJBs. EJBs don't even *have* JNDI names until they are deployed. It follows that the JNDI names can't be assigned anywhere in `ejb-jar.xml`, because this file is created when the EJBs are assembled into a JAR file, not at deployment time. This may seem like academic fussiness, but it isn't. Remember that one of the key features of J2EE is its rigorous emphasis on component-based development. It is central to this model that the specifications distinguish sharply between what happens at development time, what happens at assembly time, and what happens at deployment time. Each of these phases has its own inputs and outputs. `ejb-jar.xml` is an *output* from the assembly phase and an *input* to the deployment phase. Other inputs to the deployment phase include deployment-specific configuration, like the JNDI names of EJBs and other resources.

In this appendix, we can only consider the contents of `ejb-jar.xml`; there is nothing much to say about the structure of the vendor-specific files that will be of general usefulness. What is *usually* true is that they are XML files and they are packaged into the same `META-INF` directory as `ejb-jar.xml`.

Do we always need to provide a vendor-specific deployment descriptor for a particular package of EJBs? If it is missing, the EJB server has really only three courses of action open to it: refuse to deploy the application, prompt the deployer for the information that is missing, or use defaults for all the missing properties. Which specific response will be obtained depends on the product. In general, it is usually more efficient in the longer term to provide the vendor-specific files, even if the application can be made to work without them.

There is a bright side to all this: most graphical development tools can now provide vendor-specific deployment descriptors for a range of different server products. This, of course, is of little help to a developer who wishes to produce EJB JAR files without recourse to such tools. In practice, however, the vendor-specific deployment descriptors are uncomplicated in structure, and a developer familiar with `ejb-jar.xml` will usually have little trouble producing such other deployment descriptors as may be required.

The rest of this chapter describes the structure of `ejb-jar.xml`.

B.2   General structure

The deployment descriptor `ejb-jar.xml` has three basic XML elements, each of which has nested subelements. These elements are `enterprise-beans`, `relationships`, and `assembly-descriptor`. Here is an outline of this basic structure (the text in brackets is a description of what is to be found in each element, not part of the XML):

```
<ejb-jar>

  (...information about the package...)
```

```
 5    <enterpise −beans>
         (...information  about  the  EJBs...)
      </enterpise −beans>

      <relationships>
10       (...information  about  the
            associations  between  EJBS...)
      </relationships>

      <assembly −descriptor >
15       (... security  and  transaction
            ...)
      </assembly −descriptor >

   </ejb−jar>
```

At the top level of the `ejb-jar` element, there is optional information about the name of the package, a description, and icons to be displayed in graphical tools. For example, the deployment descriptor may well start like this:

```
<ejb−jar>
   <display −name>My EJB package</display −name>
   <enterpise −beans>
      (...  etc  ...)
```

B.3   enterprise-beans element

This is the only element that is mandatory, although in practice there is always an `assembly-descriptor` element as well. This element contains subelements describing each EJB in the package. For example:

```
   <ejb−jar>
      <enterpise −beans>
         <session >
            (...  information  about  session  EJB  1 ...)
 5       </session >
         <entity>
            (...  information  about  entity  EJB  1 ...)
         </entity>
         <entity>
10          (...  information  about  entity  EJB  2 ...)
         </entity>
         <message−driven>
            (...  information  about  message−driven  EJB  1 ...)
         </message−driven>
15    </enterpise −beans>
   </ejb−jar>
```

There can be any number of **entity** elements, any number of **session** elements, and any number of **message-driven** elements.

B.3.1   session element

This element describes a session EJB. There can be any number of these elements.
Here is an example.

```
<ejb−jar>
  <enterpise −beans>
    <session >
      <ejb −name>BookingManager </ejb−name>
      <home>BookingManagerHome</home>
      <remote>BookingManager </remote>
      <ejb−class >BookingManagerBean </ejb−class >
      <session −type>Stateless </session −type>
      <transaction −type>Container</transaction −type>
      <ejb−ref >
        <ejb−ref −name>ejb /FleetManager </ejb−ref −name>
        <ejb−ref −type>Session </ejb−ref−type>
        <home>FleetManagerHome </home>
        <remote>FleetManager </remote>
        <ejb−link >bikehire . jar#FleetManager </ejb−link >
      </ejb−ref >
    </session >
  </enterpise −beans>
</ejb−jar>
```

The `ejb-name` element denotes the internal name of the EJB. This is *not* a JNDI
name, and cannot necessarily be used by clients. JNDI names, as we have discussed,
are assigned at deployment time. The elements `home`, `remote`, and `ejb-class` define
the EJB's home interface, remote interface, and implementation class, respectively.
We might also specify `local-home` and `local` elements here if the EJB has a local
client view. `session-type` can be `Stateless` or `Stateful`; `transaction-type` can
be `Container` or `Bean`.

More interesting is the `ejb-ref` section. This denotes a reference to another
EJB. `ejb-ref-name` is the 'coded name' of the object looked up. This denotes that
the EJB whose DD this is does a lookup for another EJB using a JNDI operation
like this:

```
... = initialContext.lookup
    ("java :comp/env/ejb /FleetManager" );
```

that is, the part of the lookup after `java:comp/env` forms the contents of the
`ejb-ref-name` element. The `home` and `remote` elements denote the home and remote
interfaces of the EJB being looked up, and the `ejb-link` section gives *guidance* to
the deployer about which EJB this is a reference to. In this case, it says that the
reference is to an EJB whose internal name is `FleetManager`, which is deployed
in `bikehire.jar`. It is very important to realize that the `ejb-link` element is
optional, and will not necessarily be handled by the EJB server at deployment time.
Typically, the deployer will use the information in `ejb-link` to link to the JNDI
name of the EJB, using the EJB server vendor's tools. With the *J2EE Reference
Implementation*, this operation is performed using the deployment tool, which also

does packaging operations. This is a source of confusion to developers, because the tool is doing both 'assembly' tasks and 'deployment' tasks with the same user interface.

As well as `ejb-ref` elements, one may also declare `resource-ref` elements. These play a similar role, but for container-managed resources, rather than EJBs. As for EJBs, the `resource-ref` section defines the name by which the EJB looks up the resource, and does *not* supply the real JNDI name of the resource. The JNDI name is assigned at deployment time, and typically ends up in a vendor-specific XML file.

B.3.2   entity element

The `entity` element describes an entity EJB, and is similar in structure to the `session` element. Here is an example.

```
<ejb-jar>
  <enterpise-beans>
    <entity>
      <ejb-name>BikeModel</ejb-name>
5     <home>BikeModelHome</home>
      <remote>BikeModel</remote>
      <ejb-class>BikeModelBean</ejb-class>
      <persistence-type>Container</persistence-type>
      <prim-key-class>java.lang.String</prim-key-class>
10    <reentrant>False</reentrant>
      <cmp-version>2.x</cmp-version>
      <abstract-schema-name>bikemodel</abstract-schema-name>
      <cmp-field>
        <field-name>chargeBand</field-name>
15    </cmp-field>
      <cmp-field>
        <field-name>name</field-name>
      </cmp-field>
      <cmp-field>
20      <field-name>engineSize</field-name>
      </cmp-field>
      <cmp-field>
        <field-name>description</field-name>
      </cmp-field>
25    <primkey-field>name</primkey-field>
      <query>
        <query-method>
          <method-name>findAll</method-name>
          <method-params />
30      </query-method>
        <ejb-ql>
          select object(b) from bikemodel b
        </ejb-ql>
      </query>
35    </entity>
  </enterpise-beans>
</ejb-jar>
```

Many of the properties it specifies are the same as for the `session` element, so these won't be described again. However, the nature of container-managed persistence means that more needs to be configured than is the case for a session EJB or an entity EJB with bean-managed persistence. We know this is a CMP entity, because the `persistence-type` element has the value `Container`, rather than `Bean`.

The `entity` element can have any number of `cmp-field` elements. These denote the properties that are to be made persistent. Notice that there are no data types specified for these properties; the container works them out using reflection.

Because this EJB has a finder method (`findAll()`), an EJB QL query must be provided for it. This is in the `query` section. Here `query-method` is the name of the method for which an EJB QL query is being provided, and `ejb-ql` is the query itself.

B.3.3   message-driven element

This element specifies the properties of a message-driven EJB.

```
   <ejb−jar>
     <enterpise −beans>
       <message−driven>
         <ejb−name>LegacyReceiver </ejb−name>
5        <ejb−class>LegacyReceiverBean</ejb−class>
         <transaction −type>Container</transaction −type>
         <message−driven−destination >
           <destination −type>
           javax .jms . Queue
10         </destination −type>
         </message−driven−destination >
       </message−driven>
     </enterpise −beans>
   </ejb−jar>
```

Note that the implementation class is specified (`ejb-class`), but no interfaces, as message-driven EJBs don't have interfaces. The `message-driven-destination` element specifies that this EJB is associated with a `Queue` (rather than a `Topic`). But where do we specify the name of the queue to monitor? We don't: This, again, is a deployment-time task, so it isn't configured in here. In practice, it will be configured in a vendor-specific XML file.

B.4   relationships element

The `relationships` element specifies any number of associations between EJBs. It is optional, but will always be presented when there are container-managed associations. It has the following basic structure:

```
   <ejb−jar>

     <enterpise −beans>
       (... EJB configuration  ...)
5      </enterpise −beans>
```

```
     <relationships>
       <ejb−relation>
         <... association 1...>
10     </ejb−relation>
       <ejb−relation>
         <... association 2...>
       </ejb−relation>
       <ejb−relation>
15       <... association 3...>
       </ejb−relation>
       (... etc ...)
     </relationships>

20 </ejb−jar>
```

that is, it consists of a number of `ejb-relation` elements.

The `ejb-relation` element specifies the source and destination of a relationship, and the mutliplicity of each end. Here is an example.

```
<ejb−jar>
  <relationships>
    <ejb−relation>
      <ejb−relationship−role>
5       <ejb−relationship−role−name>
          BikeModel
        </ejb−relationship−role−name>
        <multiplicity>One</multiplicity>
        <relationship−role−source>
10        <ejb−name>BikeModel</ejb−name>
        </relationship−role−source>
        <cmr−field>
          <cmr−field−name>
            bikes
15        </cmr−field−name>
          <cmr−field−type>
            java.util.Collection
          </cmr−field−type>
        </cmr−field>
20      </ejb−relationship−role>
      <ejb−relationship−role>
        <ejb−relationship−role−name>
          Bike
        </ejb−relationship−role−name>
25      <multiplicity>Many</multiplicity>
        <relationship−role−source>
          <ejb−name>Bike</ejb−name>
        </relationship−role−source>
      </ejb−relationship−role>
30    </ejb−relation>
  </relationships>
</ejb−jar>
```

This, complicated looking declaration contains two `ejb-relationship-role` elements, each of which specifies one 'end' of the association. The first 'end' in this case is on EJB `BikeModel`, and the other is on `Bike`. The multiplicity at the `BikeModel` end is 'one,' and at the `Bike` end is 'many.' At the `BikeModel` end, we can navigate to the associated `Bike` EJBs using a `Collection`-valued property (`cmr-field`) called `bikes`. We can surmise from this that the `BikeModel` EJB defines a property `bikes` like this:

```
public abstract Collection getBikes();
```

There is no `cmr-field` element for the `Bike` end of the association, which indicates that the association is not navigable in the direction `Bike-to-BikeModel`.

B.5   assembly-descriptor element

This element is strictly optional but, as it contains transaction properties, is rarely absent in a practical deployment descriptor.

This element contains any number of `security-role`, `method-permission`, and `container-transaction` subelements (all described below). It also includes an optional list of methods (`exclude-list`) that cannot be called. This element is rarely used, and won't be described here.

B.5.1   security-role element

Each `security-role` element names (and optionally describes) one of the security roles known to the application. These role names are used in the `method-permission` elements (see below) to restrict access to certain groups of individuals. In the *Prestige Bike Hire* application, we have three roles: `Manager`, `Administrator`, and `Customer`. So we have:

```
   <ejb-jar>

     <enterpise-beans>
       (... EJB configuration ...)
5    </enterpise-beans>

     <relationships>
       (... Association configuration ...)
     </relationships>
10
     <assembly-descriptor>
       <security-role>
         <role-name>Manager</role-name>
         <role-name>Administrator</role-name>
15       <role-name>Customer</role-name>
       </security-role>
     </assembly-descriptor>

   </ejb-jar>
```

Note that although the role names are exposed in the deployment descriptor, there is no indication here of how these will be implemented as real user IDs, group names, and so on, in the real application; this is a deployment-time task.

B.5.2   method-permission element

There can be any number of `method-permission` elements in the `assembly-descriptor`. Each allows a method to be called by a certain security role, where the security roles were defined in the `security-role` elements. Here is an example.

```
    <ejb−jar>
      <assembly −descriptor >
        <method−permission >
          <role −name>Manager</role −name>
  5       <method>
            <ejb −name>CustomerManager </ejb −name>
            <method−intf >Remote</method−intf >
            <method−name>getCustomerData </method−name>
          </method>
 10       </method−permission >
      </assembly −descriptor >
    </ejb−jar>
```

This example states that the role `Manager` has access to the method `getCustomer Data` on the remote interface of the EJB `CustomerManager`. The method specifications can be given in more or less detail than this; for example, we can specify different permissions on different overloaded methods, or we can apply default permissions for all methods on a particular EJB. Rather than specifying a `role-name` we could instead have said

```
      <method−permission >
        <unchecked />
      </method−permission >
```

meaning that there is no restriction on this method. In fact, this is the default for an EJB that has no method permissions.

B.5.3   container-transaction element

This element, of which there can be any number, specifies a container-managed transaction property. Again, it is simplest to illustrate with an example:

```
    <ejb−jar>
      <assembly −descriptor >
        <container−transaction >
          <method>
  5         <ejb −name>BookingManager </ejb −name>
            <method−intf >Remote</method−intf >
            <method−name>getBookings </method−name>
          </method>
          <trans−attribute >Required </trans−attribute >
 10       </container−transaction >
```

```
</assembly-descriptor>
</ejb-jar>
```

This example says that method `getBookings()` on the remote interface of EJB `BookingManager` has transaction attribute `Requires`.

B.6   Summary

We have seen that the deployment descriptor for a package of EJBs is relatively straightforward if analyzed one piece at a time. The problem with constructing these files manually is not so much the difficulty of understanding what goes where, but the size of the file. The deployment descriptor for the *Prestige Bike Hire* application EJBs, for example, is nearly 4,000 lines long, and that's as generated by the deployment tool. If it were formatted in a nice, human-readable layout it would probably be three times as long. Using XML editors, rather than text editors, may allow some of this complexity to be managed.

Appendix C

Installing and testing the case study

> **Overview**
>
> This appendix describes how to install, configure, and test the *Prestige Bike Hire* application using the *J2EE Reference Implementation*, and demonstrates the application in operation.

Getting the *Prestige Bike Hire* application case study up and running consists of the following steps: deployment of the application as an EAR file, initialization with sample data, creation of new users and groups, and creation of the message queues. To be able to run the application, you will also need to start up the 'dummy legacy system' which handles the offline financial transactions.

To make things easy, I have set up the application in ways that would not normally be appropriate. In particular, the database mappings in the EAR file map the entity EJBs onto a database whose JNDI name is `jdbc/XACloudscape`—that is, the default database for the Reference Implementation using XA-compliant drivers.[1] The purpose of this is to avoid the necessity to configure a new database, as this one is preconfigured by the Reference Implementation installer.

C.1 Installing the application

C.1.1 Prerequisites

The *Prestige Bike Hire* application relies entirely on the EJB 2.0 model of container-managed persistence for its entity beans. Therefore, you will need either the latest version of the *J2EE Reference Implementation*, or some other application server that is fully compliant with EJB 2.0. This appendix assumes that you have installed and tested this. Information on installation and configuration of the *J2EE Reference*

---

[1]Do not attempt to use a non-XA compliant driver for this application; it exhibts transactions against multiple data sources.

Implementation can be found in Appendix F. Although other application servers might work, you're on your own: There is no space to give detailed instructions for other products.

You will also need the source code package, which is available from the accompanying Web site: `www.kevinboone.com/ejb_book`. The application can be found in the `bikehire` directory.

The compilation and initialization of the application is controlled by an Ant build script. These instructions assume that you have installed and tested Ant, and that you can run it on the command line.

C.1.2   Deploying the application

You can deploy the application using the graphical deployment tool (as has been demonstrated serveral times already in this book), or at the command line. Since we don't want to change the EAR file at this point, it is quickest to deploy at the command line. Change directory to the top of the source tree (`bikehire`), and run `deploytool` like this:

```
deploytool -deploy BikeHire.ear localhost
```

If you aren't deploying to the local machine, modify the name `localhost` as appropriate. If this doesn't work, you may need to modify your system's PATH, J2EE_HOME, and JAVA_HOME environment variables.

C.1.3   Setting up the database

The application needs some sample data to get started. Although it would be possible to use an SQL script for this, it is a better test for the EJBs to use EJB clients. Accordingly, there are a number of test clients that populate the entity EJBs (and therefore the databse) via the session EJB tier. These classes are in the `testclient` package, and have names like `InitializeCustomers`. Because the entity EJBs have dependencies on one another, these clients must be executed in the right order, thus: `InitializeFleet`, `InitializeCustomers`, and then `InitializeBookings`. The Ant script does this all automatically. Simply run:

```
ant initialize
```

There should be no error message the first time this is run. However, if you run it a second time you should expect to see errors relating to duplicate primary keys. Because the CMP system in the *Reference Implementation* clears the database every time an application is redeployed, you will need to repeat this step if you ever need to redeploy.

C.1.4   Creating users and groups

In the previous step (initializing the database), a number of customers will have been created within the application itself (e.g., as instances of the `Customer` EJB). We now need to enable them to log in, by giving them user IDs and passwords. This is done using the `realmtool` command-line utility.

```
realmtool −addGroup bikehirecustomer
realmtool −addGroup bikehireadministrator
realmtool −addGroup bikehiremanager
realmtool −add fred fred bikehirecustomer
realmtool −add mary mary bikehirecustomer
realmtool −add bill bill bikehireadministrator
realmtool −add joe joe bikehiremanager
```

As before, you may need to adjust the system PATH for it to find these commands, or change to the J2EE binaries directory. These commands create three groups, with one or more user in each. Users have passwords that are the same as their login IDs.

The supplied EAR file assumes that the groups defined above exist, but makes no assumptions about the membership of those groups. You will therefore not need to modify the EAR or to redeploy simply to add new customers to the application. You will, however, need to do both these things if you change the *group* assignments.

C.1.5   Creating message queues

The *Prestige Bike Hire* application uses JMS message queues to communicate orders to the legacy order processing system and to receive acknowledgements from that system. These queues need to exist and—as will be described below—there must be a 'dummy' legacy system attached to their ends if orders are to be submitted and acknowledged.

```
j2eeadmin −addJmsDestination jms/financialtransactionqueue queue
j2eeadmin −addJmsDestination jms/financialresponsequeue queue
```

C.2   Testing the application

C.2.1   Starting the legacy order processing system

To be able to make reservations, we need something to simulate the legacy financial processing system. The class `LegacyOrderSystem` plays this role. It is a standalone Java application, and can be run using the Ant operation:

```
ant runlegacysystem
```

It is advisable to do this in a separate command-line window, or its output will get in the way.

C.2.2   Running the application

It should now be possible to run the application using a Web browser. Point the browser at the URL: `http://[server]:[port]/BikeHire`, replacing the server name and port number with the appropiate settings for your system. The default port number is 8000; use the name `localhost` if you are running the browser on the same system as the J2EE server.

All being well, you should see the 'welcome' page (Figure 5.4), and it should be possible to view motorcycle details and make reservations.

It is also possible to interact with the application as an administrator; however, if you have already logged in as a customer, the facilities in the administrator's menu will be denied (as they should be). You will therefore have to log out (click the 'Log out' link) or restart the Web browser. To get to the administration menu, point your browser at the URL: `http://[server]:[port]/BikeHire/admin.jsp`. From this page you can search for customers, and view and edit customer details, among other things.

Appendix D

Reflection and dynamic instantiation

> ## Overview
>
> This appendix describes, as succinctly as possible, the use of the Java 're-flection' API. While EJB implementations do not usually use reflection extensively, the EJB *container* does; an understanding of reflection will help to understand why the interaction between the EJBs and the container has the form it does. In addition, with an understanding of reflection you can write some utility programs that will be of use in EJB development. For example, it is not very difficult to write a program that uses reflection to inspect an EJB's interfaces and generates a template for the implementation class dynamically.

D.1   The importance of reflection

Reflection (also called 'introspection') is a simple technique, but it is one of the cornerstones of EJB technology. The reflection API allows a Java platform class to obtain information about other classes or instances at runtime. It is reflection that makes it possible, for example, for the EJB container to generate the home object and EJB object for a deployed bean class. It also allows the generation of stubs whose published methods match those of the home and remote interfaces.

D.2   Using reflection

Reflection is done on a `Class` instance; `Class` is a Java entity for storing metadata about a Java platform class. If we have an object `obj` of any class, we can get a reference to its `Class` like this:

```
Class class = obj.getClass();
```

We can even get a `Class` reference for a noninstantiated class, like this:

```
Class class = Class.forName("com.something.MyClass");
```

From the `Class` object we can find information about the methods and instance variables declared in the class, and its superclasses. For example, the call

```
Method[] m = class.getMethods();
```

will return an array of `Method` instances, each of which provides information about a method. Once we have established that an object has a given method, we make a call on that method dynamically, by calling its `invoke()` method. For example, suppose we have a reference to an object `obj` and we want to call its method `test()`, which takes no arguments. First, we get a reference to the method like this:

```
Class class = obj.getClass();
Method m = class.getMethod("test", new Class[0]);
```

Then we can invoke it like this:

```
m.invoke(obj, new Object[0]);
```

Note that if we want to call methods with nonempty parameter lists, we can do this by assembling an appropriate array of `Class` instances instead of `new Class[0]`, and an array of `Object` instances rather than `new Object[0]`.

The important point about all this is that we don't need to know anything about the object at compile time; at runtime, if the object does not have the method requested, then `getMethod()` will throw an exception.

Listing D.1 demonstrates some of the techniques described in this appendix.

Listing D.1: **A simple demonstration of Java reflection: This code dumps information about the methods available on a class specified on the command line (rather like** `javap`**).**

```
   package com.kevinboone.ejb_book.reflection;
   import java.lang.reflect.*;

   /**
 5 This class implements a 'simple class info dumper' that
   uses the 'reflection' API. If you run its 'main()'
   method specifying a single class name as a parameter, it
   will examine that class and print information about it.
   To do this, the JVM must be able to load the class, so you
10 may need to pay attention to the CLASSPATH used at runtime
   (c)2000 Kevin Boone
   */
   public class Reflector
   {
15 /**
   The main() method does all the work of this class. There
   are no other methods. main() expects one String argument
   from the command line.  It generates output to System.out.
   */
```

```
20   public static void main (String[] args)
       {
       if (args.length != 1)
         {
         System.err.println
25         ("usage: java ejbook.reflection.Reflector [classname]");
         System.exit (-1);
         }
       try
         {
30       Class c = Class.forName (args[0]);
         Method[] m = c.getMethods();
         for (int i = 0; i < m.length; i++)
           {
           // For each method, print its signature
35         Method mm = m[i];
           String s = mm.toString();
           // And print the class that declared it (which may
           //   be a superclass of this class)
           s += " (declared in " +
40           mm.getDeclaringClass() + ")";
           System.out.println (s);
           }
         }
       catch (Exception e)
45         {
           System.err.println ("Caught exception: " + e);
           }
         }
       }
```

D.3   Dynamic instantiation

You will undoubtedly be familiar with the standard technique for instantiating new classes in Java, which is

```
MyClass myObject = new MyClass ();
```

This causes `MyClass` to be initialized, and an instance of this class to be created. Java also provides a mechanism for instantiating classes dynamically—that is, where information about the class is provided at runtime. Using the techniques described above, we can get a `Class` reference to a class identified only by its name, and then instantiate it by calling `newInstance()` on the `Class`. For example:

```
Class class = Class.forName("com.something.MyClass");
com.something.MyClass myObject = class.newInstance();
```

This will cause the class's default constructor to be executed (if it has one). If it doesn't, the class cannot be instantiated this way. This is why the *EJB Specification* states that the bean implementation class must have a default constructor [e.g., EJB2S 7.10.2].

Because we can assign the result of `Class.newInstance()` to a variable of type `Object`, the code above could be written

```
Class class = Class.forName("com.something.MyClass");
Object myObject = class.newInstance();
```

Notice that we have instantiated a class, and can now call methods on it, without that class needing to exist when the caller is compiled.

Appendix E

Java serialization

> ## Overview
>
> This appendix describes the principles of Java language serialization to what
> is probably the minimum depth required for EJB development. EJB client-
> server protocols will use serialization (probably in combination with other
> techniques) to transfer method-call information between nodes, and this
> has important implications for understanding the limitations that that *EJB
> Specification* places on argument types and the like.

E.1 The purpose of serialization

Serialization, like reflection, is a technique that is not all that widely used by Java
developers. It is, however, an important part of most schemes that allow objects
to be passed across a network. For example, serialization is often used to pass
arguments to methods of objects in RMI systems. Understanding serialization is
the key to understanding the rules on argument passing and return values in EJBs.

When an object is serialized, its complete state is converted into a stream of
bytes that can be written and read in sequence. This byte sequence can be sent
over a network, or written to a file, or passed as an argument to another method. A
serialization scheme has to account not only for the instance variables of the object
being serialized, but the instance variables of all the objects stored in its instance
variables, and the instance variables of its superclass(es) as well. It should work
whether or not the types of instance variables are known at runtime. For example,
if a class has an instance variable of type `Object`, and that variable is currently
storing a `String`, then the variable should be correctly stored as a `String` (as
known at runtime) and not an `Object` (as it is at compile time).

E.2 Serialization strategies

Fortunately, the JVM has built-in support for serialization that is adequate for most
applications, and there is a standard way to extend it for those cases where is not.

663

The Java API provides a point of access to the JVM's serialization system; the developer can either use this system in its entirety, or provide mechanisms for some or all objects to serialize themselves.

E.2.1 The standard serialization scheme

The default serialization scheme is appropriate for most applications. In this scheme, every class that is to be serialized is defined to implement the interface `java.io.Serializable`. The interface specifies no methods; it is simply used by the Java runtime engine to determine whether a class has been marked serializable. When the class is to be serialized, the runtime system uses a default format to write each of its nontransient instance variables. The instance variables do not have to be `public` for this to work. Declaring an instance variable as `transient` prevents it from being serialized; when the object is deserialized, this variable will have the value `null` or zero. The runtime engine takes care of serializing the instance variables that are themselves objects, and of the serialization of the instance variables that are declared by superclasses of the object. To succeed, all instance variables must be serializable, either by using the default scheme or by some other method.

E.2.2 Overriding default serialization with the Externalizable interface

A class can be provided with its own interface to the Java serialization architecture. This may be useful where the default serialization behavior is inappropriate. An example is the situation in which certain instance variables can contain large amounts of data, but they need not be serialized on every occasion (depending on the values of other instance variables). Using `transient` won't help here: A `transient` variable is never serialized.

The `java.io.Externalizable` interface specifies two methods: `writeExternal()` and `readExternal()`. If a class implements this interface, the Java serialization system will call `writeExternal`, when the class has to serialize itself, and `readExternal`, when it is to deserialize itself. `Externalizable` and `Serializable` classes can be mixed in one serialization operation. The `writeExternal()` method is passed an output stream onto which the object can write its state when the method is called, while the `readExternal()` method gets an input stream.

E.3 Using the serialization API

To convert an object to serializable form, a standard approach is to create an `ObjectOutputStream` and write the object to it. An `ObjectOutputStream` can be constructed on any object of a class that extends `OutputStream`. For example, if I wanted to serialize an object onto a network socket, I could do something like this:

```
Socket s = new Socket (host, port);
OutputStream os = s.getOutputStream ();
ObjectOutputStream ois = new ObjectOutputStream (os);
ois.writeObject (obj);
```

Multiple objects can be written to the stream if required. What the `writeObject` method does is to write information on the output stream about the object itself (its class, for example), then write out all its instance variables. If its instance variables are themselves instances of classes, then these are written out in much the same way as the object that contains them.

Reading an object from a serialized form is essentially the reverse of writing it. We can use, for example, an `ObjectInputStream` to read the data into objects. An `ObjectInputStream` can be constructed on any other kind of input stream—that is, any object of a class that extends `InputStream`. For example, if I wanted to read serialized object data from a network socket, I might do something like this:

```
Socket s = new Socket (host, port);
InputStream is = s.getInputStream ();
ObjectInputStream ois = new ObjectInputStream (is);
Object o = ois.readObject ();
```

Because serialization will write out all instance variables of an object, we generally don't need to write multiple objects to a `Stream`. For example, suppose we have a `Vector` object containing a number of `String` objects. We could call `writeObject` on each `String`, but it is just as quick to write the entire `Vector` in one go.

The `readObject()` method is defined to return an `Object` but, of course, the real object will be of the same type as that written by the `writeObject()` operation. Thus a `ClassCastException` will be thrown if the program tries to assign the output of `readObject` to a variable of a class different than the one written.

E.4   Controlling serialization

E.4.1   Preventing incorrect deserialization

Naturally we need to be able to prevent a serialized object from being deserialized into an object of the wrong type. The standard scheme prevents this by storing the type of the object along with its instance variables.

There is, however, a more subtle way that serialization can fail: The object being read may have the same class as an object that was written, but may have different instance variables. This can happen if, for example, the class was modified and recompiled between the `writeObject` and `readObject` calls. When using RMI, this situation arises if different versions of the class are deployed on the client and server. To avoid this problem, all classes that are marked as serializable are provided at compile time with a static instance variable containing a serialization version ID. The compiler generates a new ID every time the class changes in a way that would prevent it from being constructed from a serialized form of a previous version of the same class. For example, if an instance variable is changed in name or type, the class will no longer be compatible with previously serialized versions, and the compiler will generate a new ID.

When the JVM is asked to deserialize an object, it reads the serialization ID from the serialized data along with the class name. It checks the serialization ID in the serialized data against the serialization ID currently known for that class.

If these are different, it assumes that the class has changed since serialization, and refuses to deserialize it.

The Java JDK provides a simple way to check the serialization IDs of class files: the `serialver` command. `serialver java.lang.String` produces the following output:

```
java.lang.String: static final long
    serialVersionUID = -6849794470754667710L;
```

Because this is a standard instance variable, an object can get its own class's serialization ID if it needs to.

E.4.2   Limiting the scope of serialization

The developer can indicate that some instance variables should never be serialized simply by declaring them as 'transient.' A transient variable is never written out, and when deserialized, the variable will have the value zero or `null`.

However, we can also prevent an instance variable being serialized simply by setting it to `null`. This is the preferred approach in EJB development, when we cannot be sure that Java standard serialization will be used to serialize the object. Remember that the 'transient' keyword is only meaningful to JVM-based serialization. An EJB container is allowed, if it wishes, to use other mechanisms to passivate stateful session beans. In fact, the *EJB Specification* is very definite about the need to avoid using transient instance variables.

E.5   Non-Java serialization

The term 'serialization,' to a Java developer, probably brings to mind the standard serialization scheme implemented by the JVM and described in the preceding sections. However, the main problem with Java language serialization in the enterprise environment is that it is a *Java* language scheme. In general, the only kind of service that will be able to accept a serialized Java object as input is one that is implemented in Java. This is not good for interoperability.

So is Java serialization the only kind of serialization that is compatible with Java applications? Not at all: So long as both the producer and the consumer of the serialized object can agree on a format for its representation, then we can 'serialize' our objects however we please. Of course, some additional work will be required because the JVM will not give us much help.

An increasingly important form of serialization is defined by SOAP (simple object access protocol). This defines a scheme by which an object's state can be represented in an XML document. Developers often think of the use of techniques like SOAP as being something different from serialization but, philosophically, it's just serialization into XML. The great advantage of SOAP is that XML is accepted by just about everybody, which will have profound implications for business-to-business applications in particular.

Appendix F

Obtaining and configuring the J2EE RI

> ## Overview
>
> This appendix describes how to obtain the J2EE Reference Implementation and configure it to make following the examples in this book simple and straightforward. The information given here is intended to supplement, not to replace, the setting-up information supplied with the software.

F.1 Getting the Reference Implementation

The *J2EE Reference Implementation* (J2EE RI) is available free-of-charge from Sun Microsystems, at `http://java.sun.com/j2ee`. There are versions for Linux, Solaris, and Windows. There is also information about obtaining the software on CD-ROM, which may be useful if you are put off by the 20 Mb download.

The J2EE RI is not supplied with a Java compiler or runtime engine. It requires Java support compatible with Sun Java JDK 1.3 or later, and I will assume that you are using the standard Sun product, which is available from `http://java.sun.com/j2se`. I will also assume that it is installed and working, and is set up to be able to run from the command line. That is, if you type

```
java -version
```

at a command prompt you get a version report, and not an error message.

F.2 Setting up: Unix

Unix versions of the J2EE RI are available as compressed TAR files; installation is as simple as uncompressing and un-TARing to a suitable directory, e.g., `/usr/j2ee`. Note that the RI does not need `root` permission to execute, but by default the server does write to its installation directories when it is operating. This means that the user account that runs the server must have write access to the installation directory and its subdirectories. In short, if you install it as `root` you will have to run it as `root`. However, you should not need to be `root` in order to compile or run J2EE applications.

The software requires that the environment variables `J2EE_HOME` and `JAVA_HOME` be set: `J2EE_HOME` is the J2EE installation directory, and `JAVA_HOME` is the JDK installation directory.

For convenience, I suggest adding the `bin` subdirectory of the installation directory to your `PATH`, and creating (or extending) an environment variable `CLASSPATH` to include the file `j2ee.jar`, which is in the `lib` subdirectory. All the examples in this book assume that these two configuration recommendations have been followed.

F.3 Setting up: Windows

Windows versions of the J2EE RI are available as self-extracting executables; installation is as simple as executing the downloaded file. This will run the installation program, at which point you can decide where to install the software.

If you install the RI in a directory that is subject to access restrictions (e.g., on an NTFS partition), then the user that runs the server software must have write permission in that area.

The software requires that the environment variables `J2EE_HOME` and `JAVA_HOME` be set: `J2EE_HOME` is the J2EE installation directory, and `JAVA_HOME` is the JDK installation directory. There are various ways to do this on Windows systems. With most versions, you can create and modify the environment variables using the 'System' section of the Control Panel program.

For convenience, I suggest adding the `bin` subdirectory of the installation directory to your PATH and creating (or extending) an environment variable CLASSPATH to include the file `j2ee.jar`, which is in the `lib` subdirectory. All the examples in this book assume that these two configuration recommendations have been followed. These configuration changes can also be made using the 'System' icon in the Control Panel.

F.4 Usage hints

F.4.1 Deployment tool

- EJB applications are packaged into JAR files, which are in turn packaged into EAR files (an EAR file is also a JAR file; only the name is different). The RI deployment tool manipulates EAR files. It is important to understand that an EAR file does not contain any information about the origin of the class files it contains. That is, if you have modified and recompiled classes, and want to insert them into the EAR file, the EAR file itself does not contain information that makes this possible. To get around this problem, the RI stores additional information about the EAR file in a hidden directory. This information stays with the computer that created the EAR file. This means that it is very difficult to work on an EAR file on two different computers; copying the EAR files is not enough for the RI to work out how to keep the EAR up to date with respect to the local filesystem. Therefore, the RI deployment tool works best if the developer uses only one computer for each project. Similar problems arise if the directories containing class files are moved on the local computer: The RI will not be able to keep the EAR file in sync with the local classes. It is best to avoid moving classes or renaming directories during development.

- The deployment tool has a menu command 'Update application files' on the 'Tools' menu. This updates any files in the EAR that have been updated on the local filesystem (provided that the constraints discussed above have been adhered to). If you recompile some classes, you *must* use this procedure before redeploying the application. Note that the deployment tool provides a list of files that it knows have changed since the last deployment. If you recompile, and 'Update application files' produces the message 'All files are up to date,' then something has gone wrong. There is no point proceding with the deployment. If all else fails, you can delete the class files from the EJB JAR, and reinsert them. This will tell the deployment tool where on the local filesystem these classes are located.

- When constructing an EJB-JAR, you will be presented with about six pages of configuration settings. All of these settings can be changed later, *except* the determination of classes for the home interface, remote interface, and implementation. These settings are irrevocable, so ensure that that they are correct before going on to the next page.

F.4.2   *Cloudscape* **database**

Although it is not very well documented, you can browse and modify *Cloudscape* databases using an SQL command line client called ij; this is supplied as part of the *Cloudscape* package.

F.4.3   **j2eeadmin utility**

With the previous version of the RI, configuration changes like assigning JNDI names to databases had to be applied by editing the configuration files in the config directory. The latest version provides a command-line utility—j2eeadmin—for doing this.

F.4.4   **keytool utility**

The keytool utility is used for creating and manipulating cryptographic keys and certificates. At the time of writing, the version of keytool supplied with the RI is more up-to-date than that supplied with the latest JDK. This is important, because the examples of certificate-based authentication in Chapter 16 assume the use of the RI version of keytool. You may need to pay attention to your system's PATH setting to ensure that the correct version gets executed.

F.4.5   Verifier tool

The verifier is one of the most useful features of the RI, and is worth using even if you use a different EJB product for everything else. The verifier checks your work for compliance with the appropriate specifications. It is *very* strict. Although you can run the verifier from the deployment tool, it is often quicker and more reliable to run it from the command line:

```
verifier myapp.ear
```

This generates a file `Results.txt` (note the capital 'R') in your systems's default temporary files directory.

The verifier can check EJB JAR files, Web WAR files, EAR files, and resource adapter RAR files.

F.4.6   J2EE server

Guidelines on running and troubleshooting the server are provided in Section 4.7.

Appendix G

Overview of public key cryptography

> **Overview**
>
> This appendix provides an overview of public key cryptographic techniques, and how they are applied in the SSL (secure sockets layer) communications protocol. It discusses encryption and decryption, secure hash algorithms, digital signatures, and certificates.

G.1   Basic principles

A secure communications scheme should accomplish some or all of the following objectives:

- Protect data in transit from eavesdropping by unauthorized parties. This is usually accomplished by encryption by the sender, and decryption by the recipient.

- Allow the recipient to detect if the data has been tampered with in transit.

- Allow each party to verify the identity of the other.

- Prevent the sender later denying that the data was sent, or claiming it had different content.

SSL (secure sockets layer) and its derivative IETF-TLS (transport layer security) provide these facilities by means of public-key encryption. These schemes work at the 'transport' layer of communication—that is, they work on raw data and are not concerned what the content of that data is. This means that SSL can be used to protect browser-client communications, remote logins, or EJB method calls with equal facility.

Encrypting and decrypting data is relatively straightforward: There are any number of mathematical transformations (*ciphers*) that can be applied to a block of data that render it virtually irrecoverable without the appropriate key. Some of these techniques are, it is thought, as close to unbreakable as makes no difference.

The *strength* of a cipher (that is, how difficult it is to crack) depends on the size of the key used and the algorithm itself. Until recently most encryption schemes used 56-bit keys. A 56-bit key has 2^{56} possible values, and this is the largest number of decryption attempts that would be required to crack the key by brute force. Suppose we had a computer that could try one key every millisecond. Arithmetic reveals that it would take millions of years to try every possible combination of a 56-bit key. However, when the presence of *weak keys*[1] is taken into account, and with recent improvements in processor speed and parallel processing, many authorities now believe that it is worthwhile for criminals to attempt to break 56-bit keys by brute force. This problem is easily fixed: There are now a number of ciphers readily available that have 128-bit and 168-bit keys. The prospect of one of these being cracked by brute force is staggeringly remote. Incredibly, even the most powerful of these *cipher algorithms* can be implemented in less than a hundred or so lines of program code.

In reality, the problem with secure communication is not the strength of encryption, but with the management of keys. *Symmetric* cipher schemes (Figure G.1)— where the same key is used to decrypt as was used to encrypt—have been in use for at least 2,000 years and, right from the start, it was recognized that key management was always the weakness. The problem can be expressed simply: If you need encryption to get data safely from one place to another, then it isn't safe to send the key either.

Nearly all modern communication security systems—including SSL—are based on the notion of *asymmetric cryptography*. In an asymmetric scheme, different keys are used to encrypt and decrypt the data. In particular, a key that is used to encrypt some data cannot be used to decrypt it. Of course, the keys are mathematically related, and usually generated as a *key pair* at the same time. The process is shown in (Figure G.2). The key pair consists of 'Key A,' which is used to encrypt, and the related 'Key B,' which is capable of encrypting anything that was encrypted with Key A. If it is close to impossible to derive Key B from Key A, and Key A cannot decrypt messages it encrypted, then it is safe to send Key A across the network.

Because Key A can be transmitted, or even broadcast, from the recipient of the data, it is referred to as the *recipient's public key*, or simply 'public key' for brevity. Key B, which must be closely guarded by the recipient, is its *private key*. The use of public keys has led to these techniques to becoming known as 'public key cryptography.'

---

[1]A weak key is one for which other keys could produce the same encrypted result. That is, if a range of keys all transform the plaintext into the same ciphertext, then they are considered weak. The weakness stems from the fact that a brute force attack would not have to try all these keys: Trying one is equivalent to trying all. In practice, all cipher algorithms have weak keys, sometimes by the billion.

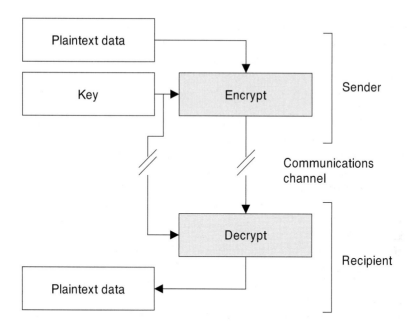

Figure G.1. Symmetric encryption: The same key is used to decrypt as was used to encrypt. In communication, this implies that we have a safe way to get the key from the sender to the recipient. If we had that, we wouldn't need encryption in the first place. In this figure, and all others in this appendix, shaded boxes indicate processes, while empty boxes indicate documents or data.

There are a number of mathematical techniques that can be used to implement an asymmetric cipher. The most widely used at present is the Rivest-Shamir-Adelmann (RSA) algorithm. In the RSA algorithm, the public key and private key are not different kinds of key; the only distinction is that one is published and one is not. The public key can decrypt messages encrypted with the private key, if necessary. The important feature is that the public key can't be used to decrypt the data it encrypts.

It is often wrongly believed that public key ciphers are 'stronger' (more difficult to crack) than symmetric ones. The strength of the cipher depends on a number of factors, particularly the number of bits in the key, and with all these factors equal there is no strength advantage to asymmetric systems. The advantage of these systems lies exclusively with the improved key management: Because the public key cannot decrypt anything it encrypted, it is safe to transmit over an insecure channel.

The scheme shown in Figure G.2 has a number of weaknesses that must be addressed.

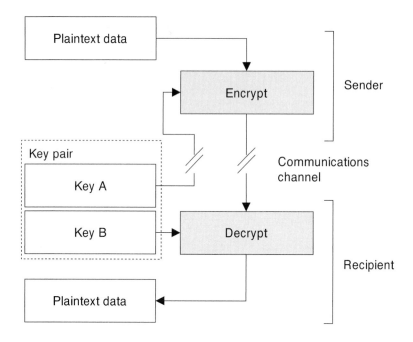

Figure G.2. Asymmetric encryption: Different keys are used to encrypt and decrypt. It is safe to transmit, or even broadcast, the encryption key (Key 'A' in the figure), as it cannot decrypt. Hence, this is usually referred to as the *public key*.

- Asymmetric encryption and decryption is much slower than symmetric, for the same level of cryptographic strength. Practical systems use a combination of symmetric and asymmetric systems.

- If the public key is intercepted by an impostor, it can be used to insert bogus data into the messages or modify the real data. This may happen after the recipient has validated the identity of the sender and assumed that it is safe to communicate. Because the whole purpose of the public key system is to enable us to send keys on insecure channels, we have to anticipate this happening and be able to deal with it.

- If the public key is intercepted by an impostor, it can be used to impersonate the real owner of the public key. In other words, we need a scheme to validate the identity of the entity that presents the public key

The rest of this appendix will discuss how these weaknesses are overcome, particularly with reference to SSL (although these techniques are generally applicable).

G.2   Combining symmetric and asymmetric techniques

Asymmetric encryption is too slow to use on large volumes of data. A much better scheme combines the use of symmetric and asymmetric schemes. Remember that the problem we are trying to overcome is that of getting a key safely from one party to another. We can use an asymmetric system to encrypt another *key* for communication and use that key for the real data. It doesn't matter what this key is (it can be a random number), so long as it can be passed safely from one party to the other.

Let's see how this is done in practice by looking at the scheme used by SSL (Figure G.3). As before, the process starts with the generation of an asymmetric key pair. This is typically carried out only once over the life of the recipient. In

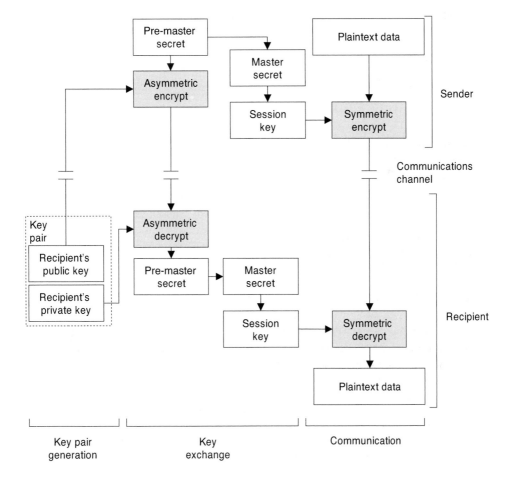

Figure G.3. The sequence of steps by which a symmetric session key is generated from a random 'pre-master secret' and shared between the sender and recipient in SSL.

the 'key exchange' phase (which is part of the SSL handshake) the sender gets the recipient's public key (which is safe to transmit) and uses it to encrypt a 'pre-master secret.' The pre-master secret is typically derived from the time and date and some random digits, but its exact content is irrelevant. The pre-master secret is encrypted with the recipient's public key and transmitted to the recipient in encrypted form. The recipient uses its private key to decrypt the pre-master secret. Both the sender and the recipient use the pre-master secret to generate the session key. This is a key that is known to both parties, and can therefore be used for symmetric encryption. Once the session key is established, it is used for the duration of that communication session. Being symmetric, the same key can be used in both directions if required.

The SSL scheme, although it appears complex, allows the benefits of both asymmetric encryption (key safety) and symmetric encryption (speed) to be realized.

Once the keys have been exchanged, the sender and recipient negotiate the symmetric cipher algorithm that will be used to handle the rest of the communication. Typically, both the sender and recipient will be able to select from a range of installed ciphers, and will settle on the one with the largest key size that both parties support.

G.3   Detecting tampering

Asymmetric cryptography makes it almost impossible for an unauthorized person to eavesdrop on communication (provided that the private keys are kept safe and are not easy to guess).

However, if an impostor knows the recipient's public key (which is very likely), then he can use it to insert spurious data in the communication between the sender and the recipient (assuming that the impostor has physical access to the data). We would, of course, like to prevent this, or at least to detect that it has occurred.

A simple approach would be for the sender to take a simple checksum of the data and transmit it along with the data itself. The recipient could also derive its own version of the checksum and compare it with the transmitted version (Figure G.4). If they are identical, then one of three things must be true:

- the data has not been tampered with;

- the data has been tampered with in such a way that the original checksum is still correct;

- the data has been tampered with, and the impostor altered the checksum to match.

Of course we hope that the first statement is true, and not one of the others, but we can't rely on this. To ensure that neither of the other alternatives is true, we can use a combination of *secure one-way hash* and (where necessary) *private key signing*.

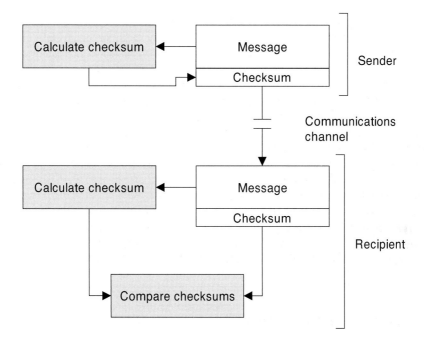

Figure G.4. Using a checksum to determine whether a message has been altered in communication. The sender computes the checksum and appends it to the message. The recipient computes its own checksum and compares it with the sender's version.

G.3.1   Secure one-way hash

A simple checksum can be calculated by adding the values of all the bytes in a message. Typically we would do this addition with some limit so that the checksum itself is a manageable size. The problem is that if we use, say, 16-bit addition, then all messages whose checksums differ by the amount of 2^{16} will have the same checksum. A sophisticated impostor could take advantage of this fact by altering the data in such a way that it will have the same checksum. To prevent this from happening, we can make use of any one of a number of secure hash algorithms. These are arithmetically more complex than a simple checksum but, again, typically require fewer than a hundred lines of code to implement. Like a checksum, the hash algorithm produces a short sequence of bytes that reflects the content of the message. This sequence is sometimes called a *message digest*. A good secure hash code algorithm is *one-way*, meaning that it has the following properties:

- Small changes to the message produce large changes in the hash code.

- It is difficult to generate a message that has a given hash code.

If the hash were not one-way, the impostor could replace the whole message with a false one that is chosen to match the checksum provided by the sender.

Two secure one-way hash algorithms are used with SSL: MD5, which produces a 16-byte hash code, and SHA-1, which produces a 21-byte hash code. Both of these have been thoroughly studied and are believed to be one-way for all practical purposes.

G.3.2   Checking the validity of the hash code

So we have a way to avoid the possibility of an impostor altering a message while keeping the same hash code. We are not yet home and dry, however, because we have to face the possibility that if the impostor has the means to tamper with the message, then he can also tamper with the hash code. In SSL, this problem is easily overcome: The hash code is derived from the data transmitted *and* the session key. Now, an impostor could replace the whole message and hash code with a new message and a hash code derived from that message. What he *can't* do, is derive the hash code from the session key, because the session key is securely locked up in the memories of the sender and recipient—it isn't stored anywhere. So if the impostor tries this, the recipient will not compute the same hash code as supplied by the impostor, because the recipient will be using the session key in the process.

In SSL, the hash code derived from the message and the session key is called a *message authentication code* (MAC). The process of generating and and verifying the MAC, and its interaction with the encryption and decryption processes, is shown in Figure G.5.

G.3.3   Private key signing

SSL is a session-based protocol, which means that the two parties in the communication begin by establishing their credentials and exchanging keys, and then the same keys are used for the duration of the communication session. This makes it relatively straightforward to validate the integrity of the data, because the two parties know something (the session key) that is not known to anyone else, and that session key can be used in the derivation of the MAC (hash code). When communication is not session-based, we still have a problem. If the sender and the recipient do not handshake, they can't establish a shared secret key, so they have nothing in common that is not known to outsiders. This applies most obviously to email communication, but is also an issue for certificate authentication, as will be discussed below.

The solution is for the sender to generate a message digest (hash code) and encrypt it with his *private* key (remember that the sender is encrypting the body of the message with the recipient's public key). The recipient uses the sender's public key to decrypt the message digest, and then compares it with a digest it generates itself. If the digests are identical, this proves that the sender has a private key that matches the public key he supplied to the recipient.

A message digest that has been encrypted with a private key is called a private key signature or, more commonly, a *digital signature*. Digital signatures are useful not only for detecting tampering, but for preventing *repudiation*. The sender cannot claim that the message was never sent, because his public key decrypts the signature.

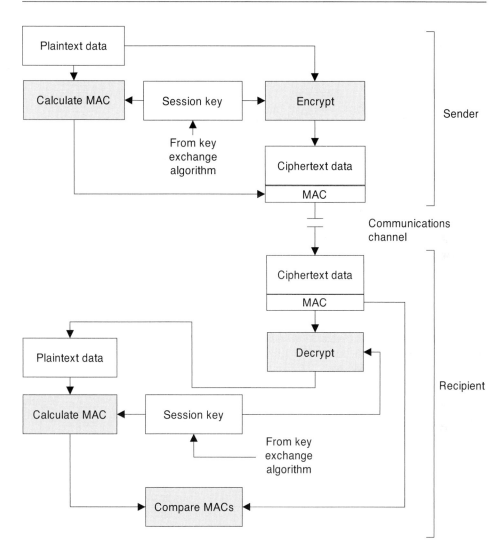

Figure G.5. Encryption and decryption, and computing and verifying the message authentication code (MAC), in an SSL session.

He can, of course, claim that his private key was compromised, which is a different matter altogether.

G.4   Identifying the communicating parties

We have seen that a message authentication code (MAC) or a digital signature (in asynchronous communication) can help to detect tampering. But before continuing, it's worth ensuring that we know *exactly* what a correct MAC or a correct signature proves. Specifically it proves these two things:

- The sender has a public key and a private key that match.

- The data was sent by the entity that has the private key, and has not been modified in transmission.

In other words, the MAC or signature proves that the data is sound and came from a particular public/private key combination. What it does *not* prove is that the key pair belongs to the person or organization that it purports to belong to. Is there anything that prevents me from presenting my public key to an online banking application, for example, and claiming it belongs to the bank manager? So far, the answer to this question is 'no.' A public key is just a string of bits that it could have come from anywhere. It's worth remembering that this problem is fundamentally insoluble. Unless we are prepared to take certain things on trust (and we'll see what these things are later), then it's impossible, even in theory, for one party in a communications link to have complete trust in another.

G.4.1   Certificates

The standard solution to the problem of authentication is the use of *public key certificates*, usually just called 'certificates' for brevity. A certificate contains the owner's public key, and some information about the owner: name, email address, and so on. If the certificate is for a service (e.g., an EJB server), rather than an individual, then it will contain the fully qualified DNS name of the server, for reasons that will be discussed below. All this in itself is of no help: A public key is exactly that—public—and can easily be inserted into a certificate of my choice. The clever part is that the certificate can have a digital signature appended by an individual or organization that the recipient is prepared to trust. Such an entity is called a *certificate authority* (CA). Suppose, for example, the sender and the recipient are both members of the same organization, and that organization acts as a CA. The organization uses its private key to generate a digital signature for the sender's certificate, and then the recipient knows that the certificate has been validated by the organization. The sender can authenticate the recipient in the same way. When SSL is secure communication between a Web server and a browser, it is usual for the server to present its certificate to the browser for authentication, but for the server to authenticate the client by means of a username and password. There are a number of reasons for this, including the fact that most individuals do not have personal certificates that are signed by an organization that the service provider would trust.

G.4.2   X.509

Most systems that use certificate-based authentication work with certificates based on the ITU-T standard X.509. Listing G.1 shows my VeriSign personal X.509 certificate (some data has been omitted for brevity). This listing is used as an example in the description that follows. An X.509 certificate contains the following information.

Version and serial number information Line 3 of the listing shows that this certificate complies with X.509 Version 3 (the latest version at the time of writing).

Algorithm information The certificate will be signed by the CA's primary key, using a particular cipher algorithm. To verify the certificate, we need to know the algorithm that was used, so that the message digest can be decrypted. In addition, the certificate will contain the owner's primary key, which is itself associated with a particular cipher. The CA and the owner need not use the same cipher algorithms. In the example, the issuer's signature algorithm is `md2WithRSAEncryption` (line 6), and the owner's public key algorithm is `rsaEncryption` (line 18). In other words, the owner's public key is to be used with the RSA algorithm, while the issuer signed the certificate by generating an MD2 checksum and encrypting it with an RSA private key.

Owner name The owner of the certificate, in X.500 format. X.500 is a scheme for naming individuals and organizations such that names are unique across the entire Internet. Because the certificate was issued directly by VeriSign, rather than being generated by myself and signed by VeriSign, VeriSign is denoted as the owner (subject) of this certificate (line 12). Note that my name does not appear anywhere. Why should it? VeriSign has no way of knowing that I am who I claim to be, and would be ill-advised to authenticate me without checking.

Issuer name The X.500 name of the organization that signed the certificate. In the example, this is VeriSign again (line 7).

Period of validity The example is valid for ten years from May 12th, 1998 (lines 10 and 11).

Owner's public key Lines 21–23 in the example

Issuer's signature Lines 37–39 in the example

Listing G.1: **My X.509 personal certificate. This listing was generated by the OpenSSL command-line utility (`www.openssl.org`).**

```
      Certificate:
        Data:
          Version: 3 (0x2)
          Serial Number:
 5            d2:76:2e:8d:14:0c:3d:7d:b2:a8:25:5d:af:ee:0d:75
          Signature Algorithm: md2WithRSAEncryption
          Issuer: C=US, O=VeriSign, Inc., OU=Class 1 \
            Public Primary Certification Authority
          Validity
10            Not Before: May 12 00:00:00 1998 GMT
```

```
              Not After : May 12 23:59:59 2008 GMT
          Subject: O=VeriSign , Inc . , OU=VeriSign Trust Network , \
            OU=www. verisign .com/repository/RPA \
            Incorp . By Ref . ,LIAB.LTD( c )98 ,\
15          CN=VeriSign Class 1 CA \
            Individual Subscriber–Persona Not Validated
          Subject Public Key Info :
              Public Key Algorithm: rsaEncryption
              RSA Public Key: (1024 bit )
20            Modulus (1024 bit ):
                  00:bb:5 a :44:8 a :04:16:bb:55: fd :03:7 a :8 a :2 d :94:
                  . . . . .
                  37:6 a : c8 :4 a : c8 :09:06: e4 :99
              Exponent: 65537 (0 x10001 )
25      X509v3 extensions :
              Netscape Cert Type :
              SSL CA, S/MIME CA
          X509v3 Certificate Policies :
              Policy : 2.16.840.1.113733.1.7.1.1
30                CPS: www. verisign .com/repository/RPA

          X509v3 Basic Constraints :
              CA:TRUE, pathlen :0
          X509v3 Key Usage :
35            Certificate Sign , CRL Sign
      Signature Algorithm: md2WithRSAEncryption
          88:b8:37:3 b :dd :da :94:37:00: ad :aa :9 f : e1 :81:01:71:1 e :92:
          . . . .
          ae :6 e
```

Although X.509 is almost universally used, there are a number of ways of storing X.509 certificates on clients and servers, along with their associated private keys. For example, most Web browsers use a format called PKCS12.

G.4.3 Authenticating a certificate

The *SSL Specification* says that the server should present its certificate to the client to be authenticated, and then, if required, the client should present its certificate to the server. Either party can choose to accept or reject the certificate. The Specification does not state explicitly how the parties should make the decision whether to accept or reject: This is at the discretion of the application developer and the system administrator. However, in practice, the procedure will be similar to the following. In this description, we assume that the client is validating the server's certificate, but the same process could be applied to the client by the server. The procedure is illustrated in Figure G.6.

First, the client checks the fundamental validity of the certificate (for example, that today's date is in the validity range of the certificate) and then attempts to verify the digital signature. If the server's certificate is 'self-signed'—that is, the owner and the issuer are the same, then the client uses the public key in the certificate to decrypt the message digest provided in the signature, and verify it

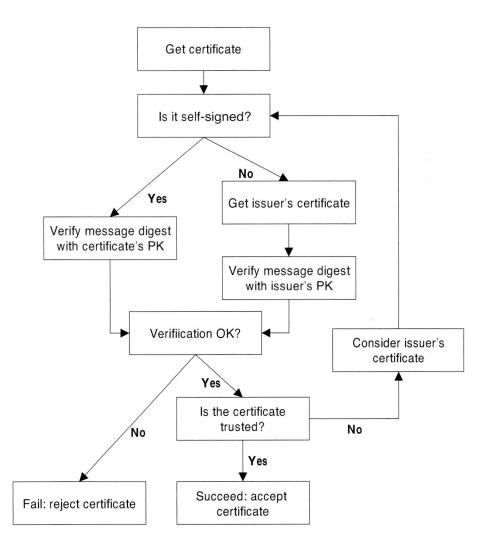

Figure G.6. A procedure for validating a certificate, by working back the certificate chain until a trusted certificate is found, or a selfsigned, nontrusted certificate is reached.

against the digest that the client itself derives from the certificate. If the message digests match, the client knows that the certificate is valid to the extent that it has not been altered since it was signed. However, the client has no way of knowing whether the certificate is from a trustworthy source. The client's administrator has to make that decision, usually by installing the serial numbers of the certificates that are considered trustworthy in a place accessible to the client.

If the certificate is not self-signed, the client finds the certificate of the organization (CA) that signed it, and uses the public key from that certificate to decrypt the message digest. If the message digest matches the one that can be derived from the message itself, then this shows that the private key that matches the CA certificate really was used to sign the server's certificate. If the CA certificate was itself self-signed, the client still has to decide whether to trust the CA. Again, it is the client's administrator that makes this decision, by installing the certificates of CAs it trusts. If the CA certificate was itself signed by a different CA, then the client can continue to verify the CA's CA. In fact, this process can continue, if the client requires, until it either finds a certificate that it trusts or the *certificate chain* runs out, ending at a self-signed certificate that it does not trust.

In a large organization, it will be difficult to ensure that all certificates are signed by the same CA. However, security is weakened if arbitrarily long certificate chains are allowed: The longer the chain, the more likely it is that an untrusted CA can find its way in. In practice, most software will only allow chains of two or three certificates. Some applications have elaborate techniques for making trust decisions, using multiple trust associations with weights, for example.

G.4.4   Organizational and public CAs

Anyone can sign a certificate, given the appropriate software (e.g., OpenSSL). If an organization wants to set up a CA to allow application components to authenticate one another, this is all that's required. The applications that use SSL simply install the organization's CA certificates in their 'trusted CA' databases and have the organization's CA sign the certificates of end users and servers. In a large organization, CA authority may have to be delegated, and SSL applications configured to accept certificate chains two or three long.

There are a number of 'public' CAs, organizations that have set themselves up to act as signing agents for other organizations. The best known of these are VeriSign and Thawte. For Web-based applications, the use of public CAs is significant, since most Web browsers are configured by default to trust server certificates that have been signed by one of the common public CAs.

Appendix H

Glossary of terms

Abstract persistence schema In EJB 2.0-style container managed persistence, the set of abstract properties that are managed by the container. These include persistent data properties ('virtual instance variables'), and persistent associations. See page 410.

Application server Anything that provides support services to a component-based application. In this book, we will usually assume that the term refers to a J2EE-compliant application server, which supports JSP, Servlets, and EJBs. However, application server technology predates J2EE and, indeed, Java. See page 553.

Bastion A server that is exposed to the Internet, but exposing a very restricted range of services. Typically the bastion will be multihomed—that is, having different network interfaces to internal and external networks. See page 534.

BMP Bean-Managed Persistence. An entity persistence scheme where persistence is handled using code supplied by the developer. See page 345.

Business method A method in an EJB implementation that is called as a direct result of a client call. See page 66.

Callback method A method in an EJB implementation that is called by the EJB container, to indicate some change in the EJB's life cycle state. See page 66.

CAS Client access services. A set of products from Sun Microsystems that support access to EJB from client that are not authored in Java. See page 9.

certificate A piece of data supplied as part of a communications handshake to allow one party to authenticate the other. Digital certificates use public-key cryptography techniques for to support their validation. See page 680.

CCI Common client interface. Part of the *J2EE Connector Specification*; defines a common set of interfaces through which clients can get access to a range of different external resources. See page 633.

CMP Container-Managed Persistence. An entity persistence scheme where persistence is handled using code generated automatically by the vendor's tools. See page 345.

Container (EJB container) The EJB container is the executing environment for an EJB. It separates the EJB from its clients and provides a range of services to the EJB. See page 69.

Client view The collection of interfaces by which EJBs interact with their clients. See page 47.

Common object request broker architecture (CORBA) A specification developed by the Object Management Group for object request brokers (ORBs). In principle, classes deployed in CORBA-compliant ORBs should be able to call methods on any other class in any other compatible ORB, regardless of the vendor or the programming language used. See page 37.

Composite primary key (or compound primary key) A primary key formed from more than one column of a database table. Used when no individual column is guaranteed to be unique. See page 353.

CORBA See 'Common Object Request Broker Architecture.'

DAO Data Access Object. A helper class that encapsulates database access logic. See page 243.

Deadlock In a database transaction, the state of complete halt reached when a number of transactions are all waiting for each other to complete. See page 251.

Deployment The process of transferring an EJB to its server and generating the supporting classes that the container uses to encapsulate the EJB. See page 82.

Deployment descriptor The XML file provided as part of an EJB that supplies configuration information to the EJB server. See page 66.

De-serialization The process of constructing an object from a form that was stored sequentially, e.g., from data passed over a network. De-serialization also allows an object's state to be retrieved from a file. See page 663.

EIS Enterprise information system. A generic term for a system that stores and manages corporate data, and is not a relational database. See page 590

EJB object The object on the EJB server that implements the EJB's remote interface. The EJB object is a proxy for the EJB's method; the client calls methods on the EJB object (via the remote stub), which delegates to the bean instance itself. The term 'remote object' is often used to describe this entity, but 'EJB object' is the preferred term, as both the home object and remote object are 'remote objects' in RMI terms. See page 71.

EJB QL EJB Query Language. The way in which the logic of finders is to be expressed in the EJB 2.0 CMP model. See page 408.

Failover Any procedure for transferring the load of a failed system to a backup system without a loss of service. See page 17.

Fully qualified Of Java classes, if a name is fully qualified, it includes the package name. For example, `java.lang.String` is the fully qualified name of the `String` class.

Home method A method on an entity EJB that does not require the caller to hold a reference to a specific EJB; the method is called on the home object, and delegated to a pooled instance of the implementation. Home objects are useful for implementing finder methods that do not return EJBs by reference but by value. See page 351.

Home object In EJB, the home object is the object created on the EJB server that implements the EJB's home interface. The client calls methods on the home object (via the home stub) to create, find, and delete EJBs. See page 70.

Home stub In EJB, the home stub is the client-side stub that implements the home interface. This stub handles the communication between the client and the home object on the server. See page 71.

IIOP See Internet intra-ORB protocol.

Internet intra-ORB protocol (IIOP) This protocol is the standard protocol for carrying remote method call information between CORBA-compliant object request brokers. See page 37.

IOR Interoperable object reference. In CORBA technology, the format in which details of a remote object are passed between ORB and client. See page 41.

JavaMail A specification for programs in the Java language to interact with email services in a protocol-independent way. Page 584.

JCA J2EE connector API. The API standardized in the *J2EE Connector Specification*, which provides interfaces between EJBs, a resource adapter, and the EJB container. See page 591.

JDBC Java DataBase Connectivity, a standard for programs in the Java language to interact with relational databases, typically using the SQL language. See page 207.

JMS Java Messaging Service. A specification for programs in the Java language to interact with asynchronous messaging products like IBMs *MQSeries*. See page 293.

JNDI Java naming and directory interface. An API and SPI for allowing programs in the Java language uniform access to data stored in naming and directory servers. There are JNDI interfaces to LDAP, COSNaming, NIS, files, and many other systems. See page 177.

JRMP Java remote method protocol. The protocol for carrying arguments and return values between the client and the remote object in the standard Java RMI scheme. See page 37.

JTA Java Transaction API. A specification for the set of interfaces and methods that must be implemented by a transaction manager. See page 287.

JVM Java virtual machine. The imaginary computer on which a program in the Java language executes. The JVM is provided as part of a Java runtime system, and provides facilities like memory management, garbage collection, and thread control.

LDAP Lightweight directory access protocol. A protocol for retrieving and searching data in a directory server. See page 178.

Load sharing (Or load balancing). The process of distributing the load of a large application between a number of different servers. See page 15.

Narrow The process of assigning a variable's value to a variable whose type has a smaller range. For example, a value stored in a long integer can be narrowed to an ordinary integer in those cases where the long integer happens to contain a value whose value is of the right range to store in an integer. In EJB technology, the term is nearly always used to refer to the process if converting the result of a JNDI lookup (which is defined to return an `Object`) to a remote reference of the desired type. See page 39.

ORB Object request broker. Any system that makes objects available for their methods to be called by remote clients. Typically an ORB will serve multiple objects, and will provide other services—such as name lookup—on behalf of those objects. There is a standard for the operation and constitution of an ORB—CORBA—and for the protocol to be used for carrying method call information between them—IIOP. See page 28.

Principal An abstract user ID; the name by which a particular user is identified in an application. This is generally *not* a login ID. See page 496.

Principal delegation The process of ensuring that the correct principal is carried forward in calls between EJBs. See page 508.

Reflection The technique that allows a Java platform class to find information about other classes at runtime. Reflection is a crucial part of EJB container operation and stub generation. See page 659.

Remote interface The interface that exposes the methods of a class that an RMI client will be able to call. The interface is used by RMI or EJB tools to generate stubs for the remote class; the client will be able to call methods on the remote class by calling methods on the stub. Because the stub implements the remote interface, the client can manipulate the stub as if it were the remote object itself. See page 30.

Remote method invocation (RMI) Any technique that allows one object to make calls on the methods of another by the medium of a network connection. Remote method invocation is a general term—it describes any such technique—but it is often used by Java developers to mean the specific technique supported by the Java JDK. See page 29.

RMI See remote method invocation.

RMI/IIOP The implementation of Java RMI with the OMG's 'IIOP' protocol as the carrier. If a Java program uses RMI/IIOP to communicate between distributed objects, then it can, in principle, make method calls on CORBA objects as well. See page 37.

Remote object In RMI, any object whose methods can be called remotely by a client. The term is also used—incorrectly—by EJB developers as a synonym for 'EJB object' (it is incorrect because EJBs don't have a remote object in the sense of Java RMI). See page 28.

Remote stub In EJB, the remote stub is the client-side stub which implements the remote interface. This stub handles the communication between the client and the EJB object on the server. Note that the term 'remote stub' is used to distinguish this stub from the 'home stub,' not to indicate that it is remote from the client. See page 71.

Resource adapter Anything that provides a Java interface to a resource manager, such as a JDBC driver. See page 287.

Resource manager Anything that controls a transactional resource; a resource manager may be a relational database or something that communicates with a relational database. Increasingly messaging systems are resource managers as well. See page 281.

Role A specification of how a user will interact with an application, including the security permissions that will be required to make that interaction possible. See page 497.

Serialization The process of converting an object to a form that can be written sequentially, e.g., over a network. Serialization also allows an object's state to be stored in a file. See page 663.

SQL Structured query language. A language for querying and modifying data in a relational database. See page 208.

SSL Secure sockets layer. A protocol for public-key encryption of data at the transport layer. By operating at the transport level, the applications do not have to implement encryption and decryption internally. See page 495.

Stub A class that acts as a proxy between an RMI client and its remote object, and implements the communications protocol between the client and the server. Ideally the stub should expose the same methods as the remote object, and implement the same interface. This allows the client to call methods on the stub as if it were making calls on the remote object itself. See page 36.

TLS Transport-layer security. A variant of the SSL secure transport defined by the Internet Engineering Task force. See page 495.

Transaction An unit of work that consists of multiple operations that must be treated as a single operation. Usually pertains to database operations, but increasingly applies to messaging operations as well. See page 248.

Transaction log A record of the operations carried out during a transaction, maintained so that the transaction can be rolled back if a later operation fails. See page 249.

Transient This term has many meanings, but in this context it usually means 'not taking part in serialization.' When an object is serialized, its transient instance variables are not stored. See page 664.

TX The interface between a transaction manager and an application, as defined by the X/Open DTP standard. See page 282.

Value object A utility class for passing a number of instance variables of an entity EJB in one method call. See page 482.

Web service A service (typically an object) exposed to its clients via XML carried on the HTTP protocol, and the supporting infrastructure for such a service. See page 43.

XA The interface between a transaction manager and a resource manager, as defined by the X/Open DTP standard. See page 282.

X/Open DTP A distributed transaction processing architecture, defined by the Open Group, a consortium of software vendors.

Appendix I

Bibliography

Ahmed and Umrysh, *Developing Enterprise Java Applications with J2EE and UML*, (Addison-Wesley, 2001) ISBN 0201738295

The EJB 2.0 Specification, final release 2, available from `java.sun.com/products/ejb`

Fields and Kolb, *Web Development with Java Server Pages*, 2nd ed. (Manning, 2000) ISBN 1884777996

Hunter *et al.*, *Java Servlet Programming* (O'Reilly, 1998) ISBN 156592391X

The JMS Specification, version 1.0.2b, available from `java.sun.com/products/jms`

The JNDI API and SPI Specifications, available from `java.sun.com/products/jndi`

Kassem *et al.*, *Designing Enterprise Applications with the Java 2 Platform, Enterprise Edition*, (Addison-Wesley, 2000) ISBN 0201702770 (known colloquially as the J2EE Blueprints, and also available from `java.sun.com/j2ee/blueprints`)

Orfali and Harkey, *Client/server Programming with Java and Corba*, 2nd ed. (Wiley, 1998) ISBN 047124578X

World-Wide Web Consortium, *Simple Object Access Protocol, Version 1.1* (2000), available from `www.w3.org/TR/SOAP`

Index